"The Beer Guide has a great beer-food pairing cheat sheet"
- Don Russell, *Philadelphia Daily News* Joe Six-Pack columnist.

"Oakes has culled the best of the brews reviews. Check it out!"
- Travis Poling, *San Antonio Express News*

Edited by Josh Oakes

RateBeer

www.RateBeer.com

Savory House Press
Fort Worth

Bulk sales of books from Savory House Press, an imprint of Great Texas Line Press, are available at special discounts for fund raising, promotions and premiums.

Barry Shlachter, Publisher
Savory House Press / Great Texas Line
Post Office Box 11105
Fort Worth, Texas 76110
1-800-738-3927 / greattexas@hotmail.com

Book design by Pinkney Media Group, LLC

For more beer information, go to www.RateBeer.com

Printed in the United States of America

Contents

RateBeer's Beer Guide

Every effort was made to create the most comprehensive and authoritative beer guide available in the United States.

It is based on tens of thousands of reviews posted on RateBeer.com, the largest and most popular beer-rating website in the world. Since 2000, it has been considered the most accurate of any beer-rating website.

This guide carries reviews and ratings of more than 2,700 beers, far more than anything else in book form. Not included are foreign beers that were not imported into the United States at the time of publication or, for the sake of fairness, U.S. and foreign beers that received 10 or fewer reviews.

THE RATINGS

RateBeer.com's 1-to 100-point ratings have been converted to a five-star system for greater ease in a published format.

The ratings contained in this book are from beer lovers like you who set down their thoughts on RateBeer.com. They eagerly try new beers and are always learning more about the brewing art. Many home brew.

They are not "experts" – the beer world is more democratic than that. Contributors learned to express clearly what their senses tell them about beer. Some approach this process in virtually a scientific manner; others are full of passion.

When you visit RateBeer.com, you'll find raters whose experience and judgment you trust and those to whom you just don't relate. With no active equivalent of wine expert Robert Parker or Hugh Johnson, RateBeer is the only place to find authoritative ratings on all of the world's beers (more than 50,000 and counting!).

Keep in mind, savoring a beer is a subjective experience. There is no one "right" way to experience beer. It fulfills a wide variety of roles in people's lives and fits into almost any situation. This is reflected in the ratings. These are real experiences from real people.

The quotes reflect the consensus view of the RateBeer community – well over 30,000 strong – on each beer. They are intended to give an idea of what to expect when you try that beer. They are not intended as the definitive experience, and you will probably find that you do not always agree with the statements.

The real power is in the collective experiences. If the general consensus holds that a certain beer is of very high quality, chances are good that you will find that too, even if you don't recognize specific flavors cited in the guide when you sample the beer.

One thing you will find is that the drinkers who make up the RateBeer community have a love for showpiece beers. They are not necessarily the easiest beers to find, but they are often among the most rewarding.

Barley Wines, Abbey-style Ales, Imperial Stouts and India Pale Ales represent the height of the brewer's art. They are the true expressions of a brewer's passion and creativity, elements that have made America's small brewers among the best in the world in a few short decades.

This guide covers "mainstream" beers as well, including all of the most popular brands. You will notice that most are not highly regarded by the RateBeer community. That reflects what reviewers believe is a lack of creative passion at the industrial brewing corporations. Mass production coupled with saturation advertising campaigns rarely appeal to beer drinkers who have discovered artisanal brews.

No particular offense is meant. In many cases, the difference is like comparing inexpensive jug wine to expertly made boutique wines. Both have their place in the marketplace, and mass-produced brands might start some people on the road to greater appreciation.

That said, some of these beers are better than others, and we attempted to capture that in the comments.

– Josh Oakes, RateBeer editor

About
RateBeer.com

RateBeer.com is the global leader in beer information and beer ratings. Whether you're planning a trip to the remotest corners of the world, or just a night downtown, we'll tell you about the beers you're about to encounter.

The website was born of a love of great beer in the spring of 2000 by a Georgian named Bill Buchanan. The site was unique in its time and quickly drew some of the most experienced amateur beer raters into the fold. One of those was Josh Oakes, who later became RateBeer's editor – and compiler of this book.

RateBeer is based in Santa Rosa, Calif., and is operated by professional Web designer and beer lover Joe Tucker, with the assistance of Oakes and a small army of volunteers.

How large is RateBeer and the world of beer it represents? Consider the following:

- 35,000+ members from all 50 states and more than 100 countries
- 52,000+ beers
- 6000+ breweries in 187 countries
- 5000+ good beer establishments
- 800,000+ ratings

Beer Styles

The first thing to know about the various styles of beer in the world is that there is no one set list of beer styles. Not only do different countries and regions interpret the world of beer differently, but within countries there is often little agreement. Some styles seem rigidly defined while others are not so much styles as they are loose categories into which a wide variety of beers fall.

All beers fall into two general categories – ales and lagers. And all are made with water, grains, (optional flavors) and yeast. It's the yeast that determines if the beer becomes an ale – if "top" fermenting varieties are used – or a lager – which uses "bottom"-fermenting yeasts. There are also hybrid varieties, such as Altbier and Kölsch from Germany, California Common beer and cream ale.

MAINSTREAM PALE LAGERS

Pale Lager

This is what most of the world understands to be "beer" – mild, fizzy, yellow brews from global macrobreweries. Includes "Light," "Dry," and "Ice."

Premium Lager

A fuller, more flavorful variation of Pale Lager; no fillers like corn or rice and lagered longer for extra smoothness.

Malt Liquor

A high-alcohol version of Pale Lager, very sweet.

European Strong Lager

Tend to be fuller, smoother and hoppier high-alcohol brews from Central Europe.

EUROPEAN PALE LAGERS

Bohemian Pilsner

The original Czech pilsner is a very bitter, creamy brew; strong malt character and a rich golden color. Think Pilsner Urquell.

German Pilsner

Very bitter, dry, quite pale in color and with a mild malt character.

Pilsner

Includes any bitter, dry, pale lager that does not conform to characteristics of the Czech or German types.

Dortmunder/Helles

Two very similar, golden, full-bodied and malt-accented German styles.

DARK LAGERS

Vienna

Copper-color with a malt accent and, generally, has a toasty, caramelly, bread crust character.

Oktoberfest/Märzen

Copper to red lager, slightly stronger and smoother than Vienna with a similar malt accent, usually with more emphasis on the toastier, earthier side of the flavor profile.

Dunkel
Red to brown lager, very smooth with a nutty, sometimes toffeeish or earthy malt character.

Schwarzbier
Literally, "black beer," these are more intense variations of the dark lager family with rich dark malt character of earthy, toasty, chocolaty notes. Similar to porter.

SPECIALTY LAGERS

Zwickel/Keller/Landbier
Three similar styles, all carbonated naturally to low levels. These can be a bit rustic, owing to their roots in the farmhouses of northern Bavaria.

Smoked
The traditional smoked beer is Rauchbier from the German town of Bamberg. The style now refers to any beer made from smoked malt, creating a malty, earthy brew with a rich smoked character.

California Common
Also known as "Steam Beer." In theory, these amber brews combine the smoothness of a lager with the fruitiness and liveliness of an ale. Few live up to that ideal. Moderately bitter and malty.

Low Alcohol
Any beer with less than 2% alcohol. Some interesting variations are found around the world.

BOCKS

Bock
A strong, dark brown lager with a sweet, earthy character and smooth body. Pale Bocks are sometimes known as Maibocks.

Doppelbock
An extra-strong dark brown lager with a very sweet character and smooth body.

Eisbock
A doppelbock frozen to concentrate alcohol and malt elements. Very sweet dessert beer with loads of dark sugar and malt character and a firm alcoholic kick.

Weizen Bock
Any extra-strong wheat beer. Often dark brown, very fruity and spicy, with a rich dark malt character and lots of carbonation.

Pale Ales

English Pale Ale

A copper or amber brew combing light, caramelly, toasty malt notes with soft, subtle character of English hops.

American Pale Ale

Amber beers that showcase the bitter, citrusy American hop varieties. Malt and yeast character are generally muted relative to English Pale in order to better complement the brash statement of American hops.

India Pale Ale

Originally made by Britain for the Indian colonial market. Today it is a strong, hoppier, drier version of American Pale Ale.

Imperial/Double India Pale Ale

Stronger, hoppier Pale Ale with very high alcohol and bitterness levels, often offset by massive quantities of chewy malt.

Bitter and Related Styles

Bitter

The most common form of English Ale is, despite the name, not necessarily all that bitter. This subtle, low-alcohol brew has a delicate hop-malt balance.

Premium Bitter/ESB

Mainly known as ESB (for Extra Special Bitter) in the United States, these are stronger versions of bitter with a bolder hop and malt statements while keeping subtleties of the basic Bitter style.

Golden/Blonde Ale

Many types of golden-hued ales exist, ranging from some virtually indistinguishable from Pale Lager to some with a fresh malt character and a subtlety not unlike Bitter.

Scottish Ale

A maltier interpretation of Bitter popular in Scotland, known overseas as Scottish Ale. Earthy, chewy flavors and heavier than its moderate alcohol suggests.

LIGHT-BODIED, DARK ANGLO-AMERICAN ALES

Amber Ale

Found in brewpubs across the land, Amber Ale has no real meaning other than the beer can be either amber or red, with a balanced character. Same as Red Ale.

Brown Ale

A nutty, malty and sweet dark brown beer generally inspired by Samuel Smith's Nut Brown or Newcastle Brown Ale. Some hoppier examples have recently emerged.

Mild

Mainly found in England, this is a dark brown brew with a light body and low bitterness. It's very refreshing like a Bitter but with earthier, nuttier flavors.

Irish Ale

Inspired by the Smithwicks and Kilkennys of the world, this ale is ideally a sweeter, caramelly version of Amber Ale.

FAMILY: STRONG ANGLO

Scotch Ale

Strong ale with malty, fruity, licorice-like and sometimes peaty characteristics. A sweet and thick beer.

Old Ale

Confusingly, there is more than one "Old Ale" style. Many will be a rich, dark, sweet brew with notes of raisins, dark fruits and brown sugar. U.S. versions are often stronger.

English Strong Ale

Not a style, but a category encompassing strong ales that feature the balanced, fruity, subtle characteristics of English brews.

American Strong Ale

A broad category with no limits, this class includes truly creative products of America's talented microbrewers. Anything goes, as long as it's strong.

Barley Wine

Massive beers that go big on malt, hops and alcohol. They will always display a degree of sweetness and heavy bodied with much hop character. Can be aged for years.

PORTERS

Porter

Dark brown brew often featuring a malt accent. Notes range from chewy dark fruits to coffee, toast and nuts. Some quite sweet, others more bitter.

Baltic Porter

Style common to Poland, the Baltic states, Denmark and nearby countries. A big, roasty lager with a molasses character, lots of alcohol and a fat, rich body.

STOUTS

Stout/Dry Stout

The most basic stout, it's coffeeish, creamy, fairly bitter and quite dry in the finish. Alcohol is low to moderate, body should be full.

Sweet Stout

A black, low-alcohol brew with only a hint of roastiness, this style emphasizes the sweetness of the malts, if not added milk sugars or oatmeal. Body should be big relative to the alcohol.

Foreign Stout

Hard to find in the United States, this stout is usually quite sweet with an acidic bite. Roast and dark malt flavors are present along with alcohol and dark fruits. Surprisingly light body.

Imperial Stout

The most massive stout, this sports big body, big alcohol, intense roastiness, bitterness and dark fruit notes. Chewy, contemplative beers that can be aged for years.

SOUTH GERMAN WHEATS

German Hefeweizen

Hefeweizen is a sweet, tart, moderately strong wheat beer with yeast added for cloudy appearance, full body and rounded flavor with notes of banana and spice.

German Kristalweizen

Same as Hefeweizen but filtered clear. This makes the beer sparkling rather than murky, but lightens the body and makes flavors a little sharper.

Dunkelweizen

A dark version of Hefeweizen that adds toasty, nutty dark malt notes to the signature banana and spice.

OTHER WHEATS

American Wheat

Typically, a golden beer with a hint of wheaty tartness but none of the complex flavors of the German wheat beers. Can be cloudy or clear.

Belgian White

A cloudy type of wheat beer spiced with orange peel and coriander seed. The result is fruity, lightly spicy and refreshing. Body is light and alcohol moderate.

Berliner Weisse

Rare beer style that is low in alcohol and body, but high in acidity. This puckering brew is extremely refreshing. Berliners often add flavoring syrup.

LAMBICS

Lambic – Unblended

A sour wheat beer that has been aged in wooden barrels. Wild yeast lends it not only acidity but also an intense, complex character.

Lambic – Gueuze

Different barrels of Lambic are blended at bottling to restart fermentation. Intense and stunning as the unblended but as effervescent and stylish as champagne.

Lambic – Faro

Rare style to which a special sugar has been added, softening acidity. Faro is generally sweet rather than sour, but with a slight acidity in the finish. Done right, very refreshing.

Lambic – Fruit

Generally, a Gueuze with added fruit. Traditionally, this meant sour cherries or raspberries. Now all sorts of fruit added.

ABBEY ALES

Abbey Dubbel

Inspired by brews crafted by Belgium's Trappist monks, these are strong, dark, sweet and fruity ales with notes of raisins, dark fruit, sometimes banana, but also toffee and brown sugar. Full bodied.

Abbey Tripel

The pale big brother to Dubbels, these are stronger but drier and have different flavors. The fruity notes are lighter and the sugar character more understated. Can be hoppy or flowery, or have a dusty yeastiness and firm alcoholic finish.

Abt/Quadrupel

Broad category for Abbey-style ales even bigger than Tripels and Dubbels, these are high in alcohol with rich, intense flavors. Highly prized, they improve in the cellar for years.

BELGIAN ALES

Saison

A rustic farmhouse brew from Flanders that has found favor with beer lovers worldwide. Stronger than average, they have very complex, idiosyncratic flavor profiles thanks to unique yeast strains.

Flemish Sour

Either red or brown, the sour ales of Flanders start with a big, sweet malt character before controlled bacterial infection (not unlike yogurt) and barrel-aging create a sweet and sour, very complex and refreshing brew.

Belgian Ale

A broad, loose category encompassing many distinctive Belgian Ales. Often, they are yeasty, sweet and quite complex, but there the similarities end.

Belgian Strong Ale

Another loose category but stronger. Attempting to categorize Belgian beers is an exercise in futility and an insult to their uniqueness. Just say, "Belgian," and leave it at that.

CONTINENTAL ALES

Altbier

A reddish-brown ale from Düsseldorf with an earthy, caramelly character. Many are somewhat sweet, but the best are rich with bitterness. Many don't live up to the style.

Kölsch

Another style whose name appears on unworthy beers, this is a sparkling Golden Ale from Cologne. Its fresh character evokes grassy German hops and fresh bread notes with a good dose of bitterness. Quite refreshing.

Bière de Garde
A name used for almost any moderately strong Northern France ale, thus no real style but a collection of often rustic, characterful brews.

FLAVORED AND TRADITIONAL BEERS

Fruit Beer
Any style beer to which fruit or fruit syrup has been added. Generally, they tend to be sweet, approachable beers intended for summer refreshment.

Spice/Herb/Vegetable
Beer of any style to which spices, herbs or vegetables (typically chiles) have been added as flavoring. Spiced ales are often sweet, dark and strong for the Christmas season.

Traditional Ale
A beer made to an ancient and almost extinct beer style. Several styles of beer exist only in one or two examples, or in a revivalist brew. These include sahti, gruit, gose, heather ale, and rustic country brews in several countries.

Beer Ratings

How to use the beer guide

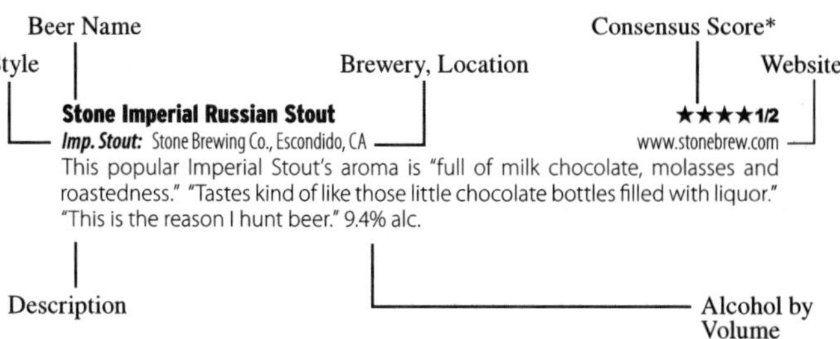

***RateBeer's 100-point rating scale has been converted to a five-star system:**

3 Monts ★★★

Biére de Garde: St. Sylvestre, St. Sylvestre-Cappel, France www.brasserie-st-sylvestre.com

"Mild herbal hops, with floral notes and a slight yeasty funk in the aroma." "Farmhouse flavor takes on an anticipated form of hearty sourdough crust with buttery lemon cream." "May be there are some things where it is worth copying the French." 8.5% alc.

33 Export ★

Pale Lager: Heineken (FRA), Schiltigheim, Alsace, France

"Smell is sweet and grainy and mildly skunky." "Corn, rice, hay, sweat socks and wet dirty dog and some other maltiness." "I could drink this for the sake of drinking it, but that is it." 4.8% alc.

A. le Coq Imperial Stout ★★★

Imp. Stout: Harvey & Son, Lewes, East Sussex, England www.harveys.org.uk

"The aroma is toasty and malty with a slight aroma of plum pudding." "Complex flavors of smoke, dried fruit (prunes and cherries), roasted malt and light sweet malt." "You either love this or hate it." 9% alc.

Aass Bock ★★★★1/2

Bock: Aass Bryggeri, Drammen, Norway www.aass.no

"Harmonic aroma of chocolate, some coffee and treacle." "Deep and firm taste of sweet malts, notes of chocolate and coffee, maybe burnt bread." "This is one of the best bocks I've had and well worth the search." 6.5% alc.

Aass Juleøl (Klasse D) ★★★★

Vienna: Aass Bryggeri, Drammen, Norway www.aass.no

"Sweet aroma of syrup, cinnamon and some roast malts." "Flavor of toasted malts, caramel and cherries." "Probably one of the best light beers I've had." 4.5% alc.

Abbaye de Floreffe Blonde ★★1/2

Belgian Ale: Brasserie Lefebvre, Rebecq-Quenast, Belgium www.brasserielefebvre.be

"Very estery aroma (lemon, apple, mango) with faint herbal hops." "Sweet grapefruit beginning, some lemon notes, faint bubblegummy phenols." "A little too quick in the finish" 6.3% alc.

Abbaye de Floreffe Double ★★★

Abbey Dubbel: Brasserie Lefebvre, Rebecq-Quenast, Belgium www.brasserielefebvre.be

"Sweet caramel and vinous aroma, with prunish notes." "Taste is a well balance mix between sweetness, strong malt with a nice touch of caramel and some subtle sourness with light funky yeast." "Unusual for the style." 6.3% alc.

Abbaye de Floreffe Prima Melior (Meilleure) ★★★★1/2

Bel. Strong Ale: Brasserie Lefebvre, Rebecq-Quenast, Belgium www.brasserielefebvre.be

"Deep fruit aroma - plum, tangerine, plus alcohol and chocolate." "Flavor is sweet, fruit-oriented (peach, tangerine), adding in hints of nut, chocolate, pepper and coriander." "Another example of why I love Belgian Ales!" 8% alc.

Abbaye de Floreffe Triple ★★★★

Abbey Tripel: Brasserie Lefebvre, Rebecq-Quenast, Belgium www.brasserielefebvre.be

"Esters dominate aroma (white grapes, pear, peach), followed by pepper and candi sugar." "Fruity flavor with some sweetness and notes of spices and alcohol." "This is too big to be a 'Belgian session' beer, but far too small to be a proper tripel." 7.5% alc.

Abbaye des Rocs Blanche des Honelles ★★★★1/2

Bel. Witbier: Brasserie de l'Abbaye des Rocs, Montignies-sur-Roc, Belgium www.abbaye-des-rocs.com

"Windmill cookie malt aroma with some spicy coriander." "Nice subtle dry orange peel aroma, some light spiciness as well. Good light and frothy mouthfeel. Very rich citrus taste complemented by some tangy maltiness." 6% alc.

Abbaye des Rocs Brune ★★★★★

Bel. Strong Ale: Brasserie de l'Abbaye des Rocs, Montignies-sur-Roc, Belgium www.abbaye-des-rocs.com
"One of the best aromas in beer - plum, fruity hops, alcohol, mandarin orange, light cocoa." "Very smooth, complex flavors that remind me of spicy dried fruits, rich toffees and caramels and some healing medicinal herbs." "Beautiful!" 9% alc.

Abbaye des Rocs Grand Cru ★★★★★

Bel. Strong Ale: Brasserie de l'Abbaye des Rocs, Montignies-sur-Roc, Belgium www.abbaye-des-rocs.com
"The aroma - big, yeasty, malty, peppery, hints of anise, pears and almost everything in between." "Cherry, raisin, plum, sour apples, pears, over some chocolate and caramel malts and a nice spicy yeast taste." "Makes for a good dessert beer." 9.5% alc.

Abbaye des Rocs La Montagnarde ★★★★

Bel. Strong Ale: Brasserie de l'Abbaye des Rocs, Montignies-sur-Roc, Belgium www.abbaye-des-rocs.com
"Aroma is deeply fruity, with lots of raisin, plum, peaches, pears and dark chocolate." "Lots of sweetness and warming alcohol, somewhat liqueur-like and vaguely reminiscent of a barley wine." "An elegant and complex beer." 9% alc.

Abbaye des Rocs Speciale Noël ★★★★★

Bel. Strong Ale: Brasserie de l'Abbaye des Rocs, Montignies-sur-Roc, Belgium www.abbaye-des-rocs.com
"Very complex fruity aroma with plum, cherry and sweet apple." "Peachy, slightly perfumey, cherryish and plummy palate with rich malty depths and a hint of chocolate." "One of the best strong ales I've sampled." 9% alc.

Abbaye des Rocs Triple Impériale ★★★★★

Bel. Strong Ale: Brasserie de l'Abbaye des Rocs, Montignies-sur-Roc, Belgium www.abbaye-des-rocs.com
"Very sweet enticing aroma of molasses, brandy, chocolate syrup and maple syrup." "There are a lot of fruits in the flavor - mostly fig and cherry. Has a honey, nutty taste with a slightly sour finish." "Another winner from des Rocs." 10% alc.

Abita Amber Lager ★

Vienna: Abita Brewing Co, Abita Springs, LA www.abita.com
"It is a malty lager, which is good, but finishes weak with a thin palate." "Soft and smooth, quite light and it has an up front light caramelized sweetness." "Could use more flavor." 5% alc.

Abita Bock ★★

Bock: Abita Brewing Co., Abita Springs, LA www.abita.com
"Predominately sweet malt with some toasty and spicy notes as well." "Malty flavor with the hops pulling through in the end to a dry and bitter aftertaste." "Interesting, but only as interesting as Pauly Shore was." 6.13% alc.

Abita Christmas Ale ★

Spice/Herb: Abita Brewing Co., Abita Springs, LA www.abita.com
"Has a very malty, spicy smell and a malty bread-like flavor." "Flavor has faint traces of raisins, dates and a bit of Christmas spice, but none are very well pronounced nor sharp." 6.13% alc.

Abita Fall Fest ★

Märzen/Oktbfst: Abita Brewing Co., Abita Springs, LA www.abita.com
"Aroma is bready, slightly fruity (ale-like)." "Flavor is toasty, bready malt with some fruit and caramel." "Oktoberfest? Come on... maybe Oktoberfest light?" 6.13% alc.

Abita Golden Lager ★★

Premium Lager: Abita Brewing Co., Abita Springs, LA www.abita.com
"Aroma got some malt and hops, grains and hints of corn." "Not much better than mass market stuff, but not cheap." "Sweetish taste." 5.25% alc.

Abita Louisiana Red ★★

Amber Ale: Abita Brewing Co., Abita Springs, LA www.abita.com

"Fairly dry, combining some light roast and background graininess with a fair amount of mildly bitter hops." "Fairly dry and malty finish." 5% alc.

Abita Purple Haze ★

Fruit Beer: Abita Brewing Co., Abita Springs, LA www.abita.com

"Definite raspberry nose." "Very light and thin, with the slightest hint of berries." "More wheaty than fruity." "Standard stuff." 4.75% alc.

Abita Turbodog ★★1/2

Brown Ale: Abita Brewing Co., Abita Springs, LA www.abita.com

"Aroma is light with a toffee sweet tone." "Surprisingly light and crisp for such a dark beer." "Sweet - also of dark fruits with hints of chocolate and a light floral hoppiness." 6.13% alc.

Abita Wheat ★

Am. Wheat: Abita Brewing Co., Abita Springs, LA www.abita.com

Taste is grassy lemon with slight hints of hops." "This is ok if you are coming in from mowing the lawn, but they really did a great job of making a tasteless brew on this one." 4.75% alc.

Achel 8 Blond ★★★★1/2

Bel. Strong Ale: Trappistenabdij De Achelse Kluis, Hamont-Achel, Belgium www.achelsekluis.org

"Hoppy aroma with yeast, peaches, leather, pepper." "Firm body - bracing alcohol but balanced by hops and underlying doughy pale malts." "Great all around brew." 8% alc.

Achel 8 Bruin ★★★★1/2

Bel. Strong Ale: Trappistenabdij De Achelse Kluis, Hamont-Achel, Belgium www.achelsekluis.org

"Aroma is full of caramel and liqorice as well as yeasty spiciness." "Sweet initial taste with caramel, fudge, a touch of dark fruit, developing into a nice chewy bitter finish." "Great sipping beer." 8% alc.

Achel Extra Bruin ★★★★★

Abt/Quadrupel: Trappistenabdij De Achelse Kluis, Hamont-Achel, Belgium www.achelsekluis.org

The aroma was fruity with a nice spicy side coming through as well as a bit of caramel in there." "Flavor is a meld of dark fruits, toffee, licorice, chocolate and spice." "That wonderful Quadrupel from Achel is to beer what Porto is to wine. 9.5% alc.

Acme California Brown Ale ★★1/2

Brown Ale: North Coast Brewing Co., Fort Bragg, CA www.northcoastbrewing.com

"Aroma and flavor dominated by smooth, lightly roasted malt." "Taste is a little watered down." "Semi-sweet caramel flavor, some malt and only a hint of bittering hops in the aftertaste." 5.6% alc.

Acme California IPA ★★1/2

IPA: North Coast Brewing Co., Fort Bragg, CA www.northcoastbrewing.com

"A floral/grapefruit citrus aroma with hops and hard candy." "Flavor is nicely bitter with piney/citrus hops, toasted, bready malt and a bit of plum." "Not up to their usual standards." 7.1% alc.

Acme California Pale Ale ★★

Am. Pale Ale: North Coast Brewing Co., Fort Bragg, CA www.northcoastbrewing.com

"Orangey-golden colored ale with a sweet, lightly malty character. Hops are only slightly noted. "Balanced and aromatic, but...zzzzz." 5% alc.

Adnams Broadside ★★★

Eng. Strong Ale: Adnams, Southwold, Suffolk, England www.adnams.co.uk

"Aroma is oak, earthy fruits, with some sweet toffee maltiness." "Rich malt taste, butterscotch, caramel, hops and pit fruits." "A lasting bitterness has you appreciating this beer for quite a while after placing the glass down." 6.3% alc.

Adnams Suffolk Strong Bitter ★★★1/2
Bitter: Adnams, Southwold, Suffolk, England www.adnams.co.uk
"Nose of wheat, chicory, berries, heavy spice, vinegar, brown sugar and dried fruit." "Not very bitter to begin with, but if finishes dry and bitter." "Didn't jump out at me with complexity, but it's a solid, well-made beer that kept my attention." 4.5% alc.

Aecht Schlenkerla Rauchbier Märzen ★★★★
Smoked: Brauerei Heller-Trum, Bamberg, Germany www.schlenkerla.de
"Incredibly well-balanced beer with a pungent smokiness and smooth, gorgeous maltiness." "Perfectly executed smoked beer." "You have to like smoke - this is not for everyone." 5.1% alc.

Aecht Schlenkerla Rauchbier Urbock ★★★★★
Smoked: Brauerei Heller-Trum, Bamberg, Germany www.schlenkerla.de
"Exceptionally rich malts with insistent smoke layered overtop." "Intense, but very well balanced." "The smoke lingers." "One of the best beers I've ever tasted." 6.5% alc.

Aecht Schlenkerla Rauchbier Weizen ★★★1/2
Smoked: Brauerei Heller-Trum, Bamberg, Germany www.schlenkerla.de
"Lots of bursting smoke in the aroma." "Vibrant, smooth smoke flavor mixes with bananas - almost dessert-like." "Definitely unique." 5.2% alc.

Afanasy Svetloe/Tver Beer ★★1/2
Pilsner: Tver Brewing, Tver, Russia www.afanasy.ru
"Aroma of bready malts, some cereal notes, slight grassiness." "The flavor is a sweet, grainy taste with perhaps just a touch of corn." "Too assertive in the finish otherwise not a bad brew." 5% alc.

Afanasy Temnoe/Tver Beer Dark ★★1/2
Dunkel: Tver Brewing, Tver, Russia www.afanasy.ru
"Aroma of caramel, brown sugar and malt." "Caramelly malt-accented lager. Clean, with hints of darker things like toffee." "Reminds me of what a Belgian brewer might do in Russia." 5% alc.

Affligem Blonde ★★1/2
Belgian Ale: Brouwerij Affligem/De Smedt (Heineken), Opwijk, Belgium www.affligem.be
"At first white pepper, then moves on to mango, banana and sweet malt." "Notes of clove, banana and lemon plus yeast, spices orange, sweet malt and some hop bitterness at the end." "Decently complex for a blond." 7% alc.

Affligem Dubbel ★★★
Abbey Dubbel: Brouwerij Affligem/De Smedt (Heineken), Opwijk, Belgium www.affligem.be
"Aroma shows plum, apple, dark rye bread, metals, phenols." "Rich dark malts, molasses and toffee, there's also some wildflower honey." "Not bad, but one of the weaker dubbels I've tried." 7% alc.

Affligem Noël Christmas Ale ★★★★
Bel. Strong Ale: Brouwerij Affligem/De Smedt (Heineken), Opwijk, Belgium www.affligem.be
Very estery aroma, cherry, some cream and caramel, milk chocolate, vinous and an underpinning of sugar coated raisins." "Very understated...if you can call a 9% Belgian strong understated." 9% alc.

Affligem Triple ★★★★1/2
Abbey Tripel: Brouwerij Affligem/De Smedt (Heineken), Opwijk, Belgium www.affligem.be
"Aroma of yeast, pepper, pear, tangerine, slight grass and banana candy." "Good flavor of yeast, citrus and hops, it finishes bitter and very dry." "All the little things are done quite well." 8.5% alc.

Aalaska Bars (green) ★
Eur Str Lager: Pivzavod AO Krasnyj Vostok, Kazan, Tatarstan, Russia www.krvostok.ru
Sweet starchy aroma." "Very caramelly, earthy flavor with sweet, sugary, alcoholic finish." "Total swill." 7% alc.

Alaskan Amber ★★★
Altbier: Alaskan Brewing Co., Juneau, AK www.Alaskanbeer.com
"A sweetish, easy-drinking amber ale with a caramelly accent and noted fruitiness. "As amber ales go, this one is tasty and pretty well done." "I have found the perfect session beer!" 5% alc.

Alaskan ESB ★★★★1/2
Prem Bitter: Alaskan Brewing Co., Juneau, AK www.Alaskanbeer.com
Dark amber with "mild sweetness and sufficient balancing bitterness." The hops have a floral, citrusy character and the malts are "a bit chewy." "Medium length bitter finish." "Worthy of two or three in a session." 5% alc.

Alaskan Pale ★★★★
Goldn/Blond Ale: Alaskan Brewing Co., Juneau, AK www.Alaskanbeer.com
"A golden-colored, refreshing example with honey-like sweetness and aromas of tangerine and honeysuckle." "The brewery Calls this a golden ale, but it can't be because I really like this beer." 4.65% alc.

Alaskan Smoked Porter ★★★★★
Smoked: Alaskan Brewing Co., Juneau, AK www.Alaskanbeer.com
"Multi-award-winning smoked black ale is probably Alaska's most famous beer. Smoke flavor and aroma dominates." "Aroma of peaty smoke erupts from the glass." "Wow, so good." 6.5% alc.

Alaskan Stout ★★★
Sweet Stout: Alaskan Brewing Co., Juneau, AK www.Alaskanbeer.com
A somewhat underwhelming oatmeal stout, at times "cloyingly sweet" with "roasted malt and a touch of coffee." Some beer lovers find it too sweet, but others find the roast balances the beer nicely. 5.65% alc.

Alaskan Summer Ale ★★★
Kölsch: Alaskan Brewing Co., Juneau, AK www.Alaskanbeer.com
Fairly well-regarded golden ale. "Light and fresh", this beer is noted for having a good balance of citrusy hop notes and pale malts. "Refreshing after an afternoon hike in Alaska. 5% alc.

Alaskan Winter Ale ★★1/2
Spice/Herb: Alaskan Brewing Co., Juneau, AK www.Alaskanbeer.com
An amber colored beer brewed with spruce tips. A malty, slightly strong beer with a spruce character that some find dominant, while others hardly notice it at all. "A simple and easy to drink winter ale." 6.4% alc.

Aldaris Porteris ★★★
Baltic Porter: Aldaris , Riga, Latvia www.aldaris.lv
Rich fruity and malty aroma with some raisins and brown sugar." "Taste is sweet, roasted malts, lots of caramel, some chocolate." "It is indeed a nice, robust, well-made porter." 6.8% alc.

Aldaris Zelta ★★1/2
Pale Lager: Aldaris , Riga, Latvia www.aldaris.lv
"Aromas of grains/corn and some hint of hops." "Light must flavor, apple notes, light grainy." "Perhaps in Latvia the best selling beer also tastes good. What a novel concept." 5.2% alc.

AleSmith Anvil ESB ★★★★★
Prem Bitter: AleSmith Brewing Co., San Diego, CA www.alesmith.com
Strange for AleSmith, this has only 5.5% ABV. "Very floral and quite aromatic with hints of orange and caramel in the nose." "Bitter flavor, but there's enough malt to back it up, some woody and spicy flavors in there too." 5.5% alc.

AleSmith Grand Cru ★★★★★
Bel. Strong Ale: AleSmith Brewing Co., San Diego, CA www.alesmith.com
A strong ale of Belgian inspiration, this has "a sweet flavor with chocolate, vanilla, grapes, with a touch of alcohol." "Like a spiced liqueur from some very obscure and sophisticated monks." 10.6% alc.

AleSmith Horny Devil ★★★1/2

Bel. Strong Ale: AleSmith Brewing Co., San Diego, CA www.alesmith.com

Funky yeasty aroma, some banana and other fruits, alcohol, black pepper and coriander, a bit sour to my nose." "It is pretty sweet, making it a little hard to consume quickly." 10% alc.

AleSmith IPA ★★★★★

IPA: AleSmith Brewing Co., San Diego, CA www.alesmith.com

"I had a rough day and this aroma alone relieved the stress of it." "Fresh and inviting hop aroma - pine, spruce and orange." "Quite bitter with some malt shyly offering support. Lots of chewy resin throughout." 7.25% alc.

AleSmith J.P. Gray's Wee Heavy Scotch Ale ★★★★★

Scotch Ale: AleSmith Brewing Co., San Diego, CA www.alesmith.com

"Aroma of alcohol, caramel, cherries, wood." "Rich malt flavor, moderate smokiness, some plum and date fruitiness." "A wonderful scotch ale and one that should be savored." 9.5% alc.

AleSmith Old Numbskull ★★★★★

Barley Wine: AleSmith Brewing Co., San Diego, CA www.alesmith.com

"Super caramel aroma with some floral hops, cotton candy, alcohol and some woodiness." "Moderate toasted malt with some hints of roasty flavor. Herbal hop and light lingering bitterness as well into the aftertaste." 10% alc.

AleSmith Speedway Stout ★★★★★

Imp. Stout: AleSmith Brewing Co., San Diego, CA www.alesmith.com

A massive stout, flavored with coffee beans. "Bitter chocolate, burnt toast, minty hops, percolated coffee." "Fairly dry for an Imperial Stout." "As we finished the bottle he looked at me and asked if I had more." The rare, barrel-aged version is extremely popular among aficionados. 12% alc.

AleSmith X ★★★★

Am. Pale Ale: AleSmith Brewing Co., San Diego, CA www.alesmith.com

An American-style pale ale that is "a bit fruity, decent ester presence, some floral and a touch of pine." "Good for what the brewer intended, but seemed unambitious." 5% alc.

AleSmith Yulesmith ★★★★★

Imp/Dbl IPA: AleSmith Brewing Co., San Diego, CA www.alesmith.com

Released both in the holiday season and again in July, this popular beer straddles the line between IPA and Double IPA. "Holy crap, there are a lot of hops going on in this beer." "An inspiration." 8.5% alc.

Alfa ★★

Pale Lager: Athenian Brewery (Heineken), Athens, Greece www.beerexports.gr

"Light floral and toasty aroma." "Cereal flavor with some hops to be found." "Amazing that the Greeks have done so many amazing things, yet never figured out beer?" 5% alc.

Alhambra Premium Lager ★★1/2

Pale Lager: Grupo Cervezas Alhambra, Granada and Cordoba, Spain www.cervezasalhambra.es

Aroma of toasted grains, slight corn, caramel, light grassy continental hop." "Body is sweet, showing slightly cloying caramel notes and DMS - creamed corn sweetness." "Easy to distinguish from a pale lager and quite refreshing". 4.6% alc.

Allagash Curieux ★★★★

Bel. Strong Ale: Allagash Brewing Co., Portland, ME www.allagash.com

"Boozy aroma with oaky vanilla notes that carry over to the flavor." "Noticeable bourbon with lots of tropical fruity flavor and plenty of spice." "Everything is in very good balance." 11% alc.

Allagash Dubbel Reserve ★★★1/2

Abbey Dubbel: Allagash Brewing Co., Portland, ME www.allagash.com

"Sweet malt, candy and chocolate are in the nose." "Quite soft and creamy in the mouth." "Subtle hints of cassis berry, sour black cherries and bitter sweet chocolate." "I like this..." 7% alc.

Allagash Four ★★★★★
Abt/Quadrupel: Allagash Brewing Co., Portland, ME www.allagash.com
"Strong alcohol and spicy malt in aroma." "Taste is strong but not crisp like most Belgian quads." "Quite spicy and while not totally blended, very appealing." "Should get even better with age." 10% alc.

Allagash Grand Cru ★★★★★
Belgian Ale: Allagash Brewing Co., Portland, ME www.allagash.com
"Great floral malts and coriander, cardamom in the nose." "Light sourness, big citric (lemon, tangerine) and some nice hops for a Belgian beer." "I like the American twist to this style here." 7.2% alc.

Allagash Summer Ale ★★★
Belgian Ale: Allagash Brewing Co., Portland, ME www.allagash.com
"Big clovey spiciness at the forefront of the aroma with lemon and a slight soapiness." "Flavor has notes of clove orange peel, lemon, spices yeast and some bubblegum." "I have a hard time imagining anyone not liking this beer." 5% alc.

Allagash Tripel Reserve ★★★★★
Abbey Tripel: Allagash Brewing Co., Portland, ME www.allagash.com
"Aroma is of sweet fruits and spices." "Flavor is an interesting blend - sweet malt, alcohol, light, juicy fruits, clove, pepper, other unknown spices and yeast." "A very nice tripel." 9% alc.

Allagash Victoria Ale
Bel. Strong Ale: Allagash Brewing Co., Portland, ME www.allagash.com
A very nice and pleasant aroma, soft grapes, light citrus. "Bright flavor, fruity and flowery, a hint of toasty malt, moderate phenolics, sweet up front with some hop bitterness showing up in the finish." 9% alc.

Allagash White ★★★★★
Bel. Witbier: Allagash Brewing Co., Portland, ME www.allagash.com
"Aromas are orange peel, coriander, some other spices." "Honey-like sweetness with bitter orange and coriander spiciness that complement." "Aftertaste is slightly sweet and a touch spicy." "Just gonna sit back and enjoy this one." 5.5% alc.

Allgäuer Büble Bier ★★★★★
Pale Lager: Allgäuer Brauhaus AG, Kempten, Germany www.allgaeuer-brauhaus.de
"Yeasty nose with hints of light/yellow citrus and some light graininess." "Taste is a skillful balance between sweet malt and herbal hopping." "No wonder the boy on the label is smiling" 5.5% alc.

Allgäuer Cambonator Doppelbock ★★★★
Doppelbock: Allgäuer Brauhaus AG, Kempten, Germany www.allgaeuer-brauhaus.de
"Surprisingly buttery malts fit pretty well into the rich earthy and dark fruits aromatic components." "Roasty for a German lager, offering plenty of dark berries, blackberries, prunes and sweet, drying earthy malt flavors." 7.2% alc.

Almaza ★★
Pale Lager: Brasserie Almaza (Heineken), Beirut, Lebanon www.almaza-beer.com
Aromas of light skunk and corn." "Taste is grainy and buttery with light hints of hops. Slightly bitter at certain points." "Overall, very smooth, yet fizzy and bland." 4% alc.

Alpine Beer Co. Pure Hoppiness ★★★★★
IPA: Alpine Beer Co. (CA), Alpine, CA www.alpinebeerco.com
Straddling the line between IPA and Imperial IPA, this has a "wonderfully explosive, pungent aroma." "The flavor is malty with floral/resin/grapefruit/ peach hoppiness." "This is a big, juicy, warming IPA." 8% alc.

Altenmunster Jubelbier Dunkel Spezial ★★★★

Dunkel: Allgäuer Brauhaus AG, Kempten, Germany www.allgaeuer-brauhaus.de

Peaty and earthy dark malts and dusty cocoa in the nose, lightly nutty with hints of tree-bark, sultanas and cinnamon spice." "There are toffee apple notes upfront and plenty of sweet dark malt, with some spicy bitterness in the finish." 5.5% alc.

Altenmunster Premium ★★★★1/2

Pale Lager: Allgäuer Brauhaus AG, Kempten, Germany www.allgaeuer-brauhaus.de

"Aroma is nice and mild, though sweet, honeyish and a bit floral." "Malt is lightly bready and lightly sweet and the hops barely makes any contribution at any point from start to finish." "Very bland and generic." 4.8% alc.

American Beer ★

Pale Lager: Pittsburgh Brewing Co., Pittsburgh, PA www.pittsburghbrewingco.com

Just a mess of corn and powdered sugar." "Huge amounts of water is what I mostly get, followed by metal and corn." "Extremely quick lagering times do not good beers make." N/A% alc.

Amstel Light ★★

Pale Lager: Heineken Nederland, Hertogenbosch, Netherlands www.heineken.com

"Little hint of anything in the smell." "Tastes weak with some hops." "I want to feel pretentious and snobby, I'll stand in a bar holding a bottle of this." 3.5% alc.

Amsterdam Mariner ★★1/2

Pale Lager: Grolsche Bierbrouwerij Ned. bv, Enschede, Netherlands www.grolsch.nl

"Weak, hoppy nose." "Zesty hay accent, grassy hops and soft pale malt flavors." "Over all there was nothing bad to say, but it was just another boring, front-bar lager." 5% alc.

Anchor Liberty Ale ★★★★★

Am. Pale Ale: Anchor Brewing Co., San Francisco, CA www.anchorbrewing.com

The first beer to showcase Cascade hops, Liberty Ale is an American classic that straddles the line between the American Pale and IPA styles. "This 1975 classic was and still remains, one of the best things to come out of that cursed decade." 6% alc.

Anchor Old Foghorn ★★★★★

Barley Wine: Anchor Brewing Co., San Francisco, CA www.anchorbrewing.com

A classic annual barley wine, Old Foghorn is a ruby-colored ale with the "aroma of syrupy malt, hop bitterness, fruit, alcohol, caramel and a trace of woodiness." "Full-bodied and rich." 9% alc.

Anchor Our Special Ale ★★★★1/2

Spice/Herb: Anchor Brewing Co., San Francisco, CA www.anchorbrewing.com

Every year brings a new mix of spices to this dark, rich winter warmer. Often drinkers find ginger, nutmeg, chocolaty malts, cinnamon and in some years pine. "This is yet another fine year of O.S.A." 5.5% alc.

Anchor Porter ★★★★★

Porter: Anchor Brewing Co., San Francisco, CA www.anchorbrewing.com

A "chocolaty, slightly sharp" example of the style, "mixing the assertiveness of a 21st century porter and the complexity of a 19th century example." "Spiffing stuff." 5.6% alc.

Anchor Small Beer ★

Bitter: Anchor Brewing Co., San Francisco, CA www.anchorbrewing.com

Made with the second runnings from Old Foghorn, in the centuries-old "small beer" tradition. The flavor is surprisingly bitter and the mouthfeel thin. "Easy drinking but boring." 3.3% alc.

Anchor Steam ★★1/2

Calif. Common: Anchor Brewing Co., San Francisco, CA www.anchorbrewing.com

A relic of a 19th century California beer style. "Sweet aroma of fruit, caramel malt, light hops and grain." "Respectable malt profile and dry finish." "Thin and kind of bland, but very drinkable." 4.9% alc.

Anchor Summer Beer ★★1/2

Am. Wheat: Anchor Brewing Co., San Francisco, CA www.anchorbrewing.com

"Nose is entirely grass, wheat and light citrus." "The body is light and soft with notes of wheat." "Not a bad beer, but closer to Coors than to Rogue." 4.6% alc.

Anderson Valley Barney Flats Oatmeal Stout ★★★★

Sweet Stout: Anderson Valley Brewing Co., Boonville, CA www.avbc.com

"A hearty but balanced flavor - moderate sweetness, hazelnut, roast, chocolate in a very drinkable blend." "This has a lot happenin'!" "Finish is long and toasty." 5.7% alc.

Anderson Valley Belk's ESB ★★★1/2

Prem Bitter: Anderson Valley Brewing Co., Boonville, CA www.avbc.com

"Fairly strong for the style, Belk's offers a "rich copper color", a "fresh, fruity aroma" and "lots of hops again in the flavor backed pretty well by a sharp light crystal malt background." 6.8% alc.

Anderson Valley Boont Amber ★★★★

Amber Ale: Anderson Valley Brewing Co., Boonville, CA www.avbc.com

Fairly highly rated for an amber, it has a "moderately hoppy aroma" and a flavor that is "very caramelly." with some deep resinous hop character. "After trying Fat Tire last night, I can see the difference. This beer tastes so much better." 5.8% alc.

Anderson Valley Brother David's Double ★★★1/2

Abbey Dubbel: Anderson Valley Brewing Co., Boonville, CA www.avbc.com

A mahogany-colored abbey-style ale with an aroma "sweet with plums and rich malts." "Malt accented, with little yeast presence, along with light chocolate, roast and nut flavors." Scores much higher than the Triple. 9% alc.

Anderson Valley Brother David's Triple ★★1/2

Abbey Tripel: Anderson Valley Brewing Co., Boonville, CA www.avbc.com

Strongish example of the style. "Pale malt and sweet vinous flavor." "Alcohol tries in vain to cut through the thick body, ultimately failing and consigning the beer to cloyingness." 10% alc.

Anderson Valley Hop Ottin IPA ★★★★1/2

IPA: Anderson Valley Brewing Co., Boonville, CA www.avbc.com

"It's got an iconoclastic West Coast IPA flavor to it." "Quite balanced and smooth." "Maintains a grapefruit sweetness and a honey-vanilla essence." "Solid IPA all around." 7% alc.

Anderson Valley Poleeko Gold ★★1/2

Am. Pale Ale: Anderson Valley Brewing Co., Boonville, CA www.avbc.com

Hazy orange pale ale. "Some hop spice is the main component, then some doughy, floury malt." "Burst of hoppiness that melts away to a watery, husky sweetness." 5.5% alc.

Anderson Valley Winter Solstice ★★★1/2

Spice/Herb: Anderson Valley Brewing Co., Boonville, CA www.avbc.com

A dark, strongish winter brew, flavored with spices and vanilla. "Aroma of vanilla, cherries, caramel and mild warm spice." "Has a small personality of ginger, clove and vanilla that reminded me of club soda." 6.9% alc.

Andrews English Pale Ale ★★1/2

Am. Pale Ale: Andrews Brewing Co., Lincolnville, ME

"Smells of clementines, lemons and brown sugar." "Flavor starts with some caramel covered toast and ends with a lovely hoppiness." "Clean and dry finish." N/A% alc.

Andrews St. Nick Porter ★★★

Porter: Andrews Brewing Co., Lincolnville, ME

"Toasty, milk chocolaty depths of aroma." "Really rich coffee taste. Very smooth and drinkable." "Slightly leafy, with bitter chocolate, nuts and toast." N/A% alc.

Angkor Beer ★★

Pale Lager: Cambrew, Sihanoukville, Cambodia

"Grassy, citrusy, sweat socks, herbal aroma and earthy hops." "Hops are crisp and slightly floral." "A little thin, weak and watery." 5% alc.

Anheuser World Lager (World Select) ★★

Pale Lager: Anheuser-Busch Companies, St. Louis, MO www.anheuser-busch.com

"Aroma is of mild bready malt, not much hops slight yeast." "Bland and a little sweet." "Most megabrews actually have more flavor." 5% alc.

Appalachian Hoppy Trails IPA ★★1/2

IPA: Appalachian Brewing Co., Harrisburg, PA www.abcbrew.com

"Hops are slightly citrus and piney and I found a light malt character with a slight roasted flavor." "Lighter body than I expect in an IPA." "A clean, middle of the road IPA, that does not take many chances." 6.2% alc.

Appalachian Jolly Scot ★★1/2

Scottish Ale: Appalachian Brewing Co., Harrisburg, PA www.abcbrew.com

"Great caramel - butterscotch flavor." "Aroma was sweet with malty doughy notes." "This is an easy drinker and will fit the bill for someone looking for real malt flavor in their beer." 5.2% alc.

Appalachian Mountain Lager ★

Helles/Dortmnd: Appalachian Brewing Co., Harrisburg, PA www.abcbrew.com

"Aroma was sweet mild malty and hoppy." "Flavor was watery hops and just about nothing else." "Very little to speak of with this brew." 4.5% alc.

Appalachian Purist Pale ★★

Am. Pale Ale: Appalachian Brewing Co., Harrisburg, PA www.abcbrew.com

"This beer has piney hops abound, mingling with some grapefruit notes as well." "Nice malty undertones, but the brew overall is too light and watery to make a good APA." 4.9% alc.

Appalachian Susquehanna Stout ★★1/2

Dry Stout: Appalachian Brewing Co., Harrisburg, PA www.abcbrew.com

"Malty, chocolate, coffee and roasty nose." " Very strong roasted coffee flavor, some bittersweet baker's chocolate lingering after." "A nice brew, could use a little more body and a little more complexity to its flavor, but nice nonetheless." 4.6% alc.

Appalachian Water Gap Wheat ★

Am. Wheat: Appalachian Brewing Co., Harrisburg, PA www.abcbrew.com

"Not much of an aroma really." "Malty fruity flavors with light hops and a fruity finish." "This is not a beer that I would drink although my friends who think Keystone Light is a good beer think this has a lot of flavor." 4.5% alc.

Arcadia Angler's Ale ★★

Eng Pale Ale: Arcadia Brewing Co., Battle Creek, MI www.arcadiabrewingcompany.com

"Smells sweet, fruity, floral, nutty and a little caramelly, but also a bit soapy." "Taste is some sharp hops up front that blend to sweet malts then back for a nice bitter finish." 5.1% alc.

Arcadia Bourbon Barrel Shipwreck Porter ★★★1/2
Porter: Arcadia Brewing Co., Battle Creek, MI www.arcadiabrewingcompany.com
"Aroma is sweet bourbon and oaky vanilla with chocolate and molasses with a touch of alcohol." "Flavor is dominated mostly by the bourbon but behind it there is some chocolate and roasted malt flavors." "Bourbon fumes kept flowing out of my glass." 7% alc.

Arcadia Imperial Stout ★★★★★
Imp. Stout: Arcadia Brewing Co., Battle Creek, MI www.arcadiabrewingcompany.com
"Port and raisin, prune fragrant floral hop aroma with dark roasted coffee and dark chocolate malt notes and a bit of oak, overall a very inviting aroma." "The flavor is huge. Charcoal, coffee, chocolate, black currants?" 8.4% alc.

Arcadia Indian Pale Ale ★★1/2
IPA: Arcadia Brewing Co., Battle Creek, MI www.arcadiabrewingcompany.com
"Strong grapefruit-orange-citrus and resiny pine hop flavors with fairly assertive finishing bitterness and a lightly toasty malt character." "Noble effort, but needs more malts." 5.9% alc.

Arcadia Lake Superior ESB ★★1/2
Prem Bitter: Arcadia Brewing Co., Battle Creek, MI www.arcadiabrewingcompany.com
"Grapefruit and oranges in the strong citrus hop flavor with underlying sweet caramel character and fair finishing bitterness." "Sweet and heavy for the style." 5.5% alc.

Arcadia London Porter ★★★★★
Porter: Arcadia Brewing Co., Battle Creek, MI www.arcadiabrewingcompany.com
"Rich smoky aroma of smoked salmon, carob, coffee, dry chocolate and some strawberries." "Taste is sweet and roasty, liked smoked chocolate, with a rather sharp hop kick toward the end." 7.2% alc.

Arcadia Nut Brown Ale ★★
Brown Ale: Arcadia Brewing Co., Battle Creek, MI www.arcadiabrewingcompany.com
"Sweet, caramel-like aroma is evident, a combination of sweet malts with a bit of nuts and a hint of chocolate as well." "Some chocolate intertwined with the nut and malt, made for a decent brew." 5.6% alc.

Arcadia Scotch Ale ★★★
Scotch Ale: Arcadia Brewing Co., Battle Creek, MI www.arcadiabrewingcompany.com
"Plums, dark fruit, soy sauce, lots of malt sweetness with a leathery tone as well." "Lots of malt in the flavor combined with brown sugar." "This is a full bodied beer, fairly thick, with a light alcohol burn." 7.5% alc.

Arcadia Starboard Stout ★★1/2
Sweet Stout: Arcadia Brewing Co., Battle Creek, MI www.arcadiabrewingcompany.com
"Nose big on roast, caramel, malts and chocolate." "Very malty, slightly ashy flavors with notes of both coffee and chocolate." "The epitome of okay." 5.6% alc.

Arcadia Whitsun ★★★★
Am. Wheat: Arcadia Brewing Co., Battle Creek, MI www.arcadiabrewingcompany.com
"Nose spicy, lots of orange, candi sugar, herbal." "Flavors revolve around lemon-banana smoothie qualities and perhaps some KFC biscuits topped with honey." "More going on than in a typical American Wheat." 6.2% alc.

Aris ★★★
Pale Lager: Mythos Breweries (Scottish & Newcastle), Sindos, Greece www.mythosbrewery.gr
"Aroma is moderately malty (bread, grain), lightly hoppy (herbs)." "Kinda like a Heineken, but much better in my opinion. Hops are evident in the aroma and flavor." "Hardly worth even wasting the time to describe it." 5% alc.

Arran Blonde ★★★
Goldn/Blond Ale: Arran, Isle of Arran, Strathclyde, Scotland www.arranbrewery.co.uk
"Apricot and orange aroma." "Crisp with slight sweet fruity notes and a decent clean hoppy finish." "A decent blond beer. Better than I expected." 5% alc.

Artevelde Grand Cru ★★1/2

Bel. Strong Ale: Brouwerij Huyghe, Melle, Belgium www.delirium.be

"Aroma is slightly chocolaty, nutty, some red wine/dark grape notes." "Initial sweet chocolate flavor is quickly replaced with a tart sugar and apple note, then into a drying bitter spicy finish." "Would be a good introduction to the style." 7.3% alc.

Asahi Black ★★1/2

Schwarzbier: Asahi Breweries, , Japan www.asahibeer.co.jp

"Some roasty notes in the aroma but also a bit of metal." "Taste is also a bit roasty, some caramel but it's all a bit thin and metallic." "Nice to see a departure from the norm for a Japanese beer." N/A% alc.

Asahi Super Dry ★★1/2

Pale Lager: Asahi Breweries, , Japan www.asahibeer.co.jp

"Aroma is faint." "Mildest of palates, you could be drinking rice water." "Not worth the import prices as it is really not much better than our own macros." 5% alc.

Aspen Meadow Vanilla Cream Stout ★

Sweet Stout: Gluek Brewing Co., Cold Spring, MN www.gluek.com

"It smells like a vanilla candle and tastes like a cream soda float which has warmed and melted all together." "As watery as a cheap Mexican lager." "I could have just had some vanilla out of the cupboard, but that may not have been as sociable." N/A% alc.

Athenian ★★1/2

Pale Lager: Athenian Brewery (Heineken), Athens, Greece www.beerexports.gr

"Aroma is sweet malts, grains, light fruitiness and light grass." "Sweet malt and floral hops dominate the flavor profile as well." "A very industrial lager." 5% alc.

Atlanta Laughing Skull Bohemian Pilsner ★

Bohem Pilsner: Atlanta Brewing Co., Atlanta, GA www.atlantabrewing.com

"Soapy, slightly funky" aroma. "It's lightly hoppy and bitter." "Mildly dry and smooth in finish, hints of citrus?" "Much more American than Bohemian." 5% alc.

Atlantic Bar Harbor Blueberry Ale ★★★

Fruit Beer: Atlantic Brewing Co., Bar Harbor, ME www.atlanticbrewing.com

"Aroma was exactly like blueberry pancake batter." "Flavor has obvious blueberries, barley and some interesting acidic tones." "Worth trying." 5.2% alc.

Atlantic Bar Harbor Real Ale ★★

Brown Ale: Atlantic Brewing Co., Bar Harbor, ME www.atlanticbrewing.com

"Nose was very light with touches of coffee, chocolate, cherry and toasted malts." "Flavor is cocoa powder, overly toasted grain flavor, floral/ spicy hop." "Verging on the edge of blandness." 5.2% alc.

Atlantic Brewing Coal Porter ★★★

Porter: Atlantic Brewing Co., Bar Harbor, ME www.atlanticbrewing.com

"Incredibly roasty aroma. Lots of cocoa, black coffee, chocolate and malts in there." "Flavor has notes of chocolate, coffee, caramel, dark roasted malt and a light presence of hops." "Good porter." 5.8% alc.

Atlantic Brother Adams Honey Bragget Ale ★★★1/2

Mead: Atlantic Brewing Co., Bar Harbor, ME www.atlanticbrewing.com

"Smells of honey and sweet mead. Caramel. Nutty, vanilla. Fruity, ripe plum. Vinous." "Flavor is rather caramel and honey and very pleasant though I think the palate lacks any lasting finish." 11.8% alc.

Atlantic Mount Desert Island Ginger ★★
Spice/Herb: Atlantic Brewing Co., Bar Harbor, ME www.atlanticbrewing.com
"Ginger-like aroma - smells like the stuff I never eat on a sushi platter." "Flavor of ginger and vanilla, up front, with a bit of wheat sour/dryness." "It's an interesting brew, but I personally wouldn't drink more than one." 5.2% alc.

Augsburger Dark ★
Dunkel: Stevens Point Brewery, Stevens Point, WI www.pointbeer.com
"Aroma is caramel and toast." "Flavors of caramelized malt, some nuttiness and a bit of smoke with a sweet finish." "This was perhaps my first 'dark' beer of any kind. Sad." N/A% alc.

Augsburger Golden ★★★★
Pale Lager: Stevens Point Brewery, Stevens Point, WI www.pointbeer.com
"Malts had elements of toasted bread with an underlying sweetness." "Finished dry and mildly bitter." "A textbook lager." N/A% alc.

Augsburger Oktoberfest ★★
Märzen/Oktbfst: Stevens Point Brewery, Stevens Point, WI www.pointbeer.com
"Aroma has some fresh lake water accents, a hint of mown grass." "Flavor has very brief caramel notes, trace of nuttiness, a bit of metal, not much else." "I like my Oktoberfest beers to be liquid bread, this falls a little short." 5.5% alc.

Augustijn ★★1/2
Abbey Tripel: Brouwerij Van Steenberge, Ertvelde, Belgium www.vansteenberge.com
"Cheesy, woody, sourish aroma with port, figs and orange zest." "Some mild fruits and some bitter malts, but it flamed out poorly in the end with notes of candi sugar." "A little too sweet and generic." 8% alc.

Augustiner Dark ★★
Am Dark Larger: Pittsburgh Brewing Co., Pittsburgh, PA www.pittsburghbrewingco.com
A beer "made primarily out of fall leaves with the burned molasses." "Watery mouthfeel with a sweet ending." "I have a feeling I'll be giving most of these away." 4.3% alc.

Augustiner Edelstoff ★★1/2
Helles/Dortmnd: Augustiner-Bräu, Münich, Germany www.augustiner-braeu.de
"Aroma of grainy malts, grassy hops and traces of citrus fruits." "Flavor is crisp, refreshing well-balanced blend of untoasted malts and noble hops." "Clean, smooth but all in all not very spectacular." 5.6% alc.

Augustiner Lager ★★★
Helles/Dortmnd: Augustiner-Bräu, Münich, Germany www.augustiner-braeu.de
"Faintly earthy aroma but completely unappealing." "Very slight malt presence and absolutely no hops to speak of." "Nothing to see here people, just another pale lager." 5.2% alc.

Augustiner Maximator ★★★★1/2
Doppelbock: Augustiner-Bräu, Münich, Germany www.augustiner-braeu.de
"Thick malt aroma with cherries, brown sugar, alcohol." "Hits all over the mouth with bitterness, sweetness and some smoky notes." "A malt-lover's delight." 7.5% alc.

Avery 14er ESB ★★1/2
Prem Bitter: Avery Brewing Co., Boulder, CO www.averybrewing.com
"Nice aroma mainly of citrus hops and a touch of malt." "Flavor is tangy hops, pale malts, some metallic notes, with somewhat of a flat finish." "A decent session beer but I prefer more hops please." 5% alc.

Avery Ellie's Brown ★★★1/2
Brown Ale: Avery Brewing Co., Boulder, CO www.averybrewing.com
"Heavily nutty nose also displays hints of firewood, earth and charred caramel." "Very smooth on the palate, with lots of chocolate, caramel, vanilla and an underlying nuttiness the flavor." 5.5% alc.

Avery Hog Heaven ★★★★★
Barley Wine: Avery Brewing Co., Boulder, CO www.averybrewing.com
"The aroma is straight up citrusy hops." "Very hoppy accent but a fair bit of sweet malts that dance with each other on the palate." "An intensely hoppy experience." 9.2% alc.

Avery IPA ★★★★
IPA: Avery Brewing Co., Boulder, CO www.averybrewing.com
"Aroma is a luscious greeting of grapefruit and citrus-like hop to my nose." "Hoppy flavor with decent maltiness." "Does not push boundaries. Would make a good starter for someone not acquainted with the style." 6% alc.

Avery Mephistopheles Stout ★★★★
Imp. Stout: Avery Brewing Co., Boulder, CO www.averybrewing.com
Nose is quite sweet with lightly roasted milk chocolate, lactose sugars, and the faintest hint of vanilla. "Nice dry and light flavor but still a good amount of roast and chocolate." "Very creamy and easy to drink. Excellent brew." 15.1% alc.

Avery New World Porter ★★★★1/2
Porter: Avery Brewing Co., Boulder, CO www.averybrewing.com
"Dark burgundy color. Robust aroma is hoppy, with chocolate and toast." "Flavor imparts a very inviting mildly sweet and creamy chocolate base, back by a mild woody and spicy hop finish." 6.7% alc.

Avery Old Jubilation Ale ★★★★1/2
Eng. Strong Ale: Avery Brewing Co., Boulder, CO www.averybrewing.com
"Roasted leathered malts over a bitter hop roasted palate." "Aroma is very strong with lots of dark caramel, sweet toffee and light citrus hops." "Easy drinking even in the summer." 8% alc.

Avery Out of Bounds Stout ★★★★
Dry Stout: Avery Brewing Co., Boulder, CO www.averybrewing.com
"Nutty, toasty, leafy, fruity aroma; lots going on; fun stuff." "Roasty flavors and astringency up front, mellows through cocoa and nutty flavors." "A paean to malt and hops." 5.1% alc.

Avery Salvation ★★★★
Bel. Strong Ale: Avery Brewing Co., Boulder, CO www.averybrewing.com
"Aromas are strong pit fruit, especially peach and some lemon." "Big, full taste, with grass and fruit notes." "Very soft and velvety." "Warm alcohol finish." 9% alc.

Avery The Beast Grand Cru Ale ★★★★1/2
Bel. Strong Ale: Avery Brewing Co., Boulder, CO www.averybrewing.com
"Rich aroma with plenty of raisins, sweet malts and musty wood." "Very sweet, liquourish flavor with lots of malt, sugar, cherries and oaky hints." "A cross between a Belgian Strong and a Barleywine." 14.9% alc.

Avery The Czar ★★★★★
Imp. Stout: Avery Brewing Co., Boulder, CO www.averybrewing.com
"Aromas are coffee, toffee, caramel malt, candied peaches. Kind of like a Heath bar." "Flavors very brandy/port wine -like supported by complexities of dark roasted malts and coffee, fig, charcoal and faint anise." 11.03% alc.

Avery The Kaiser ★★★★★
Märzen/Oktbfst: Avery Brewing Co., Boulder, CO www.averybrewing.com
The basic concept is Imperial Oktoberfest. "Malty, sweet, vineous aroma." "Complex malt, with lots of earthiness and a light flowery hop note." "They've nailed the concept and I quite like it." 8.9% alc.

Avery The Maharaja ★★★★1/2
Imp/Dbl IPA: Avery Brewing Co., Boulder, CO www.averybrewing.com
"Aroma is quite strong...flowery, with hops and fruit quite present in the mix." "The bitterness was nice but was drowned out by the sweet." "Becomes a bit cloying after some time." 9.7% alc.

Avery The Reverend ★★★1/2
Abt/Quadrupel: Avery Brewing Co., Boulder, CO www.averybrewing.com
"Very sweet and fruity aroma - apple, pear, some plum." "Very sweet and very rich." "Thick in the mouth." "Lackluster to say the least." "Good beer but simple for a quadruple." 10% alc.

Avery Thirteen ★★★1/2
Weizen Bock: Avery Brewing Co., Boulder, CO www.averybrewing.com
Aroma is chocolate-covered raisins with some cherry and smoke complexity. "Taste is also bursting with banana, dark fruit and clove flavors that are typical of a Weizenbock, and a spicy hoppiness that is not." "Well-made beer that will age gracefully." 9.5% alc.

Avery White Rascal ★★1/2
Bel. Witbier: Avery Brewing Co., Boulder, CO www.averybrewing.com
"A notice of orange in the aroma and also kind of smells like a flower that has been picked and is a day old." "Flavor is a bit muddled, wheaty spice, tart acidity." 5.5% alc.

Ayinger Altbairisch Dunkel ★★★★★
Dunkel: Ayinger, Aying, Germany www.ayinger-bier.de
"It's a mild nose, but there's peaty malt, some darker fruits, a bit raisiny." "Toasted malt on the tongue with a definite smoky aspect to it." "This beer is fantastic." 5% alc.

Ayinger Brau Weisse ★★★★★
Hefeweizen: Ayinger, Aying, Germany www.ayinger-bier.de
"Aroma has a hint of spice with a huge smell of banana, bubblegum and yeast." "Well integrated lemony, fruity flavors, with hints of banana and clove followed by a pleasantly dry finish." "I can drink this every day and never get tired of it." 5.1% alc.

Ayinger Celebrator ★★★★★
Doppelbock: Ayinger, Aying, Germany www.ayinger-bier.de
"Gorgeous malt aromas enveloped me in chocolate, caramel and dark fruits with a dash of smoke." "Semi-sweet, with dark fruits. Then come woody, earthen tones and the finish as hints of chocolate and caramel." "Tis the season for the good stuff." 6.7% alc.

Ayinger Jahrhundert ★★★★
Helles/Dortmnd: Ayinger, Aying, Germany www.ayinger-bier.de
"Sweet, honeyish aroma, with nutty and malty notes." "Comforting bitterness along with big doughy cookie flavors." "Terrific! I feel this style is very much under-rated." 5.5% alc.

Ayinger Oktober Fest-Marzen ★★★★★
Märzen/Oktbfst: Ayinger, Aying, Germany www.ayinger-bier.de
"Aromas are caramel malt, wheat bread and honeyed toast." "Finishes just dry enough to leave you wanting another sip." "Lean in body, but unfailing in flavor." 5.8% alc.

Ayinger Ur-Weisse ★★★★1/2
Dunkelweizen: Ayinger, Aying, Germany www.ayinger-bier.de
"Smoked banana smells much better than you'd imagine." "Flavor is rich with yeasty, fruity, malt sweetness, spicy notes, subtle sourness and an ever so slight roasty finish." "An exciting, unique Dunkelweizen." 5.8% alc.

Back Road Aviator ★★★1/2
Doppelbock: Back Road Brewery, LaPorte, IN www.backroadbrewery.com
"Dark fruits and bitter chocolate soaked in rum and espresso with generous amounts of anise, vanilla, cinnamon and the crusty propane torched sugar from the top of a crème brûlée." 9% alc.

Back Road Belle Gunness ★★
Dry Stout: Back Road Brewery, LaPorte, IN www.backroadbrewery.com
"Rich coffee and fresh roasted malts dominated the aroma." "This is a very thin-bodied stout but also very easy to drink." "A session stout indeed." 5% alc.

Back Road Christmas Ale ★★★★★
Smoked: Back Road Brewery, LaPorte, IN www.backroadbrewery.com
"Aroma is very strong with mocha and dark chocolates." "Roasted malts, caramel, coffee, vanilla, smoke/ash, spices, molasses, dark chocolate and some woody notes makes this a perfect beer." 8.5% alc.

Back Road Millennium Lager ★★★1/2
Helles/Dortmnd: Back Road Brewery, LaPorte, IN www.backroadbrewery.com
"Dough, grass and citrus hops aroma and some caramel malts." "Smooth malts upfront." "No traditional malt sweetness; this is grassy, dandeliony." "Yes, it's that good and I'm a freak for this style." 5% alc.

Back Road No. 9 Barleywine ★★1/2
Barley Wine: Back Road Brewery, LaPorte, IN www.backroadbrewery.com
"Starts you with the expected hefty malt, then a very sweet middle and an somewhat nutty end." "Not complex, but nonetheless enjoyable if you have no other barley wine available." 10% alc.

Backcountry Peak One Porter ★★1/2
Porter: Backcountry Brewery, Frisco, CO www.backcountrybrewery.com
"Aroma is a little sweet, with chocolate, toasted malt and hops that are a bit grassy." "Bittersweet mocha tone." "A good porter, even better would it have more esters and a bigger body." 6% alc.

Backcountry Telemark IPA ★★1/2
IPA: Backcountry Brewery, Frisco, CO www.backcountrybrewery.com
"Boasts an aroma of nice piney hoppiness and a touch of caramel malt." "The hops in this are nice." "Malt backbone is just simply plain with no distinctive flavors and not much body." 5.6% alc.

Bahia ★
Pale Lager: Cerveceria Centro Americana, Guatemala City, Guatemala www.cerveceria.com.gt
"Smells like a frathouse bedroom after a skunk died in the hamper." "Flavor is sweet malty with notes of straw and a thin body." "A mother would disown her child for less." 4.6% alc.

Baladin Nora ★★★
Traditional Ale: Le Baladin, Piozzo, Italy www.Birreria.com
"Nose of medium sweet malts, bananas and dark fruits." "Orange-pineapple-cherry esters with pepper and spruce spiciness and floral-vanilla tones." "The market's been closed for many hours, but the day's fragrances still hover." 6.8% alc.

Ballantine XXX Ale ★
Goldn/Blond Ale: Pabst Brewing Co., Chicago , IL www.pabst.com
"Slight spicy hop presence, decent balance and very light mossy, earthy nuances toward the finish." "Better than the standard macro." 5.1% alc.

Ballast Point Big Eye IPA ★★★★
IPA: Ballast Point Brewing Co., San Diego, CA www.ballastpoint.com
"Crisp, bracingly hoppy and well balanced." "Juicy aroma is piney, strongly resinous, pineapple, grapefruit." "Not the hoppiest IPA, but very good flavor and aroma with a good dry finish." 6% alc.

Ballast Point Black Marlin Porter ★★★
Porter: Ballast Point Brewing Co., San Diego, CA www.ballastpoint.com
"Nose is quite smoky right out the bottle." "Nice coffee character in the flavor with restrained sweetness, but still plenty of richness and some light bitterness." "A well balanced porter." 5.5% alc.

Ballast Point Calico Amber ★★★★1/2

Prem Bitter: Ballast Point Brewing Co., San Diego, CA www.ballastpoint.com

"Malt gives it the signature ESB backbone while something more earth centered contributes the rest." "Flavor is of abundant hops and overtoasted malt." "A very tasty amber if you can find it!" 5% alc.

Ballast Point Yellowtail Pale ★★1/2

Kölsch: Ballast Point Brewing Co., San Diego, CA www.ballastpoint.com

Described by the brewery as a Kölsch, Yellowtail has a "grainy pale malt aroma" and "sweet malty flavor almost like frosted flakes." "Perfect for someone who has never tried anything outside of the BMC [Bud-Miller-Coors] range." 4.6% alc.

Baltika 1 Lyogkoe (Light) ★★★

Pale Lager: Baltika Brewery , St. Petersburg, Russia www.baltika.ru

"Perfumed aromas on the initial pour, settling to indistinct malts." "Soft in the mouth, the sweet malts continue, along with some wispy grassiness." "Maybe my new favorite light beer." 4.4% alc.

Baltika 3 Klassicheskoe (Classic) ★★1/2

Pale Lager: Baltika Brewery , St. Petersburg, Russia www.baltika.ru

"Grainy aroma with green apple notes." "Taste is crisp with a nice mellow hop flavor." "This is truly a forgettable beer, I didn't realize I'd even drunk it until I saw the bottle weeks later!" 4.8% alc.

Baltika 4 Original ★★

Dunkel: Baltika Brewery , St. Petersburg, Russia www.baltika.ru

"Aroma is toasty and caramel like." "Clean and favorable notes of dryer caramel and whole grain toast." "Sweeter than the average Dunkel." 5.6% alc.

Baltika 5 Zolotoe (Golden) ★★★

Pale Lager: Baltika Brewery , St. Petersburg, Russia www.baltika.ru

"Crisp golden lager with faint honeyish notes and hints of malt." "Aroma is malty sweet with little detectable adjuncts." "Fairly clean and slightly heavier than most of its stablemates." 5.3% alc.

Baltika 6 Porter ★★★

Baltic Porter: Baltika Brewery , St. Petersburg, Russia www.baltika.ru

"Very malty, sweetish roasted aroma with chocolate, cold coffee." "Really dense caramel malts give this a scotch ale quality." "A little rough around the edges, which seems to be consistent with Russian beers." 7% alc.

Baltika 7 Eksportnoe (Export) ★★1/2

Pale Lager: Baltika Brewery , St. Petersburg, Russia www.baltika.ru

"Nose is archetypal lager sweet malt that is fresh, crisp and clean." "Sweetish, yet husky grain flavors." "Take an American Light beer, add sugar and dilute it to half strength and you have Baltika 7." 5.4% alc.

Baltika 8 Pshenichnoe (Wheat) ★★

Hefeweizen: Baltika Brewery , St. Petersburg, Russia www.baltika.ru

"Aroma and flavor are both simple and pleasant, with no big flaws - just an on-style wheat with a refreshing, summery character." "Quenching, wheaty, fruity character." 5% alc.

Baltika 9 Krepkoe (Strong) ★★★

Malt Liquor: Baltika Brewery , St. Petersburg, Russia www.baltika.ru

"The aroma brought back memories. Bad ones." "A better malt flavor and the warm feeling in my belly make it an improvement over the popular American corn beers, but there's not much good to say about this one." 8% alc.

Bar Harbor Cadillac Mountain Stout ★★★★★

Dry Stout: Bar Harbor Brewing Co., Bar Harbor, ME www.barharborbrewing.com

#1 Dry Stout on Ratebeer for several years. "Aroma of sweet roasty chocolate malt and subtle coffee." "The flavor is of coffee, chocolate malts, slightly sweet, some vanilla and cream." "A surprising gem." 5% alc.

Bar Harbor Lighthouse Ale ★★1/2
Mild Ale: Bar Harbor Brewing Co., Bar Harbor, ME www.barharborbrewing.com
"Tinny maltedness." "Watery mouthfeel but good malt taste. Very smooth and not bitter." "Finish gives an ever so slight cocoa flavor." 0% alc.

Bar Harbor Thunder Hole Ale ★★★
Brown Ale: Bar Harbor Brewing Co., Bar Harbor, ME www.barharborbrewing.com
"Spicy and nutty aromas." "Good flavor of malt, nuts and caramel." "Quite malty and has a nice full flavor." "Could have done without all the thunder hole jokes though." 5% alc.

Barbar Belgian Honey Ale ★★1/2
Bel. Strong Ale: Brasserie Lefebvre, Rebecq-Quenast, Belgium www.brasserielefebvre.be
"Wheat aroma, slight pepper, mildly phenolic." "Yeasty character, vaguely bananish phenols conjure images of a 'dirty Weihenstephan' yeast." "Not nearly as distinctive as I'd anticipated." 8% alc.

Barbar Winter Bok ★★★★
Bock: Brasserie Lefebvre, Rebecq-Quenast, Belgium www.brasserielefebvre.be
"Combo of sweet honey, slight tobacco, caramel and demerara (sugar)." "Deliciously spicy, lots of holiday spices, pine. Some honey, thick mouthfeel." "Tastes exactly like one would imagine a Belgian bock to taste." 8% alc.

Barbary Coast Gold Rush Style Beer ★
Calif. Common: Joseph Huber Brewing Co., Monroe, WI www.berghoffbeer.com
"Aroma is toast, caramel and the faintest of hops." "Taste is a bit worse off with sweet malts, light caramel and watery hops." "All in all it was a pleasant drinking experience." N/A% alc.

Bard's Tale Dragons Gold ★
Traditional Ale: Flying Bison Brewing, Buffalo, NY www.flyingbisonbrewing.com
"Light hops aroma. A bit of grass, some citrus and some floral notes." "Flavor is lemony, hoppy and some notes of light malt behind." "I'm sure that it will be a godsend to people who can't handle gluten.. Just not for me." 4.3% alc.

Barkley Sound Honey Almond Light ★★
Pale Lager: Gluek Brewing Co., Cold Spring, MN www.gluek.com
"Golden, near headless lager, watery and thankfully near tasteless." "No body whatsoever." "Not truly repulsive, but still distasteful and nothing resembling beer." N/A% alc.

Barley Creek Angler Black Lager (Black Widow) ★★
Schwarzbier: Barley Creek Brewing Co., Tannersville, PA www.barleycreek.com
"Aroma is light roast - weak coffee, some sweetness." "Some chocolate flavor accompanied by a slight coffee taste." "I suspect that this brewer has some quality control issues." 4.8% alc.

Barley Creek Antler Brown Ale ★★
Brown Ale: Barley Creek Brewing Co., Tannersville, PA www.barleycreek.com
"Initially a quite fruity aroma with notes of raisins and plums, it quickly picks up notes of toasty malt and a hint of roast coffee." "Austere mix of toasted malt and a hint of roast character." 4.8% alc.

Barley Creek Navigator Golden Ale (Aussie Gold) ★★1/2
Goldn/Blond Ale: Barley Creek Brewing Co., Tannersville, PA www.barleycreek.com
"Aroma is quite fruity with notes of fresh cut tart apples, banana and clove." "It has some breadiness but the sweet overtones minimize that factor." "A curious combination of slightly sweet and sour flavors at the same time." 5.6% alc.

Barley Creek Rescue IPA (SuperHOP) ★★★
IPA: Barley Creek Brewing Co., Tannersville, PA www.barleycreek.com
"Floral aroma with a bit of caramel malt mixed in." "Hop bitters stay in your mouth until you brush your teeth a half dozen times." "Quite hoppalicious." 5.8% alc.

Barley Island Bourbon Barrel-Aged Oatmeal Stout ★★1/2
Sweet Stout: Barley Island Brewing, Noblesville, IN www.barleyisland.com
"Aroma of bourbon, vanilla, oak, alcohol." "Malty sweet with noticeable oat and chocolate overtones before leading toward a vanilla and oaky midsection." "With some tweaking, this beer could rock." 4.9% alc.

Barley Island Bourbon Barrel-Aged Porter ★★★1/2
Porter: Barley Island Brewing, Noblesville, IN www.barleyisland.com
"Tastes of whisky, bourbon, light coffee and light chocolates." "Could stand to be a bit heavier." "The standard porter aromas were very obscured by the bourbon and unbalanced." 4.1% alc.

Bass Pale Ale ★★1/2
Prem Bitter: Samlesbury (InBev), Preston, Lancashire, England www.inbev.com
"Aroma is spicy and fruity - with hints of nuts and caramel." "Taste starts out bitter and gets a malty sweetness midway through the glass." "A true middle of the road beer." 5% alc.

Bavaria 8.6 ★★★
Malt Liquor: Bavaria Brouwerij (HOL), Lieshout, Netherlands www.bavaria.nl
"Sweet malty beer with lots of body for the style." "Hint of booze in the aroma and a very slight burn in the throat when it finishes." "A lot easier to put down than many other malt liquors though." 7.9% alc.

Bavaria Pilsner ★
Premium Lager: Bavaria Brouwerij (HOL), Lieshout, Netherlands www.bavaria.nl
"Heavy grassy-hoppy aroma...plus hints of graininess." "Thick bready malts blend with grassy noble hops on the palate." "One of the better beers from NETHERLANDS!" 5% alc.

Bayerischer Bahnhof Original Leipziger Gose ★★1/2
Traditional Ale: Gasthaus & Gosebrauerei Leipzig, Germany www.bayerischer-bahnhof.de
"Wheat aroma, slight pepper, mildly phenolic." "Yeasty character, vaguely bananish phenols conjure images of a 'dirty Weihenstephan' yeast." "Not nearly as distinctive as I'd anticipated." 4.6% alc.

Bayern Hefeweizen ★★1/2
Am. Wheat: Bayern Brewing, Missoula, MT www.bayernbrewery.com
"Sweet and estery nose is pleasant, but not very reminiscent of a Hefeweizen." "Very smooth and clean wheat aspect. Quite palatable, but a bit boring." 5.6% alc.

Bayern Montana Trout Slayer Ale ★
Kristallweizen: Bayern Brewing, Missoula, MT www.bayernbrewery.com
"Pale wheat nose, slight graininess, touch of cardboard." "Sweet enough and with the light hoppiness, it's not crisp at all." "I struggled to get through it but did, about one tastebud away from being a drainpour." 5.6% alc.

Bayern Oktoberfest ★★1/2
Märzen/Oktbfst: Bayern Brewing, Missoula, MT www.bayernbrewery.com
"Dark, bready aroma, slight soy, lightly spiced." "Flavor is pretty malty and a bit too much of residual sugar." "Getting harder and harder to find a good fresh lager around Oktoberfest time, this one will certainly do..." 6% alc.

Bayern Pilsner ★★★
Pilsner: Bayern Brewing, Missoula, MT www.bayernbrewery.com
"It's mildly bitter and grassy, but never hints at anything I'd consider hoppy." "Nose is yeasty, malty with the fresh aroma of noble hops springing out of the glass!" 5% alc.

Bayhawk Chocolate Porter ★
Porter: Bayhawk Ales, Irvine, CA www.bayhawkales.com
"Nose is of roasted sewage and chocolate covered roadkill." "Light chocolate with vinegar notes and vegetable-like substance." "Yep, I checked the label. It's not a vinaigrette." 5.4% alc.

Bayhawk CPA ★★

Am. Pale Ale: Bayhawk Ales, Irvine, CA www.bayhawkales.com

"Aroma is lightly sweet malts, sugar cookies, honey, clover and earthy hops." "Taste is medium sweet, herbal, some earthy, lime, light biscuit." "Hops don't quite have the bite they should." 5.4% alc.

Beamish Irish Stout ★★1/2

Dry Stout: Beamish and Crawford (Scottish & Newcastle), Cork , Ireland www.beamish.ie

"Bittersweet chocolate aroma." "Taste is all roasted malts, but with a slightly bitter hoppy finish." "Very easy to drink even for someone who is afraid of stouts." 4.1% alc.

Bear Republic Big Bear Black Stout ★★★★★

Imp. Stout: Bear Republic Brewing Co., Healdsburg, CA www.bearrepublic.com

On the lighter side for an Imperial Stout, it "brings a dry stout to Imperial size without getting too chewy or fruity." "Chocolaty, malty, at first and well-balanced by the Cascade hops and a dry, licorice-like aftertaste." 8.1% alc.

Bear Republic Hop Rod Rye ★★★★★

Am Strong Ale: Bear Republic Brewing Co., Healdsburg, CA www.bearrepublic.com

A terrific, unique beer. An IPA with a substantial portion of rye malt. "Toasty and woody with dashes of lemon juice." "Finishes with a nice bitter dry finish that keeps you coming back for more." "A steal." 7.5% alc.

Bear Republic Racer 5 ★★★★★

IPA: Bear Republic Brewing Co., Healdsburg, CA www.bearrepublic.com

Multi-award-winning IPA featuring Columbus and Cascade hops. "Floral, sweet, hoppy nose." "Flavor is malty up front, but from mid swallow on, it's all hops." "Oh Bear Republic, have I told you lately how much I love you?" 7% alc.

Bear Republic Red Rocket ★★★★1/2

Am Strong Ale: Bear Republic Brewing Co., Healdsburg, CA www.bearrepublic.com

"This is an absolutely terrific beer to look at." "Nice semi-sweet caramel malt hits your tongue and slides all around, leaving your mouth happy." "Long sticky hoppy finish." 6.8% alc.

Bear Republic XP ★★★★

Am. Pale Ale: Bear Republic Brewing Co., Healdsburg, CA www.bearrepublic.com

XP = Extra Pale. "Big aroma of fresh hops along with citrus, maple and a touch of sweet malt. Smells fantastic!" "Body is creamy and bitter. Ripe tangerines, light grapefruit, maple, sweet malts and fresh hops." 5.4% alc.

Becks ★★

Premium Lager: Brauerei Beck and Co./Becks (InBev), Bremen, Germany www.becks-beer.com

"Heavy grain and light hops aroma." "A little fruity, clean and hoppy." "Clean tasting, light malt character with faint hop flavor ." "Interchangable with Heineken to me." 4.8% alc.

Becks Alkoholfrei ★

Low Alcohol: Brauerei Beck and Co./Becks (InBev), Bremen, Germany www.becks-beer.com

"Smell and taste of a wort made entirely of pale malt." ""Flavor is like mineral water, finish is a tad bitter and a bit harsh." "The worst skunked hops I have ever tasted, stale candy corn, crackers and corn. Very bad." 0.3% alc.

Becks Dark ★

Dunkel: Brauerei Beck and Co./Becks (InBev), Bremen, Germany www.becks-beer.com

"Smells of dark malts and grains." "It has a dark roast coffee/chocolate flavor that is not very complex." "Fairly tasteless but at least not disgusting." 4.8% alc.

Becks Light ★

Pale Lager: Brauerei Beck and Co./Becks (InBev), Bremen, Germany www.becks-beer.com

"Stale, skunky faint grassy, cooked corn-dimethyl sulfide in the nose." "Flavor? What flavor? There's virtually nothing here at all, perhaps the lightest of light-struck mineral-water with vague traces of celery." 3.8% alc.

Becks Oktoberfest ★★

Märzen/Oktbfst: Brauerei Beck and Co./Becks (InBev), Bremen, Germany www.becks-beer.com

"There is a very light malt aroma but overall not much there." "It has some of that caramel-malt sweetness indicative of the style. The problem is that it's rather watery and not nearly robust enough." 5% alc.

Beer Lao ★★

Pale Lager: Lao Brewery Co (Carlsberg), Vientiane, Laos

"Hugely husky, grainy, cereal malt aroma." "Very sweet, grainy though fairly hoppy in flavor." "Not bad for a foreign lager." 5% alc.

Beermanns Lincoln Lager ★★★

Helles/Dortmnd: Beermanns Beerwerks Brewery, Lincoln, CA www.beermanns.com

"Really nice aroma - some honey sweetness, fruity/grassy hops and fresh bread." "Sweet, mellow biscuity malts, a bit of citrus, earthy and floral hoppiness." "Pretty good - far better than expected." 4.7% alc.

Beermanns Rip Roarin' Red ★★★★★

Amber Ale: Beermanns Beerwerks Brewery, Lincoln, CA www.beermanns.com

A top-10 amber ale. "My first thought upon smelling this was, 'Wow, that's different!'" "A wonderfully complex brew; constantly shifting - hoppy, malty, chocolate and back to hops, then caramel." 6.3% alc.

Belhaven Scottish Ale ★★★1/2

Bitter: Belhaven (Greene King), Dunbar, East Lothian, Scotland www.belhaven.co.uk

"Aroma is toasty, slightly breadcrusty, a little bit minerally." "Nice sweet smoky flavors, with hints of caramel and malts." "Classic bitter with a Scottish touch." "This would be a tremendous session ale." 3.9% alc.

Belhaven St. Andrews Ale ★★1/2

Prem Bitter: Belhaven (Greene King), Dunbar, East Lothian, Scotland www.belhaven.co.uk

"The aroma is toasted malt with a certain earthy element." "Flavor was malty sweet with a washed out hoppy bitterness in the finish." "Doesn't have any head turning characteristics but just a nice slurpable drop." 4.6% alc.

Belhaven Twisted Thistle IPA ★★★12

IPA: Belhaven (Greene King), Dunbar, Scotland www.belhaven.co.uk

"Cranberry, peach fruitiness, light earthiness in the aroma." "Fairly complex flavor with a cheesy, tobaccoey note, a random herbal quality and subdued fruitiness." "Interesting premium bitter but ultimately like putting a great sound system in a Tercel. It has some pretty cool features, but the overall package really isn't that enticing." 6.1% alc.

Belhaven Wee Heavy ★★★★★

Scotch Ale: Belhaven (Greene King), Dunbar, East Lothian, Scotland www.belhaven.co.uk

"Rich oat and malt aroma with an excellent sweep of cream, apples and light cinnamon." "Flavor is sweet caramel and mellowed honey, with a burst of supple fruits and chewy grains steeped in molasses and brown sugar." 6.5% alc.

Bell's Amber Ale ★★★★1/2

Amber Ale: Bells Brewery, Inc., Kalamazoo, MI www.bellsbeer.com

"Aroma is malty, caramel and a touch of hops." "Taste is sweeter than I expected from an amber, with a touch of lemon and just the slightest hop kick." "Not very complex, but it's crisp and refreshing." 6% alc.

Bell's Beer ★★★★

Premium Lager: Bells Brewery, Inc., Kalamazoo, MI www.bellsbeer.com

"It looks and smells very ale-like- cloudy with a puffy head. Nice aroma, very fruity." "Flavor was abundant of malts, some caramels and some light lemon hints." "A prototype for pale lagers." 4.5% alc.

Bell's Best Brown ★★★★★
Brown Ale: Bells Brewery, Inc., Kalamazoo, MI www.bellsbeer.com
"The quintessential brown ale - just a touch of nuttiness with a faint sour quality from the yeast, a bit of woody smoke, delicious in every way and hefty too." 6.6% alc.

Bell's Cherry Stout ★★★★1/2
Fruit Beer: Bells Brewery, Inc., Kalamazoo, MI www.bellsbeer.com
"Aroma of roasted grain and tart cherries." "Flavor is roasted malt, some chocolate, coffee and definitely some cherry tartness behind it all and very evident on the finish." "Quite different for a fruit beer." 8.5% alc.

Bell's Consecrator ★★★1/2
Doppelbock: Bells Brewery, Inc., Kalamazoo, MI www.bellsbeer.com
"Dark, fleshy fruits (cherry, etc) aroma, some toffee, some rum, some bubblegum and nuts." "Plums and brown sugariness dominate the taste immediately." "Respectable caramelly backbone." 8% alc.

Bell's Eccentric Ale ★★★★★
Spice/Herb: Bells Brewery, Inc., Kalamazoo, MI www.bellsbeer.com
"Filthy mud color." "Chocolate, cinnamon, clove and mint in the aroma." "Lots of biscuity malt and earthy yeast provide the backbone. Anise, toffee, caramel, cinnamon, clove, pine and molasses are just some of the flavor motifs." 11% alc.

Bell's Expedition Stout ★★★★★
Imp. Stout: Bells Brewery, Inc., Kalamazoo, MI www.bellsbeer.com
"Rich, vinous nose, faint hint of roast, deep fruit (cherry, plums), alcohol." "Intense flavors of alcohol, coffee, big rich fruitiness, wine, burnt cherry and Christmas fruitcake." "This one ages brilliantly - buy some extra for the cellar. 11.5% alc.

Bell's Java Stout ★★★★1/2
Stout: Bells Brewery, Inc., Kalamazoo, MI www.bellsbeer.com
"Very cappuccino/espresso like and chocolates and roastiness." "My two favorite things, beer and coffee, in one bottle." "A coffee lover's dream." 7.5% alc.

Bell's Kalamazoo Stout ★★★★★
Stout: Bells Brewery, Inc., Kalamazoo, MI www.bellsbeer.com
"Aroma is tons of roasted barley, chocolate, some coffee and some licorice." "Finish is so damn smooth." "Taste is very creamy-like with a nice dose of chocolate." 6.5% alc.

Bell's Oberon Ale ★★★★★
Am. Wheat: Bells Brewery, Inc., Kalamazoo, MI www.bellsbeer.com
"Crisp, wheaty, white bread aroma with some lemon and a bit of spice." "Quite flavorful for as light as it seems." "I may have just found a new summer session beer." 6% alc.

Bell's Pale Ale ★★★
Am. Pale Ale: Bells Brewery, Inc., Kalamazoo, MI www.bellsbeer.com
Spicy hop aroma, some citrus, light caramel underneath." "Strong hop bitterness with flavors that evoke both grapefruit and fresh vegetables." "Balance is a reductionary exposition" 5.3% alc.

Bell's Porter ★★★★1/2
Porter: Bells Brewery, Inc., Kalamazoo, MI www.bellsbeer.com
"Aroma is roasty with malts, chocolate and coffee." "Strong roastiness in the flavor, combined with caramel and chocolate." "Nice and chewy." 6% alc.

Bell's Sparkling Ale ★★★★
Bel. Strong Ale: Bells Brewery, Inc., Kalamazoo, MI www.bellsbeer.com
"Flavor is dominated by spice (mostly clove) and is very sweet with candi sugar." "Sweet, flowery finish." "Struck me like a Piraat clone." 8.2% alc.

Bell's Special Double Cream Stout ★★★★★
Sweet Stout: Bells Brewery, Inc., Kalamazoo, MI www.bellsbeer.com
"Fruity aroma with chocolate, coffee and prune notes." "The lack of roasted notes surprised me, although this allowed the chocolate and vanilla flavors to shine through." 7.5% alc.

Bell's Winter White ★★★
Bel. Witbier: Bells Brewery, Inc., Kalamazoo, MI www.bellsbeer.com
"Aroma is of wheat, yeast, banana and a little clove." "Crisp wheat flavor, with a background of soft hops, finish is fruity and yeasty." "A good hoppy spicy kick toward the end." 4.5% alc.

Bellegems Bruin ★★1/2
Flem Sour Ale: Bockor, Bellegem, Belgium www.bockor.be
"Smells of wild cherries, sugar, over ripe fruit." "Slight bit of sour wood, dark cherries, but overall weak in flavor." "More like a Flemish sour for beginners than a bruin." 5.5% alc.

Belle-Vue Kriek ★★
Fruit Lambic: Belle-Vue (InBev), Sint-Pieters-Leeuw, Belgium www.inbev.com
"Medicinal, spicy cherry taste with muted acid levels." "Mild acidity and lactic notes to start, quickly followed by sweet cherries." "My cough is doing much better, thank you." 5.2% alc.

Belzebuth ★★
Bel. Strong Ale: Brasserie Grain d'Orge , Ronchin, France www.brasserie-graindorge.com
"Very malty, slightly fruity like a strong ale." "Tastes blew up on my tongue of a bitter-sweet, hoppy alcohol. Finished with a breath of fire." "This one is a bit rough." 11.8% alc.

Berghoff Famous Bock ★★
Bock: Joseph Huber Brewing Co., Monroe, WI www.berghoffbeer.com
"Aroma is light caramel and some wood." "Flavor is more toffee than chocolate and these are introduced early in the flavor along with mild floral hops." "Body is very thin and sticky." 5.4% alc.

Berghoff Famous Red ★★
Am. Pale Ale: Joseph Huber Brewing Co., Monroe, WI www.berghoffbeer.com
"Dandelion-and-weed aroma." "Caramel malts, butter and fruity esters with some herbal hop notes and fair bitterness." "Pretty boring for a micro." 5.6% alc.

Berghoff Genuine Dark Beer ★★
Vienna: Joseph Huber Brewing Co., Monroe, WI www.berghoffbeer.com
"Sweet roasted malts on the aroma, but very weak and non-distinct." "Sweet, malty and caramelly with a slight candi sugar note." "As average as average can get." 5.4% alc.

Berghoff Hefe-Weizen ★★1/2
Hefeweizen: Joseph Huber Brewing Co., Monroe, WI www.berghoffbeer.com
"Light wheat aroma with banana/orange juice highlights." "Initially sweet taste with a quick dash of citrus and banana." "Not bad, a thin bodied example using authentic ingredients." 5.2% alc.

Berghoff OktoberFest ★★1/2
Märzen/Oktbfst: Joseph Huber Brewing Co., Monroe, WI www.berghoffbeer.com
"Caramel malt aroma with strong fruity esters." "Caramel provided much of the flavor, backed by some general toastiness and some bright hops toward the finish." "Missing the complexity of most other Oktoberfests that I have tried." 5.2% alc.

Berghoff Original Lager ★★★★
Pale Lager: Joseph Huber Brewing Co., Monroe, WI www.berghoffbeer.com
"Light hop and caramel grain aroma." "Flavor is bready, buttery, good hop bitterness, malty with a dry finish." "Nothing great here but decent for the style." 5.5% alc.

Berghoff Pale Ale ★★
Am. Pale Ale: Joseph Huber Brewing Co., Monroe, WI www.berghoffbeer.com
"Aroma has notes of grassy and floral hops, pale and bready malts, light note of grapefruit and apple, some veggie esters as well." "Mildly bitter with a good balance of malt character." 5.8% alc.

Berkshire Ale ★★1/2
Am. Pale Ale: Berkshire Brewing Co., South Deerfield, MA www.berkshirebrewingcompany.com
"Hoppy with caramel aroma." "Moderately sweet and a somewhat bitter finish." "Nice job on the malts with this beer." "Calls this a pale ale but this is really full bodied and rich." 6.3% alc.

Berkshire Cabin Fever ★★★
Am Strong Ale: Berkshire Brewing Co., South Deerfield, MA www.berkshirebrewingcompany.com
"Very earthy, with a cinnamon, maple flavor that is balanced with a mild dose of Noble hops." "Taste is very caramelly with some strange nutty elements on the finish." 6.3% alc.

Berkshire Coffeehouse Porter ★★★1/2
Porter: Berkshire Brewing Co., South Deerfield, MA www.berkshirebrewingcompany.com
Aroma was a wonderful mix of mocha, roasted malts and straight coffee." "Who knows what the underlying beer is, the coffee simply dominates." "Sessionable coffee beer for sure." 6.2% alc.

Berkshire Drayman's Porter ★★★★
Porter: Berkshire Brewing Co., South Deerfield, MA www.berkshirebrewingcompany.com
"Malty roasty dark chocolate flavors, light malt bitterness." "Medium-bodied, roasty and fairly simple, yet quaffable and tasty." "I wish I had more." 6.2% alc.

Berkshire Golden Spike ★
Kölsch: Berkshire Brewing Co., South Deerfield, MA www.berkshirebrewingcompany.com
"Aroma is slightly hoppy with hints of grass and citrus." "Tastes of lemon, grass and spices with a slightly bitter peppery finish." "Why does a Kölsch seem to mean zero malt sweetness to most American brewers?." N/A% alc.

Berkshire Holidale ★★1/2
Barley Wine: Berkshire Brewing Co., South Deerfield, MA www.berkshirebrewingcompany.com
"Quite sweet aroma with licorice hints and some piney hops." "Flavor...shows the interplay of sweet, fruity malt and strong spice." "Strong and warming." 9.5% alc.

Berkshire Imperial Stout ★★★1/2
Imp. Stout: Berkshire Brewing Co., South Deerfield, MA www.berkshirebrewingcompany.com
"Chocolate, figs, raisins, roasted malts, coffee and smoke made up the aroma." "Full-bodied with semi-sweet chocolate, malt and caramel flavors bord+B1035ering on cloying." "Watery for an Imperial Stout." 8.5% alc.

Berkshire Lost Sailor Indian Pale Ale ★★1/2
IPA: Berkshire Brewing Co., South Deerfield, MA www.berkshirebrewingcompany.com
"Aroma follows through on a medium-bodied palate with a hoppy character." "Surprising amount of fruit flavors and the malts seemed about right." "Probably the fruitiest IPA I have ever had." 5.5% alc.

Berkshire Oktoberfest ★★
Märzen/Oktbfst: Berkshire Brewing Co., South Deerfield, MA www.berkshirebrewingcompany.com
"Malty bready slightly acidic aroma." "Lacks sweetness or roastiness like I expect from the style." "It wasn't bad, just outclassed." 6% alc.

Berkshire Raspberry Strong Ale ★★★1/2
Fruit Beer: Berkshire Brewing Co., South Deerfield, MA www.berkshirebrewingcompany.com
"Raspberry jam and fresh cut grass in the somewhat medicinal (alcohol) and sugary sweet aroma." "Flavor is of raspberries, alcohol, sweet and tart/tangy." "More like a fruit wine as the alcohol is over the top." 9% alc.

Berkshire River Ale ★★1/2
Brown Ale: Berkshire Brewing Co., South Deerfield, MA www.berkshirebrewingcompany.com
"Toffee caramel-like sweetness to start, turning very mildly roasty to finish." "Mostly fruity with caramel that finishes bittersweet." "Easy, smooth drinking." 7% alc.

Berkshire Shabadoo Black and Tan ★★1/2
Porter: Berkshire Brewing Co., South Deerfield, MA www.berkshirebrewingcompany.com
"Very malty aroma." "One gulp tastes of their porter, the next tastes of a nice pale ale." "Bit tangy at the very end, with the yeast, hops and roast combined pretty well." 6.3% alc.

Berkshire Springs Stock Ale ★
Amber Ale: Joseph Huber Brewing Co., Monroe, WI www.berghoffbeer.com
"Aroma consists mostly of malt with caramel notes, along with some grassy hops and a touch of hay." "Hoppy but smooth." "Flavor is mild but respectable amber ale." 5% alc.

Berkshire Steel Rail Extra Pale ★★
Am. Pale Ale: Berkshire Brewing Co., South Deerfield, MA www.berkshirebrewingcompany.com
"Nose is fruity and malty, strength on the light side." "Medium body with mild bitterness, sweet malt and hops along with a bit of fruit flavoring." "None of the flavors are very assertive but it is a refreshing concoction." 5.3% alc.

Berliner Kindl Weisse ★★1/2
Berliner Weisse: Berliner Kindl Brauerei AG, Berlin, Germany www.berliner-kindl.de
Definitely a love it or hate it beer. "Slightly tart, yeasty aroma with a bit of lemon." "Very sour flavor, but not as extreme as I expected. Lemony notes." "Cutting acidity; quite refreshing." 2.7% alc.

BFM Abbaye de Saint Bon-Chien ★★★★
Barley Wine: Brasseries des Franches-Montagnes, Saignelégier, Switz. www.brasseriebfm.ch
Highly vinous and a touch sour, full of richness in the caramelized malts and dried fruit. "Grapes and chocolate are multifaceted, covering themselves with nuances of anise, peat, rye bread." "This is really cool stuff." 10% alc.

BFM Cuvée du 7ème ★★★1/2
Bière de Garde: Brasseries des Franches-Montagnes, Saignelégier, Switz. www.brasseriebfm.ch
Aromas are of an oaky dry tart element, with some peaty malts, spicy florals and funky grains. "Floral and hoppily bitter with more light herbal notes, yeast and dried fruits." "Strange brew. Good stuff, though." 7.5% alc.

Bière Darbyste ★★★★
Traditional Ale: Brasserie de Blaugies, Dour-Blaugies, Belgium www.brasseriedeblaugies.com
"Has a bit of everything: citrus, floral, raisins, vinous/grassy feels, barnyard." "Soft bodied, it has a refreshingly, lightly sour flavor of grapefruit, yeast and a lively spiciness." "It's smooth, yet pleasingly funky tasting." 5.8% alc.

Bière des Sans Culottes ★★★
Bière de Garde: Brasserie La Choulette, Hordain, France www.lachoulette.com
"Promising aroma has sweet malts, light fruits, hops and some spices." "Sweet malt, cherries and apples, yeast and some spicing." "Pairs well with mild cheese like American camembert." 7% alc.

Big Hole Diablo ★★1/2
Bel. Strong Ale: Big Hole Brewing Co., Belgrade, MT
"Spicy banana, clove, yeasty, sweet aroma." "Taste was very bland, sweet, light spices and chocolate." "It's got its place in the world, but I just can't seem to find it." 7.5% alc.

Big Hole Headstrong Pale Ale ★★1/2
Eng Pale Ale: Big Hole Brewing Co., Belgrade, MT
"Pine and toffee malt aroma that is not too aggressively hopped." "Potent caramel with fading, but supportive wooden hop bitterness." "I really liked this ale and will be stocking up for the summer... and for the winter." 5.7% alc.

Big Hole Mythical White Grand Cru ★★1/2

Bel. Strong Ale: Big Hole Brewing Co., Belgrade, MT

"Great aroma. Lots of lemon zest, candi sugar, earthy hops somewhat grassy in away." "Starts fruity and lightly malty. A large vane of spice run throughout and ends up peppery and papery on the finish" 7% alc.

Big Hole Wisdom Amber ★★

Amber Ale: Big Hole Brewing Co., Belgrade, MT

"Heavily burnt toffee and caramel with roasted malt tones in the nose and a touch of molasses and black currants." "Strong nutty flavor with some roasted malt following behind and a tiny bit of caramelized sugars." 5% alc.

Big Sky Crystal Ale ★★

Goldn/Blond Ale: Big Sky Brewing Co., Missoula, MT www.bigskybrew.com

"The taste has a slight herbal quality notes of bread crust and a little bit of oranges." "When 'actively sucky' is the best I can come up with for a compliment, I'm probably not having a particularly good drinking experience." 4.7% alc.

Big Sky Moose Drool ★★★★

Brown Ale: Big Sky Brewing Co., Missoula, MT www.bigskybrew.com

"Sweet chocolate malt aroma with some coffee and butterscotch notes." "Flavor is nutty, notes of toffee, caramel, a bit of chocolate and a nice dry earthy finish." "Definitely one of the top browns I've tried." 5.3% alc.

Big Sky Powder Hound Winter Ale ★★1/2

Eng. Strong Ale: Big Sky Brewing Co., Missoula, MT www.bigskybrew.com

"Aroma is a lot of roasted, nutty malt and caramel with a hint of fruity sweetness." "Sweet toffee malts with some slightly tart cherry fruitiness and a musty earthiness - kind of a strange combination." "Light for a winter ale." 6.2% alc.

Big Sky Scape Goat Pale Ale ★★1/2

Am. Pale Ale: Big Sky Brewing Co., Missoula, MT www.bigskybrew.com

"Fresh aroma of mandarin orange peel and a little bit of cedar." "Sweet malts in the flavor, with lots of the ashy, herby hoppiness that I associate with the British hops and some honey in the finish." 4.7% alc.

Big Sky Slow Elk Oatmeal Stout ★★1/2

Sweet Stout: Big Sky Brewing Co., Missoula, MT www.bigskybrew.com

"Light aroma of vanilla, milk chocolate and roast." "Chocolate notes are somewhat restrained and it all disappears by the time the finish should be making it's presence known." 4.9% alc.

Big Sky Summer Honey ★★1/2

Spice/Herb: Big Sky Brewing Co., Missoula, MT www.bigskybrew.com

"Aroma of sweet honey over caramel malts." "Some light orangey hops work with dull pale malts and a hint of sweaty yeast." "Refreshing and interesting enough not to be considered a lame lawnmower beer." N/A% alc.

Bink Bloesem ★★★

Belgian Ale: Brouwerij Kerkom, Sint-Truiden, Belgium www.brouwerijkerkom.be

"Mild chocolate, rose petals, wildflower honey, dates and moon cake in the aroma." "Flavors are subdued relative to the aroma, but still with the date-like, chocolate-accented malts." "This is a unique brew which I found quite tasty." 7.1% alc.

Bink Blond ★★1/2

Belgian Ale: Brouwerij Kerkom, Sint-Truiden, Belgium www.brouwerijkerkom.be

"Aroma was slightly sour with moderately hoppy notes of lemon and grass and a light note of cellar." "Taste reminds me of a watered down Westamalle trippel with plenty of hops." 5.5% alc.

Bink Bruin ★★1/2
Belgian Ale: Brouwerij Kerkom, Sint-Truiden, Belgium www.brouwerijkerkom.be
"A strong aroma, full of burnt sugar, raisin, honey and molasses." "Flavors of roasted malt, brown sugar and a hint of smoke with a dry finish." "Taste was watery and, I must admit, unexciting." 5.5% alc.

Birra Moretti ★★1/2
Pale Lager: Birra Moretti (Heineken), Udine, Italy www.birramoretti.it
"Aromas were floral hops and light malt." "Clean and dry, with faint malt notes and a grassy hop character in the finish." "Nothing outstanding but for a pale lager it was fair." 4.6% alc.

Birra Tirana ★★1/2
Pale Lager: Birra Malto (Peroni), Tirana, Albania www.birratirana.com
"Grassy, herbal character." "Flavor is sweet malty with notes of grain and hops." "Overall, surprised, considering where it came from." 4% alc.

Bison Organic Belgian Ale ★★
Abbey Tripel: Bison Brewing Co., Berkeley , CA www.bisonbrew.com
"A tripel made with Cascade hops. "Floral aroma with weak Belgian yeast." "The flavor is lightly sweet, straw and cake malt, coriander and a bit of yeasty spiciness." "A little on the lame side for a Belgian." 8.1% alc.

Bison Organic Chocolate Stout ★★★★
Stout: Bison Brewing Co., Berkeley , CA www.bisonbrew.com
"Rich cocoa, coffee and some nice hops.. I could sniff this one for a long time." "The chocolate is subtle, but adds so much. It's not blatantly sweet like many other chocolate stouts." 6.1% alc.

Bison Organic Gingerbread Ale ★★1/2
Spice/Herb: Bison Brewing Co., Berkeley , CA www.bisonbrew.com
"Based on a porter, Gingerbread Ale "does smell like a gingerbread man." "Taste is heavy malt with no hops, just the tingle and sizzle of the many spices." "Fairly thin feel." 6.8% alc.

Bison Organic Red ★★
Amber Ale: Bison Brewing Co., Berkeley , CA www.bisonbrew.com
"Aroma is medium sweet, caramel, chocolate, nutty, some grapefruit." "Taste is full, with sweet cocoa, pumpkin seed, bitter coffee, clove, coriander and peanuts." 6% alc.

Bitburger ★★★
Classic Ger Pils: Brauerei Th. Simon GmbH, Bitburg, Germany www.bitburger.de
Aroma is clean, bready and grassy." "Very dry; very bitter with a long, herbal finish." "Light-bodied but full of flavor." "The finish is pretty bitter, just how I like it." 4.8% alc.

Bitburger Drive ★★1/2
Low Alcohol: Brauerei Th. Simon GmbH, Bitburg, Germany www.bitburger.de
"Has a mild grassy and floral hop aroma." "Mild bitter hop aftertaste." "Fairly decent German macro lager flavor with the requisite attenuation of the body caused by missing alcohol." "There's a hole in my beer, Heidi!" 0.5% alc.

Black Boss Porter ★★★
Baltic Porter: BOSS Browar Witnica, Witnica, Poland www.browar-witnica.pl
"Rich malt aroma with almond cake, light molasses, raisin, plum, dark chocolate, peach." "Sweet, silky malt flavors, coffee, fruity (apricot orange) notes." "Delicious, a great way to warm up in the winter perhaps." 9.4% alc.

Black Sheep Ale ★★1/2
Prem Bitter: Black Sheep Brewery, Ripon, North Yorkshire, England www.blacksheep.co.uk
"Faint, harmonic aroma of resiny hops and some malts, maybe some bready notes." "Very earthy, with a complex maltiness and the delicious yeastiness derived from the use of Yorkshire Squares." "Super easy beer to drink." 4.4% alc.

Black Sheep Monty Pythons Holy Grail ★★

Prem Bitter: Black Sheep Brewery, Ripon, North Yorkshire , England www.blacksheep.co.uk

"Caramel malt and subtle autumn fruit on the nose." "Light flavored overall, but fruity and very nutty with a very mild bitterness." "Above average gimmick beer." 4.7% alc.

Black Sheep Riggwelter ★★★1/2

Eng. Strong Ale: Black Sheep Brewery, Ripon, North Yorkshire, England www.blacksheep.co.uk

"Aroma of citrus, raisins and malt." "Flavor is roasted malt, dark chocolate, sugary sweetness." "Lovely drop and a credit to this master brewer." 5.7% alc.

Black Toad Distinctive Dark Ale ★★1/2

Brown Ale: Goose Island Beer Co., Chicago, IL www.gooseisland.com

"Quite fruity (plums and cherries) atop a rich, sweet malt aroma." "Flavor is nutty with caramel and a hint of coffee. Finishes fairly bitter." "I could see myself calling this one a toned-down porter." 0% alc.

Blanche de Bruxelles ★★1/2

Bel. Witbier: Brasserie Lefebvre, Rebecq-Quenast, Belgium www.brasserielefebvre.be

"Aroma of lemon, coriander and cloves." "Taste was lemony and mild, quite a bit of wheat, some citrus and other fruits and a hint of ashy hops - very smooth." "Easy to drink - good summer beer." 4.5% alc.

Blanche de Chambly ★★★

Bel. Witbier: Unibroue (Sleeman), Chambly, Quebec www.unibroue.com

"Nose is light and exotic with notes of soft orange, pineapple and mango balanced by the typical yeast and wheat aromas." "A decent Witbier with standard orange/spice flavor." "Not up there with the classics, but very drinkable." 5% alc.

Blatz ★★

Pale Lager: Pabst Brewing Co., Chicago , IL www.pabst.com

"Vegetable and corn aroma, fairly strong." "It tasted reasonably drinkable (a la premium lager) but the finish was just awful." "A very drinkable, yet not particularly tasty, beer." Pabst brand, contract brewed by Miller. 4.89% alc.

BluCreek Blueberry Ale ★★1/2

Fruit Beer: Sand Creek Brewing Co. , Black River Falls, WI www.sandcreekbrewing.com

"Very blueberry aroma that's quite appetizing." "There was a hint of blueberry, but not enough to matter." "Not sure what's going on there but it's not pleasant." 4% alc.

BluCreek Herbal Ale ★

Spice/Herb: Sand Creek Brewing Co., Black River Falls, WI www.sandcreekbrewing.com

"Aroma of pears with some basil." "Bready medicine flavors not very pleasant." "Save the herbs for Sobe and start making some real beer." N/A% alc.

Blue Diamond Premium Beer ★

Pale Lager: Gluek Brewing Co., Cold Spring, MN www.gluek.com

"The aroma was corny and semi sweet with a light maltiness." "Bitter taste with a small bite, also a strange chemical taste." N/A% alc.

Blue Moon Belgian White ★★1/2

Bel. Witbier: Coors Brewing Co. (MolsonCoors), Golden, CO www.coors.com

"Good sweetness with coriander orange and spice tones." "Phenolic curacao and yeast sweat intermingling under a blanket of dull, plodding malts." "This is the beer I used to drink before discovering the world of RateBeer." 5.4% alc.

Blue Moon Pumpkin Ale ★

Spice/Herb: Coors Brewing Co. (MolsonCoors), Golden, CO www.coors.com

"Aroma of canned pumpkin pie filling." "Flavor is malty, sweet, hints of cinnamon and caramel. A decent, simple pumpkin brew." 5.7% alc.

Blue Point Hoptical Illusion ★★★1/2

IPA: Blue Point Brewing, Patchogue, NY www.bluepointbrewing.com

"Citrusy hoppy aroma with some sweet nutty malt presence." "Flavor was lightly malty (some caramel sweetness) with a moderate amounts of citrus hops." "A lighter sessionable IPA." 6.2% alc.

Blue Point Toasted Lager ★★★

Vienna: Blue Point Brewing, Patchogue, NY www.bluepointbrewing.com

"Pleasant mild blend of light roast malt, dry hops and generic (non-corn) grain." "Nice malt taste you would expect from a Vienna, with some additional light hops." "Nothing outstanding or unique here, just a solid take on the style." 4.8% alc.

Blue Ridge (MD) ESB Red Ale ★★★

Prem Bitter: Frederick Brewing Co (Snyder Intl), Frederick, MD www.frederickbrewing.com

"Aroma of biscuits and barley just harvested from field." "Rich spicy floral hop tone that's balanced nicely with sweet biscuity and caramel malt notes." "Surprisingly good." 4.8% alc.

Blue Ridge (MD) Hopfest Brown ★★★★

Brown Ale: Frederick Brewing Co (Snyder Intl), Frederick, MD www.frederickbrewing.com

"Earthy aroma that held some caramel and a touch of coffee along with the hops." "Flavor is very nutty, cocoa powder, mild mixed hops." "It reminded me of a small Arrogant Bastard." 5.5% alc.

Blue Ridge (MD) Porter ★★★

Porter: Frederick Brewing Co (Snyder Intl), Frederick, MD www.frederickbrewing.com

"Nose of light roast, chocolate and a hint of licorice." "Touch on the thin side." "Nice fruitiness and toasted dark malts on top of a subtle toasted hop bitterness." 5.2% alc.

Blue Ridge (MD) Snowballs Chance ★★1/2

Eng. Strong Ale: Frederick Brewing Co (Snyder Intl), Frederick, MD www.frederickbrewing.com

"Nutty and malty aroma with hints of maple syrup, caramel and vanilla." "Flavor is not sweet, more like coffee with some hint of caramel." "Lacks the spiciness that I enjoy in traditional winter ales." 6% alc.

Blue Ridge (MD) Steeple Stout ★★★★★

Dry Stout: Frederick Brewing Co (Snyder Intl), Frederick, MD www.frederickbrewing.com

"Roasty nose, notes of charcoal and some licorice." "Taste is a nice roasted malt, roasty chocolate, a bit of bitter dark roasted malt and almost a hint of grassy mint." "Awesome brew!" 6% alc.

Bluegrass Altbier ★★

Amber Ale: Bluegrass Brewing Co., Louisville, KY www.bbcbrew.com

"Lightly malty aroma, toasty and sweet with hints of nut and caramel and faint apple-like fruitiness." "Fairly mild flavors here, just some sweet, caramel maltiness and understated fruity hops, some slight bitterness on the finish, perhaps." 5% alc.

Bluegrass American Pale Ale ★★1/2

Am. Pale Ale: Bluegrass Brewing Co., Louisville, KY www.bbcbrew.com

"Hoppy nose, medium caramel body, easy drinkablity and a slightly bitter finish." "Hoppiness could've been a little stronger." "Creamy and effervescent." "Certainly worth revisiting." 6% alc.

Bluegrass Dark Star Porter ★★1/2

Porter: Bluegrass Brewing Co., Louisville, KY www.bbcbrew.com

"Aroma is the common porter dark roasted, chocolate malts and slightly sour twang." "Has a delectable bitterness to it with roasted coffee notes, bittersweet chocolate and a touch of mint." 5.8% alc.

Bluegrass Hell for Certain ★★1/2
Bel. Strong Ale: Bluegrass Brewing Co., Louisville, KY www.bbcbrew.com
"Caramel, dough, yeast, citrus, pepper and raisins aromas." "Flavor is sweet, but not near as deep nor complex as the aroma led me to hope for." "Thuds across the palate gracelessly." 7.5% alc.

Bochkarev Krepkoe Osoboe (Extra) ★★★
Malt Liquor: Bochkarev Brewery (Heineken), St. Petersburg, Russia www.bochkarev.ru
"Aroma is a strange combination of sweet corn syrup, a dash of malt, canned vegetables and alcohol." "Big maltiness, some corn in the palate followed by strong bitter metallics." "Not worth it." 8% alc.

Boddington's Pub Ale ★★
Bitter: Samlesbury (InBev), Preston, Lancashire, England
"Moderate malty, light hoppy (flower) aroma." "Tastes a bit watery and flavorless which is quite disappointing." "Light body, watery, flat carbonated." 4.8% alc.

Bohemia ★★
Pilsner: Grupo Modelo , Monterrey/Veracruz-Llave, Mexico www.gmodelo.com
"Sweet, slightly hoppy nose." "Hops come through in the crisp taste." "Has enough malt and hops for me to crown it the king of Mexican pale lagers." 5.3% alc.

Bokrijks Kruikenbier ★★1/2
Belgian Ale: Brouwerij Moortgat, Breendonk-Puurs, Belgium www.duvel.be
"Huge sweet and chewy aroma that initially showed homemade toffee and curacao but then developed strong honey notes." "Fresh, hoppy flavors, less yeast than a lot of Belgians and subtle complexity." 7.2% alc.

Boon Faro Pertotale ★★
Lambic - Faro: Brouwerij F. Boon, Lembeek , Belgium
"Nose of pure oak and hop dusted apples." "Wring some sherry out of a cardboard box, age, yeast, hops. yum!" "A lot less sweet than other faros I've had." 6% alc.

Boon Framboise ★★★1/2
Fruit Lambic: Brouwerij F. Boon, Lembeek , Belgium
"Complex aroma - raspberry, sugar, leather." "Sour raspberry dominates, with a good deal of sweetness present too and a long, dry, woody finish." "Great choice for a dessert beer or a casual summer evening." 5% alc.

Boon Kriek ★★1/2
Fruit Lambic: Brouwerij F. Boon, Lembeek , Belgium
"Sweet cherry, some funk following up and spice." "Strong sweet cherry flavors, very candied, with maybe a hint of orange and a slight acidic touch." "A candyland kriek." 5% alc.

Boon Oude Geuze ★★★1/2
Gueuze: Brouwerij F. Boon, Lembeek , Belgium
"Yeasty champagne aroma." "Taste is an incredible earthy sourness - like the bitterness of eating fresh herbs." "Quite straight ahead in flavor." 6.5% alc.

Boon Oude Geuze Mariage Parfait ★★★★1/2
Gueuze: Brouwerij F. Boon, Lembeek , Belgium
"Pears, malts and acidity balances beautifully in the aroma." "Sharp acidic flavor, fruitiness that lands between lemon and a gin and tonic." "Ends on a nutty, mild yeast note, with plenty of honey sweetness." 8% alc.

Boris ★
Pilsner: Brasserie de Saverne (Karlsbrau), Saverne, France
"Some hay-like hops, urine and vague malts in the aroma." "One of the billions of international lagers." "At least I have a Trois Pistoles to get the taste out of my mouth." 5.5% alc.

Bornem Double ★★1/2

Abbey Dubbel: Brouwerij Van Steenberge, Ertvelde, Belgium www.vansteenberge.com

"Malty aroma with fruity (plum, dark cherries), bready and yeasty notes." "Taste is ripe apple, alcohol bitterness, mild roast malt, a bit spicy - mildly sweet but a bit harsh in the finish." "Could use a little more malt complexity." 8% alc.

Bornem Triple ★★1/2

Abbey Tripel: Brouwerij Van Steenberge, Ertvelde, Belgium www.vansteenberge.com

"Aroma of coriander, black pepper, apple, mild caramel malt, muted alcohol - pretty standard mild triple." "Sweet malty and fruity taste with yeasts, dry and fruity, a bit vinous." "Average Belgian tripel." 9% alc.

Bottleworks Imagination Series 6th Anniversary Ale ★★★★1/2

Abt/Quadrupel: Far West Brewing Co, Redmond, WA www.celticbayou.com

Marzipan, bubblegum, liqorice, oak, soy and pastry dough in the complex and sweet aroma." "Nice caramel sweetness up front, followed by more dried fruitiness, kinda like dates or raisins, then finishing with more of a chocolate cherry flavor." 11.5% alc.

Bottleworks Tripel Krullekop ★★★

Abbey Tripel: De Proefbrouwerij, Lochristi, Belgium www.proefbrouwerij.com

"Honey and sweet flowers aroma." "Flavor is of candi sugar, light fruits (apples and white grapes), some grain, a little alcohol, barnyard." "A nice understated drink." 9.8% alc.

Bottleworks Van den Vern Grand Cru ★★★1/2

Bel. Strong Ale: De Proefbrouwerij, Lochristi, Belgium www.proefbrouwerij.com

"Aroma is fruity (peach, pear, plum), sweaty, dusty and alcoholic." "Fruity mustiness follows through into the flavor - sweet malts, raisins and brown sugar flavor is thick and complex with a gentle warming thanks to the alcohol." 9.8% alc.

Boulder Beer Hazed and Infused ★★★

Am. Pale Ale: Boulder Beer Co., Boulder, CO www.boulderbeer.com

"The name refers the beer being unfiltered and dry-hopped. "Aroma of fresh citrus hops. I could just sniff it all night." "Rich texture that many hop beers often are missing." 4.85% alc.

Boulder Beer Killer Penguin Ale ★★★★

Spice/Herb: Boulder Beer Co., Boulder, CO www.boulderbeer.com

"Sweet, malty (caramel, toffee, cookie dough) aroma, reasonably hoppy (tobacco, grapefruit) and spicy (allspice, ginger)." "Smelled and somewhat tasted like Gingersnaps." 9% alc.

Boulder Beer Mojo IPA ★★★★

IPA: Boulder Beer Co., Boulder, CO www.boulderbeer.com

"Aroma is dominated by hops - floral, piney and grapefruit." "Malty yet nice hop flavor and a decent bitterness balance really makes this one good." "Solid bitterness and a clean finisher." 7% alc.

Boulder Beer Never Summer Ale ★★★

Spice/Herb: Boulder Beer Co., Boulder, CO www.boulderbeer.com

"Sweet malty aroma with caramel, squash, spices and a bit of mint." "Thick with malts and a considerably larger alcohol presence than claimed at 6%." 6% alc.

Boulder Beer Pass Time Pale Ale ★★

Eng Pale Ale: Boulder Beer Co., Boulder, CO www.boulderbeer.com

"Aroma is sweet caramel with a light cherry fruitiness and some decent fuggle hops." "A very mellow ale, nicely integrated, but altogether ...BOR-ing!" 5% alc.

Boulder Beer Planet Porter ★★
Porter: Boulder Beer Co., Boulder, CO www.boulderbeer.com
"When this beer was launched in the early 80s it was one of less than 10 porters worldwide. "You can smell the roasted grains, but there is certainly a lack of focus, the rest are barely hints at coffee graininess, faint chocolate, etc." 5.5% alc.

Boulder Beer Singletrack Copper Ale ★★
Amber Ale: Boulder Beer Co., Boulder, CO www.boulderbeer.com
Singletrack is a regular at Rock Bottom brewpubs in Colorado. "Floral aroma is subtle but inviting." "Flavors consist of caramel, some diacetyl, slight grassiness from the hops." "Mild." 5% alc.

Boulder Beer Sundance Amber Ale ★★1/2
Amber Ale: Boulder Beer Co., Boulder, CO www.boulderbeer.com
"Aroma is sweet and hoppy - good, but pretty standard." "flavor quite mild, hops, a bit of generic malt, some lemon peel and grain - nothing good or bad." 4.85% alc.

Boulder Beer Sweaty Betty Blonde ★★★
Am. Wheat: Boulder Beer Co., Boulder, CO www.boulderbeer.com
"Lightly lemony and grassy with a fair exposing of wheaty tang." "Taste is lemony with wheat notes, yeast and sweet malts." "Not the boldest wheat beer ever, but actually it's quite good." 5.9% alc.

Boulevard Bob's 47 Münich-Style Lager ★★★★★
Premium Lager: Boulevard Brewing Co., KS City, MO www.blvdbeer.com
"A combination of earthiness and tasty bready malts blend in with the crisp lemony hallertauers to create a citric, yet admirably soft elixir." "Excellent stuff, I can see why it's popular." 5.5% alc.

Boulevard Bully! Porter ★★★★
Porter: Boulevard Brewing Co., KS City, MO www.blvdbeer.com
"The aroma shows a black malt acidity, the cookie part of an Oreo and hints of coffee." "Flavor is milk chocolate, roasted malts, caramel and a raisin sweetness at the end that is finished by a coffee bitterness that I really liked." 5.4% alc.

Boulevard Dry Stout ★★1/2
Dry Stout: Boulevard Brewing Co., KS City, MO www.blvdbeer.com
"Nose is of molasses, dark chocolate, coffee." "Taste was chocolate, some roasted and light toasted malt, with a faint tartness, almost metallic taste in the end." "I wanted to like it, but there's no way around this one...sorry..." 4.9% alc.

Boulevard Irish Ale ★★★★★
Irish Ale: Boulevard Brewing Co., KS City, MO www.blvdbeer.com
"Warming nutty and caramel flavor in waves accomplished by a nice light bitter kick in the middle." "A pretty good brew." 5.3% alc.

Boulevard Nutcracker ★★★1/2
Eng. Strong Ale: Boulevard Brewing Co., KS City, MO www.blvdbeer.com
"The aroma was spiced apples, cherries, some wheat and sour grapes." "Flavor is earthy, slightly minerally, with hints of molasses and mint." "The beer gets props for being different." 6.1% alc.

Boulevard Pale Ale ★★1/2
Am. Pale Ale: Boulevard Brewing Co., KS City, MO www.blvdbeer.com
"Bready aroma with some fruity undertones." "Flavor is nicely balanced between sweet caramel malts and crystal hops, with a bittersweet finish." "Lighter hops than I like but is a good session beer." 5.1% alc.

Boulevard Unfiltered Wheat Beer ★★★
Am. Wheat: Boulevard Brewing Co., KS City, MO www.blvdbeer.com
"Slight citrus based wheaty aroma, a bit musty." "Sweet and rounded with some grassy hops alongside lemon." "Light in flavor, but there is certainly something to this beer." 4.5% alc.

Boulevard Zôn ★★★1/2
Bel. Witbier: Boulevard Brewing Co., KS City, MO www.blvdbeer.com
"Very citrusy mild hop nose with a light coriander spicing and a touch of bitter orange peel." "Fairly dry finish leaves the palate clean with just a hint of a light breezy citrus and wheat." 4.4% alc.

Boundary Bay Cabin Fever ★★1/2
Eng. Strong Ale: Boundary Bay Brewery and Bistro, Bellingham, WA www.bbaybrewery.com
"Aroma of sweet caramel, wood and vinous hops." "Flavors were rich and woody with some brown sugar and oak barrels." "A fine example of a hopped up Winter Warmer." 7% alc.

Boundary Bay ESB ★★1/2
Prem Bitter: Boundary Bay Brewery and Bistro, Bellingham, WA www.bbaybrewery.com
"Woody, toasty aroma with honeyed malts." "Flavors are woody and bitter." Balanced; English wise, a bit overhopped. Pacific Northwest-wise, a bit underhopped." 5.6% alc.

Boundary Bay Imperial IPA ★★★★★
Imp/Dbl IPA: Boundary Bay Brewery and Bistro, Bellingham, WA www.bbaybrewery.com
"Aroma is very hoppy; an appetizing blend of florals, citrus and resin." "Big crystal malts propose good caramel flavors that remain dwarfed by the complex herbal, leafy and floral hops." "Good west coast style multi-dimensional hop arrogance." 9% alc.

Boundary Bay Imperial Oatmeal Stout ★★★1/2
Imp. Stout: Boundary Bay Brewery and Bistro, Bellingham, WA www.bbaybrewery.com
"Very sweet, very roasty, caramelly, malty, smoky and a fairly alcoholic." "Rich, coating bitter bakers chocolate and stinging, smoky toasted malts." "Really easy-drinking for a 1.090 beer." 8.5% alc.

Boundary Bay Inside Passage Ale ★★1/2
IPA: Boundary Bay Brewery and Bistro, Bellingham, WA www.bbaybrewery.com
"Woody, citrusy hop aroma - all hops." "Body is a bit thin and the malts underdeveloped." "Good drinking IPA; lightly musky, but fresh and good." 6.4% alc.

Boundary Bay Scotch Style Ale ★★1/2
Scotch Ale: Boundary Bay Brewery and Bistro, Bellingham, WA www.bbaybrewery.com
"Malty, caramelly nose shows a bit of smokiness, but is fairly lightly sweet." "Body is sweet - full of chewy, toffeeish malts with maybe a hint of caramel." "Fair bit of bitterness, but this blends seamlessly into the malts." 6.4% alc.

Brahma Chopp ★
Pale Lager: InBev Brasil, Rio Grande do Sul, Brazil www.inbev.com
"No significant smell, just a tiny touch of hops." "The body is of a sweet musty malt which is barely discernable." "Malt liquor is a fractal complexity compared to this stuff." 5% alc.

Breckenridge 471 Small Batch IPA ★★★★
Imp/Dbl IPA: Breckenridge Brewery, Denver, CO www.breckbrew.com
"Nose has cedar, green apples and copper notes with, of course, hops." "Starts with a sweet and toasty maltiness with tangerine and develops into a great hoppiness of the C-type as the malt fades" 9.2% alc.

Breckenridge Avalanche Amber ★
Amber Ale: Breckenridge Brewery, Denver, CO www.breckbrew.com
"Weak aroma is mostly sweet malt, but limited." "Grainy, hopless and boring." "Sweet, cerealy body with hints of caramel, balanced by earthy hops, a tad watery." 5.4% alc.

Breckenridge Christmas Ale ★★1/2

Am Strong Ale: Breckenridge Brewery, Denver, CO www.breckbrew.com

"Light caramel, light chocolate and light nuttiness." "bit of caramel sweetness, toffee and slight notes of chocolate and vanilla." "Kind of run of the mill for a Xmas ale." "The dog does seem to like this one." 7.4% alc.

Breckenridge Oatmeal Stout ★★1/2

Sweet Stout: Breckenridge Brewery, Denver, CO www.breckbrew.com

"Roasted aroma isn't very powerful; oatmeal, cocoa and licorice." "Flavor has a fair amount of coffee notes and bitter malts, with a touch of sweetness." "Overall, this beer is a mess." 5% alc.

Breckenridge Trademark Pale Ale ★★

Am. Pale Ale: Breckenridge Brewery, Denver, CO www.breckbrew.com

"Decent enough with some grapefruit pith, light cracker." "Floral hops body with hints of pine, balanced by biscuity malts." "Average, but, hey, that's not repulsive." 5.7% alc.

BridgePort Black Strap Stout ★★★1/2

Dry Stout: BridgePort Brewing (Gambrinus Co.), Portland, OR www.bridgeportbrew.com

"A little sweet with a faint vanilla taste and fades to a pretty dry finish with some chocolate hidden in the back." "The hops kick in and balance it out, giving a dry, hoppy, bitter finish that lasts quite some time." 6% alc.

BridgePort Blue Heron ★★1/2

Am. Pale Ale: BridgePort Brewing (Gambrinus Co.), Portland, OR www.bridgeportbrew.com

"Very faint slightly sweet and hoppy aroma and a fresh crisp taste up front." "Mellow, but balanced." "Run-of-the-mill micro, barely average for the style." 4.9% alc.

BridgePort Ebenezer Ale ★★1/2

Eng. Strong Ale: BridgePort Brewing (Gambrinus Co.), Portland, OR www.bridgeportbrew.com

"Nutty, malty caramel aroma with a hint of vanilla and alcohol." "Taste is somewhat complex - bittersweet chocolate, leather, peach and maybe a few tiny notes of cherry." "Ol' Ebenezer Scrooge likely lightened up a bit after a couple pints of this." 6.4% alc.

BridgePort ESB ★★★1/2

Prem Bitter: BridgePort Brewing (Gambrinus Co.), Portland, OR www.bridgeportbrew.com

"Sugary sweet, caramelly and earthy rather than genuinely malty and shows little in the way of hops." "Starts off with a very slight sweetness backed by the expected hop bitterness." "Sessionable beyond its 6.1% capacity." 6.1% alc.

BridgePort IPA ★★★★

IPA: BridgePort Brewing (Gambrinus Co.), Portland, OR www.bridgeportbrew.com

"Aroma of citrus, piney hops and a little bit of butterscotch." "Flavor dominated by sour, bitter hops, with a weak malt balance and a floral background." "Too good to pass up." 5.5% alc.

BridgePort Old Knucklehead ★★★1/2

Barley Wine: BridgePort Brewing (Gambrinus Co.), Portland, OR www.bridgeportbrew.com

"Sweet dark fruits, cinnamon sticks, brown sugar aroma." "Flavor is nicely balanced by the hops, not too sweet, not overly rich but rich enough, very smooth, malty and caramelly." "Not overly complex, but it does what it does well." 9.1% alc.

BridgePort Pintail Ale ★★

Am. Pale Ale: BridgePort Brewing (Gambrinus Co.), Portland, OR www.bridgeportbrew.com

"Light malt nose, bready." "Dry grainy malt flavors with a peppery, spicy hoppiness." "You have some flavor and then poof, it's gone." 5.2% alc.

BridgePort Ropewalk Amber ★★
Amber Ale: BridgePort Brewing (Gambrinus Co.), Portland, OR www.bridgeportbrew.com
"Sweet fruit and caramel malt aromas." "Toasty malt flavor with moderate sweetness and a mild hop character." "As memorable as coffee at the office." 4.5% alc.

Brigand ★★1/2
Bel. Strong Ale: Brouwerij Van Honsebrouck, Ertvelde, Belgium www.vanhonsebrouck.be
"Aroma is a warm toffee with a solid floral hopping, yeast and sweet cherries and apples." "Fresh notes of yellow grapes and must, discreet alcoholic rumors." "Plain but drinkable." 12% alc.

Brooklyn Ale ★★1/2
Eng Pale Ale: Brooklyn Brewery, Brooklyn, NY www.brooklynbrewery.com
"Nice tea-like hop aroma." "Taste is full-palated with those bright cascade hops really showing pine and lemon, along with the yeast rolls and malted grains." "Damn good for the style." 5.1% alc.

Brooklyn Black Chocolate Stout ★★★★★
Imp. Stout: Brooklyn Brewery, Brooklyn, NY www.brooklynbrewery.com
"Very popular winter seasonal known for an aroma that "blasts forth, with sweet runs of cherries, abbey fruitcake, apricots, a hint of pineapple and warm alcohol notes." "Thick, gooey goodness." 8.7% alc.

Brooklyn Brown Ale ★★★★
Brown Ale: Brooklyn Brewery, Brooklyn, NY www.brooklynbrewery.com
Pleasant aroma of dark and dried fruits and caramel, hints of chocolate, tobacco, oak and leather." "Nutty, malt forward flavor with some herbal citrus notes and fair finishing bitterness." 5.6% alc.

Brooklyn East Indian Pale Ale ★★★
IPA: Brooklyn Brewery, Brooklyn, NY www.brooklynbrewery.com
"Florally hops with perhaps a touch of citrus, along with some herbal tea aromas." "Rich doughy malt character with undertones of floral hops." "Taste is of a Brit IPA that's been kicked up with a slight American influence." 6.8% alc.

Brooklyn Lager ★★★★★
Vienna: Brooklyn Brewery, Brooklyn, NY www.brooklynbrewery.com
"Pleasant amount of hops, fair amount of mildly oaky sweet light roast malt." "Fragrant hops with a good chunky dry malt body." "Surprised and impressed." 5% alc.

Brooklyn Monster ★★★★
Barley Wine: Brooklyn Brewery, Brooklyn, NY www.brooklynbrewery.com
"Nice hoppy aroma at first which gives way for fruity and wooden notes as it warms." "Wine-like flavor with plenty of hops and some alcohol. Dry aftertaste with some oak wood and tobacco." 10.8% alc.

Brooklyn Oktoberfest ★★1/2
Märzen/Oktbfst: Brooklyn Brewery, Brooklyn, NY www.brooklynbrewery.com
"Classic malty aroma with notes of toasted biscuits and cereal." "Notes of caramel, grain, toasted malt, euro hops and a touch of grass then ends a bit on the bland side." "Brooklyn can do better." 5.5% alc.

Brooklyner Weisse ★★1/2
Hefeweizen: Brooklyn Brewery, Brooklyn, NY www.brooklynbrewery.com
"Great aroma of fruit, yeast and some banana and wheat." "Lots of bready wheat malt in the flavor along with a hint of citrus." "Doesn't have the same impact as the best German examples of the style." 5% alc.

Broughton Black Douglas ★★★
Prem Bitter: Broughton Ales, Biggar, The Borders, Scotland www.broughtonales.co.uk
"Aromas of burnt caramel, hint of chocolate and some nut." "Flavor is toasty, caramel, slightly woody. Finish is clean and dry with a hint of smokiness." "Enjoyable and well-balanced." 5.2% alc.

Broughton Merlin's ★★

Bitter: Broughton Ales, Biggar, The Borders, Scotland www.broughtonales.co.uk

"Softly hoppy nose with hints of caramel malt." "Taste is grassy and hoppy with sweet malts and some earthiness." "I needed help to make this beer disappear." 4.2% alc.

Broughton Old Jock ★★★1/2

Old Ale: Broughton Ales, Biggar, The Borders, Scotland www.broughtonales.co.uk

"Medium roasted sweet caramel malt (cookie) aroma with a fruity hop nose and some port." "Sweet, malty caramel flavor up front is joined by a pleasant dark fruitiness with some hints of roastiness and fair bitterness in the finish." 6.7% alc.

Broughton Scottish Oatmeal Stout ★★1/2

Sweet Stout: Broughton Ales, Biggar, The Borders, Scotland www.broughtonales.co.uk

"Hints of coffee and chocolate in the aroma but it's not very strong." "Light in flavor; notes of roasted malt and some coffee and chocolate." "Palate is quite watery and thin for a stout." 4.2% alc.

Brueghel ★★1/2

Abbey Tripel: Kross Brewing Co., Morrisville, VT www.krossbrewing.com

"Sweet aroma of butterscotch and bubble gum." "Taste is of fruit, sweet roast malt, a bit of slightly harsh grain." "A blah session beer." 5.9% alc.

Brugse Straffe Hendrik Blond ★★1/2

Belgian Ale: Riva Brouwerij (Liefmans Breweries), Dentergem, Belgium www.liefmans.be

"Fruity, lemony aroma leading to a spicy but thin body, gentle and light on the tongue." "Easy to drink." "A sessional Belgian." 6% alc.

Brugse Straffe Hendrik Brune ★★★1/2

Bel. Strong Ale: Riva Brouwerij (Liefmans Breweries), Dentergem, Belgium www.liefmans.be

"Aroma of plums and pear brandy, with traces of yeast, alcohol and Special B." "Sweet flavor with lots of spices and dried fruits with notes of alcohol and yeast." "Without being exceptional, this is a very drinkable Bruin." 8.5% alc.

B-to-the-E ★

Spice/Herb: Anheuser-Busch Companies, St. Louis, MO www.anheuser-busch.com

Almost has an apple juice look to it." "Tastes like a watered down energy drink." "I guess there is a market for this, but it isn't beer drinkers." 6.6% alc.

Buck's County Pennbrook Traditional Amber Lager ★★★

Pale Lager: River Horse Brewing Co., Lambertville, NJ www.riverhorse.com

"Slight malty aroma leads to a standard American lager bready taste." "Watery light-medium body." "This really gives macro swill a run for it's money." 4.5% alc.

Buckeye Frankenbock ★★★

Doppelbock: Buckeye Brewing Co., Bedford Heights, OH www.buckeyebrewing.com

"Unravels maple, brown sugar, caramel, Milky Ways, sugary pecans and apple juice." "Taste starts with a caramel and sugary sweet forefront supported by a nice apple like twang." "Isn't quite to style, but that is why I like it so." 8% alc.

Buckeye Hippie IPA ★★★★

IPA: Buckeye Brewing Co., Bedford Heights, OH www.buckeyebrewing.com

"Aroma has a sweet, almost sticky caramelized citrus note to it; with both a solid malt and hop contribution." "Flavors are razor sharp with spruce and pine initially, some citrus in the middle, a rich caramel malt providing good balance." 6.8% alc.

Buckeye Ho Ho Ho Magic Dubbel ★★★★

Abbey Dubbel: Buckeye Brewing Co., Bedford Heights, OH www.buckeyebrewing.com

"Yeasty nose, somewhat bready, slightly sweet, with a touch of dark pitted fruit." "Clove yeast and moderate raisin esters along with bready malts." "Not complex, but interesting enough." 7.5% alc.

Buckeye Martian Marzen Lager ★★★★
Märzen/Oktbfst: Buckeye Brewing Co., Bedford Heights, OH www.buckeyebrewing.com
"Aroma was malty sweet with fruit and caramel." "Caramel, toffee and dry chocolate make their presence known." "This is a really good marzen." 0% alc.

Buckeye Old Mammoth Stout ★★★★★
Dry Stout: Buckeye Brewing Co., Bedford Heights, OH www.buckeyebrewing.com
"Nice aroma of flame-licked chestnuts, dark chocolate and spent burr grinds." "Flavor plays off of that and is very rich and full? pecans, hazelnuts, Frangelico, espresso, oats, caramel and rapture." 6.8% alc.

Buckeye Sasquatch Pale Ale ★★★★1/2
Am. Pale Ale: Buckeye Brewing Co., Bedford Heights, OH www.buckeyebrewing.com
"Aroma is sweet honey, grapefruit and apricots, along with hints at a dew on a spring morning's grass." "Quite biscuity on the tongue, very assertive in fact. Hop bitterness only appears near the tail end." 5% alc.

Buckeye Seventy-Six ★★★★★
Imp/Dbl IPA: Buckeye Brewing Co., Bedford Heights, OH www.buckeyebrewing.com
"Succulent hoppy aroma with plenty of citrus (pineapple and grapefruit) and floral hops." "Big hops flavor, of course - grapefruit and resin, mostly, all on a smooth, viscous malt base." 7.9% alc.

Buckler ★★
Low Alcohol: Heineken Nederland, Hertogenbosch, Netherlands www.heineken.com
"Rather weak and boring aroma with not much signs of ingredients." "Flavor of malt and barley with a hint of sweetness." "I suppose it's not so bad for a NA brew, but it's still not very good at all." 0.5% alc.

Bud Dry ★
Pale Lager: Anheuser-Busch Companies, St. Louis, MO www.anheuser-busch.com
"A faint dimple of corn and sour water mixed with rice and hops, topped off with a bit of malt." "You'd think with it's hip packaging and focus group tested graphics it wouldn't make my eyes bleed." 5% alc.

Bud Ice ★
Pale Lager: Anheuser-Busch Companies, St. Louis, MO www.anheuser-busch.com
"Smell is stale corn." "Needs hops, malt and maybe a bit of time in some fermenting tanks." "The carbonation made for a disturbing mouthfeel." 5.5% alc.

Bud Ice Light ★
Pale Lager: Anheuser-Busch Companies, St. Louis, MO www.anheuser-busch.com
"Very faint smell of skunk and alcohol." "Drink it really cold so maybe it'll freeze your tongue and you won't taste how bad it really is." 4.1% alc.

Bud Light ★
Pale Lager: Anheuser-Busch Companies, St. Louis, MO www.anheuser-busch.com
"Flavors of water stirred with a sprig of barley and hop cones waved about a foot over the boil kettle." "Aging didn't help." "I poured the rest down the bathroom sink." "Desperate times call for desperate choices." 4.2% alc.

Budweiser ★
Pale Lager: Anheuser-Busch Companies, St. Louis, MO www.anheuser-busch.com
"Aroma of fusels and light acetaldehyde." "Ethereal body." "Gross imbalance of water, leans toward Wonderbread malts, fusel alcohol." "I'm not in high school anymore." 5% alc.

Budweiser Select ★
Pale Lager: Anheuser-Busch Companies, St. Louis, MO www.anheuser-busch.com
"Stale cardboard and stale hops/malts aroma. Pitiful." "Sweeter than most pale lagers and not as skunky as its European counterparts." 4.3% alc.

Buffalo Bill's Pumpkin Ale ★★

Spice/Herb: Buffalo Bills Brewery, Hayward, CA www.buffalobillsbrewery.com

Brewed with freshly roasted pumpkins and pumpkin pie spices. "Aroma is the best part of the brew. Lots of cinnamon and nutmeg." "Taste is a little watery; lots of pumpkin flavor, fall spices, wet leaves, caramel." 5% alc.

Buffalo Bill's Orange Blossom Cream Ale ★

Fruit Beer: Buffalo Bills Brewery, Hayward, CA www.buffalobillsbrewery.com

Cream ale made with orange peel orange flower extract and honey. "The aroma and taste were dominated by a candy-orange character." "Creamy mouthfeel. Tastes like an orange soda." 5% alc.

BürgerBräu Wolnzacher (Nikolausbier) Altfränkisches Dunkel ★★★★1/2

Dunkel: BürgerBräu Wolnzach, Wolnzach, Germany www.buergerbraeu-wolnzach.de

"Sweet aroma of chocolate, molasses and nuts." "Packed with brown sugar flavored malts in the fore followed by chocolate and molasses." "This is a brewery that needs to be better known!" 5.5% alc.

BürgerBräu Wolnzacher Hell Naturtrüb ★★★★★

Helles/Dortmnd: BürgerBräu Wolnzach, Wolnzach, Germany www.buergerbraeu-wolnzach.de

"Herbal-grassy Hallertau aroma; herbal palate with baguette notes and a crisper-than-expected hoppiness." "Flavor is malty, honeyish sweet with an herbal bitterness." "On paper this doesn't look like much but damn if I don't want more of it - much more." 4.9% alc.

BürgerBräu Wolnzacher Oktoberfest-Bier ★★★★★

Märzen/Oktbfst: BürgerBräu Wolnzach, Wolnzach, Germany www.buergerbraeu-wolnzach.de

"Subtle tea leaf and mash like aroma, very slight butterscotch." "Taste is medium sweet, caramel, apple, some orange, light earthy." "This beer is closer to a Dortmunder but darker with more malt character." 5.4% alc.

BürgerBräu Wolnzacher Roggenbier ★★★★1/2

Dunkelweizen: BürgerBräu Wolnzach, Wolnzach, Germany www.buergerbraeu-wolnzach.de

BürgerBräuAroma of banana, citrus, floral Hallertauer and toasted malts." "Taste is yeasty with citrus and lightly aromatic malts." "Top-quality Belgian brune - with a unique German dark cereal grain-prune twist, perhaps imparted by the rye used." 5.5% alc.

Burger Classic ★★★★★

Pale Lager: Hudepohl-Schoenling (Snyder Intl), Frederick, MD

"Mild malt aroma with a slight wheaty smell as well as a mild hopping." "Flavor is decent as hell with a light malt hop presence." "For the style, this is the best I have had." 4.7% alc.

Burger Light ★★★★1/2

Pale Lager: Hudepohl-Schoenling (Snyder Intl), Frederick, MD

"Clean, refreshing and easy to drink. This one even has flavor!" "Burger Light is a rare opportunity to combine mass consumption with non-disgusting flavor." 3.6% alc.

Burton Bridge Empire Ale ★★★1/2

Eng. Strong Ale: Burton Bridge Brewery, Burton-on-Trent, Staffordshire, England www.burtonbridgebrewery.co.uk

"Aroma of rich citrus/resin UK hops, solid malt backing - simple but appealing." "A little sweet malt undertone balanced well by hop bitterness that is refreshing." "With one of the wildest hop profiles this is sure to please 'em all." 7.5% alc.

Busch Beer ★

Pale Lager: Anheuser-Busch Companies, St. Louis, MO www.anheuser-busch.com

"Sour corn aroma." "A lot more malty than I would have expected from a cheap macro." "Hurray for a $5 hang-over." 4.6% alc.

Busch Light ★
Pale Lager: Anheuser-Busch Companies, St. Louis, MO www.anheuser-busch.com
"Faint wafts of wet cardboard and grains." "I can't believe how watery this is." "I happen to be in college, therefore I am poor and am drinking this awful beer." 4.1% alc.

Busch NA ★
Low Alcohol: Anheuser-Busch Companies, St. Louis, MO www.anheuser-busch.com
"Flat, stale, skunky; more like colored bad tasting mineral water." "If you're going to be boring at least get me drunk." 0.4% alc.

Butte Creek Organic Ale ★★
Amber Ale: Butte Creek Brewing Co., Chico, CA www.buttecreek.com
"Very mild aroma." "Appealing light fruitiness of orange and tangerine and a midling malt backbone." "Kinda like a mass market English ale." 5.4% alc.

Butte Creek Organic Indian Pale Ale ★★1/2
IPA: Butte Creek Brewing Co., Chico, CA www.buttecreek.com
"Aroma is an interesting hop." "The body is bitter through and through, with some malt character present, offering a nice backbone." "Lacks a little punch but definitely a nice beer." 6.3% alc.

Butte Creek Organic Porter ★★1/2
Porter: Butte Creek Brewing Co., Chico, CA www.buttecreek.com
"The aroma is roasted malt with some faint dry fruit." "Sweet roastiness makes a tease to the palate, but otherwise this is an empty promise." "Ends a bit thin." 5.5% alc.

Butte Creek Winter Ale ★★1/2
Brown Ale: Butte Creek Brewing Co., Chico, CA www.buttecreek.com
"A strongish version of the brown ale style, it has "sweet, malty aromas with hints of brown sugar" and "some roasted, nutty and bready flavors." "It's different and neither real good or that bad." 6.3% alc.

Buzzards Bay Golden Ale ★
Goldn/Blond Ale: Buzzards Bay Brewery, Westport, MA www.buzzardsbrew.com
"Tasted entirely generic to me, almost indistinguishable from their lager." "Flavor is hoppy, light fruit." "This was below average in all aspects." 4.3% alc.

Buzzards Bay Olde Buzzard Lager ★★
Helles/Dortmnd: Buzzards Bay Brewery, Westport, MA www.buzzardsbrew.com
"Very light floral aroma, slight graininess." "Bready taste with a barely perceptible bitterness." "Not a bad lager, just could use a little more body and flavor." 5% alc.

Buzzards Bay Olde Buzzard Pale Ale ★★1/2
Prem Bitter: Buzzards Bay Brewery, Westport, MA www.buzzardsbrew.com
"Aroma is of some caramelly malts and some herbal hops." "Flavor is herbal, doughy." "Not as hoppy as I'd expect out of a pale ale and far maltier." 5.6% alc.

Buzzards Bay Pale Ale ★
Am. Pale Ale: Buzzards Bay Brewery, Westport, MA www.buzzardsbrew.com
A "medium-bodied pale ale" with "bready malts and fruity" aroma. "Pleasant malt and honey flavors with some hop bitterness." "A cross between an amber and a pale." 5% alc.

Buzzards Bay Stock Ale ★★
Amber Ale: Buzzards Bay Brewery, Westport, MA www.buzzardsbrew.com
"Aroma is floral, earthy and sweet, a touch perfumey." "Pretty much tastes like your typical brew pub amber ale." "Floral and caramel aftertaste." 4.7% alc.

Buzzards Bay West Porter ★★1/2
Porter: Buzzards Bay Brewery, Westport, MA www.buzzardsbrew.com
"Dark with strong coffee/mocha flavor and scent." "Rich malty touch similar to doppelbocks." "Some decent character toward the end, but quite mediocre on all counts." 5.2% alc.

Cabro ★
Pale Lager: Cerveceria Nacional (Gua.), Guatemala City, Guatemala
"Corn-accented lager with heavy adjunct taste, a little bit of hop and little else." "This beer isn't heinous or anything, it's pretty much like the soulless Lager you can find in any country." 4.8% alc.

Caffrey's ★★
Bitter: Tadcaster (MolsonCoors), Tadcaster, North Yorkshire, England
www.tadcaster.uk.combreweriesCoors.htm
Yes, this is made in ENG. "Practically no aroma, what was there was a bit malty, lacking in hops." "Vague white sugar and fructose sweetness." "You could pump nitrogen through tap water and make it smooth. So what?" 4.2% alc.

Caguama ★
Pilsner: Cerveceria La Constancia (BevCo/SABMiller), San Salvador, El Salvador www.laconstancia.com
"Cheap substitute for Corona." "Slight malt aroma." "Light corny malt flavor - very watery." "Yeah, this is really foul beer." N/A0% alc.

Camo High Gravity Lager ★
Malt Liquor: City Brewery Co., La Crosse, WI www.citybrewery.com
"Very sweet grainy aroma." "Taste is sweet, grainy and tinny." "Tastes like bobbing for rotten apples in a pool of rubbing alcohol." "If your goal is a quick, cheap descent into alcohol oblivion, there's very few comparable choices on the beer market." 8.5% alc.

Cancun ★★
Pilsner: Zuma Brewing Co., Atlanta, GA www.zumaimporting.com
"The beer is refreshing but lacks body and flavor." "Thin in body with a clean malt character and dry finish." "Makes me feel like I'm chillin at tha beach, so it serves its purpose." 5% alc.

Cantillon Bruocsella 1900 Grand Cru ★★★★
Unblend Lambic: Brasserie Cantillon, Brussels, Belgium www.cantillon.be
"Nose is very fresh, nice hints of fruit, some grass and outdoorsy notes." "Quite sour, somewhat acidic flavor with apples and wheaty malt." "Just pure, unadulterated lambic glory." 5% alc.

Cantillon Cuvee des Champions ★★★★★
Gueuze: Brasserie Cantillon, Brussels, Belgium www.cantillon.be
"The aroma is quite sour, but a definite floral hopping comes through as well." "taste is sour, like a mixture of crabapple and lemons with just a hint of the usual barnyard tastes. It finishes on a dry, flowery note." "Tastes vintage and has some class." 5% alc.

Cantillon FouFoune ★★★★★
Fruit Lambic: Brasserie Cantillon, Brussels, Belgium www.cantillon.be
"Apricot aromas leaning in with refreshing lemon." "Sour and dry taste with clearly and wonderfully present apricot." "I love spontaneous fermentation. Liquid fun!" 5% alc.

Cantillon Gueuze ★★★★1/2
Gueuze: Brasserie Cantillon, Brussels, Belgium www.cantillon.be
"Aroma is green apples, old cellar and fruity acids." "Palate very acidic, astringent - it grows on you, first taste is whoa!" "A refreshingly long, dry finish." "Funky tastes that I wouldn't associate with beer. More of a wine, champagne or even cider flavor." 5% alc.

Cantillon Iris ★★★★1/2
Unblend Lambic: Brasserie Cantillon , Brussels, Belgium www.cantillon.be
"Big aroma - wood, slightly toasted hops, sour apple - typical Cantillon for the most part." "Sour and restrained, all in class, with nice malty notes, tropical fruits, first time I actually note the malt in a lambic." "Magical unexplainable moments." 5% alc.

Cantillon Kriek ★★★★
Fruit Lambic: Brasserie Cantillon, Brussels, Belgium www.cantillon.be
Light fresh sweet cherries in aroma." "Mouth puckering sourness dominates the flavor with the cherry only barely making an appearance." "One of the more complex beers I've had in a while." 5% alc.

Cantillon Lou Pepe Framboise ★★★★★
Fruit Lambic: Brasserie Cantillon , Brussels, Belgium www.cantillon.be
"Rich, authentic and elegant raspberry aroma." "Crush some sour, unripe raspberries, stick that jam into a well used baseball glove and leave it between two bales of hay during a rainy October." "Like Parliament/Funkadelic is jamming in my mouth." 5% alc.

Cantillon Lou Pepe Gueuze ★★★★★
Gueuze: Brasserie Cantillon , Brussels, Belgium www.cantillon.be
"Aroma very sour, with yeast and apples in the background." "Flavor is juicy, somewhat tart and lemony with a dry, champagne-like finish." "Earthy and sour, but not as much as the brewery's other gueuzes." 5% alc.

Cantillon Lou Pepe Pure Kriek ★★★★★
Fruit Lambic: Brasserie Cantillon , Brussels, Belgium www.cantillon.be
"Very complex aroma; definitely vinous, aromas of cherries and lemons." "Slightly puckering to start with sour, funky, barnyard notes. Turns a bit sweeter with some cherry flavors in the aftertaste." "Flat, straightforward matured kriek." 5% alc.

Cantillon Ros, de Gambrinus ★★★1/2
Fruit Lambic: Brasserie Cantillon , Brussels, Belgium www.cantillon.be
"Aroma is hay, light barnyard, horseblanket, lightly tart raspberry, plenty of tartness with a hint of some old wood." "Notes of wood, aged barrels, faint raspberries, barnyard, musty lambic, sharp acidity, hints of yeast throughout." 5% alc.

Cantillon Saint Lamvinus ★★★★★
Fruit Lambic: Brasserie Cantillon , Brussels, Belgium www.cantillon.be
"Wine-like aroma, lots of fruit, hints of sulfur, some brett and lactic acid." "Slightly less sourly acidic (only slightly!) than most Cantillons and with an extra layer of woody complexity." "Unusual, thought-provoking, enjoyable." 5% alc.

Cantillon Vigneronne ★★★★
Fruit Lambic: Brasserie Cantillon , Brussels, Belgium www.cantillon.be
"Aroma has usual Cantillon cheese, lemon, feet, wood, but there is a definite muscat presence." "Sour, fruity with grape flavor. Some notes of oak and earth." "Similar to the Gueuze, differentiated by a slight sweetness from the grapes." 5% alc.

Cantina ★
Pale Lager: Cerveceria La Constancia (SABMiller), San Salvador, El Salvador www.laconstancia.com
"Pale malt, cardboard aroma with some funky sugars." "Quite pasty across the palate, watery and a little gassy (seems to repeat on you) with odd medicinal and alcohol flavors." "Yep, it's Corona all over again." 0% alc.

Capital 1900 ★★★
Pilsner: Capital Brewery, Middleton, WI www.capital-brewery.com
"Aroma is sweet bread malts, some corn, light floral hops." "Tastes of grain, flowers with a very light grassy finish." "Nothing fancy, just plain good beer." 5.25% alc.

Capital Autumnal Fire ★★★★1/2
Doppelbock: Capital Brewery, Middleton, WI www.capital-brewery.com
"Nose is rich in caramel and even a little ripe fruit, something resembling Christmas spices." "Caramel malt and a hint of dark fruit." "I had the rare treat of letting a beer for which I had no expectations completely wow me." 8.5% alc.

Capital Bavarian Lager ★★★
Helles/Dortmnd: Capital Brewery, Middleton, WI www.capital-brewery.com
"Intoxicating aroma with spice, hopflowers and sweet fruit esters." "A distinctly German maltiness dominates this lager with an authentically bready flavor from start to finish." 5% alc.

Capital Blonde Doppelbock ★★★
Doppelbock: Capital Brewery, Middleton, WI www.capital-brewery.com
"Aroma of sweet malt, alcohol and some fruit." "Malt is assertive in the flavor - a slightly sticky, chewy caramelized pale malt like the beer had a four hour boil." "Rich yet refreshing." 8% alc.

Capital Brown Ale ★★★
Brown Ale: Capital Brewery, Middleton, WI www.capital-brewery.com
"Brown sugar and light hazelnut aroma." "Flavor is sweet lightly caramel malt some light fruits and a touch of hop in the finish definite walnut flavor as well." "A fine British ale from a brewer of primarily German lagers." 4.2% alc.

Capital Dark Doppelbock ★★★★1/2
Doppelbock: Capital Brewery, Middleton, WI www.capital-brewery.com
"Aroma is big - plummy, molassey, medjool (date) depths." "Toasted grain, a hint of black licorice and a rather complementary alcohol flavor." "Palate is lightly dry and still quite smooth and easy to drink." 8% alc.

Capital Eisphyre
Eisbock: Capital Brewery, Middleton, WI www.capital-brewery.com
Strong aroma of dark fruit, caramel, lots of herbs and spices (almost 'Christmas-like') Strong herbal qualities, makes me feel a part of nature." "Not overly sweet or dry. Just right for sipping." % alc.

Capital Fest ★★★★1/2
Märzen/Oktbfst: Capital Brewery, Middleton, WI www.capital-brewery.com
"Medium sweet, bread, some caramel, light pepper aroma." "A gentle but crisp hoppiness, shot of alcohol and clean-if-light, well-extracted bready malt triumvirate." "Would that they make them this good in Münich." 5.5% alc.

Capital Kloster Weizen ★★★★1/2
Hefeweizen: Capital Brewery, Middleton, WI www.capital-brewery.com
"Spicy hops, lots of sweet malts, very characteristically hefe." "Flavor is right there as well with banana and plenty of spiciness in the flavor." "There's no beer I'd rather be drinking on a hot summer day." 5.12% alc.

Capital Maibock ★★★1/2
Bock: Capital Brewery, Middleton, WI www.capital-brewery.com
"Bready aroma with a hint of peppery alcohol." "Sweet malts and honey flavors with a light graininess." "These pairings well reflect the Wisconsin spring of days of cool rains paired with days of warm sun." 6.2% alc.

Capital Münich Dark ★★★★
Dunkel: Capital Brewery, Middleton, WI www.capital-brewery.com
"Sweet malt, light roasted grain and slight hop spice aroma." "Flavor is big grains and some sweet malts." "A plain Dunkel fairly well done." 5.5% alc.

Capital Oktoberfest ★★★1/2
Märzen/Oktbfst: Capital Brewery, Middleton, WI www.capital-brewery.com
"Grassy, malty, sour and hop spice aroma." "Starts with hint of sweet malt, middles on dry side and finishes with dry bitterness." "Nicely done Oktoberfest." 5.5% alc.

Capital Special Pilsner ★★★
Pilsner: Capital Brewery, Middleton, WI www.capital-brewery.com
"Slightly earthy, grassy hop aroma with backing bread notes." "Flavor picked up some lighter fruits, noble hops and biscuits." "Straightforward grass and bread combo." 4.8% alc.

Capital Wild Rice ★★1/2
Spice/Herb: Capital Brewery, Middleton, WI www.capital-brewery.com
"Münich malt nose with minerals, nuts and herbal hops." "Light and lively character, with the slight nuttiness from the wild rice." "A delicious lager and a hair shy of spectacular." 5% alc.

Capital Winter Skål ★★★1/2
Vienna: Capital Brewery, Middleton, WI www.capital-brewery.com
"Caramel malt aroma, slight grain/oatiness, a tad wheat breadish." "Clean, toasty flavor with slight woody note and background caramel." "Seems like this would be a good beer for a midwinter mild spell." 5.4% alc.

Capital Wisconsin Amber ★★★★1/2
Vienna: Capital Brewery, Middleton, WI www.capital-brewery.com
"Aroma is medium sweet, malty - caramel, bread." "Flavor is bread and lightly sweet caramel malt with a hint of fresh hay in the finish." "You can tell the brewers are very confident with their recipe." 5.1% alc.

Caracole Nostradamus ★★★★1/2
Bel. Strong Ale: Brasserie La Caracole, Falmignoul, Belgium www.caracole.be
"Alcohol, spice (cinnamon) aroma but also pungent and phenolic." "Stinging alcohol palate, hint of barnyard, swirling lively fruitiness." "It really is fun and highly drinkable." 9.5% alc.

Caracole Saxo ★★1/2
Bel. Strong Ale: Brasserie La Caracole, Falmignoul, Belgium www.caracole.be
"Very dry hoppy aroma, with plenty of lemon and very light banana-candyish malt, hints of mild spices and dry grasses and flowers." "Taste is very lemony and perfumey with honey-sweet grass, pear and a whisper of hops." 8% alc.

Caracole Troublette ★★
Bel. Witbier: Brasserie La Caracole, Falmignoul, Belgium www.caracole.be
"Aroma of sweet malt, wheat, yeast and a crisp, light fruitiness." "Flavor is sweetish, some sugar, some citrus, some acidity." "An interesting brew which is very much off the mainstream." 5% alc.

Carib ★
Pale Lager: Carib Brewery, Champs-Fleurs, Trinidad www.caribbeer.com
"Malt and corn syrup like aroma with a grassy hop." "Slightly sweet taste but not a lot of real flavor." "Sweet, thin and unimpressive." 5.2% alc.

Carlow Curim Gold ★★
Wheat: Carlow Brewing Co., Carlow, Ireland www.carlowbrewing.com
"Wheaty, slightly lemony aroma." "Lots of juicy lemon wheat flavors burst on the tongue with gentle carbonation." "An easy drinking beer that doesn't need a wedge of lemon." 4.3% alc.

Carlow Molings Traditional Red Ale ★★1/2
Irish Ale: Carlow Brewing Co., Carlow, Ireland www.carlowbrewing.com
"Faint sweet malt aroma, with barely detectable hops." "Taste is medium sweet, caramel, some cookie, tea, nutty." "If you like malty beers without hop bitterness or hop flavor this one is for you." 4.3% alc.

Carlow O'haras Celtic Stout ★★1/2
Dry Stout: Carlow Brewing Co., Carlow, Ireland www.carlowbrewing.com
"Good roasted spice aroma." "The body is rather thin, but full of bitter malts and roasted coffee." "Cheers to a real Irish stout!!!" 4.3% alc.

Carlsberg Elephant ★★★1/2

Malt Liquor: Carlsberg Brewery, Copenhagen, Denmark www.carlsberg.dk

"Malty grassy aroma, not bad." "A macro on steroids ... grainy malt, vaguely medicinal hint to the unpleasantly sweet malt flavor with a pilsner-esque twang on the back end." "Definitely a malt liquor but not bad for one." 7.2% alc.

Carlsberg Lager ★★1/2

Pale Lager: Carlsberg Danmark A/S, Copenhagen, Denmark www.carlsberg.dk

"Aromas of hops, grass and maybe corn." "Light body and soft bitter flavor." "Still it's yet another example of mass marketing making something out of not very little." 5% alc.

Carnegie Porter ★★★★1/2

Porter: Carlsberg Sverige, Falkenberg, Sweden www.carlsberg.se

"Chocolate and roasted nuts aroma." "Lightly roasted with sweet malt and molasses and chocolate." "Compelling - you just want another sip." 5.6% alc.

Carta Blanca ★★

Pale Lager: Cervecería Cuauhtémoc (FEMSA), Monterrey/Veracruz-Llave, Mexico www.femsa.com

"Aromas of grass, corn and a little skunk." "Has an astringent bitterness and a sour flavor to accompany. the corn-like malt." "If I am ever in a bar and this is the best selection I'll probably choose the wine." 6% alc.

Casa Beer ★★1/2

Pale Lager: Sociétée des Brasseries du Maroc (Heineken), Casablanca, Morocco

"Sweet nose for the style and hints of crushed grains." "Silky sweetish lager with a sharp hop bite and a nice biscuity after taste." "One of the small handful of examples of this style that is actually good." 5% alc.

Casco Bay Carrabassett Pale Ale ★★1/2

Am. Pale Ale: Casco Bay Brewing, Portland, ME www.cascobaybrewing.com

"Floral hop aroma with a touch of citrus and a mild bready malt character." "Good clean crisp taste with a slightly dry aftertaste." N/A% alc.

Casco Bay Carrabassett Winter Ale ★★1/2

Eng. Strong Ale: Casco Bay Brewing, Portland, ME www.cascobaybrewing.com

"Some initial bitterness up front followed by a caramel sweetness." "Aroma is mild hops, light spice, caramel and faint fruit." "Very drinkable winter ale." 6.8% alc.

Casco Bay Pilsner ★★★

Classic Ger Pils: Casco Bay Brewing, Portland, ME www.cascobaybrewing.com

"typical hop aroma of a pils." "Bready malt notes and crisp, moderate bitterness." "Tingly, bitter, hoppy palate." "I would drink this beer if they sold it at Fenway." 5% alc.

Casco Bay Riptide ★★★1/2

Irish Ale: Casco Bay Brewing, Portland, ME www.cascobaybrewing.com

"Aroma was malty with some spicy hops mixed in." "Flavor is a hint of spice, hops and raisins. Nice and complex, but not too full bodied." "Could best be described as toasting marshmallows on the beach over a campfire." 5.4% alc.

Casco Bay Summer Ale ★★1/2

Am. Pale Ale: Casco Bay Brewing, Portland, ME www.cascobaybrewing.com

"Sweet tea, dusty, floral, lemon aroma." "Very light bitterness in the finish." "Had a heartier flavor than many summer ales but not at all overpowering." N/A% alc.

Casco Bay Winter Ale ★★1/2

Eng. Strong Ale: Casco Bay Brewing, Portland, ME www.cascobaybrewing.com

"Mild sweet malt and hops in the aroma." "The finish is much more akin to a British bitter with hop notes all about." "Perfect for ME winters." 7.3% alc.

Casta Bruna ★★1/2
Am. Pale Ale: Especialidades Cerveceras (FEMSA), Apodaca Nuevo Leon, Mexico www.cervezacasta.com.mx
"Toffeeish, tobaccoey, brown sugary aroma." "Roasted chicory, toffee, fruity yeast of cherries and plums." "Certainly more on the English side? a nice crisp brew!" 5% alc.

Casta Dorada ★★1/2
Goldn/Blond Ale: Especialidades Cerveceras (FEMSA), Apodaca Nuevo Leon, Mexico www.cervezacasta.com.mx
"Aroma has a hint of bread and a slight apricot note." "Palate has a slight caramelly accent, combined with earthy and foresty hops." "Tasty drinkable beer but the overriding thought is that it is a little too sticky and syrupy." 5% alc.

Casta Morena ★★★1/2
Scottish Ale: Especialidades Cerveceras (FEMSA), Apodaca Nuevo Leon, Mexico www.cervezacasta.com.mx
"Honey-like musty sweetness with some berry-like fruits and a very light suggestion of smoke." "Smooth palate with black cherry, crystal malt, figs, wood, slight smoke; sweet finish." 6% alc.

Casta Triguera ★★1/2
Am. Wheat: Especialidades Cerveceras (FEMSA), Apodaca Nuevo Leon, Mexico www.cervezacasta.com.mx
"Aroma has slight biscuit and toast notes." "Sweet, doughy, wheat flavor with some spices and some buttery character." "It was kind of boring." 5.5% alc.

Casta Unica ★★★1/2
Bel. Strong Ale: Especialidades Cerveceras (FEMSA), Apodaca Nuevo Leon, Mexico www.cervezacasta.com.mx
"Olfactory senses are treated from the start, with a rich, pungent, yeasty, typical Belgian aroma invading the atmosphere." "Mellow, with flavors of chocolate, dark fruits, nuts and herbs." "Damn fine beer for a Mexican brewed Belgian." 8% alc.

Castelain Blond Bière ★★★
Bière de Garde: Brasserie Castelain, Benifontaine, France www.chti.com
"Aroma is a nice smell of a barn after an apple harvest." "Flavor has some slight caramel notes, some essences of raw cookie dough and a hint of lemon." "Overall, a refreshing but underwhelming ale." 6.4% alc.

Castelain ChTi Ambrée ★★
Bière de Garde: Brasserie Castelain, Benifontaine, France www.chti.com
"Nose is rich with fruits, wood, light grass, sweet malts and brown sugar." "Soft in mouth with more candi sugar, caramel and spicy hop on finish." "I should have liked this beer, but frankly, I didn't." 5.9% alc.

Castelain Jade ★★
Goldn/Blond Ale: Brasserie Castelain, Benifontaine, France www.chti.com
"Mild, slightly sourish, sweetish-malty aroma with honey." "Grassy-honeyish, slightly sweet-sour and oaky flavor with no hops." "Surprisingly bland." 4.5% alc.

Castello ★★1/2
Pale Lager: Castello di Udine Spa, San Giorgio di Nogaro, Italy www.birracastello.it
"Aroma is moderately malty with light herbal notes." "Light bready malts, grassy hop." "A simple but inoffensive lager, average in almost anything. Still better than most Italian macros." 5% alc.

Castle Eggenberg MacQueen's Nessie ★★
Smoked: Brauerei Schloss Eggenberg (Stoehr & Co.KG), Vorchdorf, Austria www.eggenberger.at
"Sweet, candy-like aroma with some notes of grass and not much else." "Flavors are surprisingly mild, comprising sweet, gooey malts, toasted caramel and light toffee." "I tend to rather like Eggenberg so this is something of a disappointment." 7.3% alc.

Castle Eggenberg Samichlaus Bier ★★★

Doppelbock: Brauerei Schloss Eggenberg (Stoehr & Co.KG), Vorchdorf, Austria www.eggenberger.at

"Deep currant and caramel aromatics." "Thick, malt flavors. The only real nuances I'm getting are the alcohol, which comes in like Slivowicz and a honey-mead afternote." "10 years from now, this'll be great." 14% alc.

Castle Eggenberg Urbock 23 ★★1/2

Doppelbock: Brauerei Schloss Eggenberg (Stoehr & Co.KG), Vorchdorf, Austria www.eggenberger.at

"Vinous, spicy, malty nose." "Sweet, with fruity notes, hints of honey and nuts, yet ending with a yeasty dryness." "A unique beer and one any serious drinker needs to seek out." 9.6% alc.

Castle Eggenberg Urbock Dunkel Eisbock ★★★★1/2

Eisbock: Brauerei Schloss Eggenberg (Stoehr & Co.KG), Vorchdorf, Austria www.eggenberger.at

"Rich aroma like roast beef, rich Münich malts, pecans, demerara, tobacco." "Wonderful malt palate - demerara (sugar) again, chewy earth, wood." "More people should experience brews like this, maybe they'd shut the hell up about the superiority of wine." 9.8% alc.

Castle Lager ★★

Pale Lager: South African Breweries (SABMiller), Sandton, S Africa www.sab.co.za

"Some toasted malt and grassy hops but mostly tastes like a typical lager." "Not a great premium lager." "Needless to say I won't bother getting this again." 5% alc.

Cave Creek Chili Beer ★

Spice/Herb: Black Mountain Brewing Co., Cave Creek, AZ www.chilibeer.com

With its broad distribution and chile-in-the-bottle gimmick, this beer is purchased by a lot of curious beer lovers. While its continued existence means that somebody drinks it, most beer lovers revile it. "Simply horrific." 4.7% alc.

Celis Grand Cru ★★1/2

Belgian Ale: Michigan Brewing Co., Webberville, MI www.michiganbrewing.com

"Aroma with hints of malt, grapes, spices and some yeast." "Tastes of citrus lemons, coriander orange peel and light wheat. 8% alcohol content very well hidden." 8% alc.

Celis Pale Bock ★★

Belgian Ale: Michigan Brewing Co., Webberville, MI www.michiganbrewing.com

"Aroma is candy fruity with light cinnamon." "Taste is initially lightly sweet with a slightly bitter finish." "I was underwhelmed with this beer." 5% alc.

Celis Raspberry ★★1/2

Fruit Beer: Michigan Brewing Co., Webberville, MI www.michiganbrewing.com

"Sweet vinous nose, candied raspberry aroma." "Finishes very sweet and the raspberry flavor shows obvious signs of that dreaded artificial flavoring I hate so much." N/A% alc.

Celis White ★★★★

Bel. Witbier: Michigan Brewing Co., Webberville, MI www.michiganbrewing.com

"Aroma is wheat, lemon, Belgian spices." "Fairly light and soft with a good blend of cloves and wheat. Hints of citrus and subtle maltiness makes this taste like a summer day." 4.25% alc.

Central Waters Brewers Reserve Bourbon Barrel Stout ★★★★★

Imp. Stout: Central Waters Brewing Co., Junction City, WI

"Aroma is vanilla and charred oak dominated, with lesser notes of roasted malt and bourbon." "Very smooth on the palate, more vanilla and some very sweet chocolate here, light bourbon through out." "Loved every minute of it!" 9.5% alc.

Central Waters Happy Heron Pale Ale ★★★1/2

Am. Pale Ale: Central Waters Brewing Co., Junction City, WI

"Baked light fruits in the nose, sweet and yeasty and atypical." "Juicy, pungent body, cinnamon-vanilla-caramel underlying the bright apricots and spicy hops." "Only in Wisconsin will you find a gem like this." 5.2% alc.

Central Waters Junctown Brown ★★

Brown Ale: Central Waters Brewing Co., Junction City, WI

"The aroma is strange. Piney funky hay/straw/alfalfa. Really hard to describe." "Malty flavors (nuttiness, faint coffee, caramel, toffee and brown sugar) with floral hop highlights." "Decent brown, but I was thrown off a bit by the aroma." N/A% alc.

Central Waters Lac du Bay Indian Pale Ale ★★★

IPA: Central Waters Brewing Co., Junction City, WI

"Aroma quite faint, but when finally detected it reveals a spicy floral hop character and a tiny whiff of malt." "Beautiful fruity-vanilla body, bitterness develops slowly and subtly, finally crashing through into a thick, oaky, very full juicy-hoppy finish." 7.5% alc.

Central Waters Mud Puppy Porter ★★★

Porter: Central Waters Brewing Co., Junction City, WI

"Aroma of roasty chocolate and cappuccino, lactic notes and a bit of caramel." "Taste is of creamy chocolate with a mild touch of lactose and a touch of coffee. " "A very well crafted porter. This puppy ain't muddy at all." 5.5% alc.

Central Waters Ouisconsing Red Ale ★★1/2

Amber Ale: Central Waters Brewing Co., Junction City, WI

"Nutty, caramel-y aroma and a bit of medium toasted grain." "Flavors of toasted earth, caramel and some floral hoppage." "Much more flavorful than most in this category, but I'd prefer a bit more malty sweetness." 5% alc.

Central Waters Satin Solstice Imperial Stout ★★★★

Imp. Stout: Central Waters Brewing Co., Junction City, WI

"Smell is of creamy butter, coffee and chocolate malts." "Deep roasted coffee, some smoke and seared marshmallow." "Struck me as thin for an Imperial Stout and reminded me somewhat of an Imperial Porter." 7.5% alc.

Cerveza Aguila ★★

Pale Lager: Grupo Empresarial Bavaria, Bogota, Colombia www.bavaria.com.co

""Aroma is sweetish, bordering on sickly sweet." "Boring, bland, watery." "This brew was very light and clean." 4% alc.

Cerveza Cristal ★

Pale Lager: Compania Cervecerias Unidas (Heineken), , Chile www.heineken.cl

"A little floral hop, no malt taste and a nasty bitter metallic aftertaste." "Sickly corn flavor with only a hint of malt." "This one distinguished itself by gradually getting worse the more of it I drank." 4.2% alc.

Cerveza Imperial ★★

Pale Lager: Cerveceria Hondurena (SABMiller), Tegucigalpa, Honduras www.cerveceriahondurena.com

"The aroma is a huge floral hoppiness and bready." "Not much flavor, a very light hop with a light honey/syrup sweetness." "It is probably one of the most well-made of the mainstream Central American lagers." 5% alc.

Ch'Ti Blonde ★★1/2

Bière de Garde: Brasserie Castelain, Benifontaine, France www.chti.com

"Mild caramel aroma with a touch of floral scents." "Creamy malt up front with bittering hops picking up in the end." "Would like it better with more flavor and body." 6.4% alc.

Ch'Ti Brune ★

Belgian Ale: Brasserie Castelain, Benifontaine, France www.chti.com

"Medium sweet aroma, caramel, nutty, some raisin." "Nutty toffeeish flavor and a sweet aftertaste." "This should clean out the drain quite well." 6.4% alc.

Chang ★★★
Malt Liquor: Thai Beverages, , Thailand www.changbeer.com
"Aroma has light alcohol, malt, fusels, grain." "Flavor is sweet malty with some sour notes, it must be brewing cereal." "Some would say it was perfect for the frozen mug it came with." 6.4% alc.

Charles Reibenbach Lager ★
Pale Lager: Gluek Brewing Co., Cold Spring, MN www.gluek.com
"This might possibly be the most watered down beer I've drank." "Sour grains and slightly bitter citrus flavors." "Booo!" N/A% alc.

Chimay Blanche (White) ★★★★★
Abbey Tripel: Bières de Chimay SA, Baileux, Belgium www.chimay.be
"Aroma of spices, banana and other fruits, slightly sour candy malt, alcohol - very ashy and bitter as it warms up." "Finish is dry, bitter and spicy with a nice hint of alcohol coming through at the very last." "As it warms the flavors really come out." 8% alc.

Chimay Bleue (Blue) ★★★★★
Bel. Strong Ale: Bières de Chimay SA, Baileux, Belgium www.chimay.be
"Plummy, slightly bubblegummy aroma with notes of honey, pears, sweet dark malts and a little bit of yeast." "Sweet palate with pear orange and sultana notes." "Rich and complex in an impeccable harmony." 9% alc.

Chimay Rouge (Red) ★★★★★
Abbey Dubbel: Bières de Chimay SA, Baileux, Belgium www.chimay.be
"Aroma is lightly spiced and fruity with reminders of clove, pear and plum." "Starts with sharpness, fruitiness and slight sweet malt with hints of caramel, prune (raisin)." "A good Belgian anyone can enjoy." 7% alc.

Christian Moerlein Honey Almond ★★★★★
Pale Lager: Lion Brewery, Inc., Wilkes-Barre, PA www.lionbrewery.com
"The label doesn't lie - distinct honey and almond flavor." "Tastes malty, with some almonds, slight caramel and honey at the finish." "Very drinkable for about 3/4ths of the bottle, then I was ready to move on to a new flavor as an antidote." 5.4% alc.

Christian Moerlein Oktoberfest ★★
Märzen/Oktbfst: Lion Brewery, Inc., Wilkes-Barre, PA www.lionbrewery.com
Aroma mostly of toasted cereal with a slight hop perfume." "Toasty sweet caramel flavor and some bitterness in the finish." 0% alc.

Christian Moerlein Select Lager ★★★
Helles/Dortmnd: Lion Brewery, Inc., Wilkes-Barre, PA www.lionbrewery.com
"Malty, peppery nose with notes of honey and white bread." "Nice toasted grain and light caramel flavors throughout, yet it's followed up nicely with a decent German spicy hop bitterness in the end." 5% alc.

Christoffel Blond ★★★★★
Pilsner: Bierbrouwerij St. Christoffel, JB Roermond, Netherlands www.christoffelbier.nl
"Just dripping with herbal, piney hop goodness and just enough bready malt flavors to carry the hops through to the lingering bitter finish." "It is a shame it's appreciated by so few." 6% alc.

Christoffel Robertus ★★★1/2
Vienna: Bierbrouwerij St. Christoffel, JB Roermond, Netherlands www.christoffelbier.nl
"Very malty, sweet caramel aroma." "Smooth, malty palate with lots of Vienna malt and toffeeish notes." "Seems like it'd really endear itself to me if I were to have a session on it." 6% alc.

Cimes Yeti ★★★
Bel. Strong Ale: Brasserie des Cimes, Aix les Bains, France
"Dominant aroma is alcohol along with scents of sweet spices like cinnamon and nutmeg." "Apricot, white grapes, citrus fruit in the flavor with a fair bitterness." "Very interesting flavor, although I don't think I'll get hooked." 8% alc.

Cisco Baggywrinkle Barleywine ★★★
Barley Wine: Cisco Brewers Inc., Nantucket, MA ciscobrewers.com
"Very fruity up front with hints of tartness and lighter chocolate. Real big alcohol and bourbon finish." "Flavors of leather, wood and earth sit side by side quite well with chocolate, caramel, bourbon and traces of fruity esters." 12% alc.

Cisco Bailey's Ale ★★★★★
Goldn/Blond Ale: Cisco Brewers Inc., Nantucket, MA ciscobrewers.com
"Smells of cookie dough, apples and grass. Tastes bitter with some lemony and grapefruit notes, similar to an IPA." "There was a nice bready backbone for the citrus." "Much more complex than I expected it to be." 7.5% alc.

Cisco Captain Swain's Extra Stout ★★1/2
Stout: Cisco Brewers Inc., Nantucket, MA ciscobrewers.com
Aroma of "coffee, heavy cream and a touch of sourdough bread." "Thin and tangy in the mouth with a sharp bitterness in the flavor." "Not as thick as I would have liked from a stout." 8% alc.

Cisco Celebration Libation ★★1/2
Spice/Herb: Cisco Brewers Inc., Nantucket, MA ciscobrewers.com
"Fruity, spicy nose, plums anise and allspice all making appearances..." "Flavor of spice, nuts, cherries, cinnamon and orange peel." "It is like an Anchor Old Special Ale that is too timid to step forward." 8.5% alc.

Cisco Moor Porter ★★★★1/2
Porter: Cisco Brewers Inc., Nantucket, MA ciscobrewers.com
"Nice berry fruit and chocolate in the aroma." "Rich roasted flavors again that is much more on the bitter coffee side of the line than sweet chocolate side of things." "Too much fizz in there." 7% alc.

Cisco Summer of Lager ★★★★★
Helles/Dortmnd: Cisco Brewers Inc., Nantucket, MA ciscobrewers.com
"Aroma is dough, a bit of lemon and some grassy hops." "Lemongrass and fresh cut grass flavors, dandelion. Brisk and pleasant finish." "I'm sad that the bottle is now empty." 5.5% alc.

Cisco Whales Tale Pale Ale ★★1/2
Eng Pale Ale: Cisco Brewers Inc., Nantucket, MA ciscobrewers.com
"Nice clean mild hop aroma with a caramel malt aroma on the side." "Complex malt nuttiness to it, with the hops in the background." "Overall very plain." 5.6% alc.

City Festbier ★★
Märzen/Oktbfst: City Brewery (Melanie Brewing Co), La Crosse, WI www.citybrewery.com
"Earthy malt aroma with mild hops as well." "Lighter-bodied with a caramel base and some spicy, slightly bitter floral hops." "Smooth and lightly malty, much like any good Märzen and at this price, you'd be hard pressed to find a better one." 5.7% alc.

City LaCrosse Lager ★★★★1/2
Pale Lager: City Brewery (Melanie Brewing Co), La Crosse, WI www.citybrewery.com
"Wet paper bag aroma, very pale light golden appearance, soapy white head." "Light-bodied and crisp with a decent hoppy character, along with a hint of malt." "Relatively fresh, clean, reasonable body; what else do you want in a cheap lager?" N/A% alc.

City Lager ★★1/2
Pale Lager: City Brewery (Melanie Brewing Co), La Crosse, WI www.citybrewery.com
"Sweet, grainy aroma has a definite corniness to it." "Cheap corn malt taste but much more palatable than a welfare malt liquor." "If you've had on of these macro pale lagers, you've had them all." 4% alc.

City Pale Ale ★★

Am. Pale Ale: City Brewery (Melanie Brewing Co), La Crosse, WI www.citybrewery.com

"Light caramel and light grass hop scent." "Flavor is lightly bitter some grass and citrus hop touch of orange peel." "A good cheap session beer for those who prefer hops." 5.4% alc.

City Porter ★★

Porter: Tapps Brewpub and Steakhouse, La Crosse, WI

"Aroma is slightly sweet of chocolate and black malts" "Flavor is mildly sweet, with some roastiness, sour raisin and coffee." "By the end of the bottle I was enjoying this a fair bit, but it's quite forgettable a moment after the glass is empty." N/A% alc.

Clay Pipe Backfin Pale Ale ★★1/2

Am. Pale Ale: Clay Pipe Brewing Co., Westminster, MD www.cpbrewing.com

"Non-exciting - smooth, but thin; just some decent maltiness paired with a juicy citrus hop." "I think I have found the ale for me at Camden Yard." 4.8% alc.

Clay Pipe Pursuit of Happiness ★★★★1/2

Am Strong Ale: Clay Pipe Brewing Co., Westminster, MD www.cpbrewing.com

"Aroma is bread and cookie dough, some yeasty notes and loads of fruity esters, plums and raisins, light hop, pine and citrus." "The flavor is bold. Good bitterness and hops with a toffee and caramel malt balance." 8.25% alc.

Clipper City Balto MärzHon ★★

Märzen/Oktbfst: Clipper City Brewing Co., Baltimore, MD www.clippercitybeer.com

"Big, sweet, malt aroma, along with an ever-so-slight hint of pumpkin spice." "As smooth as an Oktoberfest should be, but not nearly as flavorful as I would like." 5.8% alc.

Clipper City Gold Ale ★★★

Goldn/Blond Ale: Clipper City Brewing Co., Baltimore, MD www.clippercitybeer.com

"Very subtle, lightly hoppy with a touch of crystal malt in the aroma." "Very mild, drinkable and smooth." "Undertone of hops if I went looking for it." "Just a little too timid." 4.9% alc.

Clipper City Heavy Seas Peg Leg ★★1/2

Imp. Stout: Clipper City Brewing Co., Baltimore, MD www.clippercitybeer.com

"Caramel aroma, nothing like an Imp. Stout generally gives you." "Is it good to drink? I think the answer is yes." "I can't imagine this doing very well among Imperial Stouts." 8% alc.

Clipper City Heavy Seas Red Sky at Night ★★1/2

Saison: Clipper City Brewing Co., Baltimore, MD www.clippercitybeer.com

Styled as a Belgian saison, this has an aroma "more hoppy than anticipated with a background of perfumey, alcoholic, earthy smells." "Malty, a little funky." "Not a bad beer but not a great saison." 8% alc.

Clipper City Heavy Seas Small Craft Warning ★★★★1/2

Eur Str Lager: Clipper City Brewing Co., Baltimore, MD www.clippercitybeer.com

"Aroma is very grassy, tons of saaz, some orange notes from the amarillo." "Toasted malt presence, light citrus flavor, plenty of earthy and spicy hop characteristics." "What an idea! A malty Pils" 7.5% alc.

Clipper City Heavy Seas Winter Storm ★★★1/2

Am Strong Ale: Clipper City Brewing Co., Baltimore, MD www.clippercitybeer.com

"Extremely floral aroma, well balanced with hints of citrus fruits." "Flavor is much more malty than I would have expected, with little in the way of abrasive hop tastes sometimes associated with double IPAs." 7.3% alc.

Clipper City McHenry Old Baltimore Style ★★
Premium Lager: Clipper City Brewing Co., Baltimore, MD www.clippercitybeer.com
"Aroma is moist grains, sweat, a hint of pepper and barely detectable hops." "Slightly sweet grains without much richness to them, a very light floral/grass hops." "Hopefully this "Old Baltimore Style Beer" never makes a big resurgence." 4.5% alc.

Clipper City Oxford Raspberry Wheat ★★1/2
Fruit Beer: Clipper City Brewing Co., Baltimore, MD www.clippercitybeer.com
"Malty, some caramel maybe and a very faint hint of raspberry." "Moderately sweet raspberry flavor." "The base beer used is so mild and unassuming." "Have had better beers of this style." 4.5% alc.

Clipper City Pale Ale ★★
Am. Pale Ale: Clipper City Brewing Co., Baltimore, MD www.clippercitybeer.com
"Woody, slightly piney hops meet toasty, breadcrusty malts in the nose." "Malts are sweet and caramel but kind of watery bodied." "Decent hop ending." "Overall it's alright, but has room for improvement." 4.9% alc.

Clovis ★★1/2
Bel. Strong Ale: Brasserie Dubuisson, Pipaix, Belgium www.br-dubuisson.com
"Peppery, herbal spiciness imparts its liveliness to the peachy fruitiness." "Very sweet with a lot of complexity including oranges, other fruits and different spices." "Complex cacophony of flavors." 7.5% alc.

Club Colombia ★★
Premium Lager: Grupo Empresarial Bavaria, Bogota, Colombia www.bavaria.com.co
"Sweet corn and honey aroma, vegetal, unfermented extract." "Flavor is pretty much nothing, just fizzy water with a little metallic tinge." "No wonder they all drink rum down there..." 4% alc.

Coast Range Maduro Porter ★★★1/2
Porter: Coast Range Brewing Co., Gilroy, CA
"I'm quickly taken aback by the amount of caramel malts thrown on top of the roasted ones in this beer." "Some chocolate and coffee poke through the nice smoky roasted malts that dominate the flavor of this one." 5.5% alc.

Cobra ★★1/2
Pale Lager: The Eagle Brewery (Charles Wells Ltd.), Bedford, Bedfordshire, England www.charleswells.co.uk
"Surprisingly malty aroma considering the ingredients." "Sweet and lightly fruity on the tongue with a modest bitter finish." "It's better than most of the subcontinental curry beers." 5% alc.

Colt 45 ★★
Malt Liquor: Miller Brewing Co. (SABMiller), Milwaukee, WI www.millerbrewing.com
"Slightly cidery, vaguely malty, with some higher alcohols." "Drinkable - with touches of malt alongside the expected raunch of cider and fusels." "A quick buzz totally unencumbered by taste." 5.61% alc.

Columbus Apricot Ale ★★★
Fruit Beer: Columbus Brewing Co., Columbus, OH www.columbusbrewing.com
"Huge fresh apricot aroma, some candy/syrupy notes and lightly roasted caramel malt (cookie) and yeast (dough, oak)." "Taste is definitely apricot tart, but there is also some grassy freshness." "This is your beer is you like apricots." N/A% alc.

Columbus Golden Ale ★★
Goldn/Blond Ale: Columbus Brewing Co., Columbus, OH www.columbusbrewing.com
"Aroma is slightly floral." "Taste is light grains and lots of lemon." "Definitely not CBC's best brew." "Doesn't stimulate the palate." N/A% alc.

Columbus Nut Brown ★★★★
Brown Ale: Columbus Brewing Co., Columbus, OH www.columbusbrewing.com
"Chocolate, roasted malt and light caramel aromas" "Some sweetness on the palate, toasty and chocolaty, malt dryness." N/A% alc.

 ★★★★★ SUPERIOR ★★★★ EXCELLENT ★★★ GOOD ★★ DRINKABLE ★ POOR

Columbus Pale Ale ★★1/2

Am. Pale Ale: Columbus Brewing Co., Columbus, OH www.columbusbrewing.com

"Fragrant floral hop and pine aroma, resiny with a medium roasted caramel malt (cookie) and citrus rind nose." "Solidly citrusy hoppiness shows lots hops flavor and a moderate bitterness." N/A% alc.

Concord Grape Ale ★★1/2

Fruit Beer: The Concord Brewery, Lowell, MA www.concordbrew.com

"Strong grape juice aroma right away." "Bittersweet flavors, light though, viney, unsweetened grape juice, wheat." "A fine novelty beer and one the fine folks of Massachusetts can be proud of." N/A% alc.

Concord IPA ★★★1/2

IPA: The Concord Brewery, Lowell, MA www.concordbrew.com

"Aroma is of bitter hops with a sweet malt undertone, almost like green grape." "Flavor is grassy with notes of oil oranges and peach, leading to a very hoppy end." "Easily a session ale." 5.5% alc.

Concord Junction Porter ★★★

Porter: The Concord Brewery, Lowell, MA www.concordbrew.com

"Taste is bitter coffee and chocolate finish." "Chocolate leading to hints of nuts and an ample roasted malt finish. Earthy hops balance the malts." "Kind of thin overall, but doable." 5.5% alc.

Concord Pale Ale ★★1/2

Am. Pale Ale: The Concord Brewery, Lowell, MA www.concordbrew.com

"Floral bouquet of hops." "Bitter flavors, same as aroma, little more clove and grapefruit." "Simple, but well-made." N/A% alc.

Coniston Bluebird Bitter ★★★★★

Bitter: Coniston Brewing Co. Ltd, Coniston, Cumbria, England www.conistonbrewery.com

"Aroma is a nice balance of sweet, fruity malt and floral, English hops." "Malts are caramelly and sweet, fruity with a touch of ice tea." "Damn sessionable." 3.6% alc.

Coniston Old Man Ale ★★1/2

Old Ale: Coniston Brewing Co. Ltd, Coniston, Cumbria, England www.conistonbrewery.com

"Smoke, cherry, wood in the nose." "Toasty, creamy malt, chocolate and then the heavy bitterness imparted by the challenger hops." "Nice English ale, pleasing and solid, but lacks that 'wow' factor." 4.8% alc.

Coopers Best Extra Stout ★★★1/2

Foreign Stout: Coopers Brewery Ltd., Regency Park, Australia www.coopers.com.au

"Aroma is dark chocolate, coffee grounds, mushrooms and earth." "Flavor was sweet chocolate, light coffee and a bit of vanilla." "This is a stout drinkers stout." 6.3% alc.

Coopers Dark Ale ★★

Brown Ale: Coopers Brewery Ltd., Regency Park, Australia www.coopers.com.au

"Malty, roasted chocolate, hazelnut aroma." "Body is thin, with a vague nuttiness and a metallic finish." "It needs some more body and character." 4.5% alc.

Coopers Original Pale Ale ★★

Goldn/Blond Ale: Coopers Brewery Ltd., Regency Park, Australia www.coopers.com.au

"Aroma is ordinary straw and tiny smell of hops." "Flavor is also light fruity, with a low-mid bitterness." "Sparkly, fresh with an herbal end note." 4.5% alc.

Coopers Sparkling Ale ★★★

Goldn/Blond Ale: Coopers Brewery Ltd., Regency Park, Australia www.coopers.com.au

"Initial herbal grassy aroma followed by bubblegum." "Sweet, toasted malt and bready yeast dominated the palate with a mix of herbal hop tones." "A unique beer that fits most occasions." 5.8% alc.

Coopers Vintage Ale ★★★
Eng. Strong Ale: Coopers Brewery Ltd., Regency Park, Austalia www.coopers.com.au
"Aroma has notes of ripened currants, raisin, tangerine, caramelized malting, mild vinous esters." "Sweet rich malt palate, apricot jam and cherries, noticeable alcohol warmth, mildly bitter in the finish." 7.5% alc.

Cooperstown Back Yard IPA ★★1/2
IPA: Cooperstown Brewing Co., Milford, NY www.cooperstownbrewing.com
"Flavor is dominated by sweet caramel malt and minor notes of hops." "Nice hop taste up front that gives way to a sort of sweet middle and a nice and floral, bitter hop finish." 6.1% alc.

Cooperstown Benchwarmer ★★1/2
Porter: Cooperstown Brewing Co., Milford, NY www.cooperstownbrewing.com
"Mild toasted malt nose, with hints of coffee and semi-sweet chocolate." "Flavor is almost like a slightly fruity coffee with some bitter and dry notes." "Nice, well-balanced porter." 6.3% alc.

Cooperstown Nine Man ★★
Goldn/Blond Ale: Cooperstown Brewing Co., Milford, NY www.cooperstownbrewing.com
"Aroma of pears and some citrus." "Taste is surprisingly sweet with a caramel twinge to it and a slight hoppy bite at the end." "Won't be enshrined in the Hall-of-Fame any time soon." 4.3% alc.

Cooperstown Old Slugger ★★1/2
Am. Pale Ale: Cooperstown Brewing Co., Milford, NY www.cooperstownbrewing.com
"Flavor is sweet, quite malty, very fruity, moderately alcoholic and has a very woody characteristic." "Not a landmark product but nicely done." 5.5% alc.

Cooperstown Pride of Milford Special Ale ★★★
Eng. Strong Ale: Cooperstown Brewing Co., Milford, NY www.cooperstownbrewing.com
"Begins with a sweet and buttery flavor and goes to a smooth malt backbone and a slightly sweet and fruity finish with a nice alcohol warmth." "Not what I had expected when given this treat." 7.7% alc.

Cooperstown Strike Out Stout ★★1/2
Sweet Stout: Cooperstown Brewing Co., Milford, NY www.cooperstownbrewing.com
"Fudgey, milk chocolate nose with vanilla, sweet malts." "Taste is of chocolate and coffee, but the palate is thin, fizzy." "I'd option Strike Out Stout to the 'AA' league of sweet stouts." 5.1% alc.

Coors Aspen Edge ★
Pale Lager: Coors Brewing Co. (MolsonCoors), Golden, CO www.coors.com
"The nose was... well, not there." "Slightly sweet and corn syrupy." "Virtually colorless, odorless and tasteless...just like carbon monoxide." 4.13% alc.

Coors Extra Gold ★★
Pale Lager: Coors Brewing Co. (MolsonCoors), Golden, CO www.coors.com
"Grassy and husky." "A slight sweet taste, which is pleasant, but not overwhelming." "Maybe the best of the big three's commercial offerings." 5% alc.

Coors Light ★
Pale Lager: Coors Brewing Co. (MolsonCoors), Golden, CO www.coors.com
"Pours a corpse-yellow." "A dazzlingly vacuous beer." "Although I have never tried to kill a werewolf with this beer, I'm quite sure that it must be good at killing werewolves." 4.2% alc.

Coors Original ★
Pale Lager: Coors Brewing Co. (MolsonCoors), Golden, CO www.coors.com
"Thin grain profile." "Malts and hops are all but non-existent." "Light and heavily carbonated." "Hard to believe this beer used to be smuggled east of the Mississippi!" 5% alc.

Corona Extra ★
Pale Lager: Grupo Modelo, México DF, Mexico www.gmodelo.com
"Huge skunky aroma." "No flavor." "This is the only beer that managed travel through my esophagus in both directions at the same time." 4.6% alc.

Corona Light ★
Pale Lager: Grupo Modelo , México DF, Mexico www.gmodelo.com
"Aroma of light malt, light DMS, slight woody notes." "Perfect example of what water would taste like with a beer run through it." "It does make the regular Corona seem pretty flavorful though." 3.7% alc.

Corsendonk Agnus ★★★★
Abbey Tripel: Brasserie du Bocq, Purnode-Yvoir, Belgium www.bocq.be
"Perfumed aroma of hops, fruit, yeast and lemon." "Nice, laid-back flavor with some banana, dried flowers and some slight lemony residue." "A very easy to drink beer, very mild; nicely sweet finish." 7.5% alc.

Corsendonk Christmas Ale ★★★★1/2
Bel. Strong Ale: Brasserie du Bocq, Purnode-Yvoir, Belgium www.bocq.be
"Rich and spicy aroma, reminded me of spiced rum." "A very solid malty base that features some chocolate and coffee flavors. A wheaty, fruity, tart finish with just a touch of alcohol." 8.5% alc.

Corsendonk Pater ★★★★1/2
Abbey Dubbel: Brouwerij Van Steenberge, Ertvelde, Belgium www.vansteenberge.com
"Aroma is of nuts, raisin and a surprising amount of citrus." "Taste has Christmas fruits and a little chocolate. There is sourness and some malt and wood." "Does everything you would expect, but doesn't have any distinctive character." 7.5% alc.

Cottrell Old Yankee Ale ★★★1/2
Amber Ale: Cottrell Brewing Co., Pawcatuck, CT www.cottrellbrewing.com
"Toasty, grainy, caramel malty aroma has some sugary character and a touch of hay and grassy hops." "Flavor is quite malty upfront." "This is a solid amber ale." 5% alc.

Country Club Malt Liquor ★
Malt Liquor: Pabst Brewing Co., Chicago, IL www.pabst.com
"Healthy amount of sweetness (corn, cereal, sweet grains, crackers). Light bitterness; surprisingly balanced for a malt liquor." "A very light flavor for a malt liquor." "Definitely needed a paper bag." Pabst brand, contract brewed by Miller. N/A% alc.

Crazy Stallion ★★
Malt Liquor: City Brewery (Melanie Brewing Co), La Crosse, WI www.citybrewery.com
"Aroma was sour, stale cabbage." "Taste was mostly yeast and corn it was thin and a little sour, with a little bitterness." "It just doesn't have that 'kick you in the nuts' character that I look for in a good malt liquor." 5.9% alc.

Cricket Hill American Ale ★★★
Amber Ale: Cricket Hill Brewing Co., Fairfield, NJ www.crickethillbrewery.com
"Nose was a nice blend of toasted grains, florals and touches of toffee." "Flavor was similar with floral hops and caramel malt balancing each other to near perfection." 5% alc.

Cricket Hill East Coast Lager ★★★★1/2
Pale Lager: Cricket Hill Brewing Co., Fairfield, NJ www.crickethillbrewery.com
"Aroma is fairly clean with some spicy herbal notes, a bit of lemon and a clean, sweet grainy maltiness." "Malty, sweet flavor up front followed by very light bitterness from modest hopping." 5% alc.

Cricket Hill Hopnotic IPA ★★
IPA: Cricket Hill Brewing Co., Fairfield, NJ www.crickethillbrewery.com
"Very light nose of floral hops and nutty caramel." "Weak flavor of spicy and citrusy hops with a bitter finish." "Not one of the better IPA's I've had." N/A% alc.

Crooked River Original ESB ★★★★★
Prem Bitter: Crooked River Brewery (Snyder Intl), Frederick, MD
"Exceptionally well balanced." "Juicy and hoppy and so, so quaffable." "Caramel malt aroma nicely balanced by a floral hop nose." "Wouldn't mind having it as a regular in my beer fridge." 5.8% alc.

Crooked River Robust Porter ★★★1/2
Porter: Crooked River Brewery (Snyder Intl), Frederick, MD
"Rich coffee scent with a fainter chocolate presence." "It's robust, as advertised." "Medium sweet chocolate flavors." "Good porter but also a rather basic one." 4.9% alc.

Crooked River Select Lager ★★1/2
Helles/Dortmnd: Crooked River Brewery (Snyder Intl), Frederick, MD
"Aroma is bready malts, with a touch of sweetness." "Hops are mild and slightly spicy. Light and refreshing. Crisp and clean." "It doesn't floor me, but all-in-all a solid beer." 5.4% alc.

Crooked River Yuletide ★★1/2
Spice/Herb: Crooked River Brewery (Snyder Intl), Frederick, MD
Malty, floral, piney aroma." "Figs, caramel, spiciness reminds me of eggnog, herbiness reminds me of clove or mint, sugar like brown." "I'll just assume this was brewed with the leftover nutmeg from their fall seasonal." 6.7% alc.

Cruzcampo ★★
Pale Lager: Grupo Cruzcampo SA (Heineken), Sevilla, Spain www.cruzcampo.es
"Light pale malt aroma, with a honeyish note." "Thin palate, grassy, light sulfurous aroma and flavor." "For some reason this didn't annoy me as much as it should have." 5% alc.

Cusqueña ★★
Pale Lager: Cervecera del sur del Peru (Grupo Empresarial Bavaria), Peru www.cervesur.com.pe
"Sweet corn, vegetables aroma." "Flavor maybe brings some hops and malts, but this is most of all water." "An easily forgettable brew." 5% alc.

Cusqueña Malta ★
Schwarzbier: Cervecera del sur del Peru (Grupo Empresarial Bavaria), Peru www.cervesur.com.pe
"Nose is moderately sweet, caramel, bread, light plum, metallic." "Taste is sweet, brown sugar, caramel, maple syrup, some chocolate. No bitterness, soda-ish." "Sugary, smooth and underdeveloped." 5.6% alc.

Cuvée Angelique ★★1/2
Belgian Ale: De Proefbrouwerij, Lochristi, Belgium www.proefbrouwerij.com
"Fruity aroma, somewhat alcoholic with mildly perfumey notes." "Taste is medium sweet, caramel, some orange, yeasty spicy, cherry, faint astringency." "I found this beer rather ordinary." 7% alc.

Cuvée Diabolique ★★★
Abbey Tripel: De Proefbrouwerij, Lochristi, Belgium www.proefbrouwerij.com
"Medium sweet aroma - yeasty, herbal, some lemon, light floral, paint thinner." 'Flavors are of sweet malts, spices and citrus." "Yep, a Duvel clone all the way." 8.5% alc.

Czar-Pushka ★
Pale Lager: Pivzavod AO Hamovnikov (SABMiller), Moscow, Russia www.bochka.ru
"Aroma was doughy malty and contained a mild sweaty sock note." "Little else showed up in the flavor with the exception that I could sort of detect a hop presence." "It's worth trying at least once but much more then that would be wasting money." 5.3% alc.

Czech Rebel ★★1/2
Bohemian Pilsner: Mestansky Pivovar, Czech Rep. www.hbrebel.cz
Smell is nice and grassy and really sort of smells like outdoors. "Body starts with a faint hint of maltiness and some earthy dry bittering hops and thins incredibly toward a very bland watery finish." "Better than a Heineken, I guess. But no Urquell." 4.7% alc.

Czechvar ★★★1/2
Bohemian Pilsner: Budweiser Budvar, Ceske Budejovice, Czech Rep. www.budvar.cz
Aroma is malty, a little herbal and floral. "Flavor is relatively sweet for style, with hints of bread and saaz." "Very enjoyable, though it seems I could feel that the bottle had traveled a couple thousand miles." 5% alc.

DAB Original ★★
Classic Ger Pils: Dortmunder Actien Brauerei , Dortmund , Germany www.dab.de
"Nice leafy-hoppy aroma." "Finish is dry, slight bready with grassy hops." "Surprisingly refreshing and drinkable." 5% alc.

Daleside Morocco Ale ★★1/2
Eng. Strong Ale: Daleside, Harrogate, North Yorkshire, England
"Aromas of chocolate milk, ginger and maybe some vanilla." "Flavors of dried fruits, caramel, nice roasted taste of black coffee, cloves, cardamom and lots of ginger, some hop bitterness." "Really interesting flavors and a really unique beer." 5.5% alc.

Daleside Old Legover ★★
Brown Ale: Daleside, Harrogate, North Yorkshire, England
"Slight nut and wood aroma." "A definite caramel presence exists along with some nutmeg and vanilla flavors." "When are British brewers going to understand that they have to serve their bottled beers as a live product?" 4.1% alc.

Dark Horse 3 Guys Off the Scale Old Ale ★★★★★
Barley Wine: Dark Horse Brewing Co., Marshall, MI www.darkhorsebrewery.com
"Rum soaked fruitcake, dark fruits, brandy like alcohol, brown sugar and very mild aroma hops in the nose." "Very alcoholic mouthfeel, lots of toffee-caramel and burnt brown sugar flavors, with just a hint of lingering bitterness." 12.2% alc.

Dark Horse Belgian Amber ★★1/2
Belgian Ale: Dark Horse Brewing Co., Marshall, MI www.darkhorsebrewery.com
"Aroma is fruit, cloves and hops." "Complex moderate hop and candy flavor with a medium bitter finish." "Interesting twist on an amber ale." 5.2% alc.

Dark Horse Crooked Tree IPA ★★★
IPA: Dark Horse Brewing Co., Marshall, MI www.darkhorsebrewery.com
"Sticky sweet aroma with some dusty, piney, grapefruity hops." "Biscuity tea leaf flavor, hop profile is there but somewhat light, albeit smooth." "Reminded me that summer is ending." 6% alc.

Dark Horse Double Crooked Tree IPA ★★★★1/2
Imp/Dbl IPA: Dark Horse Brewing Co., Marshall, MI www.darkhorsebrewery.com
"Aroma of fresh lemon, nectar and alcohol. There is a real sharpness to the aroma." "Thick as a brick. The syrupy malts hit me first, then a rush of citrus hops." "Damn, do I love this brewery." 13.6% alc.

Dark Horse Fore Smoked Stout ★★★★1/2
Smoked: Dark Horse Brewing Co., Marshall, MI www.darkhorsebrewery.com
"Aroma of a mix of coffee and the smell your clothes get after sitting around a campfire all night." "Taste is rich with chocolate and smoke malts. Great smoky taste, pretty unique in that the finish is a hearty, campfire smokiness." 8% alc.

Dark Horse Imperial Stout ★★★★★

Imp. Stout: Dark Horse Brewing Co., Marshall, MI www.darkhorsebrewery.com

"Richly malty aroma with an almost smokiness." "Flavor is a rush of alcohol, chocolate and a finish of powdery coffee." "Campfire finish." "Overall, nice sippin' beverage." 10.6% alc.

Dark Horse One Oatmeal Stout ★★★★

Sweet Stout: Dark Horse Brewing Co., Marshall, MI www.darkhorsebrewery.com

"Aroma is roasted malts, rich milk chocolate, a bit of plum." "Roasted malts, berries and herbal hops play off each other nicely in the flavor with fair finishing, roasty bitterness." 8% alc.

Dark Horse Reserve Special Black Bier ★★★★★

Porter: Dark Horse Brewing Co., Marshall, MI www.darkhorsebrewery.com

"A big beer for a porter, very rich with loads of molasses and other sweet notes at first taste, surprisingly smooth as it finishes, nicely balanced hops accompany this awesome beer." 8% alc.

Dark Horse Sapient Trip ★★★

Abbey Tripel: Dark Horse Brewing Co., Marshall, MI www.darkhorsebrewery.com

"Slightly meaty nose pulls together the light fruity yeast with hints of spiced pear, wildflower honey and apple." "Yeasty bread dough, the bananas and cloves really come through." "My tastebud were numbed for a few hours." 8.6% alc.

Dark Horse Too Cream Stout ★★★★★

Sweet Stout: Dark Horse Brewing Co., Marshall, MI www.darkhorsebrewery.com

"Espresso and chocolate aromas, with hints of vanilla, roast and brownies, quite the vibrant little blend of malt aromatics." "Bitter chocolate and coffee and all creamy, this was excellent." 8% alc.

Dark Horse Tres Blueberry Stout ★★★★★

Fruit Beer: Dark Horse Brewing Co., Marshall, MI www.darkhorsebrewery.com

"Aroma is roasted malt and fried blueberries - like when they are blackened in pancakes cooked on a griddle." "Blueberry flavors are in front, but they complement the stout flavors very well." 4.5% alc.

De Dolle Arabier ★★★★

Bel. Strong Ale: De Dolle Brouwers, Diksmuide, Belgium

"Citrus and yeasty aroma with hints of lemon orange, banana, melon, floral hops, honey and light spices." "Flavor is only slightly sweet with a grapefruit bitterness in the finish. It is very dry for a Belgian, with a lot of spices." 7% alc.

De Dolle Boskeun ★★★★1/2

Bel. Strong Ale: De Dolle Brouwers, Diksmuide, Belgium

"Aroma of apple orange peel, peach, yeast and spice." "Light balance of acidic cherry and sweet candi sugar, some light hops, honey and orange peels." "A lovely and surprising mouthful of good ale." 8.9% alc.

De Dolle Dulle Teve ★★★★1/2

Abbey Tripel: De Dolle Brouwers, Diksmuide, Belgium

"Soft apple and cinnamon nose with a little pepper and doughy yeast." "Powerful, broad taste of bread, coriander, yeast with quite a bit of alcohol heat and a good deal of bitterness at the end." "Has to be one of the best triples I've had, mad or sane." 11% alc.

De Dolle Dulle Teve Special Reserva ★★★★1/2

Abbey Tripel: De Dolle Brouwers, Diksmuide, Belgium

"Very winery, alcoholic and slight apply tartness." "Predominantly woody, slightly tannic, with a hint of buttery-oak and perhaps even a hint of vanilla." "Definitely enjoyable, but just not nearly the beer that the regular version is." 11% alc.

De Dolle Extra Export Stout ★★★★★

Foreign Stout: De Dolle Brouwers, Diksmuide, Belgium

"Aroma is sweet - plummy and fruitcake with roasty, nutty notes." "Rich black malt flavor, with hints of roast, toast and hop." "A most unusual stout and damned tasty!" "Only slight downer is that there is just a touch too much carbo for me." 9% alc.

De Dolle Oerbier ★★★★★

Bel. Strong Ale: De Dolle Brouwers, Diksmuide, Belgim

"Bread, raisins, plums, port, sugar, caramel, slight mint, citrus, marshmallows, cedar and vanilla." "Excellent sweet flavor that tastes like a cherry and apple tort." "A very special beer." 9% alc.

De Dolle Oerbier Special Reserva ★★★★★

Bel. Strong Ale: De Dolle Brouwers, Diksmuide, Belgium

"Aroma of pears, apples, malt, alcohol… interesting and appetizing." "Sourish, sappy body carries notes of earth, low-lov crystal malts, pear, wood, straw and late alcohol." "A real pleasure." 13% alc.

De Dolle Stille Nacht ★★★★★

Bel. Strong Ale: De Dolle Brouwers, Diksmuide, Belgium

Some red wine characteristics, caramel, honey and an overall nice sweetness." "Flavor was damn good, sweet candied orange and peach." "It brings a tear to my eye that I drank it and have none left." 12% alc.

De Koninck ★★1/2

Belgian Ale: Brouwerij De Koninck, Antwerpen, Belgium

"Aroma is dusty-toasty malts, with a dry yeastiness and herbal notes." "Sweetish toffee-like malts mingle with fruity tastes from the yeast and some mild bittering in the finish." "Not terribly exciting but still a well balanced, enjoyable and easy to drink beer." 5% alc.

De Proef Knock Out (K-O) ★★★★

Abbey Tripel: De Proefbrouwerij, Lochristi, Belgium www.proefbrouwerij.com

"Aroma is mild, slightly fruity with sweet malt and a whiff of yeast." "Sweet and grapey, candied yams, grandma's sweet potatoes, warm applesauce, citrus touches." "Strongly reminiscent of Allagash Triple Reserve." 10% alc.

De Ranke Kriek ★★★★★

Fruit Beer: Brouwerij De Ranke, Dottignies/Dottenijs, Belgium

Aroma of cherry, slight old wooden barn - dry and musty." "Very sour, but with balancing sweetness provided by the cherries. Long, dry woody aftertaste leaving the mouth dry." "A fascinating experience." 7% alc.

De Ranke Père Noël ★★★★

Belgian Ale: Brouwerij De Ranke, Dottignies/Dottenijs, Belgium

"Spicy heather, wooden and nutty aroma." "Peppery and hoppy first, mellows down then with a lots of nice malt and yeast." "Very different than expected." 7% alc.

De Ranke XX Bitter ★★★★1/2

Belgian Ale: Brouwerij De Ranke, Dottignies/Dottenijs, Belgium

"Wonderfully herbal, hoppy aroma with slight coriander." "Bitter, rooty flavors - quinine-like; aromatic malts also show through." "The hoppiest Belgian beer I've yet sampled." 6.2% alc.

Delirium Nocturnum ★★★

Bel. Strong Ale: Brouwerij Huyghe, Melle, Belgium www.delirium.be

"Aroma of prune, raisin, alcohol, nutmeg." "Flavors are a well balanced combo of malt, sugar, a hint of Belgian chocolate and sweet fruits." "Not as full-bodied or complex as expected but still quite nice." 9% alc.

Delirium Noel ★★★★

Bel. Strong Ale: Brouwerij Huyghe, Melle, Belgium www.delirium.be

"Really boozy aroma with some toffee and a little bit of ginger." "Strongly malty flavor with less sweetness than expected but with a nice warming combination of toasted biscuit, anise, cocoa and yeast." 10% alc.

Delirium Tremens ★★★1/2

Bel. Strong Ale: Brouwerij Huyghe, Melle, Belgium www.delirium.be

"Aroma is almost candy-sweet and fruity." "Taste is cloves and spices, a little lemony citrus, followed by that barnyard hay and finishing with a bit of an alcohol bite." "I may be seeing those pink elephants sooner than I thought!" 9% alc.

Deschutes Bachelor ESB ★★★1/2

Prem Bitter: Deschutes Brewery, Bend, OR www.deschutesbrewery.com

"Big, long bitterness within an equally big malt that is mostly nondescript except for malt sugar and some bubblegum-like flavor." "I like malt and balance and this one has a lot of both." "Another winner from Deschutes." 5.4% alc.

Deschutes Black Butte Porter ★★★★

Porter: Deschutes Brewery, Bend, OR www.deschutesbrewery.com

"Roasty fore which transitions quickly to smooth chocolate and mild creamed coffee notes and finishes with a hint of molasses and maple syrup." "Almost made the business trip bearable." 5.2% alc.

Deschutes Cascade Ale ★★★

Goldn/Blond Ale: Deschutes Brewery, Bend, OR www.deschutesbrewery.com

"Grapefruit type aroma lingers with this beer." "It's quite fruity, yeasty, lightly bitter and the pale malts are very light." "For a golden ale it is exceptional." 4.6% alc.

Deschutes Cinder Cone Red ★★★★★

Amber Ale: Deschutes Brewery, Bend, OR www.deschutesbrewery.com

"Balanced nose of apricots, buttery yeast, melon seeds and peppery hops." "Flavors of toffee and some roasted malt with just enough hops to balance the sweetness without being noticeable." "Stellar session brew." 5.8% alc.

Deschutes Jubelale ★★★★

Eng. Strong Ale: Deschutes Brewery, Bend, OR www.deschutesbrewery.com

"Tannic wood aroma, with some caramel." "Filled with sweet fruits and spice, toffee and candy and then some roast and a bitter finish." "A fresh and decent malt-centered holiday ale." 6.7% alc.

Deschutes Mirror Pond Pale Ale ★★★1/2

Am. Pale Ale: Deschutes Brewery, Bend, OR www.deschutesbrewery.com

"Sweet, lightly fruity aroma, some honey and flowers with the lighter scents of grapefruit and tangerine." "Supported marginally by the toasty, sweetish malts; the finish yielding juicy, citric, piney hop flavors." 5.3% alc.

Deschutes Obsidian Stout ★★★★1/2

Stout: Deschutes Brewery, Bend, OR www.deschutesbrewery.com

"Rich depth of malt flavor, more highly roasted malts, coffee and creamy chocolate to be found, very nicely balanced with a slight amount of fruity hop flavor and bitterness." "Certainly deserving of its high rank here." 6.4% alc.

Deschutes Pine Mountain Pils ★★★★1/2

Classic Ger Pils: Deschutes Brewery, Bend, OR www.deschutesbrewery.com

"Aroma is dominated by herbal, noble hops that lend a clean sharpness over a solid base of toasted, crackery malt." "Clean and crisp, with a dry firmness of body." "Well done German-style Pils that doesn't hold back on the hop flavor." 5.1% alc.

Deschutes Quail Springs IPA ★★★
IPA: Deschutes Brewery, Bend, OR www.deschutesbrewery.com
This cloudy orange IPA exudes a mild sweet citrus aroma." "It drinks balanced, with those smooth English hops and that iced-tea, you know tannic stuff, being well blended to the degree of sweetness." 5.8% alc.

Deschutes Twilight Ale ★★★
Bitter: Deschutes Brewery, Bend, OR www.deschutesbrewery.com
"Spicy, grapefruity, grassy aroma." "Grassy and floral hop flavors complemented by mild malt accents." "I could drink a lot of this while barbecuing." 5% alc.

Desperados ★
Pale Lager: Fischer, Schiltigheim, Alsace, France
"Sweet - smells of Sprite, lime and lager." "Tequila-ish, I reckon. But cloyingly sweet and artificial." "It was definitely my worst experience in Paris." 5.9% alc.

Deus ★★★★
Bel. Strong Ale: Brouwerij Bosteels, Buggenhout, Belgium
"Aroma of PineSol, cologne, spices (mace, cardamom) and occasional biscuity malts." "Brimming with elderflower, pepper, herbs and sweetish fruit." "A very special, very interesting, very expensive beer." 11.5% alc.

Diamond Bear Irish Red ★★
Irish Ale: Diamond Bear Brewing Co., Little Rock, AR www.diamondbear.com
"Clear amber color with a malty, spicy aroma. "Taste is malty with bread crust and some nuts." "The malt could be richer." N/A% alc.

Diamond Bear Pale Ale ★★1/2
Eng Pale Ale: Diamond Bear Brewing Co., Little Rock, AR www.diamondbear.com
An amber-colored brew with a leafy hop aroma. "Nicely bitter" with "rich caramel," this is a balanced brew in the English tradition. "Arkansas is lucky to have a quality beer like this available to them." N/A% alc.

Diamond Bear Southern Blonde ★
Goldn/Blond Ale: Diamond Bear Brewing Co., Little Rock, AR www.diamondbear.com
"Nice golden yellow with a decent white head. Nose is slightly sweet malt with some decent crisp hops." "Has some lager qualities flavor wise and it is a thirst quencher." "Not bad...but." N/A% alc.

Dick's Barley Wine ★★1/2
Barley Wine: Dicks Brewing Co., Centralia, WA www.dicksbeer.com
"Aroma is nicely malty with a good fruity side and maybe a hint at the up coming alcohol." "Vinous notes with tinge of caramel in malt character." "Kinda of an odd duck..." 10% alc.

Dick's Belgian Tripel ★★★
Abbey Tripel: Dicks Brewing Co., Centralia, WA www.dicksbeer.com
"Lightly sweet aroma with a backdrop of astringent herbal notes." "Sweet fruitiness on the palate, canned peaches oranges and pears, a touch of candi sugar." "Needs more balance to be very good ." 9% alc.

Dick's Best Bitter ★★1/2
Prem Bitter: Dicks Brewing Co., Centralia, WA www.dicksbeer.com
"Very floral, fruity and grassy nose is actually reminding me of a cheap, sweet white wine." "Taste is quite sweet throughout with a good spicy hop bite at the end and a long lasting bitter aftertaste." 5.6% alc.

Dick's Bottleworks IPA ★★★★
Imp/Dbl IPA: Dicks Brewing Co., Centralia, WA www.dicksbeer.com
"Aroma is big and brash, big piney hops, also alcohol and some caramel malt." "Thick, clean, crystalmalty body balanced with lots of bitterness but surprisingly understated aromatics for a Pacific Northwest IPA." 8.5% alc.

Dick's Cream Stout ★★★

Sweet Stout: Dicks Brewing Co., Centralia, WA www.dicksbeer.com

"Cocoa nose, minor charred wood, coffee bean and very light alcohol as well." "Has a certain malted chocolate shake type note going on with the body, sweetness and chocolate notes." "A very nice dessert beer." 6.25% alc.

Dick's Danger Ale ★★1/2

Brown Ale: Dicks Brewing Co., Centralia, WA www.dicksbeer.com

"Lightly roasted malt, caramel, nutty aroma, slightly funky." "Taste also is very light, lightly roasty to semi toffeeish malts, ho hopping discernable." "Pretty flavorful complex brown ale that never goes too far." 5.6% alc.

Dick's Double Diamond Winter Ale ★★★

Am Strong Ale: Dicks Brewing Co., Centralia, WA www.dicksbeer.com

"Sweet malty aroma, strong plummy fruit, dark cherry and sweet toffeeish malts." "Flavor is also quite sweet and malty up front, but is quickly drowned by a herbal, woodsy bitterness." 8.5% alc.

Dick's Grand Cru ★★1/2

Bel. Strong Ale: Dicks Brewing Co., Centralia, WA www.dicksbeer.com

"Candyish, sugary, peachy aroma with hints of caramel, bread crust and mushrooms." "Sweet up front with an fruity orange like character that is accented by a bit of acidity." "Might be too sweet for many people though." 11.1% alc.

Dick's Imperial Stout ★★★1/2

Imp. Stout: Dicks Brewing Co., Centralia, WA www.dicksbeer.com

"Roasted malt nose, slight lactose, a bit of cocoa as well." "A bit more hoppy on the tongue, semi-sweet, soft cocoa and chocolate." "It's solid, but lacking greatness." 7.3% alc.

Dick's IPA ★★1/2

IPA: Dicks Brewing Co., Centralia, WA www.dicksbeer.com

Smell is peachy and orange with lots of biscuity malt being highlighted in the background." "Big, fat blast of hop bitterness slaps my face and calls me Sally." "You definitely need to be ready for a hop onslaught though." 6% alc.

Dick's Lava Rock Porter ★★1/2

Porter: Dicks Brewing Co., Centralia, WA www.dicksbeer.com

"Decent chocolate, roast grain and coffee in aroma." "Fruity hops interplay with sweet chocolate flavors, minimal roastiness." "The ratings are all over the place on this brew." 7% alc.

Dick's Rye Ale ★★

Ale: Dicks Brewing Co., Centralia, WA www.dicksbeer.com

"Pale malt aroma, light honey, apple/pear esters, more of a wheaty spiciness than rye." "Light fruity esters with some lemon notes and a light rye flavor, some earthy bitterness." "Hop Rod Rye this ain't, but it's not bad." 5.1% alc.

Dick's Silk Lady ★★1/2

Belgian Ale: Dicks Brewing Co., Centralia, WA www.dicksbeer.com

"The aroma is probably the best aspect of this beer, with banana, clove, breadiness, grass, twigs and malt being dominant." "Fairly light version of a Belgian blonde, some spice, mild fruitiness, definite clove, very light bitterness in the finish." 4.5% alc.

Diebels ★★

Altbier: Diebels (InBev), Issum, Germany www.diebels.de

"Moderate malty aroma with some caramel and spices, some flowery aromatic hops too." "Thinly flavored malty beer with very little character." 4.9% alc.

Dillon Dam Dam Straight Lager ★★1/2
Vienna: Dillon Dam Brewery and Restaurant, Dillon, CO www.dambrewery.com
"An amber lager with aroma of "earthy malts and sweet caramel with a touch of spicy hops." "Sweet watery malts up front with a bit of a spicy lightly bitter finish." N/A% alc.

Dillon Dam Extra Pale ★★★
Am. Pale Ale: Dillon Dam Brewery and Restaurant, Dillon, CO www.dambrewery.com
"Aroma is moderate grapefruit and floral hops with a nice balance of malt (cookie)." "Coating, rich and earthy hop flavor, fresh and piney." N/A% alc.

Dillon Dam Sweet Georges Brown ★★1/2
Brown Ale: Dillon Dam Brewery and Restaurant, Dillon, CO www.dambrewery.com
"Brown sugar aroma with caramel and a little nut." "Quite sweet, but with complex nutty, toasty malt notes." "I've had much better browns but this is drinkable." N/A% alc.

Dinkelacker CD-Pils ★★
Classic Ger Pils: Dinkelacker-Schwaben Bräu AG (InBev), Stuttgart, Germany www.ds-ag.de
"Aroma of pale malt, skunk and a bit of caster sugar." "Flavor starts slightly sweet and quickly gives way to a crisp hop bitterness." "For a German beer this one is weak." 4.9% alc.

Dinkelacker Dark ★★
Dunkel: Dinkelacker-Schwaben Bräu AG (InBev), Stuttgart, Germany www.ds-ag.de
"Solid molasses and caramel aroma." "Malt flavor is definitely tasty, but the flavor lacks punch and disappears too quickly in the short-lived finish." "Watery and inoffensive." 5.5% alc.

Dixie Beer ★★1/2
Pale Lager: Dixie Brewing Co., New Orleans, LA
"Light hoppy citrus aroma. Light to medium body with a thin texture and fizzy carbonation." "typical pale lager flavor with little hops, some malt and a watery finish. Plain and simple" 4.6% alc.

Dixie Blackened Voodoo ★★
Schwarzbier: Dixie Brewing Co., New Orleans, LA
"Aroma is hard to find but some malts make an appearance." "Flavors reminded me somewhat of a weak brown ale with suggestions of coffee and roasted malt." "A well-balanced lightweight." 5% alc.

Dixie Crimson Voodoo ★★1/2
Am Dark Larger: Dixie Brewing Co., New Orleans, LA
"Light caramel malt aroma with some candied sugar." "Tasting with a touch of caramel...hmm, almost like an Oktoberfest." "Drinkable, but not exactly the kind of thing that gets you fired up." 5% alc.

Dixie Jazz ★★1/2
Pale Lager: Dixie Brewing Co., New Orleans, LA
"Yet sweet in the mouth with a gentle dry graininess." "On the whole not very memorable and easily out classed by just a regular Sam Adams Boston larger." N/A% alc.

Dock Street Amber ★★★
Amber Ale: Matt Brewing Co., Utica, NY www.saranac.com
"Smell is lightly grassy and sweet fruity aromas underlying." "Faint hops on the tongue and a slight bitter finish." 6% alc.

Doctor Diesel ★★
Eur Str Lager: Pivovarnia Ivana Taranova, Kaliningrad, Russia www.taranov.ru
"Expected this to be more malt liquorish with a name like Doctor Diesel." "Thin bodied but still sticky and cloying." "I guess the best I can say is that it's a decent slamming beer." 6.9% alc.

Dogfish Head 120 Minute IPA ★★★★★
Imp/Dbl IPA: Dogfish Head Brewery, Milton, DEL www.dogfish.com
"Piney, citric aroma, but with underlying syrupy notes." "Sweet and malty with a big orange flavored hoppiness." "Big." "Hard to believe this is 21%." 21% alc.

Dogfish Head 60 Minute IPA ★★★★1/2
IPA: Dogfish Head Brewery, Milton, DEL www.dogfish.com
"Intoxicating aroma of citrus and hoppy florals." "Tastes of grapefruit, citrus and caramel malt." "Very well balanced like the 90 - but much lighter in every way." 6% alc.

Dogfish Head 90 Minute Imperial IPA ★★★★★
Imp/Dbl IPA: Dogfish Head Brewery, Milton, DEL www.dogfish.com
"Spicy hop nose and noticeable alcohol with a subtle malt underpinning." "Sweet flavor up front, fruity with some light honey, but big, dry hoppiness at the finish." "Top shelf in the category." 9% alc.

Dogfish Head Aprihop ★★★★★
Fruit Beer: Dogfish Head Brewery, Milton, DEL www.dogfish.com
"Lightly sweet and fruity up front, more toasty bread and faint caramel, thereafter being dominated by hops, fresh, juicy, citric and spicy, with a prominently bitter close and lingering grapefruit and apricot." 7% alc.

Dogfish Head Au Courant ★★★
Fruit Beer: Dogfish Head Brewery, Milton, DEL www.dogfish.com
"A love it or hate it beer. So either "bland berries a touch sour and wateriness.. blah" or "winery and tart, somewhat champagne-like," with "strong, sour fruit flavors." 7% alc.

Dogfish Head Burton Baton ★★★★
Imp/Dbl IPA: Dogfish Head Brewery, Milton, DEL www.dogfish.com
"Alcohol up front is quickly replaced by a fruity, citrus, spicy, strongly hopped flavor." "Taste was not as hoppy as one would expect." "Flavors of caramel, light hops, pepper with a dry mellow bitter finish." 10% alc.

Dogfish Head Chicory Stout ★★★1/2
Stout: Dogfish Head Brewery, Milton, DEL www.dogfish.com
"Aroma of malt, roasted coffee, dark chocolate, vanilla, spices, hops and a little sourness. Smells wonderful." "A little milder than I like my stouts to be." "If you only want to have one or two stouts, this is great." 5.2% alc.

Dogfish Head Festina Lente ★★
Fruit Lambic: Dogfish Head Brewery, Milton, DEL www.dogfish.com
"All about tart peach, oak and hints lemon." "Nicely funky flavor of lemon drops and peaches with firm, pleasing tartness." Recent ratings suggest this beer has improved a lot since its early days. 7% alc.

Dogfish Head Golden Shower ★★★1/2
European Strong Lager: Dogfish Head Brewery, Milton, DEL www.dogfishhead.com
Smells like the malt smell that pervades the Coors plant during the tour. "Malty sweet flavor with a light bitterness on the finish." "I wouldn't mind seeing this in a 12-oz. bottle, as this 750 is gonna try to kick my ass." 9% alc.

Dogfish Head Immort Ale ★★★★★
Barley Wine: Dogfish Head Brewery, Milton, DEL www.dogfish.com
"Lush body." "It's like I'm sipping a fine port while standing in a humidor." "Rich maltiness that is full of earthy and oaken woody flavors, with hints of vanilla and maple." "Like a smoked barley wine." 11% alc.

Dogfish Head Indian Brown Ale ★★★★★
Brown Ale: Dogfish Head Brewery, Milton, DEL www.dogfish.com
Quite sticky on the palate, with lots of sweetness in there (chocolate, molasses and caramel), semi-fresh coffee grind and a roasted nuttiness." "Finishes like liquefied brown sugar and melted Roles." 7.2% alc.

Dogfish Head Liquor de Malt ★★★★★
Malt Liquor: Dogfish Head Brewery, Milton, DEL www.dogfish.com
"There truly is a finely groomed suggestion of sweet midsummer buttered corn." "Had some floaters - why do some people hate them so much?" "The smoothest malt liquor I've had." "I am going to be CRUNKED when I finish this!" 7% alc.

Dogfish Head Midas Touch ★★★1/2
Traditional Ale: Dogfish Head Brewery, Milton, DEL www.dogfish.com
"Made with malt, honey, saffron and Muscat grapes. "The flavor starts off with a mead-like sweetness, then turns vinous and slightly sour." "Very sweet flavor. It is closer to a mead than it is to what we generally think of as beer." 9% alc.

Dogfish Head Olde School Barleywine ★★★★1/2
Barley Wine: Dogfish Head Brewery, Milton, DEL www.dogfish.com
"Tastes hugely malty but not cloying as many Barley Wines, balanced nicely with a hop bitterness that accents the malt." "Not as thick and syrupy as one might imagine, but definitely on the hot side." 15% alc.

Dogfish Head Pangaea ★★1/2
Spice/Herb: Dogfish Head Brewery, Milton, DEL www.dogfish.com
"Complex, musty aroma of yeast, lemon, ginger and fresh herbs." "Flavor accents of white cranberries, grapes, ginger and cinnamon." "Unique and enjoyable after dinner quaff." 7% alc.

Dogfish Head Punkin Ale ★★★
Spice/Herb: Dogfish Head Brewery, Milton, DEL www.dogfish.com
"Dominated by nutmeg and cinnamon with a bit of brown sugar." "No pumpkin in the taste so far as I can observe." "Nicely warm finish." 7% alc.

Dogfish Head Raison D Etre ★★★★
Am Strong Ale: Dogfish Head Brewery, Milton, DEL www.dogfish.com
"Unique to say the least." "Richly complex, malty, phenolic (bubblegum), yeasty (banana), somewhat brandyish nose." "Taste is very oak-resiny, hops, prunes, some roast malt." 8% alc.

Dogfish Head Shelter Pale ★★1/2
Am. Pale Ale: Dogfish Head Brewery, Milton, DEL www.dogfish.com
"Aroma is mostly floral hops with a little mild caramel malt." Taste is "easy on the hops" and "laid back." "An average, unremarkable craft beer." 5% alc.

Dogfish Head World Wide Stout ★★★★★
Imp. Stout: Dogfish Head Brewery, Milton, DEL www.dogfish.com
One of the strongest beers in the world, this stout is "liquid obsidian," with notes of "plums, cherries, red wine, licorice." "Surprisingly smooth flavor, chocolate with caramel and vanilla." "Something to be savored." "Unique." 21% alc.

Dojlidy Magnat ★★★
Eur Str Lager: Browar Dojlidy (KP-SABMiller), Bialystok, Poland www.kp.pl
"Flowery and sweet citrus fruit with a bit of maltiness is prevalent." "Strong, clean, lightly grainy and slightly sweet malt profile with a nice fresh hop bite toward the dry finish." 7% alc.

Dojlidy Zubr (Bison) ★★
Premium Lager: Browar Dojlidy (KP-SABMiller), Bialystok, Poland www.kp.pl
"Slightly spicy hop note mixed with bready malt (as per the Polish prototype)." "Sweet toasty pale malt, caramelized malt, straw accent, with a low expression of bitterness on the finish." "Standard East European lager." 6% alc.

Dominion Ale ★★1/2
Amber Ale: Old Dominion Brewing Co., Ashburn, VA www.olddominion.com
"Medium caramel and malt flavor gives way to slightly acidic, citrus finish." "Mild malt flavors with a lagery crispness accentuated by spicy Kent Golding notes." 4.7% alc.

Dominion Lager ★★★★
Helles/Dortmnd: Old Dominion Brewing Co., Ashburn, VA www.olddominion.com
Aroma of "light bread and some nice hops." "Flavor was good; really stuck to style, caramel, malty doughy bread-like with just enough bitterness." "One of the tastier Helles that I have come across." 5.4% alc.

Dominion Millennium ★★★★★
Barley Wine: Old Dominion Brewing Co., Ashburn, VA www.olddominion.com
"A bit of sweet honey and some hints of toffee at first, strong piney hops and some cherries." "Taste is sweet caramel with a full body and a creamy texture." "Very sweet and sugary, with honey laden malts, sherry and a well aged malt flavor." 10.4% alc.

Dominion Oak Barrel Stout ★★★★
Stout: Old Dominion Brewing Co., Ashburn, VA www.olddominion.com
Aroma mixes oak, vanilla and coffee." "Sweet, roasty malt followed by coffee, there is a touch of bourbon on the finish." "An enjoyable stout, definitely a pleasant surprise." 5.2% alc.

Dominion Oktoberfest ★★★★
Märzen/Oktbfst: Old Dominion Brewing Co., Ashburn, VA www.olddominion.com
"Malty, a bit sharp and very fall like aroma." "Molasses, some biscuit, some notes of spicy noble hops." "Having compared several American Oktoberfest beers, Dominion's version easily tops my list." 6.4% alc.

Dominion Pale Ale ★★★★1/2
Am. Pale Ale: Old Dominion Brewing Co., Ashburn, VA www.olddominion.com
"Soft malty aroma, slight graininess, even slighter hop." "A solid session beer, in my mind, as it has a relatively full flavor that is not overpowering in any aspect." 5.6% alc.

Dominion Spring Brew ★★★★★
Eur Str Lager: Old Dominion Brewing Co., Ashburn, VA www.olddominion.com
The style varies on this brew. In 2004 and 2005 it was a very highly regarded Imperial Pilsner. Prior to that it was a Bock that received mediocre reviews. If 2006 is the Imperial Pilsner again, you'll want some. 8.5% alc.

Dominion Summer Wheat ★★★
Bel. Witbier: Old Dominion Brewing Co., Ashburn, VA www.olddominion.com
The style varies on this brew. The 2005 version was a Dunkelweizen. Previously it was a Witbier and a Hefeweizen. The Hefe scored very well for the style but the past two have been more mixed in their reviews. 0% alc.

Dominion Winter Brew ★★1/2
Scotch Ale: Old Dominion Brewing Co., Ashburn, VA www.olddominion.com
The style varies on this brew. In 2004, it was an Imp. Stout that garnered mixed reviews. Previous years so a very popular Polish Porter recipe and before that was Scottish Ale. 6.7% alc.

Don de Dieu ★★★★
Bel. Strong Ale: Unibroue (Sleeman), Chambly, Quebec www.unibroue.com
"Aroma of a Belgian witbier - citrus notes and spices, with a handful of sugary malts and yeast." "Touches of fruits like peaches and apples, vanilla and some curaçao liqueur." "An unusual take on something we all know well." 9% alc.

Dos Equis XX Amber ★
Vienna: Femsa, Monterrey/Veracruz-Llave, Mexico www.femsa.com
"Sweet malt aroma with a hint of fruit and some hop notes." "Flavor is mild but pleasant, with a bit of caramel." "I drink this in Mexican restaurants where it's generally the best available among a group of weak competitors." 4.7% alc.

Dos Equis XX Special Lager ★★1/2
Pale Lager: Femsa, Monterrey/Veracruz-Llave, Mexico www.femsa.com
Faint grassy aroma." "Flavor is inoffensive with a little grain, dryish, slight mineral note." "There is nothing in this beer that repulses me." 4.45% alc.

Double Diamond ★
Bitter: Leeds (Carlsberg UK), Leeds, W. Yorkshire, England www.carlsberg.co.uk
"Caramel aroma and flavor, hints of earth." "Taste is harshly metallic-bitter, some tart citrusy hops, some artificial malt sweetness." "I only got a 9-oz. glass and chugged the last half so I could leave." 5% alc.

Double Enghien Blond ★★
Bel. Strong Ale: Brasserie de Silly, Silly, Belgium www.silly-beer.com
"Aroma is medium sweet, lemon, some yeast, banana." "Earthy, dryish flavor of pale malts, dried fruit and some spices." "It is almost as if the grain bill disappears completely." 7.5% alc.

Double Enghien Brown ★★1/2
Abbey Dubbel: Brasserie de Silly, Silly, Belgium www.silly-beer.com
"Toasted malt aroma with toffee and nuts." "Sweet (fruity) flavor with a faint bitterness." "I found I quite enjoyed it by the end, just really freakin' weird." 8% alc.

Dragon Stout ★★1/2
Foreign Stout: Desnoes and Geddes Ltd (Diageo PLC), Kingston, Jamaica
"Aroma is licorice and bready malt." "Roasty licorice fades somewhat in the body leaving a perversely thin yet sweet and partly fermented feel." "Quite basic and unsubtle, but remarkably good." 7.5% alc.

Drake's Imperial Stout ★★★★
Imp. Stout: Drakes Brewing Co., San Leandro, CA www.drinkdrakes.com
"Sweet chocolate, some raisins and roasted malt and a little coffee in the aroma." "The flavor isn't overly strong." "I like this beer a lot, but it has stiff competition in a crowded field." 9% alc.

Drake's IPA ★★★★1/2
IPA: Drakes Brewing Co., San Leandro, CA www.drinkdrakes.com
"Nose of fresh cut grass sprinkled over grapefruit, nice toasted biscuit malts and spicy preludes of the bitterness to come." "The beer is quite citrusy up front." "If I had another bottle it would probably be empty." 7.2% alc.

Drax Beer ★★
Pale Lager: SC Martens SA, Galati, Romania www.martens.ro
"Aroma is lightly sweet (almost Red Bull-ish) with a hint of skunk and grass." "Euro-lager sweetness with what seems like an extra sugar kick and hints of apple." "Odd beer, like a fruit beer mixed with a pale lager." 5% alc.

Drie Fonteinen Oude Geuze ★★★★★
Gueuze: Geuzestekerij Drie Fonteinen, Beersel, Belgium www.3fonteinen.be
"The aroma is a complex, earthy wall; full of yeasty barnyard, cellar, hay, lemongrass, citrus, wood and sour apple." "Taste is sour and musty with hints of dirt, cobweb, slight bitterness and apples." "Drie Fonteinen is the session gueuze." 6.5% alc.

Drie Fonteinen Oude Kriek ★★★★1/2
Fruit Lambic: Geuzestekerij Drie Fonteinen, Beersel, Belgium www.3fonteinen.be
"Goaty, barnyard brett aromas with moderate sour cherry notes." "Simultaneously juicy and dry, with a juggling robust brett and vibrant cherry showcase." "It breaks my heart to see the last sip go." 5% alc.

Drie Fonteinen Schaerbeekse Kriek ★★★★★
Fruit Lambic: Geuzestekerij Drie Fonteinen, Beersel, Belgium www.3fonteinen.be
"Nose is of sweet cherries, cinnamon, wood and earth notes." "Very tart wild cherry flavor with sour blanket goodness; wild, earthy, woody." "Not terribly complex, but a wonderfully pure Kriek." 6% alc.

Duchesse de Bourgogne ★★★★
Flem Sour Ale: Brouwerij Verhaeghe, Vichte, West-Vlaanderen, Belgium www.brouwerijverhaeghe.be
"Mix of woody lactic notes, tomato, pomegranate, apple skins and acetic notes." "Intense sour flavor, lots of fruit, very complex and vinous." "You have to love acetic acid (vinegar) to enjoy this beer. If you don't, it'll go down the drain." 6.2% alc.

DuClaw Bad Moon Porter ★★★
Porter: DuClaw Brewing Co., Abingdon, MD www.duclaw.com
"Aroma is roasted malt, coffee and a hint of coffee." "Strong coffee taste, very bitter along with some sweetness from dark grapes and chocolate." "An awesome beer to have at a ballgame." 5.1% alc.

DuClaw Black Jack Stout ★★★★★
Imp. Stout: DuClaw Brewing Co., Abingdon, MD www.duclaw.com
"Strong doses of coffee and bourbon wafting out, along with some chocolates." "Milky-sweet chocolate milkshake body with little bitterness." "Thick, oily texture with some good, thick lacing on the glass. A stout worthy of its score." 8% alc.

DuClaw Devi's Milk ★★★★★
Barley Wine: DuClaw Brewing Co., Abingdon, MD www.duclaw.com
"Sticky sweet malty aroma, brown sugar, molasses and subtle dark pitted fruit on the nose." "Strong sweet flavor with good prunes and caramel in the taste." "A shame this only comes around once a year." 12.2% alc.

DuClaw Serum ★★★★
Imp/Dbl IPA: DuClaw Brewing Co., Abingdon, MD www.duclaw.com
"Bursting citric hops (centennial?) evoke wood, grapefruit and lemon." "Sharp tangy hop flavor with fair bitterness over a sweet, biscuity malt base." "Finish is long, bitter and somewhat earthy." 8% alc.

DuClaw Venom Pale Ale ★★★★★
Am. Pale Ale: DuClaw Brewing Co., Abingdon, MD www.duclaw.com
"Lots of hoppy notes, citrus fruits, sweet malts and light spice." "highlighting fresh hops, showing grassy, pine and light grapefruit hops, as well as a bit of light grains and malt with a bit of dough on the finish." 5.6% alc.

Duinen Dubbel ★★★1/2
Abbey Dubbel: Brouwerij Huyghe, Melle, Belgium www.delirium.be
"Piercing, rich toffee nose loaded with raisins, light fruits, dark chocolate and lively spices." "The malts, mixed with some berry sweetness, hit you right away and leave your pallet dry like a champagne with some hoppy bitterness." 8% alc.

Duinen Tripel ★★★
Abbey Tripel: Brouwerij Huyghe, Melle, Belgium www.delirium.be
"Aroma is spicy, fruity (citrus, peach and a bit pineapple) and a bit herbal." "Strong fruity flavor with a candy-like citrus character." "Not one of my favorites, especially since this one is usually more expensive than most other tripels." 9% alc.

Dunedin Apricot Peach ★★★
Fruit Beer: Dunedin Brewery, Dunedin, FL www.dunedinbrewery.com
"HUGE aromas of apricot and peach... very fruity, very real, very nice." "Hints of the apricot and peach are here but not as strong as I desired." "Almost soda-like." 5.2% alc.

Dunedin Beach Tale Brown ★★
Brown Ale: Dunedin Brewery, Dunedin, FL www.dunedinbrewery.com
"Nice smooth malt profile finishes with just a smidgeon of hops." "Palate was light and very carbonated." "Good if you like a roasty, very bitter brown ale." 5.2% alc.

Dunedin Celtic Gold ★★
Goldn/Blond Ale: Dunedin Brewery, Dunedin, FL www.dunedinbrewery.com
"Nice hoppy aroma that hints at some underlying sweetness." "Tastes more like a pale ale than just a gold ale." "Relatively bitter finish." 5.2% alc.

Dunedin Christmas Farm Ale ★★1/2
Spice/Herb: Dunedin Brewery, Dunedin, FL www.dunedinbrewery.com
"Lightly spicy, nutmeg dominated." "Palate is thin and watery." "Overtly spicy. All the flavors of x-mas!" "Although on the spicy side, its not that bad." 5.2% alc.

Dunedin Highland Games Ale ★★1/2
Porter: Dunedin Brewery, Dunedin, FL www.dunedinbrewery.com
"Hoppy aroma with chocolate and coffee." "Flavor is hops, chocolate and coffee, with a slight tartness. Smokey and roasty with a bitter finish." "Overall a good brew to share." 5.2% alc.

Dunedin Leonard Croon's Old Mean Stout ★★1/2
Stout: Dunedin Brewery, Dunedin, FL www.dunedinbrewery.com
"Flavor is of coffee, some chocolate and some bitter hops to finish it off." "This doesn't blow you away with over the top flavor but it is a pretty nice stout as far as drinkability." 5.2% alc.

Dunedin Oktoberfest Ale ★
Märzen/Oktbfst: Dunedin Brewery, Dunedin, FL www.dunedinbrewery.com
"Caramel, slight toastiness, slight vanilla in the aroma." "Mild caramel, toasted malt and an herbal hop character all try to poke through with limited success." "It's not awful it just isn't very good." 5.2% alc.

Dunedin Piper's Pale ★★1/2
Am. Pale Ale: Dunedin Brewery, Dunedin, FL www.dunedinbrewery.com
"Floral aroma with some sweet malt behind it." "Nice malt profile with plenty of floral and evergreen hops for bite." "Not super complex, but very good." 5.2% alc.

Dunedin Razzbeery Wheat ★★1/2
Fruit Beer: Dunedin Brewery, Dunedin, FL www.dunedinbrewery.com
"Aroma is of wheat and a little hint of raspberry ." "Taste is bittersweet with tart fruits, yeast, light wheat notes, hops and some sweetened malt." "Over-carbonated." "Not bad, but could use more intense raspberry flavor." 6% alc.

Dunedin Red Head ★★
Amber Ale: Dunedin Brewery, Dunedin, FL www.dunedinbrewery.com
"Sweet, malty aroma of caramel and dark bread with some leafy tobacco notes." "The hops are strong enough to add a mild punch." "It's not one of the better Dunedin's but it's certainly much better than your standard restaurant beers." 5.2% alc.

Dupont Avec Les Bons Voeux ★★★★★
Saison: Dupont Brasserie, Tourpes-Leuze, Belgium www.brasserie-dupont.com
"Yeasty, peppery aroma with pear esters." "Flavors are a beautiful melding of spices, yeasty esters (cloves and bananas), crisp spicy hops, peppermint." "This is quite simply a masterfully crafted beer and the finest 'Super-Saison' I have had." 9.5% alc.

Dupont Bière de Miel ★★★
Saison: Dupont Brasserie, Tourpes-Leuze, Belgium www.brasserie-dupont.com
"Pleasing aroma of spicy grasses, lemon, honey, melon husks, sweet candy and pepper." "Taste is a little bit dry with some light honey. There are also some grassy notes with a little bit of bread." 8% alc.

Duvel ★★★★★

Bel. Strong Ale: Brouwerij Moortgat, Breendonk-Puurs, Belgium www.duvel.be

"Simplicity of the ingredients to form such a complex beer amazes me." "Pear/apple esters, light pale malt, sweaty yeast and a hint of alcohol." "This is a unique beer." "The more of these I drink the more I like them." 8.5% alc.

EJ Phair Indian Pale Ale ★★★

IPA: E.J. Phair Brewing Co., Concord, CA www.ejphair.com

"Fruity, malty and quite sweet, with loads of orange citrus." "Hops are grapefruity and piney and very pronounced." "It's definitely a solid brew that doesn't stand out but doesn't stand down either." 7% alc.

Eau Bénite ★★★

Abbey Tripel: Unibroue (Sleeman), Chambly, Quebec www.unibroue.com

"Aroma is yeasty and peppery spicy with lemony notes." "Taste is full and spicy, very tripelish and very tasty." "Aftertaste is somewhat short for a beer so complex." 7.7% alc.

EB Premium ★

Pilsner: Elbrewery Co. Ltd. (Heineken), Elblag, Poland

"Fruity and slightly caramelly aromas, with a minor note of herbal hops." "Refreshing mouthful, a bit more body than most; with nice carbonation." "This is what Labatt's Blue would taste like if it was an all-malt commercial pilsner." 5.7% alc.

Ebulum ★★★

Traditional Ale: Williams Brothers (Heather Ales), Alloa, Central, Scotland www.fraoch.com

"Aromas of dark berries/wood and a hint of chocolate." "Sweet and malty, slightly smoky with some licorice." "Sure this wasn't a wine?" 6.5% alc.

Eddie McStiff's Chestnut Brown ★★

Brown Ale: Eddie McStiffs Restaurant and Micro Brewery, Moab, UT www.eddiemcstiffs.com

"Fruit hop (melon) and lightly roasted caramel malt aroma." "Rather nutty and bring notes of toasted honey wheat bread on top." "A barely there/slightly above average brown." N/A% alc.

Edelweiss Hefetrüb Weissbier ★★★

Hefeweizen: HofBräu Kaltenhausen (Brau Union AG), Hallein, Austria www.edelweissbier.at

"Richly banana aroma is chased by a slightly citric flavor, smooth but not especially tangy." "Flavor has some spiciness and citrus notes." "Very patio-friendly." 5.5% alc.

Edelweiss Weissbier Dark ★★1/2

Dunkelweizen: HofBräu Kaltenhausen (Brau Union AG), Hallein, Austria www.edelweissbier.at

"A bit subdued aroma but with hints of clove and light spice." "Flavor is actually pretty mellow and easy drinking with a slight lemon twist as well as bubblegum flavoring and bitter aftertaste left behind." 5.5% alc.

Edelweiss Weissbier Kristallklar ★★1/2

Kristallweizen: HofBräu Kaltenhausen (Brau Union AG), Hallein, Austria www.edelweissbier.at

"Aroma is sweet malty and dominated by wheat." "Pronounced flavors of wheat, but completely lacking the fruity esters from the Hefe." "Probably average, but felt better." 5.5% alc.

Edison Light ★★1/2

Pale Lager: New Century Brewing Co. Boston, MA www.saranac.com

"Sweet, grassy, corny and mildly spicy aroma." "Corn-like flavors. Finishes watery." "Not much flavor, but it isn't actively nasty in any way." Contract brewed by Matt Brewing Co. 4% alc.

Eel River Certified Organic Amber Ale ★★1/2

Amber Ale: Eel River Brewing Co., Fortuna, CA www.eelriverbrewing.com

"Grainy, minimally sweet and lightly roasty." "This would have been good with some traditional beer-loving food: cheese, pizza, salami, Indian food." 4.75% alc.

Eel River Certified Organic Extra Pale Ale ★
Am. Pale Ale: Eel River Brewing Co., Fortuna, CA www.eelriverbrewing.com
"This one has an evergreen and lemony nose, maybe a little flowery with some yeast hints." "Flavor has some buttery accents with a citrusy undertone." "Decent beer to have with dinner but Keystone is cheaper." 0% alc.

Eel River Certified Organic Indian Pale Ale ★★1/2
IPA: Eel River Brewing Co., Fortuna, CA www.eelriverbrewing.com
"Fairly citrusy hop aroma with a bit of malt backing and pine." "Alcohol becomes pretty evident, more so than the typical 7% ABV beer would show." "Taste is run-of-the-mill West Coast IPA." 7% alc.

Eel River Certified Organic Porter ★★★★
Porter: Eel River Brewing Co., Fortuna, CA www.eelriverbrewing.com
Complex aroma of roasted bread, chocolate and dark fruits." "The sweetness dominates early, but is countered by a moderate bitterness in the finish." "Next time, I'll buy more than just a single bottle." 5.5% alc.

Efes Dark ★★★
Am Dark Larger: Anadolu Efes, Istanbul, Turkey www.efespilsen.com.tr
"Weak aroma of roasted malt, chocolate and hops." "Flavor was sweet, malty and caramel." "Surprisingly good for a Turkish mass produced dark lager." 6.5% alc.

Efes Extra ★★★★
Malt Liquor: Anadolu Efes, Istanbul, Turkey www.efespilsen.com.tr
"Kinda skunky, but malt sweetness overrides it." "Forwardly sweet, slightly tart, with some candy corn like flavor." "To my surprise this is a pretty good malt liquor" 8% alc.

Efes Pilsen (Pilsner) ★★1/2
Pale Lager: Anadolu Efes, Istanbul, Turkey www.efespilsen.com.tr
"Aroma is of light grains and bread." "Some hints of cardboard and oxidized malt in the front of the palate but otherwise pretty tasteless." "I didn't expect much from a Turkish beer and I got what I expected." 5% alc.

Einbecker Mai-Ur-Bock ★★1/2
Bock: Einbecker Brauhaus, Einbeck, Germany www.einbecker.com
"Very floral and perfumey aroma with notes of grass, cereal and cookies." "Sweet initial flavor followed by some sugary malt and finished with a dash of hop." "Just the way you want a Maibock to taste." 6.5% alc.

EKU 28 ★★
Eisbock: Kulmbacher Brauerei , Kulmbach, Germany www.kulmbacher.de
"Big aroma - alcohol, toffee, lacquerish phenols, cashews." "Viscous body; simplistic palate with fat, cloying maltiness and alcoholic dryness." "They use alcohol to try to balance malts and this just doesn't work for me." 11% alc.

EKU Pilsner ★★1/2
Classic Ger Pils: Kulmbacher Brauerei , Kulmbach, Germany www.kulmbacher.de
"Aroma is malty and buttery with a splash of honey and grass." "Flavor is milder than expected, rather malty and sweet, little hop flavor." "On the sweet side for a German Pils." 5% alc.

El Toro IPA ★★★★1/2
IPA: El Toro Brewing Co., Morgan Hill, CA
"If I'm in California eventually there is one thing I crave, an over the top West Coast IPA." "Big piney hop nose with a light citrus note." "Great hop flavor with a tongue numbing bitterness." 6.5% alc.

El Toro Negro Oatmeal Stout ★★★★
Sweet Stout: El Toro Brewing Co., Morgan Hill, CA
"Bitter, chocolaty nose." "Flavor is rich chocolate and roasty malt." "One of the most chocolaty stouts I've had." "Decent coffee substitute this morning." 5.5% alc.

El Toro Poppy Jasper Amber ★★★★
Amber Ale: El Toro Brewing Co., Morgan Hill, CA
"Clean balanced amber with definite caramel and crystal malt." "Finishes dry and crisp with nice hop flavor." "Gets points for being far superior to other insipid American beers calling themselves 'Amber Ales.' " 5.3% alc.

Elk Rock Wapati IPA ★★
IPA: Portland Brewing Co. (Pyramid), Portland, OR www.portlandbrew.com
"Aroma is fairly pleasant with citric and piney hops and a decent malt background." "Fairly well balanced, hops become a touch harsh toward the finish but not atrocious." "A starter IPA." N/A% alc.

Ellezelloise Hercule Stout ★★★★★
Imp. Stout: Ellezelloise, Ellezelles, Belgium www.brasserie-ellezelloise.be
"Great aroma of smoke, roasted malt, chocolate, caramel and more." "Flavor of chocolate cookies, caramel and liqueur with smooth oak characters." "Distinct and more complex than the vast majority of American stouts." 9% alc.

Ellezelloise Quintine Ambr,e ★★★★
Bel. Strong Ale: Ellezelloise, Ellezelles, Belgium www.brasserie-ellezelloise.be
"Rye bread and caramel aroma from the Münich malts." "Spicy mixture of maple syrup, brown sugar, raisin and oddly, grapefruit." "It stays with you for some time - definitely a slow drinker." 8.5% alc.

Ellezelloise Quintine Blonde ★★★
Bel. Strong Ale: Ellezelloise, Ellezelles, Belgium www.brasserie-ellezelloise.be
Aroma is must, leather and fruit." "Flavor is very fruity, banana, pear, white pepper, coriander, even some clove." "Very appetizing beer." 8% alc.

Elmwood Amber Ale ★
Irish Ale: Elmwood Brewing Co., Elmwood, IL www.elmwoodbrewing.com
"Taste had toffee and dirt dominating. Then there was old apple core and hint of cardboard." "Nothing to exciting going on here." 4.59% alc.

Elmwood Nut Brown ★
Brown Ale: Elmwood Brewing Co., Elmwood, IL www.elmwoodbrewing.com
"Oh man, what went wrong here?" "Flavor was sour and mildly malty with a roasted malt note and some bitterness on the finish." "Not very good at all." 4.73% alc.

Elysian Ambrosia Maibock ★★
Bock: Elysian Brewing Co., Seattle, WA www.elysianbrewing.com
"Malty, mildly yeasty aroma." "Sweet malty sweet and light earthy smoke and spicy hops." "Clean, but not big." 6.1% alc.

Elysian Avatar Jasmine IPA ★★1/2
IPA: Elysian Brewing Co., Seattle, WA www.elysianbrewing.com
"Jasmine comes through on both the nose and mouth very clearly and plays off the hop tones." "Very fruity dry hopped taste, with a jasmine tea flavor floating on everything." "The flowers are a unique element to an IPA, but it's quite nice." 5.6% alc.

Elysian Bête Blanche Belgian Triple ★★★
Abbey Tripel: Elysian Brewing Co., Seattle, WA www.elysianbrewing.com
Aroma is fruit and spices, very floral and complex." "Flavor is a bit phenolic, coriander, clove, heavier bitterness than is typical." "Interesting, but not something I'm blown away by." 6.9% alc.

Elysian Bifröst Winter Ale ★★★
Am Strong Ale: Elysian Brewing Co., Seattle, WA www.elysianbrewing.com
"Hoppy aroma a bit stale some nice citrus and a good caramel with a twinge of alcohol." "Flavor begins with sweet malt accented by a bit of nuttiness. This is promptly gunned down by a Cascade hop barrage." "Reminds me of something from Rogue." 7.5% alc.

Elysian Cyclops Barleywine ★★★1/2
Barley Wine: Elysian Brewing Co., Seattle, WA www.elysianbrewing.com
"Rich brown sugary character with butter and nuts." "Sweet honey malt in mouth, with floral hops in attack, lingering bitterness and warm alcohol." "Nice UK style barleywine." 9.85% alc.

Elysian Dragonstooth Stout ★★★★1/2
Sweet Stout: Elysian Brewing Co., Seattle, WA www.elysianbrewing.com
"Roasty, nutty, rich aroma with dark chocolate hints and sweet dark malts." "Mix of bitter coffee grains, sweet milk chocolate, dry chocolate and caramel malts." "I am fully digging this, a must try for any stoutie." 7.2% alc.

Elysian Fields Pale Ale ★★★
Am. Pale Ale: Elysian Brewing Co., Seattle, WA www.elysianbrewing.com
"Woody, earthy bitterness balanced by toasty and pale malts." "Nose seems a bit English in nature, fruity, slightly malty and lightly hoppy." "Feel is a bit thin and the aftertaste is a steady hops bite." 4.8% alc.

Elysian Icarus Belgian-style Tripel ★★1/2
Abbey Tripel: Elysian Brewing Co., Seattle, WA www.elysianbrewing.com
"Nose is pungent with American caramel malts and citrusy American hops; faint notes of alcohol and Belgian yeast." "Overly sweet, cloying candi sugar, vanilla, lemon." "Has the alcohol and the sweetness of a barleywine" 9.8% alc.

Elysian Perseus Porter ★★★
Porter: Elysian Brewing Co., Seattle, WA www.elysianbrewing.com
Chocolate, sour apple, courant, coffee and espresso make up the taste a long with a touch of vanilla." "Very rich chocolate aroma with a very slight hint of coffee hidden in there." "An interesting, almost dessert like beer...pleasant and warming." 5.4% alc.

Elysian Polyphemus Barleywine ★★★
Barley Wine: Elysian Brewing Co., Seattle, WA www.elysianbrewing.com
"Strong malt, a touch bitter on the sides of the tongue, some burnt malt/crème brûlée style at times, perhaps a touch fruity, but really fairly one-dimensional." "Too candy sweet to be top shelf." 8.5% alc.

Elysian Saison Elysée ★★★
Saison: Elysian Brewing Co., Seattle, WA www.elysianbrewing.com
"An acidic aroma, with tart pineapple, light cardamom and light sugar cookies." "A little tart, a little funky, spicy and a touch earthy." "Quite refreshing beer with a slightly hoppy finish." 5.8% alc.

Elysian The Immortal IPA ★★★
IPA: Elysian Brewing Co., Seattle, WA www.elysianbrewing.com
"Aroma is pine and grapefruit and orange peel." "A lingering bitter, herbal and pine-like note dominates the flavor profile of this biting beer." "This beer has me planning a trip to the Northwest sometime in the not so distant future." 6.3% alc.

Elysian The Wise Extra Special Bitter ★★★★
Prem Bitter: Elysian Brewing Co., Seattle, WA www.elysianbrewing.com
"Caramel, bread, with some hop presence (pine)" in the aroma. "Tastes peppery with some mild caramel notes and a bitter blood orange." "Bitterness was more like an Indian Pale Ale than an ESB, but a nice complement to the malts." 5.9% alc.

Elysian Zephyrus Pilsner ★★★
Pilsner: Elysian Brewing Co., Seattle, WA www.elysianbrewing.com
"Aroma is a pleasant, slightly sweet grain, bready honey smell." "Taste is surprisingly bitter, with a blast of strong and bitter hops." "A different sort of pilsner." 4.7% alc.

Empyrean Burning Skye Scottish Ale ★
Scottish Ale: Empyrean Brewing Co., Lincoln, NEB
"Macro-ish hop smell with a little spice and a vague whiff of caramel malt." "Taste is thin, body is thinly malty with a little hop bitterness." "Fairly weak and uninteresting." 6.45% alc.

Empyrean Chaco Canyon Honey Gold ★★★★1/2
Pale Lager: Empyrean Brewing Co., Lincoln, NEB
"Muted aroma, slightly floral." "The flavor was light malt and a mildly sweet honey hint with just a bit of caramel and maybe some spiciness." "Light beer all round." N/A% alc.

Empyrean Dark Side Vanilla Porter ★★1/2
Porter: Empyrean Brewing Co., Lincoln, NEB
The vanilla is the main aspect of this beer." "Sweet malt flavors and a dark roast note." "A slight bit thin for the style." "If you like vanilla, here you go." N/A% alc.

Empyrean LunaSea ESB ★★1/2
Prem Bitter: Empyrean Brewing Co., Lincoln, NEB
"Aroma is pleasantly malty with biscuit being predominant." "Sweet malt with some light hop bitterness in the finish." "All Extra Special Bitters should at least try to be this good." N/A% alc.

Empyrean Third Stone Brown ★★★
Brown Ale: Empyrean Brewing Co., Lincoln, NEB
Aroma is of bark, hinting at bread crust, pecans and tobacco." "Malty front with light nuttiness leads to more iron-tasting middle. Finishes with earthy, toasty notes and an increase in hop dryness." N/A% alc.

Endurance Pale Ale (Tom Creans Ale) ★★
Am. Pale Ale: Mercury Brewing and Distribution, Ipswich, MA www.mercurybrewing.com
"Light citrus, grassy aroma and floral hops as well, rather weak." "Balance of light malt and bitter finish." "Lacks definition." N/A% alc.

Erdinger Pikantus ★★★
Weizen Bock: Erdinger WeissBräu, Erding, Belgium www.erdinger.de
"Aromas started bland with caramel and grain alcohol, but opened up to find banana, leather, apricot preserves." "Spicy and complex with a full range of dark fruits and malts and just a hint of tartness." "Different, interesting, but not dynamic." 7.3% alc.

Erdinger Weissbier ★★1/2
Hefeweizen: Erdinger WeissBräu, Erding, Germany www.erdinger.de
"Surprisingly light aroma - slight spicy, sweaty yeast note." "Watery flavor with faint bananas and a dusty yeast note." "This was sub par even for the style." 5.3% alc.

Erdinger Weissbier Dunkel ★★1/2
Dunkelweizen: Erdinger WeissBräu, Erding, Germany www.erdinger.de
"Nose is fruity with hints of tobacco, chocolate and molasses." "Body is solid with a malty front - hints of molasses and brown sugar." "Far better than the regular hefe-weiss, but nothing to either sneer or exalt." 5.6% alc.

Erdinger Weissbier Kristallklar ★★
Kristallweizen: Erdinger WeissBräu, Erding, Germany www.erdinger.de
"Aroma of light lemon and banana, a bit grassy." "Dense banana fruity taste with a malty background." "I would prefer a Hefe almost any day of the week." 5.3% alc.

Estes Park Porter ★★
Porter: Estes Park Brewery, Estes Park, CO www.epbrewery.net
"Coffee aroma, roasted, with a hop nose." "Body quite roasty and dry, initially rather beguiling but quickly becoming quite thin and merely dry and papery toward the finish." 4.6% alc.

Estes Park Renegade ★★1/2
IPA: Estes Park Brewery, Estes Park, CO www.epbrewery.net
"Fragrant floral and citrus hop aroma." "Sweet, sugary, juicy malts, with excessive bitterness and once again, dulled hop flavors." "Not a complicated or unique Indian Pale Ale, this one tastes like the standard homebrew IPA kit recipe." 5.5% alc.

Estes Park Samson Stout ★★★
Stout: Estes Park Brewery, Estes Park, CO www.epbrewery.net
"Expressive stout nose with hints of roasted malts (cocoa, chocolate, coffee, roast), along with a hint of raisins." "Sweet oatmeal and chocolate blend with a light roastiness and a generous amount of hops." 5% alc.

Estrella Galicia ★★1/2
Pale Lager: Hijos de Rivera, La Coruña, Spain www.estrellagalicia.com
"Aromas of hops, grass and grains." "Decent malt backbone gives this light-bodied lager a bit more complexity." "Sweeter than the average south European lager." 5.5% alc.

Eureka Pale Ale ★
Am. Pale Ale: Gluek Brewing Co., Cold Spring, MN www.gluek.com
"Taste is watered down hops and not much else." "Slimy, watery, thin, spit-like aftertaste." "A crappy APA wannabe at best." 5% alc.

Evil Eye (Ojo Malo) ★★
Malt Liquor: City Brewery (Melanie Brewing Co), La Crosse, WI www.citybrewery.com
"Aroma was pure swill - corn and light malt with a mild sweetness." "Toasted nutty malts, understated hops." "Committing yourself to a whole can of this stuff is a challenge I couldn't meet." 10% alc.

Falls City Beer ★★★★1/2
Pale Lager: Pittsburgh Brewing Co., Pittsburgh, PA www.pittsburghbrewingco.com
"Mildly astringent aroma with a malt hop base." "Light flavor, faint malt, bit of a bite in the finish." "Would be a good lawnmower beer as many like to call them." 4% alc.

Famosa ★
Pale Lager: Cerveceria Centro Americana, GUA City, Guatemala www.cerveceria.com.gt
"Grassy aroma with some sour pear and hay." "No malt at all and only a hint of grassy hoppiness; some plastic undertones." "Definitely sub-par by Guatemalan standards." 5% alc.

Fantôme Automne ★★★★1/2
Saison: Brasserie Fantôme, Soy-Erezée, Belgium www.fantome.be
"The aroma is yeasty horseblanket and malty with spices like coriander and cardomom." "Sweetness and herbs up front becoming fruitier about midpointand with a tart, juicy, citric, spicy, peppery and very gently warming finish. 8% alc.

Fantôme BBB Babillard ★★★★1/2
Saison: Brasserie Fantôme, Soy-Erezée, Belgium www.fantome.be
"Funky, spicy, peppery and full of nice bitter lemon notes." "Flavor is fairly tart and vinous." "So easy to drink and well put together." 8% alc.

Fantôme BBB Babillard Dark ★★★★
Saison: Brasserie Fantôme, Soy-Erezée, Belgium www.fantome.be
"Notes of raisins, chocolate, spice and yeasty bread." "Flavor has a sharp tartness as well with plenty of roasted malt, spices and hints of brown sugar." "Damn this has some unique flavors to it." 8% alc.

Fantôme BBBrr ★★★★
Saison: Brasserie Fantôme, Soy-Erezée, Belgium www.fantome.be
"Very lovely nose of flowers, cookies, fruits?" "Flavor is lemons, clover honey, cookie dough, light but apparent leather." "Every bottle is different and for me, this is the allure of Fantôme." 6.4% alc.

Fantôme Black Ghost ★★★★

Bel. Strong Ale: Brasserie Fantôme, Soy-Erezée, Belgium www.fantome.be

"Complex aroma of spices (especially black pepper), sour apples and other fruit, malt and much more" "Dry woody, funky flavors abound, with plum again and slight toffee and a faint hint of acidity." "Really unique." 8% alc.

Fantôme Brise-BonBons! ★★★★1/2

Saison: Brasserie Fantôme, Soy-Erezée, Belgium www.fantome.be

"Sweet and spicy in the nose with a slight fruitiness, herbs, some phenols and a touch of wild yeast." "Lots of funk and fruit, a nice mellow hop bite rounds this one out." "Seems to beg for a warm day in a wild flower field." 8% alc.

Fantôme Chocolat ★★★

Saison: Brasserie Fantôme, Soy-Erezée, Belgium www.fantome.be

"Lemon-pepper aroma, with apple pie and gingerbread." "Not much cocoa here, but plenty of pink pepper, piment d'espelette, stale coffee and wet socks!" "Not one of the better Fantôme in my opinion." 8% alc.

Fantôme d'Été ★★★★★

Saison: Brasserie Fantôme, Soy-Erezée, Belgium www.fantome.be

"Aromas of leather, hay, lemon and spices." "Taste of sour lemons, citrus, herbal notes, bretty yeast and a light alcohol finish." "A nice, funky, tart saison." 8% alc.

Fantôme de Noël ★★★★1/2

Saison: Brasserie Fantôme, Soy-Erezée, Belgium www.fantome.be

"Fresh sour cherries/grape/woody aroma with some noble hops and a little bit of raisin." "Sweet malt, chocolate, spice, touch of tartness, woodiness all combining in the flavor." "One of the most bizarre beers I could ever imagine drinking." 10% alc.

Fantôme Hiver ★★★★1/2

Saison: Brasserie Fantôme, Soy-Erezée, Belgium www.fantome.be

"Yeasty aroma - leather, sweat, cherry, glazed pear flan, styrians." "A bit sweet at first, like a citrus candy; some barnyard, pepper, cigar and sweaty leather." "Finish was like a fine cigar." 8% alc.

Fantôme La Gourmande ★★★★★

Saison: Brasserie Fantôme, Soy-Erezée, Belgium www.fantome.be

"Sweet, citrus zest nose, faintly spice, slightly ginger." "Incredibly dry stuff, has a restrained, punchy sourness, is a bit dusty as well." 7% alc.

Fantôme Pissenlit ★★★★★

Saison: Brasserie Fantôme, Soy-Erezée, Belgium www.fantome.be

"Slightly dry, yeasty, with a little bit of fig note and barnyard." "Flavors of leather, lemon, spice and a bit of earthiness with a with a crisp, biting finish." "Just a solid offering from a great Co.." 8% alc.

Fantôme Printemps ★★★★

Saison: Brasserie Fantôme, Soy-Erezée, Belgium www.fantome.be

"Fruity and sweet aroma like a tripel, but grassy and sharp like a lighter saison." "Flavor is tangy and musty, layered with spice." "Very refreshing, fruity enjoyable and above all else, fascinating." 8% alc.

Fantôme Saison ★★★★1/2

Saison: Brasserie Fantôme, Soy-Erezée, Belgium www.fantome.be

"Aroma is light white pepper, yeasty tangy funky citrus like kumquats and some herbal grasses." "Refreshing with some bitterness in the finish, lingering citrus flavors and no noticeable alcohol." "Perhaps the epitome of the saison style?" 8% alc.

Fantôme Strange Ghost ★★★★★
Spice/Herb: Brasserie Fantôme, Soy-Erezée, Belgium www.fantome.be
"A conundrum of scents. Licorice, anise and light bready malt are buried under a cheap cologne, massive spicy aroma." "Medium sweet, tarragon, white pepper, ginger, other herbs, light lime." "This beer is totally about contradictions." 8% alc.

Far West Connaught Ranger IPA ★★★★
IPA: Far West Brewing Co, Redmond, WA www.celticbayou.com
"Fruity (blackberry, apricot) aroma with hints of wood and toast." "Moderately bitter as the ample toasty and brown sugary malts balanced the measured hopping." "typical Pacific Northwest quaffing Indian Pale Ale." 6.7% alc.

Far West Three Threads Porter ★★★★
Porter: Far West Brewing Co, Redmond, WA www.celticbayou.com
"Big, powerful flavor, very strongly roasted (i.e., burnt), smoky, licorice, minimal sweetness and a strong bitterness that lingers on." "The perfect use of hops is what makes this stuff stand above other porters I've had." N/A% alc.

Farmington River Blonde Ale ★★★
Goldn/Blond Ale: Mercury Brewing and Distribution, Ipswich, MA www.mercurybrewing.com
"Aroma is earthy, grassy hops, mild citrus, sweet malt and bread dough." "Flavor explodes with a full malt body, sweet and lasting on the palate." "I love when American beers have clear signs of unpasteurization." N/A% alc.

Farmington River Mahogany Ale ★★★★1/2
Bitter: Mercury Brewing and Distribution, Ipswich, MA www.mercurybrewing.com
"Big caramel malt waft from the get-go, joining a honeyed hops persona." "Flavor elements revolve around salty pecans, licks of honey, whole wheat bread, bran flakes and brown sugar." N/A% alc.

Fat Cat Lager ★★★
Pale Lager: Joseph Huber Brewing Co., Monroe, WI www.berghoffbeer.com
"Aroma is fairly malty." "Flavors of malt, faint hops and all in all refreshing in nature." "I still like the can design, although it'd be nice if they had a good beer inside." N/A% alc.

Felinfoel Double Dragon ★★1/2
Bitter: Felinfoel, Llanelli, Dyfed, Wales www.felinfoel-brewery.co.uk
"Oak and apple, wine fruity hop and light caramel light malt aroma, most pleasant and inviting." "Rich malts, burnt caramel and a touch of fruit." "If you mixed a cider with a beer, this is probably exactly what it would taste like." 4.2% alc.

Firestone Double Barrel Ale ★★★★1/2
Eng Pale Ale: Firestone Walker Brewing Co., Buellton, CA www.firestonebeer.com
"Body was surprisingly light; I guess I was expecting a 'big' barrel beer." "Sweeter aromas of sugar cookies orange blossom honey and just hints of pale malt." "I like the maltiness in a pale ale." 5% alc.

Firestone Pale Ale ★★★
Am. Pale Ale: Firestone Walker Brewing Co., Buellton, CA www.firestonebeer.com
"Very pleasant APA with pine and grapefruit hoppiness." "Good hops bitterness with character, medium malt flavors and a bit of earthiness from the oak barrel fermentation." 4.6% alc.

Firestone Walker's Reserve ★★★★
Porter: Firestone Walker Brewing Co., Buellton, CA www.firestonebeer.com
"Full of dark chocolate and a bit of roasted coffee." "Notes of earthy hops." "Simple porter. It just happens to be really effin' good simple porter." 5.9% alc.

Fischer Adelscott ★
Scotch Ale: Fischer (Heineken), Schiltigheim, Alsace, France www.beerstreet.com
"Smoky, brandy-like nose, traces of caramel and burnt malts." "Sweetish flavor; short sweet finish with traces of charcoal." "Leave out the sugar next time please and thank you." 6.6% alc.

Fischer Amber ★

Amber Ale: Fischer (Heineken), Schiltigheim, Alsace, France www.beerstreet.com

"Sweet caramel aroma with faint wood, diacetyl." "Very little balance in the flavor with entirely too much malt and a hint of candy cane." "I gave this beer one point for it not killing me." 6% alc.

Fischer Bitter ★★

Pilsner: Fischer (Heineken), Schiltigheim, Alsace, France www.beerstreet.com

"Some green apple in aroma, but mainly grass with diesel fumes and a touch of powdery floral." "Flavor holds bitterness without much more." "Basically this is just a standard lager with a wee bit more bittering hops." 4.9% alc.

Fischer Tradition ★★1/2

Pale Lager: Fischer (Heineken), Schiltigheim, Alsace, France www.beerstreet.com

"Aroma is grassy, grainy-malty with an alcoholic undertone." "Tastes like a well made light lager...sweet, well balanced, but very poor at hiding the alcohol which dominates the finish." 6% alc.

Fish Tale Anniversary Ale ★★★★★

Am Strong Ale: Fish Brewing Co./Leavenworth Beers, Olympia, WA www.fishbrewing.com

"Spicy, minty aroma with hints of toffee." "The flavor has a lot of elements - toasty, bitter, woody, hints of caramel." "Nice and complex and a very fine brew!" 10% alc.

Fish Tale Blonde Ale ★★★

Goldn/Blond Ale: Fish Brewing Co./Leavenworth Beers, Olympia, WA www.fishbrewing.com

"Light bready, slightly fruity aroma." "Caramel malt flavors under a patina of herbal hop spiciness." "It gets cloying and tiring on the palate." 4% alc.

Fish Tale Detonator Doppelbock ★★★★★

Doppelbock: Fish Brewing Co./Leavenworth Beers, Olympia, WA www.fishbrewing.com

"Rich malty aroma - earthy, toffee, caramel all well extracted." "Lots of toffee, hints of wood on the palate. Really chewy, almost molasses-like." "A hint of cinnamon and vinous notes sets this apart." 8% alc.

Fish Tale Leviathan Barleywine (Batch 5+) ★★★1/2

Barley Wine: Fish Brewing Co./Leavenworth Beers, Olympia, WA www.fishbrewing.com

"Aroma is rich and malty with notes of toffee, caramel, apricot and vanilla." "Very well balanced with fruity, sugary malts and yeast attributes partially tamed by the floral hops and ever-present alcohol." 10% alc.

Fish Tale Old Woody ★★★★1/2

Old Ale: Fish Brewing Co./Leavenworth Beers, Olympia, WA www.fishbrewing.com

"Rich malty prune nose with hazelnut tones." "Pretty sweet. Mellows out to a nice smoky malty flavor with some alcohol warming. Rich and meaty." "It has my seal of approval." 10% alc.

Fish Tale Organic Amber Ale ★★★

Amber Ale: Fish Brewing Co./Leavenworth Beers, Olympia, WA www.fishbrewing.com

"Nice caramel and malt flavor mixed with well with some hop bitterness." "More complex notes of mint and mild Münich malt." "I would make this my beer in the fridge to serve to folks who visit." 4% alc.

Fish Tale Organic Indian Pale Ale ★★1/2

IPA: Fish Brewing Co./Leavenworth Beers, Olympia, WA www.fishbrewing.com

"Woody aroma with hints of caramel." "Caramel malts but the hops comes across as astringent and lacking character." "Just a fair IPA overall." 5.5% alc.

Fish Tale Poseidon's Imperial Stout ★★★★1/2

Imp. Stout: Fish Brewing Co./Leavenworth Beers, Olympia, WA www.fishbrewing.com

"Slightly earthy, deeply roasty aroma with some alcohol notes." "Bitter chocolate flavors, chewy fruitcake and light roast." "While impressive and worthy of respect, my own inclination is toward something a bit more balanced." 10% alc.

Fish Tale Wild Salmon Organic Pale Ale ★★1/2
Am. Pale Ale: Fish Brewing Co./Leavenworth Beers, Olympia, WA www.fishbrewing.com
"Aroma is lightly floral and fruity." "Flavors of caramel, dried flowers, light honey and some residual citrus from the cascade." "I'd like to down several of these with my Sunday morning bagel binge." 4% alc.

Fish Tale Winterfish Ale ★★★1/2
IPA: Fish Brewing Co./Leavenworth Beers, Olympia, WA www.fishbrewing.com
"Grapefruit orange and toasted malt aroma." "Flavor is dry toffee, fruity hops and yeast (juicy cherries, peaches, tangerines oranges)." "Another hophead joy with just enough malt to keep me interested." 7% alc.

Flag Porter ★★★1/2
Porter: Elgood & Sons Ltd., North Brink Brewery, Wisbech, Cambridgeshire, England
www.elgoods-brewery.co.uk
"Lots of yeast and molasses by the truckload, oh man. Maybe some raisins as well." "Faintly sweet caramel and coffee malt flavors with some light citrus hops." "Interesting, but I like my new world fake porters better." 5% alc.

Florisgaarden Apple ★
Fruit Beer: Brouwerij Huyghe, Melle, Belgium www.delirium.be
"Candied apple aroma with a sourish hint." "Dominant taste is of sugar with an apple background." "Only thing remotely linking this to beer for me was the burp I got at the end!" 3.5% alc.

Florisgaarden Framboise ★★★
Fruit: Brouwerij Huyghe, Melle, Belgium www.delirium.be
Raspberry aroma seems true, but there is an undertone of artificial sweetener that I can't escape. "Sweet, oily with a hint of sourness, the finish is just plain raspberry and more raspberry." "Put the palate in a diabetic coma." 3.7% alc.

Florisgaarden Ninkeberry ★
Fruit Beer: Brouwerij Huyghe, Melle, Belgium www.delirium.be
"Extremely sweet aroma of added syrups." "Sweet and sour - in a bad way and not unlike the generic sweet and sour sauce that you get from Chinese restaurants in suburban strip malls everywhere." 3% alc.

Flying Bison Aviator Red ★★1/2
Irish Ale: Flying Bison Brewing, Buffalo, NY www.flyingbisonbrewing.com
"Slightly sweet and sour aroma of malt, chocolate and some caramel coffee." "Light to medium pine and citrus hops with lightly malted notes." "Very basic and undistinguished." N/A% alc.

Flying Bison Blackbird Oatmeal Stout ★★1/2
Sweet Stout: Flying Bison Brewing, Buffalo, NY www.flyingbisonbrewing.com
"Very appealing - strong espresso/bitter chocolate/hops, some dark fruity roast malt." "While some stouts turn it up to eleven this one has the strings dampened and goes acoustic." N/A% alc.

Flying Dog Doggie Style Classic Pale Ale ★★1/2
Am. Pale Ale: Flying Dog Ales (Broadway Brewing), Denver, CO www.flyingdodales.com
"Dark amber color" may be a little off style, but this pale has a "mouthwatering Pacific Northwest hop aroma." "Flavor had a thin orange note with light fruit and slight grapefruits." 5.25% alc.

Flying Dog Horn Dog Barley Wine ★★★
Barley Wine: Flying Dog Ales (Broadway Brewing), Denver, CO www.flyingdodales.com
"Aroma of sweet malt, caramel, light hops, brown sugar and alcohol." "Sweet malt, simple barley wine taste." "Kings of mediocrity." "The ingredients just don't seem to work together." 10.5% alc.

Flying Dog In-Heat Wheat ★★
Hefeweizen: Flying Dog Ales (Broadway Brewing), Denver, CO www.flyingdodales.com
Brewed in the German style, In-Heat Wheat is "Sweet and yeasty, like bread, kinda fruity or citrusy." "For an American Hefe it's pretty good. But when I finished it, I really just wanted the real deal." 5.1% alc.

Flying Dog K-9 Cruiser ★★1/2
Eng. Strong Ale: Flying Dog Ales (Broadway Brewing), Denver, CO www.flyingdodales.com
"Caramel, toffee, plenty of malts and some dark fruit." "Leaves notes of brown sugar, sweet malt and bitter tea leaves with vanilla, but it is all watered down." "Tasty, but not good enough to make me a believer." 6.4% alc.

Flying Dog Old Scratch Amber ★★
Calif. Common: Flying Dog Ales (Broadway Brewing), Denver, CO www.flyingdodales.com
"Aroma is light and sweet." "Flavor is rich and malty, accentuated by a mild hoppiness." "A good generic brew, better than the commercial beers, but unexceptional." 5.4% alc.

Flying Dog Road Dog Scottish Porter ★★1/2
Porter: Flying Dog Ales (Broadway Brewing), Denver, CO www.flyingdodales.com
"Aromas of dark caramel malt, faint dark fruit, earthy hops and sweet roasted malt." "Flavor is sweet roasted, combined with notes of wood and nutmeg, on a slightly malty back ground. " "Body is way too watery for my tastes." 5.4% alc.

Flying Dog Snake Dog IPA ★★1/2
IPA: Flying Dog Ales (Broadway Brewing), Denver, CO www.flyingdodales.com
"No offensive flavors, little thin feeling, some spicy hops come through." "Not a very strong nose like some IPAs and definitely rather weak in hoppiness." "Enjoyable but I'm not screaming for seconds." 5.75% alc.

Flying Dog Tire Bite Golden Ale ★
Kölsch: Flying Dog Ales (Broadway Brewing), Denver, CO www.flyingdodales.com
"Smells like your average American macro." "Mild, toasty malt is nicely balanced by hop flavor and bitterness." "Flying Dog's Scottish Porter if you want some flavor from them." 5.1% alc.

Flying Dog Wild Dog Double Pale Ale ★★★★1/2
Am Strong Ale: Flying Dog Ales (Broadway Brewing), Denver, CO www.flyingdodales.com
"Big floral and citrus hop aroma fills the room as soon as the pour starts." "Taste is grapefruit and grass hops with a huge malt backbone... sticky and sweet." "Very classic American." 10.5% alc.

Flying Fish Belgian Abbey Dubbel ★★1/2
Abbey Dubbel: Flying Fish Brewing Co., Cherry Hill, NJ www.flyingfish.com
"Nose is fruity and sweet with light candy notes, yeast and a hint of flowers." "Notes of rich raisins, concentrated sweet plum and a bit of fig." "Overall this is pretty tasty, but like many Dubbels it seems to be lacking a certain something." 7.3% alc.

Flying Fish ESB ★★1/2
Prem Bitter: Flying Fish Brewing Co., Cherry Hill, NJ www.flyingfish.com
"The nose is also sweet and bready, with little else going on." "Front end is malty and back end has hints of fruit and wood." "Really bready for an Extra Special Bitter." 5.5% alc.

Flying Fish Extra Pale Ale ★★
Am. Pale Ale: Flying Fish Brewing Co., Cherry Hill, NJ www.flyingfish.com
"Exceptionally mild aroma and flavor." "Flavor is a slightly bitter earth taste upfront with a light malty sweetness." "Probably targeted for the [industrial beer] market, as it's not much better than those beers." 4.8% alc.

Flying Fish Farmhouse Summer Ale ★★1/2
Saison: Flying Fish Brewing Co., Cherry Hill, NJ www.flyingfish.com
"Aroma is of citrus, grassy malts, wheat and honey." "Lightly spiced, malty, but otherwise more like a spicy full-bodied Pilsner than a Saison." "Interesting and quite refreshing, but it's still not the real thing, so I think." 4.6% alc.

Flying Fish Grand Cru ★★1/2
Belgian Ale: Flying Fish Brewing Co., Cherry Hill, NJ www.flyingfish.com
"Nose was nice with hints of coriander, dried citrus fruit (orange and lemon peel), with lighter notes of banana and cotton candy." "Fruits and spice in the flavor with yeasty cookie dough notes and a slight bitterness at the end." 6.8% alc.

Flying Fish Oktoberfish ★★1/2
Altbier: Flying Fish Brewing Co., Cherry Hill, NJ www.flyingfish.com
"Mash aroma, grainy, but also somewhat sweet and doughy." "Flavor is slightly earthy, malty and I was even picking up a little alcohol and citrus in the taste." "I can dig it." 5.5% alc.

Flying Fish Porter ★★★
Porter: Flying Fish Brewing Co., Cherry Hill, NJ www.flyingfish.com
"Roasted malts, coffee notes, dark chocolate and a bit of the hops coming through." "Fairly nice cocoa flavors, malty, not as roasty as the nose suggested." "A little more body would make this a very nice beer." 5.5% alc.

Flying Horse ★★1/2
Pale Lager: United Breweries (Scottish & Newcastle), Bangalore, India www.kingfisherworld.com
"Honey, floral and grassy notes on the nose are followed up with a strong, sharp, mineral-like bitterness in the mouth that finishes cleanly." "Not hard to drink, but not wonderful either." 4.7% alc.

Flying Monkey Amber ★★
Amber Ale: Pony Express Brewing (Great Plains Brewing), Olathe, KS www.ponygold.com
"Vaguely nutty and biscuity" "Flavor starts with sweet malt and notes of coffee but then just dies in the middle." "Slightly comparable to Fat Tire." 0% alc.

Foggy Bottom Ale ★★
Eng. Pale Ale: Old Heurich Brewing Co., Washington, D.C. www.foggybottom.com
"Powerful fruity nose with just a touch of hops." "Flavors are hoppy, woodsy and somewhat dry." "Not a great beer, but a good local." Contract brewed by Matt Brewing Co. 5% alc.

Foggy Bottom Lager ★★1/2
Premium Lager: Old Heurich Brewing Co., Washington, D.C. www.foggybottom.com
"Sweet caramel with a dusting of hops." "Malts dominate the flavor, with a moderate yeast diacetyl character more like ale than lager." Contract brewed by Matt Brewing Co. 4.6% alc.

Fordham Copperhead Ale ★
Altbier: Fordham Brewing Co. (owns Rams Head Tavern), Rehoboth Beach, DEL www.ramsheadtavern.com
"Nutty toffee sweet taste with a moderately hoppy finish." "Nothing but an easy to drink beer." "No flaws, but a little boring." 4.7% alc.

Fordham Helles Lager ★★1/2
Helles/Dortmnd: Fordham Brewing Co. (owns Rams Head Tavern), Rehoboth Beach, DEL www.ramsheadtavern.com
"Bready, caramelly and a bit sweet and buttery." "A little to crisp for style and not enough maltiness." "Tastes like a cross between an American lager and a German Helles." 5.1% alc.

Forst Sixtus ★★★★
Doppelbock: Forst, Merano, Italy www.forst.it
"Aroma of molasses, toast and brown sugar." "Fairly full body with long, toffeeish malt notes and a hint of earthiness imparted by the dark malts." "Simple but effective structure." 6.5% alc.

Fort Collins Chocolate Stout ★★★
Stout: Fort Collins Brewery, Fort Collins, CO www.fortcollinsbrewery.com
"Light chocolate and coffee aroma." "Starts malty and bittersweet with some nice dark chocolate presence and a dry roasty finish." "Not as flavorful as it could be." N/A% alc.

Fort Collins Kidd Lager ★★★★
Schwarzbier: Fort Collins Brewery, Fort Collins, CO www.fortcollinsbrewery.com
"The aroma was nicely malty with some caramel and maybe some milk chocolate notes." "Flavors of coffee, roasted grain and smoke. Quick initial light sweetness up front then it's gone almost instantly." 4.1% alc.

Fort Collins Maj. Toms Pomegranate Wheat ★★★
Fruit Beer: Fort Collins Brewery, Fort Collins, CO www.fortcollinsbrewery.com
"Aroma is that nice fruity note of pomegranate." "The pomegranate makes it slightly tart, similar to raspberries." "Very fruity light beer." "Bubbly champagne like texture." N/A% alc.

Fort Collins Spring Bock ★★★★1/2
Bock: Fort Collins Brewery, Fort Collins, CO www.fortcollinsbrewery.com
One of the top 20 lagers in the US, with an aroma described anywhere from "sweet pipe tobacco" to "grilling pork chops." "Very rich malts, rather sweet, engaging and extremely drinkable." 9% alc.

Fort Collins Z Lager ★★1/2
Smoked: Fort Collins Brewery, Fort Collins, CO www.fortcollinsbrewery.com
"Mild smoke aroma wafts above a maple, caramel maltiness with some herbal hop notes." "Initial sweet malt flavor is joined quickly by an assertive but not overpowering smoky character." 4.5% alc.

Fosters Lager ★★1/2
Pale Lager: Fosters Brewing , Ontario, Canada www.fosters.com.au
"Taste is a little corny with a little malt coming through." "Aroma and taste are pretty similar to the major macros but a bit fuller bodied and a touch more hops presence." Brewed in Canada, by Molson, for the US market. 4.9% alc.

Fosters Special Bitter ★★★
Pale Lager: Fosters Brewing , Ontario, Canada www.fosters.com.au
"Aroma is faint and lagery with a slight amount of sweetness and breadiness." "Tastes bland, a bit bready, a vague maltiness lingering on my tongue." "This is supposed to be bitter?" Brewed in Canada, by Molson, for the US market. 4.5% alc.

Founders American Black Ale ★★★★★
Ale: Founders Brewing Co., Grand Rapids, MI www.foundersales.com
"Good complex aroma of roasted malt and caramel." "Flavor is notes of chocolate, caramel and brown sugar under a pine like hop flavor." "A bit like Bell's Double Cream Stout with most of the sweetness removed." N/A% alc.

Founders Black Rye ★★★★★
Ale: Founders Brewing Co., Grand Rapids, MI www.foundersales.com
"Aroma of roasted malt, creamy chocolate and a fair amount of hops." "The flavor is a dark roasted coffee, rye, nuts, pine/citrus hops, charcoal." "Porter-like consistency and heft." 7% alc.

Founders Breakfast Stout ★★★★★
Sweet Stout: Founders Brewing Co., Grand Rapids, MI www.foundersales.com
"Aroma is almost overpoweringly of freshly brewed coffee." "Coffee, bitter roasted barley and some bitter-sweet chocolate flavors." "Not overly complex." "Like drinking a cold thick coffee." 8.3% alc.

Founders Centennial IPA ★★★★
IPA: Founders Brewing Co., Grand Rapids, MI www.foundersales.com
"Resiny and grapefruity aroma and definitely Centennial [hops] alright!" "Taste is a nice blast of hops of front which mellow a bit on the tongue and make way for a malty and doughy experience." 7.2% alc.

Founders Devil Dancer Triple IPA ★★★★★
Imp/Dbl IPA: Founders Brewing Co., Grand Rapids, MI www.foundersales.com
"Nose is huge and I mean huge on pine, grapefruit, just pure hop madness." "This baby is thick enough to chew on." "Strong malt syrup-like base." Despite strong popularity, it should be noted that those who hate it, hate it a lot. 13% alc.

Founders Dirty Bastard Scotch Ale ★★★★
Scotch Ale: Founders Brewing Co., Grand Rapids, MI www.foundersales.com
"Caramel and butterscotch sweet malt aroma." "Good work on malt. Interesting accents." "Has a great thick chewy mouthfeel with minimal carbonation." "Never betrays the high alcohol level." 8.3% alc.

Founders Imperial Stout ★★★★★
Imp. Stout: Founders Brewing Co., Grand Rapids, MI www.foundersales.com
"Heavy aromas of roasted malts, mile chocolate oranges and a bit of licorice." "As it warms, the mocha notes enhance and I'm left with feeling as though I have dark chocolate and sugarless espresso fudge in my mouth." 12% alc.

Founders Pale Ale ★★★
Am. Pale Ale: Founders Brewing Co., Grand Rapids, MI www.foundersales.com
"Resiny hop aroma dominates with a little sweet malt and grapefruit." "The flavor is citrus hops, very wet tasting, finishing bone dry." "Stretches the limits of the pale category." 6.2% alc.

Founders Porter ★★★★★
Porter: Founders Brewing Co., Grand Rapids, MI www.foundersales.com
"Lightly smoky but full of milk chocolate, a little cinnamon, vanilla and a touch of nutty espresso." "Flavor of roasted malt, silky smooth chocolate and coffee." "This is a top quality porter." 5.1% alc.

Founders Rübæus ★★★★1/2
Fruit Beer: Founders Brewing Co., Grand Rapids, MI www.foundersales.com
"Aroma of pure raspberry is of pure enjoyment." "Flavor is a nice balançe of tart raspberries with sweet malt." "Great with chocolate deserts." 6.9% alc.

Founders Reds Rye ★★★★★
Am Strong Ale: Founders Brewing Co., Grand Rapids, MI www.foundersales.com
"Biq aroma - floral, slightly raspberry, baked apples and spicy rye notes." "Crazy rye and dark malt flavors meld well with the floral hop notes." "A really unique beer. Delicious." 6.8% alc.

Four Peaks 8th Street ★★★★1/2
Eng Pale Ale: Four Peaks Brewing Co., Scottsdale, AZ www.fourpeaks.com
An English-style pale ale with a "very mild hop aroma" with "a whiff of grapefruit." "Great balance of hop to malt with a touch of honey." "Good session beer, especially if you're sitting on the patio in Tempe enjoying a 70-degree February afternoon." 4.5% alc.

Four Peaks Kiltlifter ★★1/2
Scottish Ale: Four Peaks Brewing Co., Scottsdale, AZ www.fourpeaks.com
An amber ale with Scottish accents, Kiltlifter is "is malt dominated with notes of caramel, toasted bread, a hint of chocolate, perhaps a hint of peat smoke and just a dash of fruitiness." 6% alc.

Frankenheim Alt ★★1/2
Altbier: Privatbrauerei Frankenheim (Warsteiner), Düsseldorf, Germany frankenheim.de
"Aromas of sweet malts and herbal hops, slight mustiness." "Lots of caramel in the flavor with a touch of chocolate." "Very drinkable in a mindless way." 4.8% alc.

Franziskaner Club Weisse (Kristall Klar) ★★★★

Kristallweizen: Spaten-Franziskaner-Bräu (InBev), Münich, Germany www.spaten.de

"Malty, fruity aroma, plenty of wheat and citrus with lighter additions of white bread with butter and honey alongside touches of clove and spicy hop." "Taste is cookie, bready, lightly sweet malts." "It feels like any unique character is missing." 5% alc.

Franziskaner Hefe-Weissbier ★★★★★

Hefeweizen: Spaten-Franziskaner-Bräu (InBev), Münich, Germany www.spaten.de

"Aroma moderate malty and yeasty, light hoppy (coriander, citrus)." "Creamy slightly sweet malt with spicy flavors." "The clean, crisp finish suits this weizen perfectly." 5% alc.

Franziskaner Hefe-Weissbier Dunkel ★★1/2

Dunkelweizen: Spaten-Franziskaner-Bräu (InBev), Münich, Germany www.spaten.de

"Dusty and yeasty, slightly sweet wheat-malty aroma with cloves and a very shy banana fruitiness." "Flavor was sour and dry... yeasts open up to malts then return to finish with overripe banana and spice." 5.5% alc.

Fraoch ★★1/2

Traditional Ale: Williams Brothers (Heather Ales), Alloa, Scotland www.fraoch.com

Rather unique heather ale. "Lemony floral nose with hints of coriander, maybe cinnamon." "Odd sweet and spicy flavor with perfume, brown sugar, dried fruit and some spruce." "More intriguing than tasty." 5% alc.

Freeminer Deep Shaft Stout ★★★★★

Stout: Freeminer, Cinderford, Gloucestershire, England website.lineone.net/~freeminer.brewery/

"Aromas are robust... lots of espresso, chocolate, some molasses, mild hoppy aroma as well." "Taste is sweet, well balanced. Coffee, chocolate, brown sugar, bready, complex!" "Too bad there was only one bottle left at the store or I'd drink this every night." 6.2% alc.

Freeminer Trafalgar IPA ★★1/2

Prem Bitter: Freeminer, Cinderford, Gloucestershire, England website.lineone.net/~freeminer.brewery/

"Bready malt flavor up front with a fruity medium hopped finish." "Imagine, an IPA from someplace where hops are not citrus and where 50 seems bitter." 6% alc.

Frugal Joe's Ordinary Beer ★

Pale Lager: August Schell Brewing Co., New Ulm, MN www.schellsbrewery.com

"A reasonably strong Saazesque nose with a hint of retch." "I says it right in the name: Cheap, boring and generic." "At least it was free." N/A% alc.

Full Sail Amber ★★★★

Amber Ale: Full Sail Brewing Co., Hood River, OR www.fullsailbrewing.com

"Fantastic aroma of fruit, sticky caramel toffee and bread." "Taste-mild bakers chocolate, powder, cherry, wood, some lactic qualities and just a hint of tobacco." "This may be the best amber ale I have ever had." 6% alc.

Full Sail Capsize Double Pilsner ★★★★

Eur Str Lager: Full Sail Brewing Co., Hood River, OR www.fullsailbrewing.com

"Taste is spicy hops at first, then shows light fruits, grassy hops and cookie dough." "The pilsner style is about purity, clean lines and subtlety all of which this beer flies in the face of." 7.2% alc.

Full Sail Half Pipe Porter ★★1/2

Porter: Full Sail Brewing Co., Hood River, OR www.fullsailbrewing.com

"Very modest notes of chocolate and coffee and a little dust." "Dry toasty bitterness, some bitter-sweet chocolate, a hint of caramel. A pretty average porter." 5.4% alc.

Full Sail Hopocity ★★★★
Am. Pale Ale: Full Sail Brewing Co., Hood River, OR www.fullsailbrewing.com
"Decent bouquet of citrusy hops and some grassy notes." "Flavor is a lovely blend of hops and subdued warm grain malt, with a long finish that draws more and more bitter as it plays out." 5.2% alc.

Full Sail Imperial Porter ★★★★★
Baltic Porter: Full Sail Brewing Co., Hood River, OR www.fullsailbrewing.com
"Aroma is huge with a big mix of chocolate, coffee and dark bitter roast." "Full-bodied, rich and fully coating the mouth, slightly syrupy, with a long-lasting finish." "It's because of beers like this, that I love this style." 7% alc.

Full Sail IPA ★★1/2
IPA: Full Sail Brewing Co., Hood River, OR www.fullsailbrewing.com
"Aroma has notes of bright citrus, a grassy herbal character, a bit of astringent grain husk, toasty malt notes and perhaps a hint of caramel." "Definitely a hop focused beer; there is a nice citrus note here that reminds me of lemons and oranges." 6.5% alc.

Full Sail Old Boardhead Barleywine ★★★★★
Barley Wine: Full Sail Brewing Co., Hood River, OR www.fullsailbrewing.com
"Nice aromas of caramel, pineapple, apricot and toffee brittle, with lighter floral hop notes upon further warming." "Oranges, malts, caramel and a nice alcohol warming." "An awesome Barley Wine, although a bit atypical." 10.6% alc.

Full Sail Pale Ale ★★★
Am. Pale Ale: Full Sail Brewing Co., Hood River, OR www.fullsailbrewing.com
"Light sweet aroma with hints of toffee and light flowery hops." "Wonderfully balanced with a strong crystal malt backbone and spicy hops. Simple and so very easy to drink." 5.4% alc.

Full Sail Rip Curl ★★★
Eng Pale Ale: Full Sail Brewing Co., Hood River, OR www.fullsailbrewing.com
"Aroma is medium sweet, caramel, floral, light orange." "Very clean flavor with biscuits, toffee, vanilla, maybe some pear." 5% alc.

Full Sail Session Premium Lager ★★★
Premium Lager: Full Sail Brewing Co., Hood River, OR www.fullsailbrewing.com
"Aroma is of clean and slightly spicy hops." "Flavor is light with a tangy, citrus, wheat, bready like taste." "Import-style Pilsner made by an American Brewery." 5.1% alc.

Full Sail Slipknot Imperial IPA ★★★
Imp/Dbl IPA: Full Sail Brewing Co., Hood River, OR www.fullsailbrewing.com
"Modest piney sweet hops aroma." "Piney hop flavor dominates the sweet malt and leaves a warming hop essence." "Kind of low key for an IIPA, but drinkable none the less." 7.8% alc.

Full Sail Sunspot IPA ★★★1/2
IPA: Full Sail Brewing Co., Hood River, OR www.fullsailbrewing.com
"Huge aroma of piney and citrusy hops comes off this beer like you wouldn't believe." "I always love a big West Coast IPA and that's exactly what this brew is." 6.5% alc.

Full Sail Switchback Ale ★★1/2
Amber Ale: Full Sail Brewing Co., Hood River, OR www.fullsailbrewing.com
"Aroma is light and grassy with hints of malt, twigs, perhaps a waft of orange peel, but pretty much its just very earthy." "Flavor is a dark roasted, nutty, with a good Cascade hops zing." 5% alc.

Full Sail Wassail ★★★1/2
Old Ale: Full Sail Brewing Co., Hood River, OR www.fullsailbrewing.com
"Spicy dark fruit aroma with a touch of alcohol." "Flavor is bitter, hoppy, followed by chocolate and roast over a decent malt base." "Very full bodied beer with a sleek, very hopped finish." 6.5% alc.

Full Sail Wreck the Halls ★★★1/2

IPA: Full Sail Brewing Co., Hood River, OR www.fullsailbrewing.com

"A bit of apricot and hints of leafy hops alongside slightly toasty malts in the aroma." "Nice blend of citrus/hops, Christmas fruit cake." "A competent hoppy ale that is aimed squarely at Full Sail's existing audience." 6.5% alc.

Fuller's 1845 ★★★★★

Eng. Strong Ale: Fuller's, Griffin Brewery, London, England www.fullers.co.uk

"Toasty aroma with a hint of caramel, yeasty earthiness and light goldings." "Flavor is fairly robust, leaning toward dry malt notes like toast, as well as earthy notes." "A delicious hoppy ale that goes great with Italian sausages." 6.3% alc.

Fuller's ESB ★★★★★

Prem Bitter: Fuller's, Griffin Brewery, London, England www.fullers.co.uk

"Light hops and malt in the somewhat sweet and yeasty aroma." "Malty and spicy with a nutty character and a certain sweetness." "If you enjoy English bitters then this stuff is great." 5.9% alc.

Fuller's Honey Dew ★★1/2

Goldn/Blond Ale: Fuller's, Griffin Brewery, London, England www.fullers.co.uk

"Sweet, fruity malty aroma." "Mild honey taste with hints of malt." "Flavor is honey sweet and mellow but not cloying, fairly well balanced with the Target hops." "Better than I thought it was going to be." 5% alc.

Fuller's Indian Pale Ale ★★★

Prem Bitter: Fuller's, Griffin Brewery, London, England www.fullers.co.uk

"Aromas of grapefruit/pine/caramel." "Malts with flavors of tres leches cake, sweet biscuit, candied dates, slightly stale bread." "American IPAs are much better." 4.8% alc.

Fuller's London Porter ★★★★★

Porter: Fuller's, Griffin Brewery, London, England www.fullers.co.uk

"Complex aromas of chocolate, coffee, prunes, raisins and toast." "Flavor is very heavy with coffee with cream, hazelnut, chocolate." "This is dessert." 5.4% alc.

Fuller's London Pride ★★★1/2

Prem Bitter: Fuller's, Griffin Brewery, London, England www.fullers.co.uk

"Earthy aroma - diacetyl, wood, rotting peaches, caramel." "Flavor is sweet - slightly earthy with caramel overtones and a hint of diacetyl." "This is a good light alternative and a fantastic session beer." 4.7% alc.

Fuller's Vintage Ale ★★★

Eng. Strong Ale: Fuller's, Griffin Brewery, London, England www.fullers.co.uk

"Aroma holds notes of whiskey, wood, toffee and toasty malt." "Sweet caramel opening, some licorice and brown sugar in the middle and a lingering citric bitterness in the finish." "Lovely, should age well." 8.5% alc.

Gösser Dark ★★1/2

Dunkel: Gösser (Brau Union AG), Leoben, Austria www.goesser.at

"Slight aroma of dark chocolate." "Chocolate and caramel come through in the flavor for an enjoyable and simple beer." "Quite sweet for a Dunkel." "A good session Dunkel, if there ever was one." 4.5% alc.

Gösser Export ★

Helles/Dortmnd: Gösser (Brau Union AG), Leoben, Austria www.goesser.at

"Clean malt-driven aroma with faint lemony hops." "Sweet and malty on the tongue, with a metallic finish." "Tastes like they use a decent malt but low-quality hops." 5.2% alc.

Gaffel Kölsch ★★1/2

Kölsch: Privatbrauerei Gaffel Becker and Co., Cologne, Germany www.gaffel.de

"Fruity, malty aroma with hints of straw." "Refreshing, dry, hoppy and fruity taste with mint in the aftertaste." "This one really hits the spot on a hot day" 4.8% alc.

..e's Christmas Ale ★★1/2

..ng. Strong Ale: Gale's, Hampshire Brewery, Horndean, Hampshire, England www.gales.co.uk

"Rich fruitcake aroma, with hints of almonds and vanilla too." "Flavor is malty, spicy, fruity and vinous." "Tastes more like spiced cider and less like beer." 8.5% alc.

Gale's Festival Mild ★★★★1/2

Mild Ale: Gale's, Hampshire Brewery, Horndean, Hampshire, England www.gales.co.uk

"Pleasing malty nose with elements of Kahlua, caramel and currants." "Fore is dry black licorice, raisins and some prune notes." "It's great that a good bottle-conditioned British mild ale can be had in the U.S." 4.8% alc.

Gale's Prize Old Ale ★★1/2

Old Ale: Gale's, Hampshire Brewery, Horndean, Hampshire, England www.gales.co.uk

"Aroma is incredibly sweet. Honey, maple syrup, dark rum, apple butter, gently musky oak. Smells like dessert!" "Spicy in the fore with lots of candied fruit notes maybe a bit of brown sugar and ample alcohol." "Christmas pudding in a glass." 9% alc.

Gavroche ★★★

Bière de Garde: Brasserie St. Sylvestre, St. Sylvestre-Cappel, France www.brasserie-st-sylvestre.com

"Strong, deliciously sweet, fruity aroma of peach and strawberries, alcohol and a hint of toffee or caramel." "Spices are apparent along with bitter orange in the round, malty flavor with tea-like tannins and notes of alcohol." 8.5% alc.

Geary's Autumn Ale ★★1/2

Brown Ale: D.L. Gearys Brewing Co., Portland, ME www.gearybrewing.com

"Light and nutty." "Caramel sweetness with an almost raspberry fruitiness to it, with plum and raisin." "Been there and already done it." 5.8% alc.

Geary's Hampshire Special ★★★

Eng. Strong Ale: D.L. Gearys Brewing Co., Portland, ME www.gearybrewing.com

"A toasty caramel malt aroma is spiced with piney hop notes making for a feast for the nose." "Flavor is heavy on the malt but becomes very hoppy on the swallow and finishes with some nice belly warming alcohol." 7% alc.

Geary's London Porter ★★★

Porter: D.L. Gearys Brewing Co., Portland, ME www.gearybrewing.com

"Sweet vinous chocolate aroma, very smooth and sweet, with vanilla." "Flavors of coffee, roasted malt, light hop bitterness." "Good honest porter." 4.2% alc.

Geary's Pale Ale ★★

Eng Pale Ale: D.L. Gearys Brewing Co., Portland, ME www.gearybrewing.com

"Aroma is balanced evenly between sweet malt and floral hops, not especially strong but still pleasant." "Lightly toasted malt up front followed by flavors of biscuit orange zest, milk chocolate and hops." 4.5% alc.

Geary's Summer Ale ★★★★

Kölsch: D.L. Gearys Brewing Co., Portland, ME www.gearybrewing.com

"Moderately sweet, caramel, bread aroma" "Light-medium body, light stickiness, easy drinking." "Decent beer but didn't strike me as particularly kölsch-y." 6% alc.

Geary's Winter Ale ★★

IPA: D.L. Gearys Brewing Co., Portland, ME www.gearybrewing.com

"Sweet caramel aroma with light notes of alcohol and hops." "Weak apricot, stale Italian bread and the barest hint of nutmeg." "Holy Ringwood!" 6% alc.

Genesee Cream Ale ★

Cream Ale: High Falls Brewing Co., Rochester, NY www.highfalls.com

"Aromas of light hay and a bit of corn." "Fairly sweet malt flavor, but that's about it." "It's damn good for when you're broke." 4.9% alc.

Genny Light ★
Pale Lager: High Falls Brewing Co., Rochester, NY www.highfalls.com
"Faint, very faint malt aroma, faint, very faint coloring, faint flavor, bilious and chemically aftertaste." "Kind of fruity - lemon - with something sour and a bittersweet bready finish." 3.6% alc.

George Killian's Irish Red ★★1/2
Am Dark Larger: Coors Brewing Co. (MolsonCoors), Golden, CO www.coors.com
"Doesn't have off flavors or anything, it is pretty watery and very little going on flavor wise." "A little malty, too much carbonation and very light on the flavor." "Not great but better than many macros." 4.9% alc.

Gila Monster Amber Lager ★★★★
Pale Lager: August Schell Brewing Co., New Ulm, MN www.schellsbrewery.com
"Flavor is smooth caramel and toffee." "Sweet, dominant malts, almost no hop spice." "Trader Joe's brews are dependable fridge stockers." 4.2% alc.

Girardin Gueuze ★★★★1/2
Gueuze: Brouwerij Girardin, Sint Ulriks-Kapelle, Belgium
"Wonderful aroma, bold mixed fruit with that flowery, wet hay, barnyard brettanomyces funk." "Complex fruitiness - pears, apples, lemons, berries, a very floral/perfumey flavor." "This is an unforgettable experience, a true masterpiece." 5% alc.

Girardin Kriek ★★★★
Fruit Lambic: Brouwerij Girardin, Sint Ulriks-Kapelle, Belgium
"Lots of cherries, oak, cream, vanilla and hay with a subtle barnyard funk." "Sweet-sour cherry flavor with slight mustiness and yeast tone." "Simple and dry Kriek." 5% alc.

Gluek Honey Bock ★
Bock: Gluek Brewing Co., Cold Spring, MN www.gluek.com
"I guess you can call anything a bock nowadays." "No hops, no bitterness and this is wayyyyy too sweet to be truly bock." "Tasted like a somewhat watery amber ale with a touch of honey." 5.8% alc.

Gluek Stite Golden Pilsner ★
Pilsner: Gluek Brewing Co., Cold Spring, MN www.gluek.com
"Sweet, adjunctified American standard." "Non-existent hops aroma, light-bodied with a cloying malt/corn sweetness." "And then the corn stank hit me?" "Not as bad as expected, but I expected the worst." 4.7% alc.

Golden Eagle ★
Goldn/Blond Ale: Carlsberg Sverige, Falkenberg, Sweden www.carlsberg.se
"Slightly sour malt aroma." "Starts with hints of hops and malt, no distinct flavor, really just a watery lawnmower beer." "The most creative use of corn - they made it drinkable." 5.1% alc.

Golden Pheasant ★★
Dunkel: Zlaty Bazant (Heineken), Hurbanova, Slovakia www.zlatybazant.sk
"Saazy, grassy aroma with bready malts underneath and a slight mineral note." "Medium bodied that starts dry with light sweet malt flavor and finishes dry with light hop bitterness." "They just make a good pilsner and that is good enough for me." 4.5% alc.

Goose Island 1800 Demolition Ale ★★★1/2
Bel. Strong Ale: Goose Island Beer Co., Chicago, IL www.gooseisland.com
"Vinous flavor with touches of alcohol and moderate bitterness." "Rugged earthiness and hoppy grapefruit bitterness add good balance." "Pretty tasty stuff but more American than Belgian in style." 7.8% alc.

Goose Island Bourbon County Stout ★★★★★
Imp. Stout: Goose Island Beer Co., Chicago, IL www.gooseisland.com
"Bourbon aroma - sweet charcoal, slight vanilla, prunes and big rich malts." "Taste is bourbon, vanilla, buttery oak, dark bitter chocolate, some smoke." "A very hypnotic beer." 11% alc.

Goose Island Christmas Ale ★★★
Old Ale: Goose Island Beer Co., Chicago, IL www.gooseisland.com
"Roasty, nutty, very much like a heavy brown ale." "Some chocolate, toasted malt, caramel/toffee sweetness." "Christmas cake in a bottle." 5.4% alc.

Goose Island Hex Nut Brown ★★★★
Brown Ale: Goose Island Beer Co., Chicago, IL www.gooseisland.com
"Malt has decent complexity with some slight chocolate and some good toasted bread accents." "Heavy on sweet malts with notes of nuts and chocolate." "Very drinkable, but there is also room for improvement." 5.2% alc.

Goose Island Honkers ★★1/2
Am. Pale Ale: Goose Island Beer Co., Chicago, IL www.gooseisland.com
"Nose picked up some sweetness from caramel malt as well as a subtle spice bouquet and some floral hops." "Bitter, spicy finish with a tease of sweet caramel malt." "Finish is moderately bitter and very clean." 5% alc.

Goose Island Imperial IPA ★★★★★
Imp/Dbl IPA: Goose Island Beer Co., Chicago, IL www.gooseisland.com
"Nice malt base with smooth herbal hops and nice alcohol vapors, oily mouthfeel, lingering bitterness in mouth, very smooth and blended." "Rather sweet and very fresh with a fine bitterness." 9.2% alc.

Goose Island Indian Pale Ale ★★★1/2
IPA: Goose Island Beer Co., Chicago, IL www.gooseisland.com
"Caramel, toffee, light sweet fruity hop aroma." "Hoppy flavor with notes of pine needles and fruits." "Flavors are rather blunt - needs a punch of pale malt or a slap of citrus to come alive." 5.9% alc.

Goose Island Kilgubbin Red ★★1/2
Irish Ale: Goose Island Beer Co., Chicago, IL www.gooseisland.com
"Aroma is chock full of nuts, caramelized pecans, spruce and English toffee." "Light toasted character with some fruity flavors with a subdued citric finish." "Sweeter and lighter than most in the genre." 4.5% alc.

Goose Island Matilda ★★★★1/2
Belgian Ale: Goose Island Beer Co., Chicago, IL www.gooseisland.com
"Tart, bretty aroma with some sour cherries." "Dryish but very hoppy for a Belgian, then some honeyish malt and lemon zest in the finish." "This one surprised me by how different it was." 7% alc.

Goose Island Oatmeal Stout ★★★
Sweet Stout: Goose Island Beer Co., Chicago, IL www.gooseisland.com
"Smooth and creamy, with a quick coffee roasted aftertaste." "Not overly viscous and certainly not dry." "The finish is balanced, thick body and mouthfeel with an overall satisfying molasses character." 5% alc.

Goose Island Oktoberfest ★★★1/2
Märzen/Oktbfst: Goose Island Beer Co., Chicago, IL www.gooseisland.com
"Aroma is heavy on the malt and caramel." "Well balanced flavor with a good bittersweet finish of long duration." "If you like malt this is a beer for you." 4.4% alc.

Goose Island Pere Jacques ★★★★1/2
Bel. Strong Ale: Goose Island Beer Co., Chicago, IL www.gooseisland.com
"Full and fruity aroma - prune, ripe pear, molasses, nutmeg and clove." "Flavor is malty, slightly sweet, with caramel, vanilla, notes of alcohol in the finish and a faint bitterness." 9% alc.

Goose Island Pils ★★★★
Pilsner: Goose Island Beer Co., Chicago, IL www.gooseisland.com
"Clean aroma, floral and spicy noble hops." "Pleasant hop buzz" and "clean, smooth taste." "This is a good example of what the American giants should taste like." 5% alc.

Goose Island Summertime ★★★★

Kölsch: Goose Island Beer Co., Chicago, IL www.gooseisland.com

"Very lightly fruity yeast characteristics over the soft malty flavor with some citrus-herbal hops and fair finishing bitterness." "Accomplishes its purpose" 5% alc.

Gordon Biersch Blonde Bock ★★1/2

Bock: Gordon Biersch Brewing Co., Palo Alto, CA www.gordonbiersch.com

"Big malty aroma, sweet, slight cardboard." "Moderate body and mouthfeel." "Creamy and smooth." "Quite a fair bock from the States." 7% alc.

Gordon Biersch Golden Export ★★

Helles/Dortmnd: Gordon Biersch Brewing Co., Palo Alto, CA www.gordonbiersch.com

"I worried as soon as the waitress said this beer was their version of Bud or Miller." "Light grassy notes, sweet malts and maybe a hint of lemon." "Overall needs a malt boost." 5% alc.

Gordon Biersch Märzen ★★

Märzen/Oktbfst: Gordon Biersch Brewing Co., Palo Alto, CA www.gordonbiersch.com

"The aroma is mostly sweet malt with a touch of hop and citrus." "Flavor is toasty with some roasted grains and caramel and pleasant hops in the finish." "This is a very drinkable beer but nothing significant." 5.7% alc.

Gordon Biersch Pilsner ★★1/2

Premium Lager: Gordon Biersch Brewing Co., Palo Alto, CA www.gordonbiersch.com

"Full gold color; biscuity malts in the nose are appetizing." "Flavor is slightly malty, crisp but fades over time." "Has some good elements, but needs to expand upon them because it comes up too light overall." 5.3% alc.

Gouden Carolus Classic ★★★★★

Bel. Strong Ale: Brouwerij Het Anker, Mechelen, Belgium www.hetanker.be

"Excellent aroma of fruit, toffee, light chocolate and a hint of yeast." "Very well rounded with dark candied sugar flavors as plum, currant and raisin mix in with a lightly chewy fruit cake backing drizzled with caramel and light spices." 8.5% alc.

Gouden Carolus Grand Cru of the Emperor ★★★★★

Bel. Strong Ale: Brouwerij Het Anker, Mechelen, Belgium www.hetanker.be

"Rich fig and dark fruit aroma with a fair bit of yeasty fun as well." "Sweet flavor with a floral accent, again light hints of yeastiness." "Very wonderful treat all around!" 11% alc.

Gouden Carolus Noël ★★★★★

Bel. Strong Ale: Brouwerij Het Anker, Mechelen, Belgium www.hetanker.be

"Aroma of hard candy, vanilla, caramel and brown sugar, yeast, mild spices (nutmeg, cinnamon) - oh yeah, this says 'Christmas' to me." "Lovely, warming, spicy - a comfort beer that could make you wake up under a bridge with a huge smile on your face." 10.5% alc.

Gouden Carolus Triple ★★★★1/2

Abbey Tripel: Brouwerij Het Anker, Mechelen, Belgium www.hetanker.be

"Clean, fresh aroma with hints of lemon, butterscotch and mown grass." "Full of apples, grapes, summer flowers and some Belgian yeast." "Light, airy, but still full of flavor." 9% alc.

Grain Belt Premium ★★★★1/2

Pale Lager: August Schell Brewing Co., New Ulm, MN www.schellsbrewery.com

"Flavor starts with a surprising run of decent malt flavor, but then quickly fades into something a little skunky." "This beer produces an aura of conviviality among all who imbibe." 4.6% alc.

Grand Teton Bitch Creek ESB ★★★★
Prem Bitter: Grand Teton Brewing Co., Victor, ID www.grandtetonbrewing.com
"Rich and chewy aroma - earth, toffee, caramel and wood with light fruitcakey notes." "Brilliantly balanced between bitter, resiny hopping and toffeeish, demerara malts." "A damn fine pint." 5.5% alc.

Grand Teton Old Faithful ★★
Goldn/Blond Ale: Grand Teton Brewing Co., Victor, ID www.grandtetonbrewing.com
"Aroma is sweet with some fruitiness (orange and apple) and light floral hops." "Dryish palate with mild biscuity underbody, modest lemony hops." "An uninspired recipe well-executed." N/A% alc.

Grand Teton Sweetgrass Indian Pale Ale ★★1/2
IPA: Grand Teton Brewing Co., Victor, ID www.grandtetonbrewing.com
"The aroma is woody, citrusy with fresh bready maltiness." "Lots of citrus and sweet grapefruit throughout." "Balance is a bit too far on the sweet malty side." N/A% alc.

Grand Teton Teton Ale ★★1/2
Amber Ale: Grand Teton Brewing Co., Victor, ID www.grandtetonbrewing.com
"Pretty subtle aroma with some sugary caramel sweetness and a faint touch of cascade hops." "A middlin beer with no outstanding qualities." N/A% alc.

Grand Teton Workhorse Wheat ★★★
Am. Wheat: Grand Teton Brewing Co., Victor, ID www.grandtetonbrewing.com
"Slightly wheaty, sweaty aroma." "The taste has some light lemons with a note of clove spice at the end." "Better than most American Wheats." 4% alc.

Gray's Black and Tan ★★★
Ale: Grays Brewing Co., Janesville, WI www.graybrewing.com
"Aroma is mostly roasty, nutty (chestnut, pecan), bit of thyme and just a touch of burnt sugar, quite pleasant." "Would have been great with a steak!" 6% alc.

Gray's Honey Ale ★
Goldn/Blond Ale: Grays Brewing Co., Janesville, WI www.graybrewing.com
"A grainy, very bready and somewhat sweet golden ale with a light bitterness in the finish." "Not horrible tasting, but if this were the best beer available at a bar, I'd pay for a glass of water." 4.9% alc.

Gray's IPA ★★1/2
IPA: Grays Brewing Co., Janesville, WI www.graybrewing.com
"Mildly piney hoppy nose, touch of lemon, some wood and some dry biscuity malt." "Some nice piney/resiny flavors come out but this is not overly bitter -some nice toasty malts back this up." "A solid middle-of-the-road effort." 5.6% alc.

Gray's Irish Ale ★★1/2
Irish Ale: Grays Brewing Co., Janesville, WI www.graybrewing.com
"Smells hoppy and of sweet caramel malts." "Sweet biscuity malts dominate, little after that." "It's a bit sweeter then I like but over all it is a decent brew." 6.2% alc.

✔ **Gray's Oatmeal Stout** ★★★
Sweet Stout: Grays Brewing Co., Janesville, WI www.graybrewing.com
Drinkers truly like it or really don't like it. "Aroma is tons of brown sugared chocolate banana oatmeal brownies." "Flavor is dark, almost burnt, malt, very black coffee and bitter chocolate." 5.6% alc.

Gray's Witbier ★★
Bel. Witbier: Grays Brewing Co., Janesville, WI www.graybrewing.com
"Nose faint, fresh grass and lemons." "Sweet, fruity and lightly tart flavor profile, with generous amounts of orange and spice." "A bit stickier than this style should be." N/A% alc.

Great Divide Denver Pale Ale ★★1/2
Eng Pale Ale: Great Divide Brewing Co., Denver, CO www.greatdivide.com
"Very pleasant floral hoppage in the aroma, with just the right amount of sweet caramel behind it." "Flavor is lightly sweet to start, some brown sugar apparent, turning fruitier and floral with a freshly hoppy, lightly bitter finish." 5.4% alc.

Great Divide Hercules Double IPA ★★★★★
Imp/Dbl IPA: Great Divide Brewing Co., Denver, CO www.greatdivide.com
"Very popular beer known for its "Big hoppy nose with a piney character." "Initial flavor is a BIG HIT of mouth-puckering high alpha-acid hop bitterness along with the amped up alcohol; dry and crisp." 9.1% alc.

Great Divide Hibernation Ale ★★★★1/2
Am Strong Ale: Great Divide Brewing Co., Denver, CO www.greatdivide.com
Strong winter ale with a "deep chestnut color" and a "roasty, smoky aroma with plenty of malts, caramel, prunes." The flavor is of "malty, burnt caramel" with a "bitter hop finish." 8.1% alc.

Great Divide Hotshot ESB ★★1/2
Prem Bitter: Great Divide Brewing Co., Denver, CO www.greatdivide.com
"Soapy, piney/thymey hop aroma." "Moderately hoppy amber ale with woody, toasty notes and an even balance." "Bitter herbal finish." 5% alc.

Great Divide Oak Aged Yeti Imp. Stout ★★★★★
Imp. Stout: Great Divide Brewing Co., Denver, CO www.greatdivide.com
"Nose has elements of chocolate, anise, roasted coffee, bourbon and hints of, well, oak." "Sweet flavor - vanilla, bourbon, white chocolate and more light roasty notes." Coltrane may have even included it in 'My Favorite Things.' " 9.5% alc.

Great Divide Old Ruffian ★★★★★
Barley Wine: Great Divide Brewing Co., Denver, CO www.greatdivide.com
"Piney, slightly minty hop aroma with breadcrusty malts." "The woody bitterness is balanced by ample whole grain malts, as well as toast and caramel notes." "Easy-drinking and well-structured while maintaining stylistic integrity." 10.27% alc.

Great Divide Ridgeline Amber Ale (Arapahoe Amber) ★★1/2
Amber Ale: Great Divide Brewing Co., Denver, CO www.greatdivide.com
"The aroma is bright and yeasty with some citrusy hops." "Full of caramel, malts and some nuttiness." "A straightforward amber - and thus devoid of any particular attractions - but decently made." 5.3% alc.

Great Divide St. Bridgets Porter (St. Brigids) ★★★
Porter: Great Divide Brewing Co., Denver, CO www.greatdivide.com
Aroma of bitter chocolate, wood smoke, burnt coffee beans - very nice." "Body and flavor are full and robust while still retaining the characteristics of a true porter." "This isn't the greatest porter ever, but it's so drinkable." 6% alc.

Great Divide Titan IPA ★★★★★
IPA: Great Divide Brewing Co., Denver, CO www.greatdivide.com
"The orangey, piney aroma is very fresh." "Fairly bitter body, but with substantial malt base." "There's nothing quite like a cold, crisp, well-hopped, well-balanced Indian Pale Ale in the morning!" 6.8% alc.

Great Divide Wild Raspberry ★★1/2
Fruit Beer: Great Divide Brewing Co., Denver, CO www.greatdivide.com
"Aroma is light raspberries and light malts." "Flavor has a distinct malt underpinning with slightly juicy fruitiness playing lead." "The overall concept has limitations, but they've done a good job with it." 5.6% alc.

Great Divide Yeti Imp. Stout ★★★★★
Imp. Stout: Great Divide Brewing Co., Denver, CO www.greatdivide.com
"Pours completely black." "Huge malt aroma, with a tang of alcohol on the nose." "Molasses, dark fruit, dark chocolate, coffee, motor oil, tobacco, burnt caramel and toast." "Big burly imperial ready for the cold weather." 9.5% alc.

Great Lakes Blackout Stout ★★★★★
Imp. Stout: Great Lakes Brewing Co., Cleveland, OH www.greatlakesbrewing.com
"Rich, deep, chocolaty character with burnt fruitcake roastiness that adds accent to the background." "Finishes intensely." "I want to keep drinking this one to see if it's real." 9% alc.

Great Lakes Burning River Pale Ale ★★★★★
Am. Pale Ale: Great Lakes Brewing Co., Cleveland, OH www.greatlakesbrewing.com
"Slight citrus and pine in the nose." "Flavor is a hop oil covered orange marmalade and white bread." "Excellent example of the style." 6% alc.

Great Lakes Christmas Ale ★★★1/2
Spice/Herb: Great Lakes Brewing Co., Cleveland, OH www.greatlakesbrewing.com
"Spicy, hoppy, gingery nose." "The spicing is mixed with a nice amount of sweet malts to balance everything out." "I've come to expect the best from Great Lakes and they usually stand up to the test!" 7.5% alc.

Great Lakes Commodore Perry IPA ★★★1/2
IPA: Great Lakes Brewing Co., Cleveland, OH www.greatlakesbrewing.com
Aroma of citrus grapefruit and wildflowers over caramel malts. "Flavor is hoppy with lots of grapefruit, apricot and floral notes, but it is balanced quite well with underlying caramel malts." "Enjoyable, but not the best amongst American IPAs." 7.5% alc.

Great Lakes Conway's Irish Ale ★★★
Irish Ale: Great Lakes Brewing Co., Cleveland, OH www.greatlakesbrewing.com
"Bready and caramel malts dominate with a medium fruitiness." "Complex malt palate - chocolate chip cookies, slight tropical fruit esters, depth of toast notes and bread crust." "I think it's underrated." 6.5% alc.

Great Lakes Dortmunder Gold ★★★★★
Helles/Dortmnd: Great Lakes Brewing Co., Cleveland, OH www.greatlakesbrewing.com
"Aroma is semi-sweet with lots of grains, light citrus, mild hops, malts and light cereal notes." "Flavor starts malty, hops follow, biscuity, crackers also." "Very big and chewy for the style." 5.8% alc.

Great Lakes Edmund Fitzgerald Porter ★★★★★
Porter: Great Lakes Brewing Co., Cleveland, OH www.greatlakesbrewing.com
"Sweet dark chocolate roasted caramel malt aroma with raisin and port notes." "Flavor is wonderfully chocolaty and creamy with a nicely sweet (and somewhat hoppy) aftertaste." "I certainly wouldn't give up the opportunity to drink this beer." 5.8% alc.

Great Lakes Eliot Ness ★★★★★
Vienna: Great Lakes Brewing Co., Cleveland, OH www.greatlakesbrewing.com
"Rich, deep amber color; chewy nose of fresh malt." "Deep malt palate and sticky finish." "Simple but flawless construction typical of classic German styles." 6.2% alc.

Great Lakes Holy Moses ★★★
Bel. Witbier: Great Lakes Brewing Co., Cleveland, OH www.greatlakesbrewing.com
"Aroma is quite spicy with notes of citrus, both orange and lemon, a bit of a hot spicy pepper." "Lightly malty/bready, lightly sweet-cidery and hugely sour and cobwebby-farmy-dusty toward the back end." 5.4% alc.

Great Lakes Locktender Lager ★★1/2
Helles/Dortmnd: Great Lakes Brewing Co., Cleveland, OH www.greatlakesbrewing.com
Aroma is of clean grainy and toasty malt, light DMS." "Bready malt profile with slight spice and a hint of fruit from the hops." "Makes an excellent choice when you want to buy a good beer for guests whose tastes you are unsure of." 4.8% alc.

Great Lakes Moondog Ale ★★★
Prem Bitter: Great Lakes Brewing Co., Cleveland, OH www.greatlakesbrewing.com
"Fresh bready malt aroma mingling with flowery notes." "Dry bitterness, gets a bit bready at that point with a bit of sweetness." "Shame I can't get this brew where I live at the moment." 5% alc.

Great Lakes Nosferatu ★★★★1/2
Am Strong Ale: Great Lakes Brewing Co., Cleveland, OH www.greatlakesbrewing.com
"Nose is instantly alive and surprisingly malty sweet with caramel, nuts and overripe fruit." "Flavor starts smooth and sweet like the aroma but is rounded out by a sharp, powerful hop bitterness of citrus." 8% alc.

Great Northern Wheatfish Hefeweizen ★★
Hefeweizen: Great Northern Brewing Co., Whitefish, MT www.greatnorthernbrewing.com
"Sour wheat nose, weak wheaty flavor." "Simple for sure, but fairly clean at least." "Lingering tartness." N/A% alc.

Great Northern Wild Huckleberry ★★★
Fruit Beer: Great Northern Brewing Co., Whitefish, MT www.greatnorthernbrewing.com
"More fruit than wheat with some light sweet notes intermingled with the huckleberry tartness." "Actually rather pleasant fruit brew." N/A% alc.

Green Flash Extra Pale ★★1/2
Am. Pale Ale: Green Flash Brewing Co., Vista, CA www.greenflashbrew.com
"Light citrus aroma with some spicy notes as well with a piney/leafy almost earthy tones from the Chinook." "Crisp, west coast style hoppiness is apparent right from the first sip." 4.8% alc.

Green Flash Nut Brown ★★1/2
Brown Ale: Green Flash Brewing Co., Vista, CA www.greenflashbrew.com
"The aroma has notes of walnut and cashews, caramel and biscuity malt, some grassy hops and a bit of citrus." "A little thin and watery, but still some nice flavor components going on here." N/A% alc.

Green Flash Ruby Red ★★1/2
Amber Ale: Green Flash Brewing Co., Vista, CA www.greenflashbrew.com
"Nose is mainly malt, sweet and clean." "Flavor is lightly sweetened malt with hops and nuts." "Another enjoyable ale from Green Flash." 5.3% alc.

Green Flash West Coast IPA ★★★★1/2
IPA: Green Flash Brewing Co., Vista, CA www.greenflashbrew.com
"Well balanced, bitter, but lots of malt backing to balance it all out." "Wonderfully long bitter finish." "I would think that this one would definitely make an IPA lover very happy." 7% alc.

Greene King Abbot Ale ★★1/2
Prem Bitter: Greene King Plc, Bury St. Edmunds, Suffolk, England www.greeneking.co.uk
"Caramel and faint fruit aromas." "Sweet caramel malt palate with a non-specific fruity element that you lose as you get further into the beer." "Not as bad as a nitro-can can often be." 5% alc.

Greene King IPA ★
Bitter: Greene King Plc, Bury St. Edmunds, Suffolk, England www.greeneking.co.uk
"Mostly biscuity malt with some subtle earthy hoppiness and a slight metallic tinge." "Clean, dry finish." "This one is on the fringe of being decent, but it comes up second best." 3.6% alc.

Greene King Strong Suffolk (Olde Suffolk) ★★★★1/2
Old Ale: Greene King Plc, Bury St. Edmunds, Suffolk, England www.greeneking.co.uk
"Sweet berry fruits in the aroma, along with licorice." "Sweet and creamy, plenty of malt with lots of dark fruit (maybe cherries) and a little hint of iron." "Very characterful beer, lots of personality here." 6% alc.

Grimbergen Blonde ★★1/2
Belgian Ale: Brasserie Union (Alken-Maes / Scottish & Newcastle), Jumet, Belgium www.alkenmaes.be
"Candyish nose, reminiscent of the typical tripel....citrus zest...minor whiffs of tropical fruit." "Well-balanced, tangy flavor with apricot and coriander." "It's good but it lacks a bit of flavor." 6.7% alc.

Grimbergen Double ★★★
Abbey Dubbel: Brasserie Union (Alken-Maes / Scottish & Newcastle), Jumet, Belgium www.alkenmaes.be
"Aroma of prunes and raisons, light brown sugar, very light tartness." "Taste is yeasty, hints of toffee, a bit fruity and caramel." "Nice, but not very complex dubbel." 6.5% alc.

Grimbergen Triple ★★★
Abbey Tripel: Brasserie Union (Alken-Maes / Scottish & Newcastle), Jumet, Belgium www.alkenmaes.be
"Smells like some sort of spiced lemon pie." "A sweet liquid spice bread dough with mild floral hops stirred in." "Boring for a triple!" 9% alc.

Gritty McDuff's Best Bitter ★★1/2
Bitter: Gritty McDuffs, Portland, ME www.grittys.com
"Muted malt and hops in the aroma." "Full of caramel malts and earthy notes." "Slightly earthy hops are noticeable and very tingly." 5% alc.

Gritty McDuff's Black Fly Stout ★★1/2
Dry Stout: Gritty McDuffs, Portland, ME www.grittys.com
"Good aroma of chocolate, roasted malts and peanut butter." "Flavor is roasty nutty with coffee, but also chocolate and hints of caramel." "Middle of the road." 4.1% alc.

Gritty McDuff's Halloween Ale ★★★
Prem Bitter: Gritty McDuffs, Portland, ME www.grittys.com
"Muted fruity malt in the aroma." "Some chocolate, some nuttiness, some bitter hoppiness?" "Gritty's seasonal brews are typically better than their flagship brews." 6% alc.

Gritty McDuff's Scottish Ale ★★1/2
Scottish Ale: Gritty McDuffs, Portland, ME www.grittys.com
"Caramel, light nutty hops bitterness and butterscotch in the nose." "Great subtle smoky, toffee-ish malts, light to medium body." "It's got some nice flavors, but it just needs some more body." 6.3% alc.

Gritty McDuffs Original Pub Style ★★
Am. Pale Ale: Gritty McDuffs, Portland, ME www.grittys.com
"Toasty, fruity hops and Ringwood esters." "Flowery hops predominate taste. There is also a very fresh yeasty and malty quality overall." "One of those déjà vu beers." 4.5% alc.

Grittys Lions Pride Brown Ale ★
Brown Ale: Gritty McDuffs, Portland, ME www.grittys.com
"Mild fruity aroma." "Thin bodied caramel with some nuttiness and a smooth, butter thing going on." "Needs more everything." 4.1% alc.

Grolsch ★★1/2
Goldn/Blond Ale: Grolsche Bierbrouwerij Ned. bv, Enschede, Netherlands www.grolsch.nl
"Grassy hop aroma with hints of bready malt." "A mild hop bitterness is apparent amidst the mildly malty backline." "Fairly interesting premium lager." 5% alc.

Grolsch Amber Ale ★

Amber Ale: Grolsche Bierbrouwerij Ned. bv, Enschede, Netherlands www.grolsch.nl

"Light caramel in the nose." "Mildly sweet but very dominated by metals and chemicals." "Drinkable if somewhat pedestrian amber." 5% alc.

Grottenbier Bruin ★★★1/2

Abbey Dubbel: St. Bernardus Brouwerij, Watou, Belgium www.sintbernardus.be

"Aroma of plums, fruitcake oranges and maybe some Special B or Aromatic malt." "Fruity, yeasty flavors with date and spices." "Some plums, raisins and dates, but they aren't prominent enough to make this beer bright." 6.5% alc.

Grozet ★★

Traditional Ale: Williams Brothers (Heather Ales), Alloa, Scotland www.fraoch.com

"Aroma is light… citrus, yeast, soap?" "Taste is a bit thin and the gooseberry influence is barely discernable." "Not a bad flavor really but where is the rest of this beer?" 5% alc.

Gubernija Baltiskoe Pivo Svetloe ★★1/2

Eur Str Lager: Gubernija, Siauliai, Lithuania www.gubernija.lt

"A bit of a sour aroma with a hint of spicy hops." "Flavor is sweet and totally dominated by alcohol." "Nothing foul which is definitely a bonus." 8.2% alc.

Gubernijos Ekstra ★

Goldn/Blond Ale: Gubernija, Siauliai, Lithuania www.gubernija.lt

"Sweetish fruity/hoppy/veggie aroma with malt lingering behind it all." "Light-bodied, quite malty with a short, dry bitterness." "Didn't taste like anything other than your typical, bland yellow lager, despite being called an ale." 5.5% alc.

Guinness Draught ★★★

Dry Stout: Guinness (Diageo), Dublin, Ireland www.guinness.com

"Masked aroma of watery roasted grains." "Closed the door on the college keg parties and showed the way towards beer enlightenment." However, "the legend of the beer exceeds the experience." "Flavor a nice roasty and burnt caramel with a good balance of mild bitterness, but too watery." 4.1% alc.

Guinness Extra Stout (North America) ★★★

Dry Stout: Labatt Breweries (InBev), London, Ontario www.labatt.com

"Not bottled Draught, but regular bottled Guinness is made in Canada under contract for the US market. "Light aroma of toast, cheap coffee and macro ale." "Light roast flavor, with hints of milk chocolate." "Not bad for a mass produced stout." 5% alc.

Gulden Draak ★★★★1/2

Bel. Strong Ale: Brouwerij Van Steenberge, Ertvelde, Belgium www.vansteenberge.com

"Aroma of alcohol, chocolate, raisin, baked apples." "Smooth texture that starts with light sweet malt, caramel, grape flavors and finishes with a sweet malt aftertaste." "A real ear-warmer." 10.5% alc.

Guldenberg ★★★★

Bel. Strong Ale: Brouwerij De Ranke, Dottignies/Dottenijs, Belgium www.sheltonbrothers.com

"Scent of pear, nutmeg, cumin, pepper, very light malt-derived caramel." "Citrusy grapefruit flavor with sweet malt and woody bitterness, finished with obvious noble hops." "Reminds me of a mixture of an Orval and a Duvel." 8.5% alc.

Höss Doppel-Hirsch ★★1/2

Doppelbock: Privatbrauerei Höss der HirschBräu, Sonthofen, Germany www.hirschbraeu.de

"Standard malty doppelbock aroma-toffee, caramel, nuts, slight dark fruit and some smokiness." "Malty sweet, notes of caramel and dark bread, but a decent hoppy bitterness in the finish makes it very drinkable." 7.2% alc.

Höss Holzar-Bier ★★

Keller: Privatbrauerei Höss der HirschBräu, Sonthofen, Germany www.hirschbraeu.de

"Nice aroma of sweet malt, some sourness and dark fruit." "Crisp light hops, some malt sweetness, very smooth and enjoyable." "I won't need wood cutting as an excuse to drink this beer." 5.2% alc.

Höss Neuschwansteiner Helles Lager ★★

Helles/Dortmnd: Privatbrauerei Höss der HirschBräu, Sonthofen, Germany www.hirschbraeu.de

"Very bready aroma with a faint whiff of hops." "Very light and watery sweet flavor." "Just a mediocre beer disguised in a fancy bottle." 4.7% alc.

Höss Weisser-Hirsch (Bavarian Weissbier) ★★

Hefeweizen: Privatbrauerei Höss der HirschBräu, Sonthofen, Germany www.hirschbraeu.de

"Aroma is mostly that of yeast with strong nuances of banana and sour bubble gum." "Taste is wheat, spicy yeast and malts bordering on breadiness." "Very drinkable beer on nice sunny days or first thing in the morning." 5.2% alc.

Hacker-Pschorr Dunkle Weisse ★★★

Dunkelweizen: Hacker-Pschorr Bräu GmbH (Schörghuber), Münich, Germany www.hacker-pschorr.de

"Clove, wheat and a hint of banana" in the aroma. "Soft fruit body with caramel sweetness." "A decent Dunkelweizen, but I think next time I'd like to have it by the liter in Münich." 5.3% alc.

Hacker-Pschorr Edelhell ★★★

Helles/Dortmnd: Hacker-Pschorr Bräu GmbH (Schörghuber), Münich, Germany www.hacker-pschorr.de

"Aroma is a good mix of noble hops and fresh bready malts." "Clean, simple flavor profile is malt-accented (bready) with a moderate bitterness but little hop character beyond that." "Hits the mark pretty well." 5.5% alc.

Hacker-Pschorr Hefe Weisse ★★★★1/2

Hefeweizen: Hacker-Pschorr Bräu GmbH (Schörghuber), Münich, Germany www.hacker-pschorr.de

"Nose is very doughy and bananaish. Also slight notes of citrus, vanilla and clove." "Light sweet malt flavor with notable sharp acidity and fruitiness." "This is a textbook Hefe." 5.5% alc.

Hacker-Pschorr Oktoberfest Märzen ★★★★

Märzen/Oktbfst: Hacker-Pschorr Bräu GmbH (Schörghuber), Münich, Germany www.hacker-pschorr.de

Aroma "is heavy on the sweet, caramel malt side with a slight hazelnut-like aroma and mild hops." "Taste is mildly sweet, very crisp and clean, with notes of lightly acidic caramel, sugar, malt and dough." 5.8% alc.

Haffenreffer Private Stock Malt Liquor ★★★

Malt Liquor: Miller Brewing Co. (SABMiller), Milwaukee, WI www.millerbrewing.com

"Corny, malty aroma. Flavor is sweet malt with a touch of graininess and an alcohol aftertaste." "Not a great beer by any means but quite drinkable." 6.87% alc.

Hair of the Dog Adam ★★★★★

Traditional Ale: Hair of the Dog Brewing Co., Inc., Portland, OR www.hairofthedog.com

"Malty and softly hoppy aroma of molasses, charred oak and bourbon." "Sweet molasses, toffee, caramel and brandy flavors? bit of smoke, light roast, dark chocolate and alcohol." "I definitely see what all the fuss is about." 10% alc.

Hair of the Dog Doggie Claws ★★★★

Barley Wine: Hair of the Dog Brewing Co., Inc., Portland, OR www.hairofthedog.com

"Heavily hopped aroma, with some caramel laced pine cones swimming in cognac." "Strong alcohol and pineapple fruitiness with big, brown, malty sweetness and a moderately bitter, roasty finish." 11.5% alc.

Hair of the Dog Fred ★★★★★

Barley Wine: Hair of the Dog Brewing Co., Inc., Portland, OR www.hairofthedog.com

"Aroma is caramel long john with a lot of spicy, citrusy hops." "Hops creep up on you in the flavor, which starts innocently enough with a malty, molasses sweetness that eventually bursts with pine, grapefruit and maple sap." 10% alc.

Hair of the Dog Rose ★★★
Abbey Tripel: Hair of the Dog Brewing Co., Inc., Portland, OR www.hairofthedog.com
"Flowers and spices, some coriander, very light wheat and far more hops than I have ever smelled in a tripel." "Pleasantly bitter, flowery-hoppy flavor with lots of orange-peel and peppery spiciness with a dry finish." 8% alc.

Hair of the Dog Ruth ★★★★1/2
Goldn/Blond Ale: Hair of the Dog Brewing Co., Inc., Portland, OR www.hairofthedog.com
"Aroma of yeast and orange peel; flavor is slightly sour yeast with a soft malt touch." "Very light and refreshing flavor." "A lot of obvious Belgian characteristics; if Ruth is an All American ale, my name is Alan Sprints." 5.6% alc.

Hakim Stout ★
Foreign Stout: Harar Beer Factory, Harar, Ethiopia
"The aroma was that of roasted barley and plastic. Highly intolerable wet cardboard in there as well." "Vaguely caramelly malts, thin body, plasticy finish." "Then everything went to hell in a handbag." 5.8% alc.

Hale's Aftermath Imperial IPA ★★★1/2
Imp/Dbl IPA: Hale's Ales, Seattle, WA www.halesales.com
Aroma was mildly malty with a decent citrus side grapefruit and hops." "Piney resinous flavor with floral hop notes, some caramel malt presence." "I think I've had denser more complex regular IPA's. Drinkable, but sub par for the style." 8.4% alc.

Hale's Drawbridge Blonde ★★1/2
Goldn/Blond Ale: Hale's Ales, Seattle, WA www.halesales.com
"Mildly sweet and lightly grainy aroma, not too far removed from what a macro smells like." "Sweet grainy maltiness is a big part of the flavor, but there's a modest hop bitterness lurking in the background for some balance." N/A% alc.

Hale's El Jefe Weizen ★★1/2
Hefeweizen: Hale's Ales, Seattle, WA www.halesales.com
"Marshmallow aroma, with a little banana." "Taste of tart wheat, citrus, banana, light bubblegum and yeast as well." "Typifies the German style but doesn't stand out." N/A% alc.

Hale's Mongoose IPA ★★★
IPA: Hale's Ales, Seattle, WA www.halesales.com
"Nice spicy hop aroma, light citrus grapefruit with a sweet toasty and biscuity aroma." "Good crisp profile, caramel in the back and a juicy finish." "A very typical Pacific Northwest Indian Pale Ale both in how it tastes and the fact that it tastes pretty good." 6.2% alc.

Hale's Moss Bay Extra ★★★★
Prem Bitter: Hale's Ales, Seattle, WA www.halesales.com
"Aromatic, boasting a darkly toasted, lightly roasted maltiness and a fair amount of hops too." "Fruity melange of flavors orange rind, cherries and lemons. Some cookie dough along for the ride." "I would drink many." N/A% alc.

Hale's O'Brien's Harvest Ale ★★★★
Amber Ale: Hale's Ales, Seattle, WA www.halesales.com
"Aroma is full of piping fresh hops, very floral and simply delicious on a fall afternoon." "Flavor is quite sweet, fruity hops and fruity yeastiness as well." "Quite different than the other few fall seasonal I've had this year." N/A% alc.

Hale's Pale Ale ★★★
Am. Pale Ale: Hale's Ales, Seattle, WA www.halesales.com
"Playful nose of perfume, pineapple and a touch of grape." "Lemon zesty hoppiness balanced with some biscuity malt, slight toffee and some melons and berries." "A competent beer, but not outstanding." 5.2% alc.

Hale's Pikop Andropovs Rushin' Imperial Stout ★★★
Imp. Stout: Hale's Ales, Seattle, WA www.halesales.com
"Heavily roasted malts, apple skin, dark chocolate and bright coffee beans on the nose." "Beef jerky and chocolate body with a toasty note." "Moderate intensity and thickness for style. A good starter imply." 7.5% alc.

Hale's Red Menace Big Amber Ale ★★1/2
Amber Ale: Hale's Ales, Seattle, WA www.halesales.com
"Malty with a nice hop presence and maybe a slight fruit and caramel side coming through as well." "I liked the malty/toffee sweet flavor of this only broken up by a hint of bitterness." "I liked this beer a nice laid back sweet amber!" N/A% alc.

Hale's Wee Heavy Winter Ale ★★★1/2
Scotch Ale: Hale's Ales, Seattle, WA www.halesales.com
"Inviting, rich malty aroma. Plum and fig." "Very slight hint of smoke, fairly sweet, hint of cherry. Some nuts come through in the moderate bitter finish." "Very welcome antidote to the bitter sting of winter cold." 6.8% alc.

Hales Rudyards Rare Barleywine ★★★★
Barley Wine: Hale's Ales, Seattle, WA www.halesales.com
"Rich syrupy malt aroma. This is the stuff they ferment other beers from." "Malty flavor like burnt sweet bread or fruitcake, then gets astringent with alcohol heat and fruitiness." "Definitely more toward the English style barley wine." 9.2% alc.

Hamm's Golden Draft ★★1/2
Pale Lager: Miller Brewing Co. (SABMiller), Milwaukee, WI www.millerbrewing.com
"Light, but sweet caramelly malt and some pepper." "Lots of corn and grainy characters. The hops are now slightly bitter and a little bit sour." 4.7% alc.

Hamm's ★
Pale Lager: Miller Brewing Co. (SABMiller), Milwaukee, WI www.millerbrewing.com
"Corny light hop aroma." "Taste is slightly sour celery with some hints of sugary sweetness." "As it warms, it turns into a skunk. But I like the old bear." 4.7% alc.

Hamovnicheskoe ★
Pale Lager: Pivzavod AO Hamovnikov (SABMiller), Moscow, Russia www.bochka.ru
"Cooked vegetables in the aroma with a tad of burnt rubber." "Malty, grainy flavors, some oxidation. Finish is dry with a hint of hop spiciness." "One suspects that this beer could be used to clean drains." 5% alc.

Hampshire Pride of Romsey ★★★
Am. Pale Ale: Hampshire Brewery Ltd., Romsey, Hampshire, England www.hampshirebrewery.com
"Wonderful spicy hoppy aroma." "Apple, pear and caramel flavors with a mild hop bite." "Apple, pear and caramel flavors with a mild hop bite." 5% alc.

Hanssens Oudbeitje ★★★
Fruit Lambic: Hanssens Artisanaal, Dworp, Belgium
"Quite dry and cobwebby, with a leathery characteristic." "Lots of funk, must and barnyard flavors are sort of balanced by a sweet berry fruitiness." "Sour and intense lambic." 6% alc.

Hanssens Oude Gueuze ★★★★1/2
Gueuze: Hanssens Artisanaal, Dworp, Belgium
"Wonderful full aroma with orange zest, animal musk, soil in a cave and the inevitable horseblanket." "Very tart palate, aggressive, some stank feet, apple, lots of leather and a fair amount of barrel character." "Very nice gueuze." 6% alc.

Hanssens Oude Kriek ★★★★1/2
Fruit Lambic: Hanssens Artisanaal, Dworp, Belgium
"Aroma strong, some leather, cherries, maybe even apples and cranberries." "Tartness that is very sharp, very light on the fruit flavor, spicy, peppery, a very small amount of wood." "Not jaw dropping good, but close. I do love myself a Kriek." 6% alc.

Harmon Brown's Point ESB ★★

Prem Bitter: Harmon Brewery and Restaurant, Tacoma, WA www.harmonbrewing.com

Scents of "sour cream and malts." "Soft hop bitterness, lots of toasty malts, mango and melon, brown sugar and cotton candy." "Sweet brownsugary finish." 5.6% alc.

Harmon Point Defiance IPA ★★★

IPA: Harmon Brewery and Restaurant, Tacoma, WA www.harmonbrewing.com

"Aroma is citrusy and floral hops with a touch of earth and fruit." "Luscious sweet malts match wits with piney, grapefruity notes." "Great interplay between two well-defined elements." 5.8% alc.

Harmon Puget Sound Porter ★★★

Porter: Harmon Brewery and Restaurant, Tacoma, WA www.harmonbrewing.com

"Coffeeish, peanutty aroma with hints of almond skins." "Taste is very hoppy and juicy, lemon, limes and melons, some bitter chocolate and a bit of roastedness." "This is way under-rated!" 5.4% alc.

Harp ★★★★★

Pale Lager: Guinness (Diageo), Dublin, Ireland www.guinness.com

"Nice bread-like aroma." "Lightly biscuity maltiness and touch of hop." "While not my favorite lager, it is better than a lot of macro swill." 4.3% alc.

Harpoon Ale ★★1/2

Amber Ale: Harpoon Brewery, Boston, MA www.harpoonbrewery.com

"Aroma hints of malts, caramel and some hops, floral and orange." "Sweet malt start with a mild grass and grain component." "It's more of a beer you'd give to your less enthusiastic friends than to keep all to yourself." 4.9% alc.

Harpoon Hibernian Ale ★★

Irish Ale: Harpoon Brewery, Boston, MA www.harpoonbrewery.com

Aroma is caramel malts and slight hops ""Malts are fruity and sweet. Hops are slightly spicy." "Kind of sweet and seems thin." "A better version of Killian's." 5.4% alc.

Harpoon IPA ★★1/2

IPA: Harpoon Brewery, Boston, MA www.harpoonbrewery.com

"Light hops aroma with bitterness equivalent to a West Coast pale ale." "Straightforward IPA flavors of citrus/grapefruit hops with a solid malt backbone." "Mildly bitter and clean finish." 5.9% alc.

Harpoon Münich Dark ★★★

Dunkel: Harpoon Brewery, Boston, MA www.harpoonbrewery.com

"Quite complex.. woody, with strong malts and caramel sweetness." "Crisp mouthfeel. Interesting full textured beer for Harpoon." 5.6% alc.

Harpoon Oktoberfest ★★★

Märzen/Oktbfst: Harpoon Brewery, Boston, MA www.harpoonbrewery.com

"Toast, chocolate, toffee on the nose." "Sweet muskiness, honey vats, butter crumble cookies, hazelnut soda syrup and piney nuttiness." "Very nice 'fest!" 5.5% alc.

Harpoon Summer Beer ★★1/2

Kölsch: Harpoon Brewery, Boston, MA www.harpoonbrewery.com

"Fresh, slightly lemony, fruity hop aroma." "Slightly bitter and sour flavor at the beginning with a touch of lemon and other citrus followed by a slightly bitter and grainy finish." 5% alc.

Harpoon UFO Hefeweizen ★★

Am. Wheat: Harpoon Brewery, Boston, MA www.harpoonbrewery.com

"Very sweet and malty aroma, with hints of lemon and freshly cut grass- very potent." "Watery taste, with not a whole lot going on." "Another American Wheat that fails to induce enjoyment." 5% alc.

Harpoon Winter Warmer ★★★

Spice/Herb: Harpoon Brewery, Boston, MA www.harpoonbrewery.com

"Aroma shows orange, cinnamon, heavy nutmeg." "Flavor was once again all spices, especially the advertised cinnamon and nutmeg." "Not bad but it doesn't really distinguish itself from the rest of the holiday spiced beers out there." 5.5% alc.

Harvey's Christmas Ale ★★★

Barley Wine: Harveys, Lewes, East Sussex, England www.harveys.org.uk

"Lovely aroma of malt, raisins, wine and alcohol." "Smooth light sweet malt, caramel, spice and dried fruit (prune?) flavors." "The aroma raises expectations, the palate doesn't meet." 8.3% alc.

Harvey's Elizabethan ★★★★

Barley Wine: Harveys, Lewes, East Sussex, England www.harveys.org.uk

"Sherry and port wine dominate the aroma. Blackberry brandy?" "Starts with buttery figs and moves to rum-steeped raisins and blueberries." "A sophisticated, regal beer." 8.2% alc.

Harviestoun Bitter and Twisted ★★★★★

Goldn/Blond Ale: Harviestoun (Caledonian), Alva, Scotland

"Muted citrusy, floral hops with some caramelly malt and berries in the aroma." "hops flavors are spicy, with a somewhat oregano-like herbal quality." "Great unfolding flavors." 3.8% alc.

Harviestoun Old Engine Oil ★★★★1/2

Old Ale: Harviestoun (Caledonian), Alva, Scotland

"Porter-like aromas of dark baking chocolate and a touch of coffee." "Full-bodied palate with a malty, coffee, hint of smokiness, roasted malt, dark chocolaty flavors." "Wickedly smooth indeed; a really fine beer." 6% alc.

Harviestoun Old Engine Oil Special Reserve ★★★★

Old Ale: Harviestoun (Caledonian), Alva, Scotland

"Malty aroma - toffee, wood, molasses and Highland whisky." "Rich malt flavors of molasses and earth, melded seamlessly with light peat and whisky notes." "A fun, distinct and unusual beer." 6% alc.

Hatuey ★★1/2

Pale Lager: Cerveceria India, Mayaguez, Puerto Rico

"Aroma is skunk, corn and old sweat socks." "Flavor was faint, bland, nondescript." "Slightly fuller than your standard brews, but still with a bland character." 5.5% alc.

Hawk's D.M.'s Imperial Stout ★★★★★

Imp. Stout: Hawks Brewing, Roseburg, OR

"Loads of burnt fruit, nuts, apple… a fruitcake basically." "Palate is thick and loaded with earthy, nutty malts. Very warming." "Flavor comes at you in gentle waves." 9.9% alc.

Hawk's Imperial Gold Malt Liquor ★★★★★

Malt Liquor: Hawks Brewing, Roseburg, OR

"Yeah it was corny and somewhat fruity but it had that little something extra that the cheap ones don't… class." "Flavor is estery and fruity." "This is not your workin' man's malt liquor." 9.9% alc.

Hawk's Super Natural ESB ★★1/2

Prem Bitter: Hawks Brewing, Roseburg, OR

"Aroma was grainy and some what hoppy with maybe some light citrus in there." "Underlying toffee base along with a medicinal, herbaceous and floral hop blend. Pretty robust for the style." 6.5% alc.

Hawk's Super Natural IPA ★★1/2
IPA: Hawks Brewing, Roseburg, OR
"Citrusy aroma with a mild malty side and a juicy fruit gum thing going on as well." "Taste is nicely malty in the beginning then tapers to a nice hop finish." "Finishes balanced, tangy, definitely delicious." 7% alc.

Hawk's Super Natural Oatmeal Stout ★★★★★
Sweet Stout: Hawks Brewing, Roseburg, OR
"Rich malty, fruity aroma, roasted, nutty, chocolaty." "Lots of burnt malt flavor greets you, with a dollop of caramel and butterscotch, good Pacific Northwest hop presence, a hint of bitter dark chocolate." "Equilibrium is achieved, as is succulence." 8% alc.

Hawk's Super Natural Porter ★★★★
Porter: Hawks Brewing, Roseburg, OR
"Aroma is very herbal with some balanced hops and a moderate amount of alcohol and dark malts." "Very much British style like everything else they make and impossible to stop drinking." 6.5% alc.

Hayward's 5000 ★★1/2
Pale Lager: Shaw Wallace (SABMiller), Mumbai, India www.shawwallace.com
"Strong alcoholic sting in aroma, with weak malts also present." "Flavor is a fairly malt taste but like a cheap imitation malt along with some grain and maybe some honey and yeast." "Good fun in a one bottle sort of way." 7% alc.

He'Brew Bittersweet Lenny's R.I.P.A. ★★★★
Imp. IPA: Shmalz Brewing Co., San Francisco, CA www.shmalz.com
"Tons of caramel, tawny port and grist in the nose with lesser notes of chocolate, avocado, maybe evergreen and mango." "Solid, beefy, barley malt profile with lots of rich caramel, but it's no match for the mother lode of resinous, astringent hops." 10% alc.

He'Brew Genesis 10:10 ★★★1/2
Fruit: Shmalz Brewing Co. , San Francisco, CA www.shmalz.com
"The pomegranate gives off a faint cherry-like aroma but is hampered by a bit of chalkiness." "Flavor is malty with caramel, and fruity as well with some grapefruit and a bit of raisin." "The most unique and experimental of the He'Brew series." Contract brewed by Saratoga Springs. 10% alc.

He'Brew Genesis Ale ★
Am. Pale Ale: Shmalz Brewing Co., San Francisco, CA www.shmalz.com
"Toasty, rye-ish aroma with a slight peppery note." "Flavors of sweet, but unimpressive malts." "Not exactly sure what style this is trying to be." 6% alc.

He'Brew Messiah Bold ★★
Brown Ale: Shmalz Brewing Co., San Francisco, CA www.shmalz.com
"Very nutty aroma, with a rich chocolate and caramel sweetness." "Very roasty, nutty, highly drinkable brown ale." "A brown with more character than usual." 5.5% alc.

Heavyweight Baltus O.V.S. ★★★
Bel. Strong Ale: Heavyweight Brewing Co., Ocean Township, NJ www.heavyweight-brewing.com
"Intriguing aroma with inviting, notes of dark fruit - figs and prunes." "Sweet and slick, rolling in with bing cherry extract, brown sugar and caramel." "This a weird, but good, beer." 8.2% alc.

Heavyweight Bière d'Art ★★★★1/2
Bière de Garde: Heavyweight Brewing Co., Ocean Township, NJ www.heavyweight-brewing.com
"Aroma of floral hops, pear, grass, hay and earthiness." "Taste is dry toffee, a bit of spiciness and peppery alcohol." "A trip back in time." 7.7% alc.

Heavyweight Cinderbock ★★★1/2

Smoked: Heavyweight Brewing Co., Ocean Township, NJ www.heavyweight-brewing.com

"Strong smoked malt aroma with bready and floral notes and plenty of plum and raisin fruity esters." "The taste starts with surprising light fruit tone and some sweet malts to balance with the smoked flavors." 7% alc.

Heavyweight Lunacy ★★★

Belgian Ale: Heavyweight Brewing Co., Ocean Township, NJ www.heavyweight-brewing.com

"Aroma has a sharp fruity character to it up front that is reminiscent of apples and pears with a bit of alcohol thrown into the mix." "Flavors are a mish mash of spice, yeast, sweet malt and then a body slam of alcohol in the finish." 7.7% alc.

Heavyweight Old Salty ★★★★

Barley Wine: Heavyweight Brewing Co., Ocean Township, NJ www.heavyweight-brewing.com

"Big malty aroma with caramel, toffee, banana bread, honey, raisin and fruit (maybe cherry)." "Flavor is dark fruit, candi sugar, toffee, cookie dough, bready, very sweet, cloyingly so and a bit salty." 11% alc.

Heavyweight Perkuno's Hammer ★★★★★

Baltic Porter: Heavyweight Brewing Co., Ocean Township, NJ www.heavyweight-brewing.com

"Rich, bold and sugary aroma of dark chocolate, coffee, marzipan and peppery alcohol." "Sweet flavor starts with boysenberry and black cherry, ends with bittersweet chocolate chips and roasty black malts." 8% alc.

Heavyweight Stickenjab ★★★

Altbier: Heavyweight Brewing Co., Ocean Township, NJ www.heavyweight-brewing.com

"Dripping hop nose. Fresh, complex rhythms like multigrain bread, wood, earth, nuts...stronger caramel in the palate, full body, halvah, earth and a very caramelly finish. Robust." 6.4% alc.

Heavyweight Two Druid's Gruit ★★1/2

Traditional Ale: Heavyweight Brewing Co., Ocean Township, NJ www.heavyweight-brewing.com

"Intriguing aroma includes orange peel, herbal/medicinal, marigold, barnyard, lemon pepper, sage and pinesap qualities." "Flavor is tart and acidic, almost geueze-like, with citrus, apricots and juniper." "Unique in my experience." 6.7% alc.

Heileman's Old Style ★★

Pale Lager: Pabst Brewing Co., Chicago, IL www.oldstyle.com

"Husky aroma and husky pale malt flavor." "Fairly clean example of the style." "At this point in time, better in my opinion than most BMC [Bud-Miller-Coors-like beers]." 5% alc.

Heineken ★★1/2

Pale Lager: Heineken Nederland, Hertogenbosch, Netherlands www.heineken.com

"A fairly weak lager, a bit sweet, some hops character." "Light-bodied palate with a crisp floral hops flavors and soft pale malt sweetness." "Always skunked; how can this beer have a following?" 5% alc.

Heineken Premium Light Lager ★1/2

Pale Lager: Heineken Nederlands, Hertogenbosch, Netherlands www.heineken.com

Aroma of mostly skunk but a little light grain under it. "Taste is pure, thin, light pale lager." "I didn't regret drinking it. That's gotta be worth something." N/A% alc.

Heineken Special Dark ★

Vienna: Heineken Nederland, Hertogenbosch, Netherlands www.heineken.com

"Brown sugar and caramel malt aroma." "Boiled veg background and a sweet body, quite watery on the palate." "I like sweet beers, but this is not a quality sweetness." 5.2% alc.

Hellekapelle ★★1/2

Belgian Ale: Brouwerij de Bie, Loker, Belgium www.brijdebie.be

"Very doughy, sweet and fruity aroma with herbal, vanilla notes and candi sugar apparent." "Hoppy flavor with grapefruit, juniper berry, pine and some fruits." "Interesting brew, but nothing special." 5% alc.

Helleketelbier ★★★1/2

Belgian Ale: Brouwerij de Bie, Loker, Belgium www.brijdebie.be

"Aroma is interesting with notes of earthy spices like coriander, clove, a bit of allspice and a bit of yeastiness." "Sweet and fruity up front but finishes quite dry and earthy." "That witch's cauldron contains a truly tongue-altering tastefest." 7% alc.

Helmar Big League Brew ★★1/2

Eng Pale Ale: MI Brewing Co., Webberville, MI www.michiganbrewing.com

"Sweet up front with some caramel. Finishes with a roastiness and light floral hoppiness." "Actually dead on for an English ale imported to the US." 4.4% alc.

Henry Weinhard's Amber ★

Amber Ale: Full Sail Brewing Co., Hood River, OR www.fullsailbrewing.com

"For a while, it felt like Henry just brewed up a base ale and added artificial colors and flavors to match whatever box it was going into." "This is a really popular beer, I don't get why." N/A% alc.

Henry Weinhard's Blue Boar Pale Ale ★

Am. Pale Ale: Miller Brewing Co. (SABMiller), Milwaukee, WI www.millerbrewing.com

"Somewhat corny aroma, adjuncts similar to BMC [Bud-Miller-Coors-like] product." "Slightly grassy flavor, dull sweetness, without any hop bite." "Couldn't be less interesting." 4.6% alc.

Henry Weinhard's Hefeweizen ★

Am. Wheat: Full Sail Brewing Co., Hood River, OR www.fullsailbrewing.com

The aroma is wheaty and slightly cardboardy with sweet fruity hints." "Flavor is dull, uninteresting with some wheat character in the finish." 4.86% alc.

Henry Weinhard's Northwest Trail Blonde Lager ★★★★

Pale Lager: Full Sail Brewing Co., Hood River, OR www.fullsailbrewing.com

"Sweet malty palate, with decent carbonation and just enough hop bite to add balance." "Drinkable is the best I can say for it, but it's also more than I can say for most others at this price point." 5.1% alc.

Henry Weinhard's Private Reserve ★★★

Pale Lager: Miller Brewing Co. (SABMiller), Milwaukee, WI www.millerbrewing.com

"Aroma is faint but does give a slight hint of grain, malt and hop." "Corn and cereal flavor, but its rather smooth and it finishes fairly clean." "Certainly drinkable, but nothing outstanding." 4.46% alc.

Het Kapittel Abt ★★★

Abt/Quadrupel: Van Eecke, Poperinge-Watou, Belgium www.brouwerijvaneecke.tk

"Sweet aroma of candi sugar, almond, chocolate and alcohol." "Sweet orange and apple flavor up front with pepper and chocolate notes ending with a fairly strong alcohol and hops finish." "Nice fruit esters and decent body, but not much else going on." 10% alc.

Het Kapittel Blond ★★1/2

Belgian Ale: Van Eecke, Poperinge-Watou, Belgium www.brouwerijvaneecke.tk

"Aroma resembles characteristics of a witbier with its coriander orange and lemon shavings." "Flavor is will also touch on coriander, mandarin, yeast and also a reminder of apricot jelly while also tasting organic." 6.5% alc.

Het Kapittel Dubbel ★★1/2

Abbey Dubbel: Van Eecke, Poperinge-Watou, Belgium www.brouwerijvaneecke.tk

"Toffee and candi sugar aroma." "Has some milk-chocolate accents, again dried raisins, some smooth caramel, dry leaves from a forest, Lait-Russe with sugar, wood (cedar) and a bitter touch of herbs and hops." 7.5% alc.

Het Kapittel Pater ★★1/2
Belgian Ale: Van Eecke, Poperinge-Watou, Belgium www.brouwerijvaneecke.tk
"Aroma is medium sweet, raisin, caramel, molasses, some herbal, mango, light bread." "Gentle caramel maltiness with wood notes and some cinnamon." "Not enormously complex, but still one of the finer light abbey browns." 6% alc.

Het Kapittel Prior ★★★1/2
Bel. Strong Ale: Van Eecke, Poperinge-Watou, Belgium www.brouwerijvaneecke.tk
Nose suggests "cherries, sultanas, sweet mapley malts and hints of deeper things that whet the appetite." "Sweet, bitterish, resinous, candy, dark fruits, molasses and malt." "Alcohol surprisingly not a factor here - it warms the heart directly." 9% alc.

Hevelius Classic ★★★
Eur Str Lager: Elbrewery Co. Ltd. (Heineken), Elbland#261;g, Poland www.czasnaeb.com.pl
"Fleeting lemony sourish nose, grassy hops." "Flavor is sweet and grainy with some black pepper and a solidly bitter hop finish." "This isn't a celestial product; perhaps if enough was consumed you would see stars." 6.8% alc.

Hevelius Kaper ★★★1/2
Eur Str Lager: Elbrewery Co. Ltd. (Heineken), Elbland#261;g, Poland www.czasnaeb.com.pl
"Soft pear aroma with light toffee and alcohol notes." "Palate is an odd mix of toffee, alcohol, salt, cola, popcorn and stewed peaches." "This is a well-made Steel Reserve." 8.7% alc.

Hidden River Amber ★★1/2
Am Dark Larger: Gluek Brewing Co., Cold Spring, MN www.gluek.com
"Hops are missing and the malts have a woody taste, kind of like splinters from a tooth pick." "Sour almost to the point of skanky." "I had a hard time with this one though I have friends who truly enjoy it." Private label for grocery chain. N/A% alc.

Hidden River Black and Tan ★
Stout: Gluek Brewing Co., Cold Spring, MN www.gluek.com
"Caramel aroma with a touch of toasted malt." "For a black and tan it was awful light." "Some very artificial tasting sweetness in the finish." "I think this one could have some potential but it needs serious reworking." Private Label for grocery chain. N/A% alc.

Hidden River Pale Ale ★
Am. Pale Ale: Gluek Brewing Co., Cold Spring, MN www.gluek.com
"Aroma is very light hay-like hops and caramel malts." "Weak and metallic with an artificial hop flavor." "The finish is so bad it'll make you grab for a razor to scrape it off your tongue." Private label for grocery chain. N/A% alc.

Himalayan Blue ★★
Pale Lager: Yuksom Breweries, Ltd., Malli, Sikkim, India www.ratebeer.com
From the former Himalayan kingdom of Sikkim, this has a "faint, sweet doughy malt aroma." "Flavor has some brief bready, biscuity highlights which differentiates this from most of this ilk." "Otherwise, pretty bland and typically corny lager flavor." 4.5% alc.

Hinano ★★1/2
Pale Lager: La Brasserie de Tahiti (Heineken), Papeete, Tahiti, Tahiti www.brasseriedetahiti.pf
"Aroma of malts, corn and alcohol." "Thin bodied with a bit of floral sweetness and a dry slightly bitter finish." "Probably tastes better on the beach with a topless girl serving it to you." 5% alc.

Hitachino Nest Japanese Classic Ale ★★★
IPA: Kiuchi Brewery, Ibaraki, Japan kodawari.cc
"Pungent Orvalish aroma, winey and spicy with pale malts and fruity hops." "Long palate full of wood, pale malt and loads of bittering hops." "Cedar comes on strong late." "Unlike any I have ever come across." 7% alc.

Hitachino Nest Lacto Sweet Stout ★

Sweet Stout: Kiuchi Brewery, Ibaraki, Japan kodawari.cc

"Aroma is of sweet under-carbonated cola with a bit of roasted malt and wood smoke." "Unfermented wort on the palate, sweet sugariness, definite acidic bite." "Watery texture, quick finish." 3.8% alc.

Hitachino Nest New Year Celebration Ale ★★★★1/2

Spice/Herb: Kiuchi Brewery, Ibaraki, Japan kodawari.cc

"Orange peel and coriander are immediately and obviously apparent in the nose." "Spicy malty flavor with a nice amount of hops added to the mix." "A delight, as good in its way as Anchor Our Special Ale." 9% alc.

Hitachino Nest Red Rice ★★1/2

Traditional Ale: Kiuchi Brewery, Ibaraki, Japan kodawari.cc

"Great nutty aroma (I guess that's the red rice) with evaporated milk and soap nuances." "Unique nutty, slightly fruity (lemon, longan, rambutan) palate with almond skin notes appearing late." "I would unhesitatingly recommend it to the adventurous..." 7% alc.

Hitachino Nest Weizen ★★1/2

Hefeweizen: Kiuchi Brewery, Ibaraki, Japan kodawari.cc

"Complex aroma with banana, smoky phenols." "Palate is smooth and sweet, like apples covered in icing sugar, followed by yeast, malt and florals." "Holds its own and a fairly decent weizen." 5% alc.

Hitachino Nest White ★★★1/2

Bel. Witbier: Kiuchi Brewery, Ibaraki, Japan kodawari.cc

"All kinds of aromas here: cardamom, citrus, noble hops." "Palate brings all of these plus complex earthy malt notes - this is very stylish." "I can see why this beer has won gold medals. A must try!" 5% alc.

Hite ★

Pale Lager: Hite Co., , S Korea www.hite.com

"Grainy aroma with some biscuit, solvent." "Taste is slightly malty, with a metallic bitter aftertaste." "Thanks, Joergen, for sharing this piece of crap." 4.5% alc.

Hoegaarden Forbidden Fruit ★★★★

Belgian Ale: Brouwerij Hoegaarden (InBev), Hoegaarden, Belgium www.inbev.com

"The aroma is of dark fruit, with some malt and spice and reminds me a lot of some Trappists." "Tastes of milk chocolate, spices (coriander), hop-bitterness, alcohol." "Definitely recommended if you want to try something new." 8.8% alc.

Hoegaarden White ★★★★★

Bel. Witbier: Brouwerij Hoegaarden (InBev), Hoegaarden, Belgium www.inbev.com

"Aroma is of coriander seed and citrus." "Lightly sweet and citrusy, with finish being lightly dry and leaving a nice coriander/clove type of spicy taste." "Very mild mannered and ethereal." 5% alc.

HofBräu München Maibock ★★★

Bock: Staatliches HofBräuhaus M_nchen, Münich, Germany www.hofbraeu-muenchen.de

"Extremely malty aroma; lots of Vienna and light Münich malts." "Flavor is big sweet and malty with some hops in the aftertaste." "Nice depth to the flavor." 7.2% alc.

HofBräu München Oktoberfestbier ★★

Märzen/Oktbfst: Staatliches HofBräuhaus M_nchen, Münich, Germany www.hofbraeu-muenchen.de

"Aroma is hayish, sweet fruits, slight caramel, kinda like a mix of an Oktoberfest and a pilsner." "Flavor is light and crisp, slightly skunk aftertaste, hay and crisp hoppy finish." "A Pilsner in disguise." 5.7% alc.

HofBräu München Original ★★1/2
Helles/Dortmnd: Staatliches HofBräuhaus M_nchen, Münich, Germany www.hofbraeu-muenchen.de
"Particularly strong malt aroma with some toasted cookie." "Mainly consists of bland grain and notes of hay, grass and a slight touch of lemon." "Recommended if you want a light, clean unchallenging beer." 5.1% alc.

HofBräu Münchner Kindl Weissbier ★★
Hefeweizen: Staatliches HofBräuhaus M_nchen, Münich, Germany www.hofbraeu-muenchen.de
"Aroma has the yeasty banana and clove notes." "Moderately bready and wheaty with a sour macro tang toward the finish." 5.1% alc.

Hogs Back TEA (Traditional English Ale) ★★
Bitter: Hogs Back, Guildford, Surrey, England www.hogsback.co.uk
"Weird nose - meaty, slightly smoky, woody." "Some tobacco, a hint of smoke and perhaps some herbs." "Would love to try from cask, this promised much but delivered less." 4.2% alc.

Hollandia ★★1/2
Pale Lager: Bavaria Brouwerij (HOL), Lieshout, Netherlands www.bavaria.nl
"Floral aroma with a note of honey." "Flavor is very fresh with lots of malt and a bit of corn." "A little one dimensional." 5% alc.

Hood Canal Big Beef Stout ★
Sweet Stout: Hood Canal Brewery, Poulsbo, WA www.hoodcanalbrewery.com
"Almond and milk chocolate aroma." "Some cocoa and nuts and light coffee." "I found this just far too mellow; a liquid library; an NPR deejay stuck in a plain-labeled bottle." N/A% alc.

Hood Canal Breidablik Barley Wine ★★★★
Barley Wine: Hood Canal Brewery, Poulsbo, WA www.hoodcanalbrewery.coml
Aroma is malt, banana, molasses and brown sugar." "Toffeeish notes lead, with raisiny, plummy depths. Slight burnt raisin in the finish." "Very sweet barleywine." 8.7% alc.

Hood Canal Dabob Bay IPA ★★
IPA: Hood Canal Brewery, Poulsbo, WA www.hoodcanalbrewery.com
"Aroma is reasonable if relatively mild, with the expected pine and citrus hops." "Sweetish almost herbal flavor, grapefruit bitterness that is very mild, fairly dry finish." "Definitely not a typical Indian Pale Ale." 6.7% alc.

Hop Back Entire Stout ★★1/2
Stout: Hop Back, Salisbury, Wiltshire, England www.hopback.co.uk
"Strong milky coffee in the aroma." "Tastes of chocolate and coffee prevail with hints of caramel further into the glass." "If a bit more robust on the palate it would score much higher." 4.5% alc.

Hop Back Summer Lightning ★★★
Goldn/Blond Ale: Hop Back, Salisbury, Wiltshire, England www.hopback.co.uk
"Aroma has some citrus, light hops and iron." "Citric and sour malt and hops on the tongue, generous orange zest in the back before a dose of bitter grassy hops took control." "Nothing out of this world, but really not bad for the style." 5% alc.

Hop Pearl ★★
Pilsner: Browary Lubelskie S.A., Lublin, Poland www.perla.pl
"Butterscotch and faint stale woody hop aroma." "Flavor at the first try seems more bitter than in other Polish Pilsners, but ending gives nice sweet aftertaste." 6.2% alc.

HopTown DUIPA Imperial IPA ★★★★★
Imp/Dbl IPA: HopTown Brewing Co., Pleasanton, CA www.hoptownbrewing.com
"HopTown's Imperial Indian Pale Ale is "lively and brash with some malt smoothness to help out." "Aromas of a Colorado pine forest followed up by some citrus." "On tap @ my house." 9.5% alc.

HopTown IPA ★★★
IPA: HopTown Brewing Co., Pleasanton, CA www.hoptownbrewing.com
"Aroma is pure hops, grapefruit and pine." "Toasty, malty flavor very well balanced with resiny, spicy hop flavor and a good level of bitterness." 6.2% alc.

HopTown Oatmeal Breakfast Stout ★★★1/2
Sweet Stout: HopTown Brewing Co., Pleasanton, CA www.hoptownbrewing.com
"Big rich oatmeal stout with some milk stout qualities, the lactic properties come through in the end." "The oat patina also served to smoothen and blend the flavor characters." 0% alc.

HopTown Old Yeltsin ★★★★1/2
Imp. Stout: HopTown Brewing Co., Pleasanton, CA www.hoptownbrewing.com
"Sherry, alcohol, vanilla sugar, almonds, demerara - great aroma." "Bakers chocolate beside piney hops." "This is lighter than other Imperial Stouts I've tried but as creamy and mouth coating as any." 9% alc.

Huber Bock ★★
Bock: Joseph Huber Brewing Co., Monroe, WI www.berghoffbeer.com
"Some roasty malts and light caramel, but rather weak." "Nice malty, chewy body, but unfortunately finishes on a light metallic note." "Decent and easily drinkable, but lacking in character." 5.4% alc.

Huber Premium Beer ★★★
Pale Lager: Joseph Huber Brewing Co., Monroe, WI www.berghoffbeer.com
"Floral hops present in the flavor and a little corn." "Just a bit lighter and weaker than most other pale lagers that I have tried." 4.5% alc.

Hudy Delight ★★★★★
Pale Lager: Hudepohl-Schoenling (Snyder Intl), Frederick, MD
"Pleasant beer in that there are no offensive odors or flavors present." "Very refreshing and quite smooth, although, as expected, nearly flavorless." "This may well be the best reduced calorie 'light beer' in the country." 3.9% alc.

Hue Beer ★★
Pale Lager: Hue Brewery (Carlsberg), Hue City, Vietnam www.huda.com.vn/vi/
"Light grassy hop aroma, sweetish malts as well." "Starts sweet, fades into grainy dryness, some slight bittering hop in the finish." "Thin and light, somewhat watery and plain." "Pretty dire." 4.8% alc.

Huebert's Old Tyme Lager ★★1/2
Pale Lager: Huebert Brewing Co., OK City, OK
"Aroma was of caramel malts with a touch of lemon." "Zingy and tart, with notes of lemon and orange." "Kind of a lemonade beer." 3.2% alc.

Humboldt IPA Nectar ★★★★
IPA: Humboldt Brewing (Firestone Walker, Nectar Ales), Arcata, CA www.nectarales.com
"Pours a gorgeous ruby-orange, dark for an Indian Pale Ale." "Aroma is heavenly, sweet, nectar-like pine, pineapple, peach and melons." "Starts sweet ends bitter just like I want in an IPA." 5.28% alc.

Humboldt Red Nectar ★★★★1/2
Amber Ale: Humboldt Brewing (Firestone Walker, Nectar Ales), Arcata, CA www.nectarales.com
"One of the more highly-respected ambers in the land, Red Nectar is "sweet and malty with a plummy fruitiness with just a touch of floral hops." "One of my top 10 red ales of all time." 5.16% alc.

Hurricane ★
Malt Liquor: Anheuser-Busch Companies, St. Louis, MO www.anheuser-busch.com
"Palate was light, watery. Flavor is of corn and rice." "It's cheaper, stronger and tastier than something like a Natty Light or Keystone." 5.8% alc.

Hurricane Reef Lager ★★★★1/2
Pale Lager: Indian River Brewing Co. (Florida Beer Co.), Melbourne, FL www.floridabeer.com
"Interesting nose of bready malts and spice, maybe hops." "Floral hops, not much bitterness." "Flavor is good balance of malts and hop." N/A% alc.

Hurricane Reef Raspberry Wheat Ale ★★1/2
Fruit Beer: Indian River Brewing Co. (Florida Beer Co.), Melbourne, FL www.floridabeer.com
"Big raspberry aroma." "What flavor you get is in the finish and it is cloying and artificial." "Light body that was somewhat watery." 0% alc.

Icehouse ★
Pale Lager: Miller Brewing Co. (SABMiller), Milwaukee, WI www.millerbrewing.com
"It was the thing to drink back in '94… still a good cheap beer served ice cold." "Weak malty aroma. Taste is very bland." 5.5% alc.

Independence Bootlegger Brown Ale ★★★1/2
Brown Ale: Independence Brewing Co., Austin, TX www.independencebrewing.com
Nutty, dusty cocoa aroma with vanilla and biscuit. "Walks the line between an English and American brown." "Almond and chicory flavor. The sweetness lingers with a mocha taste developing." 6% alc.

Independence Freestyle Wheat ★★1/2
Am Wheat: Independence Brewing Co., Austin, TX www.independencebrewing.com
"Light caramel aroma with a little spiciness and a bit of earthiness." "Mildly sweet and clean with some grain flavor." "Tastes like a wheaty Bud Light." 4.70%% alc.

Independence Pale Ale ★★1/2
Am. Pale Ale: Independence Brewing Co., Austin, TX www.independencebrewing.com
"Pleasant sweet hoppy and malty aroma." "Initial citric hoppy bitterness." "Palate is as smooth as the Guadalupe River on a lazy summer day." 5.5% alc.

Il Vicino Wet Mountain Indian Pale Ale ★★★★
IPA: Il Vicino Pizzeria and Brewery, Albuquerque, NM www.ilvicino.com
"Fruity, citric and lightly sweet aroma, plenty of pineapple and orange on top of the lightly toasty, honeyish malts." "Flavor is sweet and fruity to start, malty and toasty, with hints of tangerine and pine that carry through to the juicy, bitter finish." N/A% alc.

Indian Wells Mojave Red ★★
Am Dark Larger: Indian Wells Wells Brewing, Inyokern, CA www.mojave-red.com
A red lager that has a "mildly sweet, honey, caramel flavor." "It is a bit watered downed. This beer isn't bad its just boring." 5.5% alc.

Inveralmond Blackfriar ★★★
Scotch Ale: Inveralmond, Perth, Perthshire and Kinross, Scotland www.inveralmond-brewery.co.uk
"Reminded of scotch whiskey, blended with some berries and peat and caramel." "Tastes very caramel malty, with some fruit, molasses and nuts in the finish." "Not perfect but nicely done." 7% alc.

Inveralmond Lia Fail ★★★★★
Bitter: Inveralmond, Perth, Perthshire and Kinross, Scotland www.inveralmond-brewery.co.uk
"Aroma is of dark caramel with a hint of smokiness." "Almondy, toffeeish, malty flavors lead to a dry finish with bark-like notes." "Best palindromic beer around." 4.7% alc.

Inveralmond Ossian's Ale ★★★
Bitter: Inveralmond, Perth, Perthshire and Kinross, Scotland www.inveralmond-brewery.co.uk
"Sweet malt and light floral grassy hops in the nose." "Sweet malt and the yeast-hop mix leave a lightly smoked pear cider taste." "This beer was drinkable but kind of odd." 4.1% alc.

Ipswich Dark Ale ★★★★★
Brown Ale: Mercury Brewing and Distribution, Ipswich, MA www.mercurybrewing.com
"Extremely faint malty aroma." "Semi-sweet cocoa up front, fairly malty, mildly roasted, chocolate malt perhaps." "Nice American style brown ale." N/A% alc.

Ipswich Indian Pale Ale ★★★
IPA: Mercury Brewing and Distribution, Ipswich, MA www.mercurybrewing.com
"Aroma is nicely balanced with an underlying sweetness and a more prominent floral hop aroma." "Tastes of grapefruit with some oranges and a little fruity." "A really unique IPA" N/A% alc.

Ipswich Oatmeal Stout ★★★
Sweet Stout: Mercury Brewing and Distribution, Ipswich, MA www.mercurybrewing.com
"Roasted mocha flavors dominate as well as chocolate. Pretty soft and easy going as far as stouts go, pleasant." "Kind of dry for an oatmeal stout." "A definite must try if you are in Massachusetts." N/A% alc.

Ipswich Original Ale ★★★1/2
Eng Pale Ale: Mercury Brewing and Distribution, Ipswich, MA www.mercurybrewing.com
"Big citrusy nose, touch oaky and pungently hoppy ." "Bitter flavors, grapefruit, grassy, honey, peachy." "Lightly bitter in the finish." N/A% alc.

Ipswich Porter ★★★★
Porter: Mercury Brewing and Distribution, Ipswich, MA www.mercurybrewing.com
"Aromas of light coffee/espresso foam, milk chocolate." "Definite roasted malt and coffee along with some sweetness." "Quite rich for a porter." "I just kept drinking it; yum!" N/A% alc.

Ipswich Summer Ale ★★1/2
Am. Wheat: Mercury Brewing and Distribution, Ipswich, MA www.mercurybrewing.com
"Starts with a hoppy/malt flavor, hoppy finish with a hint of sweetness, smooth very drinkable." "Finishes dry and bitter and herbal." "My kind of lawnmower beer." N/A% alc.

Ipswich Winter Ale ★★1/2
Eng. Strong Ale: Mercury Brewing and Distribution, Ipswich, MA www.mercurybrewing.com
"Nose: brandy and raisins with maybe a touch of chocolate." "The taste is shocking piney and bitter with a good dose of spice and earthiness upon the finish." "Medium body with light chewiness." N/A% alc.

Iron City Beer ★
Pale Lager: Pittsburgh Brewing Co., Pittsburgh, PA www.pittsburghbrewingco.com
"Clean pale malt, light floral hops aroma." "Sweet and lightly grassy with hints of corn." "Very simplistic lager." 4.5% alc.

Iron City Light ★
Pale Lager: Pittsburgh Brewing Co., Pittsburgh, PA www.pittsburghbrewingco.com
"Aroma of light sweet corn. Light, thin sour hop flavor." "I'm just pleased that a regional brewer would even dare continue to make a light beer in this post BMC apocalypse." 4.15% alc.

Isle of Skye Cuillin Beast ★★1/2
Scotch Ale: Isle of Skye, Uig, Isle of Skye, Scotland www.skyebrewery.co.uk
"Sugary sweet flavor aroma: tulips, powdered sugar and caramel." "Herbal, grassy bitterness comprises the bulk of the flavor with slightly ashy, dry caramel malt sulking in the background." "A weak-kneed Scotch Ale." 7% alc.

Ithaca Double IPA ★★★1/2
Imp/Dbl IPA: Ithaca Beer Co., Ithaca, NY www.ithacabeer.com
"Citrusy tea leaf on the start, somewhat hot or big as I can tell there is some heat behind it. Hop bitterness is there, but not overpowering like many IIPAs." "Not a bad double IPA, but definitely not on par with the really good ones." 10% alc.

Ithaca Finger Lakes Amber ★★1/2
Amber Ale: Ithaca Beer Co., Ithaca, NY www.ithacabeer.com
"Has a hoppy - citrusy bite to it - more akin to a California Pale Ale than an upstate NY amber." "Nice balance also of floral aromatic hoppiness at the beginning and bitter hop finish, but nothing remarkable." 4.8% alc.

Ithaca Finger Lakes Apricot Wheat ★★
Fruit Beer: Ithaca Beer Co., Ithaca, NY www.ithacabeer.com
"Nose is all tart apricot to me." "Faint maltiness in the flavor, but the first thing you notice is of course the apricots." "Not a bad apricot beer at all, though I wish it was a bit more flavorful." 4% alc.

Ithaca Finger Lakes Nut Brown ★★1/2
Brown Ale: Ithaca Beer Co., Ithaca, NY www.ithacabeer.com
"Light aromas of chocolate and black coffee. Some hop spiciness in the deep background." "Pleasant light nutty-malty character, herbal undertones near the dry finish." 5% alc.

Ithaca Finger Lakes Pale Ale ★★1/2
Am. Pale Ale: Ithaca Beer Co., Ithaca, NY www.ithacabeer.com
"Aroma is nice, peppery and hoppy, slight hint of malt." "Lightly sweet malty flavors balanced out by some light citric hops." "Needs some malt to balance it out." 4.6% alc.

Ithaca Flower Power Indian Pale Ale ★★1/2
IPA: Ithaca Beer Co., Ithaca, NY www.ithacabeer.com
"Quite hoppy and floral aroma - fits the name well, I guess." "Taste is fairly strong citrusy hops, black pepper, a hint of malt." "Very easy to drink but could use more of a hoppy kick." 0% alc.

Ithaca Gorges Smoked Porter ★★1/2
Smoked: Ithaca Beer Co., Ithaca, NY www.ithacabeer.com
"Flavor is rather sweet, milk sugar at least, with a very subtle hop presence. Smoked aspect isn't as strong on the tongue as the nose, but is quite noticeable." "A few minor adjustments could really turn this into something lovely." 6.3% alc.

JW Lees Harvest Ale ★★★★★
Barley Wine: J.W. Lees, Middleton Junction, Manchester, England www.jwlees.co.uk
"Extra strong ale with notes of "maple syrup, vanilla, scotch, good malts, earth." "great body, complex and inviting." Also available in four wood finishes - calvados, port, sherry and Lagavulin. The standard version is rated significantly higher than these. 11.5% alc.

JW Lees Moonraker ★★★
Barley Wine: J.W. Lees, Middleton Junction, Manchester, England www.jwlees.co.uk
"Aromas of dark fruit, dough and pipe tobacco." "Soft caramel and toffee flavors, very sweet and a bit cloying." "This is an adult, liquid candy bar." 7.5% alc.

Jamaca Stout ★★1/2
Foreign Stout: Big City Brewing Co., Kingston, Jamaica
"Fruity (raisin, prune) aroma with stinging alcohol." "Flavor is lactic and very sweet with more molasses and brown sugar plus a small roasted barley note." "Similar to, but less meaty than Dragon Stout." 8% alc.

James Page Boundary Waters Golden Lager ★★1/2
Pilsner: Stevens Point Brewery, Stevens Point, WI www.pointbeer.com
"A very unique aroma of freshly baked bread, vanilla extract and malts." "Really has a wild rice quality. Lightly sweet wild rice flavors mix with mild rose and lavender." N/A% alc.

James Page Burly Brown Ale ★★★
Brown Ale: Stevens Point Brewery, Stevens Point, WI www.pointbeer.com
"The aroma has the standards brown ale characteristics of walnut, caramel and toasted malting, grassy hops." "Flavors of caramel, toffee, nuts and a touch of cocoa with a slightly dry, lightly bitter finish." N/A% alc.

James Page Iron Range Amber Lager ★★1/2
Vienna: Stevens Point Brewery, Stevens Point, WI www.pointbeer.com
"Aroma has notes of grain and pale malt with a dash of caramel." "Decent balance, somewhat sweet though with toasted caramel and honey being predominate." "A tasty little lager, when you're not in the mood for anything more challenging." N/A% alc.

James Page Voyageur Pale Ale ★★1/2
Am. Pale Ale: Stevens Point Brewery, Stevens Point, WI www.pointbeer.com
"Resiny hop aroma with some fruit." "Moderate sweet caramel with some grain and a very light hop finish that is lightly bitter." N/A% alc.

James Page Winter Warmer ★★1/2
Am Strong Ale: Stevens Point Brewery, Stevens Point, WI www.pointbeer.com
"Light fruit cake aromas, with dates and raisins, sweet bread and mild spicy hops." "Palate is sweet, sticky and very chewable. Some bready notes that rise to a finish in grapefruit and some light floral." 8% alc.

James Squire Original Amber Ale ★★★
Amber Ale: Malt Shovel Brewery (Lion Nathan Co.), Sydney, Australia www.malt-shovel.com.au
"Very sweet, toasty malt aroma, a touch of caramel." "Fairly bland flavor, a bit on the sweet side, with the aroma on tasting being more of the dominant nutty malt." "Pretty simple and lacking in hops, but well-made." 5% alc.

James Squire Porter ★★1/2
Porter: Malt Shovel Brewery (Lion Nathan Co.), Sydney, Australia www.malt-shovel.com.au
"Aroma like chocolate-covered raisins, sugar, plums." "Emphasis on roasty malt and caramel on the palate, with a light coffee backdrop." "Guess it could be summed up with 'good effort, could do better'." 5% alc.

Jenlain Ambrée ★★1/2
Bière de Garde: Brasserie Duyck, Jenlain, France www.duyck.com
"Toffeeish aroma initially, after a while the more characteristic earthy, cellar aromas started to emerge together with some yeasty spiciness." "Soft interplay of malty sweetness is broadened by oranges and a light roasted malt finish." 6.5% alc.

Jenlain No. Six (Blonde 6%) ★★
Goldn/Blond Ale: Brasserie Duyck, Jenlain, France www.duyck.com
"Aroma of apple skins, white bread, grassy noble hop notes, slight corn syrup and canned peaches." "Flavors are soft caramel, buttery malts with some sweet lemon." "Pretty thin and not very interesting." 6% alc.

Jersey Harvest Ale ★★1/2
Amber Ale: River Horse Brewing Co., Lambertville, NJ www.riverhorse.com
"Cookie, caramel, light-roasted malts, bit of peanut (butter) aroma." "Flavor is mostly toasted and chocolate malt with notes of caramel and toffee." "Quite drinkable, nowhere extraordinary." N/A% alc.

Jersey Shore Gold ★
Goldn/Blond Ale: River Horse Brewing Co., Lambertville, NJ www.riverhorse.com
"Aroma is fully sweet with little hop balance." "Flavor has notes of sweet malt, corn, grain and a touch of lemon and grass." "Not the greatest offering from the Jersey breweries." N/A% alc.

Jever Pilsner ★★★★
Classic Ger Pils: Jever , Jever, Germany www.jever.de
"Hoppy, earthy aroma with some metallic hints." "Grainy maltiness is well-balanced by a classic German hoppiness, spicy and moderately bitter." "Very straightforward, balanced pils, with the sole purpose of refreshing." 4.9% alc.

John Smiths Bitter ★
Bitter: John Smiths (Scottish & Newcastle), Tadcaster, Yorkshire, England johnsmiths.co.uk
"Nose is light malt and grain with a trace of bitterness." "Dry malty flavor with a bitterness at the end and a watery and metallic taste." "Thin watery taste with only a very weak maltiness." 4% alc.

John's Generations White Ale ★★★★1/2
Bel. Witbier: Millstream Brewing Co., Amana, IA www.millstreambrewing.com
"Smell is bright and beery, with a hint of lemon, spice and hops." "Primarily spicy and acidic throughout with a slim initial sweetness and a very light finishing bitterness." "Can't find a thing wrong with this guy." N/A% alc.

Jolly Pumpkin Bière de Mars ★★★★★
Bière de Garde: Jolly Pumpkin Artisan Ales, Dexter, MI www.jollypumpkin.com
"Spicy apple cider aroma, tart fruit skins, cola, prune and plum with sour oak tannins." "Starts with nice Belgian malty sweetness, turning more oaky dry and lightly buttery toward the finish." 7% alc.

Jolly Pumpkin Calabaza Blanca ★★★★★
Bel. Witbier: Jolly Pumpkin Artisan Ales, Dexter, MI www.jollypumpkin.com
"Aromas of coriander oranges and some sugar rise from the grass with bananas and oak in the wake." "Flavors of the wood, yeast, malt are all well integrated and the hops balance in with these perfectly." 4.8% alc.

Jolly Pumpkin La Roja ★★★★
Bière de Garde: Jolly Pumpkin Artisan Ales, Dexter, MI www.jollypumpkin.com
"Oak, candied fruits, sweet malts, doughy yeast and alcohol in the aroma." "Flavor is sweet, a blend of caramel malts, molasses, vanilla, oak, cherries." "Very pleasant beer." 7.2% alc.

Jolly Pumpkin Luciernaga ★★★★★
Belgian Ale: Jolly Pumpkin Artisan Ales, Dexter, MI www.jollypumpkin.com
"Complex aroma, providing notes of big spicy florals and citrus, hops and some sourdough malts." "Taste is of smooth vanilla and light sugary citrus with a Belgian yeast that's evident in the undertones of crisp brew." 7% alc.

Jolly Pumpkin Maracaibo Especial ★★★★1/2
Abbey Dubbel: Jolly Pumpkin Artisan Ales, Dexter, MI www.jollypumpkin.com
"Aroma really develops into a wondrous spice-shop." "Flavor of alcohol, cocoa, candy, spices orange peel with lingering sweetness." "Surprisingly alcoholic, a bit drier than most dubbels." 7.5% alc.

Jolly Pumpkin Oro de Calabaza ★★★★
Bière de Garde: Jolly Pumpkin Artisan Ales, Dexter, MI www.jollypumpkin.com
"Aroma is wheat, yeast, lemon, pepper, watermelon and banana with a few fresh biscuits mixed in." "Flavor is very spicy, with lots of lemon tartness up front, waking up the palate." 8% alc.

Jopen Adriaan ★★1/2
Traditional Ale: Brouwerij Van Steenberge, Ertvelde, Belgium www.vansteenberge.com
"Honey, toasted wheat, pepper, cardamom, nutmeg, sweat aromas." "Nutty hop and vinous flavor, well balanced malt and light fruit." "A strange concoction." 5% alc.

Jopen Koyt ★★★★
Traditional Ale: Brouwerij Van Steenberge, Ertvelde, Belgium www.vansteenberge.com
"Sourish, herbs (sweet gale, sage, thyme), lots of malt and alcohol, quite sweet." "Very flavorful spice, chocolate and bread malt." "Different and enjoyable." 8.5% alc.

Josef Bierbitzch Golden Pilsner ★
Pilsner: Coast Range Brewing Co.S, Gilroy, CA www.whatalesyou.com
"Aroma is of straw and corn." "The taste is stale Cheerios with some light leaves." "Some really killer marketing on this for a rather average beer." "This one's a plain Jane." 4.5% alc.

Josef Hoffbauer Ice ★
Pale Lager: Gluek Brewing Co., Cold Spring, MN www.gluek.com
"Like someone threw some alcohol on some canned corn and lit it on fire." "Hard to choke down but sobriety was not an option." "For swillathons only." 5.8% alc.

Josef Hoffbauer Special Reserve Lager ★
Pale Lager: Gluek Brewing Co., Cold Spring, MN www.gluek.com
"Tastes like canned urine and smells even worse." "Smooth as sandpaper." "Bland and lifeless." 5% alc.

Julius Echter Hefe-Weiss Dunkel ★★★
Dunkelweizen: Würzburger HofBräu (Schörghuber), Würzburg, Germany www.wuerzburger-hofbraeu.de
"Sweet spicy caramel aroma with prunes in aroma, lightly vinous." "Notes of wheat, banana, tropical fruits, caramel, clove, light chocolate and a touch of dark fruits." "High level of sophistication and balance." 4.9% alc.

Julius Echter Hefe-Weiss Premium (Hell) ★★★
Hefeweizen: Würzburger HofBräu (Schörghuber), Würzburg, Germany www.wuerzburger-hofbraeu.de
"Fresh citrus (orange), clove and banana peel aroma." "Flavor is a rush of wheat followed by a mixture of hops and light banana." "Full bodied wheaty, spicy, fruity and very smooth." 4.9% alc.

JW Dundee's American Amber Lager ★★1/2
Am Dark Larger: High Falls Brewing Co., Rochester, NY www.highfalls.com
"Cereal, light grains, wet paper and very little hops." "Kind of reminds me of Newcastle." "Taste is caramel, malt, nobleish hops." "A Willy Wonkaish caramelly beer." 4.9% alc.

JW Dundee's American Pale ★★
Am. Pale Ale: High Falls Brewing Co., Rochester, NY www.highfalls.com
"Aroma is a nice balance of fairly dark malts and floral hops." "Taste is medium sweet, bread, caramel, grapefruit, some orange, light lime." "Finish is balanced surprisingly but it's a very subpar pale ale." 5.3% alc.

JW Dundee's Original Honey Brown Lager ★★
Am Dark Larger: High Falls Brewing Co., Rochester, NY www.highfalls.com
"Sweet, with malt, caramel, a little honey character and almost no hops or bitterness." "Artificial and separate honey infusion, added almost as an afterthought." "Better than a majority of the macros, but doesn't touch most micros." 4.5% alc.

König Pilsner (Germany) ★★1/2
Classic Ger Pils: König Brauerei (Th. Simon), Duisburg, Germany www.koenig.de
"Light-to-moderate bitterness, some grassy-herbal hop notes and faint bready malts." "Runs almost directly average to its style." "At this price, leave the domestic crap and cheaper commie pilsners on the shelf." 4.9% alc.

Köstritzer Schwarzbier ★★★
Schwarzbier: Köstritzer Schwarzbier Brauerei, Bad Köstritz/Thüringen, Germany www.koestritzer.de
"Aroma seemed smoky, with malt and grape undertones." "Subtle flavors of chocolate and coffee, but mostly a dry palate with a non-specific fruit note as it warmed." "Not the best example, but a quality one nonetheless." 4.8% alc.

Kaliber ★★
Low Alcohol: Guinness, Dublin, Ireland www.guinness.com
"Hay, caramel, hops and malt in aroma." "Flavor is light sweet and has vague fruity notes." "I'll never volunteer to be the DD again." 0.05% alc.

Kalik ★★
Pale Lager: Commonwealth Brewery (Heineken), Nassau, Bahamas www.kalik.com
"Mixture of light grassy hops and Wonderbread." "Fairly sweet, some semblance of hop bitterness." "Works better as a paper weight." 5% alc.

Kalnapilis Export ★
Helles/Dortmnd: Kalnapilis (Royal Unibrew), Panevezys, Lithuania www.kalnapilis.lt
"Odd aroma combining apples and light herbal hop." "Palatable, sort of, flavors are quite sweet and mild." "Light body and flavor, though a highly drinkable beer." 5.4% alc.

Kalnapilis Original ★★1/2
Pale Lager: Kalnapilis (Royal Unibrew), Panevezys, Lithuania www.kalnapilis.lt
"Straw and malt aroma." "Palate is balanced - grassy hop, hint of berry notes, prickly crisp finish." "Non-offensive, but, so?" 5% alc.

Kapuziner Weissbier ★★★1/2
Hefeweizen: Kulmbacher Brauerei (Schörghuber), Kulmbach, Germany www.kulmbacher.de
"Aroma is like a typical Hefeweizen - subtle fruit, pronounced spice, yeast and grassy hops." "Lots of banana and vanilla with a touch of cloves and a kick of lemon at the end." "Very quenching and refreshing though there isn't a whole lot of depth." 5.4% alc.

Karl Strauss Amber Lager ★★1/2
Vienna: Karl Strauss Breweries, Carlsbad, CA www.karlstrauss.com
"Moderately sweet caramel, grain and corn make up the base and only a slight bitterness crashes the malty party." "Flavor was rather simple, slightly sticky and on the sweet side." 4.2% alc.

Karl Strauss Endless Summer Gold ★★1/2
Premium Lager: Karl Strauss Breweries, Carlsbad, CA www.karlstrauss.com
"Aroma of light cardboard, some hops and a small maltiness." "It's light bodied and light flavored so you can just keep refreshing yourself again and again." 5.6% alc.

Karl Strauss Red Trolley ★★1/2
Amber Ale: Karl Strauss Breweries, Carlsbad, CA www.karlstrauss.com
"The aroma had malt and caramel but it was thin." "Dark amber, creamy palate with a nice malty taste." "Not much going on here." 5.6% alc.

Karlovacko ★★1/2
Pale Lager: Karlovacka Pivovara (Heineken), Karlovac, Croatia www.karlovacko.hr
"Aromas of grain, hops, straw." "Flavor is slightly more hopped up than a typical pale lager." "A good quality, very basic brew - what more can you say?" 5.4% alc.

Kasteel Kriek ★★★★★
Fruit Beer: Brouwerij Van Honsebrouck, Ingelmunster, Belgium www.vanhonsebrouck.be
"Cherry pie in a glass but more intense and balanced than that." "Spicy yeast and tart cherries abound, with a soothing creamy lactic-like texture, semi-thick body." "Anyone who doesn't like fruit beers needs to check with this one." 8% alc.

Kasteelbier Blonde ★★★
Bel. Strong Ale: Brouwerij Van Honsebrouck, Ingelmunster, Belgium www.vanhonsebrouck.be
"Aroma of fruits with notes of spices and light acidic notes." "Golden syrup flavors in mouth and then some hop on the end which is both herby and sweet tangerine." "Overall a decent, very drinkable middle of the pack strong blonde." 11% alc.

Kasteelbier Donker ★★★★
Bel. Strong Ale: Brouwerij Van Honsebrouck, Ingelmunster, Belgium www.vanhonsebrouck.be
"Has a sweet caramel sugary and earthy, bready Belgian yeasty aroma." "Sweet palate of demerara sugar, coffee, chocolate cake and only a hint of alcohol or fruit." "Sweet, fruity beer." "Good for dessert - possibly on its own." 11% alc.

Kelly's Light Irish Stone Brewed ★★
Ale: Atlanta Brewing Co., Atlanta, GA www.atlantabrewing.com
"Slightly darker than the standard light lager." "Simple breadish malt and citric/grassy hop aroma." "I could drink these all day, but at 3.8 percent, what is the point?" 3.8% alc.

Kelpie ★★★
Traditional Ale: Williams Brothers (Heather Ales), Alloa, Scotland www.fraoch.com
"Dark malt and strong salty funky aroma with a trace of chocolate in the lagoon." "A lot happening in this glass. Starts out like a brown ale, then the salt and flavors build and roll in through the finish." "This brewers collection of eclectic brews never lets me down." 4.4% alc.

KEO ★
Premium Lager: KEO Ltd., Lemesos, Cypress www.keogroup.com
"Quite a good citric hop aroma, some lemon." "The taste is pretty bland and inoffensive, just a bit of barley." "Not very impressed with the self-proclaimed hero of Cyprus." 4.5% alc.

Key West Sunset Ale ★★1/2
Goldn/Blond Ale: Indian River Brewing Co. (Florida Beer Co.), Melbourne, FL www.floridabeer.com
"Taste is malty with a crisp slightly hopped finish." "Enough malt and hops play to realize it ain't a macrobeer." "Refreshing if uneventful light ale." N/A% alc.

Keystone Light ★
Pale Lager: Coors Brewing Co. (MolsonCoors), Golden, CO www.coors.com
"This just doesn't taste like anything at all." "Very thin, watery." "The most prominent feeling associated with drinking this beer is, 'Why am I such a cheap bastard?' " 4.2% alc.

Keystone Premium ★
Pale Lager: Coors Brewing Co. (MolsonCoors), Golden, CO www.coors.com
"Creamy sweet malt with soft carbonation." "Just like every other American lager." "No party is complete without these babies strewn across the floor." 4.8% alc.

Kilkenny ★★
Irish Ale: Guinness (Diageo), Dublin, Ireland www.guinness.com
"Aroma is flowery, soft, somewhat malty, slightly sweet, creamy." "Taste is clean and light, giving way to a faintly bitter aftertaste, with a vague hop taste." "Gets downright disappointing by the time I've finished half a glass." 4.3% alc.

King Cobra ★
Malt Liquor: Anheuser-Busch Companies, St. Louis, MO www.anheuser-busch.com
"Skunky aroma, with corn and some yeast." "Almost no taste, some sweet corn and hops." "It is s-t to the nth degree." 5.9% alc.

Kingfisher ★★
Pale Lager: United Breweries (Scottish & Newcastle), Bangalore, India www.kingfisherworld.com
"Aroma of malt and corn with fruity notes." "Well balanced and smooth, you can taste the hops and the malts, with a small sign of the adjunct (corn syrup) taste of US macros." "Not unlike a firmer, more Germanic rendition of Heineken." 4.8% alc.

Kinsale Irish Lager ★★1/2
Pale Lager: Kinsale, Kinsale, County Cork, Ireland www.kinsalebrewing.com
"Earthy vegetable aroma." "Notes of hay and some sweet beets." "Very little malt flavor, just the syrupy sweetness and a touch of hops." "There are other better beers in Ireland than this swill." N/A% alc.

Kirin Ichiban ★★1/2
Pale Lager: Kirin Brewery Co., Tokyo, Japan www.kirin.com
"Slightly malt and oily, but only slightly so, like a very light Bohemian Pilsner." "Light grassy bitterness and continental hop undertones complement the malts." "At the end of the day it's still a pale lager." 4.9% alc.

Kirin Lager ★★
Pale Lager: Kirin Brewery Co., Tokyo, Japan www.kirin.com
"Aroma mixes vague continental hop notes with grains and background solvent notes." "Grainy palate with a sweetish edge." "I can't think of any good reason to drink this again." 4.9% alc.

Koch's Golden Anniversary ★
Pale Lager: High Falls Brewing Co., Rochester, NY www.highfalls.com
"What's remarkable about the taste is how it is bad going down, but then for several minutes the aftertaste in your mouth continues to get worse, to the point where you would drink just about anything to make it go away." N/A% alc.

Koff Porter ★★★★★
Baltic Porter: Sinebrychoff (Carlsberg), Kerava, Finland www.koff.fi
"Robust aroma of caramel, chocolate, coffee, vanilla, molasses, floral hops and a hint of smoke." "Taste is mostly dark roast grain with some chocolate, a dose of molasses and a slightly warming alcohol." "This is a porter to be reckoned with." 7.2% alc.

Kona Big Wave Golden ★★
Goldn/Blond Ale: Kona Brewing Co., Kailua Kona, HA www.konabrewingco.com
"Malt, hops (light) and a touch of yeast fruitiness" highlight this beer. "Bland lager flavor but reasonably drinkable." "Perfect for the bright and breezy Hawaiian weather in which it was enjoyed." 5.2% alc.

Kona Fire Rock Pale ★★1/2
Am. Pale Ale: Kona Brewing Co., Kailua Kona, HA www.konabrewingco.com
"Grassy, citrusy hop aroma with some malt sweetness." "Soft hop flavor with fruity hints." "Nice lingering mix of fruit and malt." "Flavor is fairly unique, fruity side of grapefruit bitter and well balanced." 6% alc.

Kona Longboard Lager ★★1/2
Premium Lager: Kona Brewing Co., Kailua Kona, HA www.konabrewingco.com
"Very light aroma, some hint of citrus and malt." "Crisp, lightly bitter finish." "Decent lager, but my least liked of the Konas I've had." 5.5% alc.

Kotayk ★
Pale Lager: Abovian Brewery, Abovian, Armenia www.kotayk.am
"Relatively hoppy nose - grassy." "Malts are fruity and VERY sweet. Slightly spicy hops." "Not terrible, but nothing above a cookie-cutter Euro Pale Lager either." 5.2% alc.

Kronenbourg 1664 ★
Premium Lager: Brasseries-Kronenbourg (Scottish & Newcastle), Strasbourg, France
www.brasseries-kronenbourg.com
"Aroma is flowery and citrusy." "Mild honey nose and flavor, a drying bitterness with little hop flavor." "On a positive side there are no flaws in this beer, on the negative side it's a highly carbonated bland beer." 5% alc.

Kulmbacher Eisbock ★★★★★
Eisbock: Kulmbacher Brauerei (Schörghuber), Kulmbach, Germany www.kulmbacher.de
"Beautiful dark malt aroma - so well defined it's like chewing on Münich malt." "Sweet malt flavors mixed with nuts, brown bread crust." "Straightforward, but beautiful and lingering." 9.2% alc.

Kulmbacher Münchshof Schwarzbier ★★★
Schwarzbier: Kulmbacher Brauerei (Schörghuber), Kulmbach, Germany www.kulmbacher.de
"Plenty of mocha chocolate aromas." "Flavor is mostly malty with some German hop presence in the finish." "Very drinkable light schwarzbier." 4.9% alc.

La Bavaisienne ★★★★★

Bière de Garde: Brasserie Theillier, Bavay, France

"Aroma of dark organic honey, pine nuts, maple and sweet wort." "Very pleasant caramel and honey base for the wonderful floral hop bouquet, lemon zest, fresh biscuits and so much more." "There are very few brewers who are operating at this level." 7% alc.

La Bière de Boucanier Blonde ★★1/2

Bel. Strong Ale: Brouwerij Van Steenberge, Ertvelde, Belgium www.arborbrewing.com

Nose: "Citrus, herbs, caramel and doughy yeast." "Flavor is dominated by some sweetness associated with caramel and by doughy yeast, there's also some citrus and herbs in there." "It's interesting and good but fails to really impress or amaze." 11% alc.

La Bière de Boucanier Dark ★★★

Bel. Strong Ale: Brouwerij Van Steenberge, Ertvelde, Belgium www.vansteenberge.com

"Aroma of brown sugar, candi sugar, malt and alcohol." "Flavor is strong on the sweet side with notes of brown sugar, candi sugar and malt, there's also some alcohol vapors." "Pleasant, but unremarkable." 9% alc.

La Caracole Ambrée ★★★1/2

Bel. Strong Ale: Brasserie Caracole, Falmignoul, Belgium www.caracole.be

"Fruity and spicy aroma with apricots and a bit of tartness." "Flavors of tart apricots, ripe dark plums, muscat grapes, lemons." "Another good picnic brew." 7.5% alc.

La Chouffe ★★★★1/2

Bel. Strong Ale: Brasserie dAchouffe, Achouffe, Belgium www.achouffe.be

"Fresh and flowery scent, complex and spiced." "Notes of orange peel, caramel, sugar, coriander and clove." "The finish is mellow with the spicy character of Hallertau hops." "Dangerously easy to drink." 8% alc.

La Choulette Ambrée ★★★1/2

Bière de Garde: Brasserie La Choulette, Hordain, France www.lachoulette.com

"Firm, malty, with a touch of vanilla and a good, understated yeasty note." "There are distinct wood and honey notes mixed in with a gentle hint of white wine." "This really is the kind of flavor that I think of when I think of quality Bière de Garde." 8% alc.

La Choulette Blonde ★★1/2

Bière de Garde: Brasserie La Choulette, Hordain, France www.lachoulette.com

"Aroma has sweet biscuity malts and some nice light fruit." ""Flavor is malty, yeasty and very musty." "A nondescriptive mash of flavors with no strong notes or subtle tones." 7.5% alc.

La Choulette de Noël ★★★

Bière de Garde: Brasserie La Choulette, Hordain, France www.lachoulette.com

"Mustiness amid the caramel, nut and vanilla aroma." "Sweet malts with dark, hard candy and a bit of nutty bitterness." "typical rustic Bière de Garde-character." 7% alc.

La Choulette Framboise ★★★1/2

Fruit Beer: Brasserie La Choulette, Hordain, France www.lachoulette.com

"Pleasant raspberry aroma, with notes of oak." "Flavor is that of sweet raspberries, but far more subtle and elegant than most other beers I have had." Most folks find this fairly average but those who like it tend to love it. 6.2% alc.

La Divine ★★1/2

Bel. Strong Ale: Brasserie de Silly, Silly, Belgium www.silly-beer.com

"Aroma of light roast caramel malt, lemon, cloves, banana and alcohol." "Sweet, fruity and honeyed, with a creamy mouthfeel." "An unusual beer, well worth sampling, but DIVINE? I don't think so." 9.5% alc.

La Fringante ★★★★1/2

Bel. Strong Ale: Unibroue (Sleeman), Chambly, Quebec www.unibroue.com

"Smells of bread dough and yeast alcohol, allspice and some pepper." "Tastes like a big Belgian; hot good amount of spice pepper and allspice, touch of coriander and bread dough and yeast." "OK but low on wow factor for such a strong beer." 10% alc.

La Guillotine ★★1/2

Bel. Strong Ale: Brouwerij Huyghe, Melle, Belgium www.delirium.be

"Sweet, alcoholic nose with a citrus streak, white candi sugar." "Flavor is also very sweet and very fruity with oranges and peaches coming through." "Reminds me of the Delirium." 9.3% alc.

La Moneuse ★★★★1/2

Saison: Brasserie de Blaugies, Dour-Blaugies, Belgium www.brasseriedeblaugies.com

"Sweet spicy and fruity aroma - I pick up coriander, yeast, peaches and oranges." "Spicy orange flavor. Grassy hops in finish." "Very well-done beer with lots of character." 8% alc.

La Moneuse Speciale Noël ★★★★

Saison: Brasserie de Blaugies, Dour-Blaugies, Belgium www.brasseriedeblaugies.com

"Aroma is yeasty, musty and tart at the same time with some cheese notes." "Tart on the tongue, it's got some nice juicy fruit tastes atop some soggy Wheaties with a squirt of lemon, pepper, coriander, clove and a handful of dust." 8% alc.

La Terrible ★★★★★

Bel. Strong Ale: Unibroue (Sleeman), Chambly, Quebec www.unibroue.com

"The aroma has a real red grape juiciness, quite sweet and estery." "Flavor of caramel, dark fruit, yeast, malt, spices, some chocolate, a touch of alcohol and more - so complex and delicious." "Less fruit than the similar Trois Pistoles." 10.5% alc.

La Trappe Dubbel ★★★1/2

Abbey Dubbel: De Koningshoeven, Tilburg, Netherlands www.latrappe.nl

"Aroma is pleasant, fruity and rich in malt with apples, pears, banana and small hints of nougat." "Flavor has plenty of dates, raisins, baked brown bread, sweet ripe cherries and a hint of alcohol." "Palate is nice but could be a good bit creamier." 6.5% alc.

La Trappe Quadrupel ★★★★1/2

Abt/Quadrupel: De Koningshoeven, Tilburg, Netherlands www.latrappe.nl

"A sweet, bready aroma with, I think, a little peach and some yeast." "Taste of sweet malt reminiscent of cookie dough with some dry figs." "I think maybe this isn't my favorite style, but I appreciate the craftsmanship." 10% alc.

La Trappe Tripel ★★★★

Abbey Tripel: De Koningshoeven, Tilburg, Netherlands www.latrappe.nl

"Aroma is honey sweetness with sunflowers and orange having a little say." "Sweet malt presence with a subtle mix of spice in the background." "I've had much better Tripels but it's still a damn fine beer." 8% alc.

La Tropical ★★1/2

Pilsner: Cerveceria La Tropical, Melbourne, FL www.floridabeer.com

"This blatant marketing ploy… made from the recipe of a long defunct Cuban beer." "Fairly sweet for a pils." "Put a lime in it and its drinkable… I guess." N/A% alc.

Labatt Blue ★★1/2

Pale Lager: Labatt Breweries (InBev), London, Ontario www.labatt.com

"A slightly grainy character is the only flavor in this brew." "Not nearly as watery on the palate as most macros." "At least I didn't pay for it." 5% alc.

LaConner Belgian Wit ★★★

Bel. Witbier: LaConner Brewing Co., LaConner, WA

"Fruity, apple juicy aroma with a hint of coriander." "Sweet flavor, with an almost gruity herbal note - very orangey, too." "Pretty complex version of a wit." 5% alc.

LaConner ESB ★★1/2

Prem Bitter: LaConner Brewing Co., LaConner, WA

"Aroma of cherries, wood, pears, hint of toast." "Woody bitterness mixes with caramel sweetness on the palate." "Just a light bitterness actually, very session-like, simple, but tastes good." 6% alc.

LaConner Imperial Stout ★★★★1/2

Imp. Stout: LaConner Brewing Co., LaConner, WA

"Slightly nutty aroma of coffee and cream." "Flavor of roasted barley, dark chocolate and a hint of almonds." "A very sessionable impy stout and overall excellent to boot." 8.5% alc.

LaConner Indian Pale Ale ★★★1/2

IPA: LaConner Brewing Co., LaConner, WA

"Grapefruity aroma with notes of caramel and wood." "Flavor is hoppy, resinous hops, grapefruit, not bad, but I much prefer the dry hopped version!" "Not as clean or crisp as I would have liked, but well balanced me thinks." 7% alc.

LaConner Pilsner ★★★★1/2

Pilsner: LaConner Brewing Co., LaConner, WA

"Appetizing bready malt taste with a pungent, fruity hop character." "Crisp, grassy bitterness with a hint of lemon and some honeyed, biscuity pale malts." "This is the Pacific Northwest's version of an approachable starter beer." 5% alc.

LaConner Tannenbaum ★★★★

Eng. Strong Ale: LaConner Brewing Co., LaConner, WA

"Very sweet alcohol accented aroma, brown sugar and some subtle earthy spicing." "Chewy, sweet finish." "The alcohol is noticeable and the bitterness comes through a bit." 7.5% alc.

Lagunitas #10 ★★★1/2

Belgian Ale: Lagunitas Brewing Co., Petaluma, CA www.lagunitas.com

"Made using the Westmalle yeast on a lighter, golden Belgian-style ale. "Light fruity and spicy aroma." "Flavor has a lot going on - fruity (peach), some grain, some earthiness, some herbal tones" 5.9% alc.

Lagunitas Brown Shugga ★★★★

Barley Wine: Lagunitas Brewing Co., Petaluma, CA www.lagunitas.com

Based on an aborted batch of Olde Gnarley Wine, Brown Shugga is a strong ale that is "fairly malty", with a "sweet, mildly cloying flavor of brown sugar and burnt caramelized sugar with notes of grapefruit and mint." 9.9% alc.

Lagunitas Censored ★★★

Am Strong Ale: Lagunitas Brewing Co., Petaluma, CA www.lagunitas.com

Apparently inspired by no particular style, this ale has the "sweet aroma of caramel and malts with notes of hops, pine needles and spices" and a flavor that is "rich, malty." "I was shocked to discover its relatively high alcohol content." 7.7% alc.

Lagunitas Hairy Eyeball ★★★★

Am Strong Ale: Lagunitas Brewing Co., Petaluma, CA www.lagunitas.com

Another non-style beer from Lagunitas, this is "deep reddish brown" with an aroma "approaching some of the maltier barleywines." "Flavor is malty and nicely bitter with some leafy, earthy notes in the finish." 8.8% alc.

Lagunitas Imperial Stout ★★1/2
Imp. Stout: Lagunitas Brewing Co., Petaluma, CA www.lagunitas.com
"Elegant chocolate-port-coffee liqueur aroma, enticing and sweet." "Sweetish, charred body with some port-like aspects." "This is less an Imperial Stout than a big sweet stout." 8.2% alc.

Lagunitas Indian Pale Ale ★★★1/2
IPA: Lagunitas Brewing Co., Petaluma, CA www.lagunitas.com
"The nose is wonderful - incredibly floral with a pinch of citrus and some bready goodness underneath it all." "Flavor is fruity with bready notes and an underlying bitterness." "Not the most interesting Indian Pale Ale." 5.7% alc.

Lagunitas Maximus ★★★★1/2
Imp/Dbl IPA: Lagunitas Brewing Co., Petaluma, CA www.lagunitas.com
"This has a lot of character and balance for a double Indian Pale Ale, but not the extreme hoppiness of some competitors." "Sweet malts give a honeysuckle composure, finishing with a bitterness that seems to dangle from the larynx." 7.5% alc.

Lagunitas Olde Gnarly Wine ★★★★★
Barley Wine: Lagunitas Brewing Co., Petaluma, CA www.lagunitas.com
"Pure barleywine with heavy caramelized malts, piney and spicy hops, candied fruits, earthy yeast esters, a hint of salt and wood." "Definitely underrated in my opinion." "This bomber is going to do me in." 9.7% alc.

Lagunitas Pils ★★★★
Bohem Pilsner: Lagunitas Brewing Co., Petaluma, CA www.lagunitas.com
"Citrus, mint, herbal hops over lightly toasty malts with some hints of sulfur in the nose." "Crisp hop bitterness with a light citrus, herbal character over a clean malt base." "Close to its Czech ideal." 5.3% alc.

Lagunitas Sirius ★★★
Am Strong Ale: Lagunitas Brewing Co., Petaluma, CA www.lagunitas.com
Described by the brewery as a "high-gravity cream ale," it produces an aroma reminiscent of "honey malt, apricot and hops." The flavor is "creamy and juicy with poached spiced pears subtly affecting the malty, full body." 7.6% alc.

Lake Louie Arena Premium ★★★1/2
American Pale Ale: Lake Louie Brewing Co., Arena, WI www.lakelouie.com
Aroma is fresh bread with some pancakes and a little bit of grapefruit. "Flavor finds doughy and caramelly malts across the middle with pine forest and grapefruit hop presence." "A tasty and well-balanced APA." N/A% alc.

Lake Louie Mr. Mephisto's Imperial Stout ★★★1/2
Imperial Stout: Lake Louie Brewing Co., Arena, WI www.lakelouie.com
Aromas of cocoa, roasted coffee and cream. Nice aroma, but not as big as I would expect from an Imperial Stout. "Earthy malt and raw sugars blend with 12% alc.

Lake Louie Prairie Moon Farmhouse Ale ★★★★
Saison: Lake Louie Brewing Co., Arena, WI www.lakelouie.com
"Doughy, coriander, somewhat peppery citrus aroma." "Flavor is tart mustiness, following into a bready malt finish." "Very, very tasty and remarkably drinkable." 5% alc.

Lake Louie Tommy's Porter ★★★1/2
Porter: Lake Louie Brewing Co., Arena, WI www.lakelouie.com
Nose is chocolate with some dates and raisins and other dark fruit notes. Taste is coffee with some hazelnuts and a little bit of dark chocolate." "A very smooth drinker. I liked it." N/A% alc.

Lake Louie Warped Speed ★★★1/2

Scottish Ale: Lake Louie Brewing Co., Arena, WI www.lakelouie.com

Toasted caramel and cereal malts lead the aroma, followed by smoked cedar, dried pears and dried leafy hoppage. "Flavor is a strong toasty peated smoked malt, raisin bread, milk caramels." "Another solid brew from these guys." N/A% alc.

Lake Placid 46er IPA ★★

IPA: Lake Placid Pub and Brewery, Lake Placid, NY www.ubuale.com

"Aroma of creamed honey, grain, faintly of hops - pretty sweet for an Indian Pale Ale." "More sweet than bitter." "Flavor was OK, kind of what you expect from a generic IPA." 6% alc.

Lake Placid Frostbite Pale ★★★★1/2

IPA: Lake Placid Pub and Brewery, Lake Placid, NY www.ubuale.com

"Hoppy aroma with plenty of grapefruit, pine and hay." "Bold and extremely well balanced flavors with a toasted malt center surrounded by citrus, brown sugar, a touch of pepper and plenty of hops." B1698 N/A% alc.

Lake Placid Ubu Ale ★★★

Eng. Strong Ale: Lake Placid Pub and Brewery, Lake Placid, NY www.ubuale.com

"Aroma of lightly roasted malt, tart berry fruit and a hint of mustiness." "Sweet flavor is of red wine, smoke, fruit - balanced nicely by a strong hop presence." "Well balanced beer from a fine NY brewery." 7% alc.

Lake Superior Kayak Kölsch ★★1/2

Kölsch: Lake Superior Brewing Co., Duluth, MN www.lakesuperiorbrewing.com

"Pale malt aroma with pear skin and sourdough yeast." "Notes of wheat, hops and sourness." "Fair beer, but doesn't fit the style." N/A% alc.

Lake Superior Mesabi Red ★★★★

Amber Ale: Lake Superior Brewing Co., Duluth, MN www.lakesuperiorbrewing.com

"The aroma was malty with some cherry, fruity and hoppy hints." "Lots of deep malt flavor, with dark caramel, mild licorice and rye bread coming to mind." "A change in pace from the normal reds." 6.5% alc.

Lake Superior Old Man Winter Warmer ★★★★

Barley Wine: Lake Superior Brewing Co., Duluth, MN www.lakesuperiorbrewing.com

"Unusual aroma of caramelized banana orange marmalade, brown sugar, spiced rum and something along the lines of a honey-lemon cough drop." "Fruity flavors (figs, raisins, baked apples) combined with some woody/tannin notes." 10.3% alc.

Lake Superior Seven Bridges Brown ★★1/2

Brown Ale: Lake Superior Brewing Co., Duluth, MN www.lakesuperiorbrewing.com

"Aroma is fruity malt and roasted whole grains, with a hint of alcohol." "Flavor of caramel, nuts, plum, fig, cherry and bread." "Good but uninspiring." 5% alc.

Lake Superior Sir Duluth Oatmeal Stout ★★★

Sweet Stout: Lake Superior Brewing Co., Duluth, MN www.lakesuperiorbrewing.com

"Sweet aroma with lots of chocolate." "Light roasted malt mix with some light chocolate and dark cocoa." N/A% alc.

Lake Superior Special Ale ★★★

Am. Pale Ale: Lake Superior Brewing Co., Duluth, MN www.lakesuperiorbrewing.com

"Flavor is pretty deep. Starts off with a good burst of slightly floral hops and strong orange flavor, then finishes with a good dose of malt and a strong kick of wheaty yeast." "An enjoyable session pale!" N/A% alc.

Lake Superior Split Rock Bock ★★

Bock: Lake Superior Brewing Co., Duluth, MN www.lakesuperiorbrewing.com

"Lightly burnt wheat toast aromas with some hints of light fruit in the background." "Decent dark malt character, touch of appley acidity." "Flavors from the bottle didn't quite work together." N/A% alc.

Lake Superior St. Louis Bay IPA ★★1/2
IPA: Lake Superior Brewing Co., Duluth, MN www.lakesuperiorbrewing.com
"Taste is moderately sweet, caramel, cookie, floral, light grapefruit." "Smells of pine and grapefruit, bit woody." "Hoppy finish is solid and aggressive orangey and bitter." N/A% alc.

Lakefront Beer Line Barley Wine ★★
Barley Wine: Lakefront Brewery, Inc., Milwaukee, WI www.lakefrontbrewery.com
"Sweet heavy malt nose with hints of cherry and tons of alcohol." "Tastes of caramel, light vanilla and dark fruits." "Overwhelming cloying sweetness and alcohol." 10% alc.

Lakefront Big Easy Lager ★★1/2
Bock: Lakefront Brewery, Inc., Milwaukee, WI www.lakefrontbrewery.com
"Aroma is pears with some light bread." "Rich sugary malt, that blossoms into a lightly hopped caramel sugar." "Lakefront has skillfully crafted a malt dominant beer. Hats off to them!" 6% alc.

Lakefront Bock ★★★★
Bock: Lakefront Brewery, Inc., Milwaukee, WI www.lakefrontbrewery.com
"Malty aroma has some raisins, grapes, toffee, caramel and anise in it." "Hints of roasty coffee flavors along with some raisins, grapes and pears." "A joy to drink, with considerable flavor." 5.7% alc.

Lakefront Cattail Ale ★
Mild Ale: Lakefront Brewery, Inc., Milwaukee, WI www.lakefrontbrewery.com
"Aroma is floral with bread crust and some lemon zest." "Flavor is light wheat/grain with hints of honey and banana." "A little too much like Bud-Miller-Coors for me..." 4.5% alc.

Lakefront Cherry Lager ★★1/2
Fruit Beer: Lakefront Brewery, Inc., Milwaukee, WI www.lakefrontbrewery.com
"Sweet cherry nose; bright fruit, tart, yet sweet." "Lightly spicy and tart cherries with a clean, fresh bitterness." "A crisp, clean lager with a firm tart cherry base." N/A% alc.

Lakefront Cream City Pale Ale ★★1/2
Am. Pale Ale: Lakefront Brewery, Inc., Milwaukee, WI www.lakefrontbrewery.com
"Clean caramel smell with a well balanced pine and grapefruit hop bitterness." "This is lightly biter a hint of caramel and that's about it." "Not extremely pleasing, but not offensive." N/A% alc.

Lakefront Eastside Dark ★★★1/2
Dunkel: Lakefront Brewery, Inc., Milwaukee, WI www.lakefrontbrewery.com
"Nice complex nose: coffee, dark sweet fruits, toasted grain, cola." "Sweet, malty, chocolaty and very nutty, with only a slight bitterness in the finish." "A brew that has converted many to the dark side." 5% alc.

Lakefront Fuel Café ★★1/2
Sweet Stout: Lakefront Brewery, Inc., Milwaukee, WI www.lakefrontbrewery.com
"Aroma is straight up roasted coffee." "Bitter, sour and roasty malty flavors throughout." "Good, in a 'once-in-a-while-I-like-an-espresso' kind of way." 4.4% alc.

Lakefront Holiday Spice ★★★★
Spice/Herb: Lakefront Brewery, Inc., Milwaukee, WI www.lakefrontbrewery.com
"Oranges and wintry spices were loud and proud in the sweet, warming aroma." "Taste is moderately sweet, ginger, brown sugar, candied orange, some earthy, light caramel." "This would've made my Christmas much more enjoyable." 9.5% alc.

Lakefront Klisch Pilsner ★★★1/2

Classic Ger Pils: Lakefront Brewery, Inc., Milwaukee, Wi www.lakefrontbrewery.com

"Grain, wet grass and light citrus aromas." "Creamy, medium bodied with flavors of tart fruit and sweet malt. Herbal bitter hops finish to round it out." "Great Pils." N/A% alc.

Lakefront Oktoberfest ★

Märzen/Oktbfst: Lakefront Brewery, Inc., Milwaukee, WI www.lakefrontbrewery.com

"Aroma starts out malty and fresh but takes on an interesting unripe banana tone." "Flavor is complex with brown sugar, banana and toasted malt." "Not a fan of this below average Oktoberfest." N/A% alc.

Lakefront Organic ESB ★★

Prem Bitter: Lakefront Brewery, Inc., Milwaukee, WI www.lakefrontbrewery.com

"Sweet aromas, highly caramel with alot of fruit... cherry, raisin, some orange and vanilla." "This is one of those sweet, bready, lightly toasty Extra Special Bitters that seems so common here in the States." N/A% alc.

Lakefront Pumpkin Lager ★★1/2

Spice/Herb: Lakefront Brewery, Inc., Milwaukee, WI www.lakefrontbrewery.com

"Aroma is of nutmeg, pumpkin, cinnamon and caramel malt." "Flavor of pumpkin shines through along with pie spices, cloves, chocolate and citrusy hops." "Another average pumpkin ale?" N/A% alc.

Lakefront Riverwest Stein ★★★★★

Vienna: Lakefront Brewery, Inc., Milwaukee, WI www.lakefrontbrewery.com

"Slightly acidic caramel and light fruity notes dominate the nose with the barest hint of spice, sweet grains, spicy hops." "Wonderful hop/malt balance, a nice caramel sweetness and some earth-tones." "As near to perfection as a lager can be." 6% alc.

Lakefront Snake Chaser Irish Stout ★★1/2

Dry Stout: Lakefront Brewery, Inc., Milwaukee, WI www.lakefrontbrewery.com

"Nose has typicall coffee bitterness, some sweetness." "Thin, watery texture with mild flavors of chocolate and coffee." "Very like many Irish stouts." 4.5% alc.

Lakefront White Beer ★★★

Bel. Witbier: Lakefront Brewery, Inc., Milwaukee, WI www.lakefrontbrewery.com

"Aroma of wit yeast, coriander, slight orange peel, mild white pepper." "Flavor is spicy, peppery, malty, very refreshing." "Dry in the end and ultimately a flavorful quencher." 5.25% alc.

Lammin Puhti ★★

Spice/Herb: Saimaan Panimo/Pienpanimo Naapuri, Lappeenranta/Mikkeli, Finland www.saimaanpanimo.fi

"Sweet aroma - caramel and whiff of fresh bread." "Taste is sour and stale, apple, cherry, herbs, stale hops, scorched grass." "Sahti made to have a long shelf life is the same as bread made to have a long shelf life - a shadow of the real thing." 7% alc.

Lancaster Amish Four Grain Ale ★★1/2

Am. Pale Ale: Lancaster Brewing Co., Lancaster, PA www.lancasterbrewing.com

"Smells of caramel, mellow pine and wildflowers and yogurt." "Fairly typicall amber aromas with caramel, nougat and citrus. Light fruit abounds with peaches, pears and raisins." "Definitely scored an additional point for being original." 5.6% alc.

Lancaster Gold Star Pilsner ★★★

Pilsner: Lancaster Brewing Co., Lancaster, PA www.lancasterbrewing.com

"Notes of spicy German hops, some floral and lemony aromas, with a hint of white bread." "Starts slightly peachy almost and then lingers and transforms into a dryish lemongrass-like flavor." "Nothin wrong with that!" 5.5% alc.

Lancaster Hop Hog IPA ★★★★
IPA: Lancaster Brewing Co., Lancaster, PA www.lancasterbrewing.com
Nose is caramelly, grapefruit malty hops." "Orange citrus hops and plenty of sweet caramel malts in the flavor." "If I were a Pennsylvanian, this would definitely be among my favorite locals and have a regular slot in the fridge..." 7.9% alc.

Lancaster Milk Stout ★★★★
Sweet Stout: Lancaster Brewing Co., Lancaster, PA www.lancasterbrewing.com
"Aroma of cocoa, malt and a nice roastiness." "Rich smooth body with a semi-sweet flavor of milk chocolate and coffee primarily." "Lacks the characteristic lactose sweetness of a milk stout." 5.3% alc.

Lancaster Strawberry Wheat ★★1/2
Fruit Beer: Lancaster Brewing Co., Lancaster, PA www.lancasterbrewing.com
"Very sweet aroma, a lot of wheat and an undertone of strawberries." "Flavor is a somewhat artificial strawberry. Also picking up some vanilla. Almost like a strawberry soda." 4.7% alc.

Lancaster Winter Warmer ★★1/2
Old Ale: Lancaster Brewing Co., Lancaster, PA www.lancasterbrewing.com
"Very wintry nose of thick toffee, smoke, maple and chocolate." "Very malt-forward, molasses and dark caramel, with subtle but present notes of raisin, plum and slight bubblegum yeast." 9% alc.

Landmark Indian Red Ale ★★★1/2
Am. Pale Ale: River Horse Brewing Co., Lambertville, NJ www.riverhorse.com
"Aroma of bready malt, resiny hops, some citrus and floral spice." "Plenty of toasted bread flavors, grainy in their way reminds again of rye." "Would be something to drink as a nice session ale." N/A% alc.

Lang Creek Huckleberry N' Honey ★
Fruit Beer: Lang Creek Brewing Co., Marion, MT www.langcreekbrewery.com
"The nose is sweet with some berryness and an off wheatish note that really steals the spotlight and ruins the show." "Finishes with more of a berry flavor, that lingers well after the finish." 3.2% alc.

Lang Creek Skydiver Blonde ★★★
Goldn/Blond Ale: Lang Creek Brewing Co., Marion, MT www.langcreekbrewery.com
"Light aroma is bready, slightly sweaty, with a hint of earthy hoppiness." "Straw like taste, subtle sweetness, non-existent hop, very pale malts." 4.3% alc.

Lang Creek Tri-Motor Amber Ale ★★1/2
Amber Ale: Lang Creek Brewing Co., Marion, MT www.langcreekbrewery.com
"Nicely balanced in the nose with a touch of malt, hops and a doughy sweetness." "Moderately bitter body with slight toastiness, lots of earthiness from both the Crystal/Carastan (hops) and Willamettes." 5.2% alc.

Lawson Creek Honey Wheat ★
Am. Wheat: Gluek Brewing Co., Cold Spring, MN www.gluek.com
"Very little flavor except honey." "It is trying to be sweet and simple, but it has a sort of detracting astringent grainy note to it that really does not jive." "Thin, watery mouthfeel. Bleh." Private label for grocery chain. 5% alc.

Lawson Creek Pale Ale ★
Cream Ale: Gluek Brewing Co., Cold Spring, MN www.gluek.com
"Light-bodied with a weak hops flavor undermined by grainy and doughy aspect." "A watered down attempt to mimic a Pale Ale with all the wrong ingredients." Private label for grocery chain. 5% alc.

Lawson Creek Red Ale ★
Amber Ale: Gluek Brewing Co., Cold Spring, MN www.gluek.com
"Have to strain to smell any hint of hops and a bit of caramel." "A very flat watery taste with a hint of either malt or some chemical poison." "It's a weak beer without any perks." Private label for grocery chain. 5% alc.

Lawson Creek Vanilla Cream Stout ★
Sweet Stout: Gluek Brewing Co., Cold Spring, MN www.gluek.com
"Heavily watered down with a extremely artificial flavor of vanilla." "If you dissolved a Milk Dud in alcohol you would get this." "Downright offensive." "5-1/2 beers down the drain." Private label for grocery chain. 3.2% alc.

Layla Dirty Blonde Lager ★★★
Pale Lager: Israel Beer Breweries Ltd (Carlsberg), Ashkelon, Israel www.carlsberg.co.il
"Skunky, lightly toasted grain and some dirty hops in there with a husky undertone and a touch of caramel." "Fairly sweet, grainy malt flavor with some nutty and cocoa notes, floral hop character and fair finishing bitterness." N/A% alc.

Leffe Blond ★★★
Belgian Ale: InBev , Leuven, Belgium www.inbev.com
"Average wheaty citrus aroma." "Flavor is sweet and light, with notes of lemon, pils malts and a little general sweetness." "The lightest taste of all Leffe products." 6.6% alc.

Leffe Brune ★★★
Abbey Dubbel: InBev , Leuven, Belgium www.inbev.com
"Very light dusty yeastiness, plummy slightly cherryish esters and dark malt notes." "Tasted like sweet fruit and flowers." "Feels like it's missing something. Sweetness goes unbalanced and bothers the palate." 6.5% alc.

Left Hand Black Jack Porter ★★★
Porter: Left Hand / Tabernash / Indian Peaks, Longmont, CO www.lefthandbrewing.com
"Aroma is very chocolaty and rich." "The flavor is bitter chocolate malts and almonds, especially in the finish." "Thick and dark, a good beer to sip on." 5.8% alc.

Left Hand Deep Cover Brown ★★
Brown Ale: Left Hand / Tabernash / Indian Peaks, Longmont, CO www.lefthandbrewing.com
"Light roasted malts and slight caramel aroma." "Flavor has notes of caramel, toffee and a hint of chocolate." "It's a smooth malty brew, but with little else really going on." 4.3% alc.

Left Hand Imperial Stout ★★★★1/2
Imp. Stout: Left Hand / Tabernash / Indian Peaks, Longmont, CO www.lefthandbrewing.com
"Coffee, caramel, vanilla, spices and alcohol in the aroma." Tastes of "roasted malt, currants, sherry flavors, some dark chocolate." "Very sweet and a little thin for an Imperial Stout but enjoyable nonetheless." 9.5% alc.

Left Hand Jackman's Pale Ale ★★1/2
Am. Pale Ale: Left Hand / Tabernash / Indian Peaks, Longmont, CO www.lefthandbrewing.com
"Spicy aroma for this one." "Taste is good, on the sweet side with apricot, pineapple and a bit of pine cone/needles to prick the tongue." "Not bad but it doesn't stand out at all." 5.2% alc.

Left Hand JuJu Ginger ★★
Spice/Herb: Left Hand / Tabernash / Indian Peaks, Longmont, CO www.lefthandbrewing.com
A light ale flavored with ginger. "Smells of faint ginger and not much else." "Flavor is ginger through and through not too overwhelming though. " "Tasted like a very mild, unsweetened ginger ale." 4% alc.

Left Hand Milk Stout ★★★
Sweet Stout: Left Hand / Tabernash / Indian Peaks, Longmont, CO www.lefthandbrewing.com
"Roasty aroma with a bit of coffee, milk chocolate and light hops." "This one is very sweet." "Coffee and chocolate flavor with apparent lactose sugar in it." "Very creamy mouthfeel." 5.2% alc.

Left Hand Oak Aged Imp. Stout ★★★★★
Imp. Stout: Left Hand / Tabernash / Indian Peaks, Longmont, CO www.lefthandbrewing.com
"Rich chocolate fudge, molasses and toasty wood aroma." "Tobacco, molasses and charred sugars notes linger on the palate with only a flash of plum and leafiness." "Wayyyyy better than the standard Imperial Stout." 10% alc.

Left Hand Sawtooth Ale ★★1/2
Prem Bitter: Left Hand / Tabernash / Indian Peaks, Longmont, CO www.lefthandbrewing.com
"Fruity and lightly hoppy," Sawtooth is a "simple, easy drinking brew" with taste that "is bread dough and sweet at first, fading into a citrus hop bitter finish… nice balance." 4.75% alc.

Left Hand Twin Sisters ★★★1/2
Imperial/Double IPA: Left Hand Brewing Co., Longmont, CO www.lefthandbrewing.com
Nose is quite sweet with lightly roasted milk chocolate, lactose sugars, and the faintest hint of vanilla. "Nice dry and light flavor but still a good amount of roast and chocolate." "Very creamy and easy to drink. Excellent brew." 9.6% alc.

Legend Barleywine ★★★
Barley Wine: Legend Brewing Co., Richmond, VA www.legendbrewing.com
"Deep and broad aromas of prune, plum, leather and modest amounts of oxidation." "Residual hops still remain strong in flavor, not overdominant, rather a full and balanced bitterness. Malty and pleasant with nice alcohol warmth." 11.8% alc.

Legend Brown Ale ★★1/2
Brown Ale: Legend Brewing Co., Richmond, VA www.legendbrewing.com
"Sweet, nutty nose, like pralines." "Somewhat complex flavor, with malts, light brown sugar and a prevailing woody flavor." "It has a simple sweet yet bitter style that is very appealing." 6% alc.

Legend Golden Indian Pale Ale ★★1/2
IPA: Legend Brewing Co., Richmond, VA www.legendbrewing.com
"Saffron, allspice aroma with some hops." "Flavor was dominated by the hop resin character, lots of pine, with a light malt backing." "Overall, a good, clean IPA." 7% alc.

Legend Imperial IPA ★★★★1/2
Imp/Dbl IPA: Legend Brewing Co., Richmond, VA www.legendbrewing.com
"Bright hop illuminations infuse oranges and other various citrus fruit into the dry wood." "Hops flavor is lightly grassy, citric and rife with delicious, perfectly -balanced malt sweetness, exhibiting toffee and mostly biscuit." 8% alc.

Legend Lager ★★★1/2
Premium Lager: Legend Brewing Co., Richmond, VA www.legendbrewing.com
"Nose is mostly biscuity light malt with some faint hop aromas of general summer smells - honey, lemon, grass." "Light and easy drinking with a crisp, light hop finish." "A beer your macro beer buddies would drink." 4.8% alc.

Legend Oktoberfest Amber Lager ★★★★
Märzen/Oktbfst: Legend Brewing Co., Richmond, VA www.legendbrewing.com
"Full amber malt flavor without being too sweet." "Dominated at first with sweet caramel malt and finish with a medium bitterness." "This is the kind of beer that makes me think I might like Oktoberfests after all." 5.4% alc.

Legend Pale Ale ★★1/2
Am. Pale Ale: Legend Brewing Co., Richmond, VA www.legendbrewing.com
"Good piney hop aroma, backed by bready malts and light caramel." "the hops hit you from the get-go-piney and citrusy." "Mostly just a hop vehicle without much depth of character." 6.4% alc.

Legend Pilsner ★★★★
Bohem Pilsner: Legend Brewing Co., Richmond, VA www.legendbrewing.com
"Soft slightly grassy, floral hops and pale malt aroma." "The fruit, bitter floral hoppiness and delicate pale malts layer on each other very well." "Very smooth and enjoyable." 5.8% alc.

Legend Porter ★★1/2
Porter: Legend Brewing Co., Richmond, VA www.legendbrewing.com
"Aromas of sweet chocolate, port, prunes, caramel." "A little strong on the coffee bitterness." "Liqueur-like tang in the finish." 6% alc.

Legend Tripel Ale ★★1/2
Abbey Tripel: Legend Brewing Co., Richmond, VA www.legendbrewing.com
"Smell is fragrant citrus, clove, dust, lime." "Taste was dry, spicy crisp and possessed a strong note of sourness and a distinct alcohol bite." "It is a satisfying beer but not one that I think is indicative of the style." 10.1% alc.

Legend White Ale ★★1/2
Bel. Witbier: Legend Brewing Co., Richmond, VA www.legendbrewing.com
"Aromas are excellent orange, cloves, cardamom and some light pepper." "Spicy, light bitterness, some coriander, some orange on the tongue. Wheat dominates with the hops just barely showing up." 5% alc.

Leinenkugel's Amber Light ★★★
Pale Lager: Leinenkugel Brewing Co. (SABMiller), Chippewa Falls, WI www.leinie.com
"Nice malty nose, a bit thin, but a bit peaty, some caramel, light hops." "Real maltiness in flavor, caramel and some peat, actual depth and earthiness." "I would drink this one again, an extreme rarity for light beers." 4.14% alc.

Leinenkugel's Berry Weiss ★
Fruit Beer: Leinenkugel Brewing Co. (SABMiller), Chippewa Falls, WI www.leinie.com
"Very sweet and fruity, a reddish, fizzy pink color." "Like drinking blueberry syrup." "Doesn't taste bad per se, but comes off more as a Kool Aid or wine cooler." 4.74% alc.

Leinenkugel's Big Butt Doppelbock ★★1/2
Doppelbock: Leinenkugel Brewing Co. (SABMiller), Chippewa Falls, WI www.leinie.com
"Alcohol is low, flavors are mellow and the body is mediocre." "Soft, bubble gum taste with smooth caramel malts." "Way to mellow for a doppelbock and way to uninteresting for me." 5.79% alc.

Leinenkugel's Creamy Dark ★★1/2
Dunkel: Leinenkugel Brewing Co. (SABMiller), Chippewa Falls, WI www.leinie.com
"Medium bodied lager with a slightly roasted character." "Very earthy aroma and taste, sort of like a Guinness, but a watered down one." "A little light bodied but not a bad Dunkel." 4.94% alc.

Leinenkugel's Honey Weiss ★
Am. Wheat: Leinenkugel Brewing Co. (SABMiller), Chippewa Falls, WI www.leinie.com
"Honey-colored lager with the slightest hint of honey sweetness." "Very mass market tasting, bland, without character." "I don't think I'll be buying this one again." 4.92% alc.

Leinenkugel's Northwoods Lager ★★★★★
Pale Lager: Leinenkugel Brewing Co. (SABMiller), Chippewa Falls, WI www.leinie.com
"Aromas of malts/hops and maybe a hint of some citrus." "Caramel malt flavor and more robust hop flavor." "If you happen to be in the Northwoods and want something without much commitment, this is a good choice." 4.94% alc.

Leinenkugel's Oktoberfest ★
Märzen/Oktbfst: Leinenkugel Brewing Co. (SABMiller), Chippewa Falls, WI www.leinie.com
"Muted aroma of sweet malt and breadiness." "Malty caramelly goodness lingers for a few seconds then leaves." "A slight roastedness to it." "Not bad, certainly one of Leinie's best these days." 5.1% alc.

Leinenkugel's Original ★★★★★
Pale Lager: Leinenkugel Brewing Co. (SABMiller), Chippewa Falls, WI www.leinie.com
"Aromas of light grains, grass and a hint of hops." "Flavor is a bit on the sweet side but not watery like most macros." "Would do in a pinch." 4.5% alc.

Leinenkugel's Red ★★★1/2
Am Dark Larger: Leinenkugel Brewing Co. (SABMiller), Chippewa Falls, WI www.leinie.com
"Very non-descript nose, slightly malty at best." "Grainy tongue, slight cardboard, light sweetness lingers." "A nice beer for people who don't usually drink reds or darks." 4.94% alc.

Lemp Lager ★★1/2
Pale Lager: Lion Brewery, Inc., Wilkes-Barre, PA www.lionbrewery.com
"Slightly floral and malty aroma." "Body is on the weaker side as it is a little watery for its appearance." "The legend obviously doesn't live on." N/A% alc.

Leute Bok ★★★
Belgian Ale: Brouwerij Van Steenberge, Ertvelde, Belgium www.vansteenberge.com
"Aroma is woodchips, clay, cedar, pit fruit, yeast - a little funky, but interesting." "Malty chocolate and sour grape flavor." "Neither the beer or the glass it was served in really stand on their own." 7.5% alc.

Lexington Kentucky Ale ★★
Amber Ale: Lexington Brewing Co. (Alltech), Lexington, KY www.kentuckyale.com
"Caramelized malt aroma with a little bit of brown sugar." "Flavor is grainy caramel malts and a little yeast." "Nothing offensive, nothing exciting." 4.5% alc.

Le?ajsk Pelne ★★1/2
Pilsner: Le?ajsk (Grupa Zwiec/Heineken), , Poland www.lezajsk.com.pl
"Malt (straw, hay) and grassy yeast (sweat) aroma with grape, pear and oak notes." "Quite nice: fruit and mildly hopped. Mild tea flavors." "Good and refreshing to boot." 5.5% alc.

Liefmans Frambozen ★★★★
Flem Sour Ale: Liefmans (Liefmans Breweries), Oudenaarde, Belgium www.liefmans.be
"Sweet perfumed aroma of raspberries with notes of wood." "Flavor is really nice malt and raspberry, light acidity and a soft palate." "An almost perfect balance between sweet and sour." 4.5% alc.

Liefmans Glühkriek ★★★★1/2
Fruit Beer: Liefmans (Liefmans Breweries), Oudenaarde, Belgium www.liefmans.be
"Nose is strong, very sweet and with cherries all over the place." "Tangy, mega spicy, cinnamon and cherry fruit flavor." "This tastes better room temperature or even a bit warm as it is very much like mulled wine." 6.5% alc.

Liefmans Goudenband ★★★★1/2
Flem Sour Ale: Liefmans (Liefmans Breweries), Oudenaarde, Belgium www.liefmans.be
"Dried herbs (rosemary, thyme), cola, emerging caramel notes and an underlying shiraz pepperiness." "Flavor was sourly dark fermented fruit, candy sweetness and berries." "Handcrafted by an old Belgian lady in a pinafore I am sure." 8% alc.

Liefmans Kriek ★★★★
Flem Sour Ale: Liefmans (Liefmans Breweries), Oudenaarde, Belgium www.liefmans.be
"Aroma of sour cherries, brown sugar and yeast." "Sweet juicy cherry body with a soft underlying acidity." "A lovely brew and yet another gem from Liefmans." 6% alc.

Lindemans Cassis ★★1/2
Fruit Lambic: Brouwerij Lindemans, St Pieters Leeuw-Vlezenbeek, Belgium www.lindemans.be
"Sweet lambic with an acidic underbelly, perfumey fruit, obviously blackcurrant and quite cloying." "It just tastes like a cassis soda." 4% alc.

Lindemans Framboise ★★★★
Fruit Lambic: Brouwerij Lindemans, St Pieters Leeuw-Vlezenbeek, Belgium www.lindemans.be
"Aroma is of a pint of fresh picked raspberries." "Flavor of raspberry with a sourish finish." "It's a big step up from alcopops." 2.5% alc.

Lindemans Gueuze ★★1/2

Gueuze: Brouwerij Lindemans, St Pieters Leeuw-Vlezenbeek, Belgium www.lindemans.be

"Initially sweet, sugary aroma followed by yeast, apple, pear and more candy sweetness, dry and slightly champagne like." "Flavor is sour along with a very vinous quality." "An easy going gueuze for a gueuze-beginner." 4.5% alc.

Lindemans Gueuze Cuvée Ren ★★★★1/2

Gueuze: Brouwerij Lindemans, St Pieters Leeuw-Vlezenbeek, Belgium www.lindemans.be

"Aroma consists of nice tart apple skins, earthy tones, wood and candy." "Flavors of sour lemon, pineapple and straw with a dry, tart finish." "Very engaging and physically moving. Try to drink this and not smile." 5% alc.

Lindemans Kriek ★★★

Fruit Lambic: Brouwerij Lindemans, St Pieters Leeuw-Vlezenbeek, Belgium www.lindemans.be

"Strong black cherry with a little bit of ginger. Sort of semi-dry and a tiny bit sour." "Sugar, cherries, fruit. Only a slight sourness." "Lacking somewhat in the complexity I expect from the style." 4% alc.

Lindemans Pêche Lambic ★★★

Fruit Lambic: Brouwerij Lindemans, St Pieters Leeuw-Vlezenbeek, Belgium www.lindemans.be

"Faint peach aroma with sweet character." "Sweet with peach and malt flavors." "There is lambicy funk going on with oak and brett but for the most part this is candy." 2.5% alc.

Lion Heart Stout ★★1/2

Foreign Stout: Big City Brewing Co., Kingston, Jamaica

"Sweet roasty aroma with Hershey syrup, chocolate bubblegum, chocolate wafers, heavy cream and French silk pie." "Wood smoke and burnt sugar flavor primarily but with nice coffee malt notes and mild hops finish." "Beats the holy crap out of Red Stripe." 7.6% alc.

Lion Lager ★★★

Pale Lager: Ceylon/Lion Brewery Ltd., Nuwara Eliya and Biyagama, Sri Lanka www.lionbeer.com

"Weak malty and grainy aroma with dense notes of hops." "Light sweet malty taste with notes of cardboard and citrus fruits." "A surprisingly pleasant lager." 4.1% alc.

Lion Stout ★★★★★

Foreign Stout: Ceylon/Lion Brewery Ltd., Nuwara Eliya and Biyagama, Sri Lanka www.lionbeer.com

"Aroma of burnt brown sugar, coffee, molasses, chocolate." "Well-rounded stout flavor: roasted malt with chocolate notes, subtle but assertive hops and smooth body." "Exquisite." 8% alc.

Little King's Cream Ale ★

Cream Ale: Hudepohl-Schoenling (Snyder Intl), Frederick, MD

"Oddly fruity aroma with some skunk and some corn." "There are some bready malt flavors, along with more corn." "Not as mind-bogglingly foul as expected." 5.6% alc.

Lomza Mocne ★★1/2

Eur Str Lager: Browar Lomza, Lomza, Poland www.browarlomza.com.pl

"Aromas were soapy and floral with strong, fresh herbs and light, seedy grains." "Flavor is alcoholic with a touch of malt and little hops." "Better than expected" 7.8% alc.

Lomza Wyborowe ★

Premium Lager: Browar Lomza, Lomza, Poland www.browarlomza.com.pl

Sweet and moderately alcoholic aroma." "Flavor is at first sweet but that quickly gives way to a maltier flavor with an herbal, bitter hoppiness." 6% alc.

Lone Star ★

Pale Lager: Pabst Brewing Co., Chicago, IL www.pabst.com

"Light malty, grassy aroma and a light sweet malty, fruity taste." "Cheap, lame American macrobrew in Texas-friendly packaging." Brewed by Miller under contract. 4.7% alc.

Long Trail Ale ★★1/2
Altbier: Long Trail Brewery, Bridgewater Corners, VT www.longtrail.com
"The aroma is of malt-like sweetness with some light spice." "Mildly malty and sweet, fairly nutty and lightly hoppy." "I can see drinking it on a summer afternoon with a salad or during the winter with a bowl of soup or stew." 5% alc.

Long Trail Blackbeary Wheat ★
Fruit Beer: Long Trail Brewery, Bridgewater Corners, VT www.longtrail.com
"If you're thinking to have something with a little sweet blackberry taste that is refreshing and reminiscent of beer, it's good." "Like drinking a regular pale lager with some blueberry flavoring." 3.8% alc.

Long Trail Double Bag ★★★★
Altbier: Long Trail Brewery, Bridgewater Corners, VT www.longtrail.com
"Has forward malt flavors with nice bitterness, although not hoppy and a prominent alcohol character, which is nice." "Finish a sixer of this hippie milk and you'll find yourself on all fours in mud with a moo-cow in tippin' distance." 7.2% alc.

Long Trail Harvest Ale ★★1/2
Amber Ale: Long Trail Brewery, Bridgewater Corners, VT www.longtrail.com
"Molasses, almost coffee bean aroma mixed with some brown sugar, green grape and malt." "Flavor is hay, pretzels, slight hop bitterness and some roasty malts." "Beer, just needs to be a bit more flavorful." N/A% alc.

Long Trail Hibernator ★★1/2
Scottish Ale: Long Trail Brewery, Bridgewater Corners, VT www.longtrail.com
Aroma of caramel malt, spice, some hops." "Tastes spicy and sweet. Fruity with smooth honey flavors underneath it all." "Perfectly serviceable session ale for these otherwise dreadful winter months." N/A% alc.

Long Trail Hit the Trail Ale ★★
Brown Ale: Long Trail Brewery, Bridgewater Corners, VT www.longtrail.com
"Nuts, malts and caramel aromas." "Flavor is simple, with a mild brown sugar and toffee." "Incredibly average and boring." 5.2% alc.

Long Trail Indian Pale Ale ★★1/2
IPA: Long Trail Brewery, Bridgewater Corners, VT www.longtrail.com
"Grassy aroma with a hint of citrus." "Medium-bodied palate with pale malt, hint of maltiness, grassy, herbal, hoppy accent, piney, leading to a nicely balancing pleasant hop bitterness finish." 6.1% alc.

Lost Coast 8 Ball Stout ★★★★★
Sweet Stout: Lost Coast Brewery and Cafe, Eureka, CA www.lostcoast.com
"Sweet cookie and toasted chocolate aroma." "Creamy but bitter, roasty-malty flavor." "Flavor is a bit simplistic." "Very rich, hoppy, enjoyable stout" 5.9% alc.

Lost Coast Alleycat Amber Ale ★★★
Amber Ale: Lost Coast Brewery and Cafe, Eureka, CA www.lostcoast.com
"Pleasantly mild" with "resiny hops and nutty malt." "Rounded light malt sweetness, toffeelike, with a slight hop bitterness toward the end." "On the sweeter side." 5.5% alc.

Lost Coast Downtown Brown ★★★
Brown Ale: Lost Coast Brewery and Cafe, Eureka, CA www.lostcoast.com
"Aroma of roast malt, chestnuts, caramel and a touch of wine." "Thinnish palate" is "smooth, slightly nutty, malty sweet." "Finishes creamy and barely bitter." 5% alc.

Lost Coast Great White ★★1/2
Bel. Witbier: Lost Coast Brewery and Cafe, Eureka, CA www.lostcoast.com
A Belgian-style white beer, with American accents. "Light and refreshing" with "lots of citrus." "Really sticks to the back of the tongue, crushing and crackling with flavor." 4.8% alc.

Lost Coast Indica Indian Pale Pale Ale ★★★★★
IPA: Lost Coast Brewery and Cafe, Eureka, CA www.lostcoast.com
"Quick! Somebody needs to take a picture of my beer!" "Shining, smiling C-hops mirror juicy berries and earthy oranges." "Great floral, citrus, grapefruit and pine resin flavor skimming on top of a sweet caramel base." 6.5% alc.

Lost Coast Winterbraun ★★★1/2
Brown Ale: Lost Coast Brewery and Cafe, Eureka, CA www.lostcoast.com
This beer changes from time to time. In past it's been a porter and a brown ale. Winterbraun tends to present a slightly stronger than average version of whatever style it is doing. 6.5% alc.

Lost Lake ★
Pale Lager: City Brewery (Melanie Brewing Co), La Crosse, WI www.citybrewery.com
"Sweet and adjuncty with a corny side and very faint malt side." "Pure white trash brew at its best." "A good beer to give to your teenagers to turn them off from underage consumption." N/A% alc.

Loyalhanna Pennsylvania Lager ★★1/2
Pale Lager: Latrobe Brewing Co. (Anheuser-Busch) www.rollingrock.com
"Aroma is mostly sweet and caramelly." "Tame, watery lager with minimal hops, but nice drinkability." "A bit smoother and sweeter than the Rolling Rock line." N/A% alc.

Lucifer ★★1/2
Bel. Strong Ale: Riva Brouwerij (Liefmans Breweries), Dentergem, Belgium www.liefmans.be
"Hops dominate the aroma, strong lemon, esters, light roasted malts, coriander." "Peppery character, a little bread, a little acidity." "As many have stated, this is no Duvel." 8% alc.

Maccabee ★
Pale Lager: Tempo Beer Industries Ltd., Netanya, Israel www.tempo.co.il
"Sweet maltiness with prominent notes of vegetables." "Grassy flavor up front, a bit of a sweet middle with a mild bitter finish." "typicall international lager, quite thin and uninteresting." 4.9% alc.

✓ **Mackeson XXX Stout** ★★★★1/2
Sweet Stout: Boston Beer Co., Boston, MA www.samadams.com
"Vinous, raisiny, with a hint of chocolate, licorice." "Flavor is coffee and chocolate and mostly sweet." "Not as robust as most stouts, but Mackeson instead has a pleasant, sweet, malty appeal." 4.9% alc.

MacPelican's Scottish Style Ale ★★
Scottish Ale: Pelican Pub and Brewery, Pacific City, OR www.pelicanbrewery.com
"Caramel and toasty malts with floral and bitter hops." "Sweet toffee and fairly thin." "It did feature a nice malty flavor but too many other aspects were lacking." 4.7% alc.

MacTarnahan's Amber Ale ★★1/2
Amber Ale: Portland Brewing Co. (Pyramid), Portland, OR www.portlandbrew.com
"Sweet and hoppy aroma (citrus and floral)." "Herbal hops and caramel malt flavors." "Fair for an amber ale." 5% alc.

MacTarnahan's Blackwatch Cream Porter ★★1/2
Porter: Portland Brewing Co. (Pyramid), Portland, OR www.portlandbrew.com
"Aroma has some roasted grain, light cocoa and coffee." "Fairly bitter up front with tobacco flavors and a somewhat astringent roastiness." "Not big, but somewhat smooth and flavorful." 5.3% alc.

MacTarnahan's Highlander Pale Ale ★★
Am. Pale Ale: Portland Brewing Co. (Pyramid), Portland, OR www.portlandbrew.com
"Moderate cookie malt aroma with a light floral and citrus hoppiness." "Flavor begins by with a nice malt backdrop and just a bit of light fruitiness." "Easy drinking and smooth, but lacking in any significant flavor to be great." 5.1% alc.

MacTarnahan's Mac Frost Winter Ale ★★1/2

Eng. Strong Ale: Portland Brewing Co. (Pyramid), Portland, OR www.portlandbrew.com

"Aroma is nicely caramellish, sweetish with a touch of spices and some floral/earthy hop presence." "Nicely balanced flavors with a little fruity sweetness and hop bitterness with a solid malt backbone." 6% alc.

MacTarnahan's Thunderhead Stout ★★1/2

Dry Stout: Portland Brewing Co. (Pyramid), Portland, OR www.portlandbrew.com

"Average roasted coffee and chocolate aroma." "Has a decent roast flavor to it up next to a mild hop bitterness." "Not particularly remarkable." 6% alc.

MacTarnahan's Gran Luxe Tripel Ale ★★★

Abbey Tripel: Portland Brewing Co. (Pyramid), Portland, OR www.portlandbrew.com

"Smells like an Indian Pale Ale with candi sugar. grapefruit and prunes." "Yeasty, musty and full flavor with a rather dry and slightly alcoholic and sour finish." "Not the most traditional example of the style." 9.3% alc.

MacTarnahan's Oak-Aged IPA ★★1/2

IPA: Portland Brewing Co. (Pyramid), Portland, OR www.portlandbrew.com

"Some citrus and grassy hop aroma with tannic underpinnings." "Flavor is melon, some sweet malts and some oak." "While the flavor is pleasant this was somewhat weak for an Indian Pale Ale." 6% alc.

MacTarnahan's Original Honey Beer ★

Ale: Portland Brewing Co. (Pyramid), Portland, OR www.portlandbrew.com

"Presence of honey with notes of grass." "Flavor is honey, light grains and hay-like hops finish it off." "Yet another honey beer that just isn't worth it." 4.8% alc.

Mad Anthony Ol' Woody Pale Ale ★★1/2

Am. Pale Ale: Mad Anthony Brewing Co., Fort Wayne, IN www.madbrew.com

"Notes of leafy piney hops, grapefruit, bready pale malts, pepper and dusty yeast esters." "Moderately sweet, lightly malty base is dominated by a fairly bitter, grapefruity and floral hops." N/A% alc.

Mad River Jamaica Red ★★★

Amber Ale: Mad River Brewery, Blue Lake, CA www.madriverbrewing.com

On the darker side of the red ale spectrum, this is "grapefruit peel bitterness and ample hop flavors." "Has that grapefruit flavor that often comes out in Indian Pale Ales." "Bitter to the end." 6.6% alc.

Mad River Jamaica Sunset Indian Pale Aale ★★1/2

IPA: Mad River Brewery, Blue Lake, CA www.madriverbrewing.com

"Nice hoppy aroma though quite reserved compared to other West Coast IPAs." "This refreshes because it balances the hop content." "A good one if you aren't really into the hop monster IPAs." 6.9% alc.

Mad River John Barleycorn ★★1/2

Barley Wine: Mad River Brewery, Blue Lake, CA www.madriverbrewing.com

"Malty, sugary, caramel nose with intriguing herbal notes." "Sweet malt and dark fruit flavors with a burn of alcohol and a bite of earthy hop bitterness." "Falls face first without ever exciting the tastebuds." 9% alc.

Mad River Steelhead Extra Pale ★★

Am. Pale Ale: Mad River Brewery, Blue Lake, CA www.madriverbrewing.com

This "hazy straw gold" ale has a "mild aroma, kind of a hint of malts and flowers." "Fruity beer with a nice balance of a mildly sweet and grainy maltiness coupled with a moderately bitter hoppiness." 5.7% alc.

Mad River Steelhead Extra Stout ★★★★

Stout: Mad River Brewery, Blue Lake, CA www.madriverbrewing.com

"Rich chocolate aroma with a touch of roasted grain and coffee." "Lush" and "elegant." "Creamy with full body and a dry finish." "Like drinking cool Cuban coffee." 6% alc.

Mad River Steelhead Scotch Porter ★★★★

Porter: Mad River Brewery, Blue Lake, CA www.madriverbrewing.com

A porter brewed with a hint of peated malt. "Toasty malts with lots of caramel and hints of dark chocolate, coffee and vanilla beans." "A tasty surprise." 6.43% alc.

MaDonna ★★

Bel. Witbier: SC Martens SA, Galati, Romania www.martens.ro

"Fruity and citrusy with a spicy, nutmeg character in the background from too much coriander." "Mostly yeast and lemon come through in the flavor." "Too curious and too precious in its perfume quality to really sit well for the full bottle." 5% alc.

Magic Hat #9 ★★★

Fruit Beer: Magic Hat Brewing Co., South Burlington, VT www.magichat.net

"Dried apricot and bread crust aroma." "Mild flavor, with some notes of orange, apricot and sweet malt." "If you like apricots, go for it." 4.6% alc.

Magic Hat Blind Faith ★★★

IPA: Magic Hat Brewing Co., South Burlington, VT www.magichat.net

"Slight nose of Cascade hops with drying apples." "This has the standard characteristics of Magic Hat's brews, but it still lacks the hop assault I tend to like with IPA." "A very average IPA at best." 5.6% alc.

Magic Hat Chaotic Chemistry ★★★★

Barley Wine: Magic Hat Brewing Co., South Burlington, VT www.magichat.net

"Fruity, flowery nose - vanilla, cherry, malts, booze." "Strong bourbon naturally made the first impression on my palate, the body also being leathery with musty dark fruits and caramel." "For those who like their barley wines on the sweet side." 10.8% alc.

Magic Hat Fat Angel ★★

Eng Pale Ale: Magic Hat Brewing Co., South Burlington, VT www.magichat.net

"I had trouble detecting an aroma. What I could detect was sweet with a slight hop-like scent." "Solid, subtle bitter flavor with some brief nuttiness and a hint of citrus balances this one out." "An okay beer, but clearly not one of Magic Hat's best." 5.2% alc.

Magic Hat Heart of Darkness ★★★1/2

Sweet Stout: Magic Hat Brewing Co., South Burlington, VT www.magichat.net

"Dry cocoa powder on the nose, slightly sour or tart as well." "Taste is fine bittersweet chocolate, almost like biting into chocolate chips." "Roasty espresso beans are slathered with dark chocolate." 5.3% alc.

Magic Hat Hi.P.A. ★★1/2

IPA: Magic Hat Brewing Co., South Burlington, VT www.magichat.net

"Great sweet and fruity aroma with huge hoppy oils." "Combination of citrus and pine hops with a substantial malt body." "Tastes kinda like a hoppy wheat beer." 6.8% alc.

Magic Hat Hocus Pocus ★★1/2

Am. Wheat: Magic Hat Brewing Co., South Burlington, VT www.magichat.net

"Delicate honey, cinnamon and leaf aroma." "Tastes of lemons, wheat, light yeast and a touch of a honey sweetness to it." "Overall, drinkable but why bother." 4.5% alc.

Magic Hat Jinx ★★1/2

Smoked: Magic Hat Brewing Co., South Burlington, VT www.magichat.net

"Some peat, smoke, sweet toffee and whisky notes in nice aroma." "Taste is medium sweet, cherry, earthy." "I never did get much of any smoke aspect from this, I don't know if that is good or bad??" 6.9% alc.

Magic Hat Participation Ale ★★

Brown Ale: Magic Hat Brewing Co., South Burlington, VT www.magichat.net

"Fairly roasty, moderately bitter and only lightly sweet, but the finish is nutty, quite ashy with vague hints of molasses." "Not too bad of a quaffer given its diminutive size." 4% alc.

Magic Hat Ravell ★★★★

Porter: Magic Hat Brewing Co., South Burlington, VT www.magichat.net

"The aroma is so hugely big of sweet milk chocolate that you can literally smell it at arms length." "Initial presence of vanilla and almond, then chocolate and date sugars, like an iced light vanilla flavored coffee drink, but always a porter." 5.6% alc.

Magic Hat Thumbsucker Imperial Stout ★★★★★

Imp. Stout: Magic Hat Brewing Co., South Burlington, VT www.magichat.net

"Aroma contains strong notes of bourbon and alcohol, but also has notes of caramel and burnt malt." "Flavor is loaded with roasted malts and bourbon flavors with almost a harsh smokiness in the end." 7.8% alc.

Magnum ★

Malt Liquor: Miller Brewing Co. (SABMiller), Milwaukee, WI www.millerbrewing.com

"Stale candied sugar aroma with some rotten wheat." "Taste is just plain not good, corn and very sweet with little else going for it." "I don't wanna whore no more." 5.6% alc.

Maharaja ★★1/2

Pale Lager: Associated Breweries and Distilleries, Mumbai, India

"Very skunky grassy hop aroma." "Apples and slight adjunct in the flavor." "Palate ends with a distinct crispness that would indeed help to take off some spice." 5% alc.

Mahrs Bräu Christmas Bock ★★1/2

Bock: Mahrs Bräu, Bamberg, Germany www.mahrs-braeu.de

"Deep fresh bread aroma." "Herbal butteriness blends in with the focused breadiness." "Clean and rich. Delicious." 6.5% alc.

Mahrs Bräu der Weisse Bock ★★★

Weizen Bock: Mahrs Bräu, Bamberg, Germany www.mahrs-braeu.de

"Fresh clove and banana and bubblegum aroma with hints of dark malt melanoidins." "Tastes caramel malty, with a firm, wheaty, fruity finish." "Complex, dense, fruity palate, with some spices and cognac as it warms." 7.2% alc.

Mahrs Bräu Pilsner ★★★1/2

Pilsner: Mahrs Bräu, Bamberg, Germany www.mahrs-braeu.de

"Lightly flowery hop aroma with a sweet malt background." "Very soft bitter flavor." "Sweet malt body with just a touch of hops and some toast flavors." "Finishes with surprisingly unrefined hop bite." 4.9% alc.

Mahrs Bräu Ungespundet Hefetrüb ★★★

Unfilterd Lager: Mahrs Bräu, Bamberg, Germany www.mahrs-braeu.de

"Apricots, hops in the aroma but a little bit of skunkiness too." "Orangey-citrusy background with shy malts and equally shy hops." "A mite overly subtle, but reasonably tasty." 5.2% alc.

Mahrs Bräu Weisse ★★1/2

Hefeweizen: Mahrs Bräu, Bamberg, Germany www.mahrs-braeu.de

"Aroma of banana, spice (nutmeg, mainly) and slight tobaccoey smoke phenols." "Lots of malt, but it's well-balanced with herbal hops." "Definitely hoppy for the style." "Well-made, robust wheat beer." 5.2% alc.

Maine Coast Eden Porter ★★1/2

Porter: Maine Coast Brewing Co., Bar Harbor, ME

"Milk chocolate aroma, nutty, hints of coffee - typicall porter aroma but good complexity. Palate is a let-down - oily, with lecithin chocolate flavors and dried fruit esters." N/A% alc.

Maisel's Weisse Original ★★★★★
Hefeweizen: Brauerei Gebr. Maisel, Bayreuth , Germany www.maisel.com
"Big estery nose, along with a spicy touch." "Fresh fruitiness with a soft, wheaty touch." "This really is a hefe with its own character and personality." 5.4% alc.

Malheur 10 ★★★1/2
Bel. Strong Ale: De Landtsheer, Buggenhout, Belgium www.malheur.be
"Aroma shows orange, melon, alcohol, spice (thyme, mint, anise)." "Sweet candy-like flavor with notes of spices, hops and fruits. Hoppy and alcoholic finish." "Evokes comparison to champagne." 10% alc.

Malheur Brut ★★1/2
Bel. Strong Ale: De Landtsheer, Buggenhout, Belgium www.malheur.be
"Toasty, peppery, champagne-like aroma." "Dry, white peppery body, slight acid, reasonable potency is belied by unique complexity." "The Malheur yeast likes the methode champagnoise." 9% alc.

Malheur Dark Brut (Noir) ★★★★★
Bel. Strong Ale: De Landtsheer, Buggenhout, Greece www.malheur.be
"Very nice soft roasted malt and chocolate/caramel characters, with a typical Belgian twist (yeast, estery fruit)." "Taste is dark chocolate, yeast, light sweet malts, some cola notes and light spices." 12% alc.

Marathon ★★1/2
Pale Lager: Athenian Brewery (Heineken), Athens, Greece www.beerexports.gr
"Weak aroma of hops." "Flavors are flat, cereal and light toasted wheat." "A pale lager like thousands of others but no unpleasantries here." 5% alc.

Maredsous 10 ★★★★
Abbey Tripel: Brouwerij Moortgat, Breendonk-Puurs, Belgium www.duvel.be
Nose: "Alcohol, dried peaches, white pepper, slightly musty." "Bready malts at the beginning give way to a thin line of hops separating the sweeter, fruitier (peach, bramley apple) finish." "Very tasty with my Sunday brunch." 10% alc.

Maredsous 6 Blond ★★1/2
Belgian Ale: Brouwerij Moortgat, Breendonk-Puurs, Belgium www.duvel.be
"Aroma shows pear/peach fruitiness, light hop, sweet malt." "Starts with malt, quickly fading into a peppery shot of alcohol, finishing quite dry." "Good in all categories." 6% alc.

Maredsous 8 ★★★
Bel. Strong Ale: Brouwerij Moortgat, Breendonk-Puurs, Belgium www.duvel.be
"Light fruit and nut nose (raisin, plum)." "Opens with chewy, toffeeish malt, gaining in fruit throughout." "Notes of brown sugar, toffee, dates, wood, burnt raisin bread." "Notes of brown sugar, toffee, dates, wood, burnt raisin bread." 8% alc.

Marin Eldridge Grade White Knuckle Double IPA ★★★★★
Imp/Dbl IPA: Marin Brewing Co., Larkspur, CA www.marinbrewing.com
One of the most popular of the style. "The aroma is oranges galore! Very aromatic. Very nice!" "The swing between sweet and bitter is dramatic and adds to the character of the beer." 8% alc.

Marin Indian Pale Ale ★★★★
IPA: Marin Brewing Co., Larkspur, CA www.marinbrewing.com
"Aroma is a floral, citrusy hoppy scent, pungent and enticing." "Well-balanced flavor of grapefruit and orangey hops and the caramel malts that support them." "Solid California IPA." 6.5% alc.

Marin Mt. Tam Pale Ale ★★1/2
Am. Pale Ale: Marin Brewing Co., Larkspur, CA www.marinbrewing.com
"Mild malt flavors with tangelo zest and an acrid floral hop bitterness." "Body is kinda watery, but it's not a bad pale." 5% alc.

Marin Old Dipsea Barleywine Style Ale ★★★★
Barley Wine: Marin Brewing Co., Larkspur, CA www.marinbrewing.com
"Unusual, interesting aroma, with brown sugar, fruit punch, melon and a strong alcohol presence." "All malts right up to the finish mellow, caramel, vinous, roasted pear, macerated mixed berries." 9% alc.

Marin Point Reyes Porter ★★★1/2
Porter: Marin Brewing Co., Larkspur, CA www.marinbrewing.com
"Aromas of chocolate, coffee, roast and some yeast." "Good body for a porter." "Flavor is warm and sweet with dark roasted malts, some coffee notes and a lingering dry-hoppy finish." 6% alc.

Marin San Quentin's Breakout Stout ★★★★
Stout: Marin Brewing Co., Larkspur, CA www.marinbrewing.com
"Coffee, red wine and bittersweet chocolate aromas." "Flavor is assertive, rich deep roasted malts, espresso beans and soured fruit with a puckering finish." "Coffee that's been sitting at a truck stop for five hours." 7.1% alc.

Marin Star Brew-Triple Wheat Ale ★★★★
Barley Wine: Marin Brewing Co., Larkspur, CA www.marinbrewing.com
A straw-colored, 9.5% ultra-strong take on the American Wheat style. "Nose of a sweet corn desert, an homage to wheat." "Fruit-filled, strongly alcoholic with notes of banana peels and honey covered apricots." 9.5% alc.

Marin Tripel Dipsea ★★1/2
Abbey Tripel: Marin Brewing Co., Larkspur, CA www.marinbrewing.com
"Sugar, pears, alcohol and white grapes in the aroma." "Tastes sort of like a yeasty apple juice." "Lacks a complexity demanded by the style." 9.2% alc.

Maritime Pacific Flagship Red Alt Ale ★★1/2
Amber Ale: Maritime Pacific Brewing Co., Seattle, WA www.maritimebrewery.citysearch.com
"Smells like your average red with hints of grains, malt, nuts and vegetables." "Flavor is typicall Amber except it has a bit of a metallic aftertaste." "Fairly thin, not very interesting." 5.2% alc.

Maritime Pacific Imperial Pale Ale ★★★
Am Strong Ale: Maritime Pacific Brewing Co., Seattle, WA www.maritimebrewery.citysearch.com
"Sweet light malt aroma with notes of apricots and faint citrusy hops." "Unleashes a torrent of bittering pine in the mid-sip but let out more caramel and citrusy sweet flavors as the beer warmed." 7.5% alc.

Maritime Pacific Islander Pale Ale ★★★★
Am. Pale Ale: Maritime Pacific Brewing Co., Seattle, WA www.maritimebrewery.citysearch.com
"Aroma is hoppy with a strong twist of grapefruit and a hint of yeast." "Quite a bit more floral and hop assertiveness on the tongue, with the aforementioned grapefruit." "Lovely Pacific Northwest pale ale, superbly refreshing." 5% alc.

Maritime Pacific Jolly Roger ★★★1/2
Eng. Strong Ale: Maritime Pacific Brewing Co., Seattle, WA www.maritimebrewery.citysearch.com
"Slight plummy/figgy aroma, some caramel sweetness and a hint of booze." "Flavor is spicy over sweet caramel and toffee malts." "This is a winter brew with real cojones!" 9% alc.

Maritime Pacific Nightwatch Dark ★★★
Amber Ale: Maritime Pacific Brewing Co., Seattle, WA www.maritimebrewery.citysearch.com
"Big aroma of sweet caramel and some hints of vanilla." "Rounded complex of malts with definite espresso notes and very restrained hops." "I would recommend this beer if you can get it." 5.5% alc.

Marston's Pedigree ★★
Prem Bitter: Marstons G1364, Burton-on-Trent, Staffordshire, England www.marstonsdontcompromise.com
"Aromas of light roasted malt, straw and floral hops are found in the nose." "Flavor is nothing but average, bit of non-descript malt, some ambiguous hops, boring finish." "Enjoyable, no-frills ale." 4.5% alc.

Matt Accel ★
Pale Lager: Matt Brewing Co., Utica, NY www.saranac.com
"Smells like rotting grass and maybe a bit of moldy corn." "Devoid of flavor, well except for cardboard, corn, dry grass and hint of oats." "It's apparently designed to accelerate the drain pour process." N/A% alc.

Maudite ★★★★★
Bel. Strong Ale: Unibroue (Sleeman), Chambly, Quebec www.unibroue.com
"Rich malty nose with funky, stewed fruit notes, shows good complexity." "Spicy taste with hints of coriander, nuts, bread and malty sweetness." "Smooth and complex, a beautiful experience." 8% alc.

Mc Chouffe ★★★★
Scotch Ale: Brasserie dAchouffe, Achouffe, Belgium www.achouffe.be
"Farmyard fresh wheat fields and sticky sweet honey." "Malty, caramel taste with raisin and some spices at the finish." "Like drinking a brown ale off a cowboy's leather saddle." 8.5% alc.

McEwan's Indian Pale Ale ★
Bitter: Caledonian (Scottish & Newcastle), Edinburgh, Scotland www.caledonian-brewery.co.uk
"Spicy aroma with caramel malt and some floral hoppage." "Flavors of sweet malt, toast, wood and some smokiness are noted but also very restrained and faint." "Only IPA by its name." 4.7% alc.

McEwan's Scotch Ale ★★★★
Scotch Ale: Caledonian (Scottish & Newcastle), Edinburgh, Scotland www.caledonian-brewery.co.uk
"Richly malty aroma with peat, treacle, plums." "Very sweet flavor - slightly burnt syrup primarily." "When I want malty sweetness, this cannot be beat." 8% alc.

McNeill's Extra Special Bitter ★★★★1/2
Prem Bitter: McNeill's Brewery, Brattleboro, VT
"Strong herbal hop aroma and a definite British influence with a fairly sweet malt profile and well developed light-fruit esters." "Lots of pine and citrus hoppage, with a medium caramel backbone." N/A% alc.

McNeill's Imperial Stout ★★★★★
Imp. Stout: McNeill's Brewery, Brattleboro, VT
"Quite roasty, lots of dark malts, chocolate, coffee, cream and dark fruits. quite roasty, lots of dark malts, chocolate, coffee, cream and dark fruits." "Aroma of port fruits and lots of liquid chocolate." 7.8% alc.

McNeill's Old Ringworm ★★★★
Old Ale: McNeill's Brewery, Brattleboro, VT
"Apples, pears, some yeast and some roasted malts." "Flavor was strong and hoppy, grass with bits of citrus interlaced with hints of coffee, sweet caramel malts and spices, maybe a bit of brown sugar as well." 9% alc.

McNeill's Ruby Ale ★★★★
IPA: McNeill's Brewery, Brattleboro, VT
"Hoppy, lightly citric in nature, quite earthy with chocolate." "Flavor is a bit roasty with oak, pine and dry hop finish." "Good stuff if you're looking for a hop fix..." 0% alc.

McNeill's Slop Bucket Double Brown ★★★★
Brown Ale: McNeill's Brewery, Brattleboro, VT
"Aroma of caramel, almonds, a bit of yeast and some mild hops." "Full of weak coffee, strong tea, earth, dust, cocoa, watery chocolate and marzipan." "Did I miss the point of this one?" 0% alc.

McNeill's Dead Horse Indian Pale Ale ★★★
IPA: McNeill's Brewery, Brattleboro, VT
"Smells great, lots of grass, wet hay and some hints of caramel in the aroma." "Moderately flavorful IPA with a decent hops bite and bitterness balanced by a lightly sweet, mildly bready maltiness." 5.05% alc.

McSorley's Ale ★
Goldn/Blond Ale: Miller Brewing Co. (SABMiller), Milwaukee, WI www.millerbrewing.com
"Aroma of fruity malt and just barely some spicy hops." "Flavor was malty and watery." "While one-dimensional for sure, this is surprisingly decent." N/A% alc.

Mehana Hawaii Lager ★★★★★
Vienna: Mehana Brewing Co., Hilo, HA www.mehana.com
"This has a fairly aromatic, sweet and very bready nose." "Malt, citric, floral, pleasant enough and easy drinking." "Exceeded my expectations." N/A% alc.

Mehana Mauna Kea Pale Ale ★★1/2
Am. Pale Ale: Mehana Brewing Co., Hilo, HA www.mehana.com
"Pine, resin, citrus aroma...a bit of cookie dough." "Nice hoppy initial mouthfeel." "Much more robust than I was expecting." N/A% alc.

Mehana Volcano Red Ale ★
Amber Ale: Mehana Brewing Co., Hilo, HA www.mehana.com
"Malty aroma with an off note. " "Mouthfeel is a letdown...as is the flavor...a sort of dirty dishwater mess of malt..." "A bit unrefined, this beer seems more like a crowd pleaser that a palate pleaser." N/A% alc.

Meister Brau ★
Pale Lager: Miller Brewing Co. (SABMiller), Milwaukee, WI www.millerbrewing.com
"I really don't see anyone logging on to RateBeer and saying, 'Let's see what people say about Meister Brau since I've always wanted to try that beer but could never afford it.' " "Brings back college memories of getting sick on this crap." 4.5% alc.

Melbourn Brothers Apricot ★★1/2
Fruit Lambic: Melbourn Brothers (Samuel Smith), Stamford, Lincolnshire, England
www.melbournbrothers.co.uk
"Nose was light fruits, some tannins and not much else, but yet pleasurable." "Hint of oakiness, strong peach flavor, wet wood, hint of tartness, strange!" "Not much malt character, but still rather tasty and certainly unusual." 3.4% alc.

Melbourn Brothers Cherry ★★★
Fruit Lambic: Melbourn Brothers (Samuel Smith), Stamford, Lincolnshire, England
www.melbournbrothers.co.uk
"Has a medicinal character with deep cherries, some sugary sweetness and slight phenols underneath." "Sweet fruity flavors, some clean acidic undertones." "It almost becomes like a soft drink." 3.4% alc.

Melbourn Brothers Strawberry ★★1/2
Fruit Lambic: Melbourn Brothers (Samuel Smith), Stamford, Lincolnshire, England
www.melbournbrothers.co.uk
"Slightly tart aroma with a touch of fruit." "Strawberry flavor is very prevalent but it has a nice sour/tart finish." "Slight hoppiness keeps this from sliding into strawberry wine country." 3.4% alc.

Menabrea ★★★
Pale Lager: Menabrea (Forst), Biella, Italy www.birramenabrea.it
"Nose of grain, dried grass and some citrus." "Both malt and hay-like hop emerging from its very spritzy body." "Better than I expected." 4.8% alc.

Mendocino Black Eye ★★★1/2
Ale: Mendocino Brewing Co., Hopland, CA www.mendobrew.comraptors/brewpub.html
A premixed blend of Black Hawk'stout and Eye of the Hawk. "Lots of malt in the aroma with a hint of coffee." "As nice a mix of two great tastes as Reese's Peanut Butter Cups." 6.5% alc.

Mendocino Black Hawk'stout ★★1/2
Dry Stout: Mendocino Brewing Co., Hopland, CA www.mendobrew.comraptors/brewpub.html
"Very roasty with hints of dark fruits, citrusy hops and coffee." "A hint of smokiness." "Too thin to really wow." "typicall for style." 5.2% alc.

Mendocino Blue Heron ★★
Am. Pale Ale: Mendocino Brewing Co., Hopland, CA www.mendobrew.comraptors/brewpub.html
An American Pale Ale with a "weak hop aroma" and a "somewhat sweet, lightly bitter and hoppy" flavor. "There isn't much to remember it by." 6.1% alc.

Mendocino Eye of the Hawk ★★1/2
Am Strong Ale: Mendocino Brewing Co., Hopland, CA www.mendobrew.comraptors/brewpub.html
A dark amber strong ale with a "sugary, honey, caramel and oddly leafy" aroma. "Bready, nutty, sweet honey-caramel and fruit flavors." "Actually pretty boring for such a big beer." 8% alc.

Mendocino Red Tail Ale ★★1/2
Amber Ale: Mendocino Brewing Co., Hopland, CA www.mendobrew.comraptors/brewpub.html
One of the original microbrews in the US, Red Tail is a malt-accented, like "caramel with light fruits and an appreciable amount of earthy hopping." "Crisp, not terribly clean, decent but a bit below average in my opinion." 6.1% alc.

Mendocino Summer Ale ★★
Bel. Witbier: Olde Saratoga Brewing (Mendocino Brewing Co.), Saratoga Springs, NY www.oldesaratogabrew.com
"Aroma is sweet lemons with a touch of orange." "Starts with banana, middles with spices (clove, pepper) and finishes bubblegummy." "This is pretty much a Blue Moon clone if you ask me." N/A% alc.

Mendocino Talon Barley Wine ★★★
Barley Wine: Mendocino Brewing Co., Hopland, CA www.mendobrew.comraptors/brewpub.html
typicall American-style barley wine with rich maltiness and big hops. "Alcohol is evident. Too evident." "Rough and hoppy when young and quite possibly smoothing out after four to five years." 10.5% alc.

Mendocino White Hawk Original IPA ★★1/2
IPA: Mendocino Brewing Co., Hopland, CA www.mendobrew.comraptors/brewpub.html
"Aroma of spicy, flowery hops and caramel." "Complex, if somewhat subdued hop character." "This is not disappointing (though not spectacular either)." 7% alc.

Mendocino Winter Ale ★★★★1/2
Imp/Dbl IPA: Olde Saratoga Brewing (Mendocino Brewing Co.), Saratoga Springs, NY ***www.oldesaratogabrew.com***
"Roasty aroma of sweet caramel, molasses, mocha and a definite citrusy hops presence." "Subtle hints of chocolate, coffee, vanilla and malts. Medium to thin-bodied, yet smooth and silky." "I could drink this all year long.." 9% alc.

Mestreechs Aajt ★★★
Flem Sour Ale: Gulpener Bierbrouwerij, Gulpen, Netherlands www.gulpener.nl
"Rich aroma of cherries, whiskey, with subdued oaky and vinous tones." "Flavor is mildly sour, with notes of pepper, cherry, roasted malt and a light twinge of vinegar." "It tasted very much like a typicall Belgian sour brown ale." 5% alc.

MGD Light ★
Pale Lager: Miller Brewing Co. (SABMiller), Milwaukee, WI www.millerbrewing.com
"Flavor is slightly tingly, with a dull hops presence rounded out by adjuncts of rice and stuff." "No flavor, no taste, no buzz." 4.5% alc.

Michael Shea's Irish Amber ★★1/2
Am Dark Larger: High Falls Brewing Co., Rochester, NY www.highfalls.com
"Small caramel aroma, but with a hint of metallic." "Drenched malt flavors with shy caramel notes and watery cocoa." "I need more character in a beer." 4.62% alc.

Michelob ★★
Pale Lager: Anheuser-Busch Companies, St. Louis, MO www.anheuser-busch.com
"Aroma of corn and a bit of hops. Flavor is much the same." "Kinda watery mouthfeel and flavor." "Better than most mass produced beer." 5% alc.

Michelob Amber Bock ★★
Am Dark Larger: Anheuser-Busch Companies, St. Louis, MO www.anheuser-busch.com
"Surprising amount of caramel malt for a product such as this." "This was the first "dark" beer I ever had and it is responsible for my foray into the world of dark beers." 5.2% alc.

Michelob Black and Tan ★
Porter: Anheuser-Busch Companies, St. Louis, MO www.anheuser-busch.com
"Faint caramel and chocolate come through on the nose." "Taste is slight dark roasted malt, not much hop, too carbonated." "I wouldn't drink this again, but I applaud Busch for making this." 5% alc.

Michelob Dark 
Am Dark Larger: Anheuser-Busch Companies, St. Louis, MO www.anheuser-busch.com
"Nice nut aroma followed by a nut, roasted malt and slight caramel flavor." "Awfully thin for a dark lager." "It's not too complex for those who have untrained palates." 5% alc.

Michelob Hefeweizen ★
Hefeweizen: Anheuser-Busch Companies, St. Louis, MO www.anheuser-busch.com
"Aroma is grainy with a hint of citrus." "Some citrusy, yeasty taste." "Very smooth drinking except for the fact that is not a good example of the taste you would expect from a Hefe." 5% alc.

Michelob Honey Lager ★★1/2
Pale Lager: Anheuser-Busch Companies, St. Louis, MO www.anheuser-busch.com
"Moderate sweet malt aroma." "Very drinkable but nothing bold in flavor." "Not a bad tasting beer but a bit too sweet for my taste." 4.9% alc.

Michelob Jacks Pumpkin Spice Ale 
Spice/Herb: Anheuser-Busch Companies, St. Louis, MO www.anheuser-busch.com
"Nose of faint but distinct pumpkin pie but without any complexity." "Taste is pumpkiny enough but the body is way too light." "Pretty tame compared to other pumpkin beers, but Bud is on the right track with this." 5.5% alc.

Michelob Light ★
Pale Lager: Anheuser-Busch Companies, St. Louis, MO www.anheuser-busch.com
"Golden color, with a grain and malt aroma." "A slight detectable malt flavor and no hop finish." "Probably the best Anheuser-Busch light beer." 4.3% alc.

Michelob Marzen ★
Am Dark Larger: Anheuser-Busch Companies, St. Louis, MO www.anheuser-busch.com
"Aroma is light caramel and a slight detection of hops." "Light-bodied with a sweet malt character." "Lacks real malt depth of real Märzen." 4.9% alc.

Michelob Ultra ★
Pale Lager: Anheuser-Busch Companies, St. Louis, MO www.anheuser-busch.com
"Ultra-light uric aroma with grassy hops and corn." "Taste is of carbonated water and the body is very light." "There is no joy at all drinking this beer." 4.2% alc.

Michigan Brewing High Seas Indian Pale Ale ★★★★
IPA: Michigan Brewing Co., Webberville, MI www.michiganbrewing.com
"Aroma is toasty and hints of caramelization with a note of spicy goodness." "Malty, lightly sweet and caramelly, somewhat roasty and smoky, hoppy and bitter, with modest grapefruit notes in the finish." 7% alc.

Michigan Brewing Mackinac Pale Ale ★★
Am. Pale Ale: Michigan Brewing Co., Webberville, MI www.michiganbrewing.com
"Moderately aromatic nose shows nice balance between a lightly caramelly maltiness and gentle hops." "Flavor is citrus with a bit of caramel malt at the end." "Disappointing at best." 5.5% alc.

Michigan Brewing Majestic Nut Brown Ale 
Brown Ale: Michigan Brewing Co., Webberville, MI www.michiganbrewing.com
"Flavor is very bland, some nuts and malt, hints of the alcohol but barely." "Average-some macroness to it." "Truly thin and incomplete." 5% alc.

Mickey's Fine Malt Liquor ★★

Malt Liquor: Miller Brewing Co. (SABMiller), Milwaukee, WI www.millerbrewing.com

"Let's face it, there's only one reason to buy this stuff. It's for the wide mouth bottle. I use them all over for storage - pocket change, buttons, stuff in the garage. As for the beer... tastes like sour corn." 5.6% alc.

Mickey's Ice ★★1/2

Malt Liquor: Miller Brewing Co. (SABMiller), Milwaukee, WI www.millerbrewing.com

"Aroma contains notes of malts and bread." "Grainy, sweet, mild alcohol." "This stuff was made to chug." 5.9% alc.

Middle Ages Apricot ★★1/2

Fruit Beer: Middle Ages Brewing, Syracuse, NY www.middleagesbrewing.com

"Perfumey apricot aroma, lightly soapish." "Flavor is like a nice English Pale Ale with apricot hints." "This is the proverbial girlfriend beer...there needs to be more women out there who appreciate a good smack of Cascades." 4.4% alc.

Middle Ages Beast Bitter ★★1/2

Prem Bitter: Middle Ages Brewing, Syracuse, NY www.middleagesbrewing.com

"Grapefruit, floral orange hops are up front with some sweet caramel malt character and assertive finishing bitterness." "A lighter Extra Special Bitter fine for summer." 5.3% alc.

Middle Ages Druid Fluid ★★★1/2

Barley Wine: Middle Ages Brewing, Syracuse, NY www.middleagesbrewing.com

"Lots of orange with moderate caramel and light grapefruit hoppiness." "Taste is pleasingly simple with a mild moderate display of caramel, gentle honey and light butterscotch warmth." 9.5% alc.

Middle Ages Grail Ale ★★1/2

Amber Ale: Middle Ages Brewing, Syracuse, NY www.middleagesbrewing.com

"Aroma of corn flaky malt, some almonds, cinnamon, brown sugar and dark chocolate." "Medium sweet malty flavors, caramel, earthy and lightly musty." "Boring, though not poorly brewed." 5.5% alc.

Middle Ages ImPaled Ale ★★★

IPA: Middle Ages Brewing, Syracuse, NY www.middleagesbrewing.com

Nose: "Floral hops, green apples, grapefruit, sweet malt and spices." "Bitter with citric American hops, good sweet malt and caramel and a long, dry, bitter finish." 6.5% alc.

Middle Ages Kilt Tilter ★★★★

Scotch Ale: Middle Ages Brewing, Syracuse, NY www.middleagesbrewing.com

"Caramelly aroma with berries and hints of cola, with notes of cherry and yeasty earthiness as well." "Smooth malt base, semi-sweet, definite peat and charred wood aspects." "Great stuff and bit underrated in my opinion..." 8.5% alc.

Middle Ages Syracuse Pale ★★

Eng Pale Ale: Middle Ages Brewing, Syracuse, NY www.middleagesbrewing.com

"Aroma and flavor is caramel and light fruits like apricots." "Diacetyl is overbearing in mouth, floral, peachy and weak." 5% alc.

Middle Ages The Duke Of Winship ★★★

Porter: Middle Ages Brewing, Syracuse, NY www.middleagesbrewing.com

"Mix of malt, nuts, cabernet and chocolate aroma." "Very malty, moderately bitter and roasty, fairly chocolaty, dry initially, becoming moderately sweet toward the finish." "Extra point for the Ron Jeremy look-alike on the label." 6.5% alc.

Middle Ages Tripel Crown ★★1/2

Bel. Strong Ale: Middle Ages Brewing, Syracuse, NY www.middleagesbrewing.com

"Aroma is moderately caramel apple with light flowery hops and alcohol." "Taste has noticeable alcohol burn, sweet caramelized wort taste and vague finishing bitterness." "Noble concept, but poorly executed." 10% alc.

Middle Ages Wailing Wench ★★★★
Am Strong Ale: Middle Ages Brewing, Syracuse, NY www.middleagesbrewing.com
"Really nice balanced aroma of citrusy hops and thick deep caramel malts." "Resiny hops, burnt caramel malt, some sweet buttery toffee, then stronger hops assert themselves, along with more than a hint of alcohol." 8% alc.

Midnight Sun Arctic Devil Barley Wine ★★★★1/2
Barley Wine: Midnight Sun Brewing Co., Anchorage, AK www.wildales.com
A strong (11.5%), barrel-aged winter beer. Blends the influence of the wood with lots of malt and hops, often with a distinct maple accent. "A mesmerizing dessert concoction" for barley wine aficionados. 11.5% alc.

Midnight Sun Cohoho Imperial IPA ★★★★1/2
Imp/Dbl IPA: Midnight Sun Brewing Co., Anchorage, AK www.wildales.com
Somebody really thought they were being clever when they named this holiday release. "Sweetly malty with a long hop bitter buildup." "Sweeter than other Imperial Indian Pale Ales" but "seems to be wandering around a bit." 8% alc.

Midnight Sun Kodiak Brown Ale ★★1/2
Brown Ale: Midnight Sun Brewing Co., Anchorage, AK www.wildales.com
Medium-bodied brown ale. "A tad thin" with caramel and toasty malt flavors. "Not terrible; not even close to being memorable." N/A% alc.

Midnight Sun La Mâitresse du Moine ★★★★★
Abbey Dubbel: Midnight Sun Brewing Co., Anchorage, AK www.wildales.com
The "Monk's Mistress" has a sweet, chocolaty, fruity character. "Can you say chocolate-covered bananas?" "One fantastic Belgian impersonator." The top-rated American example of the style. 9% alc.

Midnight Sun Épluche-Culotte ★★★★1/2
Abbey Tripel: Midnight Sun Brewing Co., Anchorage, AK www.wildales.com
Popular dark abbey-style beer with aroma of banana, clove and orange peel. The flavor is sweet, candyish and fruity. Some find it too sweet "lots of under-attenuated pale malt" 9% alc.

Midnight Sun Sockeye Red ★★★★
IPA: Midnight Sun Brewing Co., Anchorage, AK www.wildales.com
"Red-colored version of an IPA, bringing the usual "very bitter hop finish," but also "toffee, caramel and toasted malt." "Not cool and crisp like most Indian Pale Ales but decent brew." N/A% alc.

Miller Genuine Draft ★
Pale Lager: Miller Brewing Co. (SABMiller), Milwaukee, WI www.millerbrewing.com
"The look, smell, flavor all very watered down." "Cold wet with alcohol." "Funny, I used to think of this as quite pleasant before I discovered real beer." 4.5% alc.

Miller High Life ★
Pale Lager: Miller Brewing Co. (SABMiller), Milwaukee, WI www.millerbrewing.com
"Pours a piss pale yellow, aroma smells bad and the flavor is just bleh." "If it's the champagne of beers, then why is it so cheap at the gas station?" 4.7% alc.

Miller High Life Light ★
Pale Lager: Miller Brewing Co. (SABMiller), Milwaukee, WI www.millerbrewing.com
"Taste is vapid with absolutely no defining character other than its remarkable lack of flavor." "I am definitely worse off by having tried this beer." 4.2% alc.

Miller Lite ★
Pale Lager: Miller Brewing Co. (SABMiller), Milwaukee, WI www.millerbrewing.com
"Obviously not a beer that you drink for anything but an icy cold one or for getting drunk." "This one is just a well marketed, small flavored beer." "Goes really well with rice cakes." 4.5% alc.

Miller Sharps ★
Low Alcohol: Miller Brewing Co. (SABMiller), Milwaukee, WI www.millerbrewing.com
"The aroma is corn and almost non existent hops." "Extremely mild and nondescript." "I can't figure out why you would want to drink a bad beer with no alcohol?" 0.4% alc.

Millstream Colony Oatmeal Stout ★
Sweet Stout: Millstream Brewing Co., Amana, IA www.millstreambrewing.com
"The folks at Millstream tried to be different and use lager yeast and this time that inventiveness did not pay off." "Tastes like I just licked a freight train." "This really is a very boring and thin beer." 5.1% alc.

Millstream German Style Pilsner ★★★
Pilsner: Millstream Brewing Co., Amana, IA www.millstreambrewing.com
"Reminds me of being on the farm during harvest season." "The flavor is well balanced, lightly sweet yet restrained with just enough hops." "A clean and wonderfully drinkable pilsner." N/A% alc.

Millstream Maifest ★★1/2
Bock: Millstream Brewing Co., Amana, IA www.millstreambrewing.com
"Cereal, dark bread, cookie and slightly nutty/grainy aroma." "Light malt, caramel and hops flavors." "All in all a pleasing beer to drink despite (because of?) the simple approach." N/A% alc.

Millstream Oktoberfest ★★1/2
Märzen/Oktbfst: Millstream Brewing Co., Amana, IA www.millstreambrewing.com
"Malty nose, perhaps a touch of charred wood." "Bold caramel a touch of chocolate and a sweet toffee aftertaste that I liked." "Palate is lighter for a Märzen." N/A% alc.

Millstream Schild Brau Amber ★★1/2
Märzen/Oktbfst: Millstream Brewing Co., Amana, IA www.millstreambrewing.com
"Aroma is roasty caramel malts. Some brief German hops as well." "Sweet with light caramel malt and just enough hops presence to balance." "Solid brew without being flashy." N/A% alc.

Millstream Schokolade Bock ★★1/2
Bock: Millstream Brewing Co., Amana, IA www.millstreambrewing.com
"Pretty ordinary toasted cereal nose, slightly influences by leafy hops." "Flavor is a roast malt light bittering hints of semi sweet chocolate and wheat." 5.7% alc.

Millstream Warsh Pail Ale ★★★
Am. Pale Ale: Millstream Brewing Co., Amana, IA www.millstreambrewing.com
"Predominantly citrusy nose-grapefruit orange, with hints of mango and caramel… fairly dry and bitter body, enough brown sugary sweetness to keep the essential tartness from overwhelming." "Good stuff." N/A% alc.

Millstream Wheat ★★1/2
Am. Wheat: Millstream Brewing Co., Amana, IA www.millstreambrewing.com
"Light, sourdough-yeasty nose, touch of old lemon." "Clean but boring sweet-sour finish." "Nothing special here, but it is exactly as it claims… liquid bread." N/A% alc.

Milwaukee's Best ★
Pale Lager: Miller Brewing Co. (SABMiller), Milwaukee, WI www.millerbrewing.com
"Smells like aluminum cans and stale barley. Has that 'I'm broke' taste." "One of the worst tailgating beers yet; some of the flavors and aromas are truly pushing the boundaries of putrid." 4.3% alc.

Milwaukee's Best Ice ★
Pale Lager: Miller Brewing Co. (SABMiller), Milwaukee, WI www.millerbrewing.com
"Taste has way too much alcohol." "A friend slipped me a few of these after a six-pack of Sam Adams Black Lager. I babysat the crapper." 5.9% alc.

Milwaukee's Best Light ★
Pale Lager: Miller Brewing Co. (SABMiller), Milwaukee, WI www.millerbrewing.com
"The only thing that makes this 'beer' is the label on the can." "The taste reminds me of every college bender weekend." "It finishes with only one thing: regret." 4.2% alc.

Mishawaka Founder's Stout ★★★1/2
Dry Stout: Mishawaka Brewing Co., Mishawaka, IN www.mishawakabrewingCo..com
"Mmm... smooth semi-sweet chocolate oriented coffee flavors." "Toasted malt aroma with a rather strong coffee presence." "Mishawaka's best yet." N/A% alc.

Mishawaka Four Horsemen Ale ★★★
Irish Ale: Mishawaka Brewing Co., Mishawaka, IN www.mishawakabrewingCo..com
"Flavor department is unique, with more bang than expected - candy apples, toffee bark and light, nutty malts." "Hops are just a background bitterness here, while malts come in nicely." 5.5% alc.

Mississippi Mud Black and Tan ★
Porter blend: AriZona Beverage Co., Lake Success, NY
"Stale bread flavor through and through and mildly sour with some lightly roasty malt and honey." "If you've ever messed up making a black and tan with two average beers, you get Mississippi Mud." Contract brewed by Matt Brewing Co. N/A% alc.

Moab Brewery Dead Horse Amber Ale ★★
Mild Ale: Moab Brewery, Moab, UT themoabbrewery.com
"Mild, sweetish, vaguely caramelly flavor with mushroomy undertones." "Smell has a stale malted fruity sense, kinda like dried peaches or apples." "Appropriate moniker for such a lifeless brew." 4% alc.

Moab Brewery Scorpion Pale Ale ★★1/2
Am. Pale Ale: Moab Brewery, Moab, UT themoabbrewery.com
"Aroma is of woody, grapefruity, blood orangey hops." "Flavor has a nice toasty malt backbone, some caramel, but the finish is bitter lemon grass and dry with hops." "Crisp, zippy beer that was fairly drinkable." 4% alc.

Modelo Especial ★★
Pale Lager: Grupo Modelo (Corona), México DF, Mexico www.gmodelo.com
"Bit of citric hop, some biscuity malt." "Pleasant malt and a bit of dusky lemon." "Drinkable for a Mexican lager." 6% alc.

Mogollon Apache Trout Stout ★★★
Stout: Mogollon Brewing Co., Flagstaff, AZ
"Very generous roasted malt aroma. Very inviting." Malty, chocolaty, roasty flavor profile. "Emerging sweetness that leads to a dry finish" N/A% alc.

Mogollon Superstition Pale ★★1/2
Am. Pale Ale: Mogollon Brewing Co., Flagstaff, AZ
Has a cloudy orange-amber color. "Medium-powered hops and citrus oranges with a clean crisp hop finish." "strong example of a pale ale meant to be easy drinking with a good amount of flavor." N/A% alc.

Moinette Biologique ★★★★1/2
Saison: Dupont Brasserie, Tourpes-Leuze, Belgium www.brasserie-dupont.com
"Taste is citric, with flowery spices, malty fruits and some barnyard." "Aroma is coriander, very yeasty, light banana, lemon pineapple cake, powdered sugar." "Note to self: Must get to Belgium!" 7.5% alc.

Moinette Blonde ★★★★1/2
Abbey Tripel: Dupont Brasserie, Tourpes-Leuze, Belgium www.brasserie-dupont.com
"Aroma shows pears, lots of yeast, leather, white pepper, coriander, bread crust, herbal hops." "Palate has sweet notes of caramel flan, pepper, dried peaches, barnyard with cobwebs." "A very rustic and interesting beer." 8.5% alc.

Moinette Brune ★★★★
Abbey Dubbel: Dupont Brasserie, Tourpes-Leuze, Belgium www.brasserie-dupont.com
"Rustic, herbal hop aroma, with hints of cork, farmhouse, banana, milk chocolate and various red fruits." "Juicy, vinous fruit flavors initially, followed by a mild tartness, which leads into a spicy, peppery herbal hop finish." 8.5% alc.

Molson Canadian ★★1/2
Pale Lager: Molson Breweries (MolsonCoors), Montreal, Quebec www.molson.com
"Doesn't really smell like much of anything... maybe faintly malts or alcohol." "Some mild sweet corn flavors at first followed by some minor bitterness." "When I'd have to choose between this and a Silver Bullet, I'd go North." 5% alc.

Molson Golden ★★1/2
Pale Lager: Molson Breweries (MolsonCoors), Montreal, Quebec www.molson.com
"Very light indistinct aroma." "Grainy, cheap tasting background with little hop character." "Thin-bodied, overly sweet, underhopped and totally unappealing." 5% alc.

Molson Ice ★★
Pale Lager: Molson Breweries (MolsonCoors), Montreal, Quebec www.molson.com
"Faintly sour corn aroma. Biting carbonation on the tongue. Flavor was very watery, with some funky off stuff going on." "I would get it over US macro's but I'd stop there." 5.6% alc.

Mongozo Palmnut ★★
Traditional Ale: Brouwerij Huyghe, Melle, Belgium www.delirium.be
"Aromas of malt, apricot, peach and yeast." "Exciting, exotic spicy flavor which doesn't resemble anything I've tasted before." "A bit sweet for my tastes but pretty drinkable and definitely unique." 7% alc.

Monkshine ★★
Belgian Ale: Uinta Brewing Co., Salt Lake City, UT www.uintabrewing.com
"Flavor is moderate in intensity, balanced between fruity (pear, peach), phenolic (slight bubblegum) and light background earthy maltiness." "Finishes with some citrusy notes, yeast, hops, flowers and grains." 4% alc.

Monte Carlo ★
Pale Lager: Cerveceria Centro Americana, Guatemala, Guatemala www.cerveceria.com.gt
"Aroma is expectantly skunky, high in Saaz hoppiness and stale water." "Almost a hint of malt in the palate, with lots of corn-derived creaminess." "Beginning to make me suspect that Guatemala just isn't one of the truly great beer countries of the world." 4.9% alc.

Monte Carlo High Roller Red ★★
Amber Ale: Monte Carlo Pub & Brewery, Las Vegas, NV www.monte-carlo.com
"Lightish character with a slight caramel accent, earthy and toasty notes, minimal hopping and a sweetish finish." "Thin palate, nothing bad, nothing special." N/A% alc.

Monte Carlo Jackpot Pale Ale ★★
IPA: Monte Carlo Pub & Brewery, Las Vegas, NV www.monte-carlo.com
"Little bit of citrusy hops in aroma." "A lot of bready malt flavor in this one, with a bit of C-hops." "If this had a little better balance, it would have been much better, the flavors were not blended well." N/A% alc.

Monte Carlo Las Vegas Lites ★★1/2
Pale Lager: Monte Carlo Pub & Brewery, Las Vegas, NV www.monte-carlo.com
"Light citrusy aftertaste." "Not offensive, though, so cheers to that, I guess." "Tastes like a few drops of OE (Original Extract of the wort) added to Bud Light." N/A% alc.

Monte Carlo Silver State Stout ★★

Dry Stout: Monte Carlo Pub & Brewery, Las Vegas, NV www.monte-carlo.com

"Deep roasted aroma, black patent malt a bit overdone." "Flavor starts lightly sweet with coffee and hints of fudge and smoke finishing lightly dry and bitter." "the biggest downer for me with this beer was its very thin and watery body." N/A% alc.

Monte Carlo Winner's Wheat ★

Am. Wheat: Monte Carlo Pub & Brewery, Las Vegas, NV www.monte-carlo.com

"Lemony, candy sweet aroma." "Smooth and sweet, lacking in body and character." "This drains down easily enough, but provides little pleasure." N/A% alc.

Moorhouses Black Cat ★★1/2

Mild Ale: Moorhouses Brewery, Burnley, Lancashire, England www.moorhouses.co.uk

"Aroma is chocolate, a touch of caramel and a bit of molasses." "Some lightweight flavors of roasted malts, chocolate, caramel and nuts make a faint presence." "There's flavor but its still a run of the mill mild." 3.4% alc.

Moorhouses Pendle Witches Brew ★★1/2

Eng. Strong Ale: Moorhouses Brewery, Burnley, Lancashire, England www.moorhouses.co.uk

"Nutty, malty and sweet nose has a very earthy character to it." "Taste is fruity and earthy and malty but also kind of mild." "Very novel taste for any English beer." 5.1% alc.

Moosehead ★★★

Pale Lager: Moosehead Brewery, Saint John, Ontario www.moosehead.ca

"Some flowery, grassy hops in the aroma." "Sweet, malty flavors with notes of corn or other brewing cereals and a metallic edge." "More balanced than many of its contemporaries, but still not worth buying." 5.5% alc.

Moretti La Rossa ★★★1/2

Bock: Birra Moretti (Heineken), Udine, Italy www.birramoretti.it

"Aroma is sweet and malt with some apple and pear along with molasses notes." "Surprisingly good caramel, brown sugar, molasses flavor with hints of dried fruit." Good entry from a Co. I normally make fun of." 7.2% alc.

Morland Hen's Tooth ★★1/2

Eng. Strong Ale: Greene King Plc, Bury St. Edmunds, Suffolk, England www.greeneking.co.uk

"Zesty marmalade, citrus fruits and a little toffee; quite pleasant." "Flavors are dominated by caramel malt and some toasted - almost coffeeish - notes." "Not the kind of strong ale that I am used to." 6.5% alc.

Morland Old Speckled Hen ★★1/2

Prem Bitter: Greene King Plc, Bury St. Edmunds, Suffolk, England www.greeneking.co.uk

"Aroma is mild but rather fruity and nutty with a slight hoppiness." "Malty body with notes of nuts and caramel." "Best thing about this beer is probably the name." 5.2% alc.

Morland Tanner's Jack ★★

Bitter: Greene King Plc, Bury St. Edmunds, Suffolk, Belgium www.greeneking.co.uk

"Stale malt aroma with caramel and some hop." "Lightly malty with pear and licorice notes, dull pasteurized iron-like feel/flavor." "A very predictable ale." 4.4% alc.

Mort Subite Cassis ★★1/2

Fruit Lambic: Brouwerij de Keersmaeker (Scottish & Newcastle), Kobbegem, Belgium www.alkenmaes.be

"Rich sherbety aroma is dominated by tart blackcurrant, sugary sweetness and a hint of the barn." "Flavor is cassis somewhat artificially sweetened, some very weak lambic tartness - a bit too sweet." "A cross between a fruit beer and a lambic." 4.5% alc.

Mort Subite Framboise ★★1/2
Fruit Lambic: Brouwerij de Keersmaeker (Scottish & Newcastle), Kobbegem, Belgium www.alkenmaes.be
"Sour aroma full of raspberry and a hint of sweet malt." "Sweet-sour flavor of raspberries, quite mild, no strong aftertaste." "Very refreshing, easy drinking framboise!" 4.5% alc.

Mort Subite Gueuze Lambic ★★1/2
Gueuze: Brouwerij de Keersmaeker (Scottish & Newcastle), Kobbegem, Belgium www.alkenmaes.be
"Unexpectedly fruity sweet aroma - apple, peach, citrus." "It's sweeter than other gueuzes that I've had, still with the underlying tartness. The flavors are a hint of wheat, sour oranges, apple, straw, grasses and pollen." 4.5% alc.

Mort Subite Kriek ★★1/2
Fruit Lambic: Brouwerij de Keersmaeker (Scottish & Newcastle), Kobbegem, Belgium www.alkenmaes.be
"Aroma is lightly malty (toasted grain), with a strong note of cherry." "Sweet, flavored chewing gum taste, a bit nutty in the background." "Well balanced sweet-sour drink with neither side dominating." 4.5% alc.

Mort Subite Pêche ★★
Fruit Lambic: Brouwerij de Keersmaeker (Scottish & Newcastle), Kobbegem, Belgium www.alkenmaes.be
"Sweet and syrupy peach aroma with hints of sourness, but too artificial." "Flavor is all fruit - pleasant with the first couple of sips, but it turns syrupy and cloying very fast." "Overall below average." 4.5% alc.

Moscova ★★
Pale Lager: Ostankinsky Brewery, Moscow, Russia www.opz.ru
"Sweet grassy aroma." "Poor grassy, hay weak flavors in a carbonated mess." "Strange unclean water..." 5% alc.

Motor City Ghettoblaster ★★
Mild Ale: Motor City Brewing Works, Detroit, MI www.motorcitybeer.com
"Lightly hoppy and moderately bitter and balanced by a sweet but gently roasty maltiness." "More flavorful than I was expecting from a Mild." 5% alc.

Motor City Nut Brown ★★★
Brown Ale: Motor City Brewing Works, Detroit, MI www.motorcitybeer.com
"Aromas of nuts, light coffee and roasted malts." "Flavors of nutty maple, vanilla, corn, squash and some toasted bread." "I was not really expecting much and I got a very nice surprise." 5% alc.

Moylan's IPA ★★1/2
IPA: Moylans Brewery and Restaurant, Novato, CA www.moylans.com
"Grapefruit orange, pineapple, spring meadow and straw aromas. Flavor was malty, earthy and smoky but with a huge hop bitterness." "Flavors still come off not mixing as best as they could." 6.5% alc.

Moylan's Irish Red Ale ★★
Irish Ale: Moylans Brewery and Restaurant, Novato, CA www.moylans.com
"Aroma is sweetly caramel malt," while the flavor "is quite unique; a bit nutty to complement the malty character." "Smooth and a bit creamy." "A decent red, but there are much better ones." 6.5% alc.

Moylan's Kilt Lifter Scotch Ale ★★1/2
Scotch Ale: Moylans Brewery and Restaurant, Novato, CA www.moylans.com
"Strong malt flavor; a little bit of alcohol bite, hop bitterness peeks through" "This is an enjoyable drink, but I'm not sure why it's a Scotch Ale, except for the ever-so-original, cute name." 8% alc.

Moylan's Moylander Double IPA ★★★★★
Imp/Dbl IPA: Moylans Brewery and Restaurant, Novato, CA www.moylans.com
"Huge notes of honey and bread that match strength for strength the full-on citrus (grapefruit) and floral cascade nose." "Very straightforward example." "It still packs a kick regardless of balance." 8.5% alc.

Moylan's Old Blarney Barley Wine ★★★★1/2
Barley Wine: Moylans Brewery and Restaurant, Novato, CA www.moylans.com
"Up front spicy malty plum wave to it up front with an undercurrent of alcohol warming it." "Flavor is caramel malts and earthy/herbal hops." "An easy drinking barleywine." 10% alc.

Moylan's Tipperary ★★★
Am. Pale Ale: Moylans Brewery and Restaurant, Novato, CA www.moylans.com
"Despite it's name, this is a pale ale with the "aroma of citrus, fruit and hops." "Flavor of grapefruit, but not the bitterness you'd expect. Very fruity and balanced." "One hell of a good beer and I'm not a big APA fan." 5% alc.

Moylan's Ryan O'Sullivans Imperial Stout ★★★★★
Imp. Stout: Moylans Brewery and Restaurant, Novato, CA www.moylans.com
"Aroma is a bit hot but includes dark bittersweet chocolate, blackberries, rum raisin and caramel." "Burnt coffee and chocolate... not roasted burnt, like smores over a campfire." 10% alc.

Moza Bock ★
Bock: Cerveceria Centro Americana, Guatemala City, Guatemala www.cerveceria.com.gt
"Malty aroma with notes of toffee, smoke, charcoal and some oxidation." "Cola-textured." "Flavor is more like a sweetened San Miguel Dark." "Cheers to Guatemala! I knew they had a not-bad brew in them!" 4.5% alc.

Murphy's Irish Red ★★
Irish Ale: Magor (UK - InBev), , Wales
"Aroma of sweet mild roasted malt, some woody/nutty notes and a hint of caramel." "Flavor quite malt-sweet and nutty, with some sharply chalky flavor there, too." "Overall a decent pint, quite drinkable but nothing special and gets oddly funky when it warms." 5% alc.

Murphy's Irish Stout 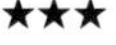
Dry Stout: Magor (UK - InBev), , Wales
"Malty, toasty and a touch nutty nose, wisps of licorice." "Flavor is somewhat roasty and coffeeish, smoky, dry, somewhat creamy." "What one would expect a dry stout to be." Made in Wales these days. 4.3% alc.

Mythos ★
Premium Lager: Mythos Breweries (Scottish & Newcastle), Sindos, Greece www.mythosbrewery.gr
"Sweetish cereal aroma." "Unclean flavor with a mild, bitter and crisp finish." "Can you make a beer with pure corn husks and wet socks?" 5% alc.

N'Ice Chouffe ★★★★★
Bel. Strong Ale: Brasserie d'Achouffe, Achouffe, Belgium www.achouffe.be
"Aroma is earthy, barnyard, spicy, with yeast." "Mostly yeasty, some spiciness that is probably both thyme and yeast. Finish is dry, with some hops and an alcoholic burn." "Not something to serve without a reason." 10% alc.

Namyslow Zamkowe Jasne (Castle) ★★★
Pale Lager: Browar Namyslow, Namyslow, Poland www.ryan.com.pl
"Clear golden Pilsner with a weak, malty aroma." "Flavor of malts and corn with notes of hops." "Very good for what it is." 5.5% alc.

Namyslow Zamkowe Mocne (Strong) ★★1/2
Eur Str Lager: Browar Namyslow, Namyslow, Poland www.ryan.com.pl
"Mild floral hops, honey and brown sugar." "Initially sharp, slightly bitter palate balanced by malt and smooth alcohol character." "I feel the need to order a cheese pie." 7% alc.

Narragansett Lager Beer ★★
Pale Lager: High Falls Brewing Co., Rochester, NY www.highfalls.com
"Smells a bit spicy and peppery with a touch of honey." "Flavor begins with apple juice, bits of powdery sugar." "Medium-bodied and a little oily with lively carbonation." N/A% alc.

Nastro Azzurro ★
Premium Lager: Birra Peroni Industriale S.p.A. (SABMiller), Roma, Italy www.peroni.it
"Slightly sweet aroma grants a whisper of hops." "Moderate bitterness; some North German lean-ness, hoppy dryness." "Italian version of Heineken." 5.2% alc.

National Bohemian ★★
Pale Lager: Miller Brewing Co. (SABMiller), Milwaukee, WI www.millerbrewing.com
"Light, creamy, hint of bready malt, gasoline." "Very crisp finish with no aftertaste." "Best when consumed alongside piles of steamed crabs and corn." N/A% alc.

Natural Ice ★
Pale Lager: Anheuser-Busch Companies, St. Louis, MO www.anheuser-busch.com
"Tasted like a mixture of sweet corn with metal flakes." "To drink this is a punishment." "Like cooked corn what's been sittin' outside the mess a day or two." 5.9% alc.

Natural Light ★
Pale Lager: Anheuser-Busch Companies, St. Louis, MO www.anheuser-busch.com
"This is the least beer tasting beer I have ever had." "Cheap, cheap, cheap. And you get what you pay for." "Slightly sweet corn and other grains very generic cheap taste." 4.2% alc.

Negra Modelo ★★1/2
Am Dark Larger: Grupo Modelo , México DF, Mexico www.gmodelo.com
"Nice roast aromas with some hops and a hint of pepper." "Biscuity malt flavor complimented nicely with German hops flavor and a raisiny hint of dark malts." "Looks darker than it tastes." 6% alc.

Nethergate Augustinian Ale ★★
Prem Bitter: Nethergate, Pentlow, Sudbury, Essex, England www.nethergate.co.uk
"Spicy aromas with hints of citrus." "Tastes fruity, spicily floral with some berries and citrus in the finish." "Lots of coriander here." "Woof, just way too much coriander in this thin, sour brew." 5.2% alc.

Nethergate Old Growler ★★1/2
Porter: Nethergate, Pentlow, Sudbury, Essex, England www.nethergate.co.uk
"Ghostly aroma with brown sugar, anise, raisins." "Slightly bitter flavor with bread crust, coffee, chocolate and some earthiness." "I could imagine gents of old English finding this a very solid everyday beer." 5.5% alc.

New Amsterdam NT Amber ★★1/2
Amber Ale: New Amsterdam Brewing Co., New York, NY www.saranac.com
"Bread and cookies with a bunch of caramel sweetness and a mostly dry finish." "Flavor is somewhat weak, light malty flavor with a slightly bitter finish." Contract brewed by Matt Brewing Co. N/A% alc.

New Belgium 1554 Brussels Style Black Ale ★★★
Traditional Ale: New Belgium Brewing Co., Fort Collins, CO www.newbelgium.com
"Interesting aroma of cherry and burnt toast." "Very earthy and slightly sweet with plenty of coffee and chocolate, with a grounding of pumpernickel bread." "good beer if you are in the mood for something a little sweeter." 5.4% alc.

New Belgium Abbey ★★★★1/2
Abbey Dubbel: New Belgium Brewing Co., Fort Collins, CO www.newbelgium.com
"Bubblegum esters dominate the sweet, rich, bready, malty aroma with some herbal notes also apparent." "Yeast, banana, bubblegum, bread." "Dusky, lowdown feel while keeping a high brow aura." 7% alc.

New Belgium Bière de Mars ★★★
Saison: New Belgium Brewing Co., Fort Collins, CO www.newbelgium.com
"Spicy, phenolic aroma of medicine, sweat, cologne... like a classic saison meeting Orval." "The palate is crisp, slightly toasty but largely perfumey, piney and phenolic." "An interesting citrus take on the Saison style." 6.2% alc.

New Belgium Blue Paddle Pilsner ★★★1/2
Pilsner: New Belgium Brewing Co., Fort Collins, CO www.newbelgium.com
"Well-balanced aroma with herbal hops and fresh bread." "Soft body is accented toward the malts." "Medium body and a crisp, clean mouthfeel." 4.8% alc.

New Belgium Fat Tire ★★1/2
Amber Ale: New Belgium Brewing Co., Fort Collins, CO www.newbelgium.com
"Grainy caramel malts balance with citrus orange and grapefruit hops in the nose." "Gentle toffee flavor with a hint of citrus hops and moderate bitterness." "This was a transition beer for me." 5.3% alc.

New Belgium Frambozen ★★★★
Fruit Beer: New Belgium Brewing Co., Fort Collins, CO www.newbelgium.com
"Aroma like a raspberry tart - very sweet and fruity." "Fresh, seedy berry flavors at the beginning, but then giving way to the more confectionary aspects." "Pleases the palate, warms the belly." 7% alc.

New Belgium La Folie ★★★★★
Flem Sour Ale: New Belgium Brewing Co., Fort Collins, CO www.newbelgium.com
Aged in wood in the style of the classic Belgian sour ale Rodenbach. "Aroma is sharp as a blade." "Dry, vinous and complex like a mofo." "Very refined flavor of cherries, wood and vinegar. I think I'm in love." 6% alc.

New Belgium Loft ★★1/2
Belgian Ale: New Belgium Brewing Co., Fort Collins, CO www.newbelgium.com
"Cake-dough, coriander and bitter orange in the sweet and malty aroma." "The flavor started off with soft malt character but as it matured, a slightly grassy, dry flavor took over." 4% alc.

New Belgium Porch Swing Single ★★★
Belgian Ale: New Belgium Brewing Co., Fort Collins, CO www.newbelgium.com
"Aroma hints of malt, earthy yeast, hayfield, lemon, pear, pepper." "Taste starts with a fruity malt hit orange candy taste up front fading to a faintly spicy hop finish." "Definitely seems unique." 6% alc.

New Belgium Saison ★★★1/2
Saison: New Belgium Brewing Co., Fort Collins, CO www.newbelgium.com
"The aroma has notes of flowery yeast esters, lavender, cardamom and coriander." "Flavor is light yet very flavorful; notes of light grain, white grapes, champagne, some caramel and light fruitiness." 6.5% alc.

New Belgium Sunshine Wheat ★★1/2
Bel. Witbier: New Belgium Brewing Co., Fort Collins, CO www.newbelgium.com
"Nice subtle spicy flavor - coriander, cinnamon and berry, citrus." "Light bitterness and a fairly sweet aftertaste." "Kind of like Budweiser with a lemon wedge." 4.8% alc.

New Belgium Transatlantique Kriek ★★★★1/2
Fruit Beer: New Belgium Brewing Co., Fort Collins, CO www.newbelgium.com
"Mix of ale from New Belgium and kriek from Frank Boon. "Highly aromatic nose; tart cherries bursting forth to pleasure my olfactory senses." "Cherry soda-like with a tart dry finish." 6.3% alc.

New Belgium Trippel ★★★★1/2
Abbey Tripel: New Belgium Brewing Co., Fort Collins, CO www.newbelgium.com
"Aroma of soft floral hops, sweet caramel malt and cloves." "Flavor is quite light and refreshing, apple, pear, peach and sweet honeyish notes." "Makes a great lens to view the world through." 7.8% alc.

New England Atlantic Amber ★★1/2
Calif. Common: New England Brewing Co., Woodbridge, CT www.newenglandbrewing.com
"Very sweet up front with lots of toffee and sugar." "Light biscuit presence, mixed bags of nuts and a watered down caramel ribbon." "Not bad for a micro brew in a can." N/A% alc.

New England Three Judges Barleywine ★★1/2
Barley Wine: New England Brewing Co., Woodbridge, CT www.newenglandbrewing.com
"Tangy, spicy aroma, like a spiced tea or perhaps fruit cake." "A rather basic toffee-caramel charged English barleywine." "Booze is too big and the flavor doesn't match it well." 11.5% alc.

New Glarus Apple Ale ★★★★★
Fruit Beer: New Glarus Brewing Co., New Glarus, WI www.newglarusbrewing.com
"Nose is dominated by apple and the spiciness smells like mulled apple cider." "Tons of apple and sweet caramel flavoring." "This has been a real treat and except for a slight hint of 'beer,' it's like drinking spiced apple cider." 3.8% alc.

New Glarus Belgian Red ★★★★★
Fruit Beer: New Glarus Brewing Co., New Glarus, WI www.newglarusbrewing.com
"Sweet fruity aroma, bright cherry and cherry pit aroma." "Nice tart sour finish over the sweet cherry character." "This has got to be the best marriage of fruit and beer I have had." 5.1% alc.

New Glarus Black Wheat ★★★★★
Dunkelweizen: New Glarus Brewing Co., New Glarus, WI www.newglarusbrewing.com
"Aroma is rich and roasty, with bitter chocolate and coffee notes and a dark brown bread yeastiness." "Taste is roasty malt, bakers chocolate and espresso initially with a dulce de leche sweetness midway and some nice fruit flavor." 5.75% alc.

New Glarus Coffee Stout ★★★1/2
Sweet Stout: New Glarus Brewing Co., New Glarus, WI www.newglarusbrewing.com
"Big coffee aroma with moderate roasted malt and chocolate." "Very nice hop bite up from and then a long, slow, coating, smooth coffee middle." "It could be more bold in its hop assertiveness or more creamy front to back, but it's very good." 5.75% alc.

New Glarus Edel-Pils ★★★★★
Pilsner: New Glarus Brewing Co., New Glarus, WI www.newglarusbrewing.com
"Wonderful slightly sweet malt and crisp, floral hop aroma." "Flavor is very clean, soft hop bitterness against a light and crisp malt backdrop." "An exceptionally well-done Pilsner." 5.3% alc.

New Glarus Fat Squirrel Nut Brown ★★★★★
Brown Ale: New Glarus Brewing Co., New Glarus, WI www.newglarusbrewing.com
"Malty aroma, redolent of toasted whole grain bread and mild, milky coffee with suggestions of hazelnut, light brown sugar." "Sweet, deliciously malty, caramelly, very toasty, slightly roasty in the finish, with just a hint of bitterness." 5.5% alc.

New Glarus Hop Hearty ★★★★1/2
IPA: New Glarus Brewing Co., New Glarus, WI www.newglarusbrewing.com
"Hop aroma, some caramel maltiness and grapefruit." "Bitterish earthy malt then dryish piney hops." "Not overhopped, just not an exceptional flavor balance either of the various hop flavor attributes or of hop vs. malt." 6.1% alc.

New Glarus Native Ale ★★1/2
Ale: New Glarus Brewing Co., New Glarus, WI www.newglarusbrewing.com
"Mostly fruity nose, a little earthy, with maybe a hint of oxidation." "Light mouthfeel and the flavor consisted of some sweet malts and a little woodiness." "I can't decide if I kind of like this or kind of hate it." 5% alc.

New Glarus Raspberry Tart ★★★★★
Fruit Beer: New Glarus Brewing Co., New Glarus, WI www.newglarusbrewing.com
"Lovely fruity tartness and a rich, thick mouthfeel." "Aroma is fresh raw raspberries and a hint of malt." "An exceptional fruit beer." 4% alc.

New Glarus Snowshoe Ale ★★★★
Amber Ale: New Glarus Brewing Co., New Glarus, WI www.newglarusbrewing.com
Straight ahead American-style amber with a fair dosage of crystal malts and earthy hops." "Bitterness is moderate and kind of hangs on the palate." "One of the only amber ales that I would seek again." 5.7% alc.

New Glarus Solstice Weiss ★★★★★
Hefeweizen: New Glarus Brewing Co., New Glarus, WI www.newglarusbrewing.com
"Large banana, vanilla aroma." "Sweet and dessert-like. Rich sweet malts, all (good) kinds of phenols. Slightly spicy finish." "I like sweet Weizens. Others may not. But for me this rocked." 5.75% alc.

New Glarus Spotted Cow ★★1/2
Cream Ale: New Glarus Brewing Co., New Glarus, WI www.newglarusbrewing.com
"Aroma of grain, corn, light hops, some citrus." "Malt flavor with a balanced hop bitterness." "Not a bad beer, but Wisconsin microbrews are much better than this." 5.1% alc.

New Glarus Staghorn Oktoberfest Beer ★★★
Märzen/Oktbfst: New Glarus Brewing Co., New Glarus, WI www.newglarusbrewing.com
"Generous amounts of Münich malt in the nose imparting a nice toffee and caramel scent." "Sweet breads and a light tea-style hops." "This is a really enjoyable example of the style." 6.25% alc.

New Glarus Uff-da Bock ★★★★
Bock: New Glarus Brewing Co., New Glarus, WI www.newglarusbrewing.com
"Aroma is nice creamy chocolate, some toffee, coffee, roasted peanuts and caramel." "Rich toasted malty goodness, heavy doses of warm roasted nuts, hazelnuts and macadamias." 7.3% alc.

New Glarus Unplugged Imperial IPA ★★★★1/2
Imp/Dbl IPA: New Glarus Brewing Co., New Glarus, WI www.newglarusbrewing.com
"Has familiar West Coast hop aroma of pine, citrus and hop spice." "Flavor is a combo of rich sweet and tart orange juice and malt syrup with grapefruit rind, ginger and pine needles, then a strong alcohol burn." 10% alc.

New Glarus Unplugged Imperial Stout ★★★1/2
Imp. Stout: New Glarus Brewing Co., New Glarus, WI www.newglarusbrewing.com
"Aroma is surprisingly not that interesting, especially for a stout, even more so for an Imperial." "Flavor is caramel sweetness with a light mix of light roast and toffee." "Mouthfeel is definitely thin and not on par with other Imperials." 8% alc.

New Glarus Unplugged Sour Brown Ale ★★★1/2
Flem Sour Ale: New Glarus Brewing Co., New Glarus, WI www.newglarusbrewing.com
"Sweet malts aroma with a balsamic note." "Flavor is wild cherries, wood, vanilla, brown sugar. There's a balance of sweetness that keeps the sourness from becoming too astringent and cloying in the back of the throat." 6% alc.

New Glarus Unplugged Triple ★★1/2
Abbey Tripel: New Glarus Brewing Co., New Glarus, WI www.newglarusbrewing.com
"Lots of fruit in here with apple, pear, apricot, some peach and banana toward the end." "Flavors are of apples and honey with very little in the way of Belgian yeastiness or intricacies." "Under-attenuated." 10% alc.

New Glarus Zwickel ★★★★1/2
Zwickel: New Glarus Brewing Co., New Glarus, WI www.newglarusbrewing.com
"German hop aroma... some orange and grass hints, on a grainy body with some slight honey sweetness." "Flavor is sweet, buttery malt with a short touch of grassy bitter." "Yummy lager." 5.3% alc.

New Holland Black Tulip ★★1/2
Abbey Tripel: New Holland Brewing Co., Netherlands, MI www.newhollandbrew.com
"Nice aroma: pears, honey, grainy malt, a bit of alcohol, a little phenolic." "Full, complex body; deep yeasty fruits work well with loads of sweet malt." 9% alc.

New Holland Blue Goat Doppelbock ★★★
Doppelbock: New Holland Brewing Co., New Holland, MI www.newhollandbrew.com
Aroma is dominated by burned sugar, maple syrup and caramel malts with the slightest hint of alcohol. "Starts off with the caramel and dark fruits, then gives way to the chocolate and roasted malts." "Lacks character." 7% alc.

New Holland Dragon's Milk ★★★★1/2
Eng. Strong Ale: New Holland Brewing Co., New Holland, MI www.newhollandbrew.com
"Somewhat like a scotch ale, smoky and strong, yet hops are present." "Flavor is tart with the oak tannins, some tobacco and fruit gluten flavors." "Unique in an old peculiar way." 10.5% alc.

New Holland Full Circle ★★★
Premium Lager: New Holland Brewing Co., New Holland, MI www.newhollandbrew.com
"The aroma was mild with malty hoppy notes." "Straightforward simply made premium lager is a unique beer in today's complicated micro-beer world." 5.25% alc.

New Holland Ichabod ★★★
Spice/Herb: New Holland Brewing Co., New Holland, MI www.newhollandbrew.com
"The pumpkin aroma is strong and is complimented by the cinnamon, all-spice and nutmeg." "Light caramel malty flavors with subtle pumpkin." "Not overly done like some I have had." 5.5% alc.

New Holland Mad Hatter ★★★1/2
IPA: New Holland Brewing Co., New Holland, MI www.newhollandbrew.com
"The nose really is quite nice with explosive scents of pine and citrus." "Big hoppy flavor with lots of sweet, sticky malts (caramel, toffee)." 5.9% alc.

New Holland Paleooza ★★★1/2
Am. Pale Ale: New Holland Brewing Co., New Holland, MI www.newhollandbrew.com
"Hop flavor jumps right out." "Dry and hoppy with mellow toasted malts backing." "I may be over-rating this beer, but frankly I can't see why not." 5% alc.

New Holland Phi ★★★
Am Strong Ale: New Holland Brewing Co., New Holland, MI www.newhollandbrew.com
"A lot going on in the aroma, light fruits, ginger, clove and allspice, honey and malt." "Wine like flavors with a smooth and fairly full palate." Note that the recipe changes from year to year. 8.7% alc.

New Holland Pilgrim's Dole ★★★
Barley Wine: New Holland Brewing Co., New Holland, MI www.newhollandbrew.com
"This wheat wine has "pine and grapefruit hoppy aroma at first, but then some dried fruit, prunes or figs " "Flavor is of dried pineapple slices and wheat with a touch of lemon and pear." "Definitely different than a barley wine." 10% alc.

New Holland Red Tulip ★★★
Amber Ale: New Holland Brewing Co., New Holland, MI www.newhollandbrew.com
"Aroma of fresh fruit, tart acids and a bit of strong malt." "Mellow flavors of sweet red malts and fruits mingle here, with faint undertones of pine, raspberry, cherry and orangey citrus." "Mild and unassuming character." 0% alc.

New Holland Sundog ★★1/2
Amber Ale: New Holland Brewing Co., New Holland, MI www.newhollandbrew.com
"Nose of banana orange, biscuits and mild earth and hops." "Flavor is of toasted malt initially, then some hop bitterness." "Nose of banana orange, biscuits and mild earth and hops." N/A % alc.

New Holland The Poet ★★★1/2

Sweet Stout: New Holland Brewing Co., New Holland, MI www.newhollandbrew.com

"Aroma of roasty malt and coffee." "Bitter fore with some very mild roastiness and even milder chocolate notes in the middle and finish." "A concentrated beer, packed with flavor." 6.5% alc.

New Holland Zoomer Wit ★★1/2

Bel. Witbier: New Holland Brewing Co., New Holland, MI www.newhollandbrew.com

"Lots of wheat and spice in the aroma." "Fresh wheat and mild spice and lemon citrus flavors, crisp carbonated mouthfeel, finishes clean and dry, a decent refreshing beer." 5.5% alc.

New Knoxville Indian Pale Ale ★★

IPA: New Knoxville Brewing Co., Knoxville, TN www.newknoxvillebrewery.com

"It's slightly sweet and flowery with a slight bitterness in the nose." "Spicy hops over a malty body." "Gross… like the Cumberland River in a bottle." N/A% alc.

New Knoxville Traditional Pale Ale ★

Eng Pale Ale: New Knoxville Brewing Co., Knoxville, TN www.newknoxvillebrewery.com

"Aroma is floral (very strong) and fruity." "Flavor was yeasty and lemon with a light bitterness." "Finishes with more citrus, light malt and light spiciness." N/A% alc.

New River Pale Ale ★★★★★

Am. Pale Ale: Old Dominion Brewing Co., Ashburn, VA www.olddominion.com

"Nose is very citrusy, grapefruit oranges, with a light caramel malt hidden behind." "Strong caramel and toffee malts balance the thick grapefruit orange floral hops in the mouth." "To the point and extremely good at it." 5.6% alc.

√ **Newcastle Brown Ale** ★★1/2

Brown Ale: Dunston (Scottish & Newcastle), Gateshead, Tyne and Wear, England www.scottish-newcastle.com

"A fruity and very mild brown ale that is an incredibly easy quaffer," Newcastle holds great appeal for many beer lovers but those who dislike it, dislike it a lot, for the same reasons so many like it. 4.7% alc.

Newport Storm '05 ★★★

Am Strong Ale: Coastal Extreme Brewing Co., Middletown, RI

"Cocoa, plum, raisin, fig, bit of soy when cold." "Smooth raspberry flavor starts off, but not overpowering. Turns chocolate-like, earthy and peat-like." "A return to the greatness of their original runs." Changes yearly. 11.7% alc.

Newport Storm Blizzard Porter ★★1/2

Porter: Coastal Extreme Brewing Co., Middletown, RI

"Notes of chocolate and some roastiness in aroma." "Taste is caramel malts, hops and a subtle toasty aftertaste." "A real Porter that is not a stout calling itself a Porter." N/A% alc.

Newport Storm Hurricane Amber ★★

Amber Ale: Coastal Extreme Brewing Co., Middletown, RI

"Aroma is dry, lightly toasty, a bit sour and fairly earthy." "Chalky malts, with notes of powdery chocolate and syrupy caramel." "There's nothing there to make it stand out." N/A% alc.

Newport Storm Maelstrom IPA ★★1/2

IPA: Coastal Extreme Brewing Co., Middletown, RI

"Fruity aroma, lightly hopped with caramel mixed in." "Tastes of light oranges and some grapefruit with light malts." "I found this to be a below average and forgettable Indian Pale Ale." 6.2% alc.

Newport Storm Regenschauer Oktoberfest ★★1/2

Märzen/Oktbfst: Coastal Extreme Brewing Co., Middletown, RI

Nutty, toasted, malty aroma." "Malty and more subdued than most American Oktoberfests." "Like the step-child of a pilsner and an Oktober." 5.5% alc.

Newport Storm Thunderhead Irish Red ★★1/2
Irish Ale: Coastal Extreme Brewing Co., Middletown, RI
"Very toasty, almost roasty maltiness with just a touch of sweetness." "Flavor is well-balanced, with some honey-cream, dry roast and well-extracted malts balancing against an easygoing hops bitterness, that is not too drying." N/A% alc.

Nimbus Brown Ale ★★★1/2
Brown Ale: Nimbus Brewing Co., Tucson, AZ www.nimbusbeer.com
A light brown ale. "Tastes of caramel, nuts, roasted malts, light chocolate and a very light coffee finish." Some find it a bit watery, but overall this is a highly regarded example of the style. 5% alc.

Nimbus Oatmeal Stout ★★★★1/2
Sweet Stout: Nimbus Brewing Co., Tucson, AZ www.nimbusbeer.com
"Aromas of chocolate and coffee blend together with caramel over roasted malts." "Refreshing, modest gravity stout." "Sweet with slight hop bitterness in the finish." "Impressive!" 6% alc.

Nimbus Palo Verde ★★1/2
Am. Pale Ale: Nimbus Brewing Co., Tucson, AZ www.nimbusbeer.com
American-style, with Cascade and Columbus hops. "Citrus/hop notes dominate the aroma." "Flavor is quite bitter for the style, border-line IPA." "Fresher, richer and bigger than Sierra Nevada Pale Ale." 5.5% alc.

Noël du Baladin ★★1/2
Bel. Strong Ale: Le Baladin Birreria, Piozzo, Italy www.birreria.com
"Aroma of lavender, pears and spices." "It's got a spiced up, sweet malt taste, yeast, with sour grapes." "Interesting concept for a Christmas ale." 9% alc.

North Coast Blue Star ★★★
Am. Wheat: North Coast Brewing Co., Fort Bragg, CA www.northcoastbrewing.com
"Nose of light Christmassy pine tree-smelling hops." "Light and sweet on the tongue with some citrus and spiciness in the flavor." "Good for a hot day, but not a standout." 4.5% alc.

North Coast Brother Thelonious ★★★1/2
Belgian Strong Ale: North Coast Brewing Co., Fort Bragg, CA www.northcoastbrewing.com
"Aroma is spices, caramel, banana, light spices." "Great full-bodied flavor with notes of chocolate, fruit, aramel maltiness and spices." 9% alc.

North Coast Old No. 38 Stout ★★★1/2
Dry Stout: North Coast Brewing Co., Fort Bragg, CA www.northcoastbrewing.com
"Just looking into the dark abyss of this beer, you know you are in for something good." "Sweet, roasty aroma with tingly hops around the edges." "Fabulous flavor of hops, dark roasted malt, coffee, chocolate and caramel." 5.6% alc.

North Coast Old Rasputin ★★★★★
Imp. Stout: North Coast Brewing Co., Fort Bragg, CA www.northcoastbrewing.com
"A bitter chocolaty Imperial Stout that is not unlike "mixing brandy, malted milk and espresso." "Creamy and rich." "Surprisingly hoppy." "Finish is a little strong, but we all like a good kick in the face, right?" 8.9% alc.

North Coast Old Stock ★★★★★
Barley Wine: North Coast Brewing Co., Fort Bragg, CA www.northcoastbrewing.com
A "fireside ale," "very thick on the palate" with a "malty sweet flavor with fruit and bread notes." "I think it has some really great potential if left for another couple of years..." 11.4% alc.

North Coast PranQster ★★★
Bel. Strong Ale: North Coast Brewing Co., Fort Bragg, CA www.northcoastbrewing.com
A strong golden ale in the style of the Belgian classic, Duvel. "Musty Belgian yeast, cloves, floral hops and a nice spice blend" in the aroma, "creamy and smooth" palate and "bubblegum, clove, candi sugar and other Belgian flavors." 7.6% alc.

North Coast Red Seal ★★★★1/2
Amber Ale: North Coast Brewing Co., Fort Bragg, CA www.northcoastbrewing.com
Golden-amber color. "Hop aroma and flavor - toasty, woody, with hints of multigrain bread and caramel." "I am not usually an amber fan, but this one has some class." 5.5% alc.

North Coast Scrimshaw ★★★
Pilsner: North Coast Brewing Co., Fort Bragg, CA www.northcoastbrewing.com
"While this rises above the average offering of the style, its not high enough to be remarkable." The character of this pils is of "biscuit malt, yeast, fruity hops, sweetness and something very spicy and tea-like." 4.4% alc.

Nutfield Auburn Ale ★★
Irish Ale: Nutfield Brewing Co., Derry, NH www.nutfield.com
"Nutty with a hint of caramel that intensifies in the finish." "Hops are understated and slightly bitter and earthy." "Flavor left quickly, with nothing great going on." 4.6% alc.

Nutfield Black 47 Stout ★★1/2
Dry Stout: Nutfield Brewing Co., Derry, NH www.nutfield.com
"Aroma of roast and burnt malts with a bitter coffee." "Nice roasted malt flavor with strong flavor of coffee and bitter chocolate." "One sip and I know this beer is way underrated." 4.1% alc.

Nutfield Old Man Ale ★★
Am. Pale Ale: Nutfield Brewing Co., Derry, NH www.nutfield.com
"Citrus, floral aroma with hops, elder and also some toffee notes. " "Ach, no complexity whatsoever, just a dry caramellish malt, with some orange flavoring." 5% alc.

O'Doul's ★
Low Alcohol: Anheuser-Busch Companies, St. Louis, MO www.anheuser-busch.com
"This is corn and water. No malt or hops. Just empty flavor." "Can I give this negative flavor points?" "I'll stick with the with alcohol varieties." 0.4% alc.

O'Doul's Amber ★★1/2
Low Alcohol: Anheuser-Busch Companies, St. Louis, MO www.anheuser-busch.com
"Malty aroma, light sweet caramel." "Sweet caramel with toasted malt and a tiny bit of bitterness." "Aside from the low alcohol, this is a complete beer." 0.4% alc.

O'Fallon Blackberry Scottish ★★1/2
Fruit Beer: o'Fallon Brewery, O'Fallon, MO www.ofallonbrewery.com
"Smell is real fruity, full of berries, hint of chocolate." "Roasted and toasted malts form a pleasurable body, accompanied by level-headed sweetness and well-integrated fruit." "Nothing spectacular, but an interesting idea nonetheless." N/A% alc.

O'Fallon Cherry Chocolate ★★
Fruit Beer: O'Fallon Brewery, O'Fallon, MO www.ofallonbrewery.com
It smells like cheapo department store chocolates with a hint of cherries." "Like a chocolate covered cherry candy." "This beats out Yoo-Hoo for the title of "thinnest body for a chocolate drink ever" title." 5.7% alc.

O'Fallon Gold ★★1/2
Goldn/Blond Ale: O'Fallon Brewery, O'Fallon, MO www.ofallonbrewery.com
"Aroma has a soapy European Saaz hoppiness and a lightly sugary maltiness." "Taste is rich and bready with some light pears and some very light clove." "Laid back." 4.9% alc.

O'Fallon Happy Holidaze ★★
Spice/Herb: O'Fallon Brewery, O'Fallon, MO www.ofallonbrewery.com
"Chocolate and peppermint aromas, candy cane and mint chocolate flavors." "Light sugary gingerbread flavor, turning more cinnamon and nutmeg spicy with a clean mint finish and hints of dark chocolate." 5.3% alc.

O'Fallon Pumpkin Ale ★★1/2

Spice/Herb: O'Fallon Brewery, O'Fallon, MO www.ofallonbrewery.com

"Solid aroma of cloves and cinnamon." "Tastes are a little of pumpkin, apple, spices (cinnamon, nutmeg, cloves) and malts." "Worth trying once." 5.5% alc.

O'Fallon Smoked Porter ★★★

Smoked: o'Fallon Brewery, O'Fallon, MO www.ofallonbrewery.com

"A pleasant campfire smell when opened, with creosote and a touch of mesquite." "Flavor is rounded between the dimensions of smoke, roast and general porter characteristics." 6% alc.

O'Fallon Wheach ★★★★

Fruit Beer: O'Fallon Brewery, O'Fallon, MO www.ofallonbrewery.com

"Fragrant aroma of peaches and yeast." "The peach aroma and flavor are present, but not obnoxious." "Wheat ale base was quite evident and kept things beery." N/A% alc.

O'Hanlon's Organic Rye ★★1/2

Ale: O'Hanlons, Whimple, Devon, England www.ohanlons.co.uk

"Aroma is fruity, sweet and spicy - kind of like a peppered caramel covered apple." "Taste is grainy and malty with light spice, more floral hops, light herbal notes, some earthiness and minute sweetness." 4.5% alc.

O'Hanlon's Wheat Beer ★★★★

Am. Wheat: O'Hanlons, Whimple, Devon, England www.ohanlons.co.uk

"Unique, bursting with herbal hoppiness, yeasty fruitiness and quenching wheaty acidity." "Taste is wheaty and yeasty with lots of earthy hops and fruits. There is lesser berries, more citrus, light melon and banana." 4% alc.

Oak Creek Amber ★

Amber Ale: Oak Creek Brewing Co., Sedona, AZ www.oakcreekbrew.com

"Pleasant mix of sweet malt, floral hops and some bitter hops." The flavor is light, with caramel notes. "There really needs to be more of something, be it malt or hops, to make this beer interesting." 5.5% alc.

Oak Creek Nut Brown ★★

Brown Ale: Oak Creek Brewing Co., Sedona, AZ www.oakcreekbrew.com

Deep brown color. "Alarmingly odorless." Some nutty flavor, "roasty but thin and light." "Hardly any hops." "I would pass on this one if offered again." 6% alc.

Oak Pond Nut Brown ★★★

Brown Ale: Oak Pond Brewery, Skowhegan, ME

"Smells of nutty sweet malt." "Hazelnut, a bit of vanilla, coffee predominate. " "I really enjoy the maltiness of this brew." "Satisfying rich mouthfeel, creamy smooth." 4.5% alc.

Oaken Barrel Gnaw Bone Pale Ale ★★

Am. Pale Ale: Oaken Barrel Brewing Co., Greenwood, IN www.oakenbarrel.com

"Dry-hopped, typically citrusy/floral Cascade approach." "A bit on the weak side hop wise for a pale ale, the malts were stronger than expected." "Good to balance with some food." 5.5% alc.

Oaken Barrel Indiana Amber ★★

Amber Ale: Oaken Barrel Brewing Co., Greenwood, IN www.oakenbarrel.com

"Aroma is malty, but not distinctive from most ambers." "Just enough hop to balance the sweetness." "It almost seems like an average of all other ales." 5.5% alc.

Oaken Barrel Razz Wheat ★★

Fruit Beer: Oaken Barrel Brewing Co., Greenwood, IN www.oakenbarrel.com

"Obvious berry aroma, wheat aroma as well." "Tastes of lightly tart raspberries with some light wheat." "Light body, some crispness." 5% alc.

OB Lager ★
Pale Lager: Oriental Brewery (InBev), S Korea www.inbev.com
"typically watery Korean lager, with a slight sour edge." "Nothing especially wrong with it, which I guess counts for something, but there isn't a whole lot right with it either." 4.5% alc.

Oberdorfer Weissbier ★★1/2
Hefeweizen: Allgäuer Brauhaus AG , Kempten, Germany www.allgaeuer-brauhaus.de
"Aroma is like Wheaties with lemon juice, a lot more citric than most of the Hefeweizens that I've had to date." "Flavor is soft malts, wheat, lemon juice and lemon zest and a touch of bubblegum." "It's OK but really not worth the effort to try this one." 4.9% alc.

Oberdorfer Weissbier Dunkel ★★
Dunkelweizen: Allgäuer Brauhaus AG , Kempten, Germany www.allgaeuer-brauhaus.de
"Big on the spices, largely clove and vanilla, zesty, uplifting, some earthy tones and notes of fruit, but quiet." "Flavors of dough with some fruit sweetness-mostly banana." "A bit heavy for my taste, but not bad at all." 4.8% alc.

Obolon Lager ★★★
Pale Lager: Obolon, Kiev, Ukraine www.obolon.kiev.ua
"Clean, sour malt and hops aroma with an underlying hint of honey." "Sugary and sweet flavor with a hint of bitterness at the end." "Reminds me a lot of a typical German pilsner." 5.2% alc.

Obolon Magnat ★★1/2
Pale Lager: Obolon, Kiev, Ukraine www.obolon.kiev.ua
"Aroma has corn and hops and is a touch metallic." "Classic European pale lager palate with mild grassy hop notes and a dry finish." "I like this style of lager but there is nothing special about this one." 5.3% alc.

Obolon Premium ★★1/2
Pale Lager: Obolon, Kiev, Ukraine www.obolon.kiev.ua
"Hints of sulfur give way to some herbally/grassy smells with a touch of grain." "Sour barley malt flavor with a light hops finish." "Another import that shouldn't be shipped halfway around the world in green bottles." 5.2% alc.

Odell 5 Barrel Pale Ale ★★1/2
Eng Pale Ale: Odell Brewing Co., Fort Collins, CO www.odells.com
Filtered through a bed of hops, 5 Barrel has a "floral aroma with strong notes of oranges." "Pleasantly hoppy, but less crisp than some of the best APAs and also less bitter than many examples of the style." 5.2% alc.

Odell 90 Shilling ★★★
Scottish Ale: Odell Brewing Co., Fort Collins, CO www.odells.com
"Light peaty aroma with clean notes of caramel and oranges." "Lightly hoppy fore followed by some sweet malt and a mellow sweet toffee finish." 5.3% alc.

Odell Curmudgeon's Nip ★★1/2
Barley Wine: Odell Brewing Co., Fort Collins, CO www.odells.com
"Very malty and slightly plummy aroma." "Taste starts quite sweet and fruity with bready background." "More toward the British style of barleywine." 7.9% alc.

Odell Cutthroat Porter ★★★1/2
Porter: Odell Brewing Co., Fort Collins, CO www.odells.com
"Aroma is sweet and very roasted combined with notes of chocolate." "Bittersweet chocolate, mild tartness and floral and bitter hop notes in the flavor." "I'm impressed that a 4.5% (alcohol) beer can taste of this much." 4.5% alc.

Odell Easy Street Wheat ★★★
Am. Wheat: Odell Brewing Co., Fort Collins, CO www.odells.com
"Has the aroma of citrus and wheat." "Tart, citrus, slightly floral, tingly mouthfeel. Refreshing without being weak." "Thin body and over-carbonation hurt this one." 4.7% alc.

Odell Isolation Ale ★★1/2
Eng. Strong Ale: Odell Brewing Co., Fort Collins, CO www.odells.com
"Aroma is chocolate malts with a nice hop tingle." "A swift hoppy cameo, then supported by hearty malt, brimming with sweet, yet dark fruit." "I don't feel like going out and hugging the Salvation Army guy, but I do feel better." 6% alc.

Offshore Amber Ale ★★
Amber Ale: Offshore Ale Co., Oak Bluffs, MA www.offshoreale.com
"Lightly malty nose, bready and lightly spicy." "Taste is caramel malt and hazelnuts with a slight hop bite at the finish." "Light bodied and cheery, light finish, very breezy, but enjoyable." 5% alc.

O'Hanlons Original Port Stout ★★1/2
Stout: O'Hanlons Brewing Co., Whimple, Devon, England www.ohanlons.co.uk
"Aroma of port, roast barley, nuts, black cherries." "Rich flavors of darkly roasted malt, charred cedar, ash and sweet plummy port." "Rather thin in the body, but full of flavor and absolutely delicious." 4.8% alc.

Okhota (Oxota) Krepkoe ★★★★
Malt Liquor: Bochkarev Brewery (Heineken), St. Petersburg, Russia www.bochkarev.ru
"Strong aroma of grassy hops and alcohol." "Some sweet grains make it slightly better than an average malt liquor." "I'm afraid half the contents will be introduced to my plumbing." 8.5% alc.

Okhota (Oxota) Svetloe ★★★
Pale Lager: Bochkarev Brewery (Heineken), St. Petersburg, Russia www.bochkarev.ru
"Aroma is sweet, grassy and a touch skunky." "Slight grass and straw along with bread dough and sweet buttery notes." "The bottom line is: really not a bad lager, there's no glaring faults at any rate." 4.5% alc.

Okocim Jasne Pelne ★★
Pilsner: Browar Okocim S.A (Carlsberg), Warszawa, Poland www.okocim.com.pl
"Fresh, herbal aroma with a mellow skunkiness to it." "Breadish malty beginning with some orange fruitiness and a short, sweet finish with a faint bitterness." "No great excitement but decent enough." 5.7% alc.

Okocim Mocne ★★1/2
Eur Str Lager: Browar Okocim S.A (Carlsberg), Warszawa, Poland www.okocim.com.pl
"A definite sharp fruit character is present in the aroma and the alcohol is apparent, too." "Caramel in the taste as well as a touch of honey, green apples and pepper." "One of the best European Strong Lagers." 7.1% alc.

Okocim OK Beer ★★★
Pale Lager: Browar Okocim S.A (Carlsberg), Warszawa, Poland www.okocim.com.pl
"Mild aroma, sweet with some grassiness." "Flavor is corn and grass." "More hops could make this good." "Slightly bolder than its American counterparts so slightly better." 5.7% alc.

Okocim Porter ★★★1/2
Baltic Porter: Browar Okocim S.A (Carlsberg), Warszawa, POLAND www.okocim.com.pl
Some find it "nauseatingly sweet", but most beer lovers are fans. "Good roasted smell, with some plums and a little coffee and chocolate." "Roasted malts, coffee and chocolate stand out at first, followed by dark fruits." "Gem of a Baltic Porter." 8.3% alc.

Old German Premium Lager ★
Pale Lager: Pittsburgh Brewing Co., Pittsburgh, PA www.pittsburghbrewingco.com
"Aroma was malty, hoppy and sweet." "Malty, sweet flavor." "Bought a case of 12-oz. cans, mainly as a joke. Got what I paid for." N/A% alc.

Old Milwaukee ★
Pale Lager: Miller Brewing Co. (SABMiller), Milwaukee, WI www.millerbrewing.com
"Slight aromas of hops and uncooked rice." "Taste is not horrific, just boring: flat, lifeless corn-grain, quick off the tongue." "On closer inspection, one could trace hints of car exhaust and a pickle smoothie. Mmm mmmm good!" 4.9% alc.

Old Milwaukee Light ★
Pale Lager: Miller Brewing Co. (SABMiller), Milwaukee, WI www.millerbrewing.com
"Faint traces of my sock drawer showed up in the aroma and, surprisingly, I got a nice hint of three-week old, rotten meatloaf in the flavor." "A masterpiece of corn and ethanol." 3.9% alc.

Olde Burnside Ten Penny Ale ★★★★
Scottish Ale: Olde Burnside Brewing Co., East Hartford, CT www.oldeburnsidebrewing.com
"Flavor has caramel, citrus, piney and floral hops." "Before you know it, you've downed four of these and you actually believe the waitress when she tells you she's heading to the club across the street when she gets off work." N/A% alc.

Olde English 800 ★
Malt Liquor: Miller Brewing Co. (SABMiller), Milwaukee, WI www.millerbrewing.com
Sharp, solvent-like flavors, "grassy and so much dimethyl sulfide it's more like vomit than corn." "This beer is like a guy with eight different diseases." "I'd rather cap myself gangsta-style than drink another bottle." 5.9% alc.

Olde English HG800 ★
Malt Liquor: Miller Brewing Co. (SABMiller), Milwaukee, WI www.millerbrewing.com
"Smells like bananas, grains, eggs, diapers (clean) and a hamster cage." "Sort of honey sweet with a light bitterness and acidity." 8% alc.

Olde Saratoga Premium Lager ★★★★1/2
Märzen/Oktbfst: Olde Saratoga Brewing (Mendocino Brewing Co.), Saratoga Springs, NY www.oldesaratogabrew.com
"Doughy aroma, some very light hops." "Tastes of toffee, caramel and some citrus." "Underrated." 6% alc.

Olde Towne Amber ★
Amber Ale: Olde Towne Brewing Co., Huntsville, AL www.oldetownebeer.com
"Dark amber ale that has, sadly, not met with the favor of beer lovers. "An odd, husky, raw, beginner-homebrew-like beer that, shall we say, needs more work." "Ass in a glass." 4.6% alc.

Olde Towne Extra Pale ★
Am. Pale Ale: Olde Towne Brewing Co., Huntsville, AL www.oldetownebeer.com
"I've never smelled beans in the aroma; that's a new one for me." "Sulfury, vegetal flavor is unappealing." That said, "apparently the earlier runnings were problematic, but the latest stuff has improved." 3.8% alc.

Olde Towne Pale Ale ★
Am. Pale Ale: Olde Towne Brewing Co., Huntsville, AL www.oldetownebeer.com
"Flavor profile of nicely balanced caramel malt sweetness underlaying a lightly bitter citrus hops is very refreshing." "As the brew warms, the grapefruit comes through." "Finishes weakly." 5% alc.

Olympia ★
Pale Lager: Pabst Brewing Co., Chicago, IL www.pabst.com
"Aromas of sweet malt and corn." "It's simply water with weak hops, straw, rice and rotten malt thrown together haphazardly for mass distribution to broke college kids and old men." Contract brewed by Miller. 4.8% alc.

Ommegang ★★★★★
Bel. Strong Ale: Brewery Ommegang (Moortgat), Cooperstown, NY www.ommegang.com
"Rich with sweet notes of fig and cherry followed by drier tones of butterscotch and toffee." "Very vinous flavor, which starts to mingle with some chocolate as it warms." 8.5% alc.

Ommegang Hennepin ★★★★1/2

Saison: Brewery Ommegang (Moortgat), Cooperstown, NY www.ommegang.com

"Aroma is tart; lemon zest, yeast, white pepper, mild hops." "Flavor came with oranges, flowers, clove and banana." "The spice, malts and earthy hop undertones blend seamlessly together - a perfect autumn quaffer." 7.5% alc.

Ommegang Rare Vos ★★★★

Belgian Ale: Brewery Ommegang (Moortgat), Cooperstown, NY www.ommegang.com

"Has aroma of fruits, caramel, spices and bubble-gum." "Flavor is slightly sweet (orange/apple?) with a smattering of spices, clove in particular." "Another solid beer from Ommegang." 6.5% alc.

Ommegang Three Philosophers ★★★★★

Abt/Quadrupel: Brewery Ommegang (Moortgat), Cooperstown, NY www.ommegang.com

"Dulled, woody cherries, toffee and chocolate in the aroma. Bit of a yeasty, candi sugar kick at the end." "It manages to walk that difficult line of carbonation, strong malt, powerful alcohol and hop finish in a careless way." 9.8% alc.

Ommegang Witte ★★★1/2

Bel. Witbier: Brewery Ommegang (Moortgat), Cooperstown, NY www.ommegang.com

"Aroma of pale malts, marshmallows, a little bit of yeast." "Flavor is of very spicy wheat, cloves, yeast and an alcoholic finish." "If you like clove flavor, this would be a good choice." 5.1% alc.

Oranjeboom ★★1/2

Pale Lager: InBev, Dommelen, Netherlands www.inbev.com

"Malty nose with a nice hop balance." "Corn, cereal, grainy taste, light malts and mild hop bite." "Unbelievably average." Acquired by InBev in 1995, brewery closed in 2003. 5% alc.

Orion Premium Draft ★★1/2

Pale Lager: Orion Breweries Limited, Urasoe-City, Okinawa, Japan www.orionbeer.co.jp

"Grassy noble hop aroma." "Typical pale lager flavor that is not meant for much description." "Not stellar, but far from objectionable." N/A% alc.

Orkney Dark Island ★★★

Old Ale: Orkney (Highlands and Islands Breweries), Stromness, Orkney Islands, Scotland www.orkneybrewery.co.uk

"Very smoky, oily and peaty." "Malty, toffeeish, smoky, whiskeyish palate." "Very surprising and interesting." "Malty session beer with abundant flavor." 4.6% alc.

Orkney Dragonhead Stout ★★1/2

Stout: Orkney (Highlands and Islands Breweries), Stromness, Orkney Islands, Scotland www.orkneybrewery.co.uk

"Dark sweet roasted caramel and chocolate malt and oat (meal, cookie) aroma." "Coffee, dark chocolate are accentuated but some hops are revealed along with the dry finish." "A good British style stout; decent flavor without a huge palate makes it drinkable." 4% alc.

Orkney Red MacGregor ★★★1/2

Bitter: Orkney (Highlands and Islands Breweries), Stromness, Orkney Islands, Scotland www.orkneybrewery.co.uk

Aroma like a dense forest of Douglas fir, meat pie and Auchentoshan (single-malt whiskey)." "Malty flavor, light caramel sweetness and a herbal hoppy finish." "Reminds me of Irish Red Ales, but not as full-bodied or malty." 4% alc.

Orkney Skullsplitter ★★★1/2

Barley Wine: Orkney (Highlands and Islands Breweries), Stromness, Orkney Islands, Scotland www.orkneybrewery.co.uk

"Has aroma of smoke, fruit and sweet malts." "Raisiny sweet but still bitter with chocolate and coffee." "The beer world's answer to Highland Park." 8.5% alc.

Orval ★★★★★
Belgian Ale: Brasserie d'Orval, Florenville - Villers-d.-Orval, Belgium www.orval.be
"The room fills with perfume, medicine, noble hops, tangerines, horseblanket." "Ample doses of malt, hops, yeast, brett, alcohol; challenging yet comforting; Orval is beer." 6.2% alc.

Oskar Blues Dale's Pale ★★★★★
Am. Pale Ale: Oskar Blues Grill and Brew, Lyons, CO www.oskarblues.com
"Resiny, woody c-hops in the aroma with crystal malts and a hint of florals." "Bountiful flavors and a dry, resinous bitterness." "It's about as big as a Pale Ale can get and still be a pale ale." 6.5% alc.

Oskar Blues Old Chub ★★★★
Scotch Ale: Oskar Blues Grill and Brew, Lyons, CO www.oskarblues.com
"Malty, slightly smoky aroma." "Sweet, malty, vinous and fruity with a roasty finish." "Velvety texture." "Nicest beer out of a can I've had." 8% alc.

Otter Creek Alpine Ale ★★1/2
Amber Ale: Otter Creek Brewing, Middlebury, VT www.ottercreekbrewing.com
"Rich malt aroma, slightly nutty and earthy hops - with a touch of the floral." "Palate is slightly sweet and nutty with an earthy hop bitterness." "Reminds me of what would have been considered a heavy hitter eight to 10 years ago." 5.9% alc.

Otter Creek Copper Ale ★★
Altbier: Otter Creek Brewing, Middlebury, VT www.ottercreekbrewing.com
"Bready, toasty and somewhat sweet." "Malty, mildly spicy with nutmeg and a metallic note." "Suggestions of coffee toward the end which I like." "Uninspiring C+ Altbier." 5.4% alc.

Otter Creek Middleberry Ale ★★
Fruit Beer: Otter Creek Brewing, Middlebury, VT www.ottercreekbrewing.com
"Nose is perfumey sweetness with a combination of jam like aromas - blueberries, blackberries, even strawberry." "The flavor isn't quite as sweet as you'd expect, but rather kinda earthy." 4.9% alc.

Otter Creek Mud Bock Spring Ale ★★★1/2
Bock: Otter Creek Brewing, Middlebury, VT www.ottercreekbrewing.com
"Some coffee notes and a very dominant malt character." "Malty with some herbal hoppy bitterness. Light notes of toffee and molasses. Slight hop spice in the finish." "Yum, yum... I like it, I like it!" 5.7% alc.

Otter Creek Oktoberfest ★
Märzen/Oktbfst: Otter Creek Brewing, Middlebury, VT www.ottercreekbrewing.com
"Aroma is caramel and some fall leaves." "Starts off nice with notes of toasted malt, caramel, grassy hops and then it just takes a nosedive and fades into watery tastelessness." "Like a mix of an Oktoberfest with an ale." 4.8% alc.

Otter Creek Otter Summer Ale ★★
Am. Wheat: Otter Creek Brewing, Middlebury, VT www.ottercreekbrewing.com
"A little wheaty and a little lemony aroma." "Flavor has notes of lemon/citrus, grain and grass with a touch of hop bitterness sneaking in at the end." "At least it wasn't disgusting." 4.9% alc.

Otter Creek Otterbahn ★★★
Weizen Bock: Otter Creek Brewing, Middlebury, NH www.ottercreekbrewing.com
Roasty, nutty, slightly smoky aroma with pleasant banana yeastiness. "Kinda bold malt character, heading toward beef stock flavors, slightly salty." "They almost got this one right." 8% alc.

Otter Creek Pale Ale ★★1/2
Am. Pale Ale: Otter Creek Brewing, Middlebury, VT www.ottercreekbrewing.com
"Littered with tons of Cascade hops." "Flavor is grapefruity, with a touch of sweet caramel and a bitter finish." "Decent, but not great." 4.6% alc.

Otter Creek Stovepipe Porter ★★★
Porter: Otter Creek Brewing, Middlebury, VT www.ottercreekbrewing.com
"Deep dark chocolate and coffee, caramel malt aroma like fresh brewed coffee and malted milk balls, Whoppers." "Dark chocolate, nuttiness and mild coffee a but overshadowed by the hops." 5.4% alc.

Otter Creek Vermont Lager ★★1/2
Premium Lager: Otter Creek Brewing, Middlebury, VT www.ottercreekbrewing.com
"Flavor had plenty of malt that nicely balanced the hefty hop hit." "Malty sweet aroma." "This would make a great summer brew, ball game, hammock and some of these, fresh cut grass..." 5% alc.

Oud Beersel Oude Geuze ★★★★★
Gueuze: Brouwerij F. Boon, Lembeek , Belgium
"Lemony, barnyard, leather, stale hay." "Complex, shifting taste: tart, sour, grapefruit, bleu cheese just for starters." "Truly the brewer's art on full display in these magnificent beers." 6% alc.

Oud Beersel Oude Kriek ★★★★★
Fruit Lambic: Brouwerij F. Boon, Lembeek , Belgium
Aromas of sour cherries, lemon and some musty barnyard." "Excellent flavor of sour cherries with mild cheese and a good dose of acidity." "Just an outrageous beer all around." 6.5% alc.

Pabst Blue Ribbon ★
Pale Lager: Pabst Brewing Co., Chicago, IL www.pabst.com
"Taste is, well, like a thin, watery, burningly fizzy sour grainy near-beer made with rice alcohol and pond water." "There's something about drinking a 24-oz. can with a straw from a paper bag that just makes you feel gloriously like a bum." 5% alc.

Pabst NA ★
Low Alcohol: Miller Brewing Co. (SABMiller), Chicago, IL www.pabst.com
"Smells absolutely awful, rotting vegetables, festering bread and regurgitated corn." "Fizzy feel with corn syrup and light beer flavors." "Tastes like papier maché. I find that extremely unfortunate." 0.5% alc.

Paceña ★
Pale Lager: Cervecería Boliviana Nacional (Quilmes), La Paz, Bolivia
"Nose is slightly grassy, bready and has a hint of buttered biscuit." "Rather a weak and slightly bitter finish." "Not nearly as dreadful as I thought it would be." 5.2% alc.

Pacifico Clara ★★1/2
Pale Lager: Grupo Modelo (Corona), México DF, Mexico www.gmodelo.com
"Rather cardboardy dead malt with some sharp citrus." "Flavors of moderate hops, some malt, corn and herbs." "Of all the really light tasting Mexican beers, I think this one's the best." 4.5% alc.

Palisade Red Truck IPA ★★★1/2
IPA: Palisade Brewery, Palisade, CO www.palisadebrewery.com
"Aroma of floral and citrus hops (grapefruit) and light pine needles." "Raw, cutting, glorious and copious amount of hops completely takeover this brew." "Damn, what a beer!" 0% alc.

Palma Louca ★
Pilsner: Kaiser (Brasil) (MolsonCoors), Diviaopolis - MG, Brazil www.kaiser.com.br
"Very watery and very thin." "Semi-sweet aroma of wheat, grains, lemons and yeast." "I think this was the first Brazilian beer that I've had but it didn't make me want to run out and find any others." 4.6% alc.

Palmetto Amber Ale ★★★
Amber Ale: Palmetto Brewing Co., Charleston, SC
"Some nice grapefruit and floral notes bite at the tongue. Underneath is a fair amount of caramel sweetness." "Clean finish, subtle malts, very minor charred wood." "Awfully righteous for what it is." N/A% alc.

Palmetto Charleston Lager ★★★★
Premium Lager: Palmetto Brewing Co., Charleston, SC
"Slight crisp hop and lemon character." "Very smooth and less grainy than many lagers." "Just a solid example to an American lager." N/A% alc.

Palmetto Pale Ale ★★1/2
Am. Pale Ale: Palmetto Brewing Co., Charleston, SC
"Caramel and mild grapefruit aroma." "At least if it's not going to be very hoppy, it does have a nice malt backbone." "Pretty much an average micro." N/A% alc.

Palmetto Porter ★★★★1/2
Porter: Palmetto Brewing Co., Charleston, SC
"Aroma is of chocolate, caramel and roasted malts." "Flavor contains a deep, rich, dark fruit and some dry chocolate, coffee and sweet caramel." "This is delicious and I'm glad I bought the six-pack!" N/A% alc.

Panil Barriquée (Sour) ★★★★★
Flem Sour Ale: Panil Birra Artigianale, Torrechiara-Parma, Italy www.panilbeer.com
"Sour cherry and wood aroma, some mild funky yeasty notes." "Strong, acidic, woody, tart, vinous flavor up front is mellowed by vanilla notes with strong underlying malt body." "Tremendous in all regards." 8% alc.

Panther Ice Ale ★★1/2
Malt Liquor: Gluek Brewing Co., Cold Spring, MN www.gluek.com
"Sweet corn and wet straw notes are most prevalent underneath the alcohol." "A little oily, like olive juice." "For the next few hours, any burping was an horrendous experience." 7.5% alc.

Paper City Cabot Street Summer Wheat ★
Am. Wheat: Paper City Brewery, Holyoke, MA www.papercity.com
"Sour aroma with banana and lemon notes in the nose." "Sweet malt flavor with subdued fruit esters." "Unspectacular American Wheat with hints of clove spiciness." 0% alc.

Paper City Denogginator ★★★
Doppelbock: Paper City Brewery, Holyoke, MA www.papercity.com
"Aroma of alcohol, toasted malt and mild hops." "Semi-sweet on the tongue, very malty, peaty, with a slight sour twang." "Slightly syrupy body. Moderately sweet finish." 8% alc.

Paper City Holyoke Dam ★★1/2
Eng Pale Ale: Paper City Brewery, Holyoke, MA www.papercity.com
"Soft nose, slight biscuity malt, subtle yet sharp hop presence." "Seems a bit more aggressive than your average English Pale." "Exhibits some characteristics of an Amber ale." N/A% alc.

Paper City Hop Monster ★★1/2
Imp/Dbl IPA: Paper City Brewery, Holyoke, MA www.papercity.com
"Very resiny hop nose, subtle pine." "It's like drinking liquid hops, but not in a good way." "Palate is both crisp and slick going down with a nice bit of tangy tartness around the mouth." 8.5% alc.

Paper City Indian Pale Ale ★★
IPA: Paper City Brewery, Holyoke, MA www.papercity.com
"Nose of resiny hop, apricots and faint butterscotch." "Taste is earthy malt and very low hops. I wouldn't even think this was an IPA." "Very easy drinking beer. Seems much more English than Pacific Northwest." N/A% alc.

Paper City Ireland Parish Golden Ale ★★★
Goldn/Blond Ale: Paper City Brewery, Holyoke, MA www.papercity.com
Aroma "is balanced a bit toward the musty hops, but is grainy, lightly sweet and perhaps just a bit caramelly." "Tastes a bit of sourdough, quite bready and grainy, ample pale malt." N/A% alc.

Paper City Riley's Stout ★★1/2
Dry Stout: Paper City Brewery, Holyoke, MA www.papercity.com
"Mixes roasty stout notes with reasonable fruity hops." "Very light on the palate." "Never really gains enough balance." "Not bad. Run of the mill." N/A% alc.

Paper City Smoked Porter ★★1/2
Smoked: Paper City Brewery, Holyoke, MA www.papercity.com
"Tangy smoked meat, roasted wood and fresh crushed malt aroma." "Whispers of anise pave the way for a rich roasted malt, unsweetened chocolate foundation." "Good, but too much roast and not enough smoke." N/A% alc.

Paper City Winter Palace Wee Heavy ★★1/2
Scotch Ale: Paper City Brewery, Holyoke, MA www.papercity.com
"Malty aroma with a slight hint of smokiness." "Sweet flavors, Chocolate, caramel, coffee/espresso with a little spruce." "Quite drinkable and no major problems." N/A% alc.

Park City Tie Die Red ★★★
Amber Ale: Moab Brewery, Moab, UT themoabbrewery.com
"Very toasty, slightly smoky aroma." "Flavor is initially roasted with some chocolate malt hints and some bitter hops." "Pretty well balanced but just an average amber ale." 4.5% alc.

Paulaner Hefeweissbier ★★★★★
Hefeweizen: Paulaner Brauerei, Münich, Germany www.paulaner.de
"Smells of citrus and honey maybe some banana in there too." "Light flavor with a refreshing hint of banana in the background." "All the elements are there, not very assertive though." 5.6% alc.

Paulaner Hefeweissbier Dunkel ★★★1/2
Dunkelweizen: Paulaner Brauerei, Münich, Germany www.paulaner.de
"Aroma of banana, toast, milk chocolate, brown sugar." "Sweet palate shows a slightly nutmeggy banana flavor with bready notes and sweaty yeast." "A light, easily drinkable, quite refreshing and balanced Dunkelweizen." 5.3% alc.

Paulaner Oktoberfest ★★★1/2
Märzen/Oktbfst: Paulaner Brauerei, Münich, Germany www.paulaner.de
Nose "of rising dough, bready cracker malts with a slightly metallic yeasty note." "Sweet malty flavor feels full and smooth, balanced out with a light hop bitterness." "This beer does indeed symbolize Oktoberfest to me." 6% alc.

Paulaner Original Münchner Hell ★★★1/2
Premium Lager: Paulaner Brauerei , Münich, Germany www.paulaner.de
"Buttery biscuits and earthy hops aroma." "Clean palate with slightly crisp hops backing up simple bready pale malts." "Has that old world flavor." 4.9% alc.

Paulaner Premium Pils ★★★
Classic Ger Pils: Paulaner Brauerei , Münich, Germany www.paulaner.de
"Aroma of grassy hops, spring water, light pale grains and a touch of honey and crisp yeast." "Some peppery flavors as well as a light and fruity peach." "Much more bitter than most German Pils." 4.9% alc.

Paulaner Salvator ★★★★
Doppelbock: Paulaner Brauerei, Münich, Germany www.paulaner.de
"Sweet malty aroma with molasses, marmalade and earthy undertones." "Flavor is also rather alcoholic, malty sweet with plenty of caramel and molasses, a herbal spiciness and moderate hops in the finish." "Definitely a blood warmer." 7.5% alc.

Pauwel Kwak ★★★1/2
Bel. Strong Ale: Brouwerij Bosteels, Buggenhout, Belgium
"Aroma of toffee and caramel malts, with some slight sour notes, some slight spiciness." "Flavors of sweet fruit, lightly toasted malt, caramel candy, spices and faint vanilla." "On the sharper end of the standard Belgian ales." 8% alc.

Pearl ★
Pale Lager: Pabst Brewing Co., Chicago, IL www.pabst.com
"It didn't taste awful, just bland with no real body or finish to speak of." "Pungent water combined with sour hops and weak malt." Pabst brand brewed by Miller. N/A% alc.

Pelican Doryman's Dark ★★★★★
Brown Ale: Pelican Pub and Brewery, Pacific City, OR www.pelicanbrewery.com
"Chewy-sweet malts with a lot of toast and roast. Mild coffee and dark chocolate." "The hoppiest brown ale that I have ever come across." 5.8% alc.

Pelican Indian Pelican Ale ★★★★★
IPA: Pelican Pub and Brewery, Pacific City, OR www.pelicanbrewery.com
"Huge Indian Pale Ale with thick and chewy malts, tropical fruit sweetness, lots of citrus and especially grapefruit." "The combination of peppery spice, grassy, plus citrusy hops is irresistible to me." 7.5% alc.

Pelican Kiwanda Cream Ale ★★1/2
Cream Ale: Pelican Pub and Brewery, Pacific City, OR www.pelicanbrewery.com
"Fruity hoppy aroma with hints of berries." "Lightly malty flavor with a good yet mild grapefruit hop taste that goes down fairly easy and smooth." 5.1% alc.

Pelican Tsunami Stout ★★★★★
Foreign Stout: Pelican Pub and Brewery, Pacific City, OR www.pelicanbrewery.com
"Very appetizing nose... a big bouquet of chocolate, roast and toast." "Perfectly balanced and very burnt with notes of dusty cocoa powder and espresso grounds." "More than I could have dreamed of." 7% alc.

Penn Dark Lager ★★1/2
Dunkel: PA Brewing Co., Pittsburgh, PA www.pennbrew.com
"Aroma contained notes of roasted malts dark malts and was mild." "Malts in the flavor grow as it warms in your mouth releasing flavors of caramel and chocolate finishing very well balanced with a light roast." 4.5% alc.

Penn Gold Lager ★★★★1/2
Pale Lager: PA Brewing Co., Pittsburgh, PA www.pennbrew.com
"Mildly malty but almost non-existent aroma." "Sweet, grainy flavor is dominant." "Mouthfeel was smooth and a tad thin." "Passable I suppose." N/A% alc.

Penn Marzen ★★★1/2
Märzen/Oktbfst: PA Brewing Co., Pittsburgh, PA www.pennbrew.com
"Slightly minerally aroma, with a light caramel sweetness and grassy hopping." "Malty, slightly nutty, soft, smooth on the tongue." "Very nice smooth Oktoberfest." N/A% alc.

Penn Oktoberfest ★★
Märzen/Oktbfst: PA Brewing Co., Pittsburgh, PA www.pennbrew.com
"Hints of cinnamon and nutmeg overlay a slightly caramel/toffee maltiness." "Flavor is full of malt with a touch of crisp spiciness." "I feel like this a standard for Märzen." 6.5% alc.

Penn Pilsner ★★1/2
Vienna: PA Brewing Co., Pittsburgh, PA www.pennbrew.com
Aroma of grassy, stale hops, some dough and faint citrus." "Extremely soft hop presence, subtle malts, grassy." "Very heavy mouthfeel for a pilsner, but lacked enough carbonation and hops to give it a crisp flavor." 5.2% alc.

Penn St. Nikolaus Bock Bier ★★★
Bock: PA Brewing Co., Pittsburgh, PA www.pennbrew.com
"Nice aroma with vanilla, malts and a bit of caramel." "Complex finish comprised of toffee, nuts, cinnamon and brown sugar." "I am not much of a bock fan but have found this one to be rather enjoyable." 6.8% alc.

Penn Weizen ★★★1/2

Hefeweizen: PA Brewing Co., Pittsburgh, PA www.pennbrew.com

"Has aromas of light cinnamon, a little banana, some pepper and some clove in for good measure." "Full and fruity, with orange and spice and loads of yeasty goodness." "This is as good as the best authentic German examples." 4.2% alc.

Peroni Gran Riserva ★★

Helles/Dortmnd: Birra Peroni Industriale S.p.A. (SABMiller), Roma, Italy www.peroni.it

"Aroma is caramel and biscuity malts with some background grassy hop aromas." "Very full bodied, with some biscuit flavors." "Nice balancing act." 6.6% alc.

Peroni Premium Lager ★★1/2

Pale Lager: Birra Peroni Industriale S.p.A. (SABMiller), Roma, Italy www.peroni.it

"Slight lemony grainy aroma." "Balanced hop character slightly rises in finish." "If I had to drink beer along a salad, Peroni might be a good pick." 4.7% alc.

Pete's Place Choc Beer ★★1/2

Am. Wheat: Petes Place, Krebs, OK www.petes.org/

"Aroma is yeasty, with hints of pear skins, light orange and dust." "Flavor contains lightly sour wheat, light pale malt sugars (honeyish)." "There's just not much here." 3.2% alc.

Pete's Wicked Ale ★★

Brown Ale: Gambrinus Co., Utica, NY www.petes.com

"Muted malt aroma with a faint floral hop character." "Taste is sweet cereal grains, caramel, some bittering hops in the finish." "'Wicked?' Don't make me laugh. Maybe 15 years ago..." Contract brewed. 5.3% alc.

Pete's Wicked Strawberry Blonde ★★

Fruit Beer: Gambrinus Co.., Utica, NY www.petes.com

"Just a small hint of strawberry, but it wasn't overpowering." "Quite sweet, but you can still taste the malt behind the fruit." "It was all I could do to choke it down." Contract brewed. 5% alc.

Petrus Aged Pale ★★★★

Flem Sour Ale: Bavik-De Brabandere, Harelbeke, Belgium www.bavik.be

"Aromas of big fruit, citrus, funky barnyard." "Brett and tannins combine on top of lemon zest and bitter honey." "Great balance and very refreshing." 7.3% alc.

Petrus Oud Bruin ★★★

Flem Sour Ale: Bavik-De Brabandere, Harelbeke, Belgium www.bavik.be

"Has a rich maltiness that is undercut by a fairly sharp acidity." "Finish is a bit dry and could have used a bit more tart fruitiness." "It's like a session wood-aged beer." 5.5% alc.

Petrus Triple ★★1/2

Abbey Tripel: Bavik-De Brabandere, Harelbeke, Belgium www.bavik.be

"Aroma is lemony with hints of spicy floral notes." "Flavor is tangy with fruit, pepper, a hint of honey finishing somewhat dry with some orange peel." "A rather standard triple in my opinion." 7.5% alc.

Petrus Winterbier ★★1/2

Belgian Ale: Bavik-De Brabandere, Harelbeke, Quebec www.bavik.be

"Sweet malty aroma with the faintest wild, lactic hint." "Fruity and spicy while being quite delicate." "Ok but quite boring." 6.5% alc.

Éphémère Cassis ★★★★

Fruit Beer: Unibroue (Sleeman), Chambly, Quebec www.unibroue.com

"Sweet black currant aroma with light yeast undertones." "Blackcurrant is the main focus, backed up by pale malt and hedgy hop notes." "A unique and refreshing beer." 5.5% alc.

Éphémère Cranberry ★★★★
Fruit Beer: Unibroue (Sleeman), Chambly, Quebec www.unibroue.com
"Cranberry aroma with vague bread, wood and hop." "Mostly cranberry on the palate, as the malt and hops both sit back and chill out." "This is a very satisfying drink for someone who (like me) isn't a real fan of fruit beers." 5.5% alc.

Piedmont Porter ★
Porter: Joseph Huber Brewing Co., Monroe, WI www.berghoffbeer.com
"Nose is a bit coffeeish and roasted with light chocolate notes." "Flavor is ok, some roastiness, caramel and molasses." "Not a bad porter, weaker than most." 5% alc.

Piels ★
Pale Lager: Miller Brewing Co. (SABMiller), Milwaukee, WI www.millerbrewing.com
"Very light toasted malt mixed with random sourness." "This is the worst beer that I have ever had." N/A% alc.

Pig's Eye Lean ★★
Pale Lager: City Brewery (Melanie Brewing Co), La Crosse, WI www.citybrewery.com
"Flavor is watery with malt and corn." "It has no noticeable flaws and goes down much easier than a light from Miller or Bud and at half the price." 4.2% alc.

Pig's Eye Pilsner ★
Pilsner: City Brewery (Melanie Brewing Co), La Crosse, WI www.citybrewery.com
Aroma was forgettable with a sign of malt (light) corn and the hops are barely noticeable." "Flavor of corn and hops." "A light beer lover might find this tolerable, I find it way too light for me." 4.55% alc.

Pike IPA ★★★
IPA: Pike Pub and Brewery, Seattle, WA www.pikebrewing.com
"Great aroma of spicy, citric hops!" "Palate is strongly woody, with plenty of toasty, whole wheat bready notes to back it up." "Even by Pacific Northwest standards this is full of the grapefruit like flavors of hops." 6.3% alc.

Pike Kilt Lifter ★★★
Scotch Ale: Pike Pub and Brewery, Seattle, WA www.pikebrewing.com
"Aroma is slightly sweet and malty." "Flavor was lightly smoked malt and caramel up front with a light hop bitterness late." "Vaguely reminds me of a few strong IPAs I've had." 6.6% alc.

Pike Naughty Nellie's ★★1/2
Goldn/Blond Ale: Pike Pub and Brewery, Seattle, WA www.pikebrewing.com
"Aromas are pretty sweet with a light hop presence." "Smooth and fruity spiced with a good balance." "All in all a pleasant diversion." 4.7% alc.

Pike Pale Ale ★★1/2
Am. Pale Ale: Pike Pub and Brewery, Seattle, WA www.pikebrewing.com
"Nose held soft notes of citrus, florals, earth, nutty caramel and toasted grains." "Light floral hop flavors blend with the nutty caramel tones almost perfectly. Medium bodied, light carbonation, dry, semi-bitter finish. An easy drinker...." 5.3% alc.

Pike Street XXXXX Stout ★★★★★
Stout: Pike Pub and Brewery, Seattle, WA www.pikebrewing.com
"Aroma is richly roasty with light fruitiness and hints of citrusy hop, toast." "Smooth as hell, with gorgeous Belgian chocolate notes, cream, vanilla sugar, Yunnan coffee." "This one is definitely in my top five for stouts. Yummalicious!" 6.2% alc.

Pils Hellas ★★1/2
Pale Lager: Hellenic Breweries of Atalanti, S.A., Atalanti, Greece
"Skunky, herbal hop aroma." "Taste is cereal grains, some cracker sweetness and decent bitterness from the hops." "A lager is a lager the world around." 4.9% alc.

Pilsen Callao ★

Helles/Dortmnd: Backus y Johnston (Grupo Empresarial Bavaria), Lima, Peru www.backus.com.pe

"Aromas of grass and light grains." "The flavor is sweet malt, may have a bit of corn and finishes on a sweet note with a dash of hop bitterness." "For a macro-brewed lager this has a lot of malt character." 5.2% alc.

Pilsner of El Salvador ★★

Pale Lager: Cerveceria La Constancia (SABMiller), San Salvador, El Salvador www.laconstancia.com

"Smells like canned corn and wet straw." "Sweet corn flavor yet is watery and bland at the same time." "Typical swill crap." N/A% alc.

Pilsner Urquell ★★★1/2

Bohemian Pilsner: Plzensky Prazdroj (SABMiller), Plzn, Czech Rep. www.prazdroz.cz

Wonderful gold with steady rising bubbles, malty aromas and moderate Saaz bitterness. "Great when fresh; could do without the green bottles." "Good firm body." "Benchmark Pilsner? Fair enough." "Amazingly full of flavor for such a light, crisp, refreshing brew." 4.4% alc.

Pinkus Alt ★★★1/2

Goldn/Blond Ale: Pinkus Muller Brauerei , Münster, Germany www.pinkus.de

"Aroma is medium sweet, bread, vegetal, light caramel, light orange." "Honey malt, lemony with some grain, gets a bit dishwatery and grassy on warming." "Tasty, enjoyable, one of the better organics I've had." 5.1% alc.

Pinkus Hefe-Weizen ★★

Hefeweizen: Pinkus Muller Brauerei , Münster, Germany www.pinkus.de

"Aroma had a light malt presence accompanied by subtle hop notes of lemon and sweet doughy yeast in the background." "Lemony flavor in a thin, wheat body." "Light bodied and actually quite watery in the finish. Wow, talk about a disappointment." 5% alc.

Pinkus Pils ★★★1/2

Classic Ger Pils: Pinkus Muller Brauerei , Münster, Germany www.pinkus.de

"Medium sweet aroma, bread/grain, light apple, caramel." "Very crisp, malty mouthfeel, slightly grainy malty taste with a citrus fruity palate and a dry and aromatic hopbitter finish." "A good and well-made Pilsner. 5.2% alc.

Pioneer Black River Red ★★

Märzen/Oktbfst: Sand Creek Brewing Co. (Pioneer/Wisconsin Brewing Co.), Black River Falls, WI www.sandcreekbrewing.com

"Aroma is caramel and vanilla." "Some roasted malt caramel and toffee flavors upfront." "In the end, it tastes like a sweeter Märzen that had a shot of dish soap dropped in it." N/A% alc.

Pioneer Groovy Brew ★

Kölsch: Sand Creek Brewing Co. (Pioneer/Wisconsin Brewing Co.), Black River Falls, WI www.sandcreekbrewing.com

"Bready and somewhat sweet, with little else in the mix to balance the beer." "Lightly sweet Euro-lager flavor with a hint of yeast. Light grassy hops in the finish." "This is a gimmick beer with a neato label, that is all." N/A% alc.

Piraat ★★★

Bel. Strong Ale: Brouwerij Van Steenberge, Ertvelde, Belgium www.vansteenberge.com

"Aroma is strong - pineapple, passion fruit, guava and brandyish alcohol." "Vanilla and lemon-candy for sweetness, doughy yeast, a light hint of herbs and spicy white wine toward the back." "Bludgeoning and yet shows some gentle, nuanced character." 9% alc.

Pizza Port Cuvée de Tomme ★★★★★

Bel. Strong Ale: Pizza Port (Solana Beach), Solana Beach, CA www.pizzaport.comontap_solana.html

OK, this is ultra-rare, but we have to laud Pizza Port for its dedication to brewing some of the most amazing and experimental brews in the US. "Palate is incredibly smooth. Body is suitably massive. Intriguing from start to finish." 11.5% alc.

Pocono Black and Tan ★★
Porter: Lion Brewery, Inc., Wilkes-Barre, PA www.lionbrewery.com
"Slight toast, cocoa, wood aroma." "Fairly sweet, mildly caramelly and quite grainy." "There are a lot of these pre-fab black and tans, but I'm not sure what the appeal is. They always come off like a half-assed Porter to me." N/A% alc.

Pocono Caramel Porter ★★★1/2
Porter: Lion Brewery, Inc., Wilkes-Barre, PA www.lionbrewery.com
"Aroma of sweet caramel." "Taste starts a tad sweet with good notes of caramel and mocha with that touch of lactic sourness on the aftertaste." "Quite drinkable, but only one at a time." N/A% alc.

Pocono Lager ★★
Premium Lager: Lion Brewery, Inc., Wilkes-Barre, PA www.lionbrewery.com
"Sweet malt extract syrup nose." "Uninteresting malt sweetness with some dark fruit flavors, caramel and white sugar." "It's like drinking wort." N/A% alc.

Pocono Pale Ale ★★
Am. Pale Ale: Lion Brewery, Inc., Wilkes-Barre, PA www.lionbrewery.com
Nose: "Floral hops, sweet orange light pine and some caramel." "Light pine, citrus, lots of caramel malts and a touch of diacetyl... really boring." N/A% alc.

Point Cascade Pale Ale ★★1/2
Am. Pale Ale: Stevens Point Brewery, Stevens Point, WI www.pointbeer.com
"Aroma leads in with fresh honey hops, ginger and a gathering of sugary, tropical Starburst assortments." "Orange peel, lemon, some roasted malt, hint of pine." "Great bang for the buck." N/A% alc.

Point Classic Amber ★★1/2
Vienna: Stevens Point Brewery, Stevens Point, WI www.pointbeer.com
"Toasted malts aroma that is quite mild and clean." "Vaguely sweet with some muted toffee flavors." "Average caramel fare with a bit of breadiness." N/A% alc.

Point Honey Light ★★★★
Pale Lager: Stevens Point Brewery, Stevens Point, WI www.pointbeer.com
"A pale lager body with the smallest addition of sweet taste." "Aromas of bread, sweet malt and a touch of citrus." "It's a little better than a macro beer." N/A% alc.

Point Pale Ale ★★
Am. Pale Ale: Stevens Point Brewery, Stevens Point, WI www.pointbeer.com
"Sugar cookie malt with resinous grassy-spicy hops in the aroma." "Just enough hops flavor at the finish to make it enjoyable." "Fairly smooth and easy to drink." N/A% alc.

Point Special Lager ★★★1/2
Pale Lager: Stevens Point Brewery, Stevens Point, WI www.pointbeer.com
"Aroma was typical of an American lager with a somewhat subtle malt component well balanced with floral hops." "Balanced with just a hint of malt sweetness up front. Light to medium-bodied, well-carbonated with a relatively clean finish." 5.1% alc.

Point Spring Bock ★★
Bock: Stevens Point Brewery, Stevens Point, WI www.pointbeer.com
"Honeyish aroma with very sweet caramel and chocolate malt notes." "Sweet caramel nicely offset by bitter chocolate and hops." "Not the best Bock but still a very good beer for the price." N/A% alc.

Point White Bière ★★1/2
Bel. Witbier: Stevens Point Brewery, Stevens Point, WI www.pointbeer.com
"Some coriander and marshmallow aroma, alongside grainy notes, oatcakes and honey." "Light, slightly honeyish, sweet, with hints of coriander and a very light yeast presence." "Spot on for the style and a good beer all-around." N/A% alc.

Polar ★★1/2

Pale Lager: Empresas Polar, Caracas, Venezuela www.empresas-polar.com

"Aroma is mildly sweet Pilsner malt, sweat, bread, dough and a light stale hops." "Almost no flavors, little grainy, some hop bitterness, very light." "This is beer? I was using it to keep my lawn green." 4.5% alc.

Pony Express Gold ★★

Goldn/Blond Ale: Pony Express Brewing (Great Plains Brewing), Olathe, KS www.ponygold.com

"Has aromas of lemons, light grassiness and some malts." "Nice appearance, but the flavor was lacking and not very complex at all." "Definitely brewed for the masses." 4.25% alc.

Pony Express Original Wheat ★★★1/2

Am. Wheat: Pony Express Brewing (Great Plains Brewing), Olathe, KS www.ponygold.com

"Aroma is crisp and wheaty with a spicy hop element." "Starts with good wheat character, light banana sweetness and some citrus." "Much more character than other American Wheats I've had." 5% alc.

Pony Express Rattlesnake Pale ★

Am. Pale Ale: Pony Express Brewing (Great Plains Brewing), Olathe, KS www.ponygold.com

"Sweetish, caramel malt flavors without enough hops to balance." "Very light almost like a lager." "Generic and boring." N/A% alc.

Pony Express Tornado Red Ale ★★

Amber Ale: Pony Express Brewing (Great Plains Brewing), Olathe, KS www.ponygold.com

"The aroma is sweet malts with a hint of nut and a light spicy hop element." "Dry maltiness, caramel notes with a light grassiness." "With the name Tornado I expected a beer that was bolder." N/A% alc.

Poperings Hommelbier ★★★1/2

Bel. Strong Ale: Van Eecke, Poperinge-Watou, Belgium www.brouwerijvaneecke.tk

"Lightly sweet malt aroma with grassy notes and light oranges." "Tangy flavor starting with yeasty citrus fruit and ending with a nice kick of hops." "Makes me want to move to Flanders." 7.5% alc.

Port Royal Export ★★1/2

Pale Lager: Cerveceria Hondureña (SABMiller), Tegucigalpa, Honduras www.cerveceriahondurena.com

"Aroma combining noble hops, solvent, creamed corn and Canadian whisky." "Vaguely malty accent with creamy sweetness, slight astringency and mucho plastic in the finish." "With all it's chemlab happenings, is too much for me to handle." 4.8% alc.

Port Townsend Barley Wine ★★★

Barley Wine: Port Townsend Brewing Co., Port Townsend, WA www.porttownsendbrewing.com

"Malty aroma with figs, plums and canned peaches." "Nice interesting yeast, blackberry/cherry, sweet plummy malts, brown sugar, bready, with a light citrus hop flavor, peppery, slightly alcoholic finish." 10.5% alc.

Portland Benchmark Old Ale ★★★★1/2

Old Ale: Portland Brewing Co. (Pyramid), Portland, OR www.portlandbrew.com

"Richly sweet in aroma with lots of molasses and brown sugar notes." "Aroma is sweet toffee, almost wort-like, with smoke and alcohol." 9.9% alc.

Portland Original Portland Ale ★★

Am. Pale Ale: Portland Brewing Co. (Pyramid), Portland, OR www.portlandbrew.com

"Fruity sweet aroma is not real strong." "Sweet caramel malt taste with some hop to it." "Reminds me of what Anheuser-Busch or Coors would make if they tried this style." N/A% alc.

Portland Pale Ale ★★

Am. Pale Ale: Portland Brewing Co. (Pyramid), Portland, OR www.portlandbrew.com

"Decent malt aroma of caramel and cookie and the slightest hint of floral hops." "Caramel and cookie up front. Light floral hoppiness." "Fairly bland pale ale." N/A% alc.

Post Road Pumpkin Ale ★★1/2
Spice/Herb: Brooklyn Brewery, Brooklyn, NY www.brooklynbrewery.com
"Aroma of pumpkin pie spices and caramel malt." "Starts with a malty palate, but not much sweetness, a touch of cinnamon and a dry earthy pumpkin finish with a subtle hint of tartness." "Nice and tasty... but not mindblowing." 5% alc.

Premium Cristal ★★
Pale Lager: Backus y Johnston (Grupo Empresarial Bavaria), Lima, Peru www.backus.com.pe
"Wet grass and light floral aroma." "Flavor is sweet malty with notes of caramel and straw, leading to a dry end." "Passable international lager." 5% alc.

Prinzregent Luitpold Weissbier Hell ★★★
Hefeweizen: Schlossbrauerei Kaltenberg, Furstenfeldbruck, Germany www.kaltenberg.de
"Aroma is light with cloves and apple." "Light yeast and citrus flavors with a hint of spiciness at the end." "Very smooth drinking and refreshing, a decent Hefeweizen." 5.5% alc.

Pyramid Amber Weizen ★★1/2
Am. Wheat: Pyramid Breweries Inc., Portland, OR www.pyramidbrew.com
"Yeasty, sweet malt aroma." "Flavor is grapes, cherries, sweetness, mild grassy hop kick to it." "Fairly watered down with wheat and a bit of crispy caramel." 5.5% alc.

Pyramid Apricot Weizen ★★★
Fruit Beer: Pyramid Breweries Inc., Portland, OR www.pyramidbrew.com
"Smells strongly of apricot." "Reminds me of that Post cereal that has the peach bits in it." "The apricot overwhelms any subtler elements that might be in there." 5.1% alc.

Pyramid Coastline Pilsner ★★1/2
Pilsner: Pyramid Breweries Inc., Portland, OR www.pyramidbrew.com
"Not much in terms of taste except for a light citrus flavor." "Bready, crisp, refreshing, grassy lager that only somewhat resembles a Pilsner." 5% alc.

Pyramid Curve Ball ★
Kölsch: Pyramid Breweries Inc., Portland, OR www.pyramidbrew.com
"Lemony flavor, very light, slightly hoppy." "Easy drinking light malty flavors that envelop you tongue with a slight tang." "This one is less of a curve ball and more of a sinker ball." 4.8% alc.

Pyramid Hefeweizen ★★1/2
Am. Wheat: Pyramid Breweries Inc., Portland, OR www.pyramidbrew.com
"Pleasant mild aromas of grain and yeast, but nothing special." "Faint lemon aroma." "Some sweetness to the fruit." "Flavor is sweet and malty, not a whole lot of character." "A refreshing Hefeweizen, but only average." 5.2% alc.

Pyramid Pale Ale ★★★
Eng Pale Ale: Pyramid Breweries Inc., Portland, OR www.pyramidbrew.com
"Aroma is sweet oranges with some bananas and a light hint of pine." "Nice hoppy flavor dominates a rather thin brew, sweet, floral." "Once you put the beer down, it will be easy for you to forget what you were drinking." 5.1% alc.

Pyramid Snow Cap ★★★
Eng. Strong Ale: Pyramid Breweries Inc., Portland, OR www.pyramidbrew.com
"Has aromas of cherry, caramel malt and a touch of hop." "Dark fruit, hops and a touch of spice." "A taste sensation, with no one element of the flavor dominating too much." 7% alc.

Pyramid Thunderhead Indian Pale Ale ★★1/2
IPA: Pyramid Breweries Inc., Portland, OR www.pyramidbrew.com
"Aroma is sweet caramel malt, honeysuckle and hops." "Assertive hop bitterness in the initial taste and in the aftertaste, but not enough to dominate the sweet honeylike malt flavor." "Even the non-hopheads will enjoy this one." 6.7% alc.

Quake Chocolate Cream Ale ★
Ale: Gluek Brewing Co., Cold Spring, MN www.gluek.com
"Very sweet chocolate and malt aroma, a bit overboard and approaching a candy bar level of sweetness." "Perhaps all its essences were too subtle for my senses but this was a very bland beer." 8.2% alc.

Quake Honey Cream Ale ★
Ale: Gluek Brewing Co., Cold Spring, MN www.gluek.com
"Mild taste, very slight maltiness, some honey sweetness." "Flavor is surprisingly thin for such a big beer." "The mouthfeel was sweet and somewhat doughy." 8.2% alc.

Quelque Chose ★★★★★
Fruit Beer: Unibroue (Sleeman), Chambly, Quebec www.unibroue.com
"Aroma - God I love this stuff - redolent with fresh sour cherry, very mild sweet malt backing, waves of allspice, nutmeg and cinnamon." "Tart hits the tongue and expands outward with clove and nutmeg and cinnamon." "Most expressive at room temp." 8% alc.

Quilmes ★★
Pale Lager: Cerveceria Malteria Quilmes SAICAY (Heineken), Buenos Aires, Argentina www.quinsa.com
"Aromas started skunked revealing grassy hops later." "Lightly bitter with a small amount of cane sugar to sweeten it at the end." "I didn't like this beer, but it wasn't as bad as I thought it would be." 4.9% alc.

Radeberger Pilsner ★★1/2
Premium Lager: Radeberger Exportbierbrauerei , Radeberg, Germany www.radeberger.de
"Pleasant aroma of malt, notes of herb and grass." "Toasted malt flavors dwell in a crisp body which seems to lack some girth." "An easy pint to down." 4.8% alc.

Raftman ★★1/2
Smoked: Unibroue (Sleeman), Chambly, Quebec www.unibroue.com
"Fruity/yeasty aroma with malts and a smoked element." "Spicy, Unibroue yeast profile but with a side order of smoke." "I expected more from this beer." 5.5% alc.

Rainier ★
Pale Lager: Pabst Brewing Co., Chicago, IL www.pabst.com
"Aromas of bread, corn and a hint of citrus." "Sort of like Miller High Life but a little less sweet; a lot of corn." "My grandpa loves this stuff, but I think he lost his taste buds in the war." Pabst brand contract-brewed by Miller. N/A% alc.

Rainier Ale ★★1/2
Malt Liquor: Pabst Brewing Co. , Chicago, IL www.pabst.com
"Wet paper bag aroma with some stale fruit notes." "Flavor is objectionable at best." "Who-boy. I really need a job." Pabst brand contract-brewed by Miller. 7.3% alc.

Ramapo Valley Passover Honey Beer ★
Mead: Ramapo Valley Brewery, Hilburn, NY www.ramapovalleybrewery.com
"Sweet, light aroma of honey, apple cider, perfume, old bread and a touch of floral hop character." "Tasted like a cheap sparkling white wine with a dash of honey tossed in." "I think I prefer gluten..." 5.2% alc.

Ramapo Valley Stud Copper ★★
Brown Ale: Ramapo Valley Brewery, Hilburn, NY www.ramapovalleybrewery.com
"Aroma is a mix between sweet caramel and intense fruity notes of prune and cherry and even perhaps a bit of sherry." "Flavor is nutty, caramel and those same hay-like hops create almost a sour aftertaste." N/A% alc.

Ramapo Valley Suffern Station Porter ★★1/2
Porter: Ramapo Valley Brewery, Hilburn, NY www.ramapovalleybrewery.com
"Sweet aroma of caramel, cocoa and a touch of fruit." "Flavor is roasted malt a touch of chocolate and some wood notes." "Short, crisp, clean finish with a blast of cocoa at the very end." 5.8% alc.

Ramapo Valley Trail Quencher IPA ★★1/2
IPA: Ramapo Valley Brewery, Hilburn, NY www.ramapovalleybrewery.com
"Citrus fruit aroma with a whisper of evergreen." "Flavor is chocolate malt, caramel and a touch of hops." "A very refreshing feel to this beer and the bitterness sticks to your tongue for awhile." N/A% alc.

Ramstein Blonde ★★1/2
Hefeweizen: High Point Wheat Beer Co., Butler, NJ www.ramsteinbeer.com
"Wheat, apple, yeast aromas with some banana and a variety of spices." "Marshmallowy sweet, with a light spiciness (cinnamon)." "Very nicely done." 5.5% alc.

Ramstein Classic ★★★★1/2
Dunkelweizen: High Point Wheat Beer Co., Butler, NJ www.ramsteinbeer.com
"Aroma is chocolate covered bananas, molasses, nutmeg and yeast." "Unsweetened chocolate bitterness and hints toward hot cocoa spiked with Irish cream liquor." "Very rich flavor without being heavy." 5.5% alc.

Ramstein Maibock ★★★★★
Bock: High Point Wheat Beer Co., Butler, NJ www.ramsteinbeer.com
"Has aromas of toasted dough, caramel malt, light hoppiness." "Tastes of yeast, bread, caramel and light fruits." "A big hit among both beer geeks and non-beer geeks alike." 7.5% alc.

Ramstein Winter Wheat ★★★★1/2
Weizen Bock: High Point Wheat Beer Co., Butler, NJ www.ramsteinbeer.com
"Aroma is gorgeous with rich malt, blackberries, blueberries, chocolate and roasted hops." "Very sweet taste, with the banana and citrus effect of the wheat going rather nicely with the chocolates." "Unique for sure." 9.5% alc.

Rapscallion Blessing ★★★1/2
Am Strong Ale: The Concord Brewery, Lowell, MA concordbrew.com
"Aroma has tons of bready yeast mixed with caramel covered oranges and juicy, pine and resin hops." "Subtle and well balanced flavor of hops, malt and burnt caramel with a roasty, bitter finish." 8% alc.

Rapscallion Creation ★★1/2
Am Strong Ale: The Concord Brewery, Lowell, MA concordbrew.com
"Anise, yeast, sweet caramel, dried fruits, vanilla and wood aromas." "Flavor is fruity with hints of cherries, raisins and prunes." "It's all enveloped in a massive wet sourdough flavor, with traces of alcohol on the end." 9.5% alc.

Rapscallion Premier ★★★
Am Strong Ale: The Concord Brewery, Lowell, MA concordbrew.com
"Yeasty, fruity aroma." "Huge hops on the palate, backed up with appropriate malt and full, sweet fruitiness that continues through the long and lovely finish." "Great tasting ale, but a bit light for it's style." 6.75% alc.

Rauchenfelser Steinbier ★★1/2
Smoked: Allgäuer Brauhaus AG, Kempten, Germany www.allgaeuer-brauhaus.de
"Fruity, mildly smoky caramel malt aroma with some bready malt character." "Smoky aroma, whiffs of burnt leaves and charred corn husks." "A taste of history, while imagining a completely different time." 4.9% alc.

RCH Ale Mary ★★1/2
Eng. Strong Ale: RCH, Weston-super-Mare, Somerset, England www.rchbrewery.com
"Aroma of cinnamon, nutmeg, ginger, toffee, sour citrus and berries." "The numerous spices are most prominent and the chocolate malt comes out in the finish." "Could see spending a long night in an English pub nursing several of these." 6% alc.

RCH Old Slug Porter ★★1/2
Porter: RCH, Weston-super-Mare, Somerset, England www.rchbrewery.com
"Very appealing nose of chocolaty dark malt with some raisins." "Sweet chocolate and roasty flavors are well-balanced." "Poor Dickens might not have much to write about on this one, but I'm sure he woulda enjoyed it." 4.5% alc.

Real Ale Brewhouse Brown Ale ★★1/2
Brown Ale: Real Ale Brewing Co., Blanco, TX www.realalebrewing.com
"Rich, nutty, bready, malt aroma." "Tastes lightly sweet, roasty, a bit caramelly, perhaps a touch nutty and moderately bitter and floral while not being noticeably hoppy." 5.4% alc.

Real Ale Full Moon Pale Rye Ale ★★★1/2
Am. Pale Ale: Real Ale Brewing Co., Blanco, TX www.realalebrewing.com
"Aroma is a flowery hops smell." "Very flavorful malty, rye, nicely balanced moderately bitter finish." "One of the best local craft brews available" in Austin and other parts of Texas. 5.6% alc.

Real Ale Rio Blanco Pale Ale ★★
Am. Pale Ale: Real Ale Brewing Co., Blanco, TX www.realalebrewing.com
"Malt aroma with a touch of fruit and some earthy hop." "Flavor is intense with tart hops and sweetish malts." "Would be a good beer to present to your Bud-Miller-Coors friends to lure them to the dark side..." 5.2% alc.

Real Ale Sisyphus ★★★★
Barley Wine: Real Ale Brewing Co., Blanco, TX www.realalebrewing.com
"Aroma of sweet malts and raisins and a touch of plum." "Taste was mostly yeasty and dry with a touch of citrus and smoky caramelly malt." "I'm about to go clean out my local store of these for the winter..." 11.5% alc.

ReaperAle Deathly Pale ★★1/2
Am. Pale Ale: ReaperAle, Vista, CA www.reaperale.com
"Sharp and juicy Pacific Northwest blended hop character of pine, grass, herbs and grapefruit with some bready and pale malts." "A fine example of an American Pale Ale in my book." 6.2% alc.

ReaperAle Mortality Stout ★★★
Stout: ReaperAle, Vista, CA www.reaperale.com
"No light shines through." "Straightforward flavors of roasted nuts, mild coffee, pale malts and a touch of roasted malt." "Should probably be given more credit than it is." 7.5% alc.

ReaperAle Redemption Red ★★1/2
Amber Ale: ReaperAle, Vista, CA www.reaperale.com
"Sweet dark caramel aromas mingle, slightly out of step, with licorice and aromatic spicy hops." "Although decently hopped, the taste leans toward the sweeter, maltier side of the spectrum." 6.6% alc.

ReaperAle Ritual Dark ★★★★
Am Strong Ale: ReaperAle, Vista, CA www.reaperale.com
"Neat aroma of roastiness, brown sugar, piney hops and caramel." "Mostly malty but with a decent, unoverbearing hoppy finish." "Finishes like a Christmas blend of pipe tobacco in cohorts with pinot noir." 8.5% alc.

ReaperAle Sleighor Double IPA ★★★★1/2
Imp/Dbl IPA: ReaperAle, Vista, CA www.reaperale.com
"Aroma is hoppy with a bit of candy sweetness." "Good balance for the style, rich malt and rich hops, no mistakes." "Not for wimps, this is a palate buster." 9.1% alc.

Red Brick Ale ★★
Brown Ale: Atlanta Brewing Co., Atlanta, GA www.atlantabrewing.combeers.htm
"Has aromas of nuts, caramel and light toffee." "Flavor starts sweet and ends hoppy - a nice earthy, tobacco-like hop." "Medium bodied, slightly dry and smooth." 6.5% alc.

Red Brick Blonde ★★
Goldn/Blond Ale: Atlanta Brewing Co., Atlanta, GA www.atlantabrewing.combeers.htm
"Aroma is lightly sweet with flowery hops." "Fresh, clean flavor, mainly light Cascades but also some balancing pale malts." "Doesn't amaze or disappoint." "It appears that ABC is improving their lineup." N/A% alc.

Red Brick Peachtree Pale Ale ★★
Am. Pale Ale: Atlanta Brewing Co., Atlanta, GA www.atlantabrewing.combeers.htm
"Lightly fruity some decent hops but thin malt flavors." "Mildly bitter." "Light grapefruit." "Simple profile, light and evenly balanced to the point of being really uneventful." N/A% alc.

Red Dog ★
Pale Lager: Miller Brewing Co. (SABMiller), Milwaukee, WI www.millerbrewing.com
"There's not much aroma other than a plain beer smell and the taste is mildly sweet and smooth." "Has a smoother taste than other Miller beers." 5% alc.

Red Stripe ★★1/2
Pale Lager: Desnoes and Geddes Ltd (Diageo PLC), Kingston, Jamaica
"Aroma of crisp hops with some sweet malt." "Flavors of bread with some light citrus and a smooth finish." "Not my style of beer, but much better than I expected." 4.7% alc.

Red Wolf ★
Pale Lager: Anheuser-Busch Companies, St. Louis, MO www.anheuser-busch.com
"A bit malty with a nice amber color." "Slightly better than Red Dog but not as good as Killians." "Clean taste, with more body than your average domestic." 5.4% alc.

Redhook Autumn Ale ★★
Amber Ale: Redhook Brewery, Woodinville, WA www.redhook.com
"Sweet toasty malt aroma with a hint of hops." "Taste is coppery, malty, soft and fresh on the palate." "Flavor was weak and watery but not offensive. A mediocre beer." N/A% alc.

Redhook Blackhook ★★1/2
Porter: Redhook Brewery, Woodinville, WA www.redhook.com
"Smells fruity and malty, a bit nutty as well." "Coffee and chocolate flavors with hints of nuts and spicy finish." "Drinkable, but not up to my standards for porters." 5.69% alc.

Redhook Blonde ★★
Goldn/Blond Ale: Redhook Brewery, Woodinville, WA www.redhook.com
"Faint but pleasant enough aroma." "Taste starts with a slight bitterness and finishes clean and neutral. This allows the malt and hops to shine through, although they are subtly intertwined to produce a mellow brew." 5.77% alc.

Redhook Chinook Copper ★★
Amber Ale: Redhook Brewery, Woodinville, WA www.redhook.com
"Bright aromas of spicy licorice, caramel, menthol and nutmeg." "A very good amber with nice balance and a good slightly hoppy finish." N/A% alc.

Redhook ESB ★★1/2
Prem Bitter: Redhook Brewery, Woodinville, WA www.redhook.com
"Mild caramel malt and muted hop aroma." "Some nice pine/ hops flavor with a tad of sweetness." "The flavor seems rather plain but has some nice malt aspects." 5.69% alc.

Redhook India Pale Ale ★★
IPA: Redhook Brewery, Woodinville, WA www.redhook.com
"Aroma is very herbal, sweet and weedy." "Flavor starts with sweet piney hops, followed by a bitter piney bite, finished by a very slight corn taste." "There are other IPAs that I like a lot more than this one." 6% alc.

Redhook Nut Brown ★★1/2

Brown Ale: Redhook Brewery, Woodinville, WA www.redhook.com

"Has aroma of fresh cut wood, pine, cedar, figs, clay." "Flavor is somewhat sweet of a brown sugar essence and also gives way of a small nutty character of hazelnut and pistachio." "This is one of the best Redhook beers I've had." 5.64% alc.

Redhook Sunrye ★★

Goldn/Blond Ale: Redhook Brewery, Woodinville, WA www.redhook.com

"Aroma of rye and lemon zest, with some bubblegum sweetness." "Flavor is light as well tasting of fruit, malt and grains." "It's pretty much what it says, very light, crisp and thirst quenching. On those merits it's not bad." 4.7% alc.

Redhook Winterhook ★★1/2

Eng. Strong Ale: Redhook Brewery, Woodinville, WA www.redhook.com

"Green hoppy aroma was unexpected." "Almost tastes like hops mixed with slightly sweetened iced tea and a strong, bitter hop finish." "Definitely the hoppiest winter ale I've ever had." 5.58% alc.

Regia Extra ★★

Pale Lager: Cerveceria La Constancia (SABMiller), San Salvador, El Salvador www.laconstancia.com

"Mild corn and grape aroma." "Fizzy, watery body has a very mild sweetness and a thin, semi-dry finish." "The bottle may look cool, but I recommend passing on this one and just buying a Colt 45 if you're looking for volume." 4.3% alc.

Reinaert Amber ★★1/2

Belgian Ale: De Proefbrouwerij, Lochristi, Belgium www.proefbrouwerij.com

"The aroma is sweet yeasty combined with fruity notes, where peaches stand out." "Light malty and has hints of stonefruits; cookies, candi sugar, spices and herbs." 7% alc.

Reinaert Flemish Wild Ale ★★★

Bel. Strong Ale: De Proefbrouwerij, Lochristi, Belgium www.proefbrouwerij.com

"Some bretty aroma notes, with nutmeg, bread and grapefruit." "Tastes slightly malty, moderate to light on the sour notes and a good amount of funkiness and hints of fruit." "Not as primitive (sour) as expected, but quite Saison-esque in nature." 9% alc.

Reissdorf Kölsch ★★★1/2

Kölsch: Brauerei Heinrich Reissdorf, Köln, Germany www.reissdorf.de

"Herbal and grassy aroma along with cereal/biscuity malts." "Crisp malt flavors to begin with some quick, sweet bready notes and juicy lemon/apple background chords that linger delicately." 4.8% alc.

Rheingold Beer ★★1/2

Pale Lager: Matt Brewing Co., Utica, NY www.saranac.com

"Sweet malty light citrus aroma and taste." "Very weak flavor with some sweetness, quite watery." "Not very good, but thanks for the memories!" 5% alc.

Rhinelander ★★1/2

Pale Lager: Joseph Huber Brewing Co., Monroe, WI www.berghoffbeer.com

"Corny, grainy aroma with a touch of toffee and wet grass." "Flavor is a bit of sweet malt with a short hop finish." "Actually not half bad for what it is." 4.4% alc.

Ringwood Old Thumper ★★★★1/2

Prem Bitter: Ringwood, Ringwood, Hampshire, England www.ringwoodbrewery.co.uk

"Toffee and sweet malt with a bit of fruitiness and a smooth moderately bitter finish." "Straightforward English ale - a step up from Bass and Double Diamond but along the same lines." 5.6% alc.

Rio Grande Desert Pils ★
Classic Ger Pils: Rio Grande Brewing Co., Alburquerque, NM www.riograndebrewing.com
"Aroma is light malt, some sour milk, some grass and some light citrus." "Flavors are mostly grainy with notes of haygrass with the diacetyl present." "Very much a lawnmower beer bringing very little to the table." N/A% alc.

Rio Grande Elfego Bock ★
Dunkel: Rio Grande Brewing Co., Alburquerque, NM www.riograndebrewing.com
"Light aroma but has wet cardboard and malt." "Flavor is sweet caramel malt." "Thin and watery and carbonated." "Little or no flavor beyond what you could get from a Bud-Miller-Coors." N/A% alc.

Rio Grande Outlaw Lager ★
Calif. Common: Rio Grande Brewing Co., Alburquerque, NM www.riograndebrewing.com
"Aroma is fruity, raisins, plums, somewhat nutty." "Flavor has a bit of a caramel tint to it with a hint of licorice as well and a finish of olive oil." "Strange combination of flavors in such a thin-bodied beer." N/A% alc.

Rio Grande Pancho Verde Chile ★
Spice/Herb: Rio Grande Brewing Co., Alburquerque, NM www.riograndebrewing.com
"Almost invisible. No head. Smells like canned jalapeño. Wet. Tastes like canned jalapeño." "What's the point of this beer again?" N/A% alc.

Rio Salado Monsoon Maerzen Amber Lager ★★★
Märzen/Oktbfst: Rio Salado Brewing Co., Tempe, AZ www.riosaladobeer.com
"Muddy amber color." Aroma of "nice toasted malts." "Smooth and well balanced." "Sweet with good mouth watering German hops and hints of a grain bread." 6.38% alc.

Rio Salado Thunderhead Schwarz ★★★★
Schwarzbier: Rio Salado Brewing Co., Tempe, AZ www.riosaladobeer.com
"Beautiful looking beer." "Burnt and roasty aroma that approaches a stout." An "ode to roastiness", this highly-regarded beer is a "fabulous example of a Schwarzbier" 5.81% alc.

River Horse Belgian Frostbite Winter Ale ★★
Bel. Strong Ale: River Horse Brewing Co., Lambertville, NJ www.riverhorse.com
"Sweet and floral aroma that is a bit estery." "Flavor is raisin, caramel, apple, raisin and a bit of plum and just a touch of toffee." "Thin mouth feel, too light bodied for the style for me." 8% alc.

River Horse Hop Hazard ★★1/2
Am. Pale Ale: River Horse Brewing Co., Lambertville, NJ www.riverhorse.com
"Aroma is citrus hops, brown sugar, very sweet caramellyness." "Nicely hopped flavor - bready caramel malt provides a characterful backing." 5.5% alc.

River Horse Special Ale ★★
Prem Bitter: River Horse Brewing Co., Lambertville, NJ www.riverhorse.com
"Fruity, earthy hops float atop caramel-covered peaches." "Watery, toasty, mildly sweet caramelly and roasted." "Like a typical bad British ale actually." 4.5% alc.

River Horse Summer Blonde ★★
Goldn/Blond Ale: River Horse Brewing Co., Lambertville, NJ www.riverhorse.com
"Aroma is light and somewhat fruity." "Light bitterness and very gentle spiciness from the hops adds balance." "Neither pleasurable nor refreshing." 4% alc.

River Horse Tripel ★★1/2
Abbey Tripel: River Horse Brewing Co., Lambertville, NJ www.riverhorse.com
"Nose is peppery and spicy with notes of yeast, citrus fruits, light melon and sweet malts." "Taste is peppery as well with spices and yeast. More citrusy notes, light candied fruits (tangerine, melon) and sweet malts." 10% alc.

Robinson's Old Tom ★★1/2

Old Ale: Robinsons (ENG), Unicorn Brewery, Stockport, Cheshire, England www.frederic-robinson.com

"The aroma is quite enticing - rich malts, toffee, dried fruits and a hint of alcohol." "Sweetness of many fruits (esp. figs), strength of a respectable amount of alcohol, mellowness from the strong dark malts." 8.5% alc.

Rochefort Trappistes 10 ★★★★★

Abt/Quadrupel: Brasserie Rochefort, Rochefort, Belgium

"Aromas of fig, raisin, port and dried flowers." "Sweet, dark chocolate, mild alcohol, oak, dark fruit - especially plum, with an underlying earthiness." "Absolute velvet coating the tongue, I could roll it around for hours." 11.3% alc.

Rochefort Trappistes 6 ★★★★1/2

Abbey Dubbel: Brasserie Rochefort, Rochefort, Belgium

"Flavor is a complex blend of figs, peat smoke, wood and molasses/burnt sugar, with a drawn out tobacco." "Sweet light roasted nutty caramel malt (cookie) aroma with candy and fruit (plum) notes, yeast (dough) and maple." 7.5% alc.

Rochefort Trappistes 8 ★★★★★

Bel. Strong Ale: Brasserie Rochefort, Rochefort, Belgium

"Aroma is of apples, raisins, a touch of caramel and chocolate." "Intensely spicy, rich and yet dry flavors of cocoa, prunes, cinnamon and light clove-like spice." "A real treat to all of the senses." 9.2% alc.

Rock Art American Red Ale ★

Amber Ale: Rock Art Brewery, Morrisville, VT www.rockartbrewery.com

"Has aroma of malt, cabernet, cherries, some brown sugar." "Flavor is slightly sour with weak roasted malt and little hop bitterness." "Something is not right with this beer." 4.8% alc.

Rock Art IPA ★

IPA: Rock Art Brewery, Morrisville, VT www.rockartbrewery.com

"Aroma of resiny hops, bready malt and some cobwebby esters." "Thin, low carbonation, resiny and lemony hops, little malt backing, no complexity, just a mess." 5% alc.

Rock Art Ridge Runner ★★

Barley Wine: Rock Art Brewery, Morrisville, VT www.rockartbrewery.com

"The taste is muddled, with hints of roasty malt, fruit, berries, dark chocolate and nutmeg." "Sweet caramel flavor with significant US hops and a nice nutty finish with low bitterness." 7.5% alc.

Rock Art Stump Jumper Gnarly Stout ★★1/2

Dry Stout: Rock Art Brewery, Morrisville, VT www.rockartbrewery.com

"Aroma is not terribly expressive, mostly roast, bitter dark chocolate." "Roasty bitterness and sweet malts contrast nicely." "Fairly simple." 5.8% alc.

Rock Art Whitetail Ale ★

Am. Wheat: Rock Art Brewery, Morrisville, VT www.rockartbrewery.com

"Aroma was of pale biscuity malts, some fruit, honey and grassy hops." "Very light in the flavor department." "Not sure what makes this a Belgian White." 5% alc.

Rock Green Light ★

Pale Lager: Latrobe Brewing Co. (Labatt - InBev), Latrobe, PA www.rollingrock.com

"Light skunky aroma and a faint taste that almost reminds me of beer." "Thin in all respects- thin hops, thin malt and even thinner taste." "What's the point in having a healthy beer when you can't enjoy drinkin' it?" 3.7% alc.

Rock River Lager ★★★

Pale Lager: Joseph Huber Brewing Co., Monroe, WI www.berghoffbeer.com

"Nose is malty with light fruit notes and grass." "Fairly complex, crisp up front, fruity midrange with malts kicking in toward the end." "Nothing spectacular about it, but it was decent enough." 5% alc.

Rodenbach Classic ★★★

Flem Sour Ale: Brouwerij Rodenbach (Palm), Roeselare, Belgium www.rodenbach.be

"Sharp aroma, fruity, tart, lightly acidic, some cherry." "Medium sweet malts, light woodiness, fairly sour and tart cherryish flavors with some cinnamony notes as well." "Very dry and lightly tart makes it very refreshing to drink in quantity." 5% alc.

Rodenbach Grand Cru ★★★★★

Flem Sour Ale: Brouwerij Rodenbach (Palm), Roeselare, Belgium www.rodenbach.be

"Fruity aroma shows cherry and black currant, but also a little bit of sugar." "Vibrant, with cherry, red currants, plums and underlying sweet malts." "Big, tangy, rounded." "A slight downgrade from perfection, but still a classic." 6.5% alc.

Rogue American Amber ★★★★1/2

Amber Ale: Rogue Ales, Newport, OR www.rogueales.com

"Very nice floral aroma, some fruity and malty notes, toffee and with creamy notes." "Taste is a silky sweet malt, nutty, with a more than expected bitterness." "A well done, high-intensity example of the style." 5.1% alc.

Rogue Brutal Bitter ★★★★★

Prem Bitter: Rogue Ales, Newport, OR www.rogueales.com

"Aroma is very strong floral hops with hints of lemon and orange and sweet malt." "Light roasted and caramel malt flavors are punctuated quickly by citrus hops and light bittering." "Lives up to its name in a pleasant and inviting way." 6.2% alc.

Rogue Buckwheat Ale ★★1/2

Spice/Herb: Rogue Ales, Newport, OR www.rogueales.com

"Interesting herbal, citrus, fruity flavor that I like." "Flavors of bread and mild spice with a moderately bitter finish." "I really like most Rogue brews and it's nice that they try different things, but it doesn't always work out for the best." 4.8% alc.

Rogue Chamomile ★★1/2

Spice/Herb: Rogue Ales, Newport, OR www.rogueales.com

"Slightly flowery aroma with clean malts backing it up. Light character with soft chamomile notes and biscuity pale malts in the background." "Very unique brew." 5.4% alc.

Rogue Charlie 1981 ★★★★★

Am Strong Ale: Rogue Ales, Newport, OR www.rogueales.com

"Citrus (grapefruit rind) flavor with a cereal-y caramel background." "Taste is hoppy, sweet and floral with some odd fruity notes." "A hop lovers' dream, but especially if you like big malty strong ales." 8.5% alc.

Rogue Chipotle Ale ★★1/2

Spice/Herb: Rogue Ales, Newport, OR www.rogueales.com

"The aroma is quite smoky and full of malts with some spicier notes." "Dry pepper and smoke flavor with some malts and a very small hop quality." "Cheers for pushing the beer world boundaries." 5.5% alc.

Rogue Chocolate Stout ★★★★★

Sweet Stout: Rogue Ales, Newport, OR www.rogueales.com

"The aroma was heavy with chocolate and roasted malt with some hints of coffee." "Bitter roasted flavor well balanced with sweet chocolaty malt, finishing bitterly leaving a smoky aftertaste. What a beer!." 6.3% alc.

Rogue Dad's Little Helper ★★1/2

Malt Liquor: Rogue Ales, Newport, OR www.rogueales.com

"Lots of creamed corn and sewage on the nose." "Tastes like corn and mild alcohol with no finish." "It would be hard to find a less-inspiring beer." 7.2% alc.

Rogue Dead Guy Ale ★★★★

Bock: Rogue Ales, Newport, OR www.rogueales.com

"Nutty roasty malts taste sweet and refreshing and smooth hops favor structure over prominence." "Rich, chewy, toffeeish character. Full body. Smooth malts, toasty and earthy." "Has very little resemblance to German bock beers." 6.6% alc.

Rogue Glen ★★★★

Am Strong Ale: Rogue Ales, Newport, OR www.rogueales.com

"Aromas of piney hops, caramelized sugar and malts and dates." "Flavorful and hoppy - chewy sticky citrus hops and creamy caramel malts." 8.2% alc.

Rogue Half-E-Weizen ★★★★1/2

Am. Wheat: Rogue Ales, Newport, OR www.rogueales.com

"Wheat and coriander with subtle malt and hops-aroma." "The ginger is unmistakable, with coriander orange citrus, mild hop bitterness and a light pale maltiness" "Much more full and hoppy than your average wheat beer." 5.2% alc.

Rogue Hazelnut Brown ★★★★★

Brown Ale: Rogue Ales, Newport, OR www.rogueales.com

"Aroma is toasted malts, plums, slightly vinous, with a nice toffee balance." "Mostly sweet, creamy flavors of hazelnut and malts - like Whoppers candy." "If you are a stout lover and you enjoy hazelnut coffee, this is a must try for you." 6.22% alc.

Rogue Imperial Pale Ale ★★★★★

Imp/Dbl IPA: Rogue Ales, Newport, OR www.rogueales.com

"Huge hop aroma with grapefruit, pine and herbs. Malt balance is there as well here, caramel." "Fairly resinous bitter flavor, with citrus, peach and apricot tones. Syrupy, biscuity malt backing." 8.4% alc.

Rogue Imperial Stout ★★★★★

Imp. Stout: Rogue Ales, Newport, OR www.rogueales.com

"Raisin, grape, fig, coffee, chocolate, cocoa...it's all there. WOW!" "Some caramel, toffee, mocha and black walnut notes come through." "This is the single most overwhelming beer I've ever tasted." 11.6% alc.

Rogue Juniper Pale Ale ★★★

Spice/Herb: Rogue Ales, Newport, OR www.rogueales.com

"The juniper berries are only an addition to the depth of the brew as opposed to the brew being a showcase for the juniper berries." "Biscuity aroma with hints of citrus hops and a slight spiciness." "Finishes dry and spicy of lemon and grass." 5.2% alc.

Rogue Kells Irish Style Lager ★★★★

Premium Lager: Rogue Ales, Newport, OR www.rogueales.com

"Nose is lightly hopped, grassy with a nice malty breadiness though fairly subdued." "Starts out creamy and malty and finishes dry and parched and hoppy/bitter." "Just a solid enjoyable lager." 5.2% alc.

Rogue Mocha Porter ★★★★

Porter: Rogue Ales, Newport, OR www.rogueales.com

"Robust aroma of bitter mocha espresso, dark chocolate, slightly souring chocolate chips, black raspberries." "Flavor also roasted malt, some coffee and an acidic mildly bitter finish." "Like Shakespeare's baby brother." 5.1% alc.

Rogue Morimoto Imperial Pilsner ★★★★★

Eur Str Lager: Rogue Ales, Newport, OR www.rogueales.com

"Gorgeous, perfumey, spicy and citrusy hop aroma." "Flavor is grainy and grassy with plenty of sweet malt, hop bitterness and a kick of alcohol." "Above average but no way will I pay the hefty price tag to try this again." 8.8% alc.

Rogue Old Crustacean ★★★★
Barley Wine: Rogue Ales, Newport, OR www.rogueales.com
"Flavor of sugar, sweet malt, alcohol, pepper, caramel and hops." "Aftertaste is incredibly bitter - way too much so." "This certainly isn't a beer for the casual drinker." 10.5% alc.

Rogue Oregon Golden Ale ★★★★
Goldn/Blond Ale: Rogue Ales, Newport, OR www.rogueales.com
"Fresh fruity aroma of mango, honey and grassy hops." "Fairly strong hop flavor with enough average malt to keep up, finishes citrusy and is on the whole still pretty hoppy." "A little subtle by Rogue's usual standards, but it's a good session beer." 5% alc.

Rogue Oyster Cloyster Stout ★★★
Stout: Rogue Ales, Newport, OR www.rogueales.com
"Chocolaty aroma with hints of coffee, almonds." "Malts are chocolate and sweet. Hops are slightly spicy." "Pretty standard stout fare, with similarities to Shakespeare but not the same intensity." 4.8% alc.

Rogue Phred's Black Soba ★★1/2
Porter: Rogue Ales, Newport, OR www.rogueales.com
"Moderately bitter chocolate, earthy malts and a ton of buckwheat." "Partially spicy, partially dry, well textured and lightly fluffy with cocoa and breads." "Though not really attempting to be a porter, it comes off as a unique twist on the style." 5% alc.

Rogue Saint Rogue Red ★★★★★
Amber Ale: Rogue Ales, Newport, OR www.rogueales.com
"Smelled slightly of floral hops, but mostly of sweet, roasted malts." "Big malt body with a moderate bitterness." "Not the most complex of beer but the high level of hops makes this more interesting than most beers in this style." 5.2% alc.

Rogue Santa's Private Reserve ★★★1/2
Am Strong Ale: Rogue Ales, Newport, OR www.rogueales.com
"Toasted malt, caramel and some grassy hops in the aroma." "Lots of caramel, notes of chocolate, coffee, lightly burnt toffee and nuts. Good hop backbone." "Highly recommended for 'hops oriented' individuals." 6% alc.

Rogue Über Pilsner ★★★★★
Pilsner: Rogue Ales, Newport, OR www.rogueales.com
"Aroma is fresh, with biscuity malts and herbal, grassy hops." "Flavor is grainy and sweet at the start, with a very nice floral and bitter back end." "Strong and hoppy lager with no pils characteristics but it is certainly enjoyable." 5.355% alc.

Rogue Shakespeare Stout ★★★★★
Stout: Rogue Ales, Newport, OR www.rogueales.com
"Has aroma of rich chocolate, light vanilla, Cascade hoppiness and roasted barley." "Bold flavor...almost espresso with a touch of roasty dark chocolate. Finishes bitter with plenty of hoppy goodness that lingers on the tongue." 6% alc.

Rogue Smoke ★★★
Smoked: Rogue Ales, Newport, OR www.rogueales.com
"Aroma produces the customary wafts - bark, goat jerky, hickory, maple syrup oak vats, caramel and butterscotch." "Light smoky flavor, with a nice underlying malt profile." "A smoked beer that is not over bearing." 5.9% alc.

Rogue Younger's Special Bitter ★★★★
Prem Bitter: Rogue Ales, Newport, OR www.rogueales.com
"Fragrant signature Rogue hop aroma with some sweet toffee." "There aren't any surprises here but the rich, earthy bitterness and sound fundamental structure make this a lovely ale." 4.8% alc.

Rolling Rock Extra Pale ★★1/2

Pale Lager: Anheuser-Busch Brewing Companies, , www.rollingrock.com

"Pretty carbonated and watery on the palate." "Flavor is sweet from the corn and malt, just a touch of hops." "This fits right in with all the other highly advertised alcohol water on the market." 4.5% alc.

Romulan Ale ★★

Pale Lager: Cerveceria La Constancia (SABMiller), San Salvador, El Salvador www.laconstancia.com

"It was blue, first of all and poured with a bluish tint to the fuzzy head." "Smells like some malts, not typical harsh or cheap hot weather pale lager." "Flavor was like a light blond ale." N/A% alc.

Roslyn Beer ★★1/2

Dunkel: Roslyn Brewing Co., Roslyn, WA www.roslynbrewery.com

"Light crystal malt aroma with some fruitiness." "Fairly light flavor profile - maybe some cocoa accents." "Despite its lightness, it's a fairly successful beer due to smooth palate and rounded flavors." N/A% alc.

Royal Challenge ★★

Pale Lager: Shaw Wallace (SABMiller), Mumbai, India www.shawwallace.com

"Smells of a stale malt and some raw sugars along with a bad hop." "Taste is weak with some skunk noticeable and some malt." "One of the most watery beers I think I have ever had." 5% alc.

Royal Oak ★★1/2

Prem Bitter: O'Hanlons, Whimple, Devon, England www.ohanlons.co.uk

"Lively aroma of passion fruit, caramel, brown sugar, plum." "Flavors are soft malts, especially caramel, with some fruit and yeast." "Entertains while waiting for the main course." 5% alc.

Ruddles County ★★1/2

Prem Bitter: Greene King Plc, Bury St. Edmunds, Suffolk, England www.greeneking.co.uk

"Sweet aroma of malts, caramel and fruits." "Moderate malty-bitter flavor, ending with a long, dry hoppy-aromatic finish." "The accountants won." 4.7% alc.

Russian River Damnation ★★★★

Bel. Strong Ale: Russian River Brewing, Santa Rosa, CA www.Russianriverbrewing.com

"Spicy and slightly phenolic nose." "Cloves, licorice, menthol and allspice blow in to mix with pears, apples and bananas." "I'd always suspected somebody could do this style as well as Moortgat..." 7% alc.

Russian River Sanctification ★★★★1/2

Belgian Ale: Russian River Brewing, Santa Rosa, CA www.Russianriverbrewing.com

"Very much flemish in the smell- lots of brett." "Light pale malt character punctuated by leather, chardonnay, wood and light brettanomyces." "It's hard not to appreciate nature's beauties." 6.25% alc.

Russian River Supplication ★★★★★

Belgian Ale: Russian River Brewing, Santa Rosa, CA www.Russianriverbrewing.com

"Orange-peach esters share the aroma with brettanomyces, leather and big Pinot Noir." "Cherry, tart and sour notes explode on the tongue and take your mouth hostage." "Just wonderful in every way." 7% alc.

Russian River Temptation ★★★★★

Belgian Ale: Russian River Brewing, Santa Rosa, CA www.Russianriverbrewing.com

"Aroma is dry, barnyardy, funky and nicely oaked with a touch of fruity tartness and brett." "Slightly toasty, highly vinous with a puckeringly tart finish." "Kick ass." 7.25% alc.

Saigon Export ★

Pale Lager: Saigon Beer Co., Saigon (Ho Chi Minh City), Vietnam

"Light flavor with discrete vegetal/grassy aroma." "Mild, sweet, lightly grainy flavor with very mild bitterness." 4.7% alc.

Saint Arnold Amber Ale ★★★

Amber Ale: Saint Arnold Brewing Co., Houston, TX www.saintarnold.com

"A nice fruity yeast aroma combined with caramel malt, a touch of toast." "Sweet up front which goes from sugary to more of a caramel in the finish with a touch of hops and some grassiness." "I liked each sip more than the previous." 5.5% alc.

Saint Arnold Brown Ale ★★★

Brown Ale: Saint Arnold Brewing Co., Houston, TX www.saintarnold.com

"Aroma - the molasses jumped right out there than came the malts, brown sugar, chocolate." "Light chocolate malts in the initial flavor with tangerine and dough." 5.3% alc.

Saint Arnold Christmas Ale ★★★1/2

Eng. Strong Ale: Saint Arnold Brewing Co., Houston, TX www.saintarnold.com

"Rich toasty caramel aroma with a hint of spices." "Taste is quite malty sweet, with some faint hop action and faint spiciness." "A quite decent, restrained English style ale, with an almost American hop flavor." 7% alc.

Saint Arnold Elissa IPA ★★★1/2

IPA: Saint Arnold Brewing Co., Houston, TX www.saintarnold.com

"Nose of fruity citrusy hops and a bit of malt, fairly hop forward." "Little grapefruit offset by a nice roasted grain flavor." "Finishes creamy and full flavored. Nice." 6.6% alc.

Saint Arnold Fancy Lawnmower Ale ★★1/2

Kölsch: Saint Arnold Brewing Co., Houston, TX www.saintarnold.com

"Smells of grapes, sugar, grass." "Kind of has a hay like flavor and uses the same hop type as Budweiser... fortunately St. Arnold made a better beer!" "Very refreshing laying by the pool in the summer." 4.9% alc.

Saint Arnold Oktoberfest ★★★

Märzen/Oktbfst: Saint Arnold Brewing Co., Houston, TX www.saintarnold.com

"Aroma is of generous amounts of caramel malt with accents of toffee." "Nicely malty toast and caramel is supported by a hint of that pruniness you sometimes get in doppelbocks." 6% alc.

Saint Arnold Spring Bock ★★★

Bock: Saint Arnold Brewing Co., Houston, TX www.saintarnold.com

"Fruity aroma, touch of caramel and sourness." "Taste is sweet up front with a rich malty finish that almost has a meatiness to it." "Definitely interesting and tasty, though it could use a bit more oomph." 6.4% alc.

Saint Arnold Summer Pils ★★1/2

Pilsner: Saint Arnold Brewing Co., Houston, TX www.saintarnold.com

"Aroma is quite citrusy, lemon, spicy hops, a touch of diacetyl as well." "Taste is lightly sweet up front with a immediate hop character that flows through to the finish of this beer." "A little too sweet and thin." 4.9% alc.

Saint Arnold Texas Wheat ★★1/2

Am. Wheat: Saint Arnold Brewing Co., Houston, TX www.saintarnold.com

"Smells grassy with light lemony notes." "Flavor is sweet malt, thin and plain otherwise." "I'd like to try something with a deeper flavor." 4.9% alc.

Saint Arnold Winter Stout ★★1/2

Stout: Saint Arnold Brewing Co., Houston, TX www.saintarnold.com

Sweet malty aroma." "Pretty thin on the body, taste is on the sweet side, heavy coffee flavor." "Needs to be much thicker." "Great on a hot day." 5.6% alc.

Saison d'Epeautre ★★★1/2

Saison: Brasserie de Blaugies, Dour-Blaugies, Belgium www.brasseriedeblaugies.com

"Semi-sweet Belgian malty and grassy, floral, yeasty aroma." "Very dry and somewhat acidic, with hints of lemon and chamomile tea." "I really like this beer - it's like a dry Hefeweizen - very nice." 6% alc.

Saison de Pipaix ★★★1/2
Saison: Brasserie à Vapeur, Leuze-Pipaix, Belgium www.vapeur.com
"Alluring aroma of curaçao, coriander, pepper, souring lemon rinds, apricots and orange skin." "Dried tangerines and lucid, lucrative pear juice give it a sharp, yet sugary twanging component." "Wonderful, classic rendition." 6% alc.

Saison Dupont ★★★★★
Saison: Dupont Brasserie, Tourpes-Leuze, Belgium www.brasserie-dupont.com
"Aroma is yeasty, with some dust, allspice, baguette crust and white pepper." "Soft palate is fruity (apricot, Asian pear), yeasty and pale malty with an underpinning of rounded, earthy, low cohumulone bitterness." "Stylish, sublime and elegant." 6.5% alc.

Saku Originaal ★★
Pale Lager: Saku Brewery , Harjumaa, Estonia www.saku.ee
"Grains and grass run amuck in the nose." "Somewhat sweet malt, wet cardboard, mild grain and cleanly free of most adjuncts." "Yeah, this sort of tastes like cardboard. But in a good way." 4.4% alc.

Saku Porter ★★1/2
Baltic Porter: Saku Brewery , Harjumaa, Estonia www.saku.ee
"Roasted aroma with notes of fruits, coffee and licorice." "Flavor was of caramel, some light malt, plums, light hops." "Much lighter than I'd expect from a Porter, especially one this strong in the booze department." 7.5% alc.

Salopian Entire Butt ★★1/2
Porter: Salopian, Shrewsbury, Shropshire, England
"Nose is sweet malt with caramel, chocolate and faint smokiness." "Palate is rich and espresso-like - very robust - with a full, creamy mouthfeel." "This is a very fine Porter - complex and surprisingly smooth." 4.8% alc.

Salva Vida ★★1/2
Pale Lager: Cerveceria Hondureña (SABMiller), Tegucigalpa, Hondura www.cerveceriahondurena.com
"So-so nose, sourdough, lemon, grass." "Not much here in the taste department, a little mossy, a little hoppy." "I drank it solely as a novelty and the novelty wore off pretty quick." 4.8% alc.

Sam Adams Light ★★1/2
Premium Lager: Boston Beer Co., Boston, MA www.samadams.com
"Rather dark for a light beer." "For all Sam Adams' hyping this beer, it still tastes like a light beer to me." "Better then most." 4.05% alc.

Sambadoro ★
Pale Lager: InBev Brasil, Rio Grande do Sul, Brazil www.inbev.com
"Mildly skunky aroma set the mood." "Start is sweet, turning thin and a bit sour." "An absolutely horrible beer to say the least." 4.9% alc.

Samuel Adams 1790 Root Beer Brew ★★1/2
Herb, Spice: Boston Beer Co., Boston, MA www.samadams.com
Nose is huge sassafras, wintergreen bubblegum and a hint of anise. "Very different but more akin to a specialty soda than a beer." "It's well-brewed, don't get me wrong, it's just not working for me." 5.5% alc.

Samuel Adams Black Lager ★★★1/2
Schwarzbier: Boston Beer Co., Boston, MA www.samadams.com
"Taste is lightly sweet, body is full, finish is lightly roasted coffee and caramel." "There's not a lot of complexity here, but this beer is very easy to drink." 4.9% alc.

Samuel Adams Boston Ale ★★★
Amber Ale: Boston Beer Co., Boston, MA www.samadams.com
"Taste is clean and herbal with a nicely set toasted dryness and smooth breadyish malty backing." "Tastes is caramel with some spicy hops, but also slightly bland." Consistent to finish. Good beer." 5.1% alc.

Samuel Adams Boston Lager ★★★

Premium Lager: Boston Beer Co., Boston, MA www.samadams.com

"There is a hint of that crispness of good lager hops." "Decent maltiness that is mildly sweet, somewhat bready and lightly grainy." "This beer is a great safety net, something I know I can count on in desperate times." 4.9% alc.

Samuel Adams Cherry Wheat ★★1/2

Fruit Beer: Boston Beer Co., Boston, MA www.samadams.com

"Reminded me of a cherry pie." "Taste started off sweet and fruity almost just like a cherry soda." "After one, then you won't want another." 5.4% alc.

Samuel Adams Chocolate Bock ★★★1/2

Bock: Boston Beer Co., Boston, MA www.samadams.com

"Great. I taste chocolate, coffee, roasted malt, vanilla and some earthiness." "There is nothing subtle about the chocolate flavors." "It's a good beer, but not for $15 a bottle." 5.5% alc.

Samuel Adams Cranberry Lambic ★★1/2

Fruit Beer: Boston Beer Co., Boston, MA www.samadams.com

"Aroma is of cranberry, but subdued, spices and yeast, banana and sugared oranges." "Flavor has a lot of cranberries and some background banana from the yeast." "Needs a great deal more tartness, especially into the finish." 5.9% alc.

Samuel Adams Cream Stout ★★★1/2

Sweet Stout: Boston Beer Co., Boston, MA www.samadams.com

"Nice nose here with caramel mocha frappacino (à la Starbucks), toasted marshmallow and hints of milk chocolate." "Ultra sweet ese coffee, light roast on the palate." "Pleasing and drinkable example of the style." 4.9% alc.

Samuel Adams Double Bock ★★★1/2

Doppelbock: Boston Beer Co., Boston, MA www.samadams.com

"Aroma is all caramel up front, with hints of toffee and dark roasted grain." "This is a beer to be sipped and enjoyed with nice hints of molasses and a deep presence of malt to cover the alcohol." "I'd drink more." 8.8% alc.

Samuel Adams James Madison Dark Wheat Ale ★★★

Dunkelweizen: Boston Beer Co., Boston, MA www.samadams.com

Nose is lightly smoky with hints of rye bread, light cocoa, toasty malts, and sweet fruit. "Body is much drier and a bit more tart than the sweet nose expects, bit of dark, sourdough breadiness." "Very interesting, but ultimately not really satisfying." 5.7% alc.

Samuel Adams Golden Pilsner ★★★

Pilsner: Boston Beer Co., Boston, MA www.samadams.com

"Very crisp and clean." "Somewhat dry." "Decent aroma of hops and a mildly spicy floral yeast, maybe a touch of honey." "An American Pils midfielder." 4.69% alc.

Samuel Adams Hefeweizen ★★1/2

Am. Wheat: Boston Beer Co., Boston, MA www.samadams.com

"Heavy on the wheat component with little if any of the traditional Hefeweizen character." "Mid-palate essentially is quite ordinary and characterless with only a hint of the citrus and spiciness of other versions of this style." 5.4% alc.

Samuel Adams Holiday Porter ★★★

Porter: Boston Beer Co., Boston, MA www.samadams.com

"Aroma is caramel and brown sugar with some dark roasted malts." "Smooth, slightly dry palate." "Mild dark roasted malt flavors and a touch of floral hops." "Nice 'gateway' brew for beginners." 5.8% alc.

Samuel Adams George Washington Porter ★★★
Porter: Boston Beer Co., Boston, MA www.samadams.com
Nose is unique. Definite molasses, some almost burnt or smoldering wood notes, light licorice and some chocolate. "Evenly balanced flavors of unsweetened bakers chocolate, molasses, licorice." "One of the better ones in the 4 pack." 5.7% alc.

Samuel Adams Octoberfest ★★★
Märzen/Oktbfst: Boston Beer Co., Boston, MA www.samadams.com
"Malty, not too sweet." "When you go big, you usually get this run-of-the-mill type boring beer." "Tasted like a crisp November morning!" 5.4% alc.

Samuel Adams Old Fezziwig ★★★
Spice/Herb: Boston Beer Co., Boston, MA www.samadams.com
"Aroma is semi-sweet and a bit spicy." "Flavor is of cinnamon, caramel and spices." "Lots of cinnamon and I can taste the orange and ginger at the end." "The taste of this beer improves with every drink." 5.9% alc.

Samuel Adams Pale Ale ★★★
Eng Pale Ale: Boston Beer Co., Boston, MA www.samadams.com
"Roasted malts and a splash of lemony hops." "Light sweet malt and caramel mix with a touch of citrus." "Leaves you wanting something with a bit more, well, something." 5.4% alc.

Samuel Adams Scotch Ale ★★★1/2
Scotch Ale: Boston Beer Co., Boston, MA www.samadams.com
"Strong malt character in the nose, smells creamy and caramel." "Flavor was of roasted malt with some hop bitterness and some smokiness in the background." "An interesting beer from a Co. whose best quality is its variety." 5.4% alc.

Samuel Adams Spring Ale ★★1/2
Kölsch: Boston Beer Co., Boston, MA www.samadams.com
"Husky malt aroma, some fresh apple, hints of grass, wheat." "A lighter taste, a little watery." "This tastes like it has smoothed out from what was intended." "Refreshing spring beer." 5.2% alc.

Samuel Adams Summer Ale ★★★
Am. Wheat: Boston Beer Co., Boston, MA www.samadams.com
"Citrus flavors dominate the profile." "Almost soda-like carbonation with a crisp refreshing citrusy taste." "A nice summer ale that, because of its peppery spice, would drink fine in the fall, too." 5.3% alc.

Samuel Adams Traditional Ginger Honey Ale ★★★
Spice, Herb: Boston Beer Co., Boston, MA www.samadams.com
Nose of lemon, honey and ginger with a light herbal spiciness. "Flavor is full-on ginger and honey at first, very reminiscent of Reeds' ginger brews." "Strange brew, but interesting." 5.5% alc.

Samuel Adams Utopias ★★★★
Barley Wine: Boston Beer Co., Boston, MA www.samadams.com
"Firm, alcoholic aroma with vanilla, bourbon, malt, nuts." "Notably phenolic palate is sweet, very mapley, with a bracing slap of alcohol." "Sweet, liqueurish finish." "Big time dessert beer." 25% alc.

Samuel Adams Vienna Style ★★★
Vienna: Boston Beer Co., Boston, MA www.samadams.com
Almost has an earth quality, some oak, toasted smoke flavors. Very good malt character." "Low in bitterness." "Not a bad offering." N/A% alc.

Samuel Adams White Ale ★★★
Bel. Witbier: Boston Beer Co., Boston, MA www.samadams.com
"Slightly sour wheat aroma." "Reasonable balance of spices orange and a slight tartness but lacking in body." "An easy, diverting spring beer." 5.4% alc.

Samuel Adams Winter Lager ★★★
Weizen Bock: Boston Beer Co., Boston, MA www.samadams.com
"Aroma shows brown sugar, spice (ginger orange peel), sweet earthy malt." "Flavor is caramel, malts, fruits and spices." "Spicy malt flavor with a short finish." 5.8% alc.

Samuel Smith's Imperial Stout ★★★★★
Imp. Stout: Samuel Smith, Yorkshire, England www.tadcaster.uk.com/breweriesSamuelSmith.htm
"Light chocolate aroma with hints of grass, white sugar and orange." "Body is thick, especially for the size of beer, with chewy malts, lots of deep fruit (plums, peaches, raisins)." "I could never turn this down." 7% alc.

Samuel Smith's Indian Ale ★★★★
Prem Bitter: Samuel Smith, Yorkshire, England www.tadcaster.uk.com/breweriesSamuelSmith.htm
"Minty, herbal, woody aroma; balanced palate with caramel and woody, rooty notes." "Good roast flavors, earthy, spicy and lots of malt." "Another nice brew from Smith and a nice match to go with a premium cigar." 5% alc.

Samuel Smith's Nut Brown Ale ★★★★1/2
Brown Ale: Samuel Smith, Yorkshire, England www.tadcaster.uk.com/breweriesSamuelSmith.htm
"Definitely nutty, with dry fruity malt and a significant bitterness." "Completely dominated by rich malts with notes of caramel and nuts." "Rich and very satisfying brew." 5% alc.

Samuel Smith's Oatmeal Stout ★★★★★
Sweet Stout: Samuel Smith, Yorkshire, England www.tadcaster.uk.com/breweriesSamuelSmith.htm
"Aroma like the finest Belgian chocolate mixed with Atholl Brose." "Silky body, fruity notes of cherry, redcurrant add an interesting layer to the silky malts and chocolate overtones." "The classic oatmeal stout - depth without compromise." 5% alc.

Samuel Smith's Old Brewery Pale Ale ★★★
Prem Bitter: Samuel Smith, Yorkshire, England www.tadcaster.uk.com/breweriesSamuelSmith.htm
"Hoppy aroma, a bit earthy." "Sweet caramel malts, with a light nuttiness and a light bitter finish." "Clean finish, this is a good pale not loaded with hops." 5% alc.

Samuel Smith's Organic Ale ★★★
Bitter: Samuel Smith, Yorkshire, England www.tadcaster.uk.com/breweriesSamuelSmith.htm
"Aroma is of sweet bready malt and fruit." "Taste is pleasant but too mild - faintly orange-juice malt, a touch of rye grain, very mild/stale hops orange pekoe tea." "Most unmemorable Sam Smith brew I've had yet." 5% alc.

Samuel Smith's Organic Lager ★★★
Premium Lager: Samuel Smith, Yorkshire, England www.tadcaster.uk.com/breweriesSamuelSmith.htm
"Dry, with some lemony citrus and a decent amount of bitterness." "Barley and even some faint malt and hops (English type)." "Good, but not worth dropping $3.29/pint." 5% alc.

Samuel Smith's Pure Brewed Lager ★★★★1/2
Premium Lager: Samuel Smith, Yorkshire, England www.tadcaster.uk.com/breweriesSamuelSmith.htm
"Aroma is very malty and clean." "More complex than most domestic lagers. Crisp up front, malty, sweet middle, dry finish." "Pretty good beer for a style I don't normally enjoy." 5% alc.

Samuel Smith's Taddy Porter ★★★★1/2
Porter: Samuel Smith, Yorkshire, England www.tadcaster.uk.com/breweriesSamuelSmith.htm
"Aroma is chocolaty, slightly vinous with vague hints of coffee and apple juice." "Fairly robust flavor profile features plums, vinous notes, hints of roast and chocolate." "A total package porter." 5% alc.

Samuel Smith's Winter Welcome Ale ★★1/2

Eng. Strong Ale: Samuel Smith, Yorkshire, England www.tadcaster.uk.com/breweriesSamuelSmith.htm

"This beer is known for having problems with skunkiness the later in the season you go. "Aroma of caramelly malts and the chalky yeastiness of Yorkshire squares." "Similar profile with more caramel, tobacco, wood - almost a dusty attic character." 6% alc.

San Lucas ★

Pale Lager: Cerveceria La Constancia (SABMiller), San Salvador, El Salvador www.laconstancia.com

"Really insipid tasting, very metallic aftertaste, very carbonated but totally lifeless in the mouth." "I expected this to be a lot like Corona and I suppose it was... It wasn't skunky, though, so that was a plus." N/A% alc.

San Miguel Dark Lager ★★★

Am Dark Larger: San Miguel, Manila, Philippines www.sanmiguel.com.ph

"Nice roast aromas with some hops and a hint of pepper." "Flavors were dark fruit, raisins, molasses, honey, slight citrus, yeast, hops and malt." "I really enjoyed this beer more than I expected I would." 5% alc.

San Miguel Premium Lager ★★1/2

Pale Lager: San Miguel, Manila, Philippines www.sanmiguel.com.ph

"Has a slight skunky smell which dissipates in a cold glass." "Sweet with notes of grain, corn, grass, hay and hop bitterness presence at the end." "A little harsh on warming." 4.8% alc.

Sand Creek English Style Special Ale ★★

Amber Ale: Sand Creek Brewing Co. (Pioneer/WI Brewing Co.), Black River Falls, WI www.sandcreekbrewing.com

"Strong toastiness and a moderate buttery flavor really jump out in this amber ale." "A moderate bitterness helps to balance the beer somewhat." "A bit more body and lasting flavors and this could be quite good." N/A% alc.

Sand Creek Oscar's Chocolate Oatmeal Stout ★★★1/2

Sweet Stout: Sand Creek Brewing Co. (Pioneer/WI Brewing Co.), Black River Falls, WI www.sandcreekbrewing.com

"Chocolate aroma mixing well with the roasted malts and coffee like notes." "Taste was full of coffee, chocolate and other fine stout flavors." "This is a solid sweet stout." N/A% alc.

Sand Creek Wood Duck Wheat ★★

Hefeweizen: Sand Creek Brewing Co. (Pioneer/WI Brewing Co.), Black River Falls, WI www.sandcreekbrewing.com

"Typical banana-clove dominant aroma, lemon-lime undercurrents and a whiff of dried grasses." "Firm malty body, sour but not lactic, doughy and sweet with subtle banana-bread/caramel character." N/A% alc.

Santa Fe Nut Brown ★

Brown Ale: Santa Fe Brewing Co., Santa Fe, NM www.santafebrewing.com

"Light malt aroma, some cookie but all in all very faint." "Flavors are light caramel, some earthy English hops and diacetyl." "Not a lot there except a little nut and some corn." 5% alc.

Santa Fe Pale Ale ★★1/2

Am. Pale Ale: Santa Fe Brewing Co., Santa Fe, NM www.santafebrewing.com

"Pale malts are woody, a touch caramelly and lightly sweet, the hops are mildly bitter with a decent hop flavor." "Reminiscent of microbrew from the early days; a standard, unimaginative example of the style." 5% alc.

Santa Fe Wheat ★

Am. Wheat: Santa Fe Brewing Co., Santa Fe, NM www.santafebrewing.com

"Nose is fairly sweet, with hints of cotton candy, caramel and dried apricots." "Floral, lemony taste and subtle hop flavors." "It was their least appealing and just above rank." 5% alc.

Sapporo Premium Draft ★★1/2
Pale Lager: Sapporo Breweries, Tokyo, Japan www.sapporobeer.com
"Aroma is a simple, sweet pale lager." "Sweet cereal grain malts, some rice. A little hop and bitterness to offset the sweet malts." "It's a light bodied pale lager - I don't expect miracles." 5% alc.

Sapporo Reserve ★★
Premium Lager: Sapporo Breweries, Tokyo, Japan www.sapporobeer.com
"Light pale malt, fusel and grassy hop aroma." "Mild bitterness from noble hop varieties, light pale malt sweetness and macroish acidity on the palate." "Mostly harmless." 5.2% alc.

Sapporo Yebisu ★★1/2
Helles/Dortmnd: Sapporo Breweries, Tokyo, Japan www.sapporobeer.com
"Aromas of grass, cheerios and a touch of flowers." "Tastes malty, with hops and a slight malty dryness at the finish." "Much better than regular Sapporo." 5% alc.

Saranac (Golden) Pilsner ★★1/2
Pilsner: Matt Brewing Co., Utica, NY www.saranac.com
"Has some slight hoppy scents, weak sweet malts." "Decent hop character; a barely-sweet, grainy maltiness." "A middle of the road beer if ever there was one." 5.2% alc.

Saranac Adirondack Amber ★★★
Vienna: Matt Brewing Co., Utica, NY www.saranac.com
"Very light, clean aroma, although not too much going on: Grape nuts and lightly spicy hoppiness." "Flavor of toast and caramel, with a moderately dry, mildly citrusy finish." 5.4% alc.

Saranac Belgian White ★★1/2
Bel. Witbier: Matt Brewing Co., Utica, NY www.saranac.com
"Aroma of oranges and white pepper, with a mild wheat sweetness in the backdrop." "Pleasantly spiced flavor - light pale malt and leafy hops along with subdued coriander." 5.3% alc.

Saranac Black and Tan ★★★
Stout: Matt Brewing Co., Utica, NY www.saranac.com
"Light roasted malty, coffee, liqorice, wet paper aroma." "Warm, earthy dark chocolate shows in the flavor along with plenty of roasted grain goodness." "I wish this was a black without the tan, it'd be a much better beer." 5.3% alc.

Saranac Black Forest ★★★
Schwarzbier: Matt Brewing Co., Utica, NY www.saranac.com
"Aroma of raisin, chocolate and a bit of caramel." "Roasted flavor with notes of fruits, berries and hops." "Light-medium body with low carbonation and a touch of acidity." 5.2% alc.

Saranac Caramel Porter ★★★
Porter: Matt Brewing Co., Utica, NY www.saranac.com
"Caramel wafts out of the bottle, very dominant in the aroma and strong in taste, along with a lot of sweetness." "Balance? Not really, sorry." "It seems like this beer is a good idea but done by the wrong brewery." 5.4% alc.

Saranac Chocolate Amber ★★1/2
Dunkel: Matt Brewing Co., Utica, NY www.saranac.com
"I got more coffee and roast out of this aroma, but there was some chocolate too." "Flavor reveals the sweet milk chocolate that the label mentions along with a bit of caramel." "Saranac couldn't make a thick beer if they tried." 5.7% alc.

Saranac ESB ★★★

Prem Bitter: Matt Brewing Co., Utica, NY www.saranac.com

"Earthy, tea-like, grapefruit nose." "Starts with some faint caramel, light malt sweetness, light body, then big citrus hops, although very thin in texture." "Lacking depth." 5.9% alc.

Saranac Hefeweizen ★★1/2

Hefeweizen: Matt Brewing Co., Utica, NY www.saranac.com

"Wheaty aroma, with pear, peach and faint coriander seed." "Flavor is banana, a hint of citrus, light malts and a bit of a sour tang toward the finish." 5.6% alc.

Saranac IPA ★★1/2

IPA: Matt Brewing Co., Utica, NY www.saranac.com

"Mild floral and orange zest hop scents dominate the soft caramel malts in the aroma." "Comes off a bit on the sweet side with moderate hop flavor and little bitterness." "Not as aggressive as the style may suggest." 5.8% alc.

Saranac Kölsch ★★1/2

Kölsch: Matt Brewing Co., Utica, NY www.saranac.com

"Bready, fairly sweet and very light on the hops." "Crisp malt and light hops, more like a non-descript lager." "Not really my idea of a Kölsch but pleasant enough anyway." 5% alc.

Saranac Marzenbier ★★1/2

Märzen/Oktbfst: Matt Brewing Co., Utica, NY www.saranac.com

"Taste is a fruity maltiness; some nice floral hops offset the maltiness." "Taste is caramel and apples along with rich bread and some wood." "A little dry and a little thin." 5.6% alc.

Saranac Mocha Stout ★★1/2

Stout: Matt Brewing Co., Utica, NY www.saranac.com

"Sweet dark chocolate and caramel." "Lots of cocoa and roasted caramel in the flavor with a tangy, cola-like metallic aftertaste." "Too thin for a stout though." 5% alc.

Saranac Mountain Berry ★★1/2

Fruit Beer: Matt Brewing Co., Utica, NY www.saranac.com

Very weak/mild aroma... slight maltiness in there, but not much of anything actually." "Flavor is mildly sweet with a light vague fruit flavor." 5% alc.

Saranac Oktoberfest ★★1/2

Märzen/Oktbfst: Matt Brewing Co., Utica, NY www.saranac.com

"Aroma of bread, slight roasty malts, light sweetness and earth." "Malty, light sweet flavor and smooth palate." "Tasted next to a Hacker-Pschorr and it got lost!" 5.4% alc.

Saranac Pale Ale ★★1/2

Eng Pale Ale: Matt Brewing Co., Utica, NY www.saranac.com

"Caramel malts aroma with floral hops." "Grassy and earthy in the flavor with some bitterness and nutty notes." "Generic, inoffensive pale ale." 5.5% alc.

Saranac Roggen Bock ★★★

Bock: Matt Brewing Co., Utica, NY www.saranac.com

"Roasty malts, creamy smooth mouthfeel, spicy, but a little thin I must say." "Faint chocolate flavor, spicy rye notes and a light graininess." "Slightly dull taste. Overall good." 5.5% alc.

Saranac Season's Best Nut Brown ★★★★

Am Dark Larger: Matt Brewing Co., Utica, NY www.saranac.com

"Subtle nut aroma with some toasted overtones." "The gentle roast, modest sweetness and mild nuttiness are nicely balanced by moderately bitter hops." "A unique beer that is nice for the style." 5.3% alc.

Saranac Single Malt ★★1/2

Scottish Ale: Matt Brewing Co., Utica, NY www.saranac.com

"Big fruit initially, on first contact with the lips and tongue, with a huge deployment of sweet malt." "Finish has a scotch character, which is quite nice, but otherwise this one misses." 5% alc.

Saranac Stout ★★★

Stout: Matt Brewing Co., Utica, NY www.saranac.com

"Aroma lightly roasty with notes of chocolate and faint coffee, appealing." "Roast notes are predominant, with a bit of chocolate and faint pine hops." "Does not compare to "real" stouts, but still pretty good for price." 5.4% alc.

Saranac Summer Ale ★★1/2

Am. Wheat: Matt Brewing Co., Utica, NY www.saranac.com

"Perfumey nose is faint spice and candied lemon." "Lightly sweet, but lots of lemony citrus and coriander and it's mildly bitter." "A refreshing brew for a hot summer day." 4.7% alc.

Saranac Traditional Lager ★★1/2

Premium Lager: Matt Brewing Co., Utica, NY www.saranac.com

"Slight aroma of apples, caramel; light and quick palate, notably bland." "Like any other light lager, just a little thicker and more featured." 4.8% alc.

Satan Red ★★★

Strong Belgian Ale: De Block Brouwerij, Peizegem, Belgium www.satanbeer.com

"A bit shy nose of fruits, sweet malts, yeasts and a spicy touch." "Yeasty flavor predominates, with a mild fruity estery quality as well." "But it is more OK to drink than try to analyze this one, I think." 8% alc.

Satan Gold ★★★

Strong Belgian Ale: De Block Brouwerij, Peizegem, Belgium www.satanbeer.com

Aroma has a skunky aspect plus citrus, old pineapples and yeasty banana esters. "Sweet and yeasty flavor with a muddled fruitiness and a noticeable plastic/chemical flavor, like the sweetness from saccarhin." "Decent beer, but toward the bottom of the barrel within its revered style." 8% alc.

Saxer Bock ★★★

Bock: Portland Brewing Co. (Pyramid), Portland, OR www.portlandbrew.com

"Malty aroma with hints of caramel, brown sugar and some yeast." "Taste is fruity and malty with light caramel." "Warming for cold wintry nights on the high seas." 7.2% alc.

Saxer Lemon Lager ★

Fruit Beer: Portland Brewing Co. (Pyramid), Portland, OR www.portlandbrew.com

"Sharp nose of old bottled lemon juice, sweet honey and a hint of malt. Strong, stale lemon character with a sweet, candy-like flavor." N/A% alc.

Scaldis / Bush Ambrée ★★★★★

Bel. Strong Ale: Dubuisson, Pipaix, Belgium www.br-dubuisson.com

"Aroma is fruity and a bit vinous, with definite alcohol notes and a lot of caramel." "Flavor is initially sweet with toffee, caramel and dark fruits (most notably prunes), but dries out quite nicely in the finish." "Lovely warming glow as it goes down." 13% alc.

Scaldis Noël ★★★★

Bel. Strong Ale: Dubuisson, Pipaix, Belgium www.br-dubuisson.com

"Aroma of alcohol, peaches, prunes, grapes and a depth of malt." "Caramel, flowery hops, Japanese apples and a medicinal, essence-like cherry note like Belle Vue Kriek." "Good for sipping slow on a winter night, definitely will keep you warm." 12% alc.

Scaldis Prestige ★★★★★

Bel. Strong Ale: Dubuisson, Pipaix, Belgium www.br-dubuisson.com

"Vanilla, wood, butterscotch and rum-soaked fruits help round out the aroma." "Notes of cherry, oak, toffee/caramel and bourbon." "One of the best beers I have had in a long, long time." 13% alc.

Schaefer ★1/2
Pale Lager: Pabst Brewing Co., Chicago, IL www.pabst.com
"It is very drinkable and predictable - don't expect anything special." "The beer brewed today has no particular aroma; yellow with a fizzy white head and tastes like corn cereal." Pabst brand contract brewed by Miller. 4.4% alc.

Schell Bock ★★★★
Bock: August Schell Brewing Co., New Ulm, MN www.schellsbrewery.com
"Aroma is clean, with small hints of caramel and nuts." "Notions of toasty caramel and bread with some very slight spice midway, notes of nuts in between the bready sweetness." "Very smooth brew." 5.6% alc.

Schell Caramel Bock ★★
Bock: August Schell Brewing Co., New Ulm, MN www.schellsbrewery.com
"As expected, aroma unfurling brown sugar, pumpernickel, copper, pepper, unsalted pecans and stale baker's chocolate." "Loose, watery and thin-bodied." "Needs some more nutty flavors and a little less sweetness." 5.75% alc.

Schell Dark ★★
Am Dark Larger: August Schell Brewing Co., New Ulm, MN www.schellsbrewery.com
"Aroma is corn and sweetness." "Very crisp, with some light roasted notes." "Just a bit of hop bitterness." "This is one of their so-so products." 4.8% alc.

Schell Doppel Bock ★★1/2
Doppelbock: August Schell Brewing Co., New Ulm, MN www.schellsbrewery.com
"Has aroma of caramel, cookie dough, licorice and fruit." "Flavors of caramel, treacle and toffee." "Clean and somewhat crisp, easy to drink, but was hoping for something more robust." 6.9% alc.

Schell Firebrick ★★★
Vienna: August Schell Brewing Co., New Ulm, MN www.schellsbrewery.com
"Some good hefty malty sweetness with caramel and a hint of bright fruit." "Has a good, sweet malty flavor for a lager with some sweet caramelly notes and a nutty undertone." 5.1% alc.

Schell Maifest ★★★
Bock: August Schell Brewing Co., New Ulm, MN www.schellsbrewery.com
"Light fruity hops, but mostly sweet and mellow with a hint of spice." "A very tasty and slightly dangerous beer that is right on for the style." 6.9% alc.

Schell Oktoberfest ★★★
Märzen/Oktbfst: August Schell Brewing Co., New Ulm, MN www.schellsbrewery.com
"Nice toasty, almond and caramel aroma with perhaps a hint of pepper." "Solid, middle of the road maltiness with some bitter, charred wood qualities and a touch of dry hops, only lightly sweet." 5.5% alc.

Schell Original ★★1/2
Pale Lager: August Schell Brewing Co., New Ulm, MN www.schellsbrewery.com
"There is a distinct dirty taste to it, like all the flavors are muddled together." "It is the quintessential American lager, the commercial description reads. This explains why I've become an ale-swigging hop-head." 4.75% alc.

Schell Pale Ale ★★★
Am. Pale Ale: August Schell Brewing Co., New Ulm, MN www.schellsbrewery.com
"Caramel and toffee up front with some citrus sneaking it's way in the middle." "Toasty finish with very light bitterness." "I never knew beers like this existed in Minneapolis!" 5.75% alc.

Schell Pilsner ★★★★1/2
Pilsner: August Schell Brewing Co., New Ulm, MN www.schellsbrewery.com
"Sweet, honeysuckle-floral aroma, hints of maple and lilac, lovely." "Distinct noble hop aroma, firm bitterness, smooth pale maltiness." "Very enjoyable European style." 5.6% alc.

Schell Schmaltz's Alt ★★★
Altbier: August Schell Brewing Co., New Ulm, MN www.schellsbrewery.com
"Caramelly malt aroma with a deep hop spiciness behind it." "Taste is some chocolate malts but very mild." "Not really a traditional Altbier, but good whatever it is." 5% alc.

Schell Snowstorm ★★1/2
Altbier: August Schell Brewing Co., New Ulm, MN www.schellsbrewery.com
"Caramel and cotton candy aroma." "Tastes very much like a British pub ale with a little less fruitiness." "Dry and drinkable but not tasty." 5% alc.

Schell Zommerfest ★★1/2
Kölsch: August Schell Brewing Co., New Ulm, MN www.schellsbrewery.com
"Aroma is heavy in wheat and Tettnang hops." "Nice clean hops taste, mildly fruity with malt sweetness." "Does not have the traditional Kölsch bite." 5% alc.

Schlafly American Lager ★★★
Pale Lager: Saint Louis Brewery, Maplewood, MO www.schlafly.com
"Big hoppy, spicy and light German funky yeast quality in the aroma." "Hops, sweet pale malt and corn in the taste." "I suppose they nailed the style, I just can't get excited about a beer that boasts of corn being added to thin it out." N/A% alc.

Schlafly American Pale Ale ★★★★
Am. Pale Ale: Saint Louis Brewery, Maplewood, MO www.schlafly.com
"Pine and grapefruit aroma revealed the hops in this beer, but the nose was not near as aromatic as other Cascade hopped beers." "The taste is grapefruit, earthy hops, held together by a honeyish maltiness." N/A% alc.

Schlafly Hefeweizen ★★1/2
Am. Wheat: Saint Louis Brewery, Maplewood, MO www.schlafly.com
"The aroma is sharp with citrus, fresh grass and pepper spice." "Malts are fruity and crisp. Slightly spicy hops. Crisp and clean." 4.1% alc.

Schlafly Kaldis Coffee Stout ★★★
Sweet Stout: Saint Louis Brewery, Maplewood, MO www.schlafly.com
"Flavors are more of the same-huge coffee bean flavors with a touch of vanilla." "Very coffee dominated beer, but fun to drink even if one dimensional." N/A% alc.

Schlafly Oatmeal Stout ★★★1/2
Sweet Stout: Saint Louis Brewery, Maplewood, MO www.schlafly.com
"Flavor is more of a blend of coffee, chocolate and a nice roasty flavor." "Quick chocolate sweetness up front. Strong roasted and burnt grain and bitter black coffee finish." 5.9% alc.

Schlafly Oktoberfest ★★★
Märzen/Oktbfst: Saint Louis Brewery, Maplewood, MO www.schlafly.com
"Woody and malty in the nose, also cocoa and slight caramel." "Medium bodied, plenty of caramel taste along with doughy bread and a dusty hop finish." "A very good domestic rendition of the type." 5.7% alc.

Schlafly Pale Ale ★★
Eng Pale Ale: Saint Louis Brewery, Maplewood, MO www.schlafly.com
"Grainy/straw malt and light flowery/perfumey hops in the nose." "Malts are fruity and sweet, with a lot of breadiness. Touch of earthiness as well." "Pleasant enough, but pretty middle of the road." 4.9% alc.

Schlafly Pilsner ★★★★
Pilsner: Saint Louis Brewery, Maplewood, MO www.schlafly.com
"Minty, slightly piney, leafy hop notes with a touch of spearmint." "Sweet malt taste with a dry hop crispness." "This is what the American premiums should be." 4.9% alc.

Schlafly Scotch Ale ★★★
Scotch Ale: Saint Louis Brewery, Maplewood, MO www.schlafly.com
"Aroma is mostly grassy hops with a hint of caramel." "Roasted malt with very little of the hop and spice notes that are detectable in the nose." "I can picture this being just the thing for sitting in front of a fire while it snows like crazy outside." 6.4% alc.

Schlafly Summer Kölsch ★★★
Kölsch: Saint Louis Brewery, Maplewood, MO www.schlafly.com
"Lightly citric aroma with some spicy hops and lemon character." "Taste is sweet malt, initially followed by a light citrus flavor. Clean, crisp, refreshing." "Very drinkable and a good example of the style!" 5.2% alc.

Schlafly Winter ESB ★★★★★
Prem Bitter: Saint Louis Brewery, Maplewood, MO www.schlafly.com
"Chewy, caramelly earthiness and mango fruitiness in the aroma." "Sort of overbalanced toward the hops (lots of 'em) but there is a nice malt backbone as well." "One of my favorite seasonals." 6.8% alc.

Schlitz ★
Pale Lager: Pabst Brewing Co., Chicago, IL www.pabst.com
"Aroma is sweet malt with no hop character. Taste is much of the same, really bland, but inoffensive." "Just another mass produced junk beer." Pabst brand contract brewed by Miller. 4.6% alc.

Schlitz Malt Liquor ★
Malt Liquor: Pabst Brewing Co., Chicago, IL www.pabst.com
"Has aromas of sweet malt, corn and soap." "Flavor is corn and malt with a sweet malty finish. Not bad as malt liquors go." "It's like watching a mime get run over." Owned by Pabst; contract brewed by Miller. 5.9% alc.

Schlitz Red Bull ★
Malt Liquor: Pabst Brewing Co., Chicago, IL www.pabst.com
"Some pale malts in the nose, with apricot and apple." "Sweet, alcoholic flavor." "Like drinking flatulence." "Frankly, it could've sucked much more." Pabst brand contract brewed by Miller. 7.1% alc.

Schmidt's Beer ★
Pale Lager: Pabst Brewing Co., Chicago, IL www.pabst.com
"Flavor was very generic lager." "Very slight grain and corn aroma and taste." "Outside of the sentimental part, there is nothing to write home about." Pabst brand contract brewed by Miller. 4.4% alc.

Schneider Aventinus ★★★★★
Weizen Bock: Weissbierbrauerei G. Schneider and Sohn, Kelheim, Germany www.schneider-weisse.de
"Luscious dark fruit aroma - banana, apple crumble, sweet malts, milk chocolate." "Smooth dark malt palate...dark malts, sweet banana esters, liberal mix of alcohol." "Complex, stylish and daring." 8% alc.

Schneider Aventinus Weizen-Eisbock ★★★★1/2
Eisbock: Weissbierbrauerei G. Schneider and Sohn, Kelheim, Germany www.schneider-weisse.de
"Nose is malty with some light dried fruits, some vanilla, light banana raisin plums." "Flavor is very sweet, very fruity and hearty, lots of raisins, cherry, prunes with a little coffee like background." "Not as good as the regular Aventinus." 12% alc.

Schneider Weisse ★★★★
Hefeweizen: Weissbierbrauerei G. Schneider and Sohn, Kelheim, Germany www.schneider-weisse.de
"Aroma of apple, banana, wheat, malts (including some light toffee)." "Sweet-tart components are complemented by a delicate spiciness, apple and banana." "Aahhhhhh .....pleasure!!" 5.2% alc.

Schneider Wiesen Edel-Weisse ★★★★1/2
Hefeweizen: Weissbierbrauerei G. Schneider and Sohn, Kelheim, Germany www.schneider-weisse.de
"Malty, very bready, fairly sweet and spicy, wow, a whole lot of clove in here and quite a bit of banana too." "I bow to this fantastic beer." 6.2% alc.

Scotch Silly ★★★
Scotch Ale: Brasserie de Silly, Silly, Belgium www.silly-beer.com
"Sweet, worty aroma with notes of molasses, hot caramel, cherry and some prominent yeast character including bubble gum." "Taste is quite rich with strong syrupy malt, caramel malts, figs dry raisins and nice subtle funky touch from the yeast." 8% alc.

Scuttlebutt Amber ★★1/2
Amber Ale: Scuttlebutt Brewing Co., Everett, WA www.scuttlebuttbrewing.com
"Aroma is nicely malty with caramel being dominant and a floral hop background." "A pretty cheap-tasting amber ale, dominated by sugary sweet caramel and a perfumey and floral hoppiness." 4.3% alc.

Scuttlebutt Gale Force IPA ★★1/2
IPA: Scuttlebutt Brewing Co., Everett, WA www.scuttlebuttbrewing.com
"Moderate aroma of citrus, wood and maybe some tobacco." "Bold citrus and floral snap up front, yet was nicely textured over smooth caramel malt notes." "A good bitter, lighter bodied IPA." 5.25% alc.

Scuttlebutt Old. No. 1 ★★1/2
Barley Wine: Scuttlebutt Brewing Co., Everett, WA www.scuttlebuttbrewing.com
"Dark chocolate aroma, caramel, toffee and dark fruits." "Rich, complex malty flavor of caramel, brown sugar maple and dark fruit." "A rare Barleywine; I wouldn't mind having more than half a pint of." 12.9% alc.

Scuttlebutt Porter ★★1/2
Porter: Scuttlebutt Brewing Co., Everett, WA www.scuttlebuttbrewing.com
"Solid, roasty, lightly sweet chocolate aroma wafts from the glass." "Flavor of heavily roasted malts, chocolate malts and a subtle hop bite." "Smooth and light bodied porter." 5.5% alc.

Sea Dog Blue Paw Wild Blueberry Wheat Ale ★★1/2
Fruit Beer: Sea Dog Brewing, Topsham, ME www.seadogbrewing.com
"Wonderful blueberry aroma." "Flavor of the beer isn't dominated by blueberries but they are definitely there." "Slightly above average for American fruit beers." 4.6% alc.

Sea Dog Old East Indian Pale Ale ★★1/2
IPA: Sea Dog Brewing, Topsham, ME www.seadogbrewing.com
"Big roasted malt nose...very inviting." "Strong malt base with caramel and toffee notes. Hop bitterness is somewhat subdued." "Nothing at all like the IPAs I'm used to here in the States; but damn tasty." 6% alc.

Sea Dog Pumpkin Ale ★
Spice/Herb: Sea Dog Brewing, Topsham, ME www.seadogbrewing.com
"No detectable pumpkin flavor, more pie spice, a little too heavy on the cinnamon, not heavy enough on the nutmeg and pumpkin." "A bit thin too support the spices." N/A% alc.

Sea Dog Raspberry Wheat ★★
Fruit Beer: Sea Dog Brewing, Topsham, ME www.seadogbrewing.com
"Aroma faintly fruity, not much else." "Tastes mostly of raspberries with touches of tart wheat and honey malt." "Too sweet to drink with food, too uninteresting to drink by itself.' 4.5% alc.

Sea Dog Riverdriver Hazelnut Porter ★★★
Porter: Sea Dog Brewing, Topsham, ME www.seadogbrewing.com
"Distinct hazelnut flavor that complements the coffee and malt." "Some sweetness at first and dry roasted bitterness at end." "Flavors are interesting but they lack intensity." 5.6% alc.

Sea Dog Windjammer Blonde Ale ★★★
Goldn/Blond Ale: Sea Dog Brewing, Topsham, ME www.seadogbrewing.com
"Malty aroma with notes of apple pie, butter and some acidic tones." "Mild flavor of citrusy hops and caramel." "Will quench your thirst but left me a bit unsatisfied." 4.8% alc.

Sea Dog Winter Stock ★★★
Eng. Strong Ale: Sea Dog Brewing, Topsham, ME www.seadogbrewing.com
"Nutty malt aroma." "Tastes rich and spicy with light hops underneath the malt." "Better than typical holiday brew." 6.3% alc.

Sebago Boathouse Brown ★★1/2
Brown Ale: Sebago Brewing Co., South Portland, ME www.sebagobrewing.com
"Roasted malts with a mildly hoppy finish." "Sweetish palate with decent malt development." "Easy drinking, not otherwise not distinctive..." N/A% alc.

Sebago Frye's Leap IPA ★★1/2
IPA: Sebago Brewing Co., South Portland, ME www.sebagobrewing.com
"Citrusy aroma, with oranges being the dominant notes." "Moderate-medium bitterness is enough to be interesting but not quite in the big leagues." "A bright, workmanlike and delicate session IPA." N/A% alc.

Sebago Lake Trout Stout ★★★
Sweet Stout: Sebago Brewing Co., South Portland, ME www.sebagobrewing.com
"Roasty flavor of strong coffee with a touch of dark chocolate." "Flavor was weaker than I expected with roasted malt, coffee and a bare hint of chocolate." "Only OK?" 5.8% alc.

Sheaf Stout ★★
Foreign Stout: Carlton and United Breweries, Melbourne, Victoria, Australia www.fosters.com.au
"Chewy, slight roasty, slight raisiny malts with a hint of alcoholic undertones in the aroma." "Tar-like, toffeeish, thick body." "Chewy but bland and probably too sweet." 5.7% alc.

Shepherd Neame Bishops Finger ★★1/2
Prem Bitter: Shepherd Neame, Faversham, Kent, England www.shepherd-neame.co.uk
"Nutty, earthy aroma, with sweetish malt notes." "Malt, caramel, citrus and tasty hops in the flavor." "A bit one-dimensional and perhaps a bit too aggressive for the lack of complexity." 5.4% alc.

Shepherd Neame Spitfire ★★
Prem Bitter: Shepherd Neame, Faversham, Kent, England www.shepherd-neame.co.uk
"Aroma is minerally, slightly caramelly." "The malt-accented palate is caramelly, quite chalky, with a late hoppy dryness." "Solid unremarkable drinking." 4.5% alc.

Shiner Blonde ★★
Pilsner: Spoetzl Brewery (Gambrinus Co.), Shiner, TX www.shiner.com
"Has aromas of grain, light grass and some light sweet malts." "Very bland with slight hops and a small hint of caramel and sweet malts." "It was OK after mowing the lawn. I gave a lil' bit to the grass. " 4.4% alc.

Shiner Bock ★★1/2
Am Dark Larger: Spoetzl Brewery (Gambrinus Co.), Shiner, TX www.shiner.com
Iconic Texas brew has "dark golden color, sometimes nutty flavor, although generally light flavor." "Tastes like a commercial macro-brewed lager with just a tiny tease of a taste that suggests it is a dark lager." 4.41% alc.

Shiner Dunkelweizen (Winter Ale) ★★★
Dunkelweizen: Spoetzl Brewery (Gambrinus Co.), Shiner, TX www.shiner.com
"Sweet nutty aroma with a hint of cocoa." "Taste is medium sweet, caramel, some nutty, light floral, raisin." "Thanks to Secret Santa for this one." N/A% alc.

Shiner Hefeweizen ★★1/2

Am. Wheat: Spoetzl Brewery (Gambrinus Co.), Shiner, TX www.shiner.com

"Spicy and yeasty in aroma with a bit of citrus and CO2." "Tastes of wheat, lemons and has a light honey sweetness." "The dude on the label is going to give me nightmares tonight." 5.28% alc.

Shiner Kölsch (Summer Stock) ★★1/2

Kölsch: Spoetzl Brewery (Gambrinus Co.), Shiner, TX www.shiner.com

"Light malt flavor, clean with light esters." "Starts dull with mild malt sweetness and no bitterness at all." "Kölners everywhere should be offended that Shiner claims this as a Kölsch." N/A% alc.

Shipyard Blue Fin Stout ★★★

Dry Stout: Shipyard Brewing Co., Portland, ME www.shipyard.com

"Smells strongly of coffee and chocolate." "Perfectly balanced bitter with very smooth dark malts and coffee undertones." "Would recommend to any stout lover." 5% alc.

Shipyard Brown Ale ★★

Brown Ale: Shipyard Brewing Co., Portland, ME www.shipyard.com

"The aroma is sweet with primary notes of caramel, but also some slight roasted nutty notes." "typical brown ale sweetness." "Starts promising but flavors fade out in the finish." 4% alc.

Shipyard Chamberlain Pale Ale ★★1/2

Eng Pale Ale: Shipyard Brewing Co., Portland, ME www.shipyard.com

"Very solid nuttiness jumps right out from the first sip of this lightly sweet beer, but moderately bitter hops comes on toward the finish." "Really nice flavor, if a bit weak." 4.8% alc.

Shipyard Export ★★1/2

Goldn/Blond Ale: Shipyard Brewing Co., Portland, ME www.shipyard.com

"Sweet and malty with some nutty notes." "Taste is grainy with a spicy bitterness." "Lager-like, good thirst quencher." "Not bad for such a dull style." 5.1% alc.

Shipyard Fuggles IPA ★★1/2

IPA: Shipyard Brewing Co., Portland, ME www.shipyard.com

"Markedly British hop flavor." "Not overly bitter." "The Fuggles make this an atypical IPA." "Too mellow to be fully enjoyable." 5.8% alc.

Shipyard Light ★

Goldn/Blond Ale: Shipyard Brewing Co., Portland, ME www.shipyard.com

"No smell... Huh?" "Taste is restricted to a mild sweetness that rides atop the moderate carbonation." "A quite awful, chemical and artificial brew. I'd rather have the calories." 3.2% alc.

Shipyard Longfellow Winter Ale ★★★★

Am Strong Ale: Shipyard Brewing Co., Portland, ME www.shipyard.com

"Aroma is dark fruits, sweet malts, caramel and light brown sugar." "Basic caramel and toffee malt flavors with some English yeast fruitiness." "An interesting brew to try." 5.8% alc.

Shipyard Prelude Ale ★★1/2

Eng. Strong Ale: Shipyard Brewing Co., Portland, ME www.shipyard.com

"Has aromas of caramel malt, cabernet, almonds, toffee." "Flavor is sweet with light traces of chocolate and a nice roasted coffee flavor." "Tastes like a brew to drink around the fire at Christmas time." 6.8% alc.

Shipyard Pumpkinhead ★★

Spice/Herb: Shipyard Brewing Co., Portland, ME www.shipyard.com

"Smells like very fresh pumpkin pie - clove, cinnamon, apple." "Pronounced pumpkin flavor accompanied by the expected spice notes." "Finish is somewhat drier than I expected." 4.5% alc.

Shipyard Summer Ale ★★1/2
Am. Wheat: Shipyard Brewing Co., Portland, ME www.shipyard.com
"Light, sweet malts with a tiny sprinkling of hops at the very finish." "Appears to be designed as a training beer for people breaking out of the Budweiser-Miller-Coors comfort zone." 5.1% alc.

Shipyard Winter Ale Special Brew ★★1/2
Amber Ale: Shipyard Brewing Co., Portland, ME www.shipyard.com
"Aroma is light and buttery with some caramel and black walnuts." "Roasted flavor with syrup, apple, almonds, meringue and fruits." "Tastes very British in nature, solidly malty and fruity; early on, a bit caramelly." 5.3% alc.

Sierra Blanca Nut Brown ★★★
Brown Ale: Sierra Blanca Brewing Co, Carrizozo, NM www.sierrablancabrewery.com
"Its aroma was roasted malt and chocolate." "Sweet malt flavor with some toasted marshmallow and a bit of chocolate at the edge." N/A% alc.

Sierra Blanca Pale Ale ★★
Am. Pale Ale: Sierra Blanca Brewing Co, Carrizozo, NM www.sierrablancabrewery.com
"Caramelly malt with some light citrus hops." "For those who find most pales overly hopped, this brew might be just what you're looking for." N/A% alc.

Sierra Blanca Pilsner ★★★1/2
Pilsner: Sierra Blanca Brewing Co, Carrizozo, NM www.sierrablancabrewery.com
"Very nice hoppy aroma with notes of malt." "Starts off with honey, turns into a delightful floral bitter hoppiness and fades slowly into a honey accented, yet dry finish." N/A% alc.

Sierra Blanca Roswell Alien Amber ★★1/2
Amber Ale: Sierra Blanca Brewing Co, Carrizozo, NM www.sierrablancabrewery.com
"The aroma is sweet and malty with a caramel note, a hint of cinnamon and perhaps a hint of hops." "Sweet malty flavor, but with a light hops presence now and then." "I don't see anyone beside Mulder going back to this one regularly." N/A% alc.

Sierra Nevada Bigfoot ★★★★★
Barley Wine: Sierra Nevada Brewing Co., Chico, CA www.sierranevada.com
"A very popular dark amber barley wine with a big hoppy aroma that is "pungent? resembles a cheap musk cologne." "VERY full beer with a long lasting bitter finish." "A truly wonderful beer." 9.6% alc.

Sierra Nevada Celebration Ale ★★★★1/2
IPA: Sierra Nevada Brewing Co., Chico, CA www.sierranevada.com
One of the most anticipated seasonal beers in the USA, this is a classic IPA with a piney, citrusy aroma. A "powerfully bitter" flavor leads to a dry finish. "Never disappoints." 6.8% alc.

Sierra Nevada Pale Ale ★★★★
Am. Pale Ale: Sierra Nevada Brewing Co., Chico, CA www.sierranevada.com
With its refined grapefruity aroma, moderate bitterness and dry finish, this quintessential American Pale Ale inspired a generation of brewers. "Cheap, easy to find beer that makes me wonder why in the world anytime has to be Miller time." 5.2% alc.

Sierra Nevada Porter ★★★★
Porter: Sierra Nevada Brewing Co., Chico, CA www.sierranevada.com
"Very nice roasty aroma, notes of chocolate, licorice, leather and oak." "Rich bitter coffee taste with chocolate undertones." "Excellent." "Delicious." "A friend of mine dubbed this beer liquid crack." 5.6% alc.

Sierra Nevada Stout ★★★1/2
Stout: Sierra Nevada Brewing Co., Chico, CA www.sierranevada.com
"Roasted and somewhat fruity aroma with coffee and dark chocolate." "Very dry, smoky, burnt, velvety dark chocolate flavor carrying a kick-ass bitterness with it." "Great day-to-day beer." 5.8% alc.

Sierra Nevada Summerfest ★★★1/2

Premium Lager: Sierra Nevada Brewing Co., Chico, CA www.sierranevada.com

"A "simple, but well-executed" Pilsner-style beer with a "moderate bitterness" and a clean character. Pleasing hoppy finish and great balance makes this a "good warm weather drink." 5% alc.

Sierra Nevada Wheat ★★1/2

Am. Wheat: Sierra Nevada Brewing Co., Chico, CA www.sierranevada.com

The lightest regularly bottled Sierra offering, with the aroma of "citrus, hops and yeast." The flavor is light - too light for some - with a bit of bitterness in the finish. "Qualifies as average, nothing more." 4.4% alc.

Siletz Black Diamond Imperial Porter ★★★1/2

Baltic Porter: Siletz Brewing and Public House, Siletz, OR www.siletzbrewing.com

"Strong malt and chocolate with a very light coffee and wood." "Chocolate up front with a roasty coffee and wood hop finish." N/A% alc.

Siletz Mojo Ale ★★1/2

Am Strong Ale: Siletz Brewing and Public House, Siletz, OR www.siletzbrewing.com

"Caramel malt aroma, piney hops, slightly minty." "Taste is moderately sweet, cherry, caramel, some grapefruit, light pine." "Thick bodied but finishes with a big malt punch and blended hops." 6.5% alc.

Siletz Noggin Knocker Barleywine ★★

Barley Wine: Siletz Brewing and Public House, Siletz, OR www.siletzbrewing.com

"Very sweet barleywine aroma with a nice caramel warmth smell and light hopping." "Divided in two distinct areas the dark fruitiness, then the spicy long lasting bitterness." "This isn't a typical Barleywine, it isn't trying to be one." 7.5% alc.

Siletz Oatmeal Cream Stout ★★★

Sweet Stout: Siletz Brewing and Public House, Siletz, OR www.siletzbrewing.com

"Fruity berry, charcoal aroma." "Over-roasted grain flavor, a touch of oatmeal and a decent hop bitterness toward the finish make this a solid stout." "It's not all that creamy and definitely not sweet." N/A% alc.

Siletz Paddle Me IPA ★★1/2

IPA: Siletz Brewing and Public House, Siletz, OR www.siletzbrewing.com

"Aroma is floral and piney, standard Indian Pale Ale fare." "Flavor is mostly pale malt with very high level of bitter citric hops - not much else." "Hopheads will not be disappointed." N/A% alc.

Siletz Spruce Ale ★★1/2

Spice/Herb: Siletz Brewing and Public House, Siletz, OR www.siletzbrewing.com

"Flavor is intensely fruity with notes of cherry and blackberry with spruce and a sweet malty finish." "Spruce tips made for an interesting ingredient." N/A% alc.

Siletz Winter Warmer ★★★★★

Amber Ale: Siletz Brewing and Public House, Siletz, OR www.siletzbrewing.com

"Aroma is richly malty with a very healthy dose of Cascade hop citrus nose." "Taste kind of brings you through an assortment of flavors finishing with a very dry spicy finish." "Musky, very unique." N/A% alc.

Siletz Wooly Bully ★★★

Keller: Siletz Brewing and Public House, Siletz, OR www.siletzbrewing.com

"Nose of fragrant fruity hops and toasty malt." "Crisp, yeasty and malty with somewhat musty fruit flavor." "Subdued German hops, truly growing on you with a rocky dryness." N/A% alc.

Silly Saison ★★1/2

Saison: Brasserie de Silly, Silly, Belgium www.silly-beer.com

"Complex aroma of with prunes, chocolate and alcohol." "Flavor is sweet, candies, light spicy with a light herbal hop note." "It's pleasant enough but I'm still wishing there was a Dupont in my glass." 5.2% alc.

Sixpoint Bolshoi! ★★★★
Imperial Stout: Sixpoint Craft Ales, Brooklyn, NY www.sixpointcraftales.com
Aroma was the usual dark malts with coffee, chocolate, roast and caramel ... and also a blast of PNW hops. "Enormously sweet and roasty flavor with plenty of alcohol and some notes of chocolate and beans." "A big hop bomb of an Imperial." 10.1% alc.

Singha ★★
Premium Lager: Boon Rawd Brewery, Bangkok, Thailand www.boonrawd.co.th
"Aroma of hops and notes of maize and malt." "Grassy hops, moderate bitterness, biscuity pale malts." "Higher alcohol." "Eh, not a terrible choice if you're facing this or Bud at a Thai restaurant. 6% alc.

SKA Buster Nut Brown ★
Brown Ale: SKA Brewing, Durango, CO www.skabrewing.com
"Odd aroma of oily nuts, lightly sweet brown sugar, toasted grains and (unidentifiable by me) off aromas." "Almost like Shiner Bock with a little extra smokiness thrown in." "An average brown ale that is easily passed over." 0% alc.

SKA Decadent Imperial IPA ★★1/2
Imp/Dbl IPA: SKA Brewing, Durango, CO www.skabrewing.com
"Dry, earthy hoppy aroma has a touch of floral grapefruit." "Loads of crystal malt caramel sweetness, warm to hot alcohol and strong hop bitterness." "It seems to be a bunch of malt and hops without a real plan." 10% alc.

SKA Nefarious Ten Pin Imperial Porter ★★★
Baltic Porter: SKA Brewing, Durango, CO www.skabrewing.com
"Blackberry and toffee-ish aroma with burnt cherries and a good alcohol twinge." "Roasted chocolate and fruit flavors with a slightly acidic finish." "Doesn't have the heft and viscosity I expected." 8% alc.

SKA Pinstripe Red ★★
Amber Ale: SKA Brewing, Durango, CO www.skabrewing.com
"Fruity hops in the fore followed by some mild graininess and then more hops." "Very mild, creamy, with slight caramel flavors." "Finish is clean and smooth." N/A% alc.

SKA Ten Pin Porter ★★1/2
Porter: SKA Brewing, Durango, CO www.skabrewing.com
"Well roasted, malty aroma, the expected coffee and dark chocolate are present, along with some mildly earthy, spicy hop." "Flavors of toasted malts, chocolate, caramel with hint of nuts." N/A% alc.

SKA True Blonde ★★
Bel. Strong Ale: SKA Brewing, Durango, CO www.skabrewing.com
"Aroma is yeasty and fruity with hints of honey and spices." "Very limited flavor range and low flavor intensity." "Perhaps they should let the graphic designer make the beer - it might be more creative." 8% alc.

Skagit River Dutch Girl Lager ★★1/2
Premium Lager: Skagit River Brewing Co., Mount Vernon, WA www.skagitbrew.com
"Leafy hops vs. biscuity malts." "Tastes fruity and sweet as well, somewhat bready, with a decent grassy, hop bitterness in the finish." "I really don't understand why there isn't more demand for a good lager like this!" 3.3% alc.

Skagit River Highwater Porter ★★★
Porter: Skagit River Brewing Co., Mount Vernon, WA www.skagitbrew.com
"Fresh coffee beans and heavily roasted (burnt is more like it) malts on the nose." "Sticky, semi-sweet raisins, dates, maple, some wood and nuts as well and an underlying sweet, resiny chocolate." 4.3% alc.

Skagit River Sculler's IPA ★★★
IPA: Skagit River Brewing Co., Mount Vernon, WA www.skagitbrew.com
"Nose is sappy with pine and sweet pineapple juice." "Very hoppy IPA; very tongue tingling some maltiness at the end, then a long rolling bitterness finished off with a good hop burp." 6.8% alc.

Skagit River Steelie Brown Ale ★★1/2
Brown Ale: Skagit River Brewing Co., Mount Vernon, WA www.skagitbrew.com
"Aromas of soft nutty woody notes." "Hints of caramel and toffee with some hops in the nose." "Room for growth, but otherwise good." 4.3% alc.

Skagit River Trumpeter Imperial Stout ★★1/2
Imp. Stout: Skagit River Brewing Co., Mount Vernon, WA www.skagitbrew.com
"Big aroma - chewy, rich, thick maltiness like a side of roast beef and a burnt fruitcake." "Very sweet sticky malts up front, treacle, molasses, lots of roasted barley and a long bitter finish." "Big, straightforward brute." 10.5% alc.

Skagit River Yellowjacket Pale Ale ★★
Am. Pale Ale: Skagit River Brewing Co., Mount Vernon, WA www.skagitbrew.com
"Hoppy aroma was sort of sweet along with a tangerine hint." "Although crisp and fresh, these hops are remarkably dry and really lack the depth that a good multi-hopping can yield." 3.5% alc.

Slavutych Mitsne ★★1/2
Eur Str Lager: Slavutych , Zaporizhzhya, Ukraine www.slavutich.ua
"Ahhhh.... the smell of coins on a cool autumn evening." "Flavor is malt sweetness, white pepper spiciness and an alcoholic burn on the tongue." "Decidedly insufficient." 7.2% alc.

Slavutych Pivo (Slavutich Premium) ★★★
Pale Lager: Slavutych , Zaporizhzhya, Ukraine www.slavutich.ua
"A light, malt-accented lager with notes of boiled broccoli, sesame oil and sweet corn." "Flavor is sweet, lightly hoppy, a bit of adjunct, but... this one is actually pretty good." 5% alc.

Slavutych Temne ★★
Dunkel: Slavutych , Zaporizhzhya, Ukraine www.slavutich.ua
"Aroma has some ripe vegetable notes with some wort-like malty essence." "Flavor has some nutty sweetness with a bit of underlying vegetable notes." "Still better than some of the other offerings from the former USSR." 4.5% alc.

Sleeman Clear ★
Pale Lager: Sleeman Brewing and Malting Co., Guelph, Ontario www.sleeman.com
"Slightly grassy, metallic aroma." "Fizzily grainy, watery, nothing." "It's like creamy water with the aftertaste of peanuts." 4% alc.

Sleeman Cream Ale ★
Cream Ale: Sleeman Brewing and Malting Co., Guelph, Ontario www.sleeman.com
"Aroma is light corn juice, not a good sign." "Very simple beer, not very flavorful." "Overall a weak, boring too-sweet ale - nothing much here." 5% alc.

Sleeman Honey Brown Lager ★★★
Am Dark Larger: Sleeman Brewing and Malting Co., Guelph, Ontario www.sleeman.com
"Light hints of honey, cereal and sweet corn in the aroma." "Mild honey did not fully compensate for the stale flavor." "Bit fizzy and harsh, not a whole lot of fun to drink." 5.2% alc.

Sleeman Original Dark ★★
Am Dark Larger: Sleeman Brewing and Malting Co., Guelph, Ontario www.sleeman.com
"A little bit of roastiness and hoppiness." "Flavors are toasted, metallic and fairly sweet. Not offensive, just nothing really to talk about." "Boring and run of the mill dark lager." 5.5% alc.

Sleeman Silver Creek Lager ★★1/2
Pale Lager: Sleeman Brewing and Malting Co., Guelph, Ontario www.sleeman.com
"Smell is malty and fruity with an initial skunkiness that leaves quickly." "Sweet grainy flavor." "Not to bad at all for a pale lager." 5% alc.

Smithwick's ★★★

Irish Ale: Guinness, Dublin, Ireland www.guinness.com

"Smells of mild malt and not much else." "Fairly balanced flavor profile of toasted malts, nuts, sweet toffee and caramel but quite restrained and limp." "Like it but nothing to freak out about." 5% alc.

Smoky Mountain Black Bear Ale ★

Brown Ale: Smoky Mountain Brewery and Restaurant, Gatlinburg, TN www.smoky-mtn-brewery.com

"Aroma is quite sweet notes of caramel and brown sugar dominate." "Flavor is very sweet with an added nuttiness." "Perhaps the great failing of this brew is the lack of excitement it offers." 5.4% alc.

Smoky Mountain Cherokee Red Ale ★

Amber Ale: Smoky Mountain Brewery and Restaurant, Gatlinburg, TN www.smoky-mtn-brewery.com

"Malty ale with a lightly hopped finish." "I was only able to drink half of my pint over the whole course of dinner." 5.5% alc.

Smoky Mountain Old Thunder Road Pilsner ★★1/2

Bohem Pilsner: Smoky Mountain Brewery - Restaurant, Gatlinburg, TN www.smoky-mtn-brewery.com

"Smells of grass, lemon and sweet caramel at the nose." "Sweet, buttery flavor with a light nutty component and a tea-like quality." "A decent American-made Pilsner." 5.1% alc.

Smoky Mountain Tuckaleechee Porter ★★

Porter: Smoky Mountain Brewery - Restaurant, Gatlinburg, TN www.smoky-mtn-brewery.com

"I wish I could rate this an N/A for aroma, but that is not an option." "Dark roasted coffee flavors with a hint of chocolate and a hint of ashy smokiness that also tastes a little sour in the end." "This was an indifferent porter." 6.3% alc.

Smoky Mountain Vela's Helles Lager ★★

Helles/Dortmnd: Smoky Mountain Brewer - Restaurant, Gatlinburg, TN

www.smoky-mtn-brewery.com

"Aroma has a bit of tangerine, light lemon, a hint of grassy hops hidden in there somewhere." "Tastes smooth, malty, with tons of honey flavor and some fruity hops." 5.2% alc.

Smuttynose Barleywine Style Ale ★★★★

Barley Wine: Smuttynose Brewing Co., Portsmouth, NH www.smuttynose.com

"Rich malty nose (brown sugar, peaches, biscuits, stroop)." "Full bodied with creamy texture that starts with sharp bitterness with hints of toffee and prunes and finishes with lingering bitterness." 10% alc.

Smuttynose Big A IPA ★★★★★

Imp/Dbl IPA: Smuttynose Brewing Co., Portsmouth, NH www.smuttynose.com

"Big aroma of pine orange, honeydew melon, plenty of hops here." "Big pine hops hit you at first and continue throughout while they merge with some grapefruit. Some sweet malt, fresh/green grain and a bit of caramel." 9.2% alc.

Smuttynose Imperial Stout ★★★★★

Imp. Stout: Smuttynose Brewing Co., Portsmouth, NH www.smuttynose.com

"Lots of chocolate with light vanilla, lighter caramel and the slightest hints of coffee." "On the sweeter side of Imp. Stouts but the bitterness does show itself in the arid finish, a remarkably creamy palate." 7.1% alc.

Smuttynose IPA ★★★★1/2

IPA: Smuttynose Brewing Co., Portsmouth, NH www.smuttynose.com

"The aroma is hoppy with fresh lemon cookies and light oranges." "Taste is citrusy hops all the way - very grapefruity - with a touch of honey and sweet malt. " "They aren't re-inventing the wheel but they make a nice wheel." 6.6% alc.

Smuttynose Maibock ★★★★★

Bock: Smuttynose Brewing Co., Portsmouth, NH www.smuttynose.com

"Fresh deep malt nose." "Maltiness reigns supreme here and hops entertain a mere tingle at the fore." "Sophisticated, truly mature." 7.7% alc.

Smuttynose Oktoberfest ★★★

Märzen/Oktbfst: Smuttynose Brewing Co., Portsmouth, NH www.smuttynose.com

"Pretty big, malty, flavorful beer for an Oktoberfest, loaded up with sweet caramel, plus a prominent toastiness." "Aroma has a nice amount of slightly roasted malts and finely selected hops." 5.2% alc.

Smuttynose Old Brown Dog ★★★1/2

Brown Ale: Smuttynose Brewing Co., Portsmouth, NH www.smuttynose.com

"Has aroma of very earthy roast malt, maybe burnt chestnut." "Flavor is a rush of roasted nut, particularly chestnut, followed by a rounding out of mildly biting hops." "A very pleasant Brown Ale, in the American style." 5.7% alc.

Smuttynose Portsmouth Lager ★★★

Vienna: Smuttynose Brewing Co., Portsmouth, NH www.smuttynose.com

"Aroma is fairly sweet, with some light hops." "Lightly sweet, toasty-malty sandwich beer." "The palate just isn't much, but still, not a bad all-around easy going drink." 4.5% alc.

Smuttynose Pumpkin Ale ★★1/2

Spice/Herb: Smuttynose Brewing Co., Portsmouth, NH www.smuttynose.com

"Big pumpkin pie aroma, with a good hop backbone." "So much more flavorful then most other pumpkin beers - it's much spicier and hoppier." "What's not to love?" 5% alc.

Smuttynose Robust Porter ★★★★★

Porter: Smuttynose Brewing Co., Portsmouth, NH www.smuttynose.com

"Good quality roast grains in the aroma, some black rye bread, wood, vanilla and a little bit of cocoa." "Wonderful balance of rich chocolate sweetness and roasty coffee bitterness." 5.7% alc.

Smuttynose Scotch Ale ★★★★

Scotch Ale: Smuttynose Brewing Co., Portsmouth, NH www.smuttynose.com

Caramel and cocoa are present in the malty aroma along with some buttery pecans." "Sweet malts on the tongue, soft bitterness, slightly thick and biscuity." "Perfect for the style." 6.2% alc.

Smuttynose Shoal's Pale Ale ★★★★★

Eng Pale Ale: Smuttynose Brewing Co., Portsmouth, NH www.smuttynose.com

"Rich malt flavor, combined with a good helping of citrusy hops, with nutty and woody notes." "A subtle beer all around; well blended and a real delight." 5% alc.

Smuttynose Weizenheimer ★★

Hefeweizen: Smuttynose Brewing Co., Portsmouth, NH www.smuttynose.com

"Light banana and clove flavors, but there's also a small hop bite at the end." "US companies are taking too many liberties with the word Hefeweizen." 0% alc.

Smuttynose Wheat Wine ★★★★

Barley Wine: Smuttynose Brewing Co., Portsmouth, NH www.smuttynose.com

"Aroma of sharp, dry wheat, lots of fruitiness (apples, pears oranges, unripened peaches), with soft, sweaty, only lightly bitter hops." "Hop resins develop from flavor to bitterness, accommodating the oranges and caramel sweetness." 11% alc.

Snake River Pale Ale ★★1/2

Am. Pale Ale: Snake River Brewing Co. (Cowfish Restaurant), Cheyenne, WY www.snakeriverpub.com

"Light hop aroma - wood orange." "Fairly moderate example of the style - some orange/wood/grapefruit hop contrasting with lightly toasty malt." "This would be an excellent gateway ale." 5.7% alc.

Snake River Vienna Style Lager ★★★

Vienna: Snake River Brewing Co. (Cowfish Restaurant), Cheyenne, WY www.snakeriverpub.com

"Aroma is a rich caramel with toffee and a smattering of herbal hops bitterness." "Flavor is of caramel malts, a touch of peat adds some earthiness." "Perfect with a slice of pizza." 6% alc.

Snake River Zonker Stout ★★★1/2
Foreign Stout: Snake River Brewing Co. (Cowfish Restaurant), Cheyenne, WY www.snakeriverpub.com
"Suave coffee engulfs the fruity esters and malt roastiness." "Creamy cocoa and coffee thrive lavishly in the sexy mouthfeel." "Primo sipping stout." 5.8% alc.

Snipes Mountain Coyote Moon ★★1/2
Brown Ale: Snipes Mountain Microbrewery and Restaurant, Sunnyside, WA www.snipesmountain.com
"Aroma is very coffee-like, some nuts." "Malty and somewhat nutty this beer almost feels watery and wet in the finish." "A cookie-cutter brown that I'm not getting much out of at all." 3.9% alc.

Snipes Mountain Indian Pale Ale ★★1/2
IPA: Snipes Mountain Microbrewery and Restaurant, Sunnyside, WA www.snipesmountain.com
"Flavor is mainly grapefruit, wood and black currant, with a light underpinning of pale malt sweetness." "Rich caramelly, toasty malt aroma, with earthy, herby hops, citrus rind and floral notes." 5.6% alc.

Snipes Mountain Porter ★★1/2
Porter: Snipes Mountain Microbrewery and Restaurant, Sunnyside, WA www.snipesmountain.com
"Coffeeish, slightly nutty, almost meaty aroma." "Woody, smoky flavor combines well with the creaminess, cheap chocolate aftertaste." "You could definitely make a good stew with this." 4.35% alc.

Snipes Mountain Red Sky ESB ★★
Prem Bitter: Snipes Mountain Microbrewery and Restaurant, Sunnyside, WA www.snipesmountain.com
"Nose of creamy malts, bread and starch." "Quite sweet brown sugar character. Hints of iron. Slight earthy note in the finish." "Taste is bitter and fruity, but a thin body really spoiled this brew." 5.2% alc.

Snipes Mountain Roza Reserve ★★★
Barley Wine: Snipes Mountain Microbrewery and Restaurant, Sunnyside, WA www.snipesmountain.com
"Sweet heavy malt with hints of cherry liqueur, brandy, caramel and hint of hops." "Nutty malt flavors mix with earthy hops and dark toffee." "Straightforward strong barley wine." 9.2% alc.

Snipes Mountain Sunnyside Pale ★★1/2
Prem Bitter: Snipes Mountain Microbrewery and Restaurant, Sunnyside, WA www.snipesmountain.com
"Nose is decently balanced with caramel and slightly floral hops." "Moderately bitter - pommelo, wood, with a clean refreshing finish." "Seems a very light Pale Ale but tasty." 4.6% alc.

Snoqualmie Falls Avalanche Ale ★★★1/2
Am Strong Ale: Snoqualmie Falls Brewing Co., Snoqualmie, WA www.fallsbrew.com
"Toasty malts and zesty, floral hops in the assertive aroma." "Hop bitterness at the forefront, albeit soft, with a mellow malt background. Slightly grainy and biscuity." "It's rather complex and I think it should age well." 7% alc.

Snoqualmie Falls Copperhead Pale ★★★★
Am. Pale Ale: Snoqualmie Falls Brewing Co., Snoqualmie, WA www.fallsbrew.com
"Lightly sweet and grainy pale malts are almost overwhelmed by the dominant grapefruity hops." "Crisp refreshingly hoppy palate, mildly fruity, biscuity undertones." "Another good offering from Snoqualmie Falls." 5.3% alc.

Snoqualmie Falls Spring Fever ★★★★1/2
Belgian Ale: Snoqualmie Falls Brewing Co., Snoqualmie, WA www.fallsbrew.com
"Strong, slightly perfumey aroma with passion fruit, mango and coriander." "tropical fruits, cumin, coriander are all beautifully balanced with sweet icing sugar malts." "A rather enjoyable beer for desert." 7% alc.

Snoqualmie Falls Steam Train Porter ★★1/2
Porter: Snoqualmie Falls Brewing Co., Snoqualmie, WA www.fallsbrew.com
"Huge aroma of bittersweet chocolate and charred malts." "Full body, light apparent hop flavoring, big chocolaty flavor with hints of roasted malt." "Tastes very similar to Rogue Mocha Porter." 5% alc.

Snoqualmie Falls Wildcat IPA ★★★★
IPA: Snoqualmie Falls Brewing Co., Snoqualmie, WA www.fallsbrew.com
"Nose of lime juice, fresh-cut green grass." "Very woody taste with lemony bitterness. Long, bitter, refreshing finish." "Has that typical Pacific Northwest IPA-in-your-face hoppiness, yet certain subtleness to it as well." 6.6% alc.

Sol ★
Pale Lager: Femsa, Monterrey/Veracruz-Llave, Mexico www.femsa.com
"Very little aroma and almost no flavor." "Thin body and corn-chip aftertaste." "I would not drink on its own unless cornered, beaten or otherwise forced." 4.5% alc.

Sonoran Burning Bird ★★★★★
Am. Pale Ale: Sonoran Brewing Co., Phoenix, AZ www.sonorabrew.com
"Golden pale ale with a floral, fruity hop aroma. The flavor is moderately hoppy with notes of grapefruit, lemon. "Fantastic APA; wish I could get more of." 5% alc.

Sonoran Desert Amber ★★★
Amber Ale: Sonoran Brewing Co., Phoenix, AZ www.sonorabrew.com
"Amber color with a malty aroma. "Very fresh bread vibe thing." "Nothing challenging or offensive, yet nothing interesting either." N/A% alc.

Sonoran Inebriator Stout ★★★★★
Imp. Stout: Sonoran Brewing Co., Phoenix, AZ www.sonorabrew.com
"Lots of dark fruit sweetness, toffee, bitter chocolate" in this strong offering. "Alcohol becomes more apparent as it warms." "Solid malt, plentiful hops, perfectly integrated, altogether nice." 9.1% alc.

Sonoran IPA ★★★★
IPA: Sonoran Brewing Co., Phoenix, AZ www.sonorabrew.com
"An amber-colored example with the aroma of fresh Cascade hops and lots of interesting tropical fruits." Flavor on the sweet side for the style, but well-balanced with a "dry finish." 6.2% alc.

Sonoran Old Saguaro Barleywine ★★★★
Barley Wine: Sonoran Brewing Co., Phoenix, AZ www.sonorabrew.com
"Dark amber color with a sweet, fruity, raisiny, nutty aroma. "This stuff is silky smooth!" The flavor is malt-accented, with dark fruit notes and just enough hops for balance. "Probably ages pretty well" 9.2% alc.

Southampton Abbot 12 ★★★★★
Abt/Quadrupel: Southampton Publick House, Southampton, NY www.publick.com
"Richly malty aroma with prunes, raisins, yeast, light caramel and a hint of alcohol." "Very sweet dark malt palate with hints of raisins and smoke. Soft, sweet finish that is slightly honeyish but never cloying." 10% alc.

Southampton Bière de Garde ★★★1/2
Bière de Garde: Southampton Publick House, Southampton, NY www.publick.com
"Aroma very skunky farmhouse, grassy and very musty." "Dry with some citric notes balanced by some sweet cookie touches." "Light, but sustentative on the palate." 7% alc.

Southampton Bière de Mars ★★★★★
Bière de Garde: Southampton Publick House, Southampton, NY www.publick.com
"Slightly sour aroma with notes of lemons." "Flavor is a bit sharp at first. Notes of grass, lemons, apples and strawberries backed by a big caramel maltiness with an almost biting dryness." 6.2% alc.

Southampton Cuvée des Fleurs ★★★★★
Saison: Southampton Publick House, Southampton, NY www.publick.com
"Aroma is like a garden. Herbs, flowers, spices and pepper come through." "Flavor is of flowers, apricots and lemons with more prominent perfumey lavender notes and some clove." 7.7% alc.

Southampton Double Ice Bock ★★★★★
Eisbock: Southampton Publick House, Southampton, NY www.publick.com
"Aroma is long on malts, plus vanilla, peach, pear and a bit of alcohol." "Thick, rich, caramel and toffee as far as the eye can see, with light raisins, vinous sherry notes and plenty of honey." 18% alc.

Southampton Double White ★★★★★
Bel. Witbier: Southampton Publick House, Southampton, NY www.publick.com
"Slight barnyard hint to the bready malt aroma." "Taste is very smooth with some good spice and wheat and some notes of citrus." "Almost reminds me of champagne on the palate." 6.8% alc.

Southampton Grand Cru ★★★★★
Bel. Strong Ale: Southampton Publick House, Southampton, NY www.publick.com
"Aroma is oranges and peaches with spices, yeast and a dominant malt profile." "Flavor was sour dark melon and citrus, a little syrupy near finish, also had a nice spiciness to balance out the sweetness." 9.5% alc.

Southampton Imperial Porter ★★★★1/2
Baltic Porter: Southampton Publick House, Southampton, NY www.publick.com
"Lighter aroma than I would like, but what is there is chocolate and molasses." "Flavor is surprisingly light, golden raisin and chocolate." "Still a good porter, I just expected a little more." 7.5% alc.

Southampton Imperial Russian ★★★★★
Imp. Stout: Southampton Publick House, Southampton, NY www.publick.com
"Excellent aroma of coffee, dark chocolate, vanilla cream and roasted grain." "Light anise, Spanish coffee, prunes, raisins and a light milk chocolate." "Pleasant but doesn't make me jump out of my seat and scream." 9.5% alc.

Southampton Old Ale ★★★★
Old Ale: Southampton Publick House, Southampton, NY www.publick.com
"Smells sweet but dark like toasted caramel. Some raisiny port notes as it warms." "Rich toffeeish malts abound, but without form nor complexity." "Enjoyable, but not what I was looking to get out of an Old Ale." 7.5% alc.

Southampton Old Herb ★★★★1/2
Barley Wine: Southampton Publick House, Southampton, NY www.publick.com
"Sweet malty, caramel aroma with a nice hoppy background." "Malty flavors up front of caramel, banana bread and light fruit." "Nice, but not as big and bold as expected in a Barley Wine." 11% alc.

Southampton Peconic County Reserve ★★★★★
Fruit Beer: Southampton Publick House, Southampton, NY www.publick.com
"Aroma is rather juicy, floral with various hints of leather, pear, grapes, juniper, heather, flowers." "Astringent, puckering grape flavor with tart notes of lemon and a creamy mouth with mild but engaging carbonation." 6.5% alc.

Southampton Saison ★★★★1/2
Saison: Southampton Publick House, Southampton, NY www.publick.com
"Yeasty to the nose with citric tartness, chamomile and white pepper." "Flavor is vaguely earthy, lemony sharp and a little sour. More spicy notes on the palate, including coriander." 6.5% alc.

Southampton Secret Ale ★★1/2
Altbier: Southampton Publick House, Southampton, NY www.publick.com
"Malty, nutty, toasty, slightly roasty, only mildly sweet and quite hoppy, citrus and bitter for excellent balance." "This beer is flavorful and well balanced without being too of anything." 5.1% alc.

Southampton Trappist-Style Triple Ale ★★★★
Abbey Tripel: Southampton Publick House, Southampton, NY www.publick.com
"Cloves and mushy bananas dominate the aroma, while straw and soft, dough yeast provide nice supporting roles." "Very unusual for a Tripel. Sour up front, more vanilla, floral (perfumey), apricot skin." 10% alc.

Southern Tier Harvest Ale ★★★★★
Am. Pale Ale: Southern Tier Brewing Co., Lakewood, NY www.southerntierbrewing.com
"Pretty malty (caramel and biscuits) paired with lemon zest and spicy hops." "Hop is pronounced but not overwhelming." "Great for a long session." 5.2% alc.

Southern Tier Hop Sun ★★★★★
Am. Wheat: Southern Tier Brewing Co., Lakewood, NY www.southerntierbrewing.com
"Aroma of rich, oily, resiny hops, with grapefruit, floral and light roast malt notes." "Very hoppy, slightly quenching wheat acidity and a hint of bread." "They call it American Wheat but more like English Summer Ale" 4.6% alc.

Southern Tier IPA ★★★★1/2
IPA: Southern Tier Brewing Co., Lakewood, NY www.southerntierbrewing.com
"Woody, leafy aroma with hints of nutmeg, minerals and orange zest." "Citric piney hop flavors predominantly, with caramel crystal malt backbone." "One of the best IPA's I've had." 6.5% alc.

Southern Tier Mild Ale ★★1/2
Mild Ale: Southern Tier Brewing Co., Lakewood, NY www.southerntierbrewing.com
"Aroma of freshly cracked malt with some caramel." "Flavor is nutty malt sweetness that rounds out nicely with just a touch of hops." 4.8% alc.

Southern Tier Old Man Winter ★★★★
Am Strong Ale: Southern Tier Brewing Co., Lakewood, NY www.southerntierbrewing.com
"Appetizing Cascade-hop aroma with toasty, caramelly malts, lemon and chocolate chip cookie dough." "Flavor starts strong with sweet caramel malt and a strange hint of grapes, develops some spiciness in the middle and finishes well with hops and pepper." 7.5% alc.

Southern Tier Phin and Matts Extraordinary Ale ★★1/2
Am. Pale Ale: Southern Tier Brewing Co., Lakewood, NY www.southerntierbrewing.com
"Strong aroma of citrus, mainly orange indicating lots of hops, but there are also hints of sweet, bready malts." "Hops, sweet malt and some tropical fruit flavors are there but are subdued." 5.2% alc.

Southern Tier Pilsner ★★★1/2
Pilsner: Southern Tier Brewing Co., Lakewood, NY www.southerntierbrewing.com
"Light malty aroma with a slight lemony appearance and a mild hop showing." "Taste starts out with floral and bitter hops, spice, with a bit of lighter malt sweetness to round it out." "I could drink (this) with some frequency." 5.5% alc.

Southern Tier Porter ★★★
Porter: Southern Tier Brewing Co., Lakewood, NY www.southerntierbrewing.com
"Aroma of coffee, alder, light grass, almonds." "Taste is a little too smoky - burnt coffee grounds and sugar, roast chestnuts, charcoal, some fruit." "Good starting point for novices, but still has enough flavor for more advanced palates." 5.2% alc.

Southern Tier Tripel ★★1/2
Abbey Tripel: Southern Tier Brewing Co., Lakewood, NY www.southerntierbrewing.com
"Yeasty aroma, with lots of fruit notes, peaches and pears come to mind." "Flavor is packed with toffee and candi sugar malt, but well balanced with mild tartness and spices." 9% alc.

Southpaw Light ★
Pale Lager: Miller Brewing Co. (SABMiller), Milwaukee , WI www.millerbrewing.com
"How many hops do they use when they double hop it? Two?" "Don't expect anything complex because it's not there." "$6 for 12 is a great price if you just want to hang out with friends and get drunk, but this one isn't for you if you are picky." 5% alc.

Spanish Peaks Black Dog ★★1/2
Eng Pale Ale: Spanish Peaks Brewing Co. (Mendocino Brewing Co.), Hopland, CA
"Aroma is pleasantly malty. Flavor is smooth and malty, with a crisp, yet light, hoppy finish." "Enough hops to overcome the sweetness and make it just right for my taste." "Not super complex but quaffable." N/A% alc.

Spanish Peaks Honey Raspberry ★★1/2
Fruit Beer: Spanish Peaks Brewing Co. (Mendocino Brewing Co.), Hopland, CA
"Flavor is of honey and raspberry and tastes pretty artificial." "Some sweetness and obviously raspberry but it doesn't form any cohesive taste structure." N/A% alc.

Spanish Peaks Monterey Pale Ale ★★1/2
Am. Pale Ale: Spanish Peaks Brewing Co. (Mendocino Brewing Co.), Hopland, CA
"This is a nice, simple Pale Ale." "Bready and caramelly, rich, with a bit of sourness and a slight hoppy bite." "A nice beer that doesn't overdo itself but does not undersell itself either." N/A% alc.

Sparhawk Golden Ale ★
Goldn/Blond Ale: Casco Bay Brewing, Portland, ME www.cascobaybrewing.com
"Gentle citrus hop aroma." "Toasted malt flavors and a faintly fruity finish." "Crisp, refreshing." "For a golden I was quite happy with this beer." 4.86% alc.

Spaten Oktoberfest Ur-Marzen ★★★1/2
Märzen/Oktbfst: Spaten-Franziskaner-Bräu (InBev), Münich, Germany www.spaten.de
"Aromas were musty, bready and herbal, with light spiciness." "Medium sweet malt flavors, caramelly, nutty and lightly bready." "This goes down too easily; drank four half liters at a local German restaurant a few weeks back." 5.9% alc.

Spaten Optimator ★★★★
Doppelbock: Spaten-Franziskaner-Bräu (InBev), Münich, Germany www.spaten.de
"Nose is malt sweet of gingerbread, butter and cinnamon." "Flavors of toast, chocolates, molasses and some toffee round this one out." "Oh so sweet, well balanced, quite complex, silky smooth. Fantastic!" 7.2% alc.

Spaten Pils ★★★★
Pilsner: Spaten-Franziskaner-Bräu (InBev), Münich, Germany www.spaten.de
"Aroma of pale malt, floral hops and some honey fruitiness." "Dry and creamy mouthfeel with herbal bitterness following light sweetness." "Easy to drink beer with a character that just screams European Lager." 5% alc.

Spaten Premium Lager ★★1/2
Helles/Dortmnd: Spaten-Franziskaner-Bräu (InBev), Münich, Germany www.spaten.de
"Light hops aroma with light grains and a bit of skunk as well." "Very nice malty flavor with a quick hop finish." "If only the macros of this country could replicate this..." 5.2% alc.

Speakeasy Big Daddy IPA ★★★
IPA: Speakeasy Ales and Lagers, San Francisco, CA www.goodbeer.com
"Clean citrusy hop aroma.... preparing me for a nice hop experience." "Not as strongly-hopped as the other IPAs that I have had." "Put 'em on ice!" 6.5% alc.

Speakeasy Prohibition Ale ★★★★★
Amber Ale: Speakeasy Ales and Lagers, San Francisco, CA www.goodbeer.com
This highly-regarded amber has "Very fresh citrus and spruce hops with some mild malt aroma" and a flavor that starts a little caramelly then finishes fairly bitter. 6.1% alc.

Speakeasy Untouchable Pale Ale ★★1/2
Am. Pale Ale: Speakeasy Ales and Lagers, San Francisco, CA www.goodbeer.com
"Good aromas of citrusy hops, some caramel and some mild spice notes." "Flavor is hop dominant." "Not terrible but it could be so much better." 5.5% alc.

Special Export ★★
Pale Lager: Miller Brewing Co. (SABMiller), Milwaukee, WI www.millerbrewing.com
"Palate was light and smooth. Flavors of sour malt and corn with a slightly bitter finish." "Stale peanuts and chewed up gum in the finish." "Just hope it didn't ruin my tasting glass." N/A% alc.

Spezial Rauchbier Lager ★★★1/2
Smoked: Brauerei Spezial, Bamberg, Germany www.brauerei-spezial.de
"Nice cigar like flavor and light spiciness." "Rich depth of stunning smoke; creamy, nutty, toasty dry malts." "Really makes me want to pay a visit to Bamberg." 4.6% alc.

Spilker Hopluia ★★1/2
IPA: Spilker Ales, Cortland, NE www.spilkerales.com
"Promising aroma of resinous hops, pine and background malts and fruity esters." "Some malt and a fairly good dose of bitter hops but nothing that screams 'IPA!' " N/A% alc.

Sprecher Abbey Triple ★★1/2
Abbey Tripel: Sprecher Brewing Co., Glendale, WI www.sprecherbrewery.com
"Sweet curaçao, coriander and globally herbal nose immediately reminds of doughy spices and caramalt." "Flavor is WOW - super sweet sugar all around." "Just too overpoweringly sweet." 8.4% alc.

Sprecher Black Bavarian ★★★★★
Schwarzbier: Sprecher Brewing Co., Glendale, WI www.sprecherbrewery.com
Full, malty aroma of roasted cocoa and slightly burnt coffee... powerful yet delicate.. really enticing." "Flavor is rich and malty, doughy/toasty with a touch of hops and a bit of vanilla flavors." "Very aromatic, very fulfilling." 5.86% alc.

Sprecher Dopple Bock ★★★1/2
Doppelbock: Sprecher Brewing Co., Glendale, WI www.sprecherbrewery.com
"Rich malt smell toffee and a touch of bitter cherry." "Chewy and creamy with flavors of honey, Butterfinger candy bar, dried cherries, subtly bitter hops and a warming alcohol taste behind." "I can see this why this was called liquid bread." 7.85% alc.

Sprecher Generation Porter ★★
Porter: Sprecher Brewing Co., Glendale, WI www.sprecherbrewery.com
"Aroma of coffee, dark chocolate and cherries." "Fruit and cocoa kind of overwhelm what would be a nice porter profile: instead of dark rich porter malts with chocolate roasties, I get a fine fruit beer." 5.73% alc.

Sprecher Hefe Weiss ★★1/2
Hefeweizen: Sprecher Brewing Co., Glendale, WI www.sprecherbrewery.com
"Wheat dominated aroma, some banana and bubblegum and lots of yeast." "Flavors of bubblegum, citrus, a bit of banana and a hint of clove with a sweet finish." "Light enough for the whole family to enjoy." 4.2% alc.

Sprecher Imperial Stout ★★★1/2
Imp. Stout: Sprecher Brewing Co., Glendale, WI www.sprecherbrewery.com
"Roasted chocolate and some caramel provided the bulk of the aroma." "Taste has some dark chocolate and cherries. There is also some light roasted coffee." "Sprecher's shown that an Imperial Stout can deliver without going over the deep end." 8% alc.

Sprecher Indian Pale Ale ★★★
IPA: Sprecher Brewing Co., Glendale, WI www.sprecherbrewery.com
"Some faint grassy, citrusy aromas and maybe a little malt." "Bitter up front taste with some honey character and some sweet malt." "Just different enough to be enjoyable." 7.5% alc.

Sprecher Irish Style Stout ★★1/2
Dry Stout: Sprecher Brewing Co., Glendale, WI www.sprecherbrewery.com
"Aroma is bitter chocolate, sweet roasted malt and a hint of coffee and hops." "Flavor is roasted coffee, dark fruits and dark semi-sweet chocolate." "Dry and tangy." 5.73% alc.

Sprecher Maibock ★★★
Bock: Sprecher Brewing Co., Glendale, WI www.sprecherbrewery.com
"Chocolate chip cookie dough aroma with slight notes of smoke and rye." "Evenly balanced, malty palate - firm, but finishing dry and smooth." "Perfect for rainy days in May." 6% alc.

Sprecher Oktoberfest ★★★1/2
Märzen/Oktbfst: Sprecher Brewing Co., Glendale, WI www.sprecherbrewery.com
"Aromas are well-malted with caramel and buttery nuts." "The flavor is floral hops and caramel with nuts. Toasted and roasted malts. Tea." "This is better than the vast majority of the American Oktoberfests." 5.75% alc.

Sprecher Pub Ale ★★1/2
Brown Ale: Sprecher Brewing Co., Glendale, WI www.sprecherbrewery.com
"Toasted malts, light caramel aromas, and a little fruity." "Good malty flavor with a decent caramel side and some latent hops in the end." "A real warmer, even though the alcohol is low." 4.5% alc.

Sprecher Special Amber ★★★1/2
Vienna: Sprecher Brewing Co., Glendale, WI www.sprecherbrewery.com
"Aroma is toffee malt, toast and a nice herbal hop fragrance." "Tastes of caramel malt and fruity, spicy hops." "This is one of those beers I could consume in MASS quantities!" 5% alc.

Sprecher Winter Brew ★★1/2
Bock: Sprecher Brewing Co., Glendale, WI www.sprecherbrewery.com
"Toast, toffee, brown sugar and earthy hops aroma, perhaps a touch of grapeskin." "Flavors of sweet caramel, toffee and nuttiness with a hint of coffee, smoke and a little floral hop bitterness at the finish." 5.75% alc.

Squatters Capt. Bastards Oatmeal Stout ★★1/2
Sweet Stout: Salt Lake Brewing Co. / Squatters Pub, Salt Lake City, UT www.squatters.com
"Aroma was roasted malt with just a little hop." "Chocolate, coffee and roasted flavors were capped with a long dry finish." 4% alc.

Squatters Full Suspension Pale Ale ★★1/2
Am. Pale Ale: Salt Lake Brewing Co. / Squatters Pub, Salt Lake City, UT www.squatters.com
"Huge fresh green hop nose. Like opening a fresh pack of hop flowers." "Sweet, light flavor, with a hoppy spice and some hedge fruits too." "Aroma is a dead ringer for cannabis… which makes this a very interesting drink." 4% alc.

Squatters Hefeweizen ★★
Hefeweizen: Salt Lake Brewing Co. / Squatters Pub, Salt Lake City, UT www.squatters.com
"Sweet and mellow with notes of apples and sweat." "Applesauce candy flavor." "Uninspired and poorly executed." N/A% alc.

Squatters Indian Pale Ale ★★1/2
IPA: Salt Lake Brewing Co. / Squatters Pub, Salt Lake City, UT www.squatters.com
"Aroma has all the classic trademarks of pine, resin and grapefruit." "Flavor is light, as are the hops... some sweet pine and mandarin oranges." "Very drinkable - which, for me, is the main purpose of beer." 6% alc.

Squatters Provo Girl Pilsner ★★★
Pilsner: Salt Lake Brewing Co. / Squatters Pub, Salt Lake City, UT www.squatters.com
"Fresh aroma of herbaceous hops, doughy yeast and fresh bready malts." "Initial sweet cereal notes in the flavor lead into a very dry, bitter and peppery finish." "Solid, spicy, German-style Pilsner." 4% alc.

St. Feuillien Cuvée de Noël ★★★★1/2
Bel. Strong Ale: Brasserie St-Feuillien / Friart, Le Roeulx, Belgium www.st-feuillien.com
"Nose of sappy sweet hops and spicy malts; notes of grapenuts, licorice, pine, toasted fennel and light alcohol." "Plum flavor, molasses with a chewy maltiness like pancake or biscuits." "Almost the quintessence of a Christmas beer." 9% alc.

St. Bernardus Abt 12 ★★★★★
Abt/Quadrupel: St. Bernardus Brouwerij, Watou, Belgium www.sintbernardus.be
"Aroma is alcohol, doughy yeast, some dark fruits (mostly raisin) and some brown sugar." "Chewy malt depths, dates, a little bit of chocolate and a sturdy alcohol backbone." "Bringing heavenly nectar within earthly grasp, indeed." 10.5% alc.

St. Bernardus Blanche (Witbier) ★★★★1/2
Bel. Witbier: St. Bernardus Brouwerij, Watou, Belgium www.sintbernardus.be
"Very complex fruity and spicy aroma." "Flavor is fruity with citrus, pears , apricots and light spicy notes, ending in a moderately sweet, slightly herbal finish." "Perfect lawnmower beer - if you are doing yard work at a monastery." 5.5% alc.

St. Bernardus Pater 6 ★★★★
Belgian Ale: St. Bernardus Brouwerij, Watou, Belgium www.sintbernardus.be
"Some spicy notes, brown sugar, caramelized malt, fruity of figs, raisins, hint of chocolate." "Flavor is fruity with raisins, chocolate, banana and light caramel tones, ending in a caramelly long finish." 6.7% alc.

St. Bernardus Prior 8 ★★★★★
Bel. Strong Ale: St. Bernardus Brouwerij, Watou, Belgium www.sintbernardus.be
"Toasty, bready, sweet caramelized malt, with a fruity nose of figs, dates, with a chocolaty hint." "This beer is much less about alcohol or even fruit than it is about malt, unlike many beers of this style." 8% alc.

St. Bernardus Tripel ★★★★1/2
Abbey Tripel: St. Bernardus Brouwerij, Watou, Belgium www.sintbernardus.be
"Loads of candy in the aroma, spicy phenolics, vanilla custard, glue and perhaps lime rind." "Flavors are somewhat fruity (a bit more banana and apricot) and sweet but are balanced by spicy yeast notes." 8% alc.

St. Druon de Sebourg ★★
Bière de Garde: Brasserie Duyck, Jenlain, France www.duyck.com
"Citric herby aroma, some creaminess." "Musty, floral, honey-like, fruity, berry flavor with herbal notes and fair finishing bitterness." "Like a really good premium lager..." 6.5% alc.

St. Feuillien Blonde ★★★
Bel. Strong Ale: Brasserie St-Feuillien / Friart, Le Roeulx, Belgium www.st-feuillien.com
"Spicy aroma (black pepper, anise, yeast) with pear." "Citrus fruity and slightly sweet malty taste with yeasts with a lemon fruity, light hop bitter and slightly alcoholic but warming finish." "Quite intense, interesting." 7.5% alc.

St. Feuillien Brune ★★★★1/2
Abbey Dubbel: Brasserie St-Feuillien / Friart, Le Roeulx, Belgium www.st-feuillien.com
"Aroma of plums, raisins, brown sugar, pears." "Tastes malty, brown sugary and figgy, with a semi-dry finish." "Great creamy aftertaste that lingers like a great chocolate banquet!" 7.5% alc.

St. Feuillien Triple ★★★★★

Abbey Tripel: Brasserie St-Feuillien / Friart, Le Roeulx, Belgium www.st-feuillien.com

"Very floral, flowery aroma with some spicy nectar hints." "Like a quarter honeydew dolloped with honey and ground black pepper and showered with parsley." "Excellent, robust Tripel." 8.5% alc.

St. George Golden Ale ★★1/2

Am. Pale Ale: St. George Brewing Co., Hampton, VA www.stgeorgebrewingco.com

"Flowery hop nose with a bit of grassiness." "Taste is citrusy, kind of grapefruit with a small hop bitter/bite." "Rather refreshing; good session beer." 5% alc.

St. George Indian Pale Ale ★★★

IPA: St. George Brewing Co., Hampton, VA www.stgeorgebrewingco.com

"Mild aroma of biscuits, tea and slightly herbaceous hops." "Flavor is initially very full, fruity and doughy with dancing carbonation and premature hints of more sylvan hops but thins out to a mildly bitter, yeast-dominated and nutty finish." 5% alc.

St. George Pils ★★★1/2

Bohem Pilsner: St. George Brewing Co., Hampton, VA www.stgeorgebrewingco.com

"Nice European hop nose along with a pleasant malt mix." "Well rounded for a pils, light flavors of grain, malt and hops." "If you're a German Pils fan, this is the US version is for you!!" 5% alc.

St. George Porter ★★★1/2

Porter: St. George Brewing Co., Hampton, VA www.stgeorgebrewingco.com

"Chocolaty, coffee, nutty nose." "Gorgeous chocolately taste in your mouth with a side of caramel." "Overall, a very nice and relatively cheap porter - a pleasant surprise!" 4.5% alc.

St. Georgen Bräu Keller Bier ★★★1/2

Keller+E2624: St. Georgen Bräu, Buttenheim, Germany www.georgenbraeu.de

"Aroma is dripping with hops - very toasty as well, with a hint of caramel." "Field-like hop notes and toasty malts dominate the flavor." "I must seek out more of this style!" 4.9% alc.

St. Ides High Gravity Malt Liquor ★

Malt Liquor: Miller Brewing Co. (SABMiller), Milwaukee, WI www.millerbrewing.com

"Fuel in a can with some corn and rice mixed in to give the texture of oil." "Has a property that makes breathing become labored." "I would call this a drain pour except that would be lying; I chucked it on my lawn." 8% alc.

St. Ides Premium Malt Liquor ★

Malt Liquor: Miller Brewing Co. (SABMiller), Milwaukee, WI www.millerbrewing.com

"When you're underage I guess you'll drink anything you can get your hands on." "Not really like beer, somewhat like apple juice." "Flavors of alcohol and corn. Finishes with stomach convulsions..." 5.9% alc.

St. Ides Special Brew - Mixed Fruit ★★1/2

Malt Liquor: Miller Brewing Co. (SABMiller), Milwaukee, WI www.millerbrewing.com

"All syrupy cherry, apple and fruit punch." "Too sweet and medicinal." "Served very cold, this could be adequately refreshing on a hot day, but I'm pretty sure that I'd end up getting very sick." 6% alc.

St. Louis Gueuze ★

Gueuze: Brouwerij Van Honsebrouck, Ingelmunster, Belgium www.vanhonsebrouck.be

"Green apples are lightly tart and contrast with citrus and wheat aromas and a mild lambic character." "Taste is moderately sweet, lemon, caramel." "How can it be so sweet?! Bleah!" 4.5% alc.

St. Louis Kriek ★

Fruit Lambic: Brouwerij Van Honsebrouck, Ingelmunster, Belgium www.vanhonsebrouck.be

"Artificial cherry aroma." "Cherry juice, avoiding any flavors or aromas that even come close to beer." 4.5% alc.

St. Pauli Girl Lager ★★1/2
Classic Ger Pils: Brauerei Beck and Co./Becks (InBev), Bremen, Germany www.becks-beer.com
"Aroma of some sour smell which masks the hop." "The flavor has hints of malty sweetness and an ever so slight hop bitterness." "Not a great beer by any means, but pretty decent for a macro-brewed light Pilsner." 4.9% alc.

St. Pauli Girl Special Dark ★★1/2
Am Dark Larger: Brauerei Beck and Co./Becks (InBev), Bremen, Germany www.becks-beer.com
"Some roasted aromas, mild nut and malt." "Taste is sweet, some roasted coffee, malt." "Watery on the palate and not much there to remember at all." 4.8% alc.

St. Pauli Non-Alcoholic ★★
Low Alcohol: Brauerei Beck and Co./Becks (InBev), Bremen, Germany www.becks-beer.com
"Light sweet aroma with a hint of hops." "Sweet with the hops coming through to give a decent bitterness." "No worse than many lagers and since this is an N/A beer that's saying a lot." 0.5% alc.

St. Peter's Cream Stout ★★★★
Sweet Stout: St. Peters (UK), Bungay, Suffolk, England www.stpetersbrewery.co.uk
"Similar aroma to Mackesons - sweet, light roast and some chocolate." "Flavor is bitter, roasty, coffee-like." "A good entry point if new to stouts." "Very good cream stout. I'll have this again." 6.5% alc.

St. Peter's Golden Ale ★★1/2
Goldn/Blond Ale: St. Peters (UK), Bungay, Suffolk, England www.stpetersbrewery.co.uk
"Aroma was malty, but also a sour fruity note, almost of orange." "I'm totally digging the smoky, malty and grassy character of this beer." "Better than I expected." 4.7% alc.

St. Peter's Old Style Porter ★★★1/2
Porter: St. Peters (UK), Bungay, Suffolk, England www.stpetersbrewery.co.uk
"Almost sour aroma, treacly, with dark cherries and light coffee." "Flavor gentle toasty, roasty malt accentuated by a balanced, chocolaty sweetness and malt bitterness throughout." "You can taste both the beers that went into making this." 5.1% alc.

St. Peters Organic Ale ★★★
Goldn/Blond Ale: St. Peters (UK), Bungay, Suffolk, England www.stpetersbrewery.co.uk
"Smells like musty clothes with some citrusy notes toward the tail end." "Earthy, pithy bitterness, lightly toasted malts, nuts, dry finish." "Quick, simple finish to a decent English ale." 4.5% alc.

St. Sebastiaan Dark ★★★
Belgian Ale: Brouwerij Moortgat, Breendonk-Puurs, Belgium www.duvel.be
"Light aroma, with treacle notes and a slight peach fruitiness." "Toffee, raisins, clove and a surprisingly strong surge of alcohol in the finish." "Overall, this is very drinkable but flawed." 6.9% alc.

St. Sebastiaan Golden ★★★
Belgian Ale: Brouwerij Moortgat, Breendonk-Puurs, Belgium www.duvel.be
"Toasty aroma, slightly peachy with additional notes of pear and a light spiciness." "A little bit of alcohol shows, as well as lively pear and apricot ester character." "Far more simple than they'd let you believe." 7.6% alc.

St. Sebastiaan Grand Reserve ★★★
Bel. Strong Ale: Brouwerij Moortgat, Breendonk-Puurs, Belgium www.duvel.be
"Aroma is citrus, fruit syrup, spice and notes of alcohol." "Sweet with lots of fruity esters, bready yeast and noticeable alcohol." "Kind of raw and unrefined." 10% alc.

Stag ★★1/2
Bel. Strong Ale: Walking Man Brewing and Public House, Stevenson, WA
"Grassy aroma with rough estery character." "Grainy-sour flavor profile with a quick finish." "Solid beer; I felt like I work in a steel mill." 9% alc.

Starr Hill Amber ★★

Brown Ale: Starr Hill Restaurant Brewery and Music Hall, Charlottesville, VA www.starrhill.com

"Subtle nose of light malt, toffee and hops." "Tastes similar to Bass - a little less yeasty but fresher. Malty, caramel, not too sweet with a subtle hop finish." 5% alc.

Starr Hill Pale ★★★

IPA: Starr Hill Restaurant Brewery and Music Hall, Charlottesville, VA www.starrhill.com

"Aroma is fruity, citrusy hops interwoven with toasty, sweet malt." "Flavor is very well balanced- sticky sweet hop citrus and bitterness, lightish caramel malt body sweetness and a slight alcohol heft with a crisp, citrus-tang finish." 5% alc.

Stary Melnik Svetloe (Lager) ★★1/2

Pilsner: Pivovar Moskva (EFES RUS), Moscow, Russia www.starymelnik.ru

"Dry, lemony hop and gritty grain aroma, fairly clean and peppery." "Biscuity palate, with a herbal-grassy hoppiness." "Quite refreshing and a standout amongst the world's pale lagers." 4.6% alc.

Steamworks Steam Engine Lager ★★★

Am Dark Larger: Steamworks Brewing Co. , Durango, CO www.steamworksbrewing.com

A dark lager with a "buttery/toasted bread nose, with hints of burnt crust and a light hop scent." "Fairly clean lager with a little too much sweetness." "Enjoyed all the dimensions by themselves, but not so much together." 5.4% alc.

Steamworks Third Eye P.A. ★★★

IPA: Steamworks Brewing Co., Durango, CO www.steamworksbrewing.com

"Aroma of citrus hops and candy." "This is a well balanced beer… not too much bittering hops and not too malty sweet." "Hop heads need not apply." 6.6% alc.

Steel Reserve 211 High Gravity ★

Malt Liquor: Miller Brewing Co. (SABMiller), Milwaukee, WI www.millerbrewing.com

"Foul, stale, metallic corn aroma." "Very sweet, cakey flavor up front replaced by mineralic corn flavor." "Keep it in the sack, don't let anyone see you drink it." 8.1% alc.

Stegmaier 1857 ★★★

Pale Lager: Lion Brewery, Inc., Wilkes-Barre, PA www.lionbrewery.com

"Grain, mild corn, moderately sweet but I actually taste a little bit of hops." "Not a great beer,but not one to pass on either." N/A% alc.

Stegmaier Porter ★★★1/2

Porter: Lion Brewery, Inc., Wilkes-Barre, PA www.lionbrewery.com

Very dark mahogany, with a plummy, fruity nose." "Sweet palate, with plum, red apples, some toffee, brown sugar notes." "I can easily see myself coming back to this beer again." 5.5% alc.

Steinlager ★★1/2

Pale Lager: Lion Breweries - NZ (Lion Nathan Co.), Auckland, New Zealand www.lion-nathan.co.nz

"Grassy aroma with hints of pale malt." "Mild bitterness with grassy notes and again a light, balancing pale malt." "This is certainly better than many American macros." 5% alc.

Stella Artois ★★1/2

Premium Lager: InBev Belgium, Leuven, Belgium www.inbev.com

"The Bud of Belgium." "White bread, spicy, grassy hops and lightly floral." "As lagers go, definitely better than most of the beer brewed for the masses in the States." 5.2% alc.

Stepan Razin Kalinkin ★★1/2

Eur Str Lager: Stepan Razin Brewery (Heineken), St. Petersburg, Russia www.razin.ru

"Smells like dirty clothes and corn meal." "Sweetness prominent with alcohol, candi sugar and bit of tartness." "Actually a high quality malt liquor." 7% alc.

Stepan Razin Porter ★★1/2
Baltic Porter: Stepan Razin Brewery (Heineken), St. Petersburg, Russia www.razin.ru
"Aroma of orange, molasses, sugar tarts, medicinal phenols." "Thinnish dark roast malt palate." "It makes for a decent porter and I would try it again." 8% alc.

Stepan Razin Zolotoye ★★
Vienna: Stepan Razin Brewery (Heineken), St. Petersburg, Russia www.razin.ru
"Corn and veggies aroma and sweet unfermented malt." "Flavor is metallic at first then mellows. Nice malt backbone with a decent amount of hops and bitterness." "Outside the Baltic Porters one of the better Russian beers." N/A% alc.

Sterkens White Ale ★★
Bel. Witbier: Brewery Ommegang (Moortgat), Cooperstown, NY www.ommegang.com
"Smell is average, sweet Belgian spices (clove, coriander), wheat and a little wet basement." "Spicy, peppery character with underlying wheat malt sweetness." "Just not very profound." 4.7% alc.

Stiegl GoldBräu ★★1/2
Premium Lager: Stieglbrauerei zu Salzburg GmbH, Salzburg, Austria www.stiegl.co.at
"Sweet grainy, unrefined aroma." "Incredibly soft and smooth mouthfeel, lots of malt and a lightly bitter finish." "Very accessible and well crafted beer for major consumption." 4.9% alc.

Stiegl Pils ★★1/2
Classic Ger Pils: Stieglbrauerei zu Salzburg GmbH, Salzburg, Austria www.stiegl.co.at
"Fresh hop nose is spicy and grassy in character with underlying grainy Pils malt aroma." "Decent malt backbone with better than expected hop character." "This would be a great everyday Pils." 4.9% alc.

Stockyard Oatmeal Stout ★★1/2
Sweet Stout: Goose Island Beer Co., Chicago, IL www.gooseisland.com
"Rich, creamy mouthfeel of true oatmeal stout is missing here." "Coffee and chocolate with a minute trace of alcohol." "I don't think Goose Island is trying their hardest with this stout." N/A% alc.

Stone Arrogant Bastard ★★★★★
Am Strong Ale: Stone Brewing Co., Escondido, CA www.stonebrew.com
One of the classic strong American ales. "Strong, stark, attack of licorice at first bite, with a symphony of woody, earthy, undertones for support." "Uhhh, sorry, I am worthy! I want some more!" 7.2% alc.

Stone Cat Barley Wine ★★★★1/2
Barley Wine: Mercury Brewing and Distribution, Ipswich, MA www.mercurybrewing.com
"Aroma is thick with dark fruits, plum, raisin, prune." "Caramel, chocolate and dark fruit up front with a big alcohol finish in flavor and warmth." "Good run of amped up hoppy goodness." 10.2% alc.

Stone Cat ESB ★★
Prem Bitter: Mercury Brewing and Distribution, Ipswich, MA www.mercurybrewing.com
"Slight dry nutty flavor (the mix of the bitter hops and the caramel malt); tinge of dry bitter orange." "Tinge of bitter/citrus hops flavor which does not go well with the watery taste." "Finishes poorly." N/A% alc.

Stone Cat IPA ★★
IPA: Mercury Brewing and Distribution, Ipswich, MA www.mercurybrewing.com
"Very dry and bitter, no real attempt at sweet malt balance here. Tastes much like pine nettles." "Really, I think it could have been much more bitter, but oh well, not bad." N/A% alc.

Stone Coast 420 Indian Pale Ale ★★★

IPA: Stone Coast Brewing Co., Bethel, ME www.stonecoast.com

"Light citrus hop aroma." "The taste is pretty mild, with some bitterness coming through balanced with maltiness." "This is a very drinkable, unique interpretation." N/A% alc.

Stone Coast Knuckleball Bock ★

Bock: Stone Coast Brewing Co., Bethel, ME www.stonecoast.com

"Rather thin beer, especially for a bock." "I found this beer to be overly sweet." "Enjoyable only for a slightly novel taste, not because its a great experience to drink." 5% alc.

Stone Double Bastard ★★★★★

Am Strong Ale: Stone Brewing Co., Escondido, CA www.stonebrew.com

"A punishingly unforgiving assault on the palate… then again I guess that's the point." "Aroma contains hops, hops, hops, hops." Flavor has a "huge robust hop taste, great caramel tones, some dry fruit notes." 10% alc.

Stone Imperial Russian Stout ★★★★1/2

Imp. Stout: Stone Brewing Co., Escondido, CA www.stonebrew.com

This popular Imperial Stout's aroma is "full of milk chocolate, molasses and roastedness." "Tastes kind of like those little chocolate bottles filled with liquor." "This is the reason I hunt beer." 9.4% alc.

Stone IPA ★★★★

IPA: Stone Brewing Co., Escondido, CA www.stonebrew.com

Championed by craft beer lovers, it has an aroma that is "pure citrus, ruby red grapefruit with nuances of orange and lemon." "Delicious flavor of fresh citrus hops with enough malt to make the taste very well balanced." 6.9% alc.

Stone Levitation Ale ★★★1/2

Amber Ale: Stone Brewing Co., Escondido, CA www.stonebrew.com

The lightest of Stone's beers, it has a "wonderful balance between citrus, grapefruit orange, herbal hops and toasty, bready malts in the inviting aroma." "Nothing outstanding or unusual, just a good, solid beer." 4.4% alc.

Stone Old Guardian ★★★★

Barley Wine: Stone Brewing Co., Escondido, CA www.stonebrew.com

This very strong ale has a "beautiful red-golden color" and aroma of "dark fruits with sappy pine hops and caramel." "Deep resiny hop palate with that tongue-scraping bitterness that extends past the taste threshold." 9.91% alc.

Stone Pale Ale ★★★★

Am. Pale Ale: Stone Brewing Co., Escondido, CA www.stonebrew.com

"Grapefruit orange, leafy, tannin-full aroma with plenty of underlying malt sweetness." "Flavor is nicely bitter a bit piney and has a very light malt with hints of citrus throughout." "The red-headed stepchild of Arrogant Bastard." 5.4% alc.

Stone Ruination IPA ★★★★

Imp/Dbl IPA: Stone Brewing Co., Escondido, CA www.stonebrew.com

"Massive hop bitterness at first. I wish I could've seen my face!" "Flavor is dominated by hoppy bitterness backed by respectable amount of malty goodness." "I hate to waste a great beer on just myself when it's more fulfilling to share, contemplate and discuss. 7.7% alc.

Stone Smoked Porter ★★★★

Porter: Stone Brewing Co., Escondido, CA www.stonebrew.com

"Understated smoke character serves to accentuate the strong roasted malt (mocha coffee), caramel, spice/citrus hop and fresh, dark fruit" flavor." "Mouthfeel is full and creamy. Overall, great porter!" 5.9% alc.

Stoney Creek Atwater Dunkel ★★

Dunkel: Stoney Creek and Atwater Block Breweries, Detroit, MI www.getstoney.com

"Very subtle aromas and flavors of toffee, chocolate, almonds and balancing, drying hops." "A bit on the weak, watery side even for a lager." 5.2% alc.

Stoney Creek Atwater Hell ★★
Helles/Dortmnd: Stoney Creek and Atwater Block Breweries, Detroit, MI www.getstoney.com
"Aroma is slightly of honey but mostly of straw." "Flavor is malty with some nuttiness." "Tad watery and thin." "An OK offering." 5% alc.

Stoney Creek Original Vanilla Porter ★★1/2
Porter: Stoney Creek and Atwater Block Breweries, Detroit, MI www.getstoney.com
"Malty aroma with a light vanilla undertone." "Plenty of vanilla as well as some chocolate and roasted malt flavor." "Very sweet." "If you like the dessert Porters, this rocks." 5.5% alc.

Stoney Creek Stoney Pale Ale ★★1/2
Am. Pale Ale: Stoney Creek and Atwater Block Breweries, Detroit, MI www.getstoney.com
"Slight hoppy bite with a soft, sweet malty backbone." "Aroma is like bread and floral hops." "The hops did not overpower the flavor and there was a nice bitterness to the finish." 5.5% alc.

Stoney Creek Stoney Red Ale ★★
Irish Ale: Stoney Creek and Atwater Block Breweries, Detroit, MI www.getstoney.com
"Sweet malt aroma mixed with spicy, noble hops." "Has some sweet caramel malt taste but also a paper taste." "Other than a trace of hops, not much else going on here" "A little on the thin side." 5% alc.

Stoney's Beer ★★1/2
Pale Lager: Pittsburgh Brewing Co., Pittsburgh , PA www.pittsburghbrewingco.com
"Touch of biscuity malt, but it's hard to find." "The taste was a well balanced mix of hops and malt with a slightly sweet yet metallic finish." "Six-pack worth every bit of the $2.99 spent on it." 4.5% alc.

Stoudt's American Pale Ale ★★★1/2
Am. Pale Ale: Stoudts Brewing Co., Adamstown, PA www.stoudtsbeer.com
"Nose has some grassy and floral notes - light toasty malt, slight lemon." "Lots of orangey bittering hops in the flavor along with a generic crystal malt background and a springy dry and bitter herbal hop finish." 5% alc.

Stoudt's Double IPA ★★★★
Imp/Dbl IPA: Stoudts Brewing Co., Adamstown, PA www.stoudtsbeer.com
"Sweet aroma of malts, caramel, pine needles and hops with notes of dried fruits." "Flavor is very similar, more malty body and generous spicy hops with a bit of orange peel and peaches." "Smooth, sticky palate." 10.6% alc.

Stoudt's Fat Dog Stout ★★★★
Imp. Stout: Stoudts Brewing Co., Adamstown, PA www.stoudtsbeer.com
Rummy, chocolately aroma with a touch of licorice." "Flavor is full of black licorice or anise or fennel, pepper and dark chocolate, oatmeal." 6% alc.

Stoudt's Gold Lager ★★★1/2
Helles/Dortmnd: Stoudts Brewing Co., Adamstown, PA www.stoudtsbeer.com
"Nose is lightly sweet and bready, hoppy and quite grassy." "Flavor is even and full, plenty of doughy breads, seasoned with brine and grassy herbs." "Mild for sure but nice stuff." 5% alc.

Stoudt's Oktoberfest ★★★
Märzen/Oktbfst: Stoudts Brewing Co., Adamstown, PA www.stoudtsbeer.com
"Light candied caramel malty aroma has a mild noble hoppy balance." "Body is creamy and full of caramel and sweet malt." "One of the better Oktoberfests I've had." 5% alc.

Stoudt's Pils ★★★1/2
Classic Ger Pils: Stoudts Brewing Co., Adamstown, PA www.stoudtsbeer.com
"Range of malt flavor from grainy, lightly toasted notes, to dry biscuity notes and a hint of honey." "Hop onslaught is somewhat tempered by a biscuit malt flavor." "Rivals its Central European forebears." 4.8% alc.

Stoudt's Weizen ★★★1/2

Hefeweizen: Stoudts Brewing Co., Adamstown, PA www.stoudtsbeer.com

"Aroma dominated by banana with a hint of cloves. Exactly how a Hefeweizen should smell." "Starts off with a soft banana-clove, followed by mellow malt-wheat, slight orange peal and citrus, spices and bitter balance." 5% alc.

Stoudt's Winter Ale ★★★1/2

Brown Ale: Stoudts Brewing Co., Adamstown, PA www.stoudtsbeer.com

"Smells like chocolate bars melted down with hops and roasted and smoked malts." "Flavor is loaded with roasted malt and light coffee." "Very good stuff." "Enjoyable." 6% alc.

Stoudts Abbey Triple ★★★1/2

Abbey Tripel: Stoudts Brewing Co., Adamstown, PA www.stoudtsbeer.com

"Very pleasant first whiff, huge malty with a vinous edge." "Taste - caramel, dark spices, sweet malt, some honey." "Pretty good in small amounts; overpowering for a 12 ounce." "Stoudts does Euro-styles very well and Tripel is a convincing example." 9% alc.

Stoudts Blonde Double Mai-bock ★★★1/2

Bock: Stoudts Brewing Co., Adamstown, PA www.stoudtsbeer.com

"Floral with background fruitiness - lots of hops for the style, especially in the finish." "Body starts lightly malty and sweet turning dry and peppery toward the finish." "A very sweet and flavorful brew." 7% alc.

Stoudts Scarlet Lady Ale ESB ★★★1/2

Prem Bitter: Stoudts Brewing Co., Adamstown, PA www.stoudtsbeer.com

"Medium roasted caramel malt (cookie) nutty aroma with a floral hop nose." "Moderately bitter hoppy floral and perfumey flavor with caramel malt body." "Something good to have when you are hopped out." 5% alc.

Stoudts Scotch Style Ale ★★★★

Scotch Ale: Stoudts Brewing Co., Adamstown, PA www.stoudtsbeer.com

"Tons of toffee and molasses, some cocoa and hazelnut, date and fig. It's marvelous!" "Rich and malty with more molasses, a hint of smoke and bitterness." "I wish I had more opportunities to try the Stoudt offerings." 7% alc.

Straub ★★1/2

Pale Lager: Straub Brewing Co., St. Marys, PA www.straubbeer.com

"Aroma of corn with some fleeting grassy hop." "Taste is sweetish, watery corn and some slight hop bitterness." "Better than your macro corn swill to be sure." "Not awful, just empty." 3.45% alc.

Stroh's ★★

Pale Lager: Pabst Brewing Co., Chicago, IL www.pabst.com

Flavor is corn a touch of rice and not much else slight hop taste and a bit of lemon." "More hops in the nose and on the tongue than most common suds merchants provide." "One of my favorite budget brews." 4.6% alc.

Sudwerk Doppel Bock ★★★1/2

Doppelbock: Sudwerk Privatbrauerei Hubsch, Davis, CA www.sudwerk.com

"Rich vanilla and caramel aroma, much like a root beer float." "Sweet caramel malts, mix with a touch of raisins and peat. Clean and slightly thin" mouthfeel. 8% alc.

Sudwerk Hefe Weizen ★★★1/2

Hefeweizen: Sudwerk Privatbrauerei Hubsch, Davis, CA www.sudwerk.com

"Aroma of bread, cloves and a hint of banana." "More robust, spritzier mouthfeel than I would expect for the style." "Flavors of bread, cloves and light banana with a crisp spicy finish." N/A% alc.

Sudwerk Marzen ★★★1/2
Märzen/Oktbfst: Sudwerk Privatbrauerei Hubsch, Davis, CA www.sudwerk.com
"It smells very malty, like a brewery tour." "Moderate body and mouthfeel, although near thin side." "Initial sweet, complex malt flavors are matched with delicate smooch of spicy Hallertauer hops." N/A% alc.

Sudwerk Pilsner ★★★1/2
Pilsner: Sudwerk Privatbrauerei Hubsch, Davis, CA www.sudwerk.com
"Aromatics with spicy hops and an underpinning of malt." "Soft and pleasing." "Rather simple, one-dimensional, easy drinking beer." N/A% alc.

Sugar Hill Golden Ale ★★1/2
Goldn/Blond Ale: Olde Saratoga Brewing (Mendocino Brewing Co.), Saratoga Springs, NY
www.oldesaratogabrew.com
"Strong grassy herbal aroma, with some malts." "Flavor has a touch of lemon, some yeast and a bit of sweet biscuity maltiness." "More interesting, more fragrant and more tasty than most (golden ales)." N/A% alc.

Summit Extra Pale ★★★1/2
Am. Pale Ale: Summit Brewing Co., Saint Paul, MN www.summitbrewing.com
"Aroma is light pine and a little bit of caramel." "Flavor is a nice blend of sweet caramel malts and bitter grapefruit hops." "Respectable and quite quaffable, but not too much character." 5.1% alc.

Summit Grand ★★★1/2
Bohem Pilsner: Summit Brewing Co., Saint Paul, MN www.summitbrewing.com
"Initially very grassy nose, pale malts, warm-sweetish aromas." "Bitter, crisp and clean." "I think this is just a step from being a really good pilsner." 5% alc.

Summit Great Northern Porter ★★★1/2
Porter: Summit Brewing Co., Saint Paul, MN www.summitbrewing.com
"Heavy roasted coffee nutty aroma." "Uniquely bitter taste to this beer, obviously lots of hops. Not quite as smooth as other Porters because of this..." 4.8% alc.

Summit Hefe Weizen ★★★1/2
Hefeweizen: Summit Brewing Co., Saint Paul, MN www.summitbrewing.com
"Pretty drinkable wheat, with strong clove, grass, banana and lemon aromas." "The flavor is citric with a mid-palate burst of malt and some banana/clove hints." "Decent middle of the pack Hefe." 4.2% alc.

Summit Indian Pale ★★★
IPA: Summit Brewing Co., Saint Paul, MN www.summitbrewing.com
Musty malt nose, subtle hop, not as aggressive as I would have thought." "Tastes bready, malty, grainy, with subdued hops and some finishing citrus notes" "Not a hop monster, that's for sure." 5.8% alc.

Summit Maibock ★★★
Bock: Summit Brewing Co., Saint Paul, MN www.summitbrewing.com
Aroma was weak to non-existent." "Caramel flavor with some spice." "A nice Maibock bock that's very true to style." 7.1% alc.

Summit Oktoberfest ★★★
Märzen/Oktbfst: Summit Brewing Co., Saint Paul, MN www.summitbrewing.com
Soft malt nose, subtle graininess, touch of sweet biscuit." "Tastes bready malty, with some dry caramel, hops and fruit." 7.7% alc.

Summit Winter Ale ★★★1/2
Eng. Strong Ale: Summit Brewing Co., Saint Paul, MN www.summitbrewing.com
Nice rich toasty caramel toffee aroma has a touch of noble hops and some milk chocolate complexity." "Flavor, also, is mostly malts, with just a hint of chocolate." 5.9% alc.

Super Bock ★★
Pale Lager: Uniao Cervejeira (Unicer), Santarém, Portugal www.superbock.pt
"Moderate malty and hoppy aroma." "Sweet and malty, developing maize and an integrated grainy bitterness." "Typical industrial lager, dominated by adjuncts." 5.6% alc.

Super du Baladin ★★★1/2
Bel. Strong Ale: Le Baladin, Piozzo, Italy www.Bièreria.com
Very aromatic. Sweet fruits...cherry and strawberry and a bit of acid tang." "Starts off with a bit of green tea, finishes with some dried fruit notes." "Possesses a self-assurance that would make it recognizable among a dozen similar products." 8% alc.

Suprema ★★1/2
Pale Lager: Cerveceria La Constancia (SABMiller), San Salvador, El Salvador www.laconstancia.com
"Aroma is lightly malty (cereal, grain), trace hops (herbs), with a note of dimethyl sulfide." "Taste has light grass notes, some sweet malt corniness and faint lemon." "More sugary carbonated corn juice than beer." 5.3% alc.

Svyturys Baltas ★★1/2
Hefeweizen: Svyturys (Baltic Beverages Holding), Klaipeda, Lithuania www.svyturys.lt
"Banana aroma with lemon cleaner." "Full body, cookie dough maltiness, leads to a sweetish finish that carries a mild yeast note." "One of the thickest Hefeweizens I have had." 5.2% alc.

Svyturys Ekstra ★★1/2
Helles/Dortmnd: Svyturys (Baltic Beverages Holding), Klaipeda, Lithuania www.svyturys.lt
"Grainy aroma with some hints of fruit and also coming off as being a little sweet." "Sweet, some light bitterness, a bit sour in the finish." "Avoid on principle a beer you must serve at the surface temperature of Neptune's moons." 5.2% alc.

Swale Whitstable Oyster Stout ★★★
Sweet Stout: Whitstable Brewery (formerly Swale), Grafty Green, Kent, England
"Rather sweet buttery and malty aroma with coffee notes." "Sweet flavor with some nice fruity notes and a good roasted tone." "Not the fullest stout but tasty and easy." 4.5% alc.

Sweetwater 420 Extra Pale Ale ★★1/2
Am. Pale Ale: Sweetwater Brewing Co., Atlanta, GA www.sweetwaterbrew.com
"Aroma is moderately hoppy with hints of fruits and flowers." "Great malt profile with a some fruitiness and some citric bitterness and flavor for balance." "This is the beer that you go to when you get home from work." 5.2% alc.

Sweetwater Blue ★★★
Fruit Beer: Sweetwater Brewing Co., Atlanta, GA www.sweetwaterbrew.com
A blueberry beer. "Two flavors and two flavors only: blueberries and dough. Sweetwater should change the name to Blueberry Muffin." "This is a good beer, for what it is." 4.8% alc.

Sweetwater Exodus Porter ★★★1/2
Porter: Sweetwater Brewing Co., Atlanta, GA www.sweetwaterbrew.com
"Lightly sweet malts, chocolate, milk chocolate and caramel backed by a light roastiness." "Very well-balanced." "Crisp slightly dry finish, but quite full and creamy." 6.2% alc.

Sweetwater Festive Ale ★★★★
Spice/Herb: Sweetwater Brewing Co., Atlanta, GA www.sweetwaterbrew.com
"Aroma of cinnamon, molasses, licorice and dark malts. Quite malty but also impressively subtle." "Flavor has piney carob, spices, molasses." "A really nice beer indeed." 8.6% alc.

Sweetwater IPA ★★★★
IPA: Sweetwater Brewing Co., Atlanta, GA www.sweetwaterbrew.com
"Big, rich hop kick, with lean and mean hoppiness." "Has a definitive hoppy bite that grabs you by the balls and forces you to take notice." "Bitterness lingers." "Excellent IPA." 6.4% alc.

Sweetwater Summer Hummer ★★★1/2
Bel. Witbier: Sweetwater Brewing Co., Atlanta, GA www.sweetwaterbrew.com
"Aroma had wheat and some kind of spice, perhaps some citrus." "Decent wit and I don't even like wheat beers!" "Spicy citric yeastiness, doughy and crusty with a hint of coriander." "Good stuff!" N/A% alc.

Sweetwater Sweet Georgia Brown ★★★
Brown Ale: Sweetwater Brewing Co., Atlanta, GA www.sweetwaterbrew.com
"Not much aroma; a hint of caramel." "Toffee flavors accompanied by faint spicy, floral flavor hop addition." "Nice beer; good session drink." 5.4% alc.

't IJ Columbus ★★★
Bel. Strong Ale: Brouwerij 't IJ , Amsterdam, Netherlands www.brouwerijhetij.nl
"Aroma is funky and fruity and dominated by apricot." "Beautiful taste, kind of peppery first followed by caramel, yeast and chocolate, finishing dry and hoppy." "A truly unusual beer." 6.5% alc.

't IJ Natte ★★1/2
Abbey Dubbel: Brouwerij 't IJ, Amsterdam, Netherlands www.brouwerijhetij.nl
"Lemon like aroma with some apricots and melon." "Tasty flavor of dried fruit and some wood, the beer ends up little sour and dry." "Underrated beer from an underrated brewery." 6.5% alc.

t IJ IJndejaars ★★★
Bel. Strong Ale: Brouwerij 't IJ , Amsterdam, Netherlands www.brouwerijhetij.nl
"A little bit of brown sugar kicks off aroma, followed by apricot and grapefruit." "Rounded candied fruit flavors mingle with large malt presence (caramel, toast) and firm alcohol backbone." "Definitely a dessert beer." 9% alc.

't IJ Plzen ★★★★1/2
Pilsner: Brouwerij 't IJ, Amsterdam, Netherlands www.brouwerijhetij.nl
"Charming, rustic hay-grass like aroma with a gentle bready, soft, lean sourdough reminiscent maltiness." "Herbal, spicy, green hop flavor with lightly vegetal character, some sugary sweetness and moderate finishing bitterness." 5% alc.

't IJ Struis ★★★★
Bel. Strong Ale: Brouwerij 't IJ, Amsterdam, Netherlands www.brouwerijhetij.nl
"The aromas are a trip: pipe tobacco, raisins and dates, cellar, alcohol and damp garden soil." "Very good flavor of leather, yeast, malt and caramel." "This beer rocked my socks." 9% alc.

't IJ (Scharrel) IJWit ★★★1/2
Bel. Witbier: Brouwerij 't IJ , Amsterdam, Netherlands www.brouwerijhetij.nl
"Malty-yeasty aroma with slight lemon, grapefruit notes." "Malty palate is slightly yeasty, with a little bit of lemon and coriander leading to a sweetish finish." "Real gem! I just wish I was sipping it on a warm summer day." 7% alc.

't IJ Zatte ★★★
Abbey Tripel: Brouwerij 't IJ, Amsterdam, Netherlands www.brouwerijhetij.nl
"Yeasty, but nonetheless interesting aroma with mango and orange peel." "Soft cookie malt flavors - musty yeast, spice and mild fruit. Dry finish." "I could drink a ton of this." 8% alc.

't Smisje BBBourgondier ★★★
Bel. Strong Ale: Brouwerij De Regenboog, Assebroek-Brugge, Belgium www.ping.betsmisje
"Huge toffee malt with a bit of raisin and earthy, woody undertones." "Flavor is yeast, alcohol, raisins, caramel. Amazingly sweet." "A very interesting nightcap." 12% alc.

't Smisje Calva Reserva ★★★
Bel. Strong Ale: Brouwerij De Regenboog, Assebroek-Brugge, Belgium www.ping.betsmisje
"Very rich aroma with some green apple hiding behind molasses, sugar, fortified wine, chocolate cake and spicy alcohol." "Sweet flavors include nutty fruitcake and cinnamon and calvados." "Too hot and the beer component too one-dimensional." 12% alc.

't Smisje Wostynje ★★★
Belgian Ale: Brouwerij De Regenboog, Assebroek-Brugge, Belgium www.ping.betsmisje
"Sweet, tart, yeasty, rich. Apricot and orange." "Very sophisticated drinking." "Slightly sugary-sweet-malty flavor with fruity hints and mustard." "Unsure what mustard seeds did here." "Different and nice." 7% alc.

Tabernash Dunkel Weiss ★★★
Dunkelweizen: Left Hand Brewing Co., Longmont, CO www.lefthandbrewing.com
"Sweetish banana and sour apple flavors work together to make a light, refreshing rendition of the style." "Nutty malt flavor, faint clover, touch of appropriate sourness." "So close to being great but will say definitely good." 4.75% alc.

Tabernash Rye Bock ★★★1/2
Bock: Left Hand Brewing Co., Longmont, CO www.lefthandbrewing.com
"Very malty and bready aroma with light fruit notes." "Flavor is malty with dark fruit and bitter finish." "A different beer for sure." 7% alc.

Tabernash Weiss ★★★
Hefeweizen: Left Hand Brewing Co., Longmont, CO www.lefthandbrewing.com
"The aroma has banana in a light toffee sauce and a very yeasty nose." "Hints of orange and lemon citrus, clove and nutmeg spice and perceptible bitterness surround a very well-defined yeast/bread flavor." 4.9% alc.

Taiwan Beer ★★
Pale Lager: Taiwan Tobacco And Wine Board, Taipei, Taiwan
"Fresh-tasting, grassy lager with a hint of malt and bready notes." "Surprisingly good for a government-managed brewery!" 4.5% alc.

Taj Mahal ★★
Pale Lager: United Breweries (Scottish & Newcastle), Bangalore, India www.kingfisherworld.com
"Aromas of caramel, malts and a touch of hops." "Sweet with a dry finish. Not much hops." "On par with mass-marketed North American lagers." 4.5% alc.

Tecate ★★
Pale Lager: Femsa, Monterrey/Veracruz-Llave, Mexico www.femsa.com
"Has aroma of sweet grass and yeast (bread, sweat) with a grainy and corny light malt." "Like most macros but slightly more bitter." "Glad wife likes pale lagers because she gets them after I take one sip." 4.55% alc.

Tejas Bock ★
Bock: Joseph Huber Brewing Co., Monroe, WI www.berghoffbeer.com
"Aroma is very grainy with just a wisp of hops." "Taste is semi-sweet and malty with mild caramel and dried fruit notes." "Overall, one-sided malt flavor." N/A% alc.

Tennent's Lager ★★
Pale Lager: Wellpark (UK - InBev), Glasgow, Scotland
"A little hay and grass in the aroma, not much else." "Flavor is lightly hoppy, lightly malty but with nothing else noticeable." "At best an average lager." 4.4% alc.

Terminal Gravity IPA ★★★1/2
IPA: Terminal Gravity Brewing Co., Enterprise, OR
"Aroma of grapefruit orange peel, pine with caramel/toffee hints." "Flavor is deliciously hoppy, but is also has a wonderful malt backbone that complement the hops really well." "Dry, bitter finish." 6.7% alc.

Terrapin Cream Ale ★★
Cream Ale: Terrapin Beer Co., Athens, GA www.terrapinbeer.com
"Light golden brew with a slight straw, grassiness on the nose." "Flavor is rather light." "Lightly sweet and malty up front; a lightly peppered, grassy hopped finish." 5% alc.

Terrapin Rye 2 ★★★★
Imp/Dbl IPA: Terrapin Beer Co., Athens, GA www.terrapinbeer.com
"Rye offers backing toasted grain notes to the deliciously piney, minty and focused herbal nose." "Taste of biscuits, caramel and juicy hops with a touch of butterscotch." "What beer's supposed to taste like." 8.5% alc.

Terrapin Rye PA ★★★1/2
Am. Pale Ale: Terrapin Beer Co., Athens, GA www.terrapinbeer.com
"Grainy rye girth forms an alluring biscuity maltiness." "Wonderful hop fragrance, very herbal and refreshing, super fresh!" "It'll be hard drinking IPAs without rye after this one!" 5.3% alc.

Tetley's English Ale ★★
Bitter: Leeds (Carlsberg UK), Leeds, W. Yorkshire, England www.carlsberg.co.uk
"Faint slightly floral aroma." "Flavor light, watered down." "To tell the truth, this beer put me to sleep. Literally. I took a nap after I drank one." 5% alc.

Thames Welsh ESB ★★★1/2
Prem Bitter: Felinfoel Brewery, Llanelli, Dyfed, Wales www.felinfoel-brewery.co.uk
"Aromas of caramel malts, dark fruits and touch of spice." "Good well balanced flavor of malt, fruit and toffee with long finish." "Nicely crafted beer on sweeter side of spectrum." 6.5% alc.

Theakston Old Peculier ★★★1/2
Old Ale: Theakston (Scottish & Newcastle), Masham, North Yorkshire, England www.theakstons.co.uk
"Splendid aroma of raisins, spice and molasses." "Some smoked notes stand out among roasted, malty, slightly coffeeish flavors." "A bit thin; even carbonation and pleasant, fulfilling finish make up for it." 5.7% alc.

Third Coast Beer ★★★
Am. Pale Ale: Bells Brewery, Inc., Kalamazoo, MI www.bellsbeer.com
"Thought the bar had Third Coast Old Ale, but, hey, no problem. This hoppy golden ale was a flavorful APA." "Thinnish but full of character." 5.2% alc.

Third Coast Old Ale ★★★★★
Barley Wine: Bells Brewery, Inc., Kalamazoo, MI www.bellsbeer.com
"Lots of rich caramel in the aroma along with some plums, raisins, soy sauce and malts." "Flavor is full bodied, rich, alcoholic and bitter. Nuances of caramel, oak and coffee." "A reason to move to Kalamazoo. Mich." 9% alc.

Thiriez La Blonde d'Esquelbecq ★★★
Bière de Garde: Brasserie Thiriez, Esquelbecq, France brasseriethiriez.iFrance.com
"Aroma is quite herbal and a bit grass in the finish." "Soft Pils maltiness, bready, corn bread like in its sweetness. Mellow floral hops, far more subtle than in the nose." "Good beer from one of the better French breweries." 6% alc.

Thirsty Dog Balto Heroic Lager ★★
Vienna: Thirsty Dog Brewing Co., Centerville, OH www.thirstydog.com
"Nose is pretty strong, sweet and fruity (apricot?) with malt and caramel." "Flavor is mildly hoppy, rather thin and also has some malty sweetness." "A brew that might grow on you after a few." 5.4% alc.

Thirsty Dog Hoppus Maximus ★★★1/2
Amber Ale: Thirsty Dog Brewing Co., Centerville, OH www.thirstydog.com
"Strong aroma with floral notes as well as a little fruit and berries." "The malty, moderately sweet, mildly earthy base is able to match brawn with the citrusy, moderately bitter and tea-like hops." "Pretty damn hoppy for an amber." 5% alc.

Thirsty Dog Old Leghumper ★★★
Porter: Thirsty Dog Brewing Co., Centerville, OH www.thirstydog.com
"Aroma is dark chocolate, coffee and roasty malts." "Flavors of chocolate, some coffee, malt and an occasional hint of something like cashews." "Flavor pops out a LOT more as it warms." 5.7% alc.

Thirsty Dog Siberian Night Imperial Stout ★★★★
Imp. Stout: Thirsty Dog Brewing Co., Centerville, OH www.thirstydog.com
"Sweet dark chocolate and dark roasted caramel malt (cookie) aroma with fragrant notes of molasses and prune/raisin and coffee." "Taste; initially a little sweet, with chocolate, coffee, roasted malts and bit of plum." "Damn fine beer." 9% alc.

Thomas Creek Amber Ale ★
Amber Ale: Thomas Creek Brewery, Greenville, SC www.thomascreekbeer.com
"Heavy dose of caramel along with some toffee and pine." "Flavor was thin and caramel in sweetness." "Lacking any real malty flavor." 5.5% alc.

Thomas Creek Dopplebock ★★1/2
Doppelbock: Thomas Creek Brewery, Greenville, SC www.thomascreekbeer.com
"Sweet caramel malt aroma with fruit hop notes (prune, plum, raisin)." "Full of honey flavored malt that kicked the backdoor of cereal toast overtones." "First drink of the night, it was pretty good - put me in a better mood." 6.3% alc.

Thomas Creek IPA ★★1/2
IPA: Thomas Creek Brewery, Greenville, SC www.thomascreekbeer.com
"The aroma had cedar and reminded me of fresh mountain air." "Hoppy and piney with a touch of sweetening caramel but not overwhelming at all." "Over the top bitterness with no balancing malt." 5.5% alc.

Thomas Creek Multi Grain ★★1/2
Ale: Thomas Creek Brewery, Greenville, SC www.thomascreekbeer.com
"Almost spicy aroma, lots of fruit and spices, almost stale." "Malty flavor, slightly buttery too. Some grain as well, light and quite palatable." "A liquid granola bar?" 4.4% alc.

Thomas Creek Pilsner ★★1/2
Pilsner: Thomas Creek Brewery, Greenville, SC www.thomascreekbeer.com
"Aroma is typical German-style with some Saaz hops with mild malt tones and dusty yeast esters." "A bit of herbal, spicy hops mixed with a little bit of pils malt." "Little more intensity and this would be some really good beer." 4.5% alc.

Thomas Creek Red Ale ★★
Amber Ale: Thomas Creek Brewery, Greenville, SC www.thomascreekbeer.com
"Somewhat malty with some walnuts, oats and a hint of citrus bitterness." "If there was such a thing as generic beer at a grocery store, you would have this beer with a plain black and white label that said Red Ale." 5.6% alc.

Thomas Hardy's Ale ★★★★★
Barley Wine: O'Hanlons, Whimple, Devon, England www.ohanlons.co.uk
"Light fruits (apricot, pear) dance with heavy but gentle sweets... Lyle's Golden Syrup sort of malts, softly sugar not at all oppressive." "A bit of heat late as well as dark chocolate and wood notes." "The potential is obvious." 11.7% alc.

Thomas Hooker Am. Pale Ale ★★1/2
Am. Pale Ale: Thomas Hooker (formerly Troutbrook), Hartford, CT www.troutbrookbeer.com
"Aroma of light brown sugar caramels with a touch of orange oil and rose petals." "Spicy, sylvan hop character that is somewhat resinous" and "medium high bitterness." "Standard example of the style." N/A% alc.

Thomas Hooker Hop Meadow IPA ★★★1/2
IPA: Thomas Hooker (formerly Troutbrook), Hartford, CT www.troutbrookbeer.com
"Really smooth, considering how hoppy it is. Sweetish malts up front that blend nicely with a sticky, pine hop flavor. Assertive, bitter, sticky finish. Very earthy, rustic flavor throughout." N/A% alc.

Thomas Hooker Imperial Porter ★★★★★
Baltic Porter: Thomas Hooker (formerly Troutbrook), Hartford, CT www.troutbrookbeer.com
"Sweet, luscious milk chocolate and coffee character with marshmallows and a little bit of roastiness." "Very rich and smooth with lots of sweet malts." "Creatively different from any other American Porters." 8% alc.

Thomas Hooker Liberator Doppelbock ★★★★★
Doppelbock: Thomas Hooker (formerly Troutbrook), Hartford, CT www.troutbrookbeer.com
Rated 4th Best American Lager. "Rich roasted malts with coffee, dark fruits (raisins and figs), baker's chocolate, caramel and some citrus Pac NW hoppage." "Quite decadent." 8% alc.

Thomas Hooker Münich-style Golden Lager ★★★★1/2
Helles/Dortmnd: Thomas Hooker (formerly Troutbrook), Hartford, CT www.troutbrookbeer.com
"Fresh baked bread and cookie nose, with hints of lemon zest and brie." "Bread and honey vs. grassy, mildly citric hops?. the perfect battle!" "It is so Nice to see this style done well!" N/A% alc.

Thomas Hooker Oktoberfest ★★★1/2
Märzen/Oktbfst: Thomas Hooker (formerly Troutbrook), Hartford, CT www.troutbrookbeer.com
"Very flavorful malt character - smoky, toffeeish and earthy, with some spicy hop in there as well." "Vibrant, lively example leans toward rusticity over cleanliness." N/A% alc.

Thomas Hooker Old Marley Barleywine ★★★★1/2
Barley Wine: Thomas Hooker (formerly Troutbrook), Hartford, CT www.troutbrookbeer.com
"Slight alcoholic nose, otherwise citrus peel, some caramel, malty/bready sweetness, with a nice hop flair." "Smooth oak properties thickly sedate the tongue, basking in a blanket of bourbon and vanilla eloquence." 9.6% alc.

Three Floyds Alpha King ★★★★
Am. Pale Ale: Three Floyds Brewing Co., Munster, IN www.3floyds.com
"This iconic American Pale Ale "smells like delicious bite size hop candy." "Flavor is orange with a nice hop and malt balance." "Absolutely beautiful." 6% alc.

Three Floyds Alpha Klaus ★★★★
Porter: Three Floyds Brewing Co., Munster, IN www.3floyds.com
"A solid, hoppy porter with a fairly robust flavor profile including chocolate, vanilla, coffee, molasses." "More hops than one expects from a porter, but it manages to stay well balanced." 7.5% alc.

Three Floyds Behemoth ★★★★
Barley Wine: Three Floyds Brewing Co., Munster, IN www.3floyds.com
"Second most attractive brew I have seen." "Amazing flavor of hops, spruce, candy, fruits, maple sugar, caramel and alcohol." "Like getting smacked in the face by a pine branch with hops duct-taped on it." 10.5% alc.

Three Floyds Brian Boru ★★★1/2
Irish Ale: Three Floyds Brewing Co., Munster, IN www.3floyds.com
"Dazzling; light hints of smoky malts, hints of caramelized brown sugar, a gentle nuttiness, but mostly a grand fruitiness and prefect balance of hops!" "Probably the best Amber Ale that I've had." 5.9% alc.

Three Floyds Dark Lord ★★★★1/2
Imp. Stout: Three Floyds Brewing Co., Munster, IN www.3floyds.com
"An oily, jet-black pour." "Incredibly rich aroma features plenty of molasses, vanilla beans, coffee and chocolate." "Assaulted with the roasts, but balanced by the other flavors." "Unfortunately it's worth every penny..." 13% alc.

Three Floyds Dreadnaught Imperial IPA ★★★★1/2
Imp/Dbl IPA: Three Floyds Brewing Co., Munster, IN www.3floyds.com
"Nose is all about grapefruit hops and brown sugar." "Explosion of citrus hops." "Chewy hops resonate in the lingering finish." "One hell of beer." "Thanks Three Floyds!" 9.5% alc.

Three Floyds Gumballhead ★★★★
Am. Wheat: Three Floyds Brewing Co., Munster, IN www.3floyds.com
"Big, fresh, hoppy aroma." "Taste is sweet grapefruit, lemon, crisp, refreshing and in the background, the wheat peeks through." "Wheat Beer? I would have guessed an IPA." 4.8% alc.

Three Floyds Pride and Joy ★★★1/2
Bitter: Three Floyds Brewing Co., Munster, IN www.3floyds.com
"Lots of hops, but not particularly bitter, ends with an interesting sweet hop finish." "Not my idea of what a mild is," but "this would make an excellent session brew." 4.88% alc.

Three Floyds Robert the Bruce ★★★1/2
Scottish Ale: Three Floyds Brewing Co., Munster, IN www.3floyds.com
"Sweet malt aroma with strong flowery hops." "Nice heady malt flavor to start, bittering a little in the middle as the hops develop the palate." "A really remarkable and balanced palate, leaving a pleasant sticky-sweet aftertaste." 9.1% alc.

Three Stooge's Beer ★★
Pale Lager: Matt Brewing Co., Utica, NY www.saranac.com
"Very light in body with some malt sweetness and a very discreet bitterness." "Nyuk nyuk nyuk, the joke is on me, Moe and every other schmo that bought this..." "Watery, thin, lifeless. Hilarious!" 4.8% alc.

Tiger ★★1/2
Pale Lager: Asia Pacific Breweries (Heineken), Singapore
"Aroma is skunky and a little sour." "Light and watery, with some slight fusel influence." "Undeservedly popular in many countries in Asia." 5% alc.

Tilburgs Dutch Brown Ale ★★1/2
Brown Ale: De Koningshoeven, Tilburg, Netherlands www.latrappe.nl
"Malty, caramel, sweet and dark fruit aroma." "Flavor is sweet, caramel malts, honey, brown sugar. Palate is somewhat watery and light." "Not a whole lot of flavor beyond the sweetness." 5% alc.

Tinkov Lager ★★★
Pale Lager: Tinkoff Brewery (InBev), Pushkin, St. Petersburg obl., Russia www.tinkoff.ru
"Aroma of yeast and grass and hay...and more hay." "Sweet up front and crisp and semi sweet in the finish with hints of sulfury yeast." "A fairly straight forward lager that is very drinkable and does have some flavor." 4.8% alc.

Toña ★
Pale Lager: Compañja Cevercera de NIC, Managua, Nicaragua www.ccn.com.ni
"Light malt corn and faint hops aroma." "Grainy character with dominant Perrier notes." "Finish is almost nonexistent." "Harsh, unbalanced and relatively horrid." 4.6% alc.

Tommyknocker Alpine Glacier Lager ★★1/2
Premium Lager: Tommyknocker Brewery, Idaho Springs, CO www.tommyknocker.com
"Aroma is refreshing, some hops and a sweet/sugary note as well." "Tastes of light grass and some sweet malts." "A very basic lager with some good hops." 4.6% alc.

Tommyknocker Butt Head Bock ★★★1/2
Doppelbock: Tommyknocker Brewery, Idaho Springs, CO www.tommyknocker.com
"Sweet malty aroma, almost sugary sweet." "Notes of maple, molasses, caramel and toasted bread." "Not bad but a little too sweet for me." 8.2% alc.

Tommyknocker Imperial Nut Brown ★★★1/2
Am Strong Ale: Tommyknocker Brewery, Idaho Springs, CO www.tommyknocker.com
"Toasty, caramel, brandy, maple malt nose." "Basic chocolate and hazelnut caramel malts are accompanied by a potentially too heavy herbal and earthy hops presence." "Good overall but not a great one." 9.8% alc.

Tommyknocker Jack Whacker Wheat ★★1/2
Am. Wheat: Tommyknocker Brewery, Idaho Springs, CO www.tommyknocker.com
Lemony citrus, a bit of light fruit, a touch of sweetness and barely any wheat malt flavor, this is entirely forgettable." "Clean dry lemony flavored beer, slightly sour with a quick clean finish." 5.4% alc.

Tommyknocker Maple Nut Brown ★★1/2
Brown Ale: Tommyknocker Brewery, Idaho Springs, CO www.tommyknocker.com
Sweet maple aroma, nutty and toasty." "Flavor not as good as aroma." "Taste is medium sweet, caramel, nutty, maple." "There's almost no body to this one and it is not good." 4.5% alc.

Tommyknocker Ornery Amber ★★1/2
Am Dark Larger: Tommyknocker Brewery, Idaho Springs, CO www.tommyknocker.com
Sweet fruity aroma of peach and hops." "Flavor is grainy and malty sweet." "I would compare this beer to hometown girlfriend, nice but glad you can go elsewhere." 5.3% alc.

Tommyknocker Pick Axe Pale ★★★
Eng Pale Ale: Tommyknocker Brewery, Idaho Springs, CO www.tommyknocker.com
Nice fresh hop aroma with a slight sweetness." "The taste was a bit of a letdown, as it seemed to just be muddled hops and bitterness stewing about in water." 6.2% alc.

Tröeg's Bavarian Lager ★★★1/2
Premium Lager: Tröegs Brewing Co., Harrisburg, PA www.troegs.com
"Aroma sends off notes of caramel malt and some nuts." "Full, sweet and bready with some bitterness in the back." "The beer sits squarely in Oktoberfest territory." 5% alc.

Tröeg's HopBack Amber Ale ★★★★★
Amber Ale: Tröegs Brewing Co., Harrisburg, PA www.troegs.com
"The aroma is full of grapefruit and lemons with some nice floral hops." "Pine and hops are dominant at first taste, then melts away for an extremely smooth finish." "If I lived in Pennsylvania, I'd drink lots of this." 5.6% alc.

Tröeg's Oatmeal Stout ★★★★1/2
Sweet Stout: Tröegs Brewing Co., Harrisburg, PA www.troegs.com
"Coffee paralyzes the nose, but there is some aroma of Ovaltine that sneaks in." "Lots of roast and espresso flavors with a nice dose of hop bitterness in there." "Wonderful. Just about everything I could want in a Stout." 6.8% alc.

Tröeg's Pale Ale ★★★★1/2
Am. Pale Ale: Tröegs Brewing Co., Harrisburg, PA www.troegs.com
"Pungent floral, grape and honey aromas. Also some grassy Sauvignon Blanc and Xmas tree notes." "Flavors are malty upfront, followed by light pine, earthy/resiny notes as well." 5.4% alc.

Tröeg's Rugged Trail Nut Brown ★★★
Brown Ale: Tröegs Brewing Co., Harrisburg, PA www.troegs.com
"Malty aroma with hints of hazelnut." "Flavor is nutty, toffee, bread, light chocolate." "Very neutral and unassertive all around." 4.4% alc.

Tröeg's Sunshine Pils ★★★★★
Pilsner: Tröegs Brewing Co., Harrisburg, PA www.troegs.com
"Smells bright, citrusy and hoppy, with mild grain." "Flavors are pretty hoppy, light citrus, some nice malt sweetness and a grassy finish." "This is a fine Pils and I like the American twist to this style." 5.3% alc.

Tröeg's Tröegenator Doublebock ★★★
Doppelbock: Tröegs Brewing Co., Harrisburg, PA www.troegs.com
"Aroma caramelly, sweet, smooth and not that strong." "Sweet bready malt flavor, burnt raisins, slightly charred dryish finish." "This is not a heavy, suffocating Doppelbock." 8.2% alc.

Tröeg's The Mad Elf Holiday Ale ★★★★
Spice/Herb: Tröegs Brewing Co., Harrisburg, PA www.troegs.com
"Light Belgian yeast accents highlight this strong ale, complementing the husky malt character, hint of spices." "Tart and fruity with a dry bitter finish." "Great replacement for wine with dinner." 11% alc.

Trader Joe's Bohemian Lager ★
Bohem Pilsner: Gordon Biersch Brewing Co., Palo Alto, CA www.gordonbiersch.com
Available at Trader Joe's. "Aroma is quite sweet, with notes of dried grass and stale malt." "Light bodied." "Very lightly malty, the sweetness is so mild." 5% alc.

Trader Joe's Hofbrau Bock ★★
Bock: Gordon Biersch Brewing Co., Palo Alto, CA www.gordonbiersch.com
Available at Trader Joe's. "Strong sweet honey aroma." "Sweet upfront taste with a little kick of spicy hops in the finish." "Body is thin and lifeless. Yawn." 7% alc.

Trader Joe's Bavarian Style Hefeweizen ★★★
Hefeweizen: Gordon Biersch Brewing Co., Palo Alto, CA www.gordonbiersch.com
"Big aroma of banana, bubblegum, marshmallows and clove - really nice! Mouthfeel is soft and creamy. flavor is spot on for the style." "Definitely the best of the four Trader Joe's brews." 5.3% alc.

Trader Joe's Vienna Style Lager ★★1/2
Vienna: Gordon Biersch Brewing Co., Palo Alto, CA www.gordonbiersch.com
Available at Trader Joe's. "Good looking amber with excellent lacing." "The aroma is malty, bread, caramel and some biscuit." "Flavor is bready up front then an earthiness kicks in finally followed by some hops." 5.7% alc.

Traquair House Ale ★★★★1/2
Eng. Strong Ale: Traquair House Brewery, Innerleithen, Borders, Scotland www.traquair.co.uk
"Notes of yeast, very malty, with a winey accent, hint of oakiness in the aroma." "The malts are in your face. Has a little smokiness to it and the caramel and vanilla really come through in the finish." 7.2% alc.

Traquair Jacobite Ale ★★★★★
Spice/Herb: Traquair House Brewery, Innerleithen, Borders, Scotland www.traquair.co.uk
"One of the best aromas in beer - flowers, coriander, the finest milk chocolate, toffee, cinnamon, bread crust..." "Flavor is sweet, with coriander, brown sugar, light molasses, chocolate and beautiful malts." "One of the world's most gorgeous brews." 8% alc.

Trinity Red Ale ★★★
Irish Ale: Goose Island Beer Co., Chicago, IL www.gooseisland.com
"Bready, very toasty, perhaps even slightly roasty, mildly sweet and partially balanced by a mild bitterness." "Flavors start malty with a bit of caramel sweetness." "Not really anything to write home about but does grow on me." N/A% alc.

Tripel Karmeliet ★★★★★
Abbey Tripel: Brouwerij Bosteels, Buggenhout, Belgium
"Incredible nose - very peachy, floral, yeasty with coriander, pepper, leather, mint, sage." "Soft palate - sweet malts, flowers, herbal hops, vinous alcoholic depth, fresh coriander." "This is what I would want a Triple to always be." 8% alc.

Trois Pistoles ★★★★★
Bel. Strong Ale: Unibroue (Sleeman), Chambly, Quebec www.unibroue.com
"Rich plummy, raisiny, port-like depths in both the palate and the aroma." "Sleek and sumptuous, these raisins, plums and malts wash over the palate." "I could kick myself for not trying this sooner." 9% alc.

Troubadour Blond ★★1/2
Saison: De Proefbrouwerij, Lochristi, Belgium www.proefbrouwerij.com
"Sweet bready aroma, pale floral and fruits as well." "Flavor is yeasty and biscuity and kind of sweet." "Very enjoyable beer, simple - yet interesting. Excellent sunny day beer." 6.5% alc.

Trout River Chocolate Oatmeal Stout ★★
Stout: Trout River Brewing Co., Lyndonville, VT www.troutriverbrewing.com
"Aroma of sweet chocolate underscored by roasted smells as well." "Tastes of strong bitter chocolate up front. Big oat flavors." "Way too watery and thin to ever be taken seriously as a true stout." N/A% alc.

Trout River Hoppin Mad Trout ★★1/2
IPA: Trout River Brewing Co., Lyndonville, VT www.troutriverbrewing.com
"IPA?! huh? Lacks the key characteristics of the style. No strong hop flavor, not very malty, very light in color." "If I were a trout, I would be insulted." 4.8% alc.

Trout River Rainbow Red Ale ★★1/2
Amber Ale: Trout River Brewing Co., Lyndonville, VT www.troutriverbrewing.com
"Pleasant nose of darker fruits and malt." "Fruity, vinous note, malty, leading to an acidic finish." "I finished it, but barely." 5% alc.

Trout River Scottish Ale ★★1/2
Scottish Ale: Trout River Brewing Co., Lyndonville, VT www.troutriverbrewing.com
"Aroma was smoky and malty sweet." "Caramel and sweet malt, hints of smokiness and a bit of spiciness/saltiness in the finish." "Like other Trout River offerings, this one seems a bit haphazard with its flavors." 5.8% alc.

Trumer Pils ★★1/2
Classic Ger Pils: Trumer Brauerei Berkeley (Gambrinus Co.), Berkeley, CA www.trumer.at
Now brewed in Berkeley for the US market. "Nose is fresh and crisp, sweet malt dominates." "Smooth and clean." "Crisp, like American pale macros claim, but this one really is." "Well-crafted German-style pils." 4.9% alc.

Tsingtao ★
Premium Lager: Tsingtao Brewery, Qinqdao, China www.tsingtaobeer.com.
"Sweet grassy aroma." "Flavor starts with a light bitterness followed by a light sweetness and a hint of grass." "I feel like I'm committing a sin against my body when I drink this." 4.8% alc.

Tuborg ★
Pale Lager: Carlsberg Brewery, Copenhagen, Denmark www.carlsberg.dk
"Aroma of malts, grain and fruits." "Some sweetness in the middle and finishing with a very mild bitterness. "Carlsberg's discount beer in Norway." 4.6% alc.

Tuborg Guld (Gold / Premium Lager) ★★1/2
Pale Lager: Carlsberg Brewery, Copenhagen, Denmark www.carlsberg.dk
"The aroma is full of yeast and malt with some grassy hops." "A thin body does what it can, suggesting citrusy, wooden hops and grainy malts." "Staring at a white wall." 5.3% alc.

Tucher Bajuvator Doppelbock ★★★1/2
Doppelbock: Tucher Brau , Nürnberg, Germany www.tucher.de
Aroma is sweet brown sugar, honey and Münich caramel malt." "Sweet and soothing with dates, raisins, raw sugar and figs, with a slight bitter herbal hop flavor and faint smoke." "Workaday doppelbock." 7.2% alc.

Tucher Dunkles Hefe Weizen ★★1/2
Dunkelweizen: Tucher Brau , Nürnberg, Germany www.tucher.de
"Yeasty and clovey aroma with toasted malts." "Almost dry, mainly wheat-malty taste, slightly toasted with a fruity tinge and yeasts. Slightly tart and bitter finish with cloves." "Clean but quite boring Dunkelweizen." 5.3% alc.

Tucher Helles Hefe Weizen ★★★
Hefeweizen: Tucher Brau , Nürnberg, Germany www.tucher.de
"Aroma of bready yeast with a weak amount of the classic clove/banana." "Taste was grapefruity, a little banana, clean, a bit metallic." "A basically a well done but not outstanding Hefeweizen." 5.3% alc.

Tucher Kristall Weizen ★★1/2
Kristallweizen: Tucher Brau , Nürnberg, Germany www.tucher.de
"Light banana and cream of wheat aroma." "Flavor is pretty light, on the sweet side with mild spice, yeast and wheat flavors and minimally bitter." "Lacking the character hoped for." 5.3% alc.

Tuckerman's Pale Ale ★★★
Am. Pale Ale: Tuckerman Brewing Co., Conway, NH www.tuckermanbrewing.com
"Lemon, sweat and light apricot aroma." "Long woody palate, some chewy earthiness, passion fruit, kumquat." "Malty body, with some fruitiness, resembles an English Pale Ale more than the typical hoppy American." 4.8% alc.

Tupper's Hop Pocket Ale ★★★1/2
Am. Pale Ale: Old Dominion Brewing Co., Ashburn, VA www.olddominion.com
Nose is instantly hoppy with sharp citrus and pine." "Bitter hoppy flavors co-mingled with lots of sweet malt and sugary fruit." "Exactly what this style should be: on the bitter side, but not overwhelmingly so." 5% alc.

Tupper's Hop Pocket Pils ★★★1/2
Pilsner: Old Dominion Brewing Co., Ashburn, VA www.olddominion.com
"Unique, lightly doughy aroma with delicate flowers." "Slightly sweet, fruity and floral with a grassy hoppiness and a piney hop finish." "Pilsners are not my favorite style as they usually lack something. Not this one though." 5% alc.

Tusker Lager ★★1/2
Pale Lager: East African Breweries, Nairobi , Kenya www.eabrew.com
"Aroma is sweetish and corny with some herbal hops." "Starts malty, quickly shows a dash of grassy hop." "Free from defects or glaring adjuncts, this pale lager is alright by me." 4.2% alc.

Twisted Pine Northstar Imperial Porter ★★★★1/2
Baltic Porter: Twisted Pine Brewing, Boulder, CO www.twistedpinebrewery.com
"Dark chocolate molasses and caramel toasted malt with a raisin hop nose." "Fairly tasty chocolate and roasted woodiness come out on the palate" "Incredibly well-balanced and approachable Porter." 8% alc.

Two Brothers Bare Tree Weiss Wine (after '01) ★★★1/2
Barley Wine: Two Brothers Brewing Co., Warrenville, IL www.twobrosbrew.com
"Flavors are pretty wild and very deep: vanilla beans, oats orange zest and sweet honey." "Oak is easily detectable on the tongue." "I found the finish a touch too short to be great." 11% alc.

Two Brothers Brown Fox Session Ale ★★★
Mild Ale: Two Brothers Brewing Co., Warrenville, IL www.twobrosbrew.com
"Earthy, showcasing the multitude of nutty malt." "Malt-centric with the dry caramel and chocolate tones." "Smooth, sweet mouthfeel." 4.2% alc.

Two Brothers Cane and Ebel ★★★1/2
American Strong Ale: Two Brothers Brewing Co., Warrenville, IL www.twobrosbrew.com
Deli rye, caraway, ginger, pepper, brown sugar in the nose. "Definitive grass-hop nose, pine and rye bread that all permeate the flavor." "The combination of rye and hops is fantastic." 7% alc.

Two Brothers Dog Days Dortmunder Style Lager ★★1/2
Helles/Dortmnd: Two Brothers Brewing Co., Warrenville, IL www.twobrosbrew.com
"Aroma has caramel, malts, easy on the hops." "Taste is full of light lager malts with a brush of Vienna and a clean German hop profile." "Quite true to the style." 4.9% alc.

Two Brothers Domaine DuPage ★★★1/2
Bière de Garde: Two Brothers Brewing Co., Warrenville, IL www.twobrosbrew.com
"Bright aroma of sweet caramel malt, bread and some floral hops in there." "Flavor is bitter dry start, moves into a sweet fruity body, caramel and toasted malt flavors." "Pretty decent overall." 5.9% alc.

Two Brothers Ebels Weiss Beer ★★★1/2
Hefeweizen: Two Brothers Brewing Co., Warrenville, IL www.twobrosbrew.com
"Sweet banana, vanilla, vaguely yeasty, some of the most definite clove flavor I've ever found." "Quite light and airy." "Good complexity." 4.9% alc.

Two Brothers Heavy Handed Indian Pale Ale ★★★1/2
IPA: Two Brothers Brewing Co., Warrenville, IL www.twobrosbrew.com
"Citrus hops seem to float on top of a layer of bready malt." "Flavor is a little yeasty, with flowery hops and decent amounts of malts." "Aftertaste is bitter and a little piney." "Easy to drink, enjoyable IPA." 5.7% alc.

Two Brothers Hop Juice ★★★1/2
Imp/Dbl IPA: Two Brothers Brewing Co., Warrenville, IL www.twobrosbrew.com
"Big Pacific Northwest nose, though hardly a blast or assault." "Nicely bitter but definitely on the mild side" "If somebody made hop juice, this is what it would be.". 9.9% alc.

Two Brothers Monarch Wit ★★★
Bel. Witbier: Two Brothers Brewing Co., Warrenville, IL www.twobrosbrew.com
"Aromas of coriander oranges and lemons." "Maybe not entirely traditional but citric and zesty with just a hint of spice." "Overall pleasant, though not the most robust or profound wit." 4.5% alc.

Two Brothers Northwind Imperial Stout ★★★1/2
Imp. Stout: Two Brothers Brewing Co., Warrenville, IL www.twobrosbrew.com
"Some lighter coffee and baker's chocolate aroma." "Cocoa and hop bitterness and hints of coffee, but not much sweet malt in the first few quaffs." "Not as rich or thick for an Imperial Stout." "Good not great." 8.5% alc.

Two Brothers Prairie Path Ale ★★★
Goldn/Blond Ale: Two Brothers Brewing Co., Warrenville, IL www.twobrosbrew.com
"Taste is thin and just a little bit dry." "Mellow malt flavor and hop bitterness." "Flavor is very mild almost to the point of being watery." "Good beer for a hot summer's day." 4.4% alc.

Two Brothers The Bitter End Pale Ale ★★★
Am. Pale Ale: Two Brothers Brewing Co., Warrenville, IL www.twobrosbrew.com
"Low levels of floral and grassy hops with some hints of caramel and vanilla." "Bittersweet flavors, grapefruit, caramel orange, some fruitiness, cherry maybe." "An average, drinkable micro." "Easy to drink and enjoyable." 5.1% alc.

✓ **Two Hearted Ale** ★★★★★
IPA: Bells Brewery, Inc., Kalamazoo, MI www.bellsbeer.com
"Lovely spicy hoppy aroma." "Bursting with honey coated spicy hops, some light alcohol and mild yeasty/bready notes." "A solid IPA deserving of its reputation." "A new favorite." 6% alc.

Tyranena Ancient Aztalan Brown Ale ★★1/2
Brown Ale: Tyranena Brewing, Lake Mills, WI www.tyranena.com
"Nice brown sugar, caramel, nutty aroma." "Flavor is toasty, fruity and nutty with caramel, brown sugar and red grape." "Balanced with enough flavor to keep it interesting." 6% alc.

Tyranena Bitter Woman from Hell ★★★★
India Pale Ale: Tyrenena Brewing Co., Lake Mills, WI www.tyranena.com
"Aroma has grapefruit, light caramel and a little woodiness." "Lightly sweet caramel maltiness and plenty of fresh citrusy-flavor hops." "Tongue-numbing." 6.25% alc.

Tyranena Bitter Woman IPA ★★★1/2

IPA: Tyranena Brewing, Lake Mills, WI www.tyranena.com

"Hoppy, juicy nose is moderately resiny, plenty of pine and citrusy notes." "Flavor is a real sound citrus bittersweetness, with a good malty backbone." "Now this is a solid, well-balanced IPA." 6.6% alc.

Tyranena Chief BlackHawk Porter ★★★1/2

Porter: Tyranena Brewing, Lake Mills, WI www.tyranena.com

"Nice coffee, dry grain, slight malt and chocolate aroma." "Bittersweet flavors, roasty." "Wonderfully made American Porter, very balanced, very tasty." 5.4% alc.

Tyranena Fargo Brothers Hefeweizen ★★1/2

Hefeweizen: Tyranena Brewing, Lake Mills, WI www.tyranena.com

"Aroma was of sweet banana, clove and maybe bubblegum." "Flavor is slightly sweet yet sour and yeasty with an underlying bitterness and a touch of citrus." "Worth a try for anyone who likes a good Hefe." 5.2% alc.

Tyranena Fighting Finches Bock ★★1/2

Bock: Tyranena Brewing, Lake Mills, WI www.tyranena.com

"Has aroma of Noble hop, a light unrecognized fruit and a touch of sweetness." "Flavor picks up to a chalky malt with some light citrus, the hops there make it a nice well rounded beer." "Nice rendition of a Maibock." 4.7% alc.

Tyranena Gemuetlichkeit Oktoberfest ★★1/2

Märzen/Oktbfst: Tyranena Brewing, Lake Mills, WI www.tyranena.com

"Nutty, dry caramel aroma with lightly citrus and grassy hops." "Flavor almost comes off as a wheat with a roasted hazelnuts and nice Vienna-like malt." "A good change, a good Oktoberfest." 4.9% alc.

Tyranena Headless Man Amber Alt ★★1/2

Altbier: Tyranena Brewing, Lake Mills, WI www.tyranena.com

"Aroma is subtle with grainy wood and some light soybeans." "Flavor has a bunch of perfume hops, light citrus, deep toasted caramel." "A great session style brew." 5% alc.

Tyranena Rocky's Revenge Bourbon Brown ★★★1/2

Brown Ale: Tyranena Brewing, Lake Mills, WI www.tyranena.com

"Sweet, malty and chocolaty with the added bonus of... bourbon barrel aging, showing nice restraint with mild vanilla and some almond." "A fine brew and equal to the sum of its parts." N/A% alc.

Tyranena Shantytown Doppelbock ★★1/2

Doppelbock: Tyranena Brewing, Lake Mills, WI www.tyranena.com

"Nose is varying shades of malty sweetness, some toffee, fruit, nuts, caramel malt aplenty." "Nice flavor of caramel and maybe a bit of coffee with a decent hop presence." "Seemed like a nice malty Oktoberfest to me, still liked it though." 6.4% alc.

Tyranena Stone Tepee Pale Ale ★★1/2

Am. Pale Ale: Tyranena Brewing, Lake Mills, WI www.tyranena.com

"Faint aroma of bitter hops, light malt and a touch of sour grass." "Flavor is tart grapefruit and pine with a light hint of caramel." "Needs to be bigger in all aspects." 5.7% alc.

Tyskie Gronie ★★1/2

Pilsner: Tyskie Browary Ksiazece (KP- SABMiller), Tychy, Poland www.kp.pleng/tyskie.html

"Bready nose with floral hints." "Flavor is malty as well with some grassiness." "Not very remarkable but somewhat drinkable Pilsner." 5.6% alc.

Uerige Alt ★★★1/2

Altbier: Obergärige Hausbrauerei GmbH, Düsseldorf, Germany www.uerige.deen_home

"Aroma of toasted malt, raisins, mild florals, licorice, cola and maple syrup." "Flavor is mostly bitter with hints of nuts and warm malts." "A very smooth, yet mildly complex and very enjoyable brew that epitomizes the style." 4.5% alc.

Uerige Doppel Sticke ★★★★★

Altbier: Obergärige Hausbrauerei GmbH, Düsseldorf, Germany www.uerige.deen_home

"Fresh hoppy aroma (grass mostly) with sticky caramel malts." "Very good flavor of rich malt, pears, spices and caramel." "Having the excellent malts found in the best of doppelbocks freaking with some crazy cool hops." 8.5% alc.

Uerige Sticke ★★★★1/2

Altbier: Obergärige Hausbrauerei GmbH, Düsseldorf, Germany www.uerige.deen_home

"Big malt aroma, some grassiness and breadiness." "Chewy, woody bitterness with caramel layers and lots of earthiness." "This is a beer that I could definitely see myself stocking up on around the holidays." 6.5% alc.

Uinta Angler's Pale Ale ★★1/2

Am. Pale Ale: Uinta Brewing Co., Salt Lake City, UT www.uintabrewing.com

"Nice refreshing Cascade aroma, clean simple malty flavors." "Nice hop flavor that is well balanced with notes of caramel malt and a gentle breadiness." 5.6% alc.

Uinta Anniversary Barley Wine ★★★

Barley Wine: Uinta Brewing Co., Salt Lake City, UT www.uintabrewing.com

"Aroma of toasted bread, toffee, caramel, chocolate and some citrus." "A very basic barley wine that is sweet and malty up front with some prominent brown sugar aspects and firm bitterness in the finish." 10.4% alc.

Uinta Cutthroat Pale Ale ★★1/2

Am. Pale Ale: Uinta Brewing Co., Salt Lake City, UT www.uintabrewing.com

"The aroma is fruity and flowery with hints of caramel and slight malts." "Delightful bitter finish with a citrus touch." "It packs some good flavor… just lacks body." 4% alc.

Uinta King?s Peak Porter ★★1/2

Porter: Uinta Brewing Co., Salt Lake City, UT www.uintabrewing.com

"Smell is of roasted malts (crystal malts and black patent jumping out) with a touch of caramel, chocolate and vanilla hidden in there." "Brown bread and Tootsie Rolls and light burnt smokiness." Multiple medallist at GABF for Schwarzbier. N/A% alc.

Uinta Solstice ★★1/2

Kölsch: Uinta Brewing Co., Salt Lake City, UT www.uintabrewing.com

"Straw-like aroma with slightly earthy hop notes." "Moderately sour-bitter body, dry herbal hoppy late qualities, quite dry." "Very little hops, but enough flavor." 4% alc.

La Fin Du Monde ★★★★1/2

Abbey Tripel: Unibroue (Sleeman), Chambly, Quebec www.unibroue.com

"Aroma of fresh bell peppers, yeast orange zest, dark German bread." "Lemon, fennel, pepper, yeast, a touch of white wine." "Half-way through, your belly is warm and you realize you've been drinking an awesome beer." 9% alc.

Ephemere Apple ★★★★

Fruit Beer: Unibroue (Sleeman), Chambly, Quebec www.unibroue.com

"Yeasty aroma with tart green apple." "Flavors of apple, black pepper, hint of orange and some coriander." "C'mon Unibroue, you can do better than this!" 5.5% alc.

Ephemere Peach ★★★
Fruit Beer: Unibroue (Sleeman), Chambly, Quebec www.unibroue.com
"Peach dominates the aroma with a little yeastiness and dried hops." "Yeasty, off-dry character with peach candy." "Disappointing to say the least, but not horrible." 5% alc.

Upland Bad Elmer's Porter ★★
Porter: Upland Brewing Co., Bloomington , IN www.uplandbeer.com
"Very thin to drink, it has mild roast barley and barley malt, coffee and some milk chocolate to taste." "Way too thin and watery for a good porter." 5.5% alc.

Upland Dragonfly IPA ★★1/2
IPA: Upland Brewing Co., Bloomington , IN www.uplandbeer.com
"Very fruity flavor, some lemons and oranges, some grassiness and lingering bitterness." "Light-to-medium bodied with a little malty sweetness present." "Good introduction to the style." 6.8% alc.

Upland Pale Ale ★★1/2
Am. Pale Ale: Upland Brewing Co., Bloomington , IN www.uplandbeer.com
"Hops were quieter than expected." "Fairly well balanced, sweet bready malts and mellow citrus hops." "Follows the generic American Pale Ale recipe that 1,000 US brewers apparently have stashed away." 5.1% alc.

Upland Valley Weizen ★★1/2
Dunkelweizen: Upland Brewing Co., Bloomington , IN www.uplandbeer.com
"Clove and over-ripe banana aroma." "Medium sweet, clove, banana, some lemon." "Some effervescence, very refreshing." 6% alc.

Upland Wheat Ale ★★1/2
Bel. Witbier: Upland Brewing Co., Bloomington , IN www.uplandbeer.com
"Very subdued clove and banana, perhaps a hint of orange." "Slightly yeasty and a little wheat character." "Fairly light bodied." 4.5% alc.

Upland Winter Warmer ★★★★
Barley Wine: Upland Brewing Co., Bloomington , IN www.uplandbeer.com
"Sweet fruity aroma penetrated by apple tones and mandarin." "Thinner than most barley wines." "Malts, diluted brown sugar and subtle dark pitted fruit." 9% alc.

Upper Canada Dark Ale ★★
Brown Ale: Sleeman Brewing and Malting Co., Guelph, Ontario www.sleeman.com
"Ever-so-slight hop and caramel aroma." "Taste was very brackish and metallic with artificially sweet darkish malt and an overriding taste of past-their-prime prunes." "Not bad but Upper Canada isn't what it was." 5% alc.

Upper Canada Lager ★★
Premium Lager: Sleeman Brewing and Malting Co., Guelph, Ontario www.sleeman.com
"Fair malty nose with bready and hoppy hints." "Taste is refreshing and quite crisp; has more flavor then your usual macro lager." "Serviceable lager." 5.2% alc.

Upstream Blackstone Stout ★★
Stout: Upstream Brewing Co., Omaha, NE www.upstreambrewing.com
"Intensity of the roast was as much as many Imperial Stouts I've had (although a bit harsh)." "Lacks depth but intensity of flavor is good." "Best of Upstream's standard brews." 5.9% alc.

Upstream Dundee 90 Shilling Scotch Ale ★★
Scotch Ale: Upstream Brewing Co., Omaha, NE www.upstreambrewing.com
"Strong caramel malt aroma with some green grape and bits of woody grains (wheat), a touch of toffee." "The pine flavor is bold upon tasting - a big hop bite, too." "Can't escape the watery base and the homebrew characteristics." 6.5% alc.

Upstream Firehouse ESB ★
Prem Bitter: Upstream Brewing Co., Omaha, NE www.upstreambrewing.com
"Very mild nose procures toasted grain and cereal." "A touch piney and grapefruity." "All the trappings of a brewer instructed to keep the beer light for the Bud-drinking beautiful people." 5.8% alc.

Upstream Indian Pale Ale ★
IPA: Upstream Brewing Co., Omaha, NE www.upstreambrewing.com
"Very underhopped for an IPA." "This is a tart brew with a very hoppy bite but not as clean as it should be and the hops are not as big." "Moderate hops, thin and not very assertively bitter." 6.5% alc.

Urthel Hibernus Quentum ★★★1/2
Abbey Tripel: Brouwerij Van Steenberge, Ertvelde, Belgium www.vansteenberge.com
"Aroma of sweet pears and hint of grapefruit, white pepper, pale malt and yeast." "A riddling complex of vanilla, wheat, butter, peaches and pears all bound by an astringent tie." "Just not fat enough to be a good tripel to me." 9% alc.

Urthel Samaranth ★★★1/2
Bel. Strong Ale: Brouwerij Van Steenberge, Ertvelde, Belgium www.vansteenberge.com
"Grapey, rummy, caramelized orange aromas." "Dates, apples, (yellow delicious) in the fairly sweet but somewhat plain flavor with alcohol apparent throughout." "Good, not great stuff." 11.5% alc.

Urthel Tonicum Finiboldhus ★★★
Bel. Strong Ale: Brouwerij Van Steenberge, Ertvelde, Belgium www.vansteenberge.com
"Nose is spicy and floral with light fruit notes, sugar and yeast." "Taste is big spices and flowers with strong yeast notes." "Very pleasant." 7.5% alc.

Utenos ★★★
Pale Lager: Utenos , Utena, Lithuania www.utenosalus.lt
"Aroma has light malts and a lightly noticeable sweetness." "Malt flavors thought the mouth and a light euro hop on the finish." "This blonde may not have everything upstairs, but she's still a pretty good time." 5.2% alc.

Utenos Porter ★★1/2
Baltic Porter: Utenos , Utena, Lithuania www.utenosalus.lt
"Aromas of dark chocolate, roasted malt and a hint of coffee." "Flavors of the dark fruit, some chocolate and a bit of nuttiness." "Sweet finish; a bit one sided but not to the point of being undrinkable." 6.8% alc.

Utica Club ★
Pale Lager: Matt Brewing Co., Utica, NY www.saranac.com
"Flavor is weak, watery and has little of what the label calls Pilsner." "It's basically a light lager with not too much of an adjunct presence, well carbonated, a very little bit of hop dryness at the end." 5% alc.

Val-Dieu Blonde ★★1/2
Belgian Ale: Brasserie de l'Abbaye du Val-Dieu, Aubel, Belgium www.val-dieu.com
"Aroma is delicate with bananas, citrus and mild spices." "Soft and lightly malty with a weak perfumey touch from the coriander." "A very accessible and pleasant 'Blonde' that hardly can offend anyone." 6% alc.

Val-Dieu Brune ★★★
Abbey Dubbel: Brasserie de l'Abbaye du Val-Dieu, Aubel, Belgium www.val-dieu.com
"Pleasant mild aroma of malt and dark fruits." "Slightly nutty, chocolately, fruity, a hint of caramel but all very subtle." "An excellent beer for introducing 'virgins' to the joys of Belgian beer - no harsh flavors but lots of subtlety." 8% alc.

Val-Dieu Triple ★★★
Abbey Tripel: Brasserie de l'Abbaye du Val-Dieu, Aubel, Belgium www.val-dieu.com
"Orange zest, either styrians or Hallertau, white pepper, apricot, pear." "Relatively soft, sweet flavors - marshmallow, pepper, cream, pear." "Not complex but very drinkable given the strength." 9% alc.

Vapeur Cochonne ★★1/2
Belgian Ale: Brasserie à Vapeur, Leuze-Pipaix, Belgium www.vapeur.com
"Aroma of almost a sour red wine, some caramel, roasted malts and sour apples." "Winey, sourish, pruney aroma; brandyish taste." "This is certainly interesting and lends itself to being a sipper." 9% alc.

Vapeur en Folie ★★1/2
Saison: Brasserie à Vapeur, Leuze-Pipaix, Belgium www.vapeur.com
"Pleasant aroma of sweet malt, yeast, fruit and alcohol." "Mild grapefruit taste, followed by lemon candy and a bready finish." "I was surprised how quickly I drank it." 8% alc.

Veltins Pilsner ★★1/2
Classic Ger Pils: Brauerei C.and A. Veltins GmbH and Co, Meschede-Grevenstein, Germany www.veltins.de
"Aroma of hay-like hops and day-old challah (bread)." "Balanced body with light bitterness and clean, sweet pale malts." "Just another German Pils." 4.8% alc.

Vergina ★★★
Pale Lager: Macedonian Thrace Brewery, Komotini, Greece www.vergina-beer.com
"Aroma of malt and a sharp spice kick." "Flavors of sweet malt and light citrus with a crisp, clean finish." "The funniest part about this beer was having the cashier call for a price check over the intercom. Even she had to laugh." 5% alc.

Verhaeghe Echt Kriek ★★1/2
Flem Sour Ale: Brouwerij Verhaeghe, Vichte, West-Vlaanderen, Belgium www.brouwerijverhaeghe.be
"Acetic, lactic aroma with cherry candies. Oaky, fat, tangy, voluptuous." "Notes of sour black cherry, must, red grape and cellar...very balsamic." "Thoroughly spanks the palate, slapping cherry-whips on the tongue." 6.8% alc.

Verhaeghe Vichtenaar ★★★★
Flem Sour Ale: Brouwerij Verhaeghe, Vichte, West-Vlaanderen, Belgium www.brouwerijverhaeghe.be
"Remarkably mild sour aroma - lactic and vinegary, quite fruity berrylike, wooden notes, barrique dryness." "Less acidic than most Flemish sours I've had before, but with a stronger bite in the end." 5.1% alc.

Victory Festbier ★★1/2
Märzen/Oktbfst: Victory Brewing Co., Downingtown, PA www.victorybeer.com
"Aroma is full of rye bread, cereal and caramel." "Caramel and oats help to carry a smooth nutty sweetness." "Not as layered as the best beers of the style and just a touch too sweet but above average." 5.6% alc.

Victory Golden Monkey ★★★★1/2
Abbey Tripel: Victory Brewing Co., Downingtown, PA www.victorybeer.com
"Lots of fruit and alcohol up front. Mostly banana but also getting some apple/pear." "Taste pretty much follows how it smells, with the cloves oranges, bananas and those Belgian yeasts." "A very enjoyable fruity sweet beer." 9.5% alc.

Victory Hop Devil IPA ★★★★★
IPA: Victory Brewing Co., Downingtown, PA www.victorybeer.com
"Orange rind and grapefruit in aroma, lemon zest, weak pine and pepper... a lovely citric nose with just a touch of acridity." "Sweet malts give rise of caramel flavor on top of grapefruit and sweet citrus." 6.7% alc.

Victory Hop Wallop ★★★★1/2
Imp/Dbl IPA: Victory Brewing Co., Downingtown, PA www.victorybeer.com
"Aroma is of earthy and spicy hops." "Interesting flavor, dominated by sweet fruits, with a huge dose of German hops." "A solid IIPA, but there are quite a few others out there that have this beat." 8.5% alc.

Victory Moonglow Weizenbock ★★★★
Weizen Bock: Victory Brewing Co., Downingtown, PA www.victorybeer.com
"Aroma is reserved yet loaded with fresh warm alcohol, over French pears sautéed with butter." "Starts with tart, sweet malt flavor with touches of spices and banana and finishes dry with slight bitterness." 8.7% alc.

Victory Old Horizontal ★★★★★
Barley Wine: Victory Brewing Co., Downingtown, PA www.victorybeer.com
"Nose is sweetly hoppy with a light caramel and citrus quality." "Beautifully balanced with loads of soft, chewy malt and flowering, citric hop." "At times this is like bathing in hop oils." 10.5% alc.

Victory Prima Pils ★★★★★
Pilsner: Victory Brewing Co., Downingtown, PA www.victorybeer.com
"The grassy, lemony aroma is the perfect prelude to this crisp refresher." "Tons of hops true to their style roots, lots of light malt taste." "Surely one of the best examples of the style anywhere in the world." 5.3% alc.

Victory St. Victorious Doppelbock ★★★1/2
Doppelbock: Victory Brewing Co., Downingtown, PA www.victorybeer.com
"Aroma is kind of light, not very distinct, sweet fruit and malt, with nuances of caramel." "Loads of caramel and maple and syrup, crystallized nuts, bread pudding, cold sweet tea, toffee." "An interesting restrained, fruity take." 7.9% alc.

Victory Storm King Imp. Stout ★★★★★
Imp. Stout: Victory Brewing Co., Downingtown, PA www.victorybeer.com
"Smoky malt, cola and dark fruit sweetness followed by an amazingly smooth, judicious hoppiness." "Aroma is glorious, raisins and dried apples and chocolate cake." "Needs to spend some time in the cellar to truly become something special." 9.1% alc.

Victory Sunrise Weissbier ★★★★1/2
Hefeweizen: Victory Brewing Co., Downingtown, PA www.victorybeer.com
"Nose is solid spice/clove and light banana, plus a bit of citrus and wheat in there too." "Tastes of bananas, lemons, wheat, yeast and light spices." "The perfect breakfast beer." 5.7% alc.

Victory Whirlwind Wit ★★★★
Bel. Witbier: Victory Brewing Co., Downingtown, PA www.victorybeer.com
"Smell is perfumey, soft banana, clove, coriander, citrus and melon." "Wheat dominates the flavor as well, but some banana, lemon and orange sneak in when the wheat isn't looking." 5% alc.

Viking Brewing Abby Normal ★★★
Abbey Dubbel: Viking Brewing Co., Dallas, WI www.vikingbrewing.com
"Aroma of raisins, pear, white grapes and lots of Granny Smith apples." "Flavor is sweet and spicy like cinnamon roll with molasses and a floral hop garnish." "It isn't as complex as the USSR was but it is a bit of a curiosity." N/A% alc.

Viking Brewing Berserk Barleywine ★★★
Barley Wine: Viking Brewing Co., Dallas, WI www.vikingbrewing.com
"Aroma weighs in heavily of dark roasty malts, molasses, prunes and raisins with hints of floral hops." "Flavor is rich, dark fruity malts, brown sugar clove and spice, big alcohol presence and a bit of bitterness." 12% alc.

Viking Brewing Big Swede ★★★★
Imp. Stout: Viking Brewing Co., Dallas, WI www.vikingbrewing.com
"Very vinous aroma, dark fruit, chocolate." "Flavor is rich milk chocolate, some coffee and a bit of raisin." "Quite different and much appreciated." 8% alc.

Viking Brewing Copperhead ★★★
Dunkel: Viking Brewing Co., Dallas, WI www.vikingbrewing.com
"Aroma of fruit, cinnamon and light toffee." "Flavor is dry chocolate, caramel, smooth vanilla, apples, pears and nutmeg." "I really admire their gumption but I question their delivery." 5.5% alc.

Viking Brewing Hot Chocolate ★★1/2
Spice/Herb: Viking Brewing Co., Dallas, WI www.vikingbrewing.com
"Smells of roasted chocolate and coffee with a touch of hops." "I have had some high quality spicy hot chocolate and truffles. Those had a lot more chocolate and were more flavorful." 5% alc.

Viking Brewing Invader Doppelbock ★★★

Doppelbock: Viking Brewing Co., Dallas, WI www.vikingbrewing.com

"Nice aroma of dark fruits and molasses." "Sweet flavors of caramel, whole wheat, cherry/ grape." "Could be thicker and more balanced, but I like the sweetness." 6.5% alc.

Viking Brewing JS Bock ★★★

Bock: Viking Brewing Co., Dallas, WI www.vikingbrewing.com

"Mildly sweet aroma, mostly malts, but just a hint of wet grass." "Sour grassy notes and also some caramel malt sweetness." "Straightforward, moderately malty lager, not overly Bockish." 6% alc.

Viking Brewing Mørketid ★★1/2

Schwarzbier: Viking Brewing Co., Dallas, WI www.vikingbrewing.com

Light malt and caramel in the aroma, followed by more caramel and smoke in the flavor. "Flavor is slightly tart, with some brown sugar and a touch of sweet smoke." "The black sheep of black biers." N/A% alc.

Viking Brewing Juleøl ★★★

Spice/Herb: Viking Brewing Co., Dallas, WI www.vikingbrewing.com

"Apple aroma with cinnamon and ginger." "Mild malty flavor, plentiful spice, apple and cinnamon, nice hop tartness in the finish." "A fascinating Christmas beer." N/A% alc.

Viking Brewing Vienna Woods ★★★

Vienna: Viking Brewing Co., Dallas, WI www.vikingbrewing.com

"Aroma of delicately toasted malt and spicy floral hops." "Smooth, malty flavor profile with a very pleasant caramel component." "As an American Heartland brew, this is a quite impressive clone of a Vienna lager." N/A% alc.

Viking Brewing Whole Stein ★★★1/2

Porter: Viking Brewing Co., Dallas, WI www.vikingbrewing.com

"Aroma is a dash of coffee, a sprinkle of red pepper and surprisingly smoky." "Flavor is roasty malty up front, with chocolate, spicy cinnamon flavors and some creaminess at the finish." "A good Porter, thick and earthy." 4.5% alc.

Virgin Islands Blackbeard Ale ★★1/2

Amber Ale: Virgin Islands Brewing Co., Christiansted, St. Croix, Virgin Islands www.blackbeardale.com

"The aroma is fairly light - slightly caramelly, earthy." "Watery start, fairly bland, very soft malts, graininess isn't as strong as I would have thought." "My #1 pirate-themed beer. " 5.2% alc.

Virgin Islands Foxy's Lager ★★

Pale Lager: Virgin Islands Brewing Co., Christiansted, St. Croix, Virgin Islands www.blackbeardale.com

"Aroma of corn syrup and herby hops." "Light malty flavor, citrus tang and grassy hops but overall watery and thin." "Drink it on a boat in the Caribbean and it won't really matter what it tastes like." N/A% alc.

Vondel ★★★

Bel. Strong Ale: Riva Brouwerij (Liefmans Breweries), Dentergem, Belgium www.liefmans.be

"Sweet caramelized malt, fruity character." "Fruity Porto accent, nutmeg spiciness, also reminiscent of a fruit-cake flavor." "The alcohol content makes itself known in the warm, sticky finish." "Nice brown… pleasant surprise." 8.5% alc.

Vuuve ★★★

Bel. Witbier: Brouwerij De Regenboog, Assebroek-Brugge, Belgium www.ping.betsmisje

"Aroma of coriander, biscuits, celery, lemon, leather and slight phenols." "Very malty, dry palate with more leather, coriander flavors are like chewing the stuff, bitter lemon rind, with a fair bit of hop in the finish and some yeasty firmness." "Had hopes for this one." 5% alc.

Wachusett Black Shack Porter ★★★1/2
Porter: Wachusett Brewing, Westminster, MA www.wachusettbrew.com
"The aroma full of milk chocolate, vanilla, coffee and toasted pecan." "Big, fat malt and not at all lacking hops. Lingering, coffeeish bitterness through finish." "Nice velvety mouthfeel and good drinkability." N/A% alc.

Wachusett Blueberry ★★1/2
Fruit Beer: Wachusett Brewing, Westminster, MA www.wachusettbrew.com
"Smells of wheat and blueberries - nice taste, not overly complex." "Flavor is well balanced but thin." "Mixed with Guinness (Black and Blue), it actually tastes a little better." N/A% alc.

Wachusett Country Ale ★★★
Goldn/Blond Ale: Wachusett Brewing, Westminster, MA www.wachusettbrew.com
"Pale malt aroma, slightly grainy. Thin body, malty but weak." "Flavors of mild pale malt with very mild peat, earth, husky grain and mild floral hints." "Unassuming brew." N/A% alc.

Wachusett IPA ★★★
IPA: Wachusett Brewing, Westminster, MA www.wachusettbrew.com
"Once on the tastebuds, a lovely hop-dance ensues. While malt is not tasted, it's presence is felt in this nicely balanced beer." "If a mild-mannered IPA is for you, this is the one." N/A% alc.

Wachusett Nut Brown ★★★
Brown Ale: Wachusett Brewing, Westminster, MA www.wachusettbrew.com
"Milk chocolate, roasted nuts and black tea constitute the nose." "Some light chocolate notes mix with a drier yeast and nutty flavor to create some semblance of balance." "Quite nice for what it is." N/A% alc.

Wachusett Oktoberfest ★★★★
Märzen/Oktbfst: Wachusett Brewing, Westminster, MA www.wachusettbrew.com
"Malty, very subtle biscuit, soft sweetness and very clean." "Delicate notes of caramel with slight hints of roastiness turning to finish with small hints of brown sugar and a slight hop flavor." "Drinkable." N/A% alc.

Wachusett Quinn's Irish Style Ale ★★1/2
Irish Ale: Wachusett Brewing, Westminster, MA www.wachusettbrew.com
"Aroma, rich and malty, sweet, herbal and fruity." "Flavor is pretty basic, similar to Smithwick's though not as much hops, quite malty and sweet" "Next..." 4.6% alc.

Wachusett Summer Breeze ★★1/2
Am. Wheat: Wachusett Brewing, Westminster, MA www.wachusettbrew.com
"Light lemon, wheat aroma." "They have found a way to take Glade Air Freshener and turn it in to a liquid!" "Good for someone whose friends aren't into better beer." "Very mild and summery." N/A% alc.

Wachusett Winter Ale ★★★1/2
Eng. Strong Ale: Wachusett Brewing, Westminster, MA www.wachusettbrew.com
"Coffee, dark fruits and spices." "Flavor unfortunately does not live up to the aroma - strong, bitter orange, light roastiness but somehow flat." "Flavor got better as it warmed." "One of the better ones from this brewer." N/A% alc.

Wagner Valley Caywood Station Stout ★★1/2
Sweet Stout: Wagner Valley Brewing Co., Lodi, NJ www.wagnervineyards.com
"Aromas of espresso, nuts and roasted malts." "Slight licorice note flavor note along with your typical roasted coffee and caramel." "Surprisingly light bland stout." "Forgettable." 5.5% alc.

Wagner Valley Dockside Amber ★★★1/2
Vienna: Wagner Valley Brewing Co., Lodi, NJ www.wagnervineyards.com
"A nutty/malty aroma with little hop influence." "Caramel malt is the dominant flavor along with some Vienna and Münich malts and some clean bitterness." "Very drinkable and full of flavor for a light lager." 5.1% alc.

Wagner Valley IPA ★★★
IPA: Wagner Valley Brewing Co., Lodi, NJ www.wagnervineyards.com
"Citrus, flowers, grapefruit aromas with some malts." "Orange peel bitterness, apple sauce sweetness and lingering grapefruit bitterness in the finish." "Rather different from usual Pacific Northwest IPAs." "Pretty good overall." 6.2% alc.

Wagner Valley Sled Dog Doppelbock ★★★
Doppelbock: Wagner Valley Brewing Co., Lodi, NJ www.wagnervineyards.com
"Aroma of big fruit, malt, slight licorice and prunes." "Tastes of burnt brown sugar, dark fruits and caramel." "Smelled, tasted great up front but lacking on the back end." 8.5% alc.

Wagner Valley Sled Dog Trippelbock ★★★
Doppelbock: Wagner Valley Brewing Co., Lodi, NJ www.wagnervineyards.com
Aroma is of sugary, mapley malts, earth and hints of molasses." "This beer is all about the dark sweetness with lots of caramel, plums, dried fruit and a warming alcohol sensation." "A stiff brew to be consumed by the snifter." 11% alc.

Wagner Valley Sugar House Maple Porter ★★1/2
Porter: Wagner Valley Brewing Co., Lodi, NJ www.wagnervineyards.com
Aroma is pretty roasty along with some caramel/maple sweetness." "Dark caramel with a hint of maple and smoke." "Body is a little thin, but this is very drinkable and not a bad change of pace." "Enjoyable." N/A% alc.

Waimea Bay Pale Ale ★★
Am. Pale Ale: Waimea Brewing Co., Waimea, Kauai, HA www.waimeabrewing.com
"Citrus aroma with light grapefruit hops and a light cookie dough aroma." "Sweet malty body… caramel and citrus followed by an overwhelming bitter finish." "Lacks richness in its malts." N/A% alc.

Waimea Luau Lager ★★1/2
Premium Lager: Waimea Brewing Co., Waimea, Kauai, HA www.waimeabrewing.com
"Rather plain lager, a bit sweet in the middle with a decent hop follow." "Smooth, crisp, light and sweet." "Better than you average lager." N/A% alc.

Warka Jasne Pelne ★★★★
Pale Lager: Browary Warka (Heineken), Warka, Poland www.warka.com.pl
"Light nose is balanced between hay and bread." "Sweetish on palate but some discernible hops there too." "Light, clean and balanced." 5.7% alc.

Warka Strong ★★
Eur Str Lager: Browary Warka (Heineken), Warka, Poland www.warka.com.pl
"Aromas of ripe soft fruit, caramel, menthol and a bit of alcohol." "Sweet flavor with hints of caramel." "It would probably go over well with the malt liquor crowd." 7% alc.

Warsteiner Premium Dunkel ★★1/2
Dunkel: Warsteiner Brauerei, Arnsberger Forestpark, Germany www.warsteiner.de
"Sweet malt aroma, a little bit of nuts and a sweet grass undertone." "Roasted caramel malt and coffee flavors." "Seriously tastes more like a slightly sweet pale lager than a Dunkel." 4.9% alc.

Warsteiner Premium Fresh ★1/2
Low Alcohol: Warsteiner Brauerei, Arnsberger Forestpark, Germany www.warsteiner.de
"Aroma is mix of wort and grassy hops." "Very faint sweet malt flavor. They could at least have added more hops." "Honestly, this isn't a total waste." 0.5% alc.

Warsteiner Premium Verum
Classic Ger Pils: Warsteiner Brauerei, Arnsberger Forestpark, Germany www.warsteiner.de
"Fresh sweet malt and hop aromas." "OK flavor with herbal bitterness in a light-bodied lager." "I could live without this." "Nice to fall back on." 4.8% alc.

Wasatch Polygamy Porter ★★

Porter: Schirf Brewing Co./Wasatch Brew Pub, Park City, UT www.wasatchbeers.com

"Aromas are light and earthy with dry roast malts." "Coffee accents come through first, then sweet malt." "Somewhat thin and watery." "Sucks when an ad campaign has more bite than the product." "Great for a wedding present." 4% alc.

Wasatch Superior Ale ★★★

Ale: Schirf Brewing Co./Wasatch Brew Pub, Park City, UT www.wasatchbeers.com

"Spicy aroma of malt and hops." "Interesting combination of flavors with a bit of chocolate, some toasted malt, hops, vanilla and a little acridness." "Not really superior." N/A% alc.

Weihenstephaner Hefe Weissbier ★★★★★

Hefeweizen: Bayerische Staatsbrauerei Weihenstephan, Freising, Germany www.brauerei-weihenstephan.de

"Light banana and moderate clove in the flavor along with mild wheat" "Creamy, viscous, citrus, spicy, banana flavors upon drinking." "The Germans know how to make the best Hefes!" 5.4% alc.

Weihenstephaner Hefeweissbier Dunkel ★★★★

Dunkelweizen: Bayerische Staatsbrauerei Weihenstephan, Freising, Germany www. brauerei-weihenstephan.de

"Aroma is very fruity, lightly wheaty, with sweet malt, apple, clove." "Flavor was thick and heavy on bitterness with a sweet wheat and yeast character resting on malted haunches." "Good complexity for the style." 5.3% alc.

Weihenstephaner Korbinian ★★★★1/2

Doppelbock: Bayerische Staatsbrauerei Weihenstephan, Freising, Germany www.brauerei-weihenstephan.de

"Has aroma of good caramel, nuts, light roast and hints of fruits such as apple and pear." "Good complexity of toasted malt, sour mash, sweet toffee and licorice." "Just a great malt-bomb of a Doppelbock." 7.4% alc.

Weihenstephaner Kristallweissbier ★★★★★

Kristallweizen: Bayerische Staatsbrauerei Weihenstephan, Freising, Germany www.brauerei-weihenstephan.de

"Lemons, banana and fruit at the nose." "Typical wheaty aroma and flavors but the banana was light." "If I was to drink a filtered Weizen, this most likely would be the one." 5.4% alc.

Weihenstephaner Original Bayrisch Mild ★★★

Helles/Dortmnd: Bayerische Staatsbrauerei Weihenstephan, Freising, Germany www.brauerei-weihenstephan.de

"Aroma was a little yeasty with a slight doughy smell." "Quite crisp, slightly sweetish flavor with a touch of bitterness." "A pleasant, decent Helles, above the average." "Tasty and refreshing." 5.1% alc.

Wells Bombardier (5.5%) ★★★1/2

Prem Bitter: The Eagle Brewery (Charles Wells Ltd.), Bedford, Bedfordshire, England www.charleswells.co.uk

"Nose of wheat and berries with an initial hint of figs and plums as brew warms." "Candied malts marrying nicely with bitter finish, some refreshing herbal notes." "Unexpectedly good, balanced, easy to drink." 5.5% alc.

Weltenburger Kloster Anno 1050 ★★★

Vienna: Weltenburg Klosterbrauerei, Kelheim, Germany www.weltenburger.de

"Gritty, dry and grainy nose like rye-bread and plain muesli with the slightest hint of orange peel underneath." "Quite sweet, piney and very malty in the mouth." 'Malt driven, generously flavored lager." 5.5% alc.

Weltenburger Kloster Asam Bock ★★★★★

Doppelbock: Weltenburg Klosterbrauerei, Kelheim, Germany www.weltenburger.de

"Nose is prunes, raisins, brown sugar, malt." "Smooth, rich malt palate - earth, wood, demerara sugar, toffee, almost smoky." "A delectable treat fit for a brisk Autumn's evening." 6.9% alc.

Weltenburger Kloster Barock Dunkel ★★★★

Dunkel: Weltenburg Klosterbrauerei, Kelheim, Germany www.weltenburger.de

"Terrific aromas of fresh brown bread and caramel." "Rich roasted malt palate with sweet flavors of brown sugar and toffee balanced by a slightly woody character." "An excellent Dunkel close to greatness." 4.7% alc.

Weltenburger Kloster Barock Hell ★★★

Helles/Dortmnd: Weltenburg Klosterbrauerei, Kelheim, Germany www.weltenburger.de

"Soft, malty with fresh bread, lychee, canned pineapple and faint pine notes." "Medium bodied, grainy, some citrus, some shortbread and a soft carbonation." "Went down so swiftly - with a constant gleaming grin on my face." 5.6% alc.

Weltenburger Kloster Hefe-Weissbier Hell ★★★

Hefeweizen: Weltenburg Klosterbrauerei, Kelheim, Germany www.weltenburger.de

"Zesty, slightly clove-like spicy, banana, apple and pear nose with strong doughy sweet, yeasty note underneath." "Taste of citrus, lemon orange, cloves and toffee with maybe some banana." "Didn't love it; liked it just fine." 5.4% alc.

Weltenburger Kloster Hefe-Weizen Dunkel ★★★

Dunkelweizen: Weltenburg Klosterbrauerei, Kelheim, Germany www.weltenburger.de

"Aroma is fruity and malty with soft caramel." "Sweet banana and dry chocolate notes in the mouth, delicately dry finish with hints of chocolate powder and roasted grains." "Pretty good Dunkelweizen." 5.3% alc.

Weltenburger Kloster Pils ★★★★

Pilsner: Weltenburg Klosterbrauerei, Kelheim, Germany www.weltenburger.de

"Yeasty, fruity, malty some sweetness, citrus notes." "Flavor dominated initially by sweet malt but there is some sharp hop cut-through in the finish." "This is Michael Bublé, I'd rather listen to Tom Waits." 4.9% alc.

Weltenburger Kloster Urtyp Hell ★★★1/2

Helles/Dortmnd: Weltenburg Klosterbrauerei, Kelheim, Germany www.weltenburger.de

"Soft, subtle peppery hops in the aroma, balanced by dry, grainy malt and haystack chaff." "Peppery, grassy and slightly herbal following on through to a mildly bitter swallow." "Another notch for simple excellence." 4.9% alc.

Weltenburger Kloster Winter-Traum ★★★

Vienna: Weltenburg Klosterbrauerei, Kelheim, Germany www.weltenburger.de

"Aroma mostly of caramel, tinge of lemongrass." "Malt accented with caramel and toffee malt flavors, soft apple and a touch of honey covered fruit." "What German winter beers should all be like." 5.2% alc.

Westmalle Dubbel ★★★★★

Abbey Dubbel: Brouwerij der Trappisten van Westmalle, Malle, Belgium www.trappistwestmalle.be

"Complex bouquet of fruity esters, spices and couple with an undercurrent of mild malt." "Lots of caramel and ever-present yeast and fruity esters." "Very warm beer :)" 7% alc.

Westmalle Tripel ★★★★★

Abbey Tripel: Brouwerij der Trappisten van Westmalle, Malle, Belgium www.trappistwestmalle.be

"Musty spicy-honey-apricot aroma." "Flavor bready and yeasty with nice burst of orangey hops in the middle. Long dry finish with a nice note of bitterness." "Good, drinkable, dry Belgian ale." 9.5% alc.

Westvleteren Abt 12 ★★★★★
Abt/Quadrupel: Westvleteren Abdij St. Sixtus, Westvleteren, Belgium www.sintsixtus.be
"Wonderfully madeirized malt with raisins, prunes and dates in aroma and nice spices wafting through." "Extremely complex taste containing notes of dried fruits, licorice, caramel roasted malt and orange." "Now I know what the fuss is about." 10.2% alc.

Westvleteren Blond ★★★★★
Belgian Ale: Westvleteren Abdij St. Sixtus, Westvleteren, Belgium www.sintsixtus.be
"Sweet candy-like fruity aroma with notes of grapefruit, pine needles, hops and spices." "Dry, yet firm malt flavors abound mixing with a hops, spice and herb backdrop." "Flavor is citrusy and lightly malty, very well balanced in bitterness as well." 5.8% alc.

Westvleteren Extra 8 ★★★★★
Bel. Strong Ale: Westvleteren Abdij St. Sixtus, Westvleteren, Belgium www.sintsixtus.be
"Flavor of alcohol, plum, chocolate in the beginning, then smoothening up to kind of caramellish, fruity and some roast too." "Aroma of malt, almost candy like sweetness, yeast, plums, dust, bubble gum, very fruity." "In a class of its own." 8% alc.

Wexford Irish Cream ★★
Irish Ale: Greene King Plc., Bury St. Edmunds, Suffolk, England www.greeneking.co.uk
"Aroma of malts, caramel and fruits." "Only faint hints of a malty sweetness." "Incredibly flat and somewhat watery." "I am beginning to wonder what Budweiser would taste like if it was offered in a nitro-can." 5% alc.

Weyerbacher Autumn Fest ★★1/2
Amber Ale: Weyerbacher Brewing Co., Easton, PA www.weyerbacher.com
"Pleasant aroma of roasted malt mixed with honey." "Oily aroma resolves into caramel malt with plenty of aged tree fruit and some woody, earthy yeast - not much bitterness here." 6.1% alc.

Weyerbacher Black Hole ★★★
Porter: Weyerbacher Brewing Co., Easton, PA www.weyerbacher.com
"Nose of vanilla, roast, dark chocolate, raison, faintly floral, dark caramel and over-ripe chocolate covered fruit." "Tastes of sweet roasted malt, sweet milk chocolate. Light cocoa bean with a bitter dark chocolate type finish." 7% alc.

Weyerbacher Blanche ★★
Bel. Witbier: Weyerbacher Brewing Co., Easton, PA www.weyerbacher.com
"Wheat and banana yeast (sweat) malt (straw) aroma with lemon hops and coriander." "Light yeasty flavor with citrus and spice." "The wateriness is very apparent by the end of the bottle." 5% alc.

Weyerbacher Blithering Idiot ★★★★
Barley Wine: Weyerbacher Brewing Co., Easton, PA www.weyerbacher.com
"Aromas of brown sugar, dark fruit and some vinous notes." "Toasty and spicy flavor with nutty malt, breadcrust, dried figs and molasses." "Not hoppy but doesn't especially need. it." 11.1% alc.

Weyerbacher Decadence ★★1/2
Am Strong Ale: Weyerbacher Brewing Co., Easton, PA www.weyerbacher.com
"Strong vinous, medicinal and menthol notes." "Strong alcohol flavor with a sweet honey finish." "Pure dessert brew." "Very nice original and substantial. I just could not drink a lot of this." 13% alc.

Weyerbacher Double Simcoe ★★★★
Imperial/Double IPA: Weyerbacher Brewing Co., Easton, PA www.weyerbacher.com
Nose on this beer is awesome with lots of big aromas of grapefruit and lemon. "Sweet and succulent maltiness, with the hops riding high — lots of tangerines and oranges, pine as well." "The ultimate aperitif beer." 9% alc.

Weyerbacher ESB ★★1/2

Prem Bitter: Weyerbacher Brewing Co., Easton, PA www.weyerbacher.com

"Aromas of caramel, flowers and a little nutty." "Body starts with a semi-sweet, dry, grainy maltiness. Thick palate and bittersweet hoppy finish." 5.25% alc.

Weyerbacher Hefeweizen ★★

Hefeweizen: Weyerbacher Brewing Co., Easton, PA www.weyerbacher.com

"Citrus and sour yeast aroma, golden body and thin head." "Taste was a big let-down here - we were all surprised at how bland it tasted." "Not a very good German Hefe." 5.2% alc.

Weyerbacher Heresy ★★★★1/2

Imp. Stout: Weyerbacher Brewing Co., Easton, PA www.weyerbacher.com

"Sweet molassesy aroma - molasses, milk chocolate, white rum and peach." "Flavor has lactose, roasted chocolate, rhubarb and oak." "Smooth, soft body but lacks a little of the depth and character necessary to be truly elite." 8.2% alc.

Weyerbacher Hops Infusion ★★★

IPA: Weyerbacher Brewing Co., Easton, PA www.weyerbacher.com

"Very aromatic." "Grapefruit and orange in the nose as well, with biscuit-like and caramel drenched malt." "One of the better balanced hophead beers." 6.2% alc.

Weyerbacher Imperial Pumpkin ★★★★★

Spice/Herb: Weyerbacher Brewing Co., Easton, PA www.weyerbacher.com

"Aromas of pumpkin, cinnamon, nutmeg and cloves." "Flavor is on the complex side, with nuances of clove, hops, nutmeg, all spice and alcohol." "Big and brash. Definitely lacks finesse." 8% alc.

Weyerbacher Indian Pale Ale ★★★

IPA: Weyerbacher Brewing Co., Easton, PA www.weyerbacher.com

"Clean citrus hop aroma with a touch of acidity." "Flavor is mildly hoppy with a rich malt base underneath." "A starter for someone who isn't into IPA's." 6% alc.

Weyerbacher Insanity ★★★★1/2

Barley Wine: Weyerbacher Brewing Co., Easton, PA www.weyerbacher.com

"Vanilla, sugar, wine, chocolate and caramel fill my nose." "Whiskey and bourbon are dominant in the flavor as well as hints of vanilla, malt, caramel and wood." "A big brew for a big man is what this amounts to, insane is right." 11.1% alc.

Weyerbacher Merry Monks ★★1/2

Abbey Tripel: Weyerbacher Brewing Co., Easton, PA www.weyerbacher.com

"Aroma is very floral and fruity… with notes of cereal and peaches." "Flavor is initially an assault of sweet malt, bubble gum and candi sugar." "Definitely one of the least realized of their styles I have had." 9.3% alc.

Weyerbacher Old Heathen (Imp. Stout) ★★★★1/2

Imp. Stout: Weyerbacher Brewing Co., Easton, PA www.weyerbacher.com

"Dark chocolate roasted caramel and chocolate malt with raisins and plum, hint of oak and port, cocoa and molasses, with a yeast nose." "A bit light overall for a big ol' Imperial." 8.2% alc.

Weyerbacher Prophecy ★★1/2

Bel. Strong Ale: Weyerbacher Brewing Co., Easton, PA www.weyerbacher.com

"Aromas of candi sugar, a little Belgian yeast, some banana and some lemon a hint of vanilla and a little orange/citrus zest." "Rich citrus malts, with pronounced bourbon and oak flavors, tart and bitter in the finish." 9.3% alc.

Weyerbacher Quad ★★★★

Abt/Quadrupel: Weyerbacher Brewing Co., Easton, PA www.weyerbacher.com

"Good aroma of fruit jam, caramel, candy and alcohol." "Flavor is candi sugar, toffee, some dark fruit, caramel, very sweet until a slightly sour finish." "In general it's not an overly complex beer." 11.9% alc.

Weyerbacher Raspberry Imperial Stout ★★★★
Imp. Stout: Weyerbacher Brewing Co., Easton, PA www.weyerbacher.com
"Intense aroma of raspberry extract." "Tastes almost like a Black Forest chocolate cake with raspberry sauce on top." "A very nice dessert beer." 8% alc.

Weyerbacher Winter Ale ★★1/2
Eng. Strong Ale: Weyerbacher Brewing Co., Easton, PA www.weyerbacher.com
"Aroma is a bit smoky, roasted malts, chocolate and coffee with hints of bourbon." "Solid roastiness and a fair amount of smokiness, with a hint of spice and modest hops in the finish." "Overall a nice addition to my stomach." 6.1% alc.

Whim Old Izaak ★★★
Eng. Strong Ale: Broughton Ales Ltd., Biggar, The Borders, Scotland www.broughtonales.co.uk
"Blended aromas of caramel and toffee with a sturdy whiff of smoked peat drifting through." "Tastes caramel malty, with big brown sugar, toffee, some figs and scotch elements." "A decent session beer." 5% alc.

Whitbread Pale Ale ★★1/2
Prem Bitter: Boston Beer Co., Boston, MA www.samadams.com
"Malty nose with a faint tinge of herbal hops." "Tastes malty, nutty, with hops and fruit in the finish." 5.7% alc.

Lamar St. Pale Ale ★★
Am. Pale Ale: Goose Island Beer Co., Chicago, IL www.gooseisland.com
"Lemony, grassy hops with grainy malt in the aroma." "Very mellow malt profile with some light hops to back it up." "It's doable but not really that good." Organic. Brewed by Goose Island for Whole Foods. N/A% alc.

Widmer Brothers Blonde Ale ★★
Goldn/Blond Ale: Widmer Brothers Brewing Co., Portland, OR www.widmer.com
"Standard light malt aroma with a faint hop hint." "Flavor features a decent malty backbone with a balance of bittering hops and a peppery finish." "Fairly unremarkable blonde ale." 4.3% alc.

Widmer Brothers Drop Top Amber ★
Amber Ale: Widmer Brothers Brewing Co., Portland, OR www.widmer.com
"Flavor has a bit of biscuit and caramel to it." "It's slightly sweet and malty with a little woodiness." "Nothing to it, very boring." 4.85% alc.

Widmer Brothers Hefeweizen ★★★
Am. Wheat: Widmer Brothers Brewing Co., Portland, OR www.widmer.com
"A little citrus and hops aroma." "The flavor is of grapefruit and orange blossom honey." "Boring, not up to the level of most Hefes." 4.7% alc.

Widmer Brothers Hop Jack ★★1/2
Am. Pale Ale: Widmer Brothers Brewing Co., Portland, OR www.widmer.com
"Fresh and fruity nose - nectarines, peaches, melons." "Taste is very clean, just a touch of hoppiness." "Just a bit thin on the palate and not very exciting brew." 5% alc.

Widmer Brothers KGB Russian Imperial Stout ★★★★★
Imp. Stout: Widmer Brothers Brewing Co., Portland, OR www.widmer.com
"Chocolate, licorice and very light coffee in the aroma." "Sweet with notes of chocolate turning toward prunes to end up like coffee on a subtle background of alcohol." "Just the thing as the evening cooled down." 9.25% alc.

Widmer Brothers Okto Festival Ale (Oktoberfest) ★★1/2
Amber Ale: Widmer Brothers Brewing Co., Portland, OR www.widmer.com
"Aroma nice sweet malt presence with honey/earthy hop notes and a touch of sour graininess." "Flavor is crisp, clean, malty, caramel with a light hoppy finish." "A tad bland as Oktoberfests go." 5% alc.

Widmer Brothers Snow Plow ★★★
Sweet Stout: Widmer Brothers Brewing Co., Portland, OR www.widmer.com
"Light aroma of roasted malt and coffee, light chocolate." "Taste is one of chocolate sweet candy, roasted nuts and coffee." "It is pretty sweet, something I could drink every now and then." 5.5% alc.

Widmer Brothers Sommerbrau ★★1/2
Kölsch: Widmer Brothers Brewing Co., Portland, OR www.widmer.com
"Pretty strong smell of zesty type hops." "Slightly sweet maltiness up front which quickly dries out. Slightly more than a touch of bitterness comes through." "Not quite as delicate as most examples of the style but still quite nice." 4.8% alc.

Widmer Brothers Spring Run IPA ★★1/2
IPA: Widmer Brothers Brewing Co., Portland, OR www.widmer.com
"Aroma of dusty leaves, some hints of citrus, pale malt." "Nice bitter flavor, a little light compared to most IPAs." "Decent beer but run of the mill for IPA's." 6% alc.

Widmer Brothers W05 Indian Pale Ale ★★1/2
IPA: Widmer Brothers Brewing Co., Portland, OR www.widmer.com
"A pleasant citrus (grapefruit) and mildly grass hop aroma." "Taste is moderately sweet, pineapple, grapefruit, some caramel, melon. Light-medium body, very drinkable." 6% alc.

Widmer Brothers Widberry ★★1/2
Fruit Beer: Widmer Brothers Brewing Co., Portland, OR www.widmer.com
"Smells of fresh berries but tastes of sugary berry flavored syrup added to the beer." "The fruit character seems a bit syrupy and artificial between swigs." "Thirst-quenching. Good summer beer." 4.6% alc.

Wieckse Witte ★★1/2
Bel. Witbier: Heineken Nederland, Hertogenbosch, Netherlands www.heineken.com
"Some soft clove notes and a touch of orange." "Dry, lightly bitter with citric notes of orange peel - and perhaps also coriander." "Very smooth and good, but wished flavor was a bit stronger." 5% alc.

Wiedemann Bohemian Special ★★1/2
Pale Lager: Pittsburgh Brewing Co., Pittsburgh, PA www.pittsburghbrewingco.com
"Kind of plain and really light for something that isn't labeled as such." "Mostly corn syrupiness with an appallingly weak, watery texture." "This may be my new favorite old man beer." 4% alc.

Wiedenmayer Jersey Lager ★★★
Märzen/Oktbfst: Olde Saratoga Brewing (Mendocino Brewing Co.), Saratoga Springs, NY www.oldesaratogabrew.com
"Nose of molasses, honey - thick and broad." "Smooth and easy drinking, like a fruity cookie, very little hop, thin sweet sticky finish." "A good more-than-one beer, so buying a six is more than justified." 5.2% alc.

Wild Goose Amber ★★1/2
Amber Ale: Frederick Brewing Co (Snyder Intl), Frederick, MD www.frederickbrewing.com
"Malty, light honey, light cocoa and hints of caramel. Mild hop profile as well." "It is still a little too sweet for its own good, but serviceable at warmer temperature." 5% alc.

Wild Goose Indian Pale Ale ★★
IPA: Frederick Brewing Co (Snyder Intl), Frederick, Russia www.frederickbrewing.com
"Aroma is weak and grassy." "Light citrus notes, faint tangerine and orange peel, some earthy notes, light chewy malt notes and light yeast." "Flavor is some what weak." 5.9% alc.

Wild Goose Nut Brown ★★1/2

Brown Ale: Frederick Brewing Co (Snyder Intl), Frederick, MD www.frederickbrewing.com

"Subtle aroma has hints of sugar, chocolate, oak, nuts and stale malts." "Flavor is a nice balance of toasty, caramelly malt and fruity, herbal hops." "Nicely rounded, without being pretentious." 5.2% alc.

Wild Goose Oatmeal Stout ★★★

Sweet Stout: Frederick Brewing Co (Snyder Intl), Frederick, MD www.frederickbrewing.com

"Nicely roasty and mildly sweet, with a coffee bean bitterness in the finish." "Roasty but mild and does not venture too far off the beaten path for the style." "Simple and straightforward, but good stuff." 5.9% alc.

Wild Goose Porter ★★★

Porter: Frederick Brewing Co (Snyder Intl), Frederick, MD www.frederickbrewing.com

"Gives off a nice roastiness, along with charred dark fruits, malted dough and a touch of anise." "Thin palate that delivers decent flavor without the full body that great Porters sport." 5.3% alc.

Wild Goose Snow Goose ★★★1/2

Eng. Strong Ale: Frederick Brewing Co (Snyder Intl), Frederick, MD www.frederickbrewing.com

Lots of sweet malt, caramel, roasted grain and some dark fruit." "Moderate hop bitterness emerging in the finish." "A good beer for a snowy day." 5.9% alc.

Williamsburg Pale Ale ★★1/2

Am. Pale Ale: Williamsburg Brewing Co., Williamsburg, VA www.williamsburgbrewing.com

"Aroma of green apples, walnuts and green leafy hops." "Flavor is sweet with clementines and apples. Pithy with a bit of earthy leaf and invert sugar." "Bitter but not as bitter as many pale ales." 5.5% alc.

Williamsburg Porter ★★★

Porter: Williamsburg Brewing Co., Williamsburg, VA www.williamsburgbrewing.com

"Vanilla, roasted nuts, cocoa and caramel in the nose." "Initially significantly smoky with a burnt bitter edge but then just more mildly port-like with a robust smoke finish." "Traditional version of the style" 6.5% alc.

Williamsburg Stock Ale ★

Brown Ale: Williamsburg Brewing Co., Williamsburg, VA www.williamsburgbrewing.com

"Sour, appley nose." "Tea more prominent in the flavor, along with some clearly roasted, even smoke notes. There's a sour edge in there, too." "Maybe the dog will like it or if not the drain." 5% alc.

Williamsburg Wheat Ale ★★1/2

Am. Wheat: Williamsburg Brewing Co., Williamsburg, VA www.williamsburgbrewing.com

"Earthy nose with notes of straw and Amaretto sugar cookies." "The flavor is mostly bland, but inoffensive, refreshing and crisp." "If you like wheat beers that have decent amounts of hops, this one isn't bad." 4.5% alc.

Winterkoninkske ★★★

Bel. Strong Ale: Brouwerij Kerkom, Sint-Truiden, Belgium www.brouwerijkerkom.be

"Sweet malty aroma with lots of raisins and molasses." "Quite sweet, very malty, somewhat toffeeish flavor with hops and some fruity cherry hints." "I wish I'd had a few more of these to stave off this un-Godly January freeze." 8.3% alc.

Wisconsin Badger Porter ★★1/2

Porter: Sand Creek Brewing Co. (Pioneer/Wisconsin Brewing Co.), Black River Falls, WI www.sandcreekbrewing.com

"Aroma a bit empty with slight roastiness, nuts and vanilla." "Taste is plain and simple with just a nudge of roastiness, very skimmed chocolate notes and old coffee." N/A% alc.

Wisconsin Cranberry Special Ale ★

Fruit Beer: Sand Creek Brewing Co. (Pioneer/Wisconsin Brewing Co.), Black River Falls, WI www.sandcreekbrewing.com

"Faint cranberries in the aroma, along with more usual grainy beer smells." "Sweet-tart flavor, syrupy and cloying." "My first and last of these..." 4.5% alc.

Wisconsin Rainbow Red ★★★1/2

Amber Ale: Sand Creek Brewing Co. (Pioneer/Wisconsin Brewing Co.), Black River Falls, WI www.sandcreekbrewing.com

"Sweet and grapefruity aroma." "Flavor is sweet, lots of caramel, some bright fruit, hops for balance at the end." "On the sweet side. Fairly decent red ale." N/A% alc.

Wittekerke ★★1/2

Bel. Witbier: Bavik-De Brabandere, Harelbeke, Belgium www.bavik.be

"Malty, wheaty, slightly spicy (styrians) aroma." "Creamy, marshmallowy maltiness; spritzy middle; herbal, off-dry finish." "A little dry, but a decent white beer." 5% alc.

Wolaver's Brown Ale ★★1/2

Brown Ale: Otter Creek Brewing, Middlebury, VT www.ottercreekbrewing.com

"Really interesting aroma and flavor of walnuts and cherries." "Taste is initially sour malt, still a bit of chocolate, somewhat hop-bitter. But as it warms, the malt mutates to a nice juicy orange flavor." "Seems more like a lite-brown." Organic. 5.7% alc.

Wolaver's Indian Pale Ale ★★★

IPA: Otter Creek Brewing, Middlebury, VT www.ottercreekbrewing.com

"Citrus hops aroma mixed with some malty sweetness." "Big pine on the flavors with subtle grapefruit, resiny hop dryness." "A funky bitter pine cone." Organic. 6.5% alc.

Wolaver's Oatmeal Stout ★★1/2

Sweet Stout: Otter Creek Brewing, Middlebury, VT www.ottercreekbrewing.com

"Aroma is maple and brown sugar oatmeal, caramel and chocolate chip cookies and some perfunctory dark chocolate." "Flavor is roasted malts, coffee, some baker's chocolate and a bit of the oats." Organic. 5.9% alc.

Wolaver's Pale Ale ★★1/2

Am. Pale Ale: Otter Creek Brewing, Middlebury, VT www.ottercreekbrewing.com

"Very bready aroma with light hints of caramel and moderate floral hops." "Flavor was heavy with both floral and fruity hops and plenty of hop bitterness." "Not really balanced, but who cares?" Organic. 5.8% alc.

Wolaver's Wit ★★1/2

Bel. Witbier: Otter Creek Brewing, Middlebury, VT www.ottercreekbrewing.com

"Fruity wheat notes with the lightest touch of orange peel eke out from an overall mild aroma." "Flavor wise this seemed a bit too toned down to compete with the classics." Organic. 4.6% alc.

Wychwood Black Wych Stout ★

Stout: Wychwood (Refresh UK), Witney, Oxfordshire, England www.wychwood.co.uk

"Aroma is bland, slight grass and malt but nothing to write home about." "Quite a thin beer with an indistinct roast malt flavor - seems like just enough to add color." "A waste of my drinking capacity." 5% alc.

Wychwood Fiddler's Elbow ★★

Prem Bitter: Wychwood (Refresh UK), Witney, Oxfordshire, England www.wychwood.co.uk

"Caramel malty, fruity aroma and a sweet fruity taste." "Flavor is grainy and slightly roasty, with some light toffee notes." "One-dimensional and occasionally cardboardy." 5.2% alc.

Wychwood Goliath Ale ★

Prem Bitter: Wychwood (Refresh UK), Witney, Oxfordshire, England www.wychwood.co.uk

"Musty, caramel and vanilla nose, lightly toasted grain note with an inkling of sour lemons." "Light amount of toasted grain and rasping, leafy hops." "The name deserves something better." 4.2% alc.

Wychwood Hobgoblin ★★1/2

Prem Bitter: Wychwood (Refresh UK), Witney, Oxfordshire, England www.wychwood.co.uk

"Caramel and earthen malt in the aroma." "First taste is light, apples, caramel, tasty malt, maybe hazelnut." "Thinner than I'd have liked but not too shabby." 5.2% alc.

Wychwood Scarecrow ★

Prem Bitter: Wychwood (Refresh UK), Witney, Oxfordshire, England www.wychwood.co.uk

"Very faint sweet hop notes." "Lighter malts in this one make this beer more one dimensionally hoppy, with the rise of bitterness in the finish." "Ended up dumping half down the drain." 4.7% alc.

Wye Valley Dorothy Goodbody's Wholesome Stout ★★1/2

Dry Stout: Wye Valley, Hereford, Herefordshire, England www.wyevalleybrewery.co.uk

"Coffee, roast and some sweet notes in the nose." "Nice coffee bitter flavor blends with some smoke over a great bitter dry background." "A little light bodied and not so interesting compared to other British/Irish dry stouts." 4.6% alc.

Xingu ★★1/2

Schwarzbier: Kaiser (BRA) (MolsonCoors), Diviaopolis - MG , Brazil www.kaiser.com.br

"Dark fruits, lighter coffee and a hint of toffee in the aroma." "Sweet malty character with notes of caramel and molasses." "Nice session beer for folks who enjoy a milder, smooth and non-bitter character." 4.4% alc.

Yards Extra Special Ale ★★1/2

Prem Bitter: Yards Brewing Co., Philadelphia, PA www.yardsbrewing.com

"Floral, heavily hopped beer offers mild citrus aromas and a peppery spiciness on a dry display." "Grapefruit and lime citrus hops are tangy in the flavor with some bready malts." 6.3% alc.

Yards General Washington Tavern Porter ★★1/2

Porter: Yards Brewing Co., Philadelphia, PA www.yardsbrewing.com

"Slight roast, some malt, some alcohol, maybe a bit of hop." "Aroma of faint roasted malt/burnt toast, chalk and some dark fruit." "Somehow I don't think that George would approve of evoking his name in regards to this beer." 7% alc.

Yards Indian Pale Ale ★★★

IPA: Yards Brewing Co., Philadelphia, PA www.yardsbrewing.com

Mild ruby red grapefruit aromas dominate and only yield slightly to sweet malt." "Snappy and crisp hop notes were earthy, citrusy and herbal. Malts had elements of soft toffee and cocoa powder." 8% alc.

Yards Love Stout ★★1/2

Stout: Yards Brewing Co., Philadelphia, PA www.yardsbrewing.com

"Aroma of sweet cocoa, mild roast and a touch of citrus." "Astringent burnt malt flavor, extremely spritzy, too much so." "Thin palate as a dry stout should have but over carbonated." 5% alc.

Yards Philadelphia Pale Ale ★★

Am. Pale Ale: Yards Brewing Co., Philadelphia, PA www.yardsbrewing.com

"Weak citrus and floral aroma." "Taste was hoppy and grapefruit rind like, but lacked much malt sweetness." "Felt a lot more West Coast influenced than most others from Pennsylvania." 4.3% alc.

Yards Saison ★★

Saison: Yards Brewing Co., Philadelphia, PA www.yardsbrewing.com

"Aroma is grassy, musty with notes of apricot and citrus." "Light spices and herbs with a mild bitterness." "Somewhat dreary in terms of flavor and finish." 4.7% alc.

Yards Thomas Jefferson Tavern Ale ★★★
Am Strong Ale: Yards Brewing Co., Philadelphia, PA www.yardsbrewing.com
"Dry aroma of honey, grassy hops, herbs oranges and caramel." "Dry aroma of honey, grassy hops, herbs oranges and caramel." "Generally an intense beer." 8% alc.

Yarpivo Elitnoye (Premium) ★★
Pale Lager: Yarpivo , Yaroslav, Russia www.yarpivo.ru
"Aroma is very sweet and malty- with some bread-like smells." "Flavor is mainly corn syrup sweetness with some malty graininess." "Quite thin." "Higher alcohol notes make the whole production rather unpleasant" 5.8% alc.

Yarpivo Krepkoe (Strong) ★★
Eur Str Lager: Yarpivo , Yaroslav, Russia www.yarpivo.ru
"Very industrial aromas with grass/hay, fusels and minerals." "Taste is slightly sweet, grainy with a distinct note of alcohol and some corn." 7.2% alc.

Yarpivo Original ★
Helles/Dortmnd: Yarpivo , Yaroslav, Russia www.yarpivo.ru
"Bready aroma with herbal balance." "Flavor is sweetly malted with an average bitter finish and a touch of metal." "Kinda industrial and thus not clean enough, but not horrible either." 4.7% alc.

Yazoo Amarillo Pale Ale ★★1/2
Am. Pale Ale: Yazoo Brewing Co., Nashville, TN www.yazoobrew.com
"Semi-citrus like sweetness with a huge malt backbone." "Flavors of caramel, a hint of spices and a small amount of orange with a smooth mildly bitter finish." "But be warned: It has a pretty strong taste for a Pale Ale." 5.8% alc.

Yazoo Dos Perros ★★
Altbier: Yazoo Brewing Co., Nashville, TN www.yazoobrew.com
"Bready yeast and malt in the aroma." "Light sweet hoppy flavor of lemon, flowers and a hint of vanilla and malts." "An easy crossover beer." 3.5% alc.

Ybor Gold Amber Lager ★★★
Premium Lager: Indian River Brewing Co. (Florida Beer Co.), Melbourne, FL www.floridabeer.com
"The aroma has a nice toasted biscuit malt note." "Body is med/light, crisp." "Light dry maltiness, bready, toasty with a light grassiness." "I put this one in the same category as Samuel Adams when it comes to quality." 4.6% alc.

Ybor Gold Brown Ale ★★1/2
Brown Ale: Indian River Brewing Co. (Florida Beer Co.), Melbourne, FL www.floridabeer.com
"Aroma of nuts, caramel and a bit of brown sugar." "Dry malt flavors with a laid back spiciness, caramel notes and a bit of nuttiness." "Not as thick and rich as I would like." "Wonderful with beef and potatoes." 4.4% alc.

Ybor Gold Gaspar's Porter ★★1/2
Porter: Indian River Brewing Co. (Florida Beer Co.), Melbourne, FL www.floridabeer.com
"Nose is mildly caramelly, lightly roasty." "Roasty malt flavor, kick of sweet chocolate in the middle, finishing out nicely bitter." "A decent all around porter." 5.2% alc.

Ybor Gold Wheat Ale ★★
Am. Wheat: Indian River Brewing Co. (Florida Beer Co.), Melbourne, FL www.floridabeer.com
"Light aroma of wheat with a lighter fruitiness and some spice." "Some Euro-lager flavors." "Needs something to make it notable." 3.9% alc.

Yellowstone Valley Black Widow Oatmeal Stout ★★1/2
Sweet Stout: Yellowstone Valley Brewing Co., Billings, MT www.yellowstonevalleybrew.com
"Oats and chocolate malt aromas with faint citrus hop nose." "Flavors were roasted coffee, bitter chocolate, roasted malt and a little brown sugar." "Not quite what I expected. Just so-so." 5.9% alc.

Yellowstone Valley Grizzly Wulff Wheat ★
Am. Wheat: Yellowstone Valley Brewing Co., Billings, MT www.yellowstonevalleybrew.com
"Not much to be spoken of in the aroma, except a touch of light grains and herbs." "Taste is mellow with a slight sharpness toward the end." N/A% alc.

Yellowstone Valley Huckle-Weizen ★★1/2
Fruit Beer: Yellowstone Valley Brewing Co., Billings, MT www.yellowstonevalleybrew.com
"Intriguing berry aroma: very fresh, awake and alive, full of fruitiness." "Light notes of yeast - wholesome and earthy. Nice level of huckleberry. Just enough to show up in the background." N/A% alc.

Yellowstone Valley Renegade Red ★★1/2
Prem Bitter: Yellowstone Valley Brewing Co., Billings, MT www.yellowstonevalleybrew.com
"Oaked caramel malt flavor with alcohol and a thin hop finish." "Malt is king here, hops bow out, true to style." "They're being a bit coy there. It's much fuller than an ESB but contains much of that style's ease of drinkability." N/A% alc.

Yellowstone Valley Wild Fly Ale ★★1/2
Amber Ale: Yellowstone Valley Brewing Co., Billings, MT www.yellowstonevalleybrew.com
"Nose is lightly hoppy and spicy with faint fruit notes." "An amber ale that isn't too sophisticated to appeal to the casual Macro drinker who might chance to try it." N/A% alc.

Young's Dirty Dick's ★★1/2
Bitter: Young and Co.'s Brewery Plc., Wandsworth, London, England www.youngs.co.uk
"Aroma is of caramel and lightly roasted malts." "Nutty sweet malts quickly overtaken by bitter hops with a sugary follow." "This type of by-the-numbers bland bottled ale is why so many Americans think English ales aren't very interesting." 4.1% alc.

Young's Double Chocolate Stout ★★★★★
Sweet Stout: Young and Co.'s Brewery Plc., Wandsworth, London, England www.youngs.co.uk
"Smells of bittersweet chocolate and toasted malts with a slight raisin and metallic aroma." "Loaded with hops, chocolate, toffee and a smooth bitter aftertaste." "Always a fully creamy stout." 5.2% alc.

Young's Oatmeal Stout ★★★1/2
Stout: Young and Co.'s Brewery Plc., Wandsworth, London, England www.youngs.co.uk
"Good malty nose of milk chocolate, oats and a touch of hops." "Tastes smooth with hints of chocolate, very thick and rich, finishes with a nice roasted flavor." "Dare I say this beer replaces Guinness as my favorite everyday drinking stout? I think so." 5% alc.

Young's Old Nick ★★★1/2
Barley Wine: Young and Co.'s Brewery Plc., Wandsworth, London, England www.youngs.co.uk
"Aroma of sweet malts and rich fruitcake." "Flavor had a nice balance between smooth fruity malts and the fuggles... there was also a good deal of caramel." "Lighter on the palate than your typical barley wine." 7.2% alc.

Young's Ram Rod ★★1/2
Prem Bitter: Young and Co.'s Brewery Plc., Wandsworth, London, England www.youngs.co.uk
"Roasty malt, caramel/toffee aroma - but not much aroma." "Sweet, nutty taste with resiny, citrusy hop notes. Soft, dry aftertaste with notes of resin and pine needles." "A sweet but mellow bitter for those who really don't like bitter ales." 5% alc.

Young's Special London ★★★1/2
Eng. Strong Ale: Young and Co.'s Brewery Plc., Wandsworth, London, England www.youngs.co.uk
"Sweet aroma with notes of raisin and treacle." "Deep, sweet, malty taste of nuts, combined with bitterness, citrus and pine needles." "This is lacking that Nth degree of complexity, but is most drinkable - an nice warmer on a gray drizzly day." 6.4% alc.

Young's Waggledance ★★
Goldn/Blond Ale: Young and Co.'s Brewery Plc., Wandsworth, London, England www.youngs.co.uk
"Some light grassy notes, bit of floral, heathery notes and a touch of graham crackers." "Stylish blend of sweet, creamy honey and soft, gentle maltiness." "Isn't much more than a filtered, pasteurized, watery concoction of honey and very light hops." 5% alc.

Young's Winter Warmer ★★1/2
Eng. Strong Ale: Young and Co.'s Brewery Plc., Wandsworth, London, England www.youngs.co.uk
"Sweet aromas with some raisin and cinnamon notes." "Sweet bitter, mild but rich, liqueur, well-balanced, drier aftertaste." "Too bad the taste and flavors couldn't quite make a beefier approach on the ol' taste buds." 5% alc.

Yuengling Dark Brewed Porter ★★1/2
Porter: Yuengling Brewery, Pottsville, PA www.yuengling.com
"Aroma of liquorice, prunes, buckwheat honey, burnt raisins." "Flavor is fruity, sweet, notes of brown sugar, a bit of cola and cherry, a touch of coffee but not much." "A good Porter even though a little light." 5% alc.

Yuengling Lord Chesterfield Ale ★
Goldn/Blond Ale: Yuengling Brewery, Pottsville, PA www.yuengling.com
"Aroma has some light honey and lots of grassy hops." "Woody malt and herbal hops flavors that seem to work against each other." "Trying to make something of nothing leaves nothing." 5.6% alc.

Yuengling Original Black and Tan ★★
Porter: Yuengling Brewery, Pottsville, PA www.yuengling.com
"Slightly nutty after taste and mild finish." "Flavor combines roasted malts, a touch of caramel, some yeast." "Not a beer to savor but has a good enough palate to enjoy briefly." 5.2% alc.

Yuengling Premium Beer ★★1/2
Pale Lager: Yuengling Brewery, Pottsville, PA www.yuengling.com
"Delicate palate, crisp, smooth." "Light watery hop aroma." "I don't know why they call it the premium." 4.9% alc.

Yuengling Premium Light ★★1/2
Pale Lager: Yuengling Brewery, Pottsville, PA www.yuengling.com
Woody, cardboard flavor and nose and minimal sweetness." "Seems to be missing a lot of the citrus tones and refreshing nature of the regular Premium beer." 4.2% alc.

Yuengling Premium Light Beer ★★1/2
Pale Lager: Yuengling Brewery, Pottsville, PA www.yuengling.com
Woody, cardboard flavor and nose and minimal sweetness." "Seems to be missing a lot of the citrus tones and refreshing nature of the regular Premium beer." 4.2% alc.

Yuengling Traditional Lager ★★★
Pale Lager: Yuengling Brewery, Pottsville, PA www.yuengling.com
Absolutely the best mass-produced, reasonably priced lager in America." "Aroma is of caramel malts and hay-like hops." "Grassy hay flavors, like chewing on a piece of straw." "A cheap decent beer." 4.9% alc.

Z Street IPA ★★1/2
IPA: Mercury Brewing and Distribution, Ipswich, MA www.mercurybrewing.com
"Juicy pineapple and melon nose, dull plasticy yeast notes." "Back bitterness shocks the palate without offering any peace or distinct flavoring." "Really too bad as I know concord can brew great stuff." N/A% alc.

Z Street Mocha Java Stout ★★★1/2
Sweet Stout: Mercury Brewing and Distribution, Ipswich, MA www.mercurybrewing.com
"Very bittersweet on the nose, cocoa and chocolate, but dry and very unsweetened." "Quite bitter in mouth, it is really concentrating on roastiness, espresso like." "This could be extraordinary with some minor adjustments." 6.8% alc.

Z Street Rollstone Red ★★★★★
Amber Ale: Mercury Brewing and Distribution, Ipswich, MA www.mercurybrewing.com
"Orangey/earthy nose with a balance leaning toward the hops." "Flavor is initially spicy, toasted malt lingering above mild sweetness." N/A% alc.

Zatte Bie ★★★
Bel. Strong Ale: Brouwerij de Bie, Loker, Belgium www.brijdebie.be
"Aroma is rich and concentrated with notes of prune, raisin, fig and toffee." "Soft dark malt base, chocolate notes, hint of honey." "Different and a fun change but not one you would want over and over." 9% alc.

Zhigulevskoye (Moscow) ★
Pale Lager: Pivzavod AO Hamovnikov (SABMiller), Moscow, Russia www.bochka.ru
"Classic Soviet style - sweet and flat. Aroma of icing sugar, apple, corn." "Flavor is sweet and somewhat unbalanced- borderline cloying." "I wonder what ingredients were used. Result is not very pleasant." 4% alc.

Zhigulevskoye (Samara) ★★1/2
Pale Lager: OAO Zhigulovskiy Pivo-Byezalkogolniy Kombinat, Samara , Russia
www.nubo.ruavm/ru/samara.htm
The original Zhigulevskoe from the Zhiguli brewery, which dates to Victorian times. "Not objectionable, strangely, given that a beer really shouldn't taste like creamed corn." 4% alc.

Ziegen Bock ★★
Am Dark Larger: Anheuser-Busch Companies, St. Louis, MO www.anheuser-busch.com
"Slight caramel aroma." "Moderate malt flavor with decent body." "One-dimensional industrial lager that lacks any real flavor or character." Brewed to compete with Texas' Shiner Bock. 5% alc.

Zigulinis ★★★
Pale Lager: AB Gubernija, Lietuva, Lithuania www.gubernija.lt
"Fresh hop aroma, with slight cat's piss." "Herbal, almost pungent (though restrained) hops and bready malt blend well." "Slightly bitter finish, light overall." 4.3% alc.

Zoetzuur Flemish Reserve ★★★★★
Flem Sour Ale: De Proefbrouwerij, Lochristi, Belgium www.proefbrouwerij.com
"Woody sourish-sweet nose, lactic acid, sour cream, fruity as wild berries, rosehips oranges, prunes." "Sweet fruity flavors, like some melon perhaps, with other earthy yeasty notes." 7% alc.

Zywiec ★★1/2
Premium Lager: Browar Zywiec (Heineken), Zywiec, Poland www.zywiec.com.pl
"Aroma is mostly hay and grains, with some maltiness." "Grainy flavor followed by a light, refreshing bitterness." "Not a world beater, but a somewhat tasty Pilsner." "Drinkable." 5.6% alc.

Zywiec Porter ★★★★★
Baltic Porter: Bracki Browar Zamkowy (Zywiec Heineken), Cieszyn, Poland www.brackie.com.pl
"Roasted malt nose with ample alcohol and some licorice, soy, burnt wood and vanilla." "Very dry, roasty and hoppy, with a big alcohol kick, some very burnt raisin flavors." "This has great depth and would make an excellent fireside beer." 9.5% alc.

Best Widely Distributed Beers

Here is a list of well-regarded beers with fairly good U.S. distribution that you can take to a store with a wide beer selection and you should be able to find at least some.

Name	Style	Cost per equivalent six-pack of 12-oz. bottles
1. Ayinger Celebrator Doppelbock	Doppelbock	$18.14
2. North Coast Old Rasputin	Russian Imperial Stout	11.95
3. Chimay Bleue (Blue)	Belgian Strong Ale	15.84
4. Samuel Smith's Oatmeal Stout	Sweet Stout	13.49
5. Arrogant Bastard Ale	American Strong Ale	12.10
6. Duvel	Belgian Strong Ale	19.80
7. Sierra Nevada Celebration Ale	India Pale Ale (IPA)	8.29
8. Youngs Double Chocolate Stout	Sweet Stout	11.88
9. Sierra Nevada Pale Ale (Bottle)	American Pale Ale	7.79
10. Hoegaarden White	Belgian White (Witbier)	8.49
11. Guinness Draught	Dry Stout	7.69
12. Rogue Dead Guy Ale	Bock	14.40
13. Anchor Steam Beer	California Common	6.99
14. Pilsner Urquell	Bohemian Pilsner	7.79
15. Bass Pale Ale	Premium Bitter/ESB	6.79
16. Samuel Adams Boston Lager	Premium Lager	5.99
17. Newcastle Brown Ale	Brown Ale	7.79

[Prices based on cheapest per-ounce bottle configuration available. Dallas-Fort Worth market, 2006]

STOP PRESS!

Updates & Corrections

Chambly Noire ★★★1/2

Belgian Ale: Unibroue (Sleeman), Chambly, Quebec www.unibroue.com

"Robust aroma ... almost black currant-like." "Flavor is sweet with brown & demerara sugar, plummy fruitiness and pinot noir. A lighter version of Trois-Pistoles?" "Just not as complex or remarkable as I've come to expect from Unibroue." 6.2%alc.

Rahr Blonde Lager ★★1/2

Helles: Rahr & Sons Brewing Co., Fort Worth, TX www. rahrbrewing.com

"Nose of husky malts and light maltiness". The flavor is lightly bitter, sweet but smooth." "Aclean version of a Helles that I really enjoyed and worth the try!"

Rahr Bucking Bock ★★★

Maibock: Rahr & Sons Brewing Co., Fort Worth, TX www. rahrbrewing.com

"Pours a clear deep gold with minimal Zhead. Aroma is faint, barely malty and sweet. Taste is lightly malty, toasty and sweet with elements of light caramel. Overall, a very clean, gentle flavor profile. Deceptive, almost too smooth: only after downing a liter did I realize it kicked me in the head. Another winner from Rahr."

Rahr's Red ★★★

Vienna: Rahr & Sons Brewing Co., Fort Worth, TX www. rahrbrewing.com

"Aroma is bready and nutty with some caramel underneath." "Decent note of toast, then pleasant piney, hoppy finish." "A good Texas brew I assume since it is easy to drink in the heat of the day."

Rahr Summertime Wheat ★★★1/2

Hefeweizen: Rahr & Sons Brewing Co., Fort Worth, TX www. rahrbrewing.com

"Aroma is heavy nutmeg, along with banana and citrus esters along with bubble gum." "Good flavor here, banana, sweet orange like flavor I can't pin down, a hint of clove, a bit of pepper on the backside." "If I ever go back to Texas I will drink more of this." 5.5% alc.

Rahr & Sons Ugly Pug ★★1/2

Schwarzbier: Rahr & Sons Brewing Co., Fort Worth, TX www. rahrbrewing.com

"Chewy raisins and maple in the nose, with some smoked maple wood scents." "Fore is waterywith some mild raisin and burnt malts on the back end and a little cocoa in the far finish." "Not bad, just seems like it's missing something."

Clarifications:

La Fin du Monde, Ephemere Apple and **Ephemere Peach** were mistakenly listed on pages 251-2.

Terrible, also a Unibroue brand, is listed as La Terrible on page 135.

Rate Beer Judging Sheet

BEER NAME: **[seasonal]**

ALCOHOL BY VOLUME: **[bottle / can / draught]**

Aroma : _____ (1 - 10)

Malty

- ☐ Light / moderate / heavy / harsh
- ☐ Bread - light / dark
- ☐ Cookie
- ☐ Grain / Hay / Straw / Cereal
- ☐ Toasted / Roasted / Burnt / Nutty
- ☐ Molasses / Caramel
- ☐ Chocolate - milk / dark
- ☐ Coffee - mild / strong
- ☐ Other: ______________________

Hoppy

- ☐ Light / moderate / heavy / harsh
- ☐ Flowers / Perfume / Herbs / Grass
- ☐ Pine / Spruce / Resin
- ☐ Citrus - grapefruit / orange
- ☐ Citrus - lemon / lime
- ☐ Other: ______________________

Yeasty

- ☐ Light / moderate / heavy / harsh
- ☐ Dough / Sweat
- ☐ Horse blanket / Barnyard / Leather
- ☐ Soap / Cheese

Head - Lacing

- ☐ Excellent
- ☐ Good
- ☐ Fair
- ☐ Virtually none

Head - Longevity

- ☐ Fully lasting
- ☐ Mostly lasting
- ☐ Mostly diminishing
- ☐ Fully diminishing

Body - Clarity

- ☐ Clear - sparkling / normal / flat
- ☐ Cloudy - hazy / murky / muddy

Body - Particles

- ☐ Size – tiny / small / medium / large / huge
- ☐ Density - thin / average / thick
- ☐ Bottle conditioned

Body - Hue

- ☐ Light / medium / dark
- ☐ Yellow
- ☐ Amber
- ☐ Orange
- ☐ Red
- ☐ Brown
- ☐ Black
- ☐ Other:______________________________

Flavor : _____ (1 - 10)

Initial flavor

- ☐ Sweet - light / moderate / heavy / harsh
- ☐ Acidic - light / moderate / heavy / harsh
- ☐ Bitter - light / moderate / heavy / harsh
- ☐ Acetic (vinegar)
- ☐ Sour (sour milk)
- ☐ Salty

Finish - Flavor

- ☐ Sweet - light / moderate / heavy / harsh
- ☐ Acidic - light / moderate / heavy / harsh
- ☐ Bitter - light / moderate / heavy / harsh

☐ Acetic (vinegar)
☐ Sour (sour milk)
☐ Salty

Finish - Duration

☐ Short
☐ Average
☐ Long

Overall Score (1-20): _____

Comments:

Palate : _____ **(1 - 5)**

Body

☐ Light
☐ Light to medium
☐ Medium
☐ Medium to full
☐ Full

Texture

☐ Dry
☐ Watery
☐ Oily
☐ Creamy
☐ Syrupy
☐ Other: ______________________________

Carbonation

☐ Fizzy
☐ Lively
☐ Soft
☐ Flat
☐ Other: ______________________________

Finish - Feel

☐ Metallic
☐ Chalky
☐ Astringent - light / moderate / heavy / harsh
☐ Alcoholic - light / moderate / heavy / harsh
☐ Other: ______________________________

- ☐ Earth / Mold / Cobwebs
- ☐ Meat / Broth
- ☐ Other: ______________________________

Miscellaneous

- ☐ Banana / Bubble gum
- ☐ Grape / Raisin / Plum / Prune / Date
- ☐ Apple / Pear / Peach / Pineapple
- ☐ Cherry / Raspberry / Cassis
- ☐ Wine - white / red
- ☐ Port - tawny / ruby
- ☐ Cask wood (e.g., oak)
- ☐ Smoke / Tar / Charcoal / Soy sauce
- ☐ Toffee / Butter / Butterscotch
- ☐ Honey / Brown sugar / Maple syrup
- ☐ Coriander / Ginger
- ☐ Allspice / Nutmeg / Clove / Cinnamon
- ☐ Vanilla / Pepper / Licorice / Cola
- ☐ Alcohol
- ☐ Dust / Chalk
- ☐ Vegetable / Cooked corn
- ☐ Cardboard / Paper
- ☐ Medicine / Solvent / Band-aid
- ☐ Soured milk / Vinegar
- ☐ Sulfur / Skunk
- ☐ Other: ______________________________

BREWER:
Date:

Appearance : _____ (1 - 5)

Head - Initial appearance

- ☐ Size - small / average / large / huge
- ☐ Rocky
- ☐ Creamy
- ☐ Frothy
- ☐ Fizzy
- ☐ Virtually none

Head - Color

- ☐ White
- ☐ Off-white
- ☐ Light brown

Food-to-beer
pairing guide

By Stan Hieronymus

APPETIZERS & BREAD	
Beer bread	Brown Ale
Couscous	Belgian Tripel
Eggs, quiche	Belgian Wit
Hummus	Oktoberfest
Nachos	American Brown
Paté	Porter
Salad, mixed greens	American Pale
Salad, Caesar	IPA
Salad, Walnut	English Brown
Salsa	American IPA
SOUPS	
Cheese	American IPA
Chicken cream	Gueuze
Chili	American Brown
Gumbo	Dark Abbey
Meat stew	Bock

	Amber Ale	Irish Red
	American Pale	Saison
	Belgian Blond	Kölsch
	Bock	Wheat beer
	American IPA	Märzen
	Dark Abbey	German Alt
	Brown Ale	Doppelbock
	Wheat	Helles
	Dark Abbey	Premium Lager
	American Brown	Porter
	Premium Lager	Dunkel
	English Pale	Pilsner
	Porter	Wheat
	Strong Scottish	Porter
	Biere de Garde	Märzen

MEAT & GAME	
Bacon	Smoked beer
Chicken, roasted	Märzen
Chicken, fried	American Brown
Duck	Dark Abbey
Ham	Pilsner
Hamburgers	Amber/Vienna
Lamb	Biere de Garde
Pork	Irish Red
Sausage	Märzen
Roast beef	British Pale
Steak	Brown Ale
Turkey	Märzen
Veal	Belgian Strong Golden
Venison	German Dunkel

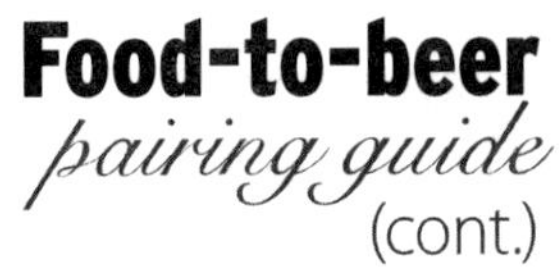

	Wheat	Saison
	Porter	Wheat
	American Pale	German Alt
	Doppelbock	Biere de Garde
	Dry Stout	Belgian Strong Golden
	American Brown	American Pale
	Scottish	Brown Ale
	Märzen	Dark Abbey
	German Alt	Saison
	German Dunkel	Dry Stout
	Porter	Dark Abbey
	Biere de Garde	German Dunkel
	Wheat	Saison
	Brown Ale	Amber Ale

SEAFOOD	
Caviar	Wheat
Crab	Belgian Blond
Fish & Chips	English Pale
Halibut	Belgian Wit
Herring, pickled	Flemish Red
Lobster	Pilsner
Mussels	Belgian Wit
Oysters	Dry Stout
Salmon, grilled	Märzen
Salmon, smoked	Smoked Beer
Scallops	Wheat
Shrimp	Pale Ale
Trout	Wheat Beer
Tuna	Fruit Beer
ETHNIC & REGIONAL	
Barbecue	Amber Ale

	Saison	Pilsner
	Pilsner	Wheat
	Porter	English IPA
	Kölsch	Helles
	Old Ale	Pilsner
	Helles	Wheat
	Stout	Gueuze
	Porter	Helles
	Wheat	Continental Lager
	Belgian Strong Golden	Pilsner
	Saison	Kölsch
	Wheat	Dark Abbey
	Premium Lager	Doppelbock
	Wheat	American Pale
	Porter	Smoked Beer

Cajun	American Dark Lager
Caribbean	Pilsner
Chile rellenos	American Brown
Chinese	Wheat
Indian, curry	IPA
Mexican, molé	Bock
Pasta, cream sauce	Belgian Tripel
Pasta, pesto	Belgian Strong Golden
Pizza, cheese	American Pale
Pizza, pepperoni	Amber Lager/Vienna
Shepherd's Pie	British Pale
Thai	Saison
VEGETABLES	
Asparagus	Belgian Tripel
Avocado/guacomole	American Brown
Carrots	IPA
Corn on the cob	Helles

	American Pale	Saison
	Saison	Porter
	American IPA	Dry Stout
	Belgian Tripel	Continental Lager
	Saison	Pilsner
	German Dunkel	American Pale
	Biere de Garde	Brown Ale
	British IPA	Belgian Blond
	Amber Ale	Oatmeal Stout
	German Dunkel	American Pale
	Oatmeal Stout	Porter
	IPA	Wheat
	Saison	Wheat
	American IPA	German Alt
	Porter	Bock
	Wheat	Kölsch

Peas	Wheat
Potatoes, baked or mashed	IPA
Potatoes, chips	British Pale
Sweet potato fries	Porter
NUTS	
Almonds	Doppelbock
Cashews	American Pale
Peanuts	American Pale
Walnuts	Doppelbock
CHEESES	
Macaroni & cheese	British Pale
Blue/Gorgonzola	English Brown
Brie	Imperial Stout
Cheddar	IPA
Goat	Saison
Muenster	Premium Lager
Smoked gouda	Bock
Stilton	Barleywine

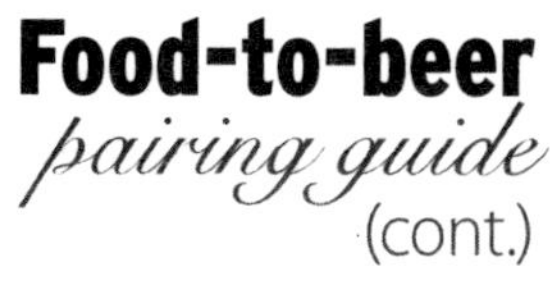

Food-to-beer *pairing guide* (cont.)

	Saison	British Pale
	British Pale	Dry Stout
	Amber Ale	Cream Ale
	German Dunkel	Smoked Beer
	American Brown	Old Ale
	English Barleywine	Weizenbock
	Continental Lager	Belgian Blond
	Brown Ale	Oatmeal Stout
	German Dunkel	Porter
	Porter	Fruit Lambic
	Baltic Porter	Doppelbock
	Dry Stout	German Alt
	Belgian Blond	Wheat
	Amber Lager/ Vienna	Kölsch
	German Dunkel	Smoked Beer
	Old Ale	Dark Abbey

DESSERTS & FRUITS	
Apple pie	Imperial stout
Cheesecake	Imperial Stout
Chocolate (in general)	Dark Abbey
Christmas cake	Old Ale
Crème Brule	Fruit Lambic
Key lime pie	Hefeweizen
Pecan pie	Oatmeal Stout
Raspberry, strawberries	Imperial Stout

	Doppelbock	Fruit beer
	Fruit Beer	Baltic Porter
	Imperial Stout	Fruit Lambic
	Doppelbock	British IPA
	Barleywine	Imperial Stout
	American Wheat	Belgian Tripel
	Imperial Stout	Dark Abbey
	Belgian Blond	Oatmeal Stout

Beer-to-food
pairing guide

Style	Example
Amber Ale	Fat Tire
Amber Lager/Vienna	Great Lakes Eliot Ness
American Brown	Saint Arnold Brown
American Dark Lager	Shiner Bock
American IPA	Stone IPA
American Pale	Sierra Nevada Pale Ale
American Wheat	Widmer Hefeweizen
Baltic Porter	Baltika Porter
Barleywine	Avery Hog Heaven
Belgian Blond	Leffe Blond
Belgian Strong Golden	Duvel
Belgian Tripel	Westmalle Tripel
Belgian Wit	Hoegaarden
Biere de Garde	Jenlain French Farmhouse Ale
Bock	Mahr's Bock
Continental Lager	Heineken

	Seafood soup	Barbecue
	Lasagna	Pork Roulade
	Almonds	Green chile hamburger
	Sausage	Macaroni & cheese
	Thai	Spicy Nachos
	Fried chicken	Cashews
	Tuna	Goat cheese
	Creamy brie	Pierogies
	Stilton	Chocolate bonbons
	Crab	Pasta with cream sauce
	Sausage	Pasta with pesto sauce
	Asparagus	Chinese
	Eggs/quiche	Halibut
	Lamb	Munster
	Meat stew	Hummus
	Shellfish	Corn on the cob

Cream Ale	Genesee Cream Ale
Dark Abbey/Dubbel	Ommegang Ale
Doppelbock	Ayinger Celebrator
Dry Stout	Guinness Draught
English Barleywine	Young's Old Nick
English Brown	Newcastle Brown
English IPA	Brooklyn EIPA
English Pale/Bitter	Fuller's London Pride
Flanders Red	Rodenbach Grand Cru
Fruit Beer	Pyramid Apricot Ale
Fruit Lambic	Boon Framboise
German Alt	Southampton Secret Ale
German Dunkel	Ayinger Altbairisch
German Weizen	Schneider Weisse
Gueuze	Cantillon Gueuze
Helles	Spaten Premium Lager
Imperial Stout	North Coast Old Rasputin
Irish Red	Smithwick's

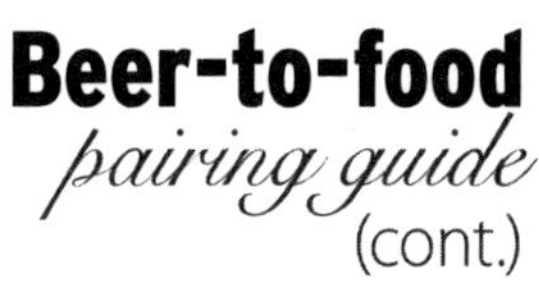

	Potato chips	Grilled salmon
	Flemish beef stew	Chocolate dessert
	Duck	Mixed green salad
	Oysters	Mashed potatoes
	Wild Game	Cashews
	Walnut salad	Roast beef
	Fish & chips	Fried calmari
	Lasagna	Roast beef
	Pickled herring	Mussels and frites
	Shrimp quesadillas	Duck
	Chocolate dessert	Cheesecake
	Fried chicken	Roast pork
	Venison	Macaroni & Cheese
	Key Lime Pie	Smoked trout
	Mussels	Smoked salmon
	Lobster	Caesar salad
	Chocolate dessert	Dessert with bananas
	Pork	Pizza

Kölsch	Goose Island Summertime
Light	Bud Light
Oatmeal Stout	Samuel Smith Oatmeal Stout
Oktoberfest/Märzen	Paulaner Oktoberfest
Old Ale	Gale's Prize Old Ale
Pilsner	Pilsner Urquell
Porter	Deschutes Black Butte
Premium Lager	Sam Adams Boston Lager
Saison	Saison Dupont
Scottish	Belhaven Scottish
Smoked	Schlenkerla Rauchbier
Steam Beer	Anchor Steam
Strong Scotch	McEwan's Scotch Ale

	Steamed halibut	Grilled pork chops
	Potato chips	Crab
	Plantains mole	Tiramisu
	Turkey	Hummus
	Robust cake	Meatloaf
	Salmon	Cajun cuisine
	Grilled steak	Gorgonzola
	Trout	Eggplant pasta
	Blackened redfish	Couscous
	Lamb	Cheddar
	Smoked fish	Bacon
	Pulled pork	Maytag Blue Cheese
	Cream Brule	Toffee bread pudding

How to use the beer guide

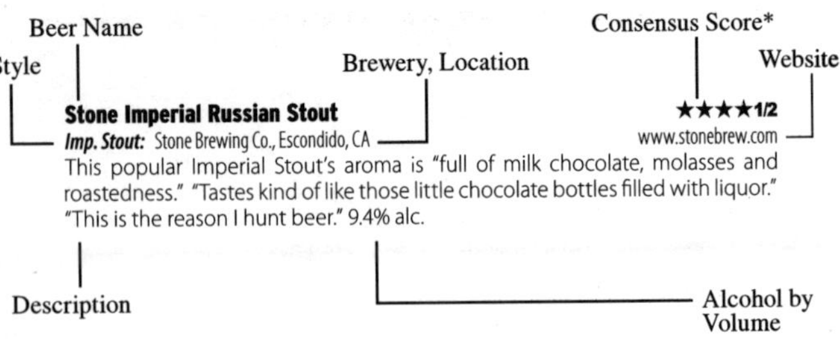
Beer Name
Consensus Score*
Style
Brewery, Location
Website
Stone Imperial Russian Stout
★★★★1/2
Imp. Stout: Stone Brewing Co., Escondido, CA
www.stonebrew.com
This popular Imperial Stout's aroma is "full of milk chocolate, molasses and roastedness." "Tastes kind of like those little chocolate bottles filled with liquor." "This is the reason I hunt beer." 9.4% alc.
Description
Alcohol by Volume

***RateBeer's 100-point rating scale has been converted to a five-star system:**

★★★★★	SUPERIOR
★★★★	EXCELLENT
★★★	GOOD
★★	DRINKABLE
★	POOR

RateBeer

Enjoyed the book?

Join the RateBeer community.

Basic membership is free.

Visit www.RateBeer.com

Savory House Press / Great Texas Line

Post Office Box 11105

Fort Worth, Texas 76110

greattexas@hotmail.com

1-800-738-3927